Lecture Notes in Computer Science 12569

More information about this subseries at http://www.springer.com/series/7407

Manuel A. Martins · Igor Sedlár (Eds.)

Dynamic Logic

New Trends and Applications

Third International Workshop, DaLí 2020
Prague, Czech Republic, October 9–10, 2020
Revised Selected Papers

Springer

Editors
Manuel A. Martins
Department of Mathematics
University of Aveiro
Aveiro, Portugal

Igor Sedlár
Institute of Computer Science
Czech Academy of Sciences
Praha 8, Czech Republic

ISSN 0302-9743 ISSN 1611-3349 (electronic)
Lecture Notes in Computer Science
ISBN 978-3-030-65839-7 ISBN 978-3-030-65840-3 (eBook)
https://doi.org/10.1007/978-3-030-65840-3

LNCS Sublibrary: SL1 – Theoretical Computer Science and General Issues

This Springer imprint is published by the registered company Springer Nature Switzerland AG
The registered company address is: Gewerbestrasse 11, 6330 Cham, Switzerland

Preface

Building on the pioneer intuitions of Floyd-Hoare logic, dynamic logic was introduced in the 1970s as a suitable logic to reason about, and verify, classic imperative programs. Since then, the original intuitions grew to an entire family of logics, which became increasingly popular for assertional reasoning about a wide range of computational systems. Simultaneously, their object (i.e. the very notion of a program) evolved in unexpected ways. This led to dynamic logics tailored to specific programming paradigms and extended to new computing domains, including probabilistic, continuous, and quantum computation. Variants of dynamic logic also became popular in formalizing epistemic events involving change of information available to cognitive agents. Both its theoretical relevance and practical potential make dynamic logic a topic of interest in a number of scientific venues, from wide-scope software engineering conferences to modal logic specific events. However, no specific event is exclusively dedicated to it. The DaLí workshop series aims at filling this gap and creating a heterogeneous community of colleagues, from academia to industry, from mathematics to computer science.

The third edition of the DaLí workshop was held online, due to the COVID-19 pandemic, during October 9–10, 2020, and organized by the Institute of Computer Science and the Institute of Philosophy of the Czech Academy of Sciences, Czech Republic. In comparison to the previous two editions, held in Brasília in 2017 and in Porto in 2019, the third edition offered a two-day program with two invited speakers. The workshop series clearly reached a state of maturity and DaLí 2020 attracted a number of submissions from different groups and trends in the dynamic logic community.

The Program Committee (PC) received 31 submissions, from which 17 were accepted for regular presentation and publication in the proceedings volume and 6 were accepted for short presentation. The decisions were made based on single-blind peer review by at least two reviewers. Conflicts of interest within the PC were dealt with using conflict of interest declarations. Invited lectures were given by Natasha Alechina (Utrecht University, The Netherlands) and Johan van Benthem (University of Amsterdam, The Netherlands, Stanford University, USA, and Tsinghua University, China).

Organization of the workshop was supported by the grant no. 18-19162Y of the Czech Science Foundation.

The editors would like to express their sincere gratitude to all authors who submitted their work to DaLí 2020, all authors of papers published in these proceedings for their cooperation during the editorial process, and to all members of the PC and additional reviewers for their time. This volume would not have been possible without their effort and commitment.

November 2020

Manuel A. Martins
Igor Sedlár

Organization

Program Committee Chairs

Manuel A. Martins	University of Aveiro, Portugal
Igor Sedlár	Czech Academy of Sciences, Czech Republic

Program Committee

Carlos Areces	University of Cordoba, Argentina
Guillaume Aucher	IRISA, France
Alexandru Baltag	University of Amsterdam, The Netherlands
Luis Barbosa	University of Minho, Portugal
Mário Benevides	Federal University of Rio de Janeiro, Brazil
Patrick Blackburn	Roskilde University, Denmark
Thomas Bolander	Danish Technical University, Denmark
Johan van Benthem	University of Amsterdam, The Netherlands, Stanford University, USA, and Tsinghua University, China
Philippe Balbiani	IRIT, France
Marta Bílková	Czech Academy of Sciences, Czech Republic
Fredrik Dahlqvist	University College London, UK
Hans van Ditmarsch	LORIA, France
Sabine Frittella	LIFO, France
Nina Gierasimczuk	Danish Technical University, Denmark
Reiner Hähnle	Technical University Darmstadt, Germany
Rolf Hennicker	Ludwig Maximilian University of Munich, Germany
Clemens Kupke	University of Strathclyde, UK
Alexandre Madeira	University of Aveiro, Portugal
Stefan Mitsch	Carnegie Mellon University, USA
Renato Neves	University of Minho, Portugal
Aybüke Özgün	University of Amsterdam, The Netherlands
Alessandra Palmigiano	Vrije Universiteit Amsterdam, The Netherlands
Olivier Roy	Bayreuth University, Germany
Lutz Schröder	University of Erlangen-Nuremberg, Germany
Sonja Smets	University of Amsterdam, The Netherlands
Fernando Velázquez Quesada	University of Amsterdam, The Netherlands
Thomas Ågotnes	University of Bergen, Norway

Additional Reviewers

Wojciech Buszkowski
Lukas Grätz
Giuseppe Greco
Sebastian Enqvist
Xiaolong Wang
Isaque Lima
Asta Halkjær From
Fei Liang
Wesley Fussner
Ronald de Haan
Eduard Kamburjan
Vitor Machado

Contents

Expedition in the Update Universe

Guillaume Aucher(✉)

Univ Rennes, CNRS, IRISA,
263, Avenue du Général Leclerc, 35042 Rennes Cedex, France
guillaume.aucher@irisa.fr

Abstract. Dynamic epistemic logic (DEL) is a logic dealing with knowledge and belief change based on the concepts of event model and product update. The product update accounts for the way we update our knowledge and beliefs about situations when events occur. However, DEL does not account for the way we update our knowledge and beliefs about events when other events occur. Indeed, events are assumed to occur instantaneously in DEL and this idealization precludes to study this kind of update. We provide a logical analysis of updates without this assumption. It leads us to identify a graph structure for events based on their relative dependence of occurence and to introduce a generic product update. The DEL product update is a specific instance of this generic product update.

1 Introduction

It is commonly believed that only our knowledge and beliefs *about situations* can be updated, whereas our knowledge and beliefs *about events* cannot. This common belief implies that what we represent has always a manichean nature: on the one hand we have situations and on the other hand we have events, and the occurrence of events update our knowledge and beliefs about situations. The most prominent logical formalisms of knowledge representation and reasoning are all based on this approach [13,14].

As we shall see, this manichean distinction is not fine enough to account for the dynamics of knowledge and beliefs. In fact, our knowledge and beliefs *about events* can also be updated and this can be demonstrated by the following scenario. Assume that there are two barrels of wine: barrel 1 and barrel 2. Barrel 1 is being filled with wine but Ann and Bob do not know which of these barrels is being filled. Clearly, this filling of barrel 1 with wine is an event, perceived identically by Ann and Bob. Now, assume that the wine waiter privately announces to Bob that it is actually barrel 1 which is being filled. Again, clearly, this announcement is another event, perceived differently by Ann and Bob. Then, as a result of this second event, Bob knows that barrel 1 is being filled but Ann still does not know which barrel is being filled. So, Bob's knowledge and beliefs of the first event (the filling with wine) has been updated by his perception of the second event (the announcement).

M. A. Martins and I. Sedlár (Eds.): DaLí 2020, LNCS 12569, pp. 1–16, 2020.
https://doi.org/10.1007/978-3-030-65840-3_1

This scenario cannot be directly represented in DEL because only situations, and not events, can be updated by events. This stems from the assumption that events are implicitly assumed to be instantaneous in DEL, thus leading to a new situation, and our perception of an event can be updated only if this event lasts long enough, obviously. Hence, this idealization precludes the study of important logical dynamics like the one of the barrel example. However, this assumption can be perfectly removed from the DEL framework. Once we remove it, we realize that the fact that events and not only situations can be updated by other events is only the 'tip of the iceberg' and many other logical dynamics start to appear. In particular, we realize that events have an internal and rich structure based on their relative dependence of occurrence. Moreover, this structure constrains and determines the updates which are possible and a generic kind of product updates can then be identified. A contribution of this article is to provide a formal account of these logical dynamics by eliciting a series of principles. These principles will guide us for defining our formal framework.

Organization of the Article. In Sect. 2, we briefly recall DEL. In Sect. 3, we analyze the structure of events by means of various examples and we elicit a number of intuitive principles about events. We use them in Sect. 4 for motivating our formal definitions of event structures and generic product updates. We end Sect. 4 by providing an example of scenario which cannot (or hardly) be modeled in DEL. We conclude and discuss our approach in Sect. 5.

2 Dynamic Epistemic Logic

Dynamic epistemic logic (DEL) is a relatively recent non-classical logic introduced by [4]. It extends ordinary modal epistemic logic [11] by the inclusion of *event models* to describe actions/events, and a *product update* operator that defines how epistemic models are updated as the consequence of executing actions described through event models. For more details about DEL, see [3,14].

2.1 Epistemic Models

In the rest of this article, $\mathbb{A} := \{1, \ldots, N\}$ is a finite set of indices called *agents* and $\mathbb{P}_0$ is a set of propositional letters called *atomic facts* which describe static situations.

Definition 1 (Language $\mathcal{L}(\mathbb{P})$). *Let $\mathbb{P}$ be a set of propositional letters. We define the* language $\mathcal{L}(\mathbb{P})$ *inductively by the following grammar in BNF:*

$$\mathcal{L}(\mathbb{P}) : \quad \varphi \ ::= \ p \ \mid \ \neg\varphi \ \mid \ (\varphi \wedge \varphi) \ \mid \ \Box_j \varphi$$

where p ranges over $\mathbb{P}$ and j over $\mathbb{A}$. When $\mathbb{P} = \mathbb{P}_0$, $\mathcal{L}(\mathbb{P}_0)$ is called the epistemic language. *We will use the following abbreviations: $\varphi \vee \psi := \neg(\neg\varphi \wedge \neg\psi)$ and $\varphi \to \psi := \neg\varphi \vee \psi$. To save parenthesis, we use the following ranking of binding strength: $\Box_j, \neg, \wedge, \vee, \to$ (*i.e., *$\Box_j$ binds stronger than $\neg$, which binds stronger than $\wedge$,* etc.*). For example, $\Box_j \neg p \wedge q \to r \vee s$ means $((\Box_j(\neg p)) \wedge q) \to (r \vee s)$. If $E = \{\varphi_1, \ldots, \varphi_n\}$, we write $\bigwedge E := \varphi_1 \wedge \ldots \wedge \varphi_n$ and $\bigvee E := \varphi_1 \vee \ldots \vee \varphi_n$.*

A (pointed) epistemic model $(\mathcal{M}, w)$ represents how the actual world represented by w is perceived by the agents. Atomic facts are used to state properties of this actual world. Intuitively, wR_jv means that in world w agent j considers that world v might be the actual world w.

Definition 2 ($\mathbb{P}$–model and epistemic model). *Let $\mathbb{P}$ be a set of propositional letters. A* $\mathbb{P}$–model *is a tuple $\mathcal{M} = (W, R, V)$ where:*

- *W is a non-empty set;*
- *$R : \mathbb{A} \to 2^{W \times W}$ assigns an* accessibility relation *to each agent;*
- *$V : \mathbb{P} \to 2^W$ is a* valuation *which assigns a subset of W to each atomic event of $\mathbb{P}$.*

If $w, v \in W$, we write wR_jv for $(w, v) \in R(j)$, and $R_j(w)$ denotes $\{v \in W \mid wR_jv\}$. We write $w \in \mathcal{M}$ for $w \in W$ and $(\mathcal{M}, w)$ is called a pointed $\mathbb{P}$–model. *When $\mathbb{P} = \mathbb{P}_0$, $\mathcal{M}$ is called an* epistemic model *and $(\mathcal{M}, w)$ is called a* pointed epistemic model *(w often represents the actual world). The class of pointed $\mathbb{P}$–models is denoted $\mathcal{C}(\mathbb{P})$.*

As one can easily notice, a $\mathbb{P}$–model is an 'ordinary' Kripke model. Then, the epistemic language can be used to describe and state properties of epistemic models.

Definition 3 (Epistemic logic). *Let $\mathbb{P}$ be a set of propositional letters. We define the* satisfaction relation *$\models\ \subseteq \mathcal{C}(\mathbb{P}) \times \mathcal{L}(\mathbb{P})$ inductively as follows. In the truth conditions below, $(\mathcal{M}, w) \in \mathcal{C}(\mathbb{P})$ is any pointed $\mathbb{P}$–model and $\varphi, \psi \in \mathcal{L}(\mathbb{P})$.*

$$\begin{array}{lll}
\mathcal{M}, w \models p & \textit{iff} & w \in V(p) \\
\mathcal{M}, w \models \neg\psi & \textit{iff} & \textit{it is not the case that } \mathcal{M}, w \models \psi \\
\mathcal{M}, w \models \varphi \wedge \psi & \textit{iff} & \mathcal{M}, w \models \varphi \textit{ and } \mathcal{M}, w \models \psi \\
\mathcal{M}, w \models \Box_j\varphi & \textit{iff} & \textit{for all } v \in R_j(w), \textit{ we have } \mathcal{M}, v \models \varphi
\end{array}$$

We write $\mathcal{M} \models \varphi$ when $\mathcal{M}, w \models \varphi$ for all $w \in \mathcal{M}$. If $S \subseteq \mathcal{L}(\mathbb{P})$, we write $\mathcal{M}, w \models S$ ($\mathcal{M} \models S$) when for all $\varphi \in S$, $\mathcal{M}, w \models \varphi$ (resp. $\mathcal{M} \models \varphi$). The triple $(\mathcal{L}(\mathbb{P}), \mathcal{C}(\mathbb{P}), \models)$ is a logic called the epistemic logic based on $\mathbb{P}$.

The formula $\Box_j\varphi$ reads as "agent j believes φ". Its truth conditions are defined in such a way that agent j believes φ holds in a possible world when φ holds in all the worlds agent j considers possible in this possible world.

Example 1 ('Barrel' example). Assume that there are two agents Ann and Bob and that there are two barrels of wine: barrel 1 and barrel 2. So, we have $\mathbb{A} := \{A, B\}$ with A standing for Ann and B standing for Bob, and $\mathbb{P}_0 := \{p_0, q_0\}$ with p_0 standing for 'barrel 1 is full' and q_0 for 'barrel 2 is full'. The situation is such that barrel 1 is not full and barrel 2 is full, but Ann and Bob do not know which one is full. This situation is depicted in the pointed epistemic model $(\mathcal{M}_0, w_0) = (W, R, V, w_0)$ of Fig. 1 (left). We have $W = \{w_0, v_0\}$ and the circled world w represents the actual world. Possible worlds are labeled by the propositional letters of $\mathbb{P}_0$ that are true at these worlds. The accessibility relations are represented by arrows indexed by A or B: an arrow indexed by A (or B) from a world u to a world u' means that $(u, u') \in R_A$ (resp. $(u, u') \in R_B$). So, we have $\mathcal{M}_0, w_0 \models \Box_A(p_0 \vee q_0) \wedge \Box_B(p_0 \vee q_0)$: 'Ann and Bob both know that one of the two barrels is full'. The situation where both barrels are full and both Ann and Bob know it is represented in the pointed epistemic model $(\mathcal{N}_0, u_0)$ of Fig. 1 (right).

Fig. 1. Pointed epistemic models $(\mathcal{M}_0, w_0)$ and $(\mathcal{N}_0, u_0)$

2.2 Event Models

A pointed event model $(\mathcal{E}, e)$ represents how the actual event represented by e is perceived by the agents. Intuitively, $eR^\alpha_j f$ means that while the possible event represented by e is occurring, agent j considers possible that the possible event represented by f is actually occurring.

Definition 4 (Event model). *An* event model *is a tuple* $\mathcal{E} = (W^\alpha, R^\alpha, \text{PRE}, \text{POST})$ *where:*

- W^α *is a finite and non-empty set of* possible events*;*
- $R^\alpha : \mathbb{A} \to 2^{W^\alpha \times W^\alpha}$ *assigns an* accessibility relation *to each agent;*
- $\text{PRE} : W^\alpha \to \mathcal{L}(\mathbb{P}_0)$ *is a* precondition function *which assigns to each possible event a formula of* $\mathcal{L}(\mathbb{P}_0)$*;*
- $\text{POST} : W^\alpha \to (\mathbb{P}_0 \to \mathcal{L}(\mathbb{P}_0))$ *is a* postcondition function *which assigns to each possible event a function from* $\mathbb{P}_0$ *to* $\mathcal{L}(\mathbb{P}_0)$.

If $e, f \in W^\alpha$, *we write* $eR^\alpha_j f$ *for* $(e, f) \in R^\alpha(j)$, *and* $R^\alpha_j(e)$ *denotes* $\{f \in W^\alpha \mid eR^\alpha_j f\}$. *We write* $e \in \mathcal{E}$ *for* $e \in W^\alpha$, *and* $(\mathcal{E}, e)$ *is called a* pointed event model *(e often represents the actual event).*

Our definition of event models corresponds to the definition of [16]. It embeds the definition of [15] based on the notion of substitutions.

Example 2 ('barrel' example). Assume that barrel 1 is being filled with wine. Ann and Bob do not know whether it is barrel 1 or barrel 2 which is being filled. This event and its perception by the agents Ann and Bob is represented in Fig. 2 (left). We use the same notations for the possible events and the accessibility relations as in Fig. 1. The preconditions are such that $\text{PRE}(e) = \neg p_0$ (and $\text{PRE}(f) = \neg q_0$): barrel 1 (resp. barrel 2) is not full when barrel 1 (resp. barrel 2) is being filled with wine. The postconditions are such that $\text{POST}(e)(p_0) = \top$ and $\text{POST}(e)(q_0) = q_0$ (and $\text{POST}(f)(p_0) = p_0$ and $\text{POST}(f)(q_0) = \top$): when the filling of barrel 1 (resp. barrel 2) terminates, barrel 1 (resp. barrel 2) is full, the other barrel remaining in the same state.

Fig. 2. Pointed event models $(\mathcal{E}, e)$ and $(\mathcal{F}, g)$

2.3 Product Update

The DEL product update of [4] is defined as follows. This update yields a new epistemic model $\mathcal{M} \otimes \mathcal{E}$ representing how the new situation which was previously represented by $\mathcal{M}$ is perceived by the agents after the occurrence of the event represented by $\mathcal{E}$.

Definition 5 (Product update). *Let $\mathcal{M} = (W, R, V)$ be an epistemic model and let $\mathcal{E} = (W^\alpha, R_1^\alpha, \ldots, R_N^\alpha, \textsc{Pre}, \textsc{Post})$ be an event model. We define the epistemic model $\mathcal{M} \otimes \mathcal{E} = (W^\otimes, R^\otimes, V^\otimes)$ as follows (with the proviso that $W^\otimes$ is not empty): for all $p \in \mathbb{P}_0$ and all $j \in \mathbb{A}$,*

- $W^\otimes := \{(w, e) \in W \times W^\alpha \mid \mathcal{M}, w \models \textsc{Pre}(e)\}$;
- $(v, f) \in R_j^\otimes(w, e)$ *iff* $v \in R_j(w)$ *and* $f \in R_j^\alpha(e)$;
- $(w, e) \in V^\otimes(p)$ *iff* $\mathcal{M}, w \models \textsc{Post}(e)(p)$.

If $(\mathcal{M}, w)$ and $(\mathcal{E}, e)$ are pointed epistemic and event models. If $\mathcal{M}, w \models \textsc{Pre}(e)$, we define the pointed epistemic model $(\mathcal{M}, w) \otimes (\mathcal{E}, e) = (\mathcal{M} \otimes \mathcal{E}, (w, e))$.

Example 3. The product update of $(\mathcal{M}_0, w_0)$ by $(\mathcal{E}, e)$ results in the epistemic model represented on the extreme right of Fig. 3. This epistemic model is in fact bisimilar to the epistemic model $(\mathcal{N}_0, u_0)$ of Fig. 1. In this epistemic model, we have that $\mathcal{N}_0, u_0 \models (p_0 \wedge q_0) \wedge \Box_A(p_0 \wedge q_0) \wedge \Box_B(p_0 \wedge q_0)$: 'both barrels are full and Ann and Bob both know it'.

2.4 DEL

Definition 6 ([4]). *We define the* language $\mathcal{L}_{\text{DEL}}$ *inductively by the following grammar in BNF:*

$$\mathcal{L}_{\text{DEL}}: \quad \varphi \quad ::= \quad p \quad | \quad \neg\varphi \quad | \quad (\varphi \wedge \varphi) \quad | \quad \Box_j \varphi \quad | \quad [\mathcal{E}, e]\varphi$$

where p ranges over $\mathbb{P}_0$, j over $\mathbb{A}$ and $(\mathcal{E}, e)$ over $\mathcal{C}^\alpha$.

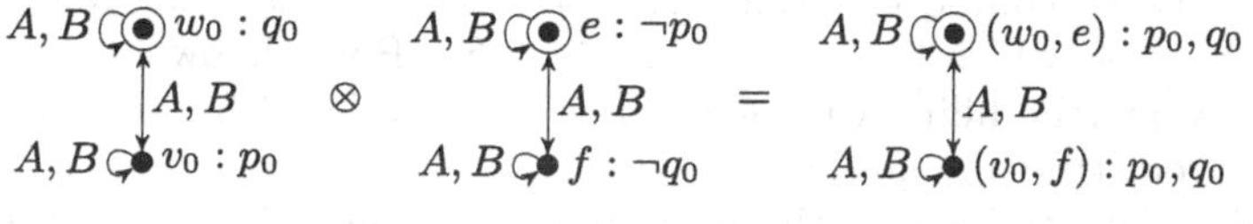

Fig. 3. Product update of $(\mathcal{M}_0, w_0)$ by $(\mathcal{E}, e)$

Intuitively, $[\mathcal{E}, e]\varphi$ reads as 'φ will hold after the occurence of the event represented by $(\mathcal{E}, e)$' and $\langle\mathcal{E}, e\rangle\varphi$ reads as 'the event represented by $(\mathcal{E}, e)$ is executable in the current situation and φ will hold after its execution'.

Definition 7 (Dynamic epistemic logic). *We define the* satisfaction relation $\models \subseteq \mathcal{C}(\mathbb{P}_0) \times \mathcal{L}_{\text{DEL}}$ *inductively as follows. In the truth conditions below,* $(\mathcal{M}, w) \in \mathcal{C}(\mathbb{P})$ *is any pointed* $\mathbb{P}$*–model and* $\varphi \in \mathcal{L}(\mathbb{P})$*.*

$$\mathcal{M}, w \models [\mathcal{E}, e]\varphi \textit{ iff if } \mathcal{M}, w \models \textsc{Pre}(e) \textit{ then } (\mathcal{M}, w) \otimes (\mathcal{E}, e) \models \varphi$$

The other truth conditions for the Boolean and modal cases are identical to those of Definition 3. The triple $(\mathcal{L}_{\text{DEL}}, \mathcal{C}(\mathbb{P}_0), \models)$ *is a logic called* dynamic epistemic logic *(DEL).*

Proposition 1 ([4])**.** *DEL is as expressive as the epistemic logic based on* $\mathbb{P}_0$*.*

3 Analyzing the Structure of Events

In this section, we discuss and analyze two examples from which we elicit a series of principles about events. These principles, whose some of them are obvious, are introduced to motivate the formal definitions of Sect. 4. They will allow us to show that the dependence graph of Definition 8 can be any directed graph, and not necessarily a tree or a bipartite graph for example.

In philosophy, the exact definition of an event is a moot topic [17] and we do not intend to take any stance in this debate. Here, we are not so much interested in the nature of events but rather in their logical and internal structure. Our examples will always be chosen so that events are indisputable events.

3.1 The 'Barrel' Example

Assume at time t_1 that there are two barrels of wine: barrel 1 and barrel 2. Barrel 2 is full and barrel 1 is being filled with wine, but Ann and Bob do not know which of these barrels is being filled. However, they know that one of them is full (and therefore cannot be filled) but they do not know which one. Clearly, this filling of barrel 1 with wine is an event, perceived identically by Ann and Bob. We consider two Scenarios from which we are going to elicit a series of principles.

Scenario 1. Assume that during barrel 1 is filled the wine waiter privately announces to Bob that it is actually barrel 1 which is being filled. Again, clearly, this announcement is another event, perceived differently by Ann and Bob. Then, as a result of this second event, Bob knows that barrel 1 is being filled but Ann still does not know which barrel is being filled. So, Bob's knowledge and beliefs of the first event (the filling with wine) has been updated by his perception of the second event (the announcement).

It is important to modify the event model while it is being executed, as opposed to modifying the Kripke model that is obtained by applying the event model because if we sever the relation between (w, e_1) and (w, e_2) after the update, this means that the event modeled by e_1 has already ended and therefore the update is on the resulting situation and not on the perception of the event. What we want to model is an update about the perception of the event itself while this event is occuring, not after. This example leads us to state the following principle:

PRINCIPLE 1: Our knowledge about ongoing events can be updated by the perception of other events.

Moreover, this announcement depends on the fact that barrel 1 is being filled and not on the precondition of this event, *i.e.* the fact that barrel 1 is not full. In this scenario, the nature of the event is "barrel 1 is being filled with wine", its precondition is "barrel 1 is not full" and its postcondition is "barrel 1 is full". This example entails that the very nature of events has to be taken into account when knowledge of events is updated by the perception of other events. This is captured by the following principle:

PRINCIPLE 2: The occurrence of events sometimes depends on the nature of other events and not on their preconditions.

Scenario 2. Assume at time t_2 that the wine waiter publicly announces that barrel 1 is not full. As a result of this announcement, at time t_3, Ann and Bob both know that barrel 2 *is* full. From this new piece of information, they can infer at time t_5 that it is barrel 1 which is being filled and not barrel 2 (since the latter is full). Hence, from this example, we can state the following principle:

PRINCIPLE 3: Our knowledge about a *situation* or an event can update our knowledge of another event while this other event is occuring.

Moreover, Ann and Bob may not make immediately the inference that it is barrel 1 which is being filled, but only as an afterthought at time t_4. Hence,

PRINCIPLE 4: After learning a new piece of information, we do not always update immediately our knowledge to take it into account.

Note that PRINCIPLE 4 is very much related to well-known problems in epistemic logic dealing with bounded rationality and logical omniscience (for more details on these problems, see [7, Chap. 9], [8, p. 157–168] or [9]). In fact, for some time, Ann and Bob may entertain the inconsistent possibility that barrel 2 is full and that at the same time it is being filled. So,

PRINCIPLE 5: We may consider possible at the same time that some event is occurring and that its precondition does not hold.

Formalizing the 'Barrel' Example. We can formalize the example by introducing the following sets of propositional letters:

- $\mathbb{P}_0 := \{p_0, q_0\}$, where p_0 stands for "Barrel 1 is full" and q_0 for "Barrel 2 is full".

- $\mathbb{P}_1 := \{p_1\}$, where p_1 stands for "The wine waiter truthfully announces that barrel 1 is not full".
- $\mathbb{P}_2 := \{p_2, q_2\}$, where p_2 stands for "Barrel 1 is being filled" and q_2 for "Barrel 2 is being filled".
- $\mathbb{P}_3 := \{p_3\}$, where p_3 stands for "The wine waiter truthfully announces that barrel 1 is being filled".

Then, we can represent the dependence between these sets of propositional letters by the graph $(\mathcal{P}, \mathcal{S})$ of Fig. 4 (where $\mathcal{P} := \{\mathbb{P}_0, \mathbb{P}_1, \mathbb{P}_2, \mathbb{P}_3\}$ and $\mathcal{S} \subseteq \mathcal{P} \times \mathcal{P}$ is defined in Fig. 4). An edge $(\mathbb{P}_i, \mathbb{P}_j) \in \mathcal{S}$ means that the events described by $\mathbb{P}_i$ depend on the events/situations described by $\mathbb{P}_j$. More precisely, an edge is set from $\mathbb{P}_i$ to $\mathbb{P}_j$ when the preconditions for the occurrence of any atomic event of $\mathbb{P}_i$ depends on the truth value of formula(s) of $\mathcal{L}(\mathbb{P}_j)$ or that the occurrence of the atomic events of $\mathbb{P}_i$ will affect in some way or another the occurrence of the atomic events of $\mathbb{P}_j$ or their knowledge and beliefs (to be more concrete, see all subsequent examples, and in particular the 'traffic lights' example).

Note that we have an arrow from $\mathbb{P}_0$ to $\mathbb{P}_2$. This arrow is motivated by the example that we used to introduce PRINCIPLE 3: our knowledge about a situation can also update our perception/knowledge about an ongoing event.

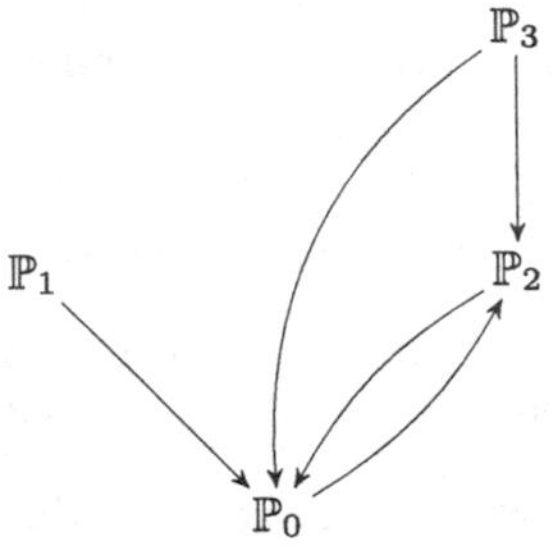

Fig. 4. Dependence graph for the 'barrel' example

For each edge $(\mathbb{P}', \mathbb{P}) \in \mathcal{S}$, we can define $(\mathbb{P}', \mathbb{P})$–preconditions functions $\text{PRE}_{\mathbb{P}',\mathbb{P}} : \mathbb{P}' \to 2^{\mathcal{L}(\mathbb{P})}$ and $(\mathbb{P}', \mathbb{P})$–postconditions functions $\text{POST}_{\mathbb{P}',\mathbb{P}} : \mathbb{P}' \to (\mathbb{P}- > 2^{\mathcal{L}(\mathbb{P})})$. The reading of $\text{PRE}_{\mathbb{P}',\mathbb{P}}(p) := \varphi$ is 'the precondition of the atomic event p is φ'; the reading of $\text{POST}_{\mathbb{P}',\mathbb{P}}(q)(p) := \varphi$ is 'p holds after the occurrence of the atomic event q if, and only if, φ held before this occurrence'.

- $\text{PRE}_{\mathbb{P}_1,\mathbb{P}_0}(p_1) := \neg p_0$: the wine waiter can truthfully announce that barrel 1 is not full only if it is indeed not full.
  $\text{POST}_{\mathbb{P}_1,\mathbb{P}_0}(p_1)(p) := p$ for all $p \in \mathbb{P}_0$: the announcement of the wine waiter does not change the actual state of the world.
- $\text{PRE}_{\mathbb{P}_2,\mathbb{P}_0}(p_2) := \neg p_0$ and $\text{PRE}_{\mathbb{P}_2,\mathbb{P}_0}(q_2) := \neg q_0$: barrel 1 and barrel 2 can be filled only if they are not full.
  $\text{POST}_{\mathbb{P}_2,\mathbb{P}_0}(p_2)(p_0) := \top$ and $\text{POST}_{\mathbb{P}_2,\mathbb{P}_0}(p_2)(q_0) := q_0$: after the filling of barrel 1, it is full, the status of barrel 2 remains unchanged.

$\text{POST}_{\mathbb{P}_2,\mathbb{P}_0}(q_2)(p_0) := p_0$ and $\text{POST}_{\mathbb{P}_2,\mathbb{P}_0}(q_2)(q_0) := \top$: after the filling of barrel 2, it is full, the status of barrel 1 remains unchanged.
- $\text{PRE}_{\mathbb{P}_3,\mathbb{P}_2}(p_3) := p_2$: the wine waiter can truthfully announce that barrel 1 is being filled only if it is indeed being filled.
  $\text{POST}_{\mathbb{P}_3,\mathbb{P}_2}(p_3)(p) := p$ for all $p \in \mathbb{P}_2$: the announcement of the wine waiter does not change the actual state of the world.
- $\text{PRE}_{\mathbb{P}_3,\mathbb{P}_0}(p_3) := \neg p_0$: the wine waiter can truthfully announce that barrel 1 is being filled only if it is not full (so that it can indeed be filled).
  $\text{POST}_{\mathbb{P}_3,\mathbb{P}_0}(p_3)(p) := p$ for all $p \in \mathbb{P}_0$: the announcement of the wine waiter does not change the actual state of the world.
- $\text{PRE}_{\mathbb{P}_0,\mathbb{P}_2}(p_0) := \neg p_2$ and $\text{PRE}_{\mathbb{P}_0,\mathbb{P}_2}(q_0) := \neg q_2$: if one of the barrels is full, it is not possible that it is being filled.
  $\text{POST}_{\mathbb{P}_0,\mathbb{P}_2}(p')(p) := p$ for all $p \in \mathbb{P}_2$ and $p' \in \mathbb{P}_0$.

Note that there is no arrows towards $\mathbb{P}_1$ nor $\mathbb{P}_3$. This is because these announcements are instantaneous, and therefore it is not possible that the agents' beliefs about them change *while* they are occurring, unlike the filling event of $\mathbb{P}_2$. This said, we could add arrows from, say, $\mathbb{P}_0$ to $\mathbb{P}_1$ if we considered that the agents can assess the truthfulness of the announcement, which can be a lie, before applying the product update on the event model, and may then revise it beforehand, based on their beliefs about the barrels.

3.2 The 'Traffic Lights' Example

We consider a naïve representation of a traffic lights system on a road. This example would be classically modeled by means of timed–automata [2], but we follow here the modeling approach of DEL to investigate what this example implies in term of representational requirements (formalized by our principles) for a DEL style modeling approach based on event models and product updates.

Assume that there are n traffic lights on a road. Each traffic light can be either 'green', 'yellow' or 'red' and only one of them at the same time. The color changes and goes from green via yellow to red and then back to green. Between any two of these states, a timer counts the time that elapses and eventually changes the traffic light from one state to the next after a certain amount of time. Then, each time the state of a light changes (from 'green' to 'yellow', from 'yellow' to 'red', or from 'red' to 'green'), the corresponding timer starts (timer 'yellow', timer 'red' or timer 'green'). Multiple timers run at the same time and they can be arbitrarily many. So,

PRINCIPLE 6: Arbitrary many events can occur at the same time and in parallel.

Moreover, we assume that there is a synchronization between the different traffic lights: when the 'red' timer of light k starts, the 'green' timer of traffic light $k+1$ ends and the traffic light $k+1$ goes to state 'yellow' (and then the yellow timer of traffic light $k+1$ starts). This synchronization is set in order to ease the flow of cars on the road so that cars do not stop at each traffic light.

When a pedestrian comes at traffic light k and presses the 'crossing button', the 'green' timer changes its timer mode and goes to another mode in order to shorten the amount of time that the pedestrian will have to wait. As a result, and in order to synchronize the other traffic lights on the road, the timer mode of traffic light $k+1$ also changes mode if its timer is currently in its usual 'green' mode, so as to keep the synchronization between the different traffic lights. (To be really precise, this change of timer mode of traffic light k should also affect the timer mode of traffic light $k-1$ in order to keep the system fully synchronized.) Hence,

PRINCIPLE 7: There can be an arbitrarily long chain of events, each event depending on the occurrence of the previous one.

Moreover, if the pedestrian presses the 'crossing button' of traffic light k when it is green, the new green timer mode will affect not only the green timer mode of traffic light $k+1$ but also the color of traffic light k (when the new green timer of traffic light k ends). Therefore,

PRINCIPLE 8: The occurrence of an event can have effects on multiple situations or types of events.

Formalizing the 'Traffic Lights' Example. We can formalize the example by introducing the following sets of propositional letters: for all $k \in \{1, \ldots, n\}$,

- $\mathbb{P}_k := \{\text{GTIMER}_k, \text{YTIMER}_k, \text{RTIMER}_k, \text{GTIMER}'_k\}$, where GTIMER_k (resp. YTIMER_k, RTIMER_k, GTIMER'_k) stands for "the green (resp. yellow, red, modified green) timer of traffic light k is running".
- $\mathbb{P}_{n+k} := \{\text{PRESS}_k\}$, where PRESS_k stands for "a pedestrian is pressing the crossing button of traffic light k while it is green".
- $\mathbb{P}_0 := \{\text{GREEN}_k, \text{YELLOW}_k, \text{RED}_k \mid k \in \{1, \ldots, n\}\}$, where GREEN_k (resp. YELLOW_k, RED_k) stands for "traffic light k is green (resp. yellow, red)".

Then, we can represent the dependence between these sets of propositional letters by the graph $(\mathcal{P}, \mathcal{S})$ of Fig. 5 (where $\mathcal{P} := \{\mathbb{P}_i \mid i \in \{0, \ldots, 2n\}\}$ and $\mathcal{S} \subseteq \mathcal{P} \times \mathcal{P}$ is defined in Fig. 5). An edge $(\mathbb{P}', \mathbb{P}) \in \mathcal{S}$ means that the events described by $\mathbb{P}'$ depend on the events/situations described by $\mathbb{P}$. We spell out the precondition and postcondition functions. We only do it for the edges of the form $(\mathbb{P}_k, \mathbb{P}_0)$ and $(\mathbb{P}_0, \mathbb{P}_k)$, where $k \in \{1, \ldots, n\}$. We define $(\mathbb{P}', \mathbb{P})$–preconditions functions $\text{PRE}_{\mathbb{P}',\mathbb{P}} : \mathbb{P}' \to 2^{\mathcal{L}(\mathbb{P})}$ and $(\mathbb{P}', \mathbb{P})$–postconditions functions $\text{POST}_{\mathbb{P}',\mathbb{P}} : \mathbb{P}' \to (\mathbb{P}- > 2^{\mathcal{L}(\mathbb{P})})$ as follows: for all $k \in \{1, \ldots, n\}$,

- $\text{PRE}_{\mathbb{P}_k,\mathbb{P}_0}(\text{GTIMER}_k) := \text{GREEN}_k$,
  $\text{PRE}_{\mathbb{P}_k,\mathbb{P}_0}(\text{YTIMER}_k) := \text{YELLOW}_k$,
  $\text{PRE}_{\mathbb{P}_k,\mathbb{P}_0}(\text{RTIMER}_k) := \text{RED}_k$,
  $\text{PRE}_{\mathbb{P}_k,\mathbb{P}_0}(\text{GTIMER}'_k) := \text{GREEN}_k$,

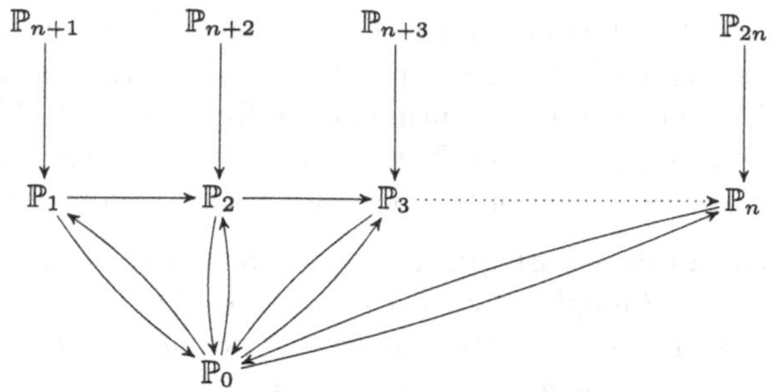

Fig. 5. Dependence graph for the 'Traffic lights' example

$$\text{POST}_{\mathbb{P}_k,\mathbb{P}_0}(x)(p_0) := \begin{cases} \top & \text{if } p_0 = y \\ \bot & \text{otherwise} \end{cases}$$
for all $(x, y) \in \{(\text{GTIMER}_k, \text{YELLOW}_k), (\text{YTIMER}_k, \text{RED}_k), (\text{RTIMER}_k, \text{GREEN}_k)\}$ and for all $p_0 \in \mathbb{P}_0$.

- $\text{PRE}_{\mathbb{P}_0,\mathbb{P}_k}(\text{GREEN}_k) := \text{GTIMER}_k \vee \text{GTIMER}'_k$,
  $\text{PRE}_{\mathbb{P}_0,\mathbb{P}_k}(\text{YELLOW}_k) := \text{YTIMER}_k$,
  $\text{PRE}_{\mathbb{P}_0,\mathbb{P}_k}(\text{RED}_k) := \text{RTIMER}_k$,
  $$\text{POST}_{\mathbb{P}_0,\mathbb{P}_k}(x)(p_k) := \begin{cases} \top & \text{if } p_k = y \\ \bot & \text{otherwise} \end{cases}$$
  for all $(x, y) \in \{(\text{GREEN}_k, \text{GTIMER}_k), (\text{YELLOW}_k, \text{YTIMER}_k), (\text{RED}_k, \text{RTIMER}_k)\}$ and for all $p_k \in \mathbb{P}_k$.

4 The Update Universe

The principles that we have elicited in Sect. 3 lead us to define what we call an *event structure* and a *generic product update*. An event structure captures the dependence relation between different types of events, based on their relative pre/postconditions, while the generic product update deals with the dynamics of knowledge and beliefs within the frame of a given event structure.

4.1 Event Structure

Because of PRINCIPLE 2, the very nature of events plays a role in the dynamics of knowledge and beliefs. Our idea is to define formally an 'event' model completely identically to the way we define an epistemic model. The propositional letters for 'event' models will determine the factual nature of events, just as they determine the factual nature of situations in epistemic models. Also, we 'externalize' the precondition and postcondition functions that were fused with the event model in DEL. So, on the one hand, we have event types represented by nodes in the dependence graph and on the other hand we have the different pre/postconditions between these events. These relative pre/postconditions determine in general the different edges of the dependence graph: an edge is set from a node $\mathbb{P}'$ to a node $\mathbb{P}$ when the preconditions for the occurrence of any atomic event of $\mathbb{P}'$ depends on the truth value of formulas of $\mathcal{L}(\mathbb{P})$ or when the occurrence of the atomic events of $\mathbb{P}'$ will affect in some way or another the occurrence of the atomic events of $\mathbb{P}$. This leads us to the following definition.

Definition 8 (Dependence graph, event structure). *A* dependence graph *is an irreflexive directed graph* $(\mathcal{P}, \mathcal{S})$ *such that* $\mathcal{P}$ *is a family of disjoint sets of propositional letters. These sets are called* event types *and their elements* atomic events or facts*. Let* $(\mathcal{P}, \mathcal{S})$ *be a dependence graph. If* $(\mathbb{P}', \mathbb{P}) \in \mathcal{S}$,

- *a* $(\mathbb{P}', \mathbb{P})$–precondition function *is a mapping* $\text{PRE}_{\mathbb{P}',\mathbb{P}} : \mathbb{P}' \to 2^{\mathcal{L}(\mathbb{P})}$*. We denote by* $\text{PRE}_{\mathbb{P}',\mathbb{P}}$ *the set of all* $(\mathbb{P}', \mathbb{P})$*–precondition functions;*
- *a* $(\mathbb{P}', \mathbb{P})$–postcondition function *is a mapping* $\text{POST}_{\mathbb{P}',\mathbb{P}} : \mathbb{P}' \to \left(\mathbb{P} \to 2^{\mathcal{L}(\mathbb{P})}\right)$*. We denote by* $\text{POST}_{\mathbb{P}',\mathbb{P}}$ *the set of all* $(\mathbb{P}', \mathbb{P})$*–postcondition functions.*

An event structure $(\mathcal{P}, \mathcal{S}, \text{PRE}, \text{POST})$ *is a dependence graph* $(\mathcal{P}, \mathcal{S})$ *together with two sets of precondition and postcondition functions* $\text{PRE} := \{\text{PRE}_{\mathbb{P}',\mathbb{P}} \in \text{PRE}_{\mathbb{P}',\mathbb{P}} \mid (\mathbb{P}', \mathbb{P}) \in \mathcal{S}\}$ *and* $\text{POST} := \{\text{POST}_{\mathbb{P}',\mathbb{P}} \in \text{POST}_{\mathbb{P}',\mathbb{P}} \mid (\mathbb{P}', \mathbb{P}) \in \mathcal{S}\}$.

A dependence graph is a directed graph without specific constraint except its irreflexivity. It seems natural to wonder whether it is in fact a specific kind of graph: a tree, a chain, a clique, ... The other principles can help us answering this question. Indeed, we learn from PRINCIPLE 1 that there can be more than three event types. In fact, PRINCIPLE 7 even indicates us that the number of nodes in the dependence graph can be arbitrary. Moreover, from PRINCIPLE 3, we infer that there can be cycles in the dependence graph and it turns out that our two examples illustrate this phenomenon. Hence, the dependence graph is in general not a tree. Finally, we learn from PRINCIPLE 8 that there can be multiple outgoing edges from a given node of the dependence graph. Therefore, it is not a chain either in general. So, from this analysis, we conclude that we cannot impose any particular constraint on the definition of this dependence graph and we state that it can be any kind of directed graph.

4.2 A Generic Product Update

In this section, $(\mathcal{P}, \mathcal{S}, \text{PRE}, \text{POST})$ is an event structure and $(\mathbb{P}', \mathbb{P}) \in \mathcal{S}$. Each edge of an event structure induces a product update. To define it, we first need to recover the pre/postconditions for each world of a $\mathbb{P}'$–model from the $(\mathbb{P}', \mathbb{P})$–pre/postcondition functions associated to an event structure.

Definition 9 ($(\mathbb{P}', \mathbb{P})$–precondition and postcondition functions of a $\mathbb{P}'$–model). *Let* $\mathcal{M}' := (W', R', V')$ *be a* $\mathbb{P}'$*–model.*

- *The* $(\mathbb{P}', \mathbb{P})$–precondition function of $\mathcal{M}'$, $\text{PRE}^{\mathcal{M}'}_{\mathbb{P}',\mathbb{P}} : W' \to 2^{\mathcal{L}(\mathbb{P})}$*, is such that for all* $w' \in W'$,

$$\text{PRE}^{\mathcal{M}'}_{\mathbb{P}',\mathbb{P}}(w') := \bigcup_{p' \in \mathbb{P}'} \{\text{PRE}_{\mathbb{P}',\mathbb{P}}(p') \mid w' \in V'(p')\}$$

– *The* $(\mathbb{P}', \mathbb{P})$–postcondition function of $\mathcal{M}'$, $\text{Post}^{\mathcal{M}'}_{\mathbb{P}',\mathbb{P}} : W' \to \left(\mathbb{P} \to 2^{\mathcal{L}(\mathbb{P})}\right)$, *is such that for all* $w' \in W'$, *all* $p \in \mathbb{P}$,

$$\text{Post}^{\mathcal{M}'}_{\mathbb{P}',\mathbb{P}}(w')(p) := \bigcup_{p' \in \mathbb{P}'} \{\text{Post}_{\mathbb{P}',\mathbb{P}}(p')(p) \mid w' \in V'(p')\} \tag{1}$$

Note that the range of our precondition and postcondition functions are *sets* of formulas, and not single formulas like for event models (see Definition 4). This generalization of the DEL framework is meaningful. Indeed, there is no particular reason that the occurrence of an event depends on a property definable in modal logic by a single formula. The precondition of an event is implicitly determined by the class of pointed epistemic models in which this event can occur.[1] This class of epistemic models is often infinite and there is no reason that it should be definable by a single formula. In general, and especially in an infinite setting, it is quite possible that an event occurs in a class of epistemic models which is only definable by an *infinite set* of formulas [6, Sect. 2.6–3.3].

Definition 10 (Generic product update). *Let* $\mathcal{M} = (W, R, V)$ *be a* $\mathbb{P}$–*model and let* $\mathcal{M}' = (W', R', V')$ *be a* $\mathbb{P}'$–*model. The* $(\mathbb{P}', \mathbb{P})$–product update of $\mathcal{M}$ and $\mathcal{M}'$ *is the* $\mathbb{P}$–*model* $\mathcal{M} \odot \mathcal{M}' = (W^{\odot}, R^{\odot}, V^{\odot})$ *defined as follows (with the proviso that* $W^{\odot}$ *is not empty): for all* $p \in \mathbb{P}_0$ *and all* $j \in \mathbb{A}$,

- $W^{\odot} := \left\{(w, w') \in W \times W' \mid \mathcal{M}, w \models \text{Pre}^{\mathcal{M}'}_{\mathbb{P}',\mathbb{P}}(w')\right\}$;
- $(v, v') \in R^{\odot}_j(w, w')$ *iff* $v \in R_j(w)$ *and* $v' \in R_j(w')$;
- $(w, w') \in V^{\odot}(p)$ *iff* $\mathcal{M}, w \models \varphi$ *for some* $\varphi \in \text{Post}^{\mathcal{M}'}_{\mathbb{P}',\mathbb{P}}(w')(p)$.

The following example is a concrete example that the standard event update cannot account for: if everything was put on the same level, we could not account for the update of events by other events and then subsequently the update of events by the situation. This example will be discussed once again in the next section.

Example 4 ('Barrel' example). In Fig. 6 we represent the generic product update that occurred in Scenario 1 of Sect. 3.1, whereby Ann and Bob's perception of the ongoing event was updated by their perception of another event (namely the fully private announcement to Bob that barrel 1 is being filled). In Fig. 7, we represent the Scenario 2 of Sect. 3.1. At each line, we represent the situations and the events that occur at the corresponding time stamp as they are defined in Scenario 2. To simplify notations, edges are represented without arrows, so the reader must assume that all arrows are bidirectional and that there are reflexive arrows indexed by all agents at each node. When there are no arrows, this means that edges are bidirectional and reflexive. We start at time t_1 with two models, one showing knowledge and beliefs concerning q_0, p_0, the other one concerning p_2 and q_2 (which actually represent events). Then an announcement is added

[1] [5] defined independently from the DEL community a variant of the DEL framework where preconditions are replaced by classes of pointed epistemic models.

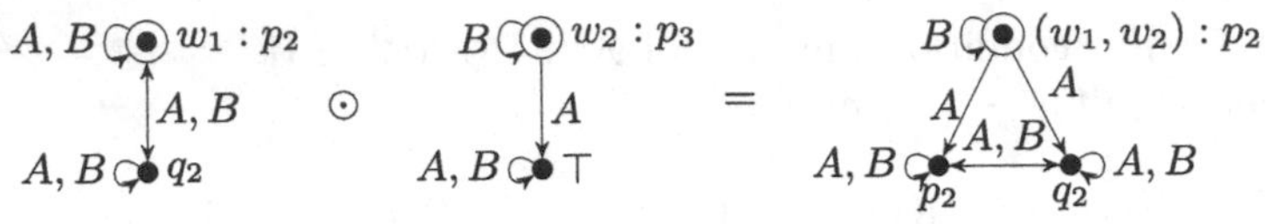

Fig. 6. Barrel example: Scenario 1

(represented by $w_1 : p_1$) such that in the system state at time t_2 we have three models. Then two of the models "amalgamate" by a product update leading to the next system state at time t_3 with two models. At time t_4, the situation updates in a backward fashion the perception of the event, leading to the final situation at time t_5.

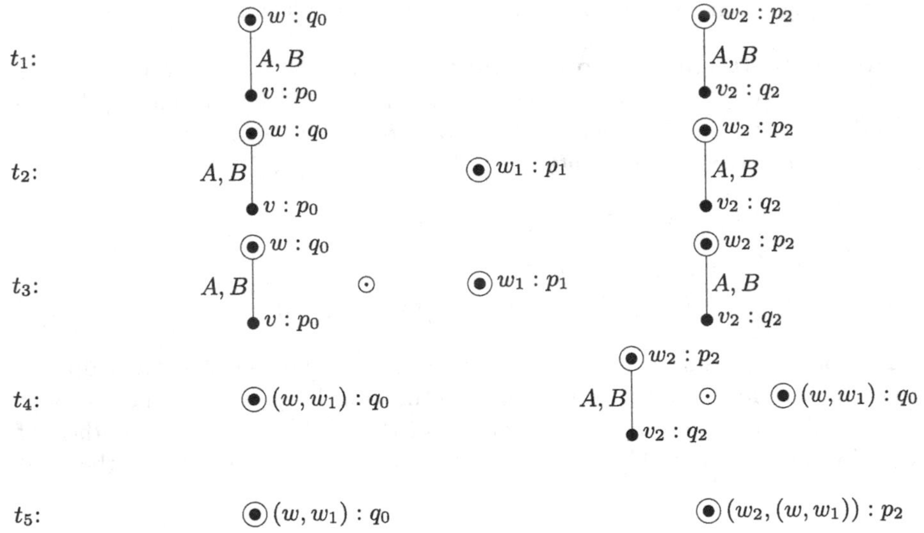

Fig. 7. Barrel example: Scenario 2

5 Discussion

One may still argue that DEL can already handle our examples. Because we deal with lasting events, what seems to be needed are propositions stating the status of events in the epistemic models, such as "(the filling of barrel 1) has ended", "(the filling of barrel 2) is still happening" together with constraints such as "(the filling of barrel 2) is still happening" $\rightarrow$ "barrel 2 is not full". Then, the standard DEL setting can also handle the updates of knowledge of events by the perception of other events. In our approach, the uncertainty of the occurrences of the events and the uncertainty of basic facts are captured in separate models initially and the updates are on each model separately. However, they can be put in the same model if the propositions about the events can be expressed in the language. In a sense, our whole framework and the event structure that we have elicited could simply be 'flattened' by adding some sort of predicates about events that would be formalized by specific propositional letters. Even if that would work out from a formal point of view, this *ad hoc* solution is very far to be satisfactory from a conceptual and modeling point of view. Indeed, the intuitive insights that we have elicited by means of our principles would then be disguised under the form of (meta-)predicates and constraints between propositional letters. These predicates in disguise and constraints would actually encode our dependence graphs and event structures.

One may then argue that our examples could be dealt with by existing extensions of DEL such as temporal DEL with past. In particular, Scenario 2 of the 'barrel' example could be reformulated in terms of uncertainty about which actual event *history* the agents are in. This kind of modeling is however subject to problems which are inherent to any state–based models such as all dynamic and process logics [10, 12]. It is hardly possible to express in these logics that "barrel 1 is being filled" and to model Scenario 1. One could express it in an *ad hoc* way by adding the propositional letter "barrel 1 is being filled" in the language, but we would need to also update its truth value when the filling ends and we would need another specific update to formalize this ending of the filling event. Likewise, Scenario 1 would be possible in temporal DEL with past only if we had that propositional letter in our model and language. In fact, we would need again to somehow encode our event structure. Moreover, the kind of modular reasoning with bounded rationality which occurs in Scenario 2 at time t_4 would not be really captured with this type of state–based and history–based logic.

One may then argue that it is not clear exactly how specific scenarios are supposed to be modeled with dependence graphs and event structures. The answer is that this problem is not inherent to our approach but applies to any modeling approach of epistemic scenarios and in particular already with epistemic and event models. There is no procedure or algorithm for constructing neither epistemic or event models nor dependence graphs or event structure. So it is a general problem of epistemic modeling. We have striven to give some guidelines that would help modelers to build their models and dependency graphs, but the general problem of how to model epistemic situations is still more at the stage of an art than a science for the moment.

We have demonstrated that the current modeling approach of DEL is not adequate enough to account for certain information dynamics. This defect should not be ignored and dismissed, even if the examples that we have chosen to illustrate it were, intentionally, extreme, borderline and different from the usual examples encountered in DEL.

Extending [1], we identified various principles that events fulfill, by means of examples. They led us to motivate the formal definitions of dependence graph and event structure. These should be the main ingredients for a genuine logical framework. Yet, before defining this general framework, the preliminary logical analysis presented so far was necessary to be carried out in order to identify the key features that needed to be formalized and included as well as highlight the weaknesses of the current application of the DEL modeling approach, based on event models and product updates.

Acknowledgments. I thank Johan van Benthem and two anonymous referees for helpful comments. I thank Sabine Frittella for a discussion which enabled to find out a defect.

References

1. Aucher, G.: BMS revisited. In: Heifetz, A. (ed.) TARK, pp. 24–33 (2009)
2. Baier, C., Katoen, J.P.: Principles of Model Checking. MIT Press, Cambridge (2008)
3. Baltag, A., Moss, L.S.: Logic for epistemic programs. Synthese **139**(2), 165–224 (2004)
4. Baltag, A., Moss, L.S., Solecki, S.: The logic of public announcements and common knowledge and private suspicions. In: Gilboa, I. (ed.) TARK, pp. 43–56. Morgan Kaufmann (1998)
5. Billot, A., Vergnaud, J.-C., Walliser, B.: Multiagent belief revision. J. Math. Econ. **59**, 47–57 (2015)
6. Blackburn, P., de Rijke, M., Venema, Y.: Modal Logic. Cambridge Tracts in Computer Science, vol. 53. Cambridge University Press, Cambridge (2001)
7. Fagin, R., Halpern, J., Moses, Y., Vardi, M.: Reasoning About Knowledge. MIT Press, Cambridge (1995)
8. Gochet, P., Gribomont, P.: Epistemic logic. In: Gabbay, D., Woods, J. (eds.) Handbook of the History of Logic. Twentieth Century Modalities, vol. 7, pp. 99–195. Elsevier, Amsterdam (2006)
9. Halpern, J.Y., Pucella, R.: Dealing with logical omniscience: expressiveness and pragmatics. Artif. Intell. **175**(1), 220–235 (2011)
10. Harel, D., Kozen, D., Tiuryn, J.: Dynamic Logic. MIT Press, Cambridge (2000)
11. Hintikka, J.: Knowledge and Belief, An Introduction to the Logic of the Two Notions. Cornell University Press, Ithaca and London (1962)
12. Pratt, V.R.: Process logic. In: Proceedings of the 6th ACM Symposium on Principles of Programming Languages, San Antonio (1979)
13. Reiter, R.: Knowledge in Action: Logical Foundations for Specifying and Implementing Dynamical Systems. MIT Press, Cambridge (2001)
14. van Benthem, J.: Logical Dynamics of Information and Interaction. Cambridge University Press, Cambridge (2011)
15. van Benthem, J., van Eijck, J., Kooi, B.: Logics of communication and change. Inf. Comput. **204**(11), 1620–1662 (2006)
16. van Ditmarsch, H., Kooi, B.: Semantic results for ontic and epistemic change. In: Bonanno, G., van der Hoek, W., Wooldridge, M. (eds.) Logic and the Foundations of Game and Decision Theory (LOFT 7). Texts in Logic and Games, vol. 3, pp. 87–117. Amsterdam University Press (2008)
17. Wilson, G., Shpall, S.: Action. In: Zalta, E.N. (ed.) The Stanford Encyclopedia of Philosophy. Summer 2012 edn. (2012)

Thinking About Causation: A Causal Language with Epistemic Operators

Fausto Barbero[1], Katrin Schulz[2], Sonja Smets[2,3],
Fernando R. Velázquez-Quesada[2](✉), and Kaibo Xie[2]

[1] University of Helsinki, Helsinki, Finland
fausto.barbero@helsinki.fi
[2] ILLC, Universiteit van Amsterdam, Amsterdam, The Netherlands
{K.Schulz,S.J.L.Smets,F.R.VelazquezQuesada,K.Xie}@uva.nl
[3] Department of Information Science and Media Studies, University of Bergen, Bergen, Norway

Abstract. In this paper we propose a formal framework for modeling the interaction of causal and (qualitative) epistemic reasoning. To this purpose, we extend the notion of a causal model [11,16,17,26] with a representation of the epistemic state of an agent. On the side of the object language, we add operators to express knowledge and the act of observing new information. We provide a sound and complete axiomatization of the logic, and discuss the relation of this framework to causal team semantics.

Keywords: Causal reasoning · Epistemic reasoning · Counterfactuals · Team semantics · Dependence

1 Introduction

In recent years a lot of effort has been put in the development of formal models of causal reasoning. A central motivation behind this is the importance of causal reasoning for AI. Making computers take into account causal information is currently one of the central challenges of AI research [9,27]. There has also been tremendous progress in this direction after the earlier groundbreaking work in [23] and [28]. Advanced formal and computational tools have been developed for modelling causal reasoning and learning causal information, with applications in many different scientific areas. In this paper we want to extend this work further. The direction we want to explore is that of developing formal models of the interaction between causal and epistemic reasoning.

Even though the standard logical approach to causal reasoning [17,18,23] can model epistemic uncertainty[1], it does not permit reasoning about the interaction between causal and epistemic reasoning in the object language. Although recently there have been proposals adding probabilistic expressions to the object language (e.g., [21]), very little has been done on combining causal and qualitative epistemic reasoning.[2]

[1] E.g., by adding a probability distribution over a causal model's exogenous variables.
[2] See [5] for an exception, though the epistemic element is not made fully explicit in the language. We will come back to this approach in Sect. 6.

M. A. Martins and I. Sedlár (Eds.): DaLí 2020, LNCS 12569, pp. 17–32, 2020.
https://doi.org/10.1007/978-3-030-65840-3_2

However, this kind of reasoning occurs frequently in our daily life, especially in connection with counterfactual thinking.

Example 1. *In front of Billie there is a button, which is connected to a circuit breaker and a sprinkler. If the circuit is closed, the sprinkler works if and only if the button is pushed. If the circuit is not closed, the sprinkler won't work, independently of the state of the button. Billie knows these causal laws. She can also see the button and the sprinkler, but she does not know the state of the circuit breaker. Suppose that at the moment the circuit is closed and the button is not pushed; as a result, the sprinkler is not working.*

We want to derive that Billie is not sure that if the button had been pushed, the sprinkler would have been working. Thus, we want to make inferences involving epistemic attitudes towards counterfactuals, which in turn explore causal dependencies. We also want to reason counterfactually about such epistemic attitudes. For instance, in the example, we also want to infer that if Billie had pushed the button and saw that the sprinkler works, then she would have known that the circuit is closed. To formalize this type of reasoning, we need a framework that combines causal reasoning with a model of epistemic attitudes.

Given the vast literature on epistemic logic, there is a lot of work that we can build on. This paper makes a start on combining the standard approach to causal reasoning [17,18,23] with tools from Dynamic Epistemic Logic (DEL; [4,8,13]). The main motivation for this choice is the dynamic character of both systems, even though this aspect will not be explored at depth here. For now we will only consider a very simple extension of the standard system of causal reasoning. But, as we will show, this basic extension already allows us to formalise some interesting concepts and formulate concrete questions for further research.

Outline. Section 2 introduces the standard approach to causal reasoning, and then Sect. 3 motivates in more detail the extension proposed here. Section 4 extends the standard causal modeling with means to express knowledge and external communication, and Sect. 5 provides a sound and complete axiomatization for the new system. Section 6 concludes the paper discussing the relationship with Causal Team Semantics [5,6]. For space reasons, some proofs have been omitted; they can be found in the paper's full version.[3]

2 The Standard Causal Modelling Approach

What we refer to as the standard logic of causal reasoning was presented on [24], extended in [16], and then further developed in, among others, [11,17,25]. This section recall briefly the most important concepts and tools. The starting point is a formal representation of causal dependencies. This is done through *causal models*, which represent the causal relationships between a finite set of variables. These variables as well as their ranges of values are given by a *signature*. Throughout this text, let $\mathcal{S} = \langle \mathcal{U}, \mathcal{V}, \mathcal{R} \rangle$ be the *finite* signature where

[3] arXiv:2010.16217 [cs.AI].

- $\mathcal{U} = \{U_1, \ldots, U_m\}$ is a finite set of *exogenous* variables (those whose value is causally independent from the value of every other variable in the system),
- $\mathcal{V} = \{V_1, \ldots, V_n\}$ is a finite set of *endogenous* variables (those whose value is completely determined by the value of other variables in the system), and
- $\mathcal{R}(X)$ is the finite non-empty range of the variable $X \in \mathcal{U} \cup \mathcal{V}$.[4]

A causal model is formally defined as follows.

Definition 1 (Causal model). *A* causal model *is a triple* $\langle \mathcal{S}, \mathcal{F}, \mathcal{A} \rangle$ *where*

- $\mathcal{S} = \langle \mathcal{U}, \mathcal{V}, \mathcal{R} \rangle$ *is the model's signature,*
- $\mathcal{F} = \{f_{V_j} \mid V_j \in \mathcal{V}\}$ *assigns, to each endogenous variable* V_j*, a map*

$$f_{V_j} : \mathcal{R}(U_1, \ldots, U_m, V_1, \ldots, V_{j-1}, V_{j+1}, \ldots, V_n) \to \mathcal{R}(V_j).$$

The map f_V *is sometimes called* V*'s* structural function, *and the set* $\mathcal{F}$ *is called a set of structural functions for* $\mathcal{V}$.

- $\mathcal{A}$ *is the* valuation *function, assigning to every* $X \in \mathcal{U} \cup \mathcal{V}$ *a value* $\mathcal{A}(X) \in \mathcal{R}(X)$*. For each endogenous variable, the valuation should* comply *with the variable's structural function. In other words, for every* $V_j \in \mathcal{V}$*, the following should hold:*

$$\mathcal{A}(V_j) = f_{V_j}\big(\mathcal{A}(U_1), \ldots, \mathcal{A}(U_m), \mathcal{A}(V_1), \ldots, \mathcal{A}(V_{j-1}), \mathcal{A}(V_{j+1}), \ldots, \mathcal{A}(V_n)\big).$$

In a causal model $\langle \mathcal{S}, \mathcal{F}, \mathcal{A} \rangle$, the functions in $\mathcal{F}$ describe the causal relationship between the variables. Using these functional dependencies, we can define what it means for a variable to directly causally affect another variable.[5]

Definition 2 (Causal dependency). *Let* $\mathcal{F}$ *be a set of structural functions for* $\mathcal{V}$*. Given an endogenous variable* $V_j \in \mathcal{V}$*, rename each other variable in* $\mathcal{S}$*, the variables* $U_1, \ldots, U_m, V_1, \ldots, V_{j-1}, V_{j+1}, \ldots, V_n$*, as* $X_1, \ldots, X_{m+n-1}$*, respectively.*

We say that, under the structural functions in $\mathcal{F}$*, an endogenous variable* $V_j \in \mathcal{V}$ *is* directly causally affected *by a variable* $X_i \in (\mathcal{U} \cup \mathcal{V}) \setminus \{V_j\}$ *(in symbols,* $X_i \hookrightarrow_{\mathcal{F}} V_j$*) if and only if there is a tuple*

$$(x_1, \ldots, x_{i-1}, x_{i+1}, \ldots, x_{m+n-1}) \in \mathcal{R}(X_1, \ldots, X_{i-1}, X_{i+1}, \ldots, X_{m+n-1})$$

and there are $x'_i \neq x''_i \in \mathcal{R}(X_i)$ *such that*

$$f_{V_j}(x_1, \ldots, x'_i, \ldots, x_{m+n-1}) \neq f_{V_j}(x_1, \ldots, x''_i, \ldots, x_{m+n-1}).$$

When $X_i \hookrightarrow_{\mathcal{F}} V_j$*, we will also say that* X_i *is a* causal parent *of* V_j*. The relation* $\hookrightarrow^{+}_{\mathcal{F}}$ *is the transitive closure of* $\hookrightarrow_{\mathcal{F}}$.

---

[4] Given $(X_1, \ldots, X_k) \in (\mathcal{U} \cup \mathcal{V})^k$, abbreviate $\mathcal{R}(X_1) \times \cdots \times \mathcal{R}(X_k)$ as $\mathcal{R}(X_1, \ldots, X_k)$.

[5] This notion of a *direct cause* is adopted from [16]; it is related to the notion of a variable having a *direct effect* on another, as discussed in [23] in the context of Causal Bayes Nets. The notions defined here differ from Halpern's notion of *affect* [17], and this affects the axiomatization: axiom HP6 (Table 1) has the same function as C6 in [17] (ensuring that the canonical model is recursive), but does so in a slightly different way.

As it is common in the literature, we restrict ourselves to causal models in which circular causal dependencies do not occur.[6]

Definition 3 (Recursive causal model). *A set of structural functions* $\mathcal{F}$ *is* recursive *if and only if* $\hookrightarrow^{+}_{\mathcal{F}}$ *is a strict partial order (i.e., an asymmetric [hence irreflexive] and transitive relation, so there are no cycles). A causal model* $\langle \mathcal{S}, \mathcal{F}, \mathcal{A} \rangle$ *is* recursive *if and only if* $\mathcal{F}$ *is recursive. In this text, a recursive causal model will be called simply a* causal model.

The most important notion of this formalisation of causal reasoning is that of an *intervention*. This notion refers to the action of changing the values of variables in the system. Before we define an intervention formally, let us first introduce the notion of assignment.

Definition 4 (Assignment). *Let* $\mathcal{S} = \langle \mathcal{U}, \mathcal{V}, \mathcal{R} \rangle$ *be a signature. An* assignment *on* $\mathcal{S}$ *is an expression* $\vec{X} = \vec{x}$ *where* $\vec{X}$ *is a tuple of different variables in* $\mathcal{U} \cup \mathcal{V}$ *(that is,* $\vec{X} = (X_1, \ldots, X_k) \in (\mathcal{U} \cup \mathcal{V})^k$ *for some* $k \in \mathbb{N}$*, with* $X_i \neq X_j$ *for* $i \neq j$*), and* $\vec{x} \in \mathcal{R}(\vec{X})$*.*

Now, an intervention that sets a variable X to the value x can be defined as an operation that maps a given model M to a new model $M_{X=x}$, which is the same except that the function determining the value of X is replaced by the constant function mapping X to x. In other words, X is cut off from all its causal dependencies and fixed to the value x.

Definition 5 (Intervention). *Let* $M = \langle \mathcal{S}, \mathcal{F}, \mathcal{A} \rangle$ *be a causal model; let* $\vec{X} = \vec{x}$ *be an assignment on* $\mathcal{S}$*. The causal model* $M_{\vec{X}=\vec{x}} = \langle \mathcal{S}, \mathcal{F}_{\vec{X}=\vec{x}}, \mathcal{A}^{\mathcal{F}}_{\vec{X}=\vec{x}} \rangle$*, resulting from an intervention setting the values of variables in* $\vec{X}$ *to* $\vec{x}$*, is such that*

- $\mathcal{F}_{\vec{X}=\vec{x}}$ *is as* $\mathcal{F}$ *except that, for each endogenous variable* X_i *in* $\vec{X}$*, the function* f_{X_i} *is replaced by a* constant *function* f'_{X_i} *that returns the value* x_i *regardless of the values of all other variables.*
- $\mathcal{A}^{\mathcal{F}}_{\vec{X}=\vec{x}}$ *is the unique valuation where* **(i)** *the value of each exogenous variable not in* $\vec{X}$ *is exactly as in* $\mathcal{A}$*,* **(ii)** *the value of each each exogenous variable* X_i *in* $\vec{X}$ *is the provided* x_i*, and* **(iii)** *the value of each endogenous variable complies with its* new *structural function (that in* $\mathcal{F}_{\vec{X}=\vec{x}}$*).*[7]

Building on the notion of intervention, we can now extend a propositional language with a new type of sentence. The expression $[\vec{X}=\vec{x}]\gamma$ should be read as the counterfactual conditional *if the variables in* $\vec{X}$ *were set to the values* $\vec{x}$*, respectively, then* γ *would be the case.*

---

[6] The reason behind this restriction is that only acyclic relations are thought to have a causal interpretation (see [29] for an argument). The counterfactuals satisfy different logical laws if cyclic dependencies are allowed (see [17]).

[7] Note that, since $\mathcal{F}$ is recursive, the valuation $\mathcal{A}^{\mathcal{F}}_{\vec{X}=\vec{x}}$ is uniquely determined. First, the value of every exogenous variable U is uniquely determined, either from $\vec{x}$ (if U occurs in $\vec{X}$) or else from $\mathcal{A}$ (if U does not occur in $\vec{X}$). Second, the value of every endogenous variable V is also uniquely determined, either from $\vec{x}$ (if V occurs in $\vec{X}$, as V's new structural function is a constant) or else from the (recall: recursive) structural functions in $\mathcal{F}_{\vec{X}=\vec{x}}$ (if V does not occur in $\vec{X}$).

Definition 6. *Formulas ϕ of the language $\mathcal{L}_C$ based on the signature $\mathcal{S}$ are given by*

$$\gamma ::= Z = z \mid \neg\gamma \mid \gamma \wedge \gamma \qquad \text{for } Z \in \mathcal{U} \cup \mathcal{V} \text{ and } z \in \mathcal{R}(Z)$$
$$\phi ::= Z = z \mid \neg\phi \mid \phi \wedge \phi \mid [\vec{X}=\vec{x}]\gamma \qquad \text{for } \vec{X}=\vec{x} \text{ an assignment on } \mathcal{S}$$

The language makes free use of Boolean operators, but it forbids the nesting of intervention operators $[\vec{X}=\vec{x}]$ (see [11] for a way to extend the system with nested interventions). Formulas of $\mathcal{L}_C$ are evaluated in causal models $\langle \mathcal{S}, \mathcal{F}, \mathcal{A} \rangle$. The semantic interpretation for Boolean operators is the usual; for the rest,

$$\langle \mathcal{S}, \mathcal{F}, \mathcal{A} \rangle \models Z{=}z \quad \text{iff} \quad \mathcal{A}(Z) = z$$
$$\langle \mathcal{S}, \mathcal{F}, \mathcal{A} \rangle \models [\vec{X}=\vec{x}]\gamma \quad \text{iff} \quad \langle \mathcal{S}, \mathcal{F}_{\vec{X}=\vec{x}}, \mathcal{A}^{\mathcal{F}}_{\vec{X}=\vec{x}} \rangle \models \gamma$$

3 Limitations of the Standard System

The notion of a causal model contains an incredible amount of extra information compared to classical models. Not only does it tell us which variables depend causally on which other variables, but it also determines the exact character of this dependence. On the side of the language this wealth of information is then explored in terms of counterfactual conditionals using the concept of an intervention. This is where the actual causal reasoning happens. The standard logic of causal reasoning is in fact a logic of counterfactual reasoning. This is no accident: Judea Pearl, founder of the approach to causal reasoning introduced above, sees both concepts as intimately related. He argues that only when an agent can evaluate counterfactual conditionals does she fully engage with causal reasoning [26, 27]. Counterfactual reasoning *is* the highest level of causal reasoning – a level that even the most advanced AI technology doesn't reach.[8]

Still, the basic causal framework has some limitations. An important one is that causal (or counterfactual) reasoning does not stand on its own: it does interact with other forms of reasoning. For instance, and as we illustrated in the introduction, counterfactual reasoning also considers the effect interventions have on the epistemic state of (observing) agents. We can reason that *If Peter had pushed the button, he would have known that his flashlight is broken*, which involves thinking about Peter's epistemic state after observing a causal intervention. This type of reasoning allows us to plan our actions (try out a flashlight before we take it for a night walk), and also influences our interaction with other agents (if you want Peter to come back from his walk, you should tell him to test his flashlight before he leaves). Therefore, a full account of the logic of causal reasoning needs to model its interaction with epistemic reasoning as well. The next section takes a first step in this direction: it adds a representation of the epistemic state of an agent to the model, extending the language with expressions that can talk about knowledge and knowledge-update in the context of causal reasoning.

[8] The other two levels that Pearl distinguishes are the level of association, which is based on observation, and the level of intervention, which is based on doing. Modern AI technology is for him still at the first level: association. Counterfactual reasoning is not possible without a true understanding of *why* things happen – in our terminology, it is not possible without knowing the causal relationships as determined by $\mathcal{F}$.

There is another perspective from which such an epistemic extension of the standard framework can be motivated. In recent years there has been growing interest in the logic of dependence/determinacy. For instance, the IF logic of [22] expresses dependence by decorations of the quantifiers. Then, [30] and [2] use a primitive expression indicating that the value of one variable depends on that of another. In all these cases, the discussed notion of dependence/determinacy relies on considering a multiplicity of valuations in the model: the variable Y depends on (it is determined by) the variables $X_1, \ldots, X_n$ when, in all valuations that are being considered, fixing the value of the latter also fixes the value of the former. This gives rise to the question of how the notion of causal dependence modelled by the just introduced framework interacts with the notions of dependence/determinacy modelled by these alternative frameworks, and how causal dependence fits into a general picture of reasoning with and about dependencies. Interestingly, extending the standard causal reasoning approach with basic epistemic notions gives us another way to express the same notion of dependence as studied in the works just cited. This, then, allows us to compare different notions of dependency within one logical system. We will come back to this connection in Sect. 6.

4 Epistemic Causal Models

The first step towards a framework that combines causal with epistemic reasoning is adding a representation of the epistemic state of an agent to the causal model. This is done by adding a set of valuations $\mathcal{T}$, representing the alternatives the agent considers possible.

Definition 7 (Epistemic causal model). *An* epistemic (note: recursive) causal model *is a tuple $\langle \mathcal{S}, \mathcal{F}, \mathcal{T} \rangle$ where $\mathcal{S} = \langle \mathcal{U}, \mathcal{V}, \mathcal{R} \rangle$ is a signature, $\mathcal{F}$ is a (note: recursive) set of structural functions for $\mathcal{V}$, and $\mathcal{T}$ is a non-empty set of valuation functions for $\mathcal{U} \cup \mathcal{V}$, each one of them complying with $\mathcal{F}$.*

Example 1 can now be modelled as follows. We define an epistemic causal model $\mathrm{E} = \langle \mathcal{S}, \mathcal{F}, \mathcal{T} \rangle$ whose signature $\mathcal{S}$ has three variables: the exogenous B for the button and C for the circuit breaker, and the endogenous S for the sprinkler. All three variables can take two values, 0 or 1. The set of functions $\mathcal{F}$ contains only one element: the function mapping S to 1 iff both B and C also have value 1. Because the agent can observe the value of the variables B and S, the set $\mathcal{T}$ contains the assignment $\mathcal{A}_1$ that maps C to 0, B to 0 and S to 0, and the assignment $\mathcal{A}_2$ that maps C to 1, B to 0 and S to 0. Note how $\mathcal{T}$ cannot contain the assignment $C = 1$, $B = 1$ and $S = 0$, for instance, because this assignment does not comply with the causal law in $\mathcal{F}$. This observation highlights an important feature of this notion of epistemic model: it cannot model uncertainty about the causal dependencies. Investigating the consequences of lifting this restriction is left for future research. The next step is to extend the notion of an intervention to epistemic causal models.

Definition 8 (Intervention). *Let $\mathrm{E} = \langle \mathcal{S}, \mathcal{F}, \mathcal{T} \rangle$ be an epistemic causal model; let $\vec{X} = \vec{x}$ be an assignment on $\mathcal{S}$. The epistemic causal model $\mathrm{E}_{\vec{X}=\vec{x}} = \langle \mathcal{S}, \mathcal{F}_{\vec{X}=\vec{x}}, \mathcal{T}^{\mathcal{F}}_{\vec{X}=\vec{x}} \rangle$, resulting from an intervention setting the values of variables in $\vec{X}$ to $\vec{x}$, is such that*

- $\mathcal{F}_{\vec{X}=\vec{x}}$ *is defined from* $\mathcal{F}$ *just as in Definition 5,*
- $\mathcal{T}^{\mathcal{F}}_{\vec{X}=\vec{x}} := \{\mathcal{A}'^{\mathcal{F}}_{\vec{X}=\vec{x}} \mid \mathcal{A}' \in \mathcal{T}\}$ *(see Definition 5).*

Note how $\langle \mathcal{S}, \mathcal{F}_{\vec{X}=\vec{x}}, \mathcal{T}^{\mathcal{F}}_{\vec{X}=\vec{x}} \rangle$ *is indeed an epistemic causal model, as* $\mathcal{F}_{\vec{X}=\vec{x}}$ *is recursive and all valuations in* $\mathcal{T}^{\mathcal{F}}_{\vec{X}=\vec{x}}$ *comply with it.*

In the just introduced model E for Example 1, we can now calculate the effects of considering the intervention that sets $B = 1$. According to Definition 8, an intervention on an epistemic causal model amounts to intervening on each of the assignments contained in the epistemic state. Thus, for our concrete example, we need to calculate the effects of an intervention with $B = 1$ on the assignments $\mathcal{A}_1$ and $\mathcal{A}_2$ that make up the epistemic state $\mathcal{T}$. The new epistemic state $\mathcal{T}^{\mathcal{F}}_{B=1}$ will now contain the assignment $\mathcal{A}^{\mathcal{F}}_{1,B=1}$ that maps C to 0, B to 1 and S to 0 and the assignment $\mathcal{A}^{\mathcal{F}}_{2,B=1}$ that maps C to 1, B to 1 and S to 1. Thus, the consequences of the intervention are calculated for all epistemic possibilities the agent considers. In other words, Definition 8 assumes that the agent has full epistemic access to the effect of the intervention on the model. In particular, she knows that the intervention takes place (in the counterfactual scenario considered). This makes a lot of sense if you think of the agent whose epistemic state is modelled as the one engaging in the counterfactual thinking. It is less plausible in connection to counterfactual thinking about the knowledge states of other agents. But this is something that we can leave for now, as we will not consider epistemic causal models for multiple agents in this paper. Based on these changes on the semantic side, we can now extend the object language with expressions that talk about the epistemic state of the agent. More specifically, we add the operator K for knowledge and "!" for information update. In other words, we understand "!" as expressing the action of observing or receiving information.

Definition 9. *Formulas* ϕ *of the language* $\mathcal{L}_{PAKC}$ *based on* $\mathcal{S}$ *are given by*

$$\gamma ::= Z = z \mid \neg\gamma \mid \gamma \wedge \gamma \mid K\gamma \mid [\gamma!]\gamma \qquad \text{for } Z \in \mathcal{U} \cup \mathcal{V} \text{ and } z \in \mathcal{R}(Z)$$
$$\phi ::= Z = z \mid \neg\phi \mid \phi \wedge \phi \mid K\phi \mid [\phi!]\phi \mid [\vec{X}=\vec{x}]\gamma \quad \text{for } \vec{X}=\vec{x} \text{ an assignment on } \mathcal{S}$$

Other Boolean operators ($\vee, \rightarrow, \leftrightarrow$) can be defined as usual. Note how, although the language makes free use of Boolean, epistemic and announcement operators (K and $[\phi!]$, for the latter two), nested intervention is again not allowed.[9] Note also how the tuple vector $\vec{X}$ can be empty, in which case $[\vec{X}=\vec{x}]\gamma$ becomes γ. The semantics for this extended language is straightforward.

Definition 10. *Formulas of* $\mathcal{L}_{PAKC}$ *are evaluated in a pairs* $(\mathrm{E}, \mathcal{A})$ *with* $\mathrm{E} = \langle \mathcal{S}, \mathcal{F}, \mathcal{T} \rangle$ *an epistemic causal model and* $\mathcal{A} \in \mathcal{T}$. *The semantic interpretation for Boolean operators is the usual; for the rest,*

$$\begin{array}{lll} (\mathrm{E}, \mathcal{A}) \models Z{=}z & \textit{iff} & \mathcal{A}(Z) = z \\ (\mathrm{E}, \mathcal{A}) \models K\phi & \textit{iff} & (\mathrm{E}, \mathcal{A}') \models \phi \textit{ for every } \mathcal{A}' \in \mathcal{T} \\ (\mathrm{E}, \mathcal{A}) \models [\psi!]\phi & \textit{iff} & (\mathrm{E}, \mathcal{A}) \models \psi \textit{ implies } (\mathrm{E}^{\psi}, \mathcal{A}) \models \phi \\ (\mathrm{E}, \mathcal{A}) \models [\vec{X}=\vec{x}]\gamma & \textit{iff} & (\mathrm{E}_{\vec{X}=\vec{x}}, \mathcal{A}^{\mathcal{F}}_{\vec{X}=\vec{x}}) \models \gamma \end{array}$$

[9] However, notice that the semantics already allows for nested occurrences of all dynamic operators. We will extend the proofs of sound- and completeness to the unrestricted language in the future.

with $E^{\psi} = \langle \mathcal{S}, \mathcal{F}, \mathcal{T}^{\psi} \rangle$ *such that* $\mathcal{T}^{\psi} := \{\mathcal{A}' \in \mathcal{T} \mid (E, \mathcal{A}') \models \psi\}$. *Note how* E^{ψ} *is an epistemic causal model:* $\mathcal{F}$ *is recursive, and all valuations in* $\mathcal{T}^{\psi}$ *comply with it.*

Let us illustrate this definition with the help of the epistemic model E we introduced for Example 1. In order to evaluate a concrete formula with respect to this model we need to select, next to E, an assignment representing the actual world. In the example this is assignment $\mathcal{A}_2$: in the actual world, the circuit breaker is closed, but because the button has not been pushed, the sprinkler is not working. We can calculate that the counterfactual $[B = 1]S = 1$ comes out as true given E and $\mathcal{A}_2$, just as in the non-epistemic approach discussed in Sect. 2. But because we now also have a representation of the epistemic state of some agent, we can additionally consider epistemic attitudes the agent has towards this counterfactual. For instance, we can check that $K([B = 1]S = 1)$ is not true given E and $\mathcal{A}_2$. For the sentence to be true, the formula $[B = 1]S = 1$ needs to be true over both $(E, \mathcal{A}_1)$ and $(E, \mathcal{A}_2)$, because $\mathcal{A}_1$ and $\mathcal{A}_2$ are the two elements of $\mathcal{T}$. Thus, we need both $(E_{B=1}, \mathcal{A}^{\mathcal{F}}_{1,B=1}) \models S = 1$ and $(E_{B=1}, \mathcal{A}^{\mathcal{F}}_{2,B=1}) \models S = 1$. We already calculated $\mathcal{T}_{B=1}$ above: $\mathcal{T}_{B=1} = \{\mathcal{A}^{\mathcal{F}}_{1,B=1}, \mathcal{A}^{\mathcal{F}}_{2,B=1}\}$. But the content of $\mathcal{T}_{B=1}$ does not matter for the truth of the consequent $S = 1$ of the counterfactual that we are considering here, since this consequent does not contain epistemic operators. However, while in $\mathcal{A}^{\mathcal{F}}_{1,B=1}$ the sprinkler is still off, in $\mathcal{A}^{\mathcal{F}}_{2,B=1}$ it is on. This means that $(E_{B=1}, \mathcal{A}^{\mathcal{F}}_{1,B=1}) \not\models S = 1$, while $(E_{B=1}, \mathcal{A}^{\mathcal{F}}_{2,B=1}) \models S = 1$. Thus, the agent cannot predict the outcome of the intervention, just as intended in this case.

Finally, we define an operator $\rightsquigarrow$ in terms of the existing vocabulary as a way to express causal dependency in the object language.

Definition 11. *Take* X *and* Z *in* $\mathcal{U} \cup \mathcal{V}$. *The formula* $X \rightsquigarrow Z$ *is defined as*

$$\bigvee_{\substack{\vec{w} \in \mathcal{R}((\mathcal{U} \cup \mathcal{V}) \setminus \{X, Z\}),\\ \{x_1, x_2\} \subseteq \mathcal{R}(X),\, x_1 \neq x_2,\\ \{z_1, z_2\} \subseteq \mathcal{R}(Z),\, z_1 \neq z_2}} [\vec{W}{=}\vec{w}, X{=}x_1]Z = z_1 \;\wedge\; [\vec{W}{=}\vec{w}, X{=}x_2]Z = z_2,$$

A formula $X \rightsquigarrow Z$ should be read as *"X has a direct causal effect on Z"*. It holds when there is a vector $\vec{w}$ of values for variables in $\mathcal{R}(\mathcal{U} \cup \mathcal{V} \setminus \{X, V\})$ and two different values x_1, x_2 for X that produce two different values z_1, z_2 for Z (cf. [17]). When $Z \in \mathcal{V}$, it is clear that $\rightsquigarrow$ is the syntactic counterpart of the relation "$\hookrightarrow$" of Definition 2.

5 Axiomatization

The axiom system L_{PAKC} is presented in Table 1. The *intervention* axioms, HP1-HP6, RH1 and RH2, are the standard axiomatization for the intervention operator over recursive causal models, with EX an additional axiom indicating that an exogenous variable is immune to interventions to any other variables. Then, the *epistemic* part contains the standard modal S5 axiomatization for truthful knowledge with positive and negative introspection.

Axiom CM indicates that what the agent will know after an intervention ($[\vec{X}=\vec{x}]K\phi$) is exactly what she knows now about the effects of the intervention ($K[\vec{X}=\vec{x}]\phi$). Although maybe novel in the literature on causal models, the axiom is simply an instance of the more general DEL pattern of interaction between knowledge and a deterministic action without precondition. Axiom KR states that the agent knows how each endogenous variable $Y \in \mathcal{V}$ is affected when *all other variables* are intervened. Finally, axioms RP1-RP4 and rule RE in the *announcement* part are a *reduction-based* axiomatisation for public announcements in the DEL style. Here, axioms RP4 and RP1 are the most important. The first, RP4, is the well-known reduction axiom for announcement and knowledge, stating that knowing ϕ after an announcement of ψ is equivalent to knowing, conditionally on ψ, that the announcement of ψ would make ϕ true.[10] The second, RP1, establishes the reduction for 'atoms' of the form $[\vec{X}=\vec{x}]Z = z$; when $\vec{X}$ is not empty, it states that a public announcement does not change the causal rules in the model.

Table 1. Axiom system L_{PAKC}

Propositional:	
P $\vdash \phi$ for ϕ an instance of a tautology	MP From $\phi \to \psi$ and ϕ derive ψ
Intervention:	
HP1 $\vdash [\vec{X}=\vec{x}]Z = z \to \neg[\vec{X}=\vec{x}]Z = z'$ for $z \neq z' \in \mathcal{R}(Z)$	
HP2 $\vdash \bigvee_{z \in \mathcal{R}(Z)} [\vec{X}=\vec{x}]Z = z$	
HP3 $\vdash \left([\vec{X}=\vec{x}]Z = z \wedge [\vec{X}=\vec{x}]W = w\right) \to [\vec{X}=\vec{x}, Z{=}z]W = w$	
HP4 $\vdash [\vec{X}=\vec{x}, Z{=}z]Z = z$	
HP5 $\vdash \left([\vec{X}=\vec{x}, Z{=}z]W = w \wedge [\vec{X}=\vec{x}, W{=}w]Z = z\right) \to [\vec{X}=\vec{x}]W = w$ for $W \neq Z$	
HP6 $\vdash (Z_0 \rightsquigarrow Z_1 \wedge \cdots \wedge Z_{k-1} \rightsquigarrow Z_k) \to \neg(Z_k \rightsquigarrow Z_0)$	
RH1 $\vdash [\vec{X}=\vec{x}](\gamma_1 \wedge \gamma_2) \leftrightarrow ([\vec{X}=\vec{x}]\gamma_1 \wedge [\vec{X}=\vec{x}]\gamma_2)$	
RH2 $\vdash [\vec{X}=\vec{x}]\neg\gamma \leftrightarrow \neg[\vec{X}=\vec{x}]\gamma$	
EX $\vdash U = u \leftrightarrow [\vec{X}=\vec{x}]U = u$ for $U \in \mathcal{U}$ with $U \notin \vec{X}$	
Epistemic:	
K $\vdash K(\phi \to \psi) \to (K\phi \to K\psi)$	T $\vdash K\phi \to \phi$
N From $\vdash \phi$ derive $\vdash K\phi$	4 $\vdash K\phi \to KK\phi$
	5 $\vdash \neg K\phi \to K\neg K\phi$
Epistemic+Intervention:	
CM $\vdash [\vec{X}=\vec{x}]K\gamma \leftrightarrow K[\vec{X}=\vec{x}]\gamma$	
KR $\vdash [\vec{X}=\vec{x}]Y{=}y \to K[\vec{X}=\vec{x}]Y{=}y$ for $Y \in \mathcal{V}$ and $\vec{X} = (\mathcal{U} \cup \mathcal{V}) \setminus \{Y\}$	
Announcement:	
RP1 $\vdash [\psi!][\vec{X}=\vec{x}]Z = z \leftrightarrow (\psi \to [\vec{X}=\vec{x}]Z = z)$	RP3 $\vdash [\psi!](\phi \wedge \chi) \leftrightarrow ([\psi!]\phi \wedge [\psi!]\chi)$
RP2 $\vdash [\psi!]\neg\phi \leftrightarrow (\psi \to \neg[\psi!]\phi)$	RP4 $\vdash [\psi!]K\phi \leftrightarrow (\psi \to K(\psi \to [\psi!]\phi))$
RE If $\vdash \psi_1 \leftrightarrow \psi_2$ and $\phi[\psi_2/\psi_1] \in \mathcal{L}_{PAKC}$, then $\vdash \phi \leftrightarrow \phi[\psi_2/\psi_1]$, where $\phi[\psi_2/\psi_1]$ is a formula obtained by replacing one or more non-announcement occurrences of ψ_1 in ϕ with ψ_2.[a]	

A non-announcement occurrence of ψ in ϕ is an occurrence of ψ in ϕ where ψ is not inside the *brackets* of an announcement operator.

The axiom system L_{PAKC} is sound and complete for $\mathcal{L}_{PAKC}$ in epistemic causal models. Here is the argument for soundness.

Theorem 1. *The axiom system L_{PAKC} is sound for $\mathcal{L}_{PAKC}$ in epistemic causal models.*

[10] Note how the announcement of ψ is a deterministic action *with precondition* ψ. Hence the similarities and differences between RP4 and CM.

Proof. For the soundness of HP1-HP6, RH1 and RH2 on causal models (enough for soundness on epistemic causal models, as evaluating the formulas does not require a change in valuation), see [17]. For the soundness of K, N, T, 4, and 5 on relational structures with an equivalence relation (equivalent to having a simple set of epistemic alternatives, as epistemic causal models have), see [10, 15]. For the soundness of RP1-RP4 when $[\psi!]$ describes the effect of a deterministic domain-reducing model operation, see [31].

For axioms EX, CM and KR, take any $(\langle \mathcal{S}, \mathcal{F}, \mathcal{T}\rangle, \mathcal{A})$. For EX note how, for any $\vec{X} = \vec{x}$, the valuations $\mathcal{A}$ and $\mathcal{A}^{\mathcal{F}}_{\vec{X}=\vec{x}}$ assign the same value to *exogenous* variables not occurring in $\vec{X}$ (Definition 5). For CM, note how ***(i)*** $K[\vec{X}=\vec{x}]\phi$ holds at $(\langle \mathcal{S}, \mathcal{F}, \mathcal{T}\rangle, \mathcal{A})$ iff ϕ holds at $(\langle \mathcal{S}, \mathcal{F}_{\vec{X}=\vec{x}}, \mathcal{T}^{\mathcal{F}}_{\vec{X}=\vec{x}}\rangle, \mathcal{A}'^{\mathcal{F}}_{\vec{X}=\vec{x}})$ for every $\mathcal{A}' \in \mathcal{T}$, and ***(ii)*** $[\vec{X}=\vec{x}]K\phi$ holds at $(\langle \mathcal{S}, \mathcal{F}, \mathcal{T}\rangle, \mathcal{A})$ iff ϕ holds at $(\langle \mathcal{S}, \mathcal{F}_{\vec{X}=\vec{x}}, \mathcal{T}^{\mathcal{F}}_{\vec{X}=\vec{x}}\rangle, (\mathcal{A}^{\mathcal{F}}_{\vec{X}=\vec{x}})')$ for every $(\mathcal{A}^{\mathcal{F}}_{\vec{X}=\vec{x}})' \in \mathcal{T}^{\mathcal{F}}_{\vec{X}=\vec{x}}$. Then it is enough to notice how, by Definition 8, the set of relevant valuations for the second, $\mathcal{T}^{\mathcal{F}}_{\vec{X}=\vec{x}}$, is exactly the set of relevant valuations for the first, $\{\mathcal{A}'^{\mathcal{F}}_{\vec{X}=\vec{x}} \mid \mathcal{A}' \in \mathcal{T}\}$. For KR, simply recall that all valuations in $\mathcal{T}$ comply with the same structural functions. Finally, soundness of RE follows from two facts: the truth-value of every formula depends on the truth-value of its subformulas, and model operations (intervention and announcements) produce epistemic causal models. Thus, substituting a non-announcement subformula for a formula that is semantically equivalent in the given class of structures does not affect the final result. □

The argument for completeness uses two steps. ***(i)*** First, using the reduction axioms technique, we show that L_{PAKC} allow us to translate any formula in $\mathcal{L}_{PAKC}$ into a logically equivalent one without public announcements.[11] ***(ii)*** Then, relying on the canonical model construction for both causal models [17] and epistemic models [15, Chap. 3], we argue that L_{PAKC} is complete for the language without public announcements.

Theorem 2. *The axiom system* L_{PAKC} *is complete for* $\mathcal{L}_{PAKC}$ *in epistemic causal models.*

6 Discussion

In this section we will compare our proposal to the Causal Team Semantics developed in [5–7]. Causal Team Semantics was proposed with the intention of supporting languages that discuss both accidental and causal dependencies. This is a topic that has gained quite some interest in recent years (see, e.g., [12, 21]). Causal Team Semantics was developed along the lines of a non-modal tradition of logics of dependence and independence (e.g. [22, 30]) by extending the so-called *team semantics* [20] with elements taken from causal inference. Even though the focus there is not on combining

[11] Readers familiar with DEL might have noticed that L_{PAKC} does not have a reduction axiom for nested announcements $[\phi_1!][\phi_2!]\phi$. There are (at least) two strategies for dealing with such formulas. The first follows an 'outside-in' approach, reducing two announcements in a row into a single one. This requires an axiom for nested announcements. The second follows an 'inside-out' strategy, applying the reduction over the innermost announcement operator in the formula until the operator disappears, and then proceeding to the next. For this, the rule of substitution of equivalents (our rule RE) is enough [31, Theorem 11].

causal with epistemic reasoning, this framework bears many similarities to the one we are using, which is why we will discuss it here in detail. Furthermore, this also allows us to say a bit more on the topic of dependence from the perspective of our proposal.

Let us quickly introduce the central notions of Causal Team Semantics to facilitate a comparison of the two frameworks. A causal team[12] is a tuple $T = \langle \mathcal{T}, \mathcal{F} \rangle$ where $\mathcal{F}$ is defined similarly as in our paper[13] and $\mathcal{T}$ is a possibly empty set of valuations that comply with $\mathcal{F}$. Papers on Causal Team Semantics consider a variety of languages. The focus here is the one we shall call $\mathcal{L}_{COD}$, which is similar to the standard causal language (thus allowing to express various notions of causal dependence in terms of counterfactuals) except for the additional *dependence atoms* "$=(X_1, ..., X_n; Y)$", which expresses (accidental) dependency of the variable Y on the variables X_1 to X_n. A sentence $=(X_1, ..., X_n; Y)$ is interpreted as the claim that any two states s and s' that agree on the valuation of the variables $X_1, ..., X_n$ also have to agree on the value they assign to Y. Let us describe the syntax of $\mathcal{L}_{COD}$ in more detail. The signatures used in [5] are pairs of the form $\langle Dom, Ran \rangle$, where *Dom* is a set of variables (*not* encoding the distinction between exogenous and endogenous variables) and *Ran* is defined analogously as the $\mathcal{R}$ used in this paper. For any such fixed signature $\mathcal{S}$, the language $\mathcal{L}_{COD}$ is defined as

$$\alpha ::= Z{=}z \mid Z{\neq}z \mid \alpha \wedge \alpha \mid \alpha \vee \alpha \mid \alpha \supset \alpha \mid \vec{X}{=}\vec{x} \;\Box\!\!\rightarrow \alpha$$

$$\phi ::= Z{=}z \mid Z{\neq}z \mid {=}(\vec{X}; Y) \mid \phi \wedge \phi \mid \phi \vee \phi \mid \alpha \supset \phi \mid \vec{X}{=}\vec{x} \;\Box\!\!\rightarrow \phi$$

for $Z, Y, \vec{X} \in Dom$ and $z \in Ran(Z)$; and where the expression $\vec{X} = \vec{x}$ is an abbreviation for a conjunction of the form $X_1 = x_1 \wedge \cdots \wedge X_n = x_n$.[14] Below the complete semantics of $\mathcal{L}_{COD}$ is given, using the notation of this manuscript. Notice that formulas are evaluated on a causal team *globally*: no valuation in $\mathcal{T}$ is isolated as being 'the actual world'. At the atomic level, this is done by means of a *universal* quantification. Indeed, while formulas of the form $Z = z$ and $Z{\neq}z$ indicate, semantically, that Z's value is (different from) z in *all valuations* in $\mathcal{T}$, a dependence atom $=(X_1, ..., X_n; Y)$ indicates, as stated, that *all pairs* of valuations agreeing on the values of all X_i also agree on the value of Y. To keep the global perspective through the rest of the formulas, the interpretation of some connectives ($\vee$ and $\supset$) differs from the traditional one (and, in particular, from that given on epistemic causal models). However, these connectives behave classically if applied to subformulas without occurrences of dependence atoms, and also when $\mathcal{T}$ is a singleton (the quantification plays no relevant role).

---

[12] We are presenting here the definition from [7], which, save for implementation details, corresponds to what are called *fully defined* causal teams in [5] (where a more general notion is considered).

[13] With some additional machinery, which is not worth exploring here.

[14] Notice that the syntax allows negation only at the atomic level. Adding contradictory negation (defined by $T \models \sim\psi$ iff $T \not\models \psi$) would lead to a more expressive language and to an unintended reading of negation. As observed in [6], the language can be extended – without changes in expressivity – with a *dual negation*, defined by the clause: $(\mathcal{T}, \mathcal{F}) \models \neg\psi$ iff, for all $s \in \mathcal{T}$, $(s, \mathcal{F}) \not\models \psi$. The dual negation has the intended reading on formulas without dependence atoms. Neither negation allows the usual interdefinability of $\wedge$ and $\vee$ via the De Morgan laws; for this reason, both $\wedge$ and $\vee$ are included in the syntax.

$$\begin{array}{lll}
T \models Z{=}z & \text{iff} & s(Z) = z \text{ for all } s \in \mathcal{T} \\
T \models Z{\neq}z & \text{iff} & s(Z) \neq z \text{ for all } s \in \mathcal{T} \\
T \models {=}(X_1, \ldots, X_n; Y) & \text{iff} & \text{for all } s, s' \in \mathcal{T}, \text{ if } s(X_i) = s'(X_i) \text{ for } 1 \leqslant i \leqslant n, \text{ then } s(Y) = s'(Y) \\
T \models \phi \wedge \psi & \text{iff} & T \models \phi \text{ and } T \models \psi \\
T \models \phi \vee \psi & \text{iff} & \text{there are } \mathcal{T}_1 \cup \mathcal{T}_2 = \mathcal{T} \text{ such that } \langle \mathcal{T}_1, \mathcal{F} \rangle \models \phi \text{ and } \langle \mathcal{T}_2, \mathcal{F} \rangle \models \psi \\
T \models \alpha \supset \psi & \text{iff} & \langle \mathcal{T}^{\alpha}, \mathcal{F} \rangle \models \psi, \text{ for } \mathcal{T}^{\alpha} := \{s \in \mathcal{T} \mid (\{s\}, \mathcal{F}) \models \alpha\} \text{ and } \alpha \text{ without} \\
 & & \text{dependence atoms} \\
T \models \vec{X}{=}\vec{x} \,\Box\!\!\rightarrow \psi & \text{iff} & \langle \mathcal{T}^{\mathcal{F}}_{\vec{X}=\vec{x}}, \mathcal{F}_{\vec{X}=\vec{x}} \rangle \models \psi, \text{ with } \mathcal{T}^{\mathcal{F}}_{\vec{X}=\vec{x}} \text{ and } \mathcal{F}_{\vec{X}=\vec{x}} \text{ as in Definition 8.}
\end{array}$$

From their definitions, it is clear that an epistemic causal model and a causal team are identical objects; the only difference is that, for evaluating formulas, the former requires an 'actual world'. On the syntactic side, even though the truth clauses of the logical operators differ in various respects, we can find several equivalences. For instance, the notion of dependence from team semantics can be expressed in our formal language as well.[15] Indeed, interpret the object $\mathcal{T}$ of a causal team as the epistemic state of some agent. Then, the statement $Y = y$ of causal team semantics can be understood as a claim about the knowledge of the agent, written in our language as $K(Y = y)$. Building on this translation, we can express that variable Y depends on the variables $\vec{X}$ as the following claim: for all possible valuations $\vec{x}$ of $\vec{X}$ there is some value y of Y such that the agent knows that if she would observe $\vec{X} = \vec{x}$, she would know that Y has value y.

$$\bigwedge_{\vec{x} \in \mathcal{R}(\vec{X})} \bigvee_{y \in \mathcal{R}(Y)} [(X_1 = x_1 \wedge \cdots \wedge X_n = x_n)!]K(Y = y).$$

With this idea in mind we can define a translation of the non-nested formulas of $\mathcal{L}_{COD}$.[16] Setting aside for a moment the case of the operator $\supset$, and using A to denote the set of all possible valuations for $\mathcal{U} \cup \mathcal{V}$, the translation is given by the following clauses.

$$tr(Y{=}y) := K(Y{=}y) \qquad\qquad tr(\phi_1 \wedge \phi_2) := tr(\phi_1) \wedge tr(\phi_2)$$

$$tr(Y{\neq}y) := K(\neg(Y{=}y)) \qquad\qquad tr(\vec{X}{=}\vec{x} \,\Box\!\!\rightarrow \phi) := [\vec{X}{=}\vec{x}]tr(\phi)$$

$$tr(\phi \vee \psi) := \bigvee_{S \subseteq A} K\Big([(\bigvee_{\vec{Y}=\vec{y} \in S} \vec{Y} = \vec{y})!]tr(\phi) \wedge [(\neg \bigvee_{\vec{Y}=\vec{y} \in S} \vec{Y} = \vec{y})!]tr(\psi)\Big)$$

$$tr({=}(X_1, \ldots, X_n; Y)) := \bigwedge_{\vec{x} \in \mathcal{R}(\vec{X})} \bigvee_{y \in \mathcal{R}(Y)} [(X_1{=}x_1 \wedge \cdots \wedge X_n{=}x_n)!]K(Y{=}y)$$

A short note on the not-so-intuitive translation clause for $\vee$. First note that, in the semantic clause for $\vee$, the sets $\mathcal{T}_1$ and $\mathcal{T}_2$ can equivalently be required to form a *partition*

[15] As far as we know, this has been first observed, independently, in [14] and [1], in the context of epistemic languages with modalities for the knowledge of values.

[16] A formula is non-nested if, in every subformula of the form $\vec{X}{=}\vec{x} \,\Box\!\!\rightarrow \phi$, no $\Box\!\!\rightarrow$ occurs inside ϕ. Providing a translation for these formulas is sufficient, since every formula of the causal team language is provably equivalent to a non-nested one.

of $\mathcal{T}$, i.e. to be disjoint. The translation clause uses the fact that a partition of $\mathcal{T}$ (say, $\mathcal{T} \cap S$ and $\mathcal{T} \setminus S$) can be characterized by the pair of formulas $\bigvee_{\vec{Y}=\vec{y}\in S} \vec{Y} = \vec{y}$ (defining $\mathcal{T} \cap S$ as a subset of $\mathcal{T}$) and $\neg \bigvee_{\vec{Y}=\vec{y}\in S} \vec{Y} = \vec{y}$ (defining $\mathcal{T} \setminus S$). The conjunction $[(\bigvee_{\vec{Y}=\vec{y}\in S} \vec{Y} = \vec{y})!]tr(\phi) \wedge [(\neg \bigvee_{\vec{Y}=\vec{y}\in S} \vec{Y} = \vec{y})!]tr(\psi)$ then ensures that the current assignment either is in S and satisfies the translation of ϕ, or it is in $\mathcal{T} \setminus S$ and satisfies the translation of ψ. The K operator, placed *after* the disjunction $\bigvee_{S\subseteq A}$, ensures that, fixing a partition, this property holds for all the assignments (i.e. the partition is not picked out as a function of the assignment). Notice also that this translation clause – as well as that for dependence atoms – is well-defined relative to a fixed, finite signature, since the translation uses an enumeration of the variables and of their corresponding allowed values.

Formulas of the form $\alpha \supset \psi$ translate into public announcement formulas. However, in order to play the role of announcement, α cannot be translated using tr, as announcements are evaluated according to the classical meaning. We need instead a simpler translation e which just replaces logical operators with their counterparts in $\mathcal{L}_{PAKC}$ ($X \neq x$ is replaced by $\neg(X = x)$; $\beta \supset \gamma$ by $\beta \rightarrow \gamma$; $\vec{X} = \vec{x} \;\Box\!\!\rightarrow \phi$ by $[\vec{X} = \vec{x}]\phi$; $\wedge$ and $\vee$ are left unaltered, or, more precisely, $\beta \vee \gamma$ is replaced by $\neg(\neg\beta \wedge \neg\gamma)$). Then we can define tr for $\supset$ as follows:

$$tr(\alpha \supset \phi) := [e(\alpha)!]tr(\phi)$$

This translation satisfies the following.

Proposition 1 (Global translation). *For any causal team $\langle \mathcal{T}, \mathcal{F} \rangle$ over a* finite *signature $\mathcal{S}$ and any formula $\phi \in \mathcal{L}_{COD}$, we have $\langle \mathcal{T}, \mathcal{F} \rangle \models \phi$ if and only if, for all $\mathcal{A} \in \mathcal{T}$, we have $(\langle \mathcal{S}, \mathcal{F}, \mathcal{T} \rangle, \mathcal{A}) \models tr(\phi)$.*

This result compares truth on a causal team with validity over an epistemic causal model. On the other hand, a different translation of the dependence atom from [1, 14] suggests an alternative, "local" translation. Let tr^* be as tr, except for the following clauses (notice the additional K operator in both clauses):

$$tr^*(=(X_1, ..., X_n; Y)) := \bigwedge_{\vec{x}\in\mathcal{R}(\vec{X})} \bigvee_{y\in\mathcal{R}(Y)} K[(X_1 = x_1 \wedge \cdots \wedge X_n = x_n)!]K(Y = y)$$

$$tr^*(\alpha \supset \phi) := K[e(\alpha)!]tr(\phi)$$

Now we have the following result.

Proposition 2 (Local translation). *For any causal team $\langle \mathcal{T}, \mathcal{F} \rangle$ over a* finite *signature $\mathcal{S}$ and any formula $\phi \in \mathcal{L}_{COD}$, we have:*

***(i)** If $\langle \mathcal{T}, \mathcal{F} \rangle \models \phi$, then, for all $\mathcal{A} \in \mathcal{T}$, $(\langle \mathcal{S}, \mathcal{F}, \mathcal{T} \rangle, \mathcal{A}) \models tr(\phi)$.*
***(ii)** If* there is *an $\mathcal{A} \in \mathcal{T}$ such that $(\langle \mathcal{S}, \mathcal{F}, \mathcal{T} \rangle, \mathcal{A}) \models tr(\phi)$, then $\langle \mathcal{T}, \mathcal{F} \rangle \models \phi$.*

This result shows that, *in the finite case*, $\mathcal{L}_{PAKC}$ is at least as expressive as $\mathcal{L}_{COD}$. Despite this, the way the notion of (accidental) dependence is spelled out in the two languages differs in an interesting way. While it is a primitive element in the language of Causal Team Semantics, the way it is definable in our epistemic framework emphasises what we can *do* with such a concept of dependence: we can make predictions based on what we observe. Furthermore, it is interesting to notice the similarity between this translation of (accidental) dependence and the way causal dependence is expressed. It is also not defined as a primitive in the language, but can be expressed using counterfactuals, which work based on the concept of intervention. These counterfactuals, in turn, focus on what you can do with causal information: prediction based on intervention.

Based on the counterfactual expression, various notions of causal dependence can be defined. We saw one already in Sect. 4, Definition 11: $X \rightsquigarrow Z$, which expresses that X is a causal parent of Z (if Z is an endogenous variable). The local translation of the notion of dependence from Causal Team Semantics into our framework suggests a different notion of causal dependence. We repeat the local translation below under the name of e-dependence. C-dependence defines the corresponding causal notion.[17]

- Y *e-depends* on X in $(E, \mathcal{A})$ iff $(E, \mathcal{A}) \models \bigwedge_{x \in \mathcal{R}(X)} \bigvee_{y \in \mathcal{R}(Y)} K([(X = x)!]K(Y = y))$
- Y *c-depends* on Y in $(E, \mathcal{A})$ iff $(E, \mathcal{A}) \models \bigwedge_{x \in \mathcal{R}(X)} \bigvee_{y \in \mathcal{R}(Y)} [X = x]K(Y = y)$

Given an epistemic causal model, C-dependence holds between a list of variables $X_1, \ldots, X_n$ and a variable Y if any intervention fixing the value of the variables $X_1, \ldots, X_n$ also determines the value of Y *within the epistemic state of the agent*. While this notion is certainly more robust than the notion of e-dependence, it still takes into account the epistemic state of the agent. The less the agent knows about the values of the variables, the more variables she needs to control to make sure that a variable Y is in a particular state. If the agent knows more about the actual causal history of Y, she can predict the state of Y already from smaller interventions. These kind of hybrid notions between causal and epistemic dependence that our framework allows to define deserve certainly some attention in future research.

7 Conclusions

In this paper we have moved some steps towards the integration of causal and epistemic reasoning, providing an adequate semantics, a language combining interventionist counterfactuals with (dynamic) epistemic operators and a sound and complete system of inference. Our deductive system models the thought of an agent reasoning about the consequences of hypothetical interventions and observations. It describes what the agent may deduce from her/his *a priori* pool of knowledge about a system of variables. It is therefore a logic of thought experiments. Going back to Example 1 from the introduction, the approach allows us to account for the inference that Billie is not sure that

[17] The additional K operator in the definition of e-dependence is needed to deal with the fact that information update always checks first whether the information that the information state is updated with is true. This problem disappears in the case of interventions, because the formula you intervene with is *made* true in the hypothetical scenario you consider.

if the button had been pushed, the sprinkler would have been working. However, the logic is not yet able to also model the second inference discussed in connection with this example: if Billie had pushed the button and saw that the sprinkler works, then she would have known that the circuit is closed. In order to account for this kind of reasoning we need to model how an agent may reason about (from her perspective) actual experiments. Things change significantly in such a setting: because of unobserved factors, the agent may fail to predict the outcome of an experiment; yet the outcome may sometimes be recovered from direct observation of the consequences of the experiment. The development of a such a framework will involve a more careful distinction between *observable* and *unobservable* variables. The resulting logic must necessarily abandon the right-to-left implication of axiom CM ($[\vec{X}=\vec{x}]K\phi \rightarrow K[\vec{X}=\vec{x}]\phi$), which expresses the fact that interventions cannot increase the knowledge of the agent.

Our framework has many points in common with the earlier causal team semantics, and we provided a translation between the two approaches. For the purpose of modeling causal reasoning, our semantics has the advantage, over causal team semantics, of encoding explicitly a notion of actual state of the world (and in particular, of actual value of variables). Actual values seem to be crucial for the attempt of defining notions of *token causation* [18, 19, 32], i.e. causation between events. In order to fully appreciate this advantage, though, we will need to consider richer languages with hybrid features that allow to explicitly refer to the actual values of variables.

Finally, in future work we plan to extend the setting to a multi-agent system. This involves considering not only different agents with potentially different knowledge, but also epistemic attitudes for groups (e.g., distributed and common knowledge) and the effect of inter-agent communication. One advantage this will bring is the potential to contribute to the discussion about causal agency and the role of causation in the study of responsibility within AI (f.i. [3]).

References

1. Baltag, A.: To know is to know the value of a variable. Adv. Modal Log. **11**, 135–155 (2016)
2. Baltag, A., van Benthem, J.: A simple logic of functional dependence. J. Philos. Log. (2020)
3. Baltag, A., Canavotto, I., Smets, S.: Causal agency and responsibility: a refinement of STIT logic. In: Giordani, A., Malinowski, J. (eds.) Logic in High Definition. Trends in Logical Semantics (forthcoming)
4. Baltag, A., Moss, L.S., Solecki, S.: The logic of public announcements, common knowledge, and private suspicions. In: Gilboa, I. (ed.) TARK, pp. 43–56. Morgan Kaufmann, San Francisco (1998). http://dl.acm.org/citation.cfm?id=645876.671885
5. Barbero, F., Sandu, G.: Interventionist counterfactuals on causal teams. In: Finkbeiner, B., Kleinberg, S. (eds.) Proceedings 3rd Workshop on Formal Reasoning about Causation, Responsibility, and Explanations in Science and Technology, Thessaloniki, Greece, 21st April 2018. Electronic Proceedings in Theoretical Computer Science, vol. 286, pp. 16–30. Open Publishing Association (2019)
6. Barbero, F., Sandu, G.: Team semantics for interventionist counterfactuals: observations vs. interventions. J. Philos. Log. (2020, to appear)
7. Barbero, F., Yang, F.: Counterfactuals and dependencies on causal teams: expressive power and deduction systems. Adv. Modal Log. (2020, accepted, forthcoming)

8. van Benthem, J.: Logical Dynamics of Information and Interaction. Cambridge University Press, Cambridge (2011)
9. Bergstein, B.: What AI still can't do (2020). https://www.technologyreview.com/2020/02/19/868178/what-ai-still-cant-do/. Accessed June 2020
10. Blackburn, P., de Rijke, M., Venema, Y.: Modal Logic. No. 53 in Cambridge Tracts in Theoretical Computer Science. Cambridge University Press, Cambridge (2001). https://doi.org/10.1017/CBO9781107050884
11. Briggs, R.: Interventionist counterfactuals. Philos. Stud. **160**(1), 139–166 (2012)
12. Chockler, H., Halpern, J.Y.: Responsibility and blame: a structural-model approach. J. Artif. Int. Res. **22**(1), 93–115 (2004)
13. van Ditmarsch, H., van der Hoek, W., Kooi, B.: Dynamic Epistemic Logic. Synthese Library Series, vol. 337. Springer, Dordrecht (2008). https://doi.org/10.1007/978-1-4020-5839-4
14. van Eijck, J., Gattinger, M., Wang, Y.: Knowing values and public inspection. In: Ghosh, S., Prasad, S. (eds.) ICLA 2017. LNCS, vol. 10119, pp. 77–90. Springer, Heidelberg (2017). https://doi.org/10.1007/978-3-662-54069-5_7
15. Fagin, R., Halpern, J.Y., Moses, Y., Vardi, M.Y.: Reasoning About Knowledge. The MIT Press, Cambridge (1995)
16. Galles, D., Pearl, J.: An axiomatic characterisation of causal counterfactuals. Found. Sci. **1**, 151–182 (1998)
17. Halpern, J.Y.: Axiomatizing causal reasoning. J. Artif. Intell. Res. **12**, 317–337 (2000)
18. Halpern, J.Y.: Actual Causality. MIT Press, Cambridge (2016)
19. Hitchcock, C.: A tale of two effects. Philos. Rev. **110**(3), 361–396 (2001). https://doi.org/10.1215/00318108-110-3-361
20. Hodges, W.: Compositional semantics for a language of imperfect information. Log. J. IGPL **5**, 539–563 (1997)
21. Ibeling, D., Icard, T.: Probabilistic reasoning across the causal hierarchy. arXiv preprint arXiv:2001.02889 (2020)
22. Mann, A.L., Sandu, G., Sevenster, M.: Independence-Friendly Logic - Agame-Theoretic Approach. London Mathematical Society Lecture Note Series, vol. 386. Cambridge University Press, Cambridge (2011)
23. Pearl, J.: Causality. Models, Reasoning, and Inference. Cambridge University Press, Cambridge (2000)
24. Pearl, J.: Causal diagrams for empirical research. Biometrika **82**(4), 669–688 (1995)
25. Pearl, J.: Causality: models, reasoning, and inference. IIE Trans. **34**(6), 583–589 (2002)
26. Pearl, J.: Causality. Models, Reasoning, and Inference, 2nd edn. Cambridge University Press, Cambridge (2009)
27. Pearl, J., Mackenzie, D.: The Book of Why. The New Science of Cause and Effect. Penguin Books, London (2019)
28. Spirtes, P., Glymour, C., Scheines, R.: Causation, Prediction, and Search, 1st edn. MIT Press, Cambridge (1993)
29. Strotz, R.H., Wold, H.O.: Recursive vs. nonrecursive systems: an attempt at synthesis (part I of a triptych on causal chain systems). Econ.: J. Econ. Soc. 417–427 (1960)
30. Väänänen, J.: Dependence Logic: A New Approach to Independence Friendly Logic. London Mathematical Society Student Texts, vol. 70. Cambridge University Press, Cambridge (2007)
31. Wang, Y., Cao, Q.: On axiomatizations of public announcement logic. Synthese **190**(1), 103–134 (2013)
32. Woodward, J.: Making Things Happen. Oxford Studies in the Philosophy of Science, vol. 114. Oxford University Press, Oxford (2003)

Awareness Logic: A Kripke-Based Rendition of the Heifetz-Meier-Schipper Model

Gaia Belardinelli(✉) and Rasmus K. Rendsvig

Center for Information and Bubble Studies, University of Copenhagen, Copenhagen, Denmark
{belardinelli,rasmus}@hum.ku.dk

Abstract. Heifetz, Meier & Schipper (HMS) present a lattice model of awareness. The HMS model is syntax-free, which precludes the simple option to rely on formal language to induce lattices, and represents uncertainty and unawareness with one entangled construct, making it difficult to assess the properties of either. Here, we present a model based on a lattice of Kripke models, induced by atom subset inclusion, in which uncertainty and unawareness are separate. We show the models to be equivalent by defining transformations between them which preserve formula satisfaction, and obtain completeness through our and HMS' results.

1 Introduction

Awareness has been studied with vigor in logic and game theory since its first formal treatment by Halpern and Fagin in [8]. In these fields, awareness is added as a complement to uncertainty in models for knowledge and rational interaction. In short, where uncertainty concerns an agent's ability to distinguish possible states of the world based on its available information, awareness concerns the agent's ability to even contemplate aspects of a state, where such inability stems from the *unawareness* of the concepts that constitute said aspects. Thereby, models that include awareness avoid problems of logical omniscience (at least partially) and allows modeling game theoretic scenarios where the possibility of some action may come as an utter surprise.

To model awareness, the seminal [8] introduces the Logic of General Awareness (LGA), taking a syntax-based approach: an agent a's awareness in state w is given by an *awareness function* assigning (a, w) a set of formulas. This approach has since been inherited by a multitude of models.

In contrast, Heifetz, Meier and Schipper (HMS) construct a syntax-free framework [15], which is the main topic of this paper. In their *unawareness frames*, both "atomic" and epistemic events are defined without any appeal to atomic propositions or other syntax.

The backbone of an unawareness frame is a complete lattice of state-spaces $(\mathcal{S}, \preceq)$, with the intuition that the higher a space is, the richer the "vocabulary"

M. A. Martins and I. Sedlár (Eds.): DaLí 2020, LNCS 12569, pp. 33–50, 2020.
https://doi.org/10.1007/978-3-030-65840-3_3

it has to describe its states. Since the approach is syntax-free, this intuition is not modeled using a formal language. It is represented using $\preceq$ and a family of maps $r_S^{S'}$ which projects state-space S' down to S, with $r_S^{S'}(s)$ interpreted as the representation of s in the more limited vocabulary available in S. Uncertainty and unawareness are represented *jointly* by a *possibility correspondence* Π_a for each $a \in Ag$, which maps a state weakly downwards to the set of states the agent considers possible. If the mapped-to space is strictly less expressive, this represents that the agent does not have full awareness of the mapped-from state.

That HMS keep their model syntax-free is motivated in part by its applicability among economists [15, p. 79]. We think their lattice-based conceptualization of awareness is both elegant, interesting and intuitive—but we also find its formalization cumbersome. Exactly the choice to go fully syntax-free robs the model of the option to rely on formal language to induce lattices and to specify events, resulting in constructions which we find less than very easy to follow. This may, of course, be an artifact of us being accustomed to non-syntax-free models used widely in epistemic logic.

Another artifact of our familiarity with epistemic logic models is that we find HMS' joint definition of uncertainty and unawareness difficult to relate to other formalizations of knowledge. When HMS propose properties of their Π_a maps, it is not clear to us which aspects concern knowledge and which concern awareness. They merge two dimensions which, to us, would be clearer if left separated.[1]

With these two motivations, this paper proposes a non-syntax-free, Kripke model-based rendition of the HMS model. Roughly, we suggest to start from a Kripke model $\mathtt{K}$ for a set of atoms At, spawn a lattice containing restrictions of $\mathtt{K}$ to subsets of At, and finally add maps π_a on the lattice that take a world to a copy of itself in a restricted model. This keeps the epistemic and awareness dimensions separate: accessibility relations R_a of $\mathtt{K}$ encode epistemics while maps π_a encode awareness. We show that under three assumptions on π_a and when each R_a is an equivalence relation, the result is equivalent to the HMS model, in the sense that the two satisfy the same formulas of the language of knowledge and awareness, defined below.

Defining an equivalent model, we do not aim to generalize that of HMS, but we do include an additional perspective. [15,20] argue that the HMS model allows agents to reason about their unawareness, as possibility correspondences Π_a provide them a subjective perspective, while LGA-based approaches only present an outside perspective, as the full model must be taken into account when assigning knowledge and awareness.[2] Oppositely, Halpern and Rêgo [13] point out that the HMS model includes no objective state, and so no outside

---

[1] As a reviewer points out, then HMS take *explicit* knowledge as foundational, and derive awareness from it. This makes the one-dimensional representation justified, if not even desirable. In contrast, epistemic logic models are standardly interpreted as taking *implicit* knowledge as foundational. We think along the second line, and add awareness as a second dimension. We are not taking a stand on whether one interpretation is superior, but provide results to move between them.

[2] [13] argues that this boils down to a difference in philosophical interpretation.

perspective. The present model has both: the starting Kripke model provides an outsider perspective on agents' knowledge, while the submodel obtained by following π_a presents the subjective perspective. We remark further on this below.

The paper progresses as follows. Sects. 2 and 3 present respectively the HMS model and our rendition. Sections 4 and 5 contain our main technical results: Sect. 4 introduces transformations between the two models classes, while Sect. 5 shows that they preserve formula satisfaction. Section 6 presents a logic due to HMS [14], and shows, as a corollary to our results, that it is complete with respect to our rendition. Section 7 holds concluding remarks.

Throughout the paper, we assume that Ag is a finite, non-empty set of agents, and that At is a countable, non-empty set of atoms.

2 The HMS Model

This section presents HMS unawareness frames [15], their syntax-free notions of knowledge and awareness, and their augmentation with HMS valuations, producing HMS models [14]. For context, the HMS model is a multi-agent generalization of the Modica-Rustichini model [19] which is equivalent to Halpern's model in [10], generalized by Halpern and Rêgo to multiple agents [13], resulting in a model equivalent to the HMS model, cf. [14]. See [20] for an extensive review.

The following definition introduces the basic structure underlying the HMS model, as well as the properties of the Π_a map that controls the to-be-defined notions of knowledge and awareness. The properties are described after Definition 1. Following Definition 4 of HMS models, Fig. 1 illustrates a full HMS model, including its unawareness frame.

Definition 1. *An* ***unawareness frame*** *is a tuple* $\mathsf{F} = (\mathcal{S}, \preceq, \mathcal{R}, \Pi)$ *where* $(\mathcal{S}, \preceq)$ *is a complete lattice with* $\mathcal{S} = \{S, S', ...\}$ *a set of disjoint, non-empty* ***state-spaces*** $S = \{s, s', ...\}$ *s.t.* $S \preceq S'$ *implies* $|S| \leq |S'|$. *Let* $\Omega_{\mathsf{F}} := \bigcup_{S \in \mathcal{S}} S$ *be the disjoint union of state-spaces in* $\mathcal{S}$. *For* $X \subseteq \Omega_{\mathsf{F}}$, *let* $S(X)$ *be the state-space containing* X, *if such exists (else* $S(X)$ *is undefined). Let* $S(s)$ *be* $S(\{s\})$.

$\mathcal{R} = \{r_S^{S'} : S, S' \in \mathcal{S}, S \preceq S'\}$ *is a family of* ***projections*** $r_S^{S'} : S' \to S$. *Each* $r_S^{S'}$ *is surjective,* r_S^S *is Id, and* $S \preceq S' \preceq S''$ *implies commutativity:* $r_S^{S''} = r_S^{S'} \circ r_{S'}^{S''}$. *Denote* $r_S^T(w)$ *also by* w_S.

$D^{\uparrow} = \bigcup_{S' \succeq S} (r_S^{S'})^{-1}(D)$ *is the* ***upwards closure*** *of* $D \subseteq S \in \mathcal{S}$.[3]

Π *assigns each* $a \in Ag$ *a* ***possibility correspondence*** $\Pi_a : \Omega_{\mathsf{F}} \to 2^{\Omega_{\mathsf{F}}}$ *satisfying*

Conf ***(Confinement)*** *If* $w \in S'$, *then* $\Pi_a(w) \subseteq S$ *for some* $S \preceq S'$.
Gref ***(Generalized Reflexivity)*** $w \in (\Pi_a(w))^{\uparrow}$ *for every* $w \in \Omega_{\mathsf{F}}$.
Stat ***(Stationarity)*** $w' \in \Pi_a(w)$ *implies* $\Pi_a(w') = \Pi_a(w)$.
PPI ***(Projections Preserve Ignorance)*** *If* $w \in S'$ *and* $S \preceq S'$, *then* $(\Pi_a(w))^{\uparrow} \subseteq (\Pi_a(r_S^{S'}(w)))^{\uparrow}$.

[3] To avoid confusion, note that for $d \in S$, $(r_S^{S'})^{-1}(d) = \{s' \in S' : r_S^{S'}(s') = d\}$ and for $D \subseteq S$, $(r_S^{S'})^{-1}(D) = \bigcup_{d \in D} (r_S^{S'})^{-1}(d)$.

PPK *(Projections Preserve Knowledge) If $S \preceq S' \preceq S''$, $w \in S''$ and $\Pi_a(w) \subseteq S'$, then $r_S^{S'}(\Pi_a(w)) = \Pi_a(r_S^{S''}(w))$.*

Jointly call these five properties of Π_a the ***HMS properties.***

Conf ensures that agents only consider possibilities within one fixed "vocabulary"; Gref induces factivity of knowledge and Stat yields introspection for knowledge and awareness. PPI entails that at down-projected states, agents neither "miraculously" know or become aware of something new, while PPK implies that at down-projected states, the agent can still "recall" all events she knew before, if they are still expressible. Jointly PPI and PPK imply that agents preserve awareness of all events at down-projected states, if they are still expressible.

Remark 2. Unawareness frames include no objective perspective, as agents do not—unless they are fully aware—have a range of uncertainty defined for the maximal state-space. Taking the maximal state-space to contain a designated 'actual world' and as providing a full and objective description of states, one can still not evaluate agents "true" uncertainty/implicit knowledge. See e.g. Fig. 1 below: In $(\neg i, \ell)$, the dashed agent's "true" uncertainty about ℓ is not determined.

2.1 Syntax-Free Unawareness

Unawareness frames provide sufficient structure to define syntax-free notions of knowledge and awareness. These are defined directly as events on Ω_{F}.

Definition 3. *Let $\mathsf{F} = (\mathcal{S}, \preceq, \mathcal{R}, \Pi)$ be an unawareness frame. An* ***event*** *in F is any pair $(D^\uparrow, S)$ with $D \subseteq S \in \mathcal{S}$ with S also denoted $S(D^\uparrow)$. Let Σ_{F} be the set of events of F.*

The ***negation*** *of the event $(D^\uparrow, S)$ is $\neg(D^\uparrow, S) = ((S \setminus D)^\uparrow, S)$.*

The ***conjunction*** *of events $\{(D_i^\uparrow, S_i)\}_{i\in I}$ is $((\bigcap_{i\in I} D_i^\uparrow), \sup_{i\in I} S_i)$.*

The events that a ***knows*** *event $(D^\uparrow, S)$ and where a is* ***aware*** *of it are*

$$\boldsymbol{K}_a((D^\uparrow, S)) = \begin{cases} (\{w \in \Omega_{\mathsf{F}} : \Pi_a(w) \subseteq D^\uparrow\}, S(D)) & \text{if } \exists w \in \Omega_{\mathsf{F}}. \Pi_a(w) \subseteq D^\uparrow \\ (\emptyset, S(D)) & \text{else} \end{cases}$$

$$\boldsymbol{A}_a((D^\uparrow, S)) = \begin{cases} (\{w \in \Omega_{\mathsf{F}} : \Pi_a(w) \subseteq S(D^\uparrow)^\uparrow\}, S(D)) & \text{if } \exists w \in \Omega_{\mathsf{F}}. \Pi_a(w) \subseteq S(D^\uparrow)^\uparrow \\ (\emptyset, S(D)) & \text{else} \end{cases}$$

Negation, conjunction, knowledge and awareness events are well-defined [15,20]. To illustrate the definitions, some intuitions behind them: *i*) an event modeled as a pair $(D^\uparrow, S)$ captures that *a*) if the event is expressible in S, then it is also expressible in any $S' \succeq S$, hence $D^\uparrow$ is the set of all states where the event is expressible and occurs, and *b*) the event is expressible in the"vocabulary" of S, but not the "vocabulary" of lower state-spaces: $D \subseteq S$ are the states with the lowest "vocabulary" where the event is expressible and occurs. [20] remarks that for $(D^\uparrow, S)$, if $D \neq \emptyset$, then S is uniquely determined by $D^\uparrow$. *ii*) Events are given a non-binary understanding: an event $(D^{\uparrow}, S)$ and it's negation does not partition Ω_{F}, as $s \in S' \prec S$ is in neither, but they do partition every $S'' \succeq S$. *iii*) Conjunction defined using supremum captures that the state-space required to express the conjunction of two events is the least expressive state-space that can express both events. *iv*) Knowledge events are essentially defined as in Aumann structures/state-space models: the agent knows an event if its "information cell" is a subset of the event's states. *v*) Awareness events captures that "*an agent is aware of an event if she considers possible states in which this event is "expressible"*." [20, p. 97]

2.2 HMS Models

Though unawareness frames provide a syntax-free framework adequate for defining awareness, HMS [14] use them as a semantics for a formal language in order to identify their logic. The language and logic are topics of Sects. 5 and 6.

Instead, the models we will later define are not syntax-free. As Kripke models, they include a valuation of atomic propositions. Therefore, they do not corre-

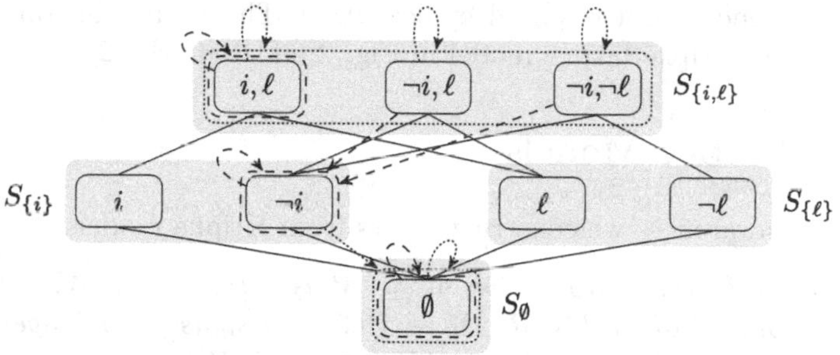

Fig. 1. An HMS model with four state-spaces (gray rectangles), ordered spatially as a lattice. States (smallest rectangles) are labeled with their true literals, over the set $At = \{i, \ell\}$. Thin lines between states show projections. There are two possibility correspondences (dashed and dotted): arrow-to-rectangle shows a mapping from state to set (information cell). Omitted arrows go to $S_{\emptyset}$ and are irrelevant to the story.

Story: Buyer (dashed) and Owner (dotted) consider trading a firm, the price influenced by whether i (a value-raising innovation) and ℓ (a value-lowering lawsuit) occurs. Assume both occur and take (i, ℓ) as actual. Then Buyer has full information, while Owner has factual uncertainty and uncertainty about Buyer's awareness and higher-order information, ultimately considering it possible that Buyer holds Owner fully unaware. *In detail:* Buyer's (i, ℓ) information cell has both i and ℓ defined (and is also singleton), so Buyer is aware of them (and also knows everything). Owner is also aware of i and ℓ, but their (i, ℓ) information cell contains also $\neg i$ and $\neg \ell$ states, so Owner knows neither. Owner is also uncertain about Buyer's information: Owner knows that either Buyer knows i and ℓ (cf. Buyer's (i, ℓ) information cell), or Buyer knows $\neg i$, but is unaware of ℓ (cf. the dashed arrows from $\neg i$ states to the less expressive state space $S_{\{i\}}$) and then only holds it possible that Owner is unaware of both i and ℓ (cf. the dotted map to $S_{\emptyset}$). See also Remark 6 concerning $S_{\{\ell\}}$.

spond to unawareness frames directly, but to the models that result by augmenting such frames with valuations. To compare the two model classes, we define such valuations here, postponing HMS syntax and semantics to Sect. 5. Figure 1 illustrates an HMS model, using an example inspired by [15, p. 87]

Definition 4. *Let* $\mathsf{F} = (\mathcal{S}, \preceq, \mathcal{R}, \Pi)$ *be an unawareness frame with events* Σ_{F}*. An **HMS valuation** for At and* F *is a map* $V_{\mathsf{M}} : At \rightarrow \Sigma_{\mathsf{F}}$*, assigning to every atom from At an event in* F*. An **HMS model** is an unawareness frame augmented with an HMS valuation, denoted* $\mathsf{M} = (\mathcal{S}, \preceq, \mathcal{R}, \Pi, V_{\mathsf{M}})$*.*

Remark 5. HMS valuations only partially respect the intuitive interpretation of state-spaces lattices, where $S \preceq S'$ represents that S' is at least as expressive as S. If $S \preceq S'$, then $p \in At$ having defined truth value at S entails that it has defined truth value at S', but if S is strictly less expressive than S', then this does not entail that there is some atom q with defined truth value in S', but undefined truth value in S. Hence, there can exist two spaces defined for the same set of atoms, but where one is still "strictly more expressive" than the other.

Remark 6. Concerning Fig. 1, then the state-space $S_{\{\ell\}}$ is, in a sense, redundant: its presence does not affect the knowledge or awareness of agents in the state (i, ℓ), and it presence is not required by definition. This stands in contrast with the corresponding Kripke lattice model in Fig. 2, cf. Remark 12.

3 Kripke Lattice Models

The models for awareness we construct starts from Kripke models:

Definition 7. *A **Kripke model** for* $At' \subseteq At$ *is a tuple* $\mathtt{K} = (W, R, V)$ *where* W *is a non-empty set of worlds,* $R : Ag \rightarrow \mathcal{P}(W^2)$ *assigns to each agent* $a \in Ag$ *an accessibility relation denoted* R_a*, and* $V : At' \rightarrow \mathcal{P}(W)$ *is a valuation.*

*The **information cell** of* $a \in Ag$ *at* $w \in W$ *is* $I_a(w) = \{v \in W : wR_a v\}$*.*

The term 'information cell' hints at an epistemic interpretation. For generality, R may assign non-equivalence relations. Some results explicitly assume otherwise.

As counterpart to the HMS state-space lattice, we build a lattice of restricted models. The below definition of the set of worlds W_X ensures that for any $X, Y \subseteq At$, $X \neq Y$, the sets W_X and W_Y are disjoint, mimicking the same requirement for state-spaces. In the restriction $\mathtt{K}_X$ of $\mathtt{K}$, it is required that $(w_X, v_X) \in R_{aX}$ iff $(w, v) \in R_a$. Each direction bears similarity to an HMS property: left-to-right to PPK and right-to-left to PPI. They also remind us, resp., of the *No Miracles* and *Perfect Recall* properties from Epistemic Temporal Logic, cf. e.g., [3,17].

Definition 8. *Let* $\mathtt{K} = (W, R, V)$ *be a Kripke model for At. The **restriction** of* $\mathtt{K}$ *to* $X \subseteq At$ *is the Kripke model* $\mathtt{K}_X = (W_X, R_X, V_X)$ *for* X *where*

$W_X = \{w_X : w \in W\}$ *where* w_X *is the ordered pair* (w, X)*,*

$R_{Xa} = \{(w_X, v_X) : (w, v) \in R_a\}$ *and*

$V_X : X \rightarrow \mathcal{P}(W_X)$ *such that, for all* $p \in X$*,* $w_X \in V_X(p)$ *iff* $w \in V(p)$*.*

For the R_{Xa} *information cell of* a *at* w_X*, write* $I_a(w_X)$*.*

To construct a lattice of restricted models, we simply order them in accordance with subset inclusion of the atoms. This produces a complete lattice.

Definition 9. *Let* K *be a Kripke model for At. The* **restriction lattice** *of* K *is* $(\mathcal{K}(\mathtt{K}), \trianglelefteq)$ *where* $\mathcal{K}(\mathtt{K}) = \{\mathtt{K}_X\}_{X \subseteq At}$ *is the set of restrictions of* K, *and* $\mathtt{K}_X \trianglelefteq \mathtt{K}_Y$ *iff* $X \subseteq Y$.

Projections in unawareness frames are informally interpreted as mapping states to alternates of themselves in less expressive spaces. Restriction lattices offer the same, but implemented w.r.t. *At*: if $Y \subseteq X \subseteq At$, then w_Y is the alternate of w_X formally described by the smaller vocabulary of atoms, Y.

The accessibility relations of the Kripke models in a restriction lattice accounts for the epistemic dimension of the HMS possibility correspondence Π_a. For the awareness dimension, each agent $a \in Ag$ is assigned an *awareness map* π_a that maps a world w_X down to $\pi_a(w_X) = w_Y$ for some $Y \subseteq X$. We think of $\pi_a(w_X)$ as a's *awareness image* of w_X—i.e., w_X as it occurs to a given her (un)awareness; the submodel from $\pi_a(w_X)$ is thus a's subjective perspective.

In the following definition, we introduce three properties of awareness maps, which we will assume. Intuitions follow the definition.

Definition 10. *With* $\mathsf{L} = (\mathcal{K}(\mathtt{K}), \trianglelefteq)$ *a restriction lattice, let* $\Omega_{\mathsf{L}} = \bigcup \mathcal{K}(\mathtt{K})$ *and let* π *assign to each agent* $a \in Ag$ *an* **awareness map** $\pi_a : \Omega_{\mathsf{L}} \to \Omega_{\mathsf{L}}$ *satisfying*

D *(**Downwards**) For all* $w_X \in \Omega_{\mathsf{L}}$, $\pi_a(w_X) = w_Y$ *for some* $Y \subseteq X$.
II *(**Introspective Idempotence**) If* $\pi_a(w_X) = w_Y$, *then for all* $v_Y \in I_a(w_Y)$, $\pi_a(v_Y) = u_Y$ *for some* $u_Y \in I_a(w_Y)$.
NS *(**No Surprises**) If* $\pi_a(w_X) = w_Z$, *then for all* $Y \subseteq X$, $\pi_a(w_Y) = w_{Y \cap Z}$.

Call $\mathsf{K} = (\mathcal{K}(\mathtt{K}), \trianglelefteq, \pi)$ *the* ***Kripke lattice model*** *of* K.

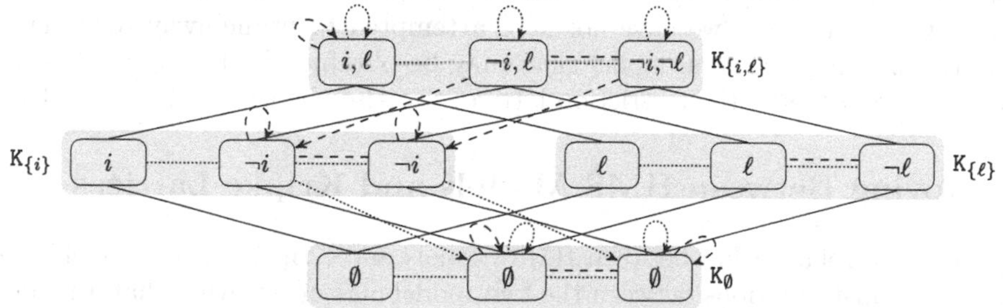

Fig. 2. A Kripke lattice model of the Fig. 1 example. See four restrictions (gray rectangles), ordered spatially as a lattice. States (smallest rectangles) are labeled with their true literals, over the set $At = \{i, \ell\}$. Horizontal dashed and dotted lines *inside restrictions* represent Buyer and Owner's accessibility relations (omitted are links obtainable by reflexive-transitive closure), while dotted and dashed arrows *between restrictions* represent their awareness maps (some arrows are omitted: they go to states' alternates in $\mathtt{K}_\emptyset$, and are irrelevant from (i, l)). Thin lines connect states with their alternate in lower restrictions. See also Remark 12 concerning $\mathtt{K}_{\{\ell\}}$.

D ensures that an agent's awareness image of a world is a restricted representation of that same world. Hence the awareness image does not conflate worlds, and does not allow the agent to be aware of a more expressive vocabulary than that which describes the world she views from. With II and accessibility assumed reflexive, it entails that π_a is idempotent: for all w_X, $\pi_a(\pi_a(w_X)) = \pi_a(w_X)$. Alone, II states that in her awareness image, the agent knows, and is aware of, the atoms that she is aware of. Given that accessibility is distributed by inheritance through the Kripke models in restriction lattices, the property implies that the same holds for every such model. NS guarantees that awareness remains "consistent" down the lattice, so that awareness of an atom does not appear or disappear without reason. Consider the consequent $\pi_a(w_Y) = w_{Y \cap Z}$ and its two subcases $\pi_a(w_Y) = w_{Y^*}$ with $Y^* \subseteq Y \cap Z$ and $Y^* \supseteq Y \cap Z$. Colloquially, the first states that if atoms are removed from the description of the world from which the agent views, then they are also removed from her awareness. Oppositely, the second states that if atoms are removed from the description of the world from which the agent views, then no more than these should be removed from her awareness. Jointly, no awareness should "miraculously" appear, and all awareness should be "recalled".[4]

Remark 11. Contrary to HMS models (cf. Remark 2), Kripke lattice models have an objective perspective: designating an 'actual world' in K_{At} allows one to check agents' uncertainty about the possible states of the world described by the maximal language, i.e., from K_{At} we can read off their "actual implicit knowledge". See e.g. Fig. 2: In the $(\neg i, \ell)$ state, the dashed agent's "true" uncertainty about ℓ *is* determined, contrary to the same state in the HMS model of Fig. 1.

Remark 12. In Remark 6, we mentioned that the HMS state-space $S_{\{\ell\}}$ of Fig. 1 is redundant. Similarly, $\mathsf{K}_{\{\ell\}}$ is redundant in Fig. 2 (from (i, ℓ), $\mathsf{K}_{\{\ell\}}$ is unreachable.) However, contrary to the HMS case, it is here required by definition, as a restriction lattice contains all restrictions of the original Kripke model. For simplicity of constructions, we have not here attempted to prune away redundant restrictions. A more general model class may be obtained by letting models be based on sub-orders of the restriction lattice. See also the concluding remarks.

4 Moving Between HMS Models and Kripke Lattices

To clarify the relationship between HMS models and Kripke lattice models, we introduce transformations between the two model classes, showing that a model from one class encodes the structure of a model from the other. The core idea is to think of a possibility correspondence Π_a as the composition of I_a and π_a: $\Pi_a(w)$ is the information cell of the awareness image of w.

The propositions of this section show that the transformations produce models of the desired class. Additionally, their proofs shed partial light on the relationship between the HMS properties and those assumed for awareness maps π_a and accessibility relations R_a: we discuss this shortly in the concluding remarks.

[4] Again, we are reminded of *No Miracles* and *Perfect Recall.*

4.1 From HMS Models to Kripke Lattice Models

Moving from HMS models to Kripke lattice models requires a somewhat involved construction as it must tease apart unawareness and uncertainty from the possibility correspondences, and track the distribution of atoms and their relationship to awareness. For an example, then the Kripke lattice model in Fig. 2 is the HMS model of Fig. 1 transformed.

Definition 13. *Let* $\mathsf{M} = (\mathcal{S}, \preceq, \mathcal{R}, \Pi, V_{\mathsf{M}})$ *be an HMS model with maximal state-space* T. *For any* $O \subseteq \Omega_{\mathsf{M}}$, *let* $At(O) = \{p \in At\colon O \subseteq V_M(p) \cup \neg V_M(p)\}$.[5]
The ***L-transform model of*** M *is* $L(\mathsf{M}) = (\mathcal{K}(\mathtt{K}), \trianglelefteq, \pi)$ *where the Kripke model* $\mathtt{K} = (W, R, V)$ *for* At *given by*
$W = T$;
R *maps each* $a \in Ag$ *to* $R_a \subseteq W^2$ *s.t.* $(w, v) \in R_a$ *iff* $r^T_{S(\Pi_a(w))}(v) \in \Pi_a(w)$;
$V : At \rightarrow \mathcal{P}(W)$, *defined by* $V(p) \ni w$ *iff* $w \in V_{\mathsf{M}}(p)$, *for every* $p \in At$;
π *assigns each* $a \in Ag$ *a map* $\pi_a : \Omega_{L(\mathsf{M})} \rightarrow \Omega_{L(\mathsf{M})}$ *s.t. for all* $w_X \in \Omega_{L(\mathsf{M})}$,
$\pi_a(w_X) = w_Y$ *where* $Y = At(S_Y)$ *for the* $S_Y \in \mathcal{S}$ *with* $S_Y \supseteq \Pi_a(r^T_{S_X}(w))$
where $S_X = \min\{S \in \mathcal{S}\colon At(S) = X\}$.

The ***state correspondence*** *between* M *and* $L(\mathsf{M})$ *is the map* $\ell : \Omega_{\mathsf{M}} \rightarrow 2^{\Omega_{L(\mathsf{M})}}$ *s.t. for all* $s \in \Omega_{\mathsf{M}}$
$\ell(s) = \{w_X \in W_X : w \in (r^T_{S(s)})^{-1}(s)$ *for* $X = At(S(s))\}$.

Intuitively, in the L-transform model, a world $v \in W$ is accessible from a world $w \in W$ for an agent if, and only if, v's restriction to the agent's vocabulary at w is one of the possibilities she entertains.[6] In addition, the awareness map π_a of agent a relates a world w_X to its less expressive counterpart w_Y if, and only if, Y is the vocabulary agent a adopts when describing what she considers possible.

Remark 14. The L-transform model $L(\mathsf{M})$ of M is well-defined as the object $\mathtt{K} = (W, R, V)$ is in fact a Kripke model for At: *i)* By def. of HMS models, $W = T \in \mathcal{S}$ is non-empty; *ii)* for each a, $R_a \subseteq W^2$ is well defined: if $w \in T = W$, then by Conf, $\Pi_a(w) \subseteq S$, for some $S \in \mathcal{S}$. Hence, $U = \{v \in T\colon r^T_S(v) \in \Pi_a(w)\}$ is well-defined, and so is $\{(w, v) \in T^2\colon v \in U\} = R_a$; *iii)* As V_{M} is an HMS valuation $V_{\mathsf{M}} : At \rightarrow \Sigma$ for At, clearly V is valuation for At. Hence $\mathtt{K} = (W, R, V)$ is a Kripke model for At.

Remark 15. The min used in defining S_X is due to the issue of Remark 5.

Remark 16. The state correspondence map ℓ is also well-defined. That it maps each state in Ω_{M} to a *set* of worlds in $\Omega_{L(\mathsf{M})}$ points to a construction difference between HMS models and Kripke lattice models: in the former, the downwards projections of two states may 'merge' them, so state-spaces may shrink when moving down the lattice; in the latter, distinct worlds remain distinct, so all world sets in a restriction lattice share cardinality.

5 $At(O)$ contains the atoms that have a defined truth value in every $s \in O$.
6 We thank a reviewer for this wording.

As unawareness and uncertainty are separated in Kripke lattice models, we show two results about L-transforms. The first shows that the Conf, Stat and PPK entail that π_a assigns awareness maps, and the second that the five HMS properties entail that R assigns equivalence relations. In showing the first, we make use of the following lemma, which intuitively shows that the information cell of an agent contains a state described with a certain vocabulary if, and only if, the agent considers possible the corresponding state described with the same vocabulary:

Lemma 17. *For every* $w_Y \in \Omega_{\mathsf{K}}$, *if* $\Pi_a(w) \subseteq S$ *and* $At(S) = Y$, *then* $v_Y \in I_a(w_Y)$ *iff* $v_S \in \Pi_a(w)$.

Proof. Let $w_Y \in \Omega_{L(\mathsf{M})}$. Consider the respective $w \in T = W$ and let $\Pi_a(w) \subseteq S$, with $At(S) = Y$. Assume that $v_Y \in I_a(w_Y)$. This is the case iff (def. of I_a) $(w_Y, v_Y) \in R_{Ya}$ iff (def. of restriction lattice) $(w, v) \in R_a$ iff (Definition 13) $v_S \in \Pi_a(w)$.

Proposition 18. *For any HMS model* M, *its* L*-transform* $L(\mathsf{M})$ *is a Kripke lattice model.*

Proof. Let $\mathsf{M} = (\mathcal{S}, \preceq, \mathcal{R}, \Pi, V_{\mathsf{M}})$ be an HMS model with maximal state-space T. We show that $L(\mathsf{M}) = (\mathcal{K}(\mathsf{K}), \trianglelefteq, \pi)$ is a Kripke lattice model by showing that π_a satisfies the three properties of an awareness map:

D: Consider an arbitrary $w_X \in \Omega_{L(\mathsf{M})}$. By def. of L-transform, $X = At(S)$ for some $S \in \mathcal{S}$. Let $S_X = \min\{S \in \mathcal{S} \colon At(S) = X\}$. If $w_X \in W_X$ then for some $w \in W = T$, $w_{S_X} \in S_X$. By Conf, $\Pi_a(w_{S_X}) \subseteq S_Y$, for some $S_Y \preceq S_X$. Let $Y = At(S_Y)$. Then, by def. of π_a, $\pi_a(w_X) = w_Y$ and $Y \subseteq X$.

II: Let $\pi_a(w_X) = w_Y$. By def. of π_a, it holds that $\Pi_a(r^T_{S_X}(w)) \subseteq S_Y$ with $At(S_Y) = Y$ and $S_X = \min\{S \in \mathcal{S} \colon At(S) = X\}$. For a contradiction, suppose there exists a $v_Y \in I_a(w_Y)$ s.t. for all $u_Y \in I_a(w_Y)$, $\pi_a(v_Y) \neq u_Y$. Then $\pi_a(v_Y) = t_Z$ for some $Z \subseteq Y$ and $t_Z \notin I_a(w_Y)$. By def. of π_a, $\pi_a(v_Y) = t_Z$ iff $\Pi_a(r^T_{S_Y}(v)) \subseteq S_Z$, where $Z = At(S_Z)$. Then, by Lemma 17, $t_Z \in I_a(v_Z)$ iff $t_{S_Z} \in \Pi_a(r^T_{S_Y}(v))$. Moreover, as $\Pi_a(r^T_{S_X}(w)) \subseteq S_Y$ and $At(S_X) = X$, by Lemma 17, it also follows that $v_Y \in I_a(w_Y)$ iff $v_{S_Y} \in \Pi_a(r^T_{S_X}(w))$. Since $v_Y \in I_a(w_Y)$ then $v_{S_Y} \in \Pi_a(r^T_{S_X}(w))$. Hence, by Stat, $\Pi_a(r^T_{S_X}(w)) = \Pi_a(r^T_{S_Y}(v))$, which implies $t_{S_Z} \in \Pi_a(r^T_{S_X}(w))$. But then $t_Z \in I_a(v_Z)$, contradicting the assumption that $t_Z \notin I_a(w_Y)$. Thus, for all $v_Y \in I_a(w_Y)$, $\pi_a(v_Y) = u_Y$ for some $u_Y \in I_a(w_Y)$.

NS: Let $\pi_a(w_X) = w_Y$. By D (cf. item 1. above), $Y \subseteq X$. Consider an arbitrary $Z \subseteq X$. We have two cases: either $i)$ $Z \subseteq Y$ or $ii)$ $Y \subseteq Z$. $i)$: then $Z \subseteq Y \subseteq X$. Let $Z = At(S_Z)$, $Y = At(S_Y)$, and $X = At(S_X)$. Then $S_Z \preceq S_Y \preceq S_X$. By PPK, $\left(\Pi_a(r^T_{S_X}(w))\right)_Z = \Pi_a(r^T_{S_Z}(w))$. As $\pi_a(w_X) = w_Y$, by def. of π_a, $\Pi_a(r^T_{S_X}(w)) \subseteq S_Y$. Then $\left(\Pi_a(r^T_{S_X}(w))\right)_Z = r^{S_Y}_{S_Z}\left(\Pi_a(r^T_{S_X}(w))\right) \subseteq S_Z$. Hence $\Pi_a(r^T_{S_Z}(w)) \subseteq S_Z$, and by def. of π_a, $\pi_a(w_Z) = w_Z$. As $Z \subseteq Y$, $\pi_a(w_Z) = w_Z = w_{Z \cap Y}$. $ii)$: then $Y \subseteq Z \subseteq X$. By analogous reasoning, we have $\pi_a(w_Y) = w_Y = w_{Y \cap Z}$ as $Y \subseteq Z$. We can conclude that if $\pi_a(w_X) = w_Y$, then for all $Z \subseteq X$, $\pi_a(w_Z) = w_{Z \cap X}$.

Proposition 19. *If* $L(\mathsf{M}) = (\mathcal{K}(\mathtt{K} = (W, R, V)), \trianglelefteq, \pi)$ *is the* L*-transform of an HMS model* M*, then for every* $a \in Ag$*,* R_a *is an equivalence relation.*

Proof. Let $\mathsf{M} = (\mathcal{S}, \preceq, \mathcal{R}, \Pi, V_{\mathsf{M}})$ have maximal state-space T.

Reflexivity: Let $w \in T$ and $\Pi_a(w) \subseteq S$, for some $S \in \mathcal{S}$. By def. of upwards closure, $(\Pi_a(w))^{\uparrow} = \bigcup_{S' \succeq S} (r^{S'}_S)^{-1}(\Pi_a(w))$, and by Gref, $w \in (\Pi_a(w))^{\uparrow} = \bigcup_{S' \succeq S} (r^{S'}_S)^{-1}(\Pi_a(w))$. Since $T \succeq S$, then $r^T_S(w) \in \Pi_a(w)$. Thus, $(w, w) \in R_a$, by def. L-transform. By def. of restriction lattices, this holds for all $A \subseteq At$, i.e. $(w_A, w_A) \in R_{Aa}$.

Transitivity: Let w, v, u be in T. By Conf, there are $S, S' \in \mathcal{S}$ such that $\Pi_a(w) \subseteq S$ and $\Pi_a(v) \subseteq S'$. Assume that $(w, v) \in R_a$ and $(v, u) \in R_a$. By def. of R_a, then $r^T_S(v) \in \Pi_a(w)$ and $r^T_{S'}(u) \in \Pi_a(v)$. By Stat, $\Pi_a(w) = \Pi_a(r^T_S(v))$ and $\Pi_a(v) = \Pi_a(r^T_{S'}(u))$. As $v \in T$ and $S \preceq T$, by PPI, $\Pi_a(v)^{\uparrow} \subseteq \Pi_a(r^T_S(v))^{\uparrow} = \Pi_a(w)^{\uparrow}$. Hence, as $r^T_{S'}(u) \in \Pi_a(v)^{\uparrow}$, also $r^T_{S'}(u) \in \Pi_a(w)^{\uparrow}$. By def. of upwards closure, $r^T_S(u) \in \Pi_a(w)$. Finally, $(w, u) \in R_a$ by def. of R_a.

Symmetry: Let $w, v \in T$ be in T. Assume that $(w, v) \in R_a$. By Conf, there are $S, S' \in \mathcal{S}$ such that $\Pi_a(w) \subseteq S$ and $\Pi_a(v) \subseteq S'$. Then $r^T_S(v) \in \Pi_a(w)$ (def. of L-transform), and by Stat, $\Pi_a(w) = \Pi_a(r^T_S(v))$. As $v \in T$ and $T \succeq S$, by PPI, by $\Pi_a(v)^{\uparrow} \subseteq \Pi_a(r^T_S(v))^{\uparrow}$. Then, by def. of upwards closure, $T \succeq S' \succeq S$. As $v \in T$, by PPK, $r^{S'}_S(\Pi_a(v)) = \Pi_a(r^T_S(v))$. By Gref, $x \in \Pi_a(w)^{\uparrow}$, and since $\Pi_a(w) \subseteq S$ then $r^T_S(w) \in \Pi_a(w)$, by def. of upward closure. Then $r^T_S(w) \in \Pi_a(w) = \Pi_a(r^T_S(v)) = r^{S'}_S(\Pi_a(v))$. So $r^T_S(w) \in r^{S'}_S(\Pi_a(v))$, i.e. $r^T_{S'}(w) \in \Pi_a(v)$, by def. of r. Hence, $(v, w) \in R_a$, by def. of R_a.

4.2 From Kripke Lattice Models to HMS Models

Moving from Kripke lattice models to HMS models requires a less involved construction, as the restriction lattice almost encode projections, and unawareness and uncertainty are simply composed to form possibility correspondences:

Definition 20. *Let* $\mathsf{K} = (\mathcal{K}(\mathtt{K} = (W, R, V)), \trianglelefteq, \pi)$ *be a Kripke lattice model for* At*. The* ***H-transform*** *of* K *is* $H(\mathsf{K}) = (\mathcal{S}, \preceq, \mathcal{R}, \Pi, V_{H(\mathsf{K})})$ *where*
$\mathcal{S} = \{W_X \subseteq \Omega_{\mathsf{K}} : \mathtt{K}_X \in \mathcal{K}(\mathtt{K})\}$;
$W_X \preceq W_Y$ *iff* $\mathtt{K}_X \trianglelefteq \mathtt{K}_Y$;
$\mathcal{R} = \{r^{W_X}_{W_Y} : r^{W_X}_{W_Y}(w_X) = w_Y$ *for all* $w \in W$, *and all* $X, Y \subseteq At\}$;
$\Pi = \{\Pi_a \in (2^{\Omega_{\mathsf{K}}})^{\Omega_{\mathsf{K}}} : \Pi_a(w_X) = I_a(\pi_a(w_X))$ *for all* $w \in W, X \subseteq At, a \in Ag\}$;
$V_{H(\mathsf{K})}(p) = \{w_X \in \Omega_{\mathsf{K}} : X \ni p$ *and* $w_X \in V_X(p)\}$ *for all* $p \in At$.

As HMS models lump together unawareness and uncertainty, we show only one result in this direction:

Proposition 21. *For any Kripke lattice model* $\mathsf{K} = (\mathcal{K}(\mathtt{K} = (W, R, V)), \trianglelefteq, \pi)$ *s.t.* R *assigns equivalence relations, the* H*-transform* $H(\mathsf{K})$ *is an HMS model.*

Proof. Let K be as stated and let $H(\mathsf{K}) = (\mathcal{S}, \preceq, \mathcal{R}, \Pi, V_{H(\mathsf{K})})$ be its H-transform.

$\mathcal{S} = \{W_X, W_Y, ...\}$ is composed of non-empty disjoint sets by construction and $(\mathcal{S}, \preceq)$ is a complete lattice as $(\mathcal{K}(\mathsf{K}), \trianglelefteq)$ is so. $\mathcal{R}$ is clearly a family of well-defined, surjective and commutative projections. As Π assigns to each $a \in Ag$, $\Pi_a(w_X) = I_a(\pi_a(w_X))$, for all $w \in W$, $X \subseteq At$, it assigns a a map $\Pi_a : \Omega_{H(\mathsf{K})} \to 2^{\Omega_{H(\mathsf{K})}}$, which is a possibility correspondence as it satisfies the HMS properties:

Conf: For $w_X \in W_X$, $\Pi_a(w_X) = I_a(\pi_a(w_X))$, by Definition 20. By D, $\pi_a(w_X) = w_Y$ for some $Y \subseteq X$, and $I_a(\pi_a(w_X)) = I_a(w_Y)$. So, $\Pi_a(w_X) \subseteq W_Y$ for some $Y \subseteq X$.

Gref: Let $w_X \in \Omega_{\mathsf{K}}$, $X \subseteq At$. By D, $\pi_a(w_X) = w_Y$ for some $Y \subseteq X$. By def. of Π_a and I_a, $\Pi_a(w_X) = I_a(w_Y) = \{v_Y \in \Omega_{\mathsf{K}} : (w_Y, v_Y) \in R_{Ya}\}$. Hence $\Pi_a(w_X) \subseteq W_Y$. By def. of upward closure, $(\Pi_a(w_X))^{\uparrow} = (I_a(w_Y))^{\uparrow} = \{u_Z \in \Omega_{\mathsf{K}} : Y \subseteq Z$ and $u_Y \in \{v_Y \in \Omega_{\mathsf{K}} : (w_Y, v_Y) \in R_{Ya}\}\}$, with the last identity given by the def. of $r^{W_Z}_{W_Y}$. As R_a is an equivalence relation, so is R_{Ya}, by def. So $w_Y \in \{v_Y \in \Omega_{\mathsf{K}} : (w_Y, v_Y) \in R_{Ya}\}$, and since $Y \subseteq X$, then $w_X \in (\Pi_a(w_X))^{\uparrow}$.

Stat: For $w_X \in \Omega_{\mathsf{K}}$, assume $v \in \Pi_a(w_X) = I_a(\pi_a(w_X))$. By D, $v \in I_a(w_Y)$, for some $Y \subseteq X$. With R_{Ya} an equivalence relation, $v \in I_a(w_Y)$ iff $w_Y \in I_a(v)$, i.e., $I_a(v) = I_a(w_B)$. II and D entails that for all $u_Y \in I_a(w_Y)$, $\pi_a(u_Y) = u_Y$, so $\pi_a(v) = v$. Therefore $\Pi_a(v) = I_a(\pi_a(v)) = I_a(v) = I_a(w_Y) = I_a(\pi_a(w_X)) = \Pi_a(w_X)$. Thus, if $v \in \Pi_a(w_X)$, then $\Pi_a(v) = \Pi_a(w_X)$.

PPI: Let $w_X \in W_X$ and $W_Y \preceq W_X$, i.e. $Y \subseteq X \subseteq At$. Let $q_Q \in (\Pi_a(w_X))^{\uparrow}$ with $Q \subseteq At$. By def. of Π_a and D, $\Pi_a(w_X) = I_a(\pi_a(w_X)) = I_a(w_Z)$ for some $Z \subseteq X$. By def. of upwards closure, it follows that $q_Z \in I_a(w_Z) = \Pi_a(w_X)$. Now let $\pi_a(w_Y) = w_P$ for some $P \subseteq Y$. Then, by NS, $P = Z \cap Y$, so $P \subseteq Z$. As $q_Z \in I_a(w_Z)$, then $q_P \in I_a(w_P) = I_a(\pi_a(w_Y)) = \Pi_a(w_Y)$, by def. of restriction lattice. Since $q_Q \in (\Pi_a(w_X))^{\uparrow} = (I_a(w_Z))^{\uparrow}$, then $Z \subseteq Q$. It follows that $P \subseteq Z \subseteq Q$, which implies $q_Q \in (\Pi_a(w_Y))^{\uparrow}$. Hence, if $q_Q \in (\Pi_a(w_X))^{\uparrow}$, then $q_Q \in (\Pi_a(w_Y))^{\uparrow}$, i.e., $(\Pi_a(w_X))^{\uparrow} \subseteq (\Pi_a(w_Y))^{\uparrow}$.

PPK: Suppose that $W_Z \preceq W_Y \preceq W_X$, $w_X \in W_X$ and $\Pi_a(w_X) \subseteq W_Y$, i.e. $\Pi_a(w_X) = I_a(w_Y)$ and $\pi_a(w_X) = w_Y$. As $Z \subseteq Y \subseteq X$, NS implies $\pi_a(w_Z) = w_{Z \cap Y} = w_Z$. Hence, $\Pi_a(w_Z) = I_a(w_Z) \subseteq W_Z$. Hence PPK is established if $(I_a(w_Y))_Z = I_a(w_Z)$. As $(I_a(w_Y))_Z = \{x_Z \in \Omega_{\mathsf{K}} : x_Y \in I_a(w_Y)\}$, then clearly $(I_a(w_Y))_Z = I_a(w_Z)$. Thus, $(\Pi_a(w_X))_Z = \Pi_a(w_Z)$.

Finally, $V_{H(\mathsf{K})}$ is an HMS valuation as for each $p \in At$, $V_{H(\mathsf{K})}(p)$ is an event $(D^{\uparrow}, S)$ with $D = \{w_{\{p\}} \in W_{\{p\}} : w_{\{p\}} \in V_{\{p\}}(p)\}$ and $S = W_{\{p\}}$.

5 Language for Awareness and Model Equivalence

Multiple languages for knowledge and awareness exist. The Logic of General Awareness (LGA, [8]) takes implicit knowledge and awareness as primitives, and define explicit knowledge as 'implicit knowledge $\wedge$ awareness'; other combinations are discussed in [4]. Variations of LGA include quantification over objects [5], formulas [1,11,12], and even unawareness [7], alternative operators informed through cognitive science [2], and dynamic extensions [4,7,9,16].

HMS [14] follow instead Modica and Rustichini [18,19] and take explicit knowledge as primitive and awareness as defined: an agent is aware of φ iff she either explicitly knows φ, or explicitly knows that she does not explicitly know φ.

Definition 22. *Let Ag be a finite, non-empty set of agents and At a countable, non-empty set of atoms. With $a \in Ag$ and $p \in At$, define the language $\mathcal{L}$ by*

$$\varphi ::= \top \mid p \mid \neg\varphi \mid \varphi \wedge \varphi \mid K_a\varphi$$

and define $A_a\varphi := K_a\varphi \vee K_a\neg K_a\varphi$.

Let $At(\varphi) = \{p \in At\colon p \text{ is a subformula of } \varphi\}$, for all $\varphi \in \mathcal{L}$.

5.1 HMS Models as a Semantics

The satisfaction of formulas over HMS models is defined as follows. The semantics are three-valued, so formulas may have undefined truth value: there may exist a $w \in \Omega_{\mathsf{M}}$ such that neither $\mathsf{M}, w \models \varphi$ nor $\mathsf{M}, w \models \neg\varphi$. This happens if and only if φ contains atoms with undefined truth value in w.

Definition 23. *Let $\mathsf{M} = (\mathcal{S}, \preceq, \mathcal{R}, \Pi, V_{\mathsf{M}})$ be an HMS model and let $w \in \Omega_{\mathsf{M}}$. Satisfaction of $\mathcal{L}$ formulas is given by*

$$\begin{array}{llll}
\mathsf{M}, w \models \top & \textit{for all } w \in \Omega_{\mathsf{M}} & & \\
\mathsf{M}, w \models p & \textit{iff} \;\; w \in V_{\mathsf{M}}(p) & \mathsf{M}, w \models \varphi \wedge \psi & \textit{iff} \;\; w \in [\![\varphi]\!] \cap [\![\psi]\!] \\
\mathsf{M}, w \models \neg\varphi & \textit{iff} \;\; w \in \neg[\![\varphi]\!] & \mathsf{M}, w \models K_a\varphi & \textit{iff} \;\; w \in \boldsymbol{K}_a([\![\varphi]\!])
\end{array}$$

where $[\![\varphi]\!] = \{v \in \Omega_{\mathsf{M}}\colon \mathsf{M}, v \models \varphi\}$ for all $\varphi \in \mathcal{L}$.

With the HMS semantics being three-valued, they adopt a non-standard notion of validity which requires only that a formula be always satisfied *if its has a defined truth value.* The below is equivalent to the definition in [14], but is stated so that it also works for Kripke lattice models:

Definition 24. *A formula $\varphi \in \mathcal{L}$ is valid over a class of models $\boldsymbol{C}$ iff for all models $M \in \boldsymbol{C}$, for all states w of M which satisfy p or $\neg p$ for all $p \in At(\varphi)$, w also satisfies φ.*

5.2 Kripke Lattice Models as a Semantics

We define semantics for $\mathcal{L}$ over Kripke lattice models. Like the HMS semantics, the semantics are three-valued, as it is possible that a pointed Kripke lattice model (M, w_X) satisfies neither φ nor $\neg\varphi$. This happens exactly when φ contains atoms not in X.

Definition 25. *Let $\mathsf{K} = (\mathcal{K}(K = (W, R, V)), \trianglelefteq, \pi)$ be a Kripke lattice model with $w_X \in \Omega_{\mathsf{K}}$. Satisfaction of $\mathcal{L}$ formulas is given by*

$$\begin{array}{llll}
\mathsf{K}, w_X \Vdash \top & & \textit{for all } w_X \in \Omega_{\mathsf{K}} & \\
\mathsf{K}, w_X \Vdash p & \textit{iff} & w_X \in V_X(p) & \textit{and } p \in X \\
\mathsf{K}, w_X \Vdash \neg\varphi & \textit{iff} & \textit{not } \mathsf{K}, w_X \Vdash \varphi & \textit{and } At(\varphi) \subseteq X \\
\mathsf{K}, w_X \Vdash \varphi \wedge \psi & \textit{iff} & \mathsf{K}, w_X \Vdash \varphi \textit{ and } \mathsf{K}, w_X \Vdash \psi & \textit{and } At(\varphi \wedge \psi) \subseteq X \\
\mathsf{K}, w_X \Vdash K_a\varphi & \textit{iff} & \pi_a(w_X) R_{Ya} v_Y \textit{ implies } \mathsf{K}, v_Y \Vdash \varphi, & \\
 & & \textit{for } Y \subseteq At \textit{ s.t. } \pi_a(w_X) \in W_Y & \textit{and } At(\varphi) \in X
\end{array}$$

5.3 The Equivalence of HMS and Kripke Lattice Models

L- and H-transforms not only produce models of the correct class, but also preserve finer details, as any model and its transform satisfy the same formulas.

Proposition 26. *For any HMS model* M *with* L*-transform* $L(\mathsf{M})$*, for all* $\varphi \in \mathcal{L}$*, for all* $w \in \Omega_{\mathsf{M}}$*, and for all* $v \in \ell(w)$*,* $\mathsf{M}, w \vDash \varphi$ *iff* $L(\mathsf{M}), v \Vdash \varphi$*.*

Proof. Let Σ_{M} be the events of $\mathsf{M} = (\mathcal{S}, \preceq, \mathcal{R}, \Pi, V_{\mathsf{M}})$ with maximal state-space T and let $L(\mathsf{M}) = (\mathcal{K}(\mathsf{K} = (W, R, V)), \trianglelefteq, \pi)$. The proof is by induction on formula complexity. Let $\varphi \in \mathcal{L}$ and let $w \in \Omega_{\mathsf{M}}$ with $At(S(w)) = X$.

Base: i) $\varphi := p \in At$ or *ii)* $\varphi := \top$. *i)* $\mathsf{M}, w \vDash p$ iff $w \in V_{\mathsf{M}}(p)$. As $V_{\mathsf{M}}(p) \in \Sigma_{\mathsf{M}}$, $(r^T_{S(w)})^{-1}(w) \subseteq V_{\mathsf{M}}(p)$. By def. of $L(\mathsf{M})$, if $v \in T = W$, then $v \in V_{\mathsf{M}}(p)$ iff $v \in V(p)$, so $v \in (r^T_{S(w)})^{-1}(w)$ iff $v \in V(p)$ iff $v_X \in V_X(p)$, with $p \in X$ (def. of Kripke lattice models). Hence, by def. of ℓ, $v \in \ell(w) = \{u_X \in W_X : u \in (r^T_{S(w)})^{-1}(w)$ for $X = At(S(w))\}$ iff $v \in V_X(p)$, i.e., iff $L(M), v \Vdash p$ for all $v \in \ell(w)$. *ii)* is trivial.

Step. Assume $\psi, \chi \in \mathcal{L}$ satisfy Proposition 26.

$\varphi := \neg\psi$. There are two cases: *i)* $At(\psi) \subseteq At(S(w))$ or *ii)* $At(\psi) \nsubseteq At(S(w))$. *i)* $\mathsf{M}, w \vDash \neg\psi$ iff (def. of $\vDash$) $w \in \neg[\![\psi]\!]$ iff (def. of V_{M}) $(r^T_{S(w)})^{-1}(w) \subseteq \neg[\![\psi]\!]$ iff (def. of $[\![\psi]\!]$) for all $v \in (r^T_{S(w)})^{-1}(w)$, $\mathsf{M}, v \nvDash \psi$ iff (Definition 13) for all $v \in (r^T_{S(w)})^{-1}(w)$, not $L(\mathsf{M}), v \Vdash \psi$ iff (def. of $\ell(w)$) for all $v_X \in \ell(w)$, not $L(\mathsf{M}), v_X \Vdash \psi$, with $At(\psi) \subseteq X$ iff (def. of $\Vdash$) for all $v_X \in \ell(w)$, $L(\mathsf{M}), v_X \Vdash \neg\psi$. *ii)* is trivial: φ is undefined in (M, w) iff it is so in $(L(\mathsf{M}), w_X)$.

$\varphi := \psi \wedge \chi$. The case follows by tracing *iff*s through the definitions of $\vDash$, V_{M}, $[\![\cdot]\!]$, $\left(r^T_{S(w)}\right)^{-1}$, L-transform, ℓ, and $\Vdash$.

$\varphi := K_a\psi$. $\mathsf{M}, w \vDash K_a\psi$ iff (def. of $\vDash$) $w \in \boldsymbol{K}_a([\![\psi]\!])$ iff (def. of $\boldsymbol{K}_a$) $\Pi_a(w) \subseteq [\![\psi]\!]$. Let $\Pi_a(w) \subseteq S$, for some $S \in \mathcal{S}$, and let $X = At(S(w))$ and $Y = At(S)$. Then $v_S \in \Pi_a(w) \subseteq [\![\psi]\!]$ iff (def. of $[\![\psi]\!]$) for all $v_S \in \Pi_a(w)$, $\mathsf{M}, v_S \vDash \psi$ iff (def. of V_{M}) for all $(r^T_S)^{-1}(v_S)$ with $v_S \in \Pi_a(w)$, $\mathsf{M}, v_T \vDash \psi$ iff (def. of L-transform) for all v_{At} with $r^T_S(v) \in \Pi_a(w)$, $L(\mathsf{M}), v_{At} \Vdash \psi$ and $At(\psi) \subseteq At$ iff (def. of L-transform) for all v_{At} with $(w_{At}, v_{At}) \in R_{Ata}$, $L(\mathsf{M}), v_{At} \Vdash \psi$ and $At(\psi) \subseteq At$ iff (def. of restriction lattice) for all v_Y with $(w_Y, v_Y) \in R_{Ya}$, $L(\mathsf{M}), v_Y \Vdash \psi$ and $At(\psi) \subseteq Y$ iff (def. of π_a and $\pi_a(w_X) = w_Y$), for all v_Y with $(\pi_a(w_X), v_Y) \in R_{Ya}$, $L(\mathsf{M}), v_Y \Vdash \psi$ and $At(\psi) \subseteq Y$ iff (def. of $\Vdash$) $L(\mathsf{M}), w_X \Vdash K_a\psi$ and $At(\psi) \subseteq Y$.

Proposition 27. *For any Kripke lattice model* K *with* H*-transform* $H(\mathsf{K})$*, for all* $\varphi \in \mathcal{L}$*, for all* $w_X \in \Omega_{\mathsf{K}}$*,* $\mathsf{K}, w_X \Vdash \varphi$ *iff* $H(\mathsf{K}), w_X \vDash \varphi$*.*

Proof. Let $\mathsf{K} = (\mathcal{K}(K = (W, R, V)), \trianglelefteq, \pi)$ with $w_X \in \Omega_{\mathsf{K}}$, $\pi_a(w_X) \in W_Y$ with $Y \subseteq At$, and let $H(\mathsf{K}) = (\mathcal{S}, \preceq, \mathcal{R}, \Pi, V_{H(\mathsf{K})})$. Let $\varphi \in \mathcal{L}$ and proceed by induction on formula complexity.

Base: i) $\varphi := p \in At$ or *ii)* $\varphi := \top$. *i)* $\mathsf{K}, w_X \Vdash p$ iff (def. of $\Vdash$) $w_X \in V_X(p)$ with $p \in X$ iff (def. of H-transform) $w_X \in V_{H(\mathsf{K})}(p)$ iff (def. of $\vDash$) $H(\mathsf{K}), w_X \vDash p$. *ii)* is trivial.

Step. Assume $\psi, \chi \in \mathcal{L}$ satisfy Proposition 27.

$\varphi := \neg\psi$. There are two cases: *i)* $At(\psi) \subseteq X$ or *ii)* $At(\psi) \not\subseteq X$. *i)* $\mathsf{K}, w_X \Vdash \neg\psi$ iff (def. of $\Vdash$) not $\mathsf{K}, w_X \Vdash \psi$ iff (def. of $[\![\psi]\!]$) $w_X \notin [\![\psi]\!]$ iff (def. of $[\![\psi]\!]$ and $At(\psi) \subseteq X$) $w_X \in \neg[\![\psi]\!]$ iff (def. of $\vDash$) $H(\mathsf{K}), w_X \vDash \neg\psi$. *ii)* is trivial: φ is undefined in (K, w_X) iff it is so in $(H(\mathsf{M}), w_X)$.

$\varphi := \psi \wedge \chi$. The case follows by tracing *iff*s through the definitions of $\Vdash$, H-transform, and $\Vdash$.

$\varphi := K_a\psi$. $\mathsf{K}, w_X \Vdash K_a\psi$ iff (def. of $\Vdash$) $\pi_a(w_X) R_{Ya} v_Y$ implies $\mathsf{K}, v_Y \Vdash \varphi$ iff (def. of π_a, i.e. $\pi_a(w_X) = w_Y$ and def. of I_a), for all v_Y s.t. $(w_Y, v_Y) \in R_{Ya}$, i.e. for all $v_Y \in I_a(w_Y)$, $\mathsf{K}, v_Y \Vdash \varphi$ iff (def. of Π_a, i.e. $\Pi_a(w_X) = I_a(\pi_a(w_X)) = I_a(w_Y)$) $\Pi_a(w_X) \subseteq [\![\psi]\!]$ iff (def. of $\boldsymbol{K}_a$) $w \in \boldsymbol{K}_a([\![\psi]\!])$ iff (def. of $\vDash$) $H(\mathsf{K}), w_X \vDash K_a\psi$.

6 The HMS Logic of Kripke Lattice Models with Equivalence Relations

As we may transition back-and-forth between HMS models and Kripke lattice models with equivalence relations in a manner that preserve satisfaction of formula of $\mathcal{L}$, soundness and completeness of a $\mathcal{L}$-logic is also transferable between the model classes. We thereby show such results for Kripke lattice models with equivalence relations as a corollary to results by HMS [14].

Definition 28. *The logic Λ_{HMS} is the smallest set of $\mathcal{L}$ formulas that contain the axioms in, and is closed under the inference rules of,* Table 1.

Table 1. Axioms and inference rules of the HMS logic of unawareness, Λ_{HMS}.

All substitution instances of propositional logic, including the formula $\top$	
$A_a\neg\varphi \leftrightarrow A_a\varphi$	(Symmetry)
$A_a(\varphi \wedge \psi) \leftrightarrow A_a\varphi \wedge A_a\psi$	(Awareness Conjunction)
$A_a\varphi \leftrightarrow A_aK_b\varphi$, for all $b \in Ag$	(Awareness Knowledge Reflection)
$K_a\varphi \rightarrow \varphi$	(T, Axiom of Truth)
$K_a\varphi \rightarrow K_aK_a\varphi$	(4, Positive Introspection Axiom)
From φ and $\varphi \rightarrow \psi$, infer ψ	(Modus Ponens)
For $\varphi_1, \varphi_2, ..., \varphi_n, \varphi$ that satisfy $At(\varphi) \subseteq \bigcup_{i=1}^n At(\varphi_i)$, from $\bigwedge_{i=1}^n \varphi_i \rightarrow \varphi$, infer $\bigwedge_{i=1}^n K_a\varphi_i \rightarrow K_a\varphi$	(RK-Inference)

As the L-transform of an HMS model has equivalence relations, one may be surprised by the lack of the standard negative introspection axiom $5 : (\neg K_a\varphi \rightarrow K_a\neg K_a\varphi)$ among the axioms of Λ_{HMS}. However, including 5 would make collapse awareness [18]. In [14], HMS remarks that Λ_{HMS} imply the weakened version $K_a\neg K_a\neg K_a\varphi \rightarrow (K_a\varphi \vee K_a\neg K_a\varphi)$, which by the Modici-Rustichini definition of awareness is $K_a\neg K_a\neg K_a\varphi \rightarrow A_a\varphi$. Defining unawareness by $U_a\varphi := \neg A_a\varphi$, this again equates $U_a\varphi \rightarrow \neg K_a\neg K_a\neg K_a\varphi$. Additionally, HMS notes that if φ is a theorem, then $A_a\varphi \rightarrow K_a\varphi$ is a theorem, that 4 implies introspection of awareness ($A_a\varphi \rightarrow K_aA_a\varphi$), while Λ_{HMS} entails that *awareness is generated by primitives propositions*, i.e., that $A_a\varphi \leftrightarrow \bigwedge_{p\in At(\varphi)} A_ap$ is a theorem. The latter two properties entails that HMS awareness is *propositionally determined*, in the terminology of [13].

Using the above given notion of validity and standard notions of proof, soundness and strong completeness, HMS [14] state that, as standard,

Lemma 29. *The logic Λ_{HMS} is strongly complete with respect to a class of structures $\mathfrak{S}$ iff every set of Λ_{HMS} consistent formulas is satisfied in some $\mathfrak{s} \in \mathfrak{S}$.*

Let $\boldsymbol{M}$ be the class of HMS modes. Using a canonical model, HMS show:

Theorem 30 ([14]). *Λ_{HMS} is sound and strongly complete with respect to $\boldsymbol{M}$.*

Let $\boldsymbol{KLM}_{EQ}$ be the class of Kripke lattice models where all accessibility relations are equivalence relations. As a corollary to Theorem 30 and our transformation and equivalence results, we obtain

Theorem 31. *Λ_{HMS} is sound and strongly complete with respect to $\boldsymbol{KLM}_{EQ}$.*

Proof. Soundness: The axioms of Λ_{HMS} are valid $\boldsymbol{KLM}_{EQ}$. We show the contrapositive. Let $\varphi \in \mathcal{L}$. If φ is not valid in $\boldsymbol{KLM}_{EQ}$, then for some $\mathsf{K} \in \boldsymbol{KLM}_{EQ}$ and some w from K, $\mathsf{K}, w \Vdash \neg\varphi$. Then its H-transform $H(\mathsf{K})$ is an HMS model cf. Proposition 21, and $H(\mathsf{K}), w \vDash \neg\varphi$ cf. Proposition 27. Hence φ is not valid in the class of HMS models. The same reasoning implies that the Λ_{HMS} inference rules preserve validity.

Completeness: Assume $\Phi \subseteq \mathcal{L}$ is a consistent set, and let $\mathfrak{M}$ be the canonical model of HMS, with $\mathfrak{w}$ a state in $\mathfrak{M}$ that satisfies Φ. This exists, cf. [14]. By Propositions 18 and 19, $L(\mathfrak{M})$ is in $\boldsymbol{KLM}_{EQ}$. By Proposition 26, for all $v \in \ell(\mathfrak{w})$, $L(\mathfrak{M}), v \Vdash \Phi$. By Lemma 29, Λ_{HMS} is thus strongly complete w.r.t. $\boldsymbol{KLM}_{EQ}$.

7 Concluding Remarks

This paper has presented a Kripke model-based rendition of the HMS model of awareness, and shown the two model classes equally general w.r.t. $\mathcal{L}$, by defining transformations between the two that preserve formula satisfaction. A corollary to this result is completeness of the HMS logic for the introduced model class.

There are several issues we would like to study in future work:

In recasting the HMS model, we teased apart the epistemic and awareness dimensions merged in the HMS possibility correspondences, and Propositions 18, 19 and 21 about L- and H-transforms show that the HMS properties are satisfied iff each π_a satisfies D, II and NS, and each R_a is an equivalence relation. For a more fine-grained property correspondence, the propositions' proofs show that each property of one model is entailed by a strict subset of the properties of the other. In some cases, the picture emerging is fairly clear: e.g., HMS' Conf is shown only using the restrictions lattice construction (RLC) plus D and *vice versa*; PPK uses only NS and RLC, while PPK and Conf entail NS. In other cases, the picture is more murky, e.g., when we use Stat, PPI and PPK to show the seemingly simple symmetry of R_a. We think it would be interesting to decompose properties on both sides to see if clearer relationships arise.

There are two issues with redundant states in Kripke lattice models. One concerns redundant restrictions, cf. Remark 12, which may be solved by working with a more general model class, where models may also be based on sub-orders of the restriction lattice. A second one concerns redundant states. For example, in Fig. 2, $\mathtt{K}_\emptyset$ contains three 'identical' states where no atoms have defined truth values—$\mathtt{K}_\emptyset$ is bisimilar to a one-state Kripke model. As bisimulation contracting each $\mathtt{K}_X$ may collapse states from which awareness maps differ, one must define a notion of bisimulation that takes awareness maps into consideration (notions of bisimulation for other awareness models exists, e.g. [6]). Together with a more general modal class definition, this could hopefully solve the redundancy issues.

Though [13,14,20] provide comparisons of the HMS and LGA [8,13] models, we would like to make a direct comparison with the latter to understand Kripke lattice models from an awareness function perspective. It would then be natural to use the LGA language with awareness and implicit knowledge as primitives over Kripke lattice models, which is possible as they include objective states.

The HMS logic is complete for HMS models and Kripke lattice models with equivalence relations. [13] prove completeness for HMS models using a standard validity notion, a 'φ is at least as expressive as ψ' operator and variants of axioms T, 4 and 5. We are very interested in considering this system and its weaker variants for Kripke lattice models, also with less assumptions on the relations.

Finally, issues of dynamics spring forth: first, whether existing awareness dynamics may be understood on Kripke lattice models; second, whether DEL action models may be applied lattice-wide with reasonable results; and third, whether the π_a maps may be thought in dynamic terms, as they map between models.

Acknowledgments. We thank the reviewers for their keen eyes and productive comments. The Center for Information and Bubble Studies is funded by the Carlsberg Foundation. RKR was partially supported by the DFG-ANR joint project *Collective Attitude Formation* [RO 4548/8-1].

References

1. Ågotnes, T., Alechina, N.: A logic for reasoning about knowledge of unawareness. J. Logic Lang. Inf. **23**(2), 197–217 (2014). https://doi.org/10.1007/s10849-014-9201-4
2. Pietarinen, A.: Awareness in logic and cognitive neuroscience. In: Proceedings of IEEE International Conference on Cognitive Informatics, pp. 155–162 (2002)
3. van Benthem, J., Gerbrandy, J., Hoshi, T., Pacuit, E.: Merging frameworks for interaction. J. Philos. Logic **38**(5), 491–526 (2009). https://doi.org/10.1007/s10992-008-9099-x

4. van Benthem, J., Velázquez-Quesada, F.R.: The dynamics of awareness. Synthese **177**, 5–27 (2010). https://doi.org/10.1007/s11229-010-9764-9
5. Board, O., Chung, K.S.: Object-based unawareness. In: Bonanno, G., van der Hoek, W.M.W. (ed.) Proceedings of LOFT 7, pp. 35–41 (2006)
6. van Ditmarsch, H., French, T., Velázquez-Quesada, F.R., Wang, Y.: Knowledge, awareness, and bisimulation. In: TARK 2013 - Proceedings of the 14th Conference on Theoretical Aspects of Rationality and Knowledge, vol. 1, pp. 61–70. Institute of Mathematical Sciences (2013)
7. van Ditmarsch, H., French, T.: Semantics for knowledge and change of awareness. J. Logic Lang. Inf. **23**(2), 169–195 (2014). https://doi.org/10.1007/s10849-014-9194-z
8. Fagin, R., Halpern, J.Y.: Belief, awareness, and limited reasoning. Artif. Intell. **34**, 39–76 (1988)
9. Grossi, D., Velázquez-Quesada, F.R.: Syntactic awareness in logical dynamics. Synthese **192**(12), 4071–4105 (2015). https://doi.org/10.1007/s11229-015-0733-1
10. Halpern, J.Y.: Alternative semantics for unawareness. Games Econ. Behav. **37**(2), 321–339 (2001)
11. Halpern, J.Y., Rêgo, L.C.: Reasoning about knowledge of unawareness. Games Econ. Behav. **67**(2), 503–525 (2009)
12. Halpern, J.Y., Rêgo, L.C.: Reasoning about knowledge of unawareness revisited. Math. Soc. Sci. **65**(2), 73–84 (2013)
13. Halpern, J.Y., Rêgo, L.C.: Interactive unawareness revisited. Games Econ. Behav. **62**(1), 232–262 (2008)
14. Heifetz, A., Meier, M., Schipper, B.: A canonical model for interactive unawareness. Games Econ. Behav. **62**, 304–324 (2008)
15. Heifetz, A., Meier, M., Schipper, B.C.: Interactive unawareness. J. Econ. Theory **130**(1), 78–94 (2006)
16. Hill, B.: Awareness dynamics. J. Philos. Logic **39**(2), 113–137 (2010)
17. van Lee, H.S., Rendsvig, R.K., van Wijk, S.: Intensional protocols for dynamic epistemic logic. J. Philos. Logic **48**(6), 1077–1118 (2019). https://doi.org/10.1007/s10992-019-09508-w
18. Modica, S., Rustichini, A.: Awareness and partitional information structures. Theory Decis. **37**(1), 107–124 (1994). https://doi.org/10.1007/BF01079207
19. Modica, S., Rustichini, A.: Unawareness and partitional information structures. Games Econ. Behav. **27**(2), 265–298 (1999)
20. Schipper, B.C.: Awareness. In: van Ditmarsch, H., Halpern, J.Y., van der Hoek, W., Kooi, B.P. (eds.) Handbook of Epistemic Logic. College Publications (2014)

Dealing with Unreliable Agents in Dynamic Gossip

Line van den Berg[1(✉)] and Malvin Gattinger[2]

[1] Univ. Grenoble Alpes, Inria, CNRS, Saint-Martin-d'Hères, France
line.van-den-berg@inria.fr
[2] University of Groningen, Groningen, The Netherlands
malvin@w4eg.eu

Abstract. Gossip describes the spread of information throughout a network of agents. It investigates how agents, each starting with a unique secret, can efficiently make peer-to-peer calls so that ultimately everyone knows all secrets. In Dynamic Gossip, agents share phone numbers in addition to secrets, which allows the network to grow at run-time.

Most gossip protocols assume that all agents are reliable, but this is not given for many practical applications. We drop this assumption and study Dynamic Gossip with unreliable agents. The aim is then for agents to learn all secrets of the reliable agents and to identify the unreliable agents.

We show that with unreliable agents classic results on Dynamic Gossip no longer hold. Specifically, the Learn New Secrets protocol is no longer characterised by the same class of graphs, so-called sun graphs. In addition, we show that unreliable agents that do not initiate communication are harder to identify than agents that do. This has paradoxical consequences for measures against unreliability, for example to combat the spread of fake news in social networks.

1 Introduction

The internet has led to great changes in the distribution of news. Recently, 'fake news' received attention, possibly having influenced the 2016 US presidential election [1]. Besides the challenge to identify fake news, a question is how to treat it: should false information be removed or is marking it as false sufficient?

Dynamic Gossip is a formal model how information can spread throughout a changing network of agents. It investigates how agents, each with a unique secret, decide, based on their own knowledge about the network, what calls to make so that ultimately everyone knows all the secrets. A gossip protocol can help agents to decide on a call sequence to perform. Examples from the literature are ANY ("call any agent"), CMO ("call me once") and LNS ("learn new secrets") [7]. In a dynamic setting, additional to secrets, agents share phone numbers, allowing the network to grow at run-time.

Traditionally these systems assume that *everybody is reliable*, but this assumption is not justified for many practical applications. Therefore, we adapt

M. A. Martins and I. Sedlár (Eds.): DaLí 2020, LNCS 12569, pp. 51–67, 2020.
https://doi.org/10.1007/978-3-030-65840-3_4

Dynamic Gossip to account for unreliable agents. Of course, the possibilities for agents to be unreliable are numerous: agents can lie about their own secret or about secrets of others, agents can have a memory of whom they have lied to or not, agents can always lie or with a certain probability, and agents can lie merely about secrets or also about phone numbers, etc. With any such form of unreliability, the aim of the reliable agents should still be to learn all the secrets (of the reliable agents) and, in addition, to identify the unreliable agents.

We show that, already with relatively simple unreliable agent a known result in Dynamic Gossip from [7] breaks down. Specifically, the Learn New Secrets protocol is no longer characterised by sun graphs. This emphasises the need to discard the assumption that everyone is reliable for any practical application. In addition, we show that unreliable agents that do not initiate communication are harder to identify than those that do. This has seemingly paradoxical consequences for security measures taken against unreliable agents: blocking as a measure against false information has the adverse effect of securing the anonymity of the unreliable agents. New protocols are needed to properly cope with unreliable agents in Dynamic Gossip.

Our article is structured as follows. We give a short summary of related work in Sect. 2. In Sect. 3 we recall the definitions of Dynamic Gossip. We then define Unreliable Gossip and unreliable agents in Sect. 4 and 5, respectively. The new setting then motivates a new notion of success which we define and examine in Sect. 6. We conclude with future work ideas and a discussion the relevance of Unreliable Gossip for social networks in Sect. 7.

2 Related Work

Gossip has first been studied in combinatorics and graph-theory [11]. The classical question, also known as the "telephone problem" is: Given n agents who each start with a unique secret, how many phone calls are needed to spread all secrets? For $n > 3$ agents that all have the phone number of all other agents, $2n - 4$ calls are necessary and sufficient to make everyone learn all secrets [15]. For networks in which not every agent has the phone number of all other agents, these numbers are naturally higher [10]. Besides communication networks, gossip has also been used for the study of epidemics [9], power grids [17] and neural networks [17].

Most results on classical gossip assume a *central* and *all-knowing scheduler* deciding who should call whom and when. This is not realistic for practical applications in which agents have to decide autonomously what (communication) action to take. Hence, *distributed* gossip has been studied in which agents decide autonomously, on their own, whom to call using *epistemic* protocols [2,3].

More recently, another assumption has been lifted, namely the assumption that the graph representing who can call whom is constant, i.e. agents have a static phone book or contact list. In *dynamic* gossip agents also exchange phone numbers, adding edges in the reachability graph [7]. This means that the network may grow at run-time. This is the setting which we use and extend here.

Most work on the classical telephone problem and on Dynamic Gossip assumes that all agents are reliable and follow the same protocol. However, gossip with unreliability has been studied extensively in other areas. One direction of research is about settings where communication links are unreliable, as studied in [14] and [16]. In contrast, here we assume that communication works perfectly but that agents are unreliable. Our setting is thus more comparable to having faulty or malicious agents, as in distributed storage [6] or consensus protocols [4].

Similar to our work is also the proposal of 'corrected gossip' in [12]. The authors study failing nodes and define a gossip protocol which tries to reduce latency of the total group communication. A big difference to our setting is that their networks are static and no links are added at run-time.

3 Dynamic Gossip

We now give a short introduction to Dynamic Gossip, following [7]. We assume a finite set of agents, $\mathcal{A}$. Initially, each agent knows only their own secret and some set of phone numbers including their own. If an agent a has the phone number of an agent b, then the phone call ab can take place. During a call, the two agents exchange secrets and phone numbers — including those they learned in previous calls. One might wonder what else agents learn in such a call, but for all results we discuss here higher-order knowledge such as "a knows that b knows the secret of c" is irrelevant, hence we will not model it and refer to [8].

Example 1. Suppose agent a knows the number of b, and agents b and c know each other's number and no other numbers are known. We draw this situation below. Note that we use dashed arrows for the binary relation of knowing the number of someone (N). Now if a calls b then a and b learn each other's secret, which we draw with solid arrows (S). We also add another dashed arrow: in the call ab agent a also learns the number of c.

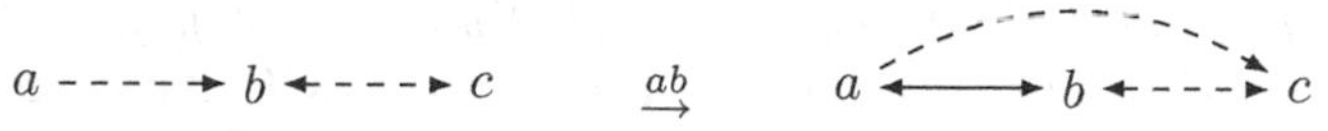

We formally define gossip graphs, calls and sequences as follows.

Definition 1 (Gossip Graph). *For any set $\mathcal{A}$, let $I_{\mathcal{A}} := \{(a,a) \mid a \in \mathcal{A}\}$. A* gossip graph *is a triple $G = (\mathcal{A}, N, S)$ where $\mathcal{A}$ is a finite set of agents, $N \subseteq \mathcal{A} \times \mathcal{A}$ and $S \subseteq \mathcal{A} \times \mathcal{A}$ such that $I_{\mathcal{A}} \subseteq N$ and $I_{\mathcal{A}} \subseteq S$. Given any G, let $S_a := \{b \in \mathcal{A} \mid (a,b) \in S\}$ and $N_a := \{b \in \mathcal{A} \mid (a,b) \in N\}$.*

A graph is initial *iff $S = I_{\mathcal{A}}$. A graph is* complete *iff $S = \mathcal{A} \times \mathcal{A}$.*

An agent a is an expert *iff $S_a = \mathcal{A}$. An agent a is* terminal *iff $N_a = \{a\}$.*

We say that "agent a knows the number of agent b" iff $(a,b) \in N$. Similarly, we say "agent a knows the secret of agent b" iff $(a,b) \in S$.

We now define calls ab, in which agent a and b share all their information.

Definition 2 (Call). *Suppose* $G = (\mathcal{A}, N, S)$, $a, b \in \mathcal{A}$ *and* $(a, b) \in N$. *The* call ab *maps* G *to* $G^{ab} := (\mathcal{A}, N^{ab}, S^{ab})$ *where*

$$N_c^{ab} := \begin{cases} N_a \cup N_b & \textit{if } c \in \{a, b\} \\ N_c & \textit{otherwise} \end{cases} \quad \textit{and} \quad S_c^{ab} := \begin{cases} S_a \cup S_b & \textit{if } c \in \{a, b\} \\ S_c & \textit{otherwise} \end{cases}$$

Definition 3 (Call sequences). *A* call sequence σ *is a sequence of calls. We use the following notation:* ϵ *is the empty sequence and* $\sigma; \tau$ *is the concatenation of two sequences* σ *and* τ*; Moreover,* $\sigma \sqsubseteq \tau$ *denotes that* σ *is a prefix of* τ.

We say that call ab *is* possible *on a graph* $G = (\mathcal{A}, N, S)$ *iff* $(a, b) \in N$. *The call sequence* ϵ *is possible on any graph, and a call sequence* $ab; \sigma$ *is possible on* G *iff the call* ab *is possible on* G *and* σ *is possible on* G^{ab}. *If a call sequence* σ *is possible on a graph* G*, then* G^σ *is defined by:* $G^\epsilon := G$ *and* $G^{ab;\sigma} := (G^{ab})^\sigma$.

It is an easy exercise to show by induction on σ that "if a knows the secret of b, then a also knows the number of b" is an invariant when making calls.

Lemma 1. *For any initial graph* $G = (\mathcal{A}, N, S)$ *and any call sequence* σ *that is possible on* G*, we have in the resulting graph* $G^\sigma = (\mathcal{A}, N^\sigma, S^\sigma)$ *that* $S^\sigma \subseteq N^\sigma$.

A protocol for Dynamic Gossip is a rule how agents decide whom they should call. The goal of a gossip protocol is to reach a complete graph, where everybody knows all secrets. Moreover, good protocols will use fewer calls and avoid superfluous or redundant calls. Here we will focus on the LNS protocol from [7]. For a general definition of protocols in a formal language, see [8].

Definition 4 (LNS Protocol). *A call* ab *is* LNS-permitted *iff* $(a, b) \in N$ *and* $(a, b) \notin S$.

We now define when a protocol is successful on a graph. Intuitively, this means all possible executions of the protocol lead to a complete graph.

Definition 5 (Success). *Let* P_G *bet the set of all call sequences possible on* G *and permitted by protocol* P. *We also call such call sequences* P-permitted.

Let a graph $G = (\mathcal{A}, N, S)$ *and a protocol* P *be given. A finite call sequence* $\sigma \in P_G$ *is* successful *iff* G^σ *is complete. A sequence* σ *is* P-maximal *on* G *iff* σ *is* P*-permitted on* G *and there is no call* P*-permitted on* G^σ*, i.e. no call* ab *can be added to* σ *such that* $\sigma; ab$ *is still* P*-permitted.*

- P *is* strongly successful *on* G *if all* P*-maximal* $\sigma \in P_G$ *are successful.*
- P *is* weakly successful *on* G *if there is a* $\sigma \in P_G$ *that is successful.*
- P *is* unsuccessful *on* G *if there is no* $\sigma \in P_G$ *that is successful.*

Given a certain class $\mathcal{G}$ of networks (graphs) and a protocol P, we can ask the question: is P (strongly, weakly, un-) successful on $\mathcal{G}$. That is, does P lead to a complete network? This question, the *gossip problem*, is used to characterise networks both by their graph-theoretical properties and by the protocols that are (strongly, weakly, un-) successful on them.

It is easy to see that on any graph that consists of disconnected parts no protocol is successful. Hence, graphs need to be weakly connected to allow any of the protocols to be successful [7].

Definition 6. *A graph* $G = (\mathcal{A}, N, S)$ *is* weakly connected *iff for all agents* $a, b \in \mathcal{A}$ *there is a undirected* N*-path between* a *and* b. *We say that* G *is* strongly connected *iff for all agents* $a, b \in \mathcal{A}$ *there is an* N*-path from* a *to* b.

A graph $G = (\mathcal{A}, N, S)$ *is a* sun graph *iff* N *is strongly connected on* $s(G)$, *where* $s(G)$ *is the result of removing all terminal agents from* G.

Informally, one can think of sun graphs as 'almost' strongly connected graphs.

Example 2. The following graph is a sun graph: if we remove the only terminal agent a, then we obtain a strongly connected graph (consisting of b and c).

$$a \dashleftarrow b \dashleftarrow\!\!\dashrightarrow c$$

Theorem 1 (Theorem 13 in [7]). *Suppose* G *is an initial gossip graph. Then* LNS *is strongly successful on* G *iff* G *is a sun graph.*

4 Unreliable Gossip

It is easy to define reliable agents: they do exactly what they are expected to do. In particular, reliable agents communicate truthfully about their own secret, about secrets of others and share all the phone numbers they have.

However, when unreliability is allowed, there are numerous different options. There may be noise on the communication channel causing the communication between agents to fail; agents may (intentionally or unintentionally) follow a different protocol; agents may actively spread lies, either about their own secret, about other agents' secrets or both; agents may sabotage connections between other agents; unreliable agents may form coalitions to manipulate the network; the degree of unreliability may evolve over time, via peer pressure or other mechanisms; unreliable agents might have a memory of whom they have lied to; etc. This gives rise to many different types of unreliable behaviour.

In this article we only consider a basic form of unreliability: unreliability in the form of unintended random memoryless noise. A real-world example for this kind of unreliability could be a network of sensors that communicate with each other, but where one or more of the sensors are faulty. We therefore assume:

- Agents all follow the same protocol;
- Unreliable agents only lie about their own secret;
- Connections are not sabotaged;
- Unreliability does not evolve;
- Unreliable agents do not remember to whom they lied;
- Agents consider all new information as true until proven otherwise.

In the standard model of (dynamic) gossip, an agent either knows a secret or not. For settings with unreliable agents we need more: agents can also have obtained a wrong secret and thus have a false belief.

To model this, we let secrets be bits and replace the former set of secrets S_a with two sets: X_a for agents of which a received secret 1, and Y_a for agents of which a received secret 0. When an agent is in either X_a or Y_a, then a considers that agent to be reliable. But when an agent is both in X_a and Y_a, then a will consider that agent unreliable.

Definition 7 (UG Graph). *A gossip graph with unreliable agents, short* Unreliable Gossip graph *or* UG graph, *is a quadruple* $G = (\mathcal{A}, R, N, S)$ *where* A *is a finite set of agents,* $R \subseteq \mathcal{A}$ *is the set of reliable agents,* $N \subseteq \mathcal{A} \times \mathcal{A}$ *is the network relation and* $S \colon \mathcal{A} \to \mathcal{P}(\mathcal{A}) \times \mathcal{P}(\mathcal{A})$ *assigns to each agent* $a \in \mathcal{A}$ *a pair* (X_a, Y_a)*. We say that* a has a positive secret of b *iff* $b \in X_a$*, that* a has a negative secret of b *iff* $b \in Y_a$*, and that* a knows that b is unreliable *iff* $b \in X_a \cap Y_a$.

We also write S_a for $X_a \cup Y_a$, which intuitively is the set of all agents of which a knows any secret. When all agents are reliable ($R = \mathcal{A}$), a UG graph can be identified with a gossip graph by setting $S_a := X_a \cup Y_a$ for each $a \in \mathcal{A}$.

Definition 8 (Initial UG Graph). *A UG graph* $G = (\mathcal{A}, R, N, S)$ *is* initial *iff for all* $a \in \mathcal{A}$ *we have* $X_a \cup Y_a = \{a\}$.

In a regular call ab, where both agents speak the truth, information is shared as follows. This means that both agents update their contact lists (N_a and N_b, respectively) and update their sets X, Y by taking unions. In particular, if before the call agent a had a positive and secret agent b had a negative secret of some agent c, then after the call both a and b know that agent c is unreliable.

Definition 9 (UG Call between reliable agents). *Let* $G = (\mathcal{A}, R, N, S)$ *be a UG Graph and let* $a, b \in \mathcal{A}$ *such that* $(a, b) \in N$*. The* call ab *maps* G *to* $G^{ab} = (\mathcal{A}, R, N^{ab}, S^{ab})$ *where* N^{ab} *is as in Definition 2 and*

$$S_c^{ab} := \begin{cases} (X_a \cup X_b, Y_a \cup Y_b) & \text{if } c \in \{a, b\} \\ (X_c, Y_c) & \text{otherwise} \end{cases}$$

Analogous to Definition 3 we write G^σ *for the result of executing a sequence of calls* σ *on a UG graph* G.

Note that in the definition of a call, agents are naive: they consider all new information completely trustworthy and update their knowledge accordingly. In other settings where unreliable agents may lie about secrets of other agents, one can imagine that agents would adopt a more sceptic approach or prefer first hand information (an agent sharing their own secret) over second hand information (and agent sharing a secret of another agent).

5 Unreliable Agents

We now formally define unreliable agents that satisfy the constraints given in Sect. 4. An unreliable agent may report a wrong value of their own secret in a call. We do not assume any rules about when and how often an unreliable agent reports the wrong value of their secret, only that the probability to lie is non-zero (for when the probability is zero, it is a reliable agent).

In addition to the call ab from Definition 9, we now define three calls Ab, aB or AB in which respectively a, b or both agents report the wrong value of their own secret. That is, the agents denoted with a capital letter are lying about their own secrets in this call. For example, in a call Ab all secrets are shared normally, *apart from agent a's secret.* More specifically, if $a \in X_a$ then the new set of secrets for b is not given by merging X_a with X_b, and Y_a with Y_b, but by merging $X_a \setminus \{a\}$ with X_b, and $Y_a \cup \{a\}$ with Y_b. The lying of agent a is thus represented by acting as if her own secret was in Y_a and not in X_a (or vice versa).

Note that Ab, Ba and AB can only occur if, respectively, a, b or both agents do not belong to the set of reliable agents R. On the other hand, note that in the call Ab agent b does not necessarily belong to R, but might still be unreliable and just happen to speak the truth in this call.

Definition 10 (UG Call with unreliable agents). *Let $G = (\mathcal{A}, R, N, S)$ be a UG Graph and let $a, b \in \mathcal{A}$ such that $(a, b) \in N$. We define four calls.*

ab *The call ab maps G to $G^{ab} = (\mathcal{A}, R, N^{ab}, S^{ab})$ from Definition 2.*

Ab *Suppose $a \notin R$. The* call *Ab maps G to $G^{Ab} = (\mathcal{A}, R, N^{Ab}, S^{Ab})$ where $N^{Ab} := N^{ab}$ from Definition 2, and for agents a and b:*

$$S_a^{Ab} := (X_a \cup X_b, Y_a \cup Y_b) \tag{1}$$

$$S_b^{Ab} := \begin{cases} ((X_a \setminus \{a\}) \cup X_b, Y_a \cup \{a\} \cup Y_b) & \text{if } a \in X_a \setminus Y_a \\ (X_a \cup \{a\} \cup X_b, (Y_a \setminus \{a\}) \cup Y_b) & \text{if } a \in Y_a \setminus X_a \\ (X_a \cup X_b, Y_a \cup Y_b) & \text{if } a \in X_a \cap Y_a \end{cases} \tag{2}$$

and $S_c^{Ab} := (X_c, Y_c)$ for all other agents $c \notin \{a, b\}$.

aB *Vice versa, suppose $b \notin R$. The* call *aB maps G to G^{aB} which is defined symmetrically, i.e. the same as G^{Ba}.*

AB *Finally, suppose $a \notin R$ and $b \notin R$. The* call *AB maps G to $G^{AB} = (\mathcal{A}, R, N^{AB}, S^{AB})$ where $N^{AB} := N^{ab}$ from Definition 2 and for a and b:*

$$S_a^{AB} := \begin{cases} (X_a \cup (X_b \setminus \{b\}), Y_a \cup Y_b \cup \{b\}) & \text{if } b \in X_b \setminus Y_b \\ (X_a \cup X_b \cup \{b\}, Y_a \cup (Y_b \setminus \{b\})) & \text{if } b \in Y_b \setminus X_b \\ (X_a \cup X_b, Y_a \cup Y_b) & \text{if } b \in X_b \cap Y_b \end{cases} \tag{3}$$

$$S_b^{AB} := \begin{cases} ((X_a \setminus \{a\}) \cup X_b, Y_a \cup \{a\} \cup Y_b) & \text{if } a \in X_a \setminus Y_a \\ (X_a \cup \{a\} \cup X_b, (Y_a \setminus \{a\}) \cup Y_b) & \text{if } a \in Y_a \setminus X_a \\ (X_a \cup X_b, Y_a \cup Y_b) & \text{if } a \in X_a \cap Y_a \end{cases} \tag{4}$$

and $S_c^{AB} := (X_c, Y_c)$ for all other agents $c \notin \{a, b\}$.

Analogous to Definition 3 we write G^σ for the result of executing a sequence of reliable or unreliable calls σ on a UG graph G.

We stress that an unreliable agent will not always report the wrong value. In fact, then it would be the same as a reliable agent with the opposite secret value, and the other agents would never find out that the unreliable agent is lying.

To illustrate the different types of calls, consider the following example.

Example 3. Consider the UG graph $G = (\mathcal{A}, R, N, S)$ where $\mathcal{A} = \{a, b, c, d\}$, $R = \{c, d\}$, $N = \mathcal{A} \times \mathcal{A}$ and $S_x = (X_x, Y_x) = (\{x\}, \varnothing)$ for each $x \in \mathcal{A}$. The (LNS-permitted) call sequence $AB; ac; Ad; cd; bc$ changes G as follows:

	(X_a, Y_a)	(X_b, Y_b)	(X_c, Y_c)	(X_d, Y_d)
	$(\{a\}, \varnothing)$	$(\{b\}, \varnothing)$	$(\{c\}, \varnothing)$	$(\{d\}, \varnothing)$
$\xrightarrow{AB}$	$(\{a\}, \{b\})$	$(\{b\}, \{a\})$	$(\{c\}, \varnothing)$	$(\{d\}, \varnothing)$
$\xrightarrow{ac}$	$(\{a, c\}, \{b\})$	$(\{b\}, \{a\})$	$(\{a, c\}, \{b\})$	$(\{d\}, \varnothing)$
$\xrightarrow{Ad}$	$(\{a, c, d\}, \{b\})$	$(\{b\}, \{a\})$	$(\{a, c\}, \{b\})$	$(\{c, d\}, \{a, b\})$
$\xrightarrow{cd}$	$(\{a, c, d\}, \{b\})$	$(\{b\}, \{a\})$	$(\{a, c, d\}, \{a, b\})$	$(\{a, c, d\}, \{a, b\})$
$\xrightarrow{bc}$	$(\{a, c, d\}, \{b\})$	$(\{a, b, c, d\}, \{a, b\})$	$(\{a, b, c, d\}, \{a, b\})$	$(\{a, c, d\}, \{a, b\})$

In particular, after the fourth call cd the agents c and d learn that a is unreliable. However, even after the last call, agent d does not know this about b and no more call is permitted according to the LNS protocol.

Interestingly, a consequence of Definition 10 is that agents may find out themselves that they are unreliable. This is what happens after the call bc in Example 3 for agent b: after this call, $b \in X_b \cap Y_b$, hence she considers herself unreliable. But this also informs her that she is uncovered by agent c, who learns the same information about the unreliability of b. If now another agent e enters the network and the call be (or Be) takes place, e will be informed by agent b of her own unreliability. This results from Definition 10: the last clauses of Eqs. 2, 3 and 4 enforce that, in a call between a and b, whenever a is uncovered, i.e. $a \in X_a \cap Y_a$, the sets X_a and X_b and Y_a and Y_b are merged without adjustments. Hence afterwards $a \in X_b \cap Y_b$, i.e. b learns that a is unreliable.

In our setting where unreliability is unintended random memoryless noise this definition is not problematic, but in fact can help the network to perform better. In a network of sensors for instance, the unreliable sensor could then give a signal that it needs to be fixed.

If agents are intentionally unreliable, it might be more realistic to change their behavior once they learn they are uncovered. To model this we could easily change the last clauses of Eqs. 2, 3 and 4 in Definition 10 to

$$(X_a \cup X_b, Y_a \setminus \{a\} \cup Y_b) \tag{2'}$$

$$(X_a \cup X_b, Y_a \setminus \{a\} \cup Y_b) \tag{3'}$$

$$(X_a \cup X_b, Y_a \cup Y_b \setminus \{b\}) \tag{4'}$$

respectively. Similarly, we could do the same but remove a (resp. b) from X_a (resp. X_b) instead of Y_a (resp. Y_b), but the effect would be analogous. In that situation, an uncovered agent will only continue to communicate one value of her secret (here X_a). In other words, once uncovered she will change her behavior.

A simple example of an unreliable agent is an *alternating bluffer* that "lies" in every second call. It provides a first approach to random unintended noise, but it is deterministic and thus easier to simulate and reason about. We note that agent a in Example 3 behaves as an alternating bluffer.

In our model there is no "curing" or "going back" from unreliability. Once an agent is unreliable and consequently (possibly) uncovered, there is no way for agents to change their behavior. This is sufficient to introduce unreliability into Dynamic Gossip and explore whether the known results continue to hold. But of course, for practical applications, it would be desirable to enable agents to be cured. For example for the application of this framework to the spread of diseases [9]. An important question is then how agents can convince others that they have improved their behavior, from unreliable to reliable.

6 Unreliable Success

We now define what it means to be successful in Unreliable Gossip. Completeness on UG graphs is reached when all agents know all secrets, now in the sense that each agent knows at least one secret of each other agent. We note that this is equivalent to completeness on gossip graphs as defined in Definition 1 with $S_a = X_a \cup Y_a$.

Definition 11. *A UG graph* $G = (\mathcal{A}, R, N, S)$ *is* complete *iff for all agents* $a \in \mathcal{A}$ *we have* $X_a \cup Y_a = \mathcal{A}$.

However, for Unreliable Gossip this kind of completeness and success according to Definition 5 is not a useful goal. Instead, *the aim of the reliable agents should be to reach completeness among themselves and to identify all unreliable agents.* We now define *reliable completeness* formally and argue that it is a more intuitive goal in the setting of Unreliable Gossip than (mere) completeness.

Definition 12. *A UG graph* $G = (\mathcal{A}, R, N, S)$ *is* reliably complete *iff for all* $a \in R$ *we have (i)* $X_a \cup Y_a \setminus (X_a \cap Y_a) = R$*, and (ii)* $X_a \cap Y_a = \mathcal{A} \setminus R$.

That is, a graph is reliably complete iff each reliable agent (i) knows the secrets of all reliable agents and (ii) knows for all unreliable agents that they are unreliable. We note that in the presence of (ii) the condition (i) is equivalent to $X_a \cup Y_a = \mathcal{A}$. To make it easier to refer to the second condition we also say that *an agent a identifies the unreliable agents* iff $X_a \cap Y_a = \mathcal{A} \setminus R$.

Note that reliably complete does not imply complete, because in a reliably complete graph the unreliable agents do not have to know all secrets. Reliable agents should learn all secrets and identify all unreliable agents, but we do not care at all about what unreliable agents learn. Also vice versa, completeness does not imply reliable completeness, because completeness says nothing about knowing which other agents are unreliable.

In order to compare completeness on unreliable networks to completeness on normal networks, we define *reliable counter-graphs* and *reliable subgraphs.*

Definition 13. *Let* $G = (\mathcal{A}, R, N, S)$ *be a UG Graph. Then we define its* reliable counter-graph $G^* := (\mathcal{A}, N, S^*)$ *where* $S^*_a := (X_a \cup Y_a) \setminus (X_a \cap Y_a)$. *And we define its* reliable subgraph $G|_R := (\mathcal{A}|_R, N|_R, S|_R)$ *where* $\mathcal{A}|_R := R$, $N|_R := N \cap (R \times R)$ *and* $(S|_R)_a := (X_a \cup Y_a) \cap R$.

A sanity check shows that indeed both G^* and $G|_R$ are gossip graphs. Definition 13 allows us to rephrase the definition of reliable completeness: a graph G is reliably complete if and only if the reliable subgraph of G is complete and all reliable agents identify the unreliable agents.

To conclude this section, we define success for Unreliable Gossip, both for the original notion of completeness and reliable completeness.

Definition 14. *Suppose we have a UG graph* G *and a call sequence* σ *which can be executed on* G. *We say that* σ *is* successful *on* G *iff* G^σ *is complete and we say that* σ *is* reliably successful *on* G *iff* G^σ *is reliably complete.*

A protocol is (reliably) weakly/strongly/un-successful *on a graph* G *iff all/some/no sequences permitted by the protocol and executable on* G *are (reliably) successful on* G.

6.1 LNS Is Not Reliably Successful on Sun Graphs

Here we show that, already with a small amount of unreliability, for example in the form of the alternating bluffer, a known result about LNS [7] fails to hold. Specifically, we show that on UG graphs that are sun graphs with only terminal unreliable agents, LNS fails to identify the unreliable agents in the sense that it is not reliably successful as defined in the previous section. Before the general result we give an example where the classification of LNS fails to hold.

Example 4. Consider again the sun graph from Example 2 and suppose a is unreliable. Now consider the sequence $bc; ba; cA$. This is an LNS sequence resulting in a complete graph. However, if a is an alternating bluffer, then b will learn one value of the secret of a and c the other. Formally, in the resulting graph $G^{bc;ba;cA}$ we have $a \in X_c \setminus Y_c$ and $a \in Y_b \setminus X_b$. Unfortunately, LNS allows no further calls. Hence b and c may no longer communicate and will not notice that a is unreliable.

Consider $ba; Ac; bc$. This is also an LNS sequence which can be executed on the graph above. But in this case b and c talk to each other *after* having learned different values from a and will thus find out that a is unreliable. Formally, in the resulting graph $G^{ba;Ac;bc}$ we have $a \in (X_b \cap Y_b)$ and $a \in (Z_c \cap Y_c)$.

Hence, whether b and c find out that a is unreliable depends on the sequence.

Example 4 already suffices to show that LNS is not reliably successful on all sun graphs when we have unreliable agents. However, we now prove something slightly stronger, namely that for all graphs of a similar shape there is a maximal sequence which is not successful.

Theorem 2. *Consider any initial UG graph with at least one unreliable agent. If all unreliable agents are terminal then LNS is not reliably strongly successful.*

Intuitively, Theorem 2 holds because there are call sequences in which the unreliable agents are called too late, so that the reliable agents cannot verify the secrets of these unreliable agents with each other. This is the case in Example 4: the reliable agents b and c first learn each others' secrets before calling the unreliable agent a. But then b and c cannot call each other again in LNS and hence cannot verify the secret of a with each other. That is why they fail to identify c as unreliable.

We now first prove a lemma.

Lemma 2. *Suppose $G = (\mathcal{A}, R, N, S)$ is an initial UG graph with at least one unreliable agent. Moreover, suppose that all unreliable agents in G are terminal. Then for any LNS-permitted call sequence σ we have: if there is a prefix $\tau \sqsubseteq \sigma$ such that $G^\tau|_R$ is complete but G^τ is not reliably complete, then also G^σ is not reliably complete and thus σ is not reliably successful on G.*

Lemma 2 states that any LNS sequence cannot become reliably successful any more as soon as it reaches a complete reliable subgraph. Intuitively, once the reliable subgraph becomes complete, the reliable agents can no longer call each other to compare secrets they received from the unreliable agents.

Proof (of Lemma 2). Let G be an initial UG graph with at least one unreliable agent and where all unreliable agents are terminal. Let σ be an LNS-permitted call sequence with a prefix $\tau \sqsubseteq \sigma$ such that $G^\tau|_R$ is complete. Then $\forall r \in R$: $X_r^\tau \cup Y_r^\tau \supseteq R$ and therefore also $\forall r \in R : X_r^\sigma \cup Y_r^\sigma \supseteq R$ because no contradictory information can be learned about reliable agents.

Now note that after the call sequence τ no more calls from an unreliable agent to a reliable agent can take place: just after τ the unreliable agents are still terminal, and in all later calls where they learn the number of a reliable agent they will also learn the secret of that same agent (because $G^\tau|_R$ is complete). Moreover, we can ignore calls between unreliable agents because they do not affect reliable completeness.

Hence, let ab be the last call to take place in σ from a reliable agent a to an unreliable agent b. Let $\sigma \setminus ab$ denote the sequence without this last call. That means before the call a knew no secret of b, i.e. $b \notin X_a^{\sigma\setminus ab} \cup Y_a^{\sigma\setminus ab}$. But then, because a will not be involved in any later calls, we have that $b \in X_a^\sigma \cup Y_a^\sigma$. Hence agent b will not be identified by agent a and σ is not reliably successful on G.

Proof (of Theorem 2). Let $G = (\mathcal{A}, R, N, S)$ be an initial UG graph that is a sun graph where all unreliable agents are terminal. Because all unreliable agents are terminal, the reliable subgraph $G|_R$ of G must be a sun graph too. By Theorem 1, any maximal LNS-permitted call sequence τ consisting of calls ab with $a, b \in R$ will complete $G|_R$, i.e. $G^\tau|_R$ is complete. Now by Lemma 2, any LNS-permitted call sequence σ extending τ will fail to identify all unreliable agents and hence fail to reliably complete the network.

Thus, we cannot extend the sun graph characterisation of LNS to Unreliable Gossip. This already holds for a small amount of unreliability: one terminal alternating bluffer. Of course, this is because we now also demand that reliable agents identify the unreliable agents. If we only care about completeness in the original sense, then LNS is still strongly successful on UG graphs *with respect to the reliable agents*. In particular, even if unreliable agents are involved in earlier calls (i.e. if there is no τ as in the proof above), the reliable subgraph will still be completed.

6.2 Blocking Unreliable Agents Hides and Helps Them

How can we "repair" LNS to deal with unreliable agents? Intuitively, blocking unreliable agents seems a good measure against the spread of false information in networks because it would prevent unreliable agents from spreading their false information. This would mean that, when an unreliable agent performs a call to another agent, her call will be rejected.

By blocking unreliable agents, their communicative power is restricted: they will not be able to initiate calls – whenever they do, they are rejected. Of course, conceptually, there is a difference between blocked agents and agents that are not able to initiate communication. The latter may rather occur whenever their communicating device is broken. Yet, mathematically, these situations are analogous: in both situations, the unreliable agents cannot successfully make a call to another agent. Therefore we evaluate the following protocol that limits the unreliable agents in their ability to make calls to discuss whether blocking unreliable agents is indeed a good measure.

Definition 15 (Protocol LNSR). *A call ab is* LNSR-permitted *iff* $(a, b) \in N$, $a \in R$ *and* $(a, b) \notin S$.

But, against the intuition, the protocol LNSR does not only prevent false information from spreading, it might also prevent unreliable agents from being detected by the reliable agents. Specifically, we prove that unreliable agents that are not allowed to initiate any form of communication are harder to identify than unreliable agents that are. In other words, unreliability can be easier detected when it is spread more. Therefore the restriction to disable, via blocking, the unreliable agents from initiating calls is not desirable.

Theorem 3. *LNSR is a proper strengthening of LNS in the following sense:*

(i) For any UG graph G we have: If LNSR is (reliably) weakly successful on G, then also LNS is (reliably) weakly successful on G.

(ii) There is a UG graph G where LNSR is not reliably weakly unsuccessful, but where LNS is reliably weakly successful.

Proof. (i) Note that any LNSR-permitted call sequence σ is also LNS-permitted. If LNSR is (reliably) weakly successful on some UG graph G, then there is an LNSR-permitted call sequence σ such that G^σ is (reliably) complete. But then σ is also LNS-permitted, and hence LNS is also (reliably) weakly successful on G.

(ii) Consider the UG graph $G = (\mathcal{A}, R, N, S)$ below with $\mathcal{A} = \{a, b, c\}$, $R = \{a, b\}$, $N = \{(b, a), (b, c)\}$ and $S_x = (\{x\}, \varnothing)$ for all $x \in \mathcal{A}$.

$$a \dashleftarrow b \dashrightarrow c$$

Then the following are all the LNS-permitted call sequences on G. For each sequence we list four variants, depending on where c is lying.

1. $ba; ac; bc$ or $ba; aC; bc$ or $ba; ac; bC$ or $ba; aC; bC$
2. $ba; bc; ac$ or $ba; bC; ac$ or $ba; bc; aC$ or $ba; bC; aC$
3. $bc; ca; ba$ or $bC; ca; ba$ $(*)$ or $bc; Ca; ba$ or $bC; Ca; ba$
4. $bc; ba; ca$ or $bC; ba; ca$ or $bc; ba; Ca$ or $bC; ba; Ca$

Only the call sequences under 1 and 2 are LNSR-permitted. But only the sequence marked with $*$ reliably completes the network: first the agents a and b need to learn different values from agent c and after that they should communicate with each other to learn that c is unreliable. None of the other sequences reliably complete the network and in particular no LNSR-permitted call sequence reliably completes G. Hence LNS is reliably weakly successful on G, but $LNSR$ is not.

It is crucial in part (ii) of Theorem 3 that reliable agents are the last to communicate in order to identify the unreliable agent as such. Thus the success of the protocol is dependent on the call sequence, and in particular on the position of calls between reliable agents: they need to verify the secrets of the unreliable agents. But, agents do not know which agents are the unreliable agents (this is the goal of the protocol), hence they do not know which secrets need to be verified nor with whom to verify this.

This problem of verification is similar to the Byzantine Generals Problem [13] developed to describe a situation in which agents must agree on a joint strategy to avoid catastrophic failure of the system, but where some of the agents or some are unreliable. In a simple form, multiple generals are threatened by a common enemy and they each have to decide whether to attack or to retreat with a preferred outcome of a coordinated attack or coordinated retreat. A good solution to the problem is an algorithm that can both guarantee that all reliable generals decide upon the same plan and that a small number of unreliable generals cannot cause the reliable generals to adopt a bad strategy. Such solutions have been studied in the literature under the name of Byzantine Fault Tolerance, starting with [6] and more recently including [4].

Theorem 3 illustrates that there are networks on which unreliable agents remain unidentified when they are not allowed to initiate calls, but can be identified when they do initiate calls. This has direct consequences for the security measure to block unreliable agents and raises questions about their effectiveness for real-life applications and gossip-like settings. For example, a faulty sensor should not be shut down immediately but continue to communicate such that it will be identified as faulty by a larger number of other sensors. As another example, fake news articles shared in social networks will be easier to uncover and identify if they are *not* removed or blocked, but instead marked as fake and continued to be actively shared.

Formally, we define the ideas of blocking and deleting as follows. Deleting means that an agent removes those agents she knows to be unreliable from her own phone book. Blocking means that, in addition to deleting, the agent removes her own number from the phone book of agents she knows to be unreliable.

Definition 16 (Delete and Block). *Let $G = (\mathcal{A}, R, N, S)$ be a UG graph and let $a \in \mathcal{A}$. The* delete *action λ_a maps G to $G^{\lambda_a} = (\mathcal{A}, R, N^{\lambda_a}, S)$ and the* block *action μ_a maps G to $G^{\mu_a} = (\mathcal{A}, R, N^{\mu_a}, S)$, which are defined by*

$$N_c^{\lambda_a} := \begin{cases} N_c & \text{if } c \neq a \\ N_c \setminus (X_c \cap Y_c) & \text{if } c = a \end{cases}$$

$$N_c^{\mu_a} = \begin{cases} N_c & \text{if } c \neq a \text{ and } c \notin X_a \cap Y_a \\ N_c \setminus \{a\} & \text{if } c \neq a \text{ and } c \in X_a \cap Y_a \\ N_c \setminus (X_c \cap Y_c) & \text{if } c = a \end{cases}$$

As Theorem 3 shows, blocking unreliable agents, though seemingly a good approach to prevent the spread of false information, comes at a cost. Blocking unreliable agents seems analogous to restricting their communicative power because the effects are the same: unreliable agents will not be able to initiate communication. This is exactly what has been shown to help them remain unidentified.

However, in contrast to LNSR, let us now assume that agents only block other agents once they have identified them as unreliable. They will then be able to forward the information that agents are unreliable to others. The following example illustrates how this can prevent the unwanted effect of hiding unreliable agents.

Example 5. Consider the following network of four agents with one unreliable agent, agent b, i.e. $\mathcal{A} = \{a, b, c, d\}$ and $R = \{a, c, d\}$:

Suppose that the reliable agents block the unreliable agents as soon as they identify them. Consider the LNS-permitted call sequence $ab; cB; ac; cd$. After the subsequence $ab; cB; ac$ the agents a and c will identify agent b as unreliable and this will then be communicated to agent d in the final call cd. Hence also agent d will block b after this and the whole sequence is reliably successful.

A disadvantage of both LNSR and blocking known-to-be-unreliable agents is that it might exclude other reliable agents "behind" unreliable ones. Whenever there is a reliable agent a that is only able to communicate with an unreliable agent, blocking this unreliable agent also prevents agent a to contact the rest of the network. She is therefore excluded from the rest of the network. Consider the following example.

Example 6. Let $G = (\mathcal{A}, R, N, S)$ be the network drawn below where $R = \mathcal{A} \setminus \{b\}$ and $\mathcal{A} \setminus \{a, b\}$ forms a complete cluster, i.e. $\forall r \in \mathcal{A} \setminus \{a, b\}$: $X_r \cup Y_r = \mathcal{A} \setminus \{b\}$. Suppose further that all agents in the cluster consider b unreliable, i.e. $\forall r \in \mathcal{A} \setminus \{a, b\} : b \in X_r \cap Y_r$, and have no information about a, that b has all the information about $\mathcal{A} \setminus \{a\}$ and that a only has the phone number of b, as drawn below. Then blocking agent b effectively blocks agent a and the network will not be reliably completed. We argue that this is a realistic scenario for LNS: the call ab might come too late in the call sequence. Then, because the other reliable agents block agent b, agent a is also blocked indirectly.

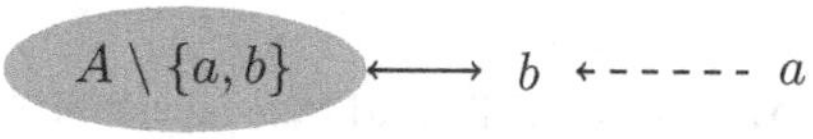

7 Discussion and Conclusion

We extended the formal model of Dynamic Gossip from [7] to include unreliable agents. To better capture success in Dynamic Gossip with unreliable agents we defined the notion of reliable success: all reliable agents should learn all secrets and they should identify the unreliable agents. We have then shown that, already with a single unreliable agent, we cannot extend the results about the success of the LNS protocol: LNS is successful in the old sense, but not reliably successful on sun graphs with unreliable terminal agents. This shows that the assumption that *everybody is reliable* is crucial for the success of LNS and that LNS should be adapted for practical applications where agents might fail.

We then examined a way to counter the spread of false information, namely to restrict communication of unreliable agents. It turns out that unreliable information that is not actively spread is harder to identify than unreliable information that is actively spread. This has seemingly paradoxical consequences for measures against unreliable agents: blocking can have a contrary effect and help unreliable agents to remain unidentified. Thus, there is a pay-off between identifying and containing false information.

Our framework and in particular the alternating bluffer are of course simplistic and there are many ways to extend this work: agents can also be unreliable or (with intent) lie about other agents' secrets, about phone numbers, about their own knowledge, etc. Yet, we see this work as a starting point for the discussion of reliability and unreliability in dynamic gossip and its real life applications. We thus end this article with the following open questions.

- What is the class of unreliable gossip graphs characterized by LNS?
- Is there any limitation on the position of unreliable agents in this class?
- Is there an LNS weakening or strengthening (in the sense of [8]) that performs better in situations with unreliability?

Further research will show how Dynamic Gossip protocols can be adapted to deal with other forms of unreliability.

Finally, we want to stress that this work is not purely theoretical: social media and the spread of fake news can be seen as an instance of gossip with unreliable agents. Some social networks already use hybrid strategies where false information is not blocked but just marked as such.

Acknowledgements. This work is based on the master's thesis of the first author [5], supervised by Jan van Eijck. We thank Hans van Ditmarsch and the anonymous reviewers at the DaLí workshop for helpful feedback.

References

1. Allcott, H., Gentzkow, M.: Social media and fake news in the 2016 election. J. Econ. Perspect. **31**(2), 211–268 (2017). https://doi.org/10.1257/jep.31.2.211
2. Apt, K.R., Grossi, D., van der Hoek, W.: Epistemic protocols for distributed gossiping. In: Proceedings TARK 2015. EPTCS, vol. 215, pp. 51–66 (2015). https://doi.org/10.4204/EPTCS.215.5
3. Attamah, M., van Ditmarsch, H., Grossi, D., van der Hoek, W.: Knowledge and gossip. In: Proceedings of the Twenty-first European Conference on Artificial Intelligence, pp. 21–26 (2014). https://doi.org/10.3233/978-1-61499-419-0-21
4. Baird, L.: The swirlds hashgraph consensus algorithm: fair, fast, Byzantine fault tolerance (2017). https://www.swirlds.com/downloads/SWIRLDS-TR-2016-01.pdf
5. van den Berg, L.: Unreliable gossip (2018). https://eprints.illc.uva.nl/1597/, Master's thesis, University of Amsterdam
6. Castro, M., Liskov, B.: Practical Byzantine fault tolerance. In: Proceedings of the Third Symposium on Operating Systems Design and Implementation, OSDI 1999, pp. 173–186 (1999). https://www.usenix.org/legacy/events/osdi99/castro.html
7. van Ditmarsch, H., van Eijck, J., Pardo, P., Ramezanian, R., Schwarzentruber, F.: Dynamic gossip. Bull. Iran. Math. Soc. **45**(3), 701–728 (2018). https://doi.org/10.1007/s41980-018-0160-4
8. van Ditmarsch, H., Gattinger, M., Kuijer, L.B., Pardo, P.: Strengthening gossip protocols using protocol-dependent knowledge. J. Appl. Logics - IfCoLog J. Logics Appl. **6**(1) (2019). https://arxiv.org/abs/1907.12321
9. Eugster, P.T., Guerraoui, R., Kermarrec, A.M., Massoulié, L.: Epidemic information dissemination in distributed systems. Computer **37**, 60–67 (2004). https://doi.org/10.1109/MC.2004.1297243
10. Harary, F., Schwenk, A.J.: The communication problem on graphs and digraphs. J. Franklin Inst. **297**, 491–495 (1974). https://doi.org/10.1016/0016-0032(74)90126-4

11. Hedetniemi, S.M., Hedetniemi, S.T., Liestman, A.L.: A survey of gossiping and broadcasting in communication networks. Networks **18**(4), 319–349 (1988). https://doi.org/10.1002/net.3230180406
12. Hoefler, T., Barak, A., Shiloh, A., Drezner, Z.: Corrected gossip algorithms for fast reliable broadcast on unreliable systems. In: 2017 IEEE International Parallel and Distributed Processing Symposium (IPDPS), pp. 357–366 (2017). https://doi.org/10.1109/IPDPS.2017.36
13. Lamport, L., Shostak, R., Pease, M.: The Byzantine generals problem. ACM Trans. Program. Lang. Syst. (TOPLAS) **4**(3), 382–401 (1982). https://doi.org/10.1145/3335772.3335936
14. Shi, G., Johansson, M., Johansson, K.H.: Randomized gossiping with unreliable communication: dependent or independent node updates. In: 2012 IEEE 51st IEEE Conference on Decision and Control (CDC), pp. 4846–4851 (2012). https://doi.org/10.1109/CDC.2012.6426729
15. Tijdeman, R.: On a telephone problem. Nieuw Archief voor Wiskunde **3**(19), 188–192 (1971)
16. Wang, H., Liao, X., Wang, Z., Huang, T., Chen, G.: Distributed parameter estimation in unreliable sensor networks via broadcast gossip algorithms. Neural Netw. **73**, 1–9 (2016). https://doi.org/10.1016/j.neunet.2015.09.008
17. Watts, D.J., Strogatz, S.H.: Collective dynamics of 'small-world' networks. Nature **393**(6684), 440–442 (1998). https://doi.org/10.1038/30918

Belief Based on Inconsistent Information

Marta Bílková[1], Sabine Frittella[2(✉)], Ondrej Majer[3], and Sajad Nazari[2]

[1] The Czech Academy of Sciences, Institute of Computer Science, Prague, Czech Republic
bilkova@cs.cas.cz

[2] INSA Centre Val de Loire, Univ. Orléans, LIFO EA 4022, Bourges, France
{sabine.frittella,sajad.nazari}@insa-cvl.fr

[3] The Czech Academy of Sciences, Institute of Philosophy, Prague, Czech Republic
majer@flu.cas.cz

Abstract. A recent line of research has developed around logics of belief based on evidence [4,6]. The approach of [6] understands belief as based on information confirmed by a reliable source. We propose a finer analysis of how belief can be based on information, where the confirmation comes from multiple possibly conflicting sources and is of a probabilistic nature. We use Belnap-Dunn logic and its probabilistic extensions to account for potentially contradictory information on which belief is grounded. We combine it with an extension of Łukasiewicz logic, or a bilattice logic, within a two-layer modal logical framework to account for belief.

Keywords: Epistemic logics · Non-standard probabilities · Belnap-Dunn logic · Two-layer modal logic

1 Introduction

To form beliefs about the world, we collect and process data of different origins to provide us with reliable information concerning particular issues. Information derived from data typically is of a probabilistic nature, and, as obtained from multiple sources of different origins, it inevitably is incomplete and often conflicting concerning the issues we wish to resolve. In this context, we propose logics to formalize how an agent can build beliefs based on information (uncertain, incomplete, and sometimes inconsistent) provided from the available collected data, and how to reason with and about such beliefs.

Incompleteness of information alone is ever-present when reasoning about data. Applications, such as relational databases, often use many-valued logics to properly account for indefiniteness. Namely, Kleene's three-valued logic [23] became the design choice of SQL and similar systems (the use of Kleene's logic

The research of Marta Bílková was supported by the grant GA17-04630S of the Czech Science Foundation. The research of Sabine Frittella and Sajad Nazari was funded by the grant ANR JCJC 2019, project PRELAP (ANR-19-CE48-0006). The research of Ondrej Majer was supported by the grant GA16-15621S.

M. A. Martins and I. Sedlár (Eds.): DaLí 2020, LNCS 12569, pp. 68–86, 2020.
https://doi.org/10.1007/978-3-030-65840-3_5

in this context was first proposed by [8], and argued optimal in [9].) In [5], Belnap introduced a four-valued logic with intended database applications (see e.g. [18]), which extends Kleene's logic, but also allows to model reasoning with non-trivial *inconsistencies*. Further developed by Dunn [13], Belnap-Dunn four-valued logic BD, also referred to as First Degree Entailment, became a prominent logical framework which encompasses reasoning with both incomplete and inconsistent information. This logic evaluates formulas to Belnap-Dunn square – a lattice built over an extended set of truth values $\{t, f, b, n\}$ (true, false, both, neither), where b and n correspond to inconsistent and incomplete information respectively (Fig. 1, middle). One of the underlying ideas of this logic is that not only truth, but also amount of information that formulas carry (reflected by the four semantical values) matters. This idea was generalized by introducing the algebraic notion of bilattices by Ginsberg [17] in the context of AI, and studied further in [22,26]. Bilattices contain two lattice orders simultaneously: a truth order, and a knowledge (or an information) order. Belnap-Dunn square, the smallest interlaced bilattice, can be seen as the product bilattice of the two-element lattice (Fig. 1, left) where the truth-values are pairs of classical values which can be naturally interpreted as representing two independent dimensions of information – positive and negative one[1]. We can understand them as providing positive and negative support for statements independently. It was used to provide the logic with the double-valuation frame semantics by Dunn [13].

The problem of dealing with inconsistency concerns probabilistic information as well. There are essentially two ways out. One way is to get rid of inconsistencies, the other way is to develop systems with inference rules which can work with inconsistent premises. While on the logic side there are systems providing both kinds of solutions, for example belief revision or paraconsistent logics, the majority of solutions on the probability side go for the first solution – getting rid of inconsistency (cf. the Dempster–Shafer theory of belief functions [11]) – and the attempts of the second kind emerged only relatively recently. Zhou [28] extends the theory of belief functions to the setting of distributive lattices, in particular bilattices and de Morgan lattices, and provides a complete logic to reason about belief functions based on BD. Michael Dunn [14] defines a probabilistic framework over four-valued logic and studies properties of the resulting probabilistic entailment. The idea of an independent account for positive and negative information, underlying the double-valuation semantics of BD, naturally generalizes to probabilistic extensions of Belnap-Dunn four-valued logic proposed in [24], which we will use in this paper. It generalizes Belnap–Dunn logic in a similar way as classical probability theory generalizes propositional logic, and is referred to as theory of non-standard probabilities.

When it comes to management of *uncertainty*, probability and other measures of uncertainty can be understood as graded notions, as one tries to quantify the plausibility of unverified events typically over the interval [0,1]. Graded notions are one of the subjects traditionally studied by methods of fuzzy logics. As

[1] This independence assumption has in fact a support in scientific practice – if an experiment confirming a hypothesis fails, does not automatically mean it is rejected.

probability is not truth-functional, it does not admit a straightforward treatment by logical methods. However, one may deal with probability as a modal operator in logical systems (cf. [21]), for example in the systems of modal fuzzy logic [19]. There are two main approaches to probabilistic modalities over classical logic: two-layered and intensional. The two-layered logical formalism introduced in [15,20] separates the non-modal lower language of events from the modal upper language of probabilities. The system divides into three parts: lower level of classical propositional reasoning, reasoning about probabilities consisting of the axioms that characterize probability measures in finite spaces, and the upper level of reasoning about (Boolean combinations of) linear inequalities. Hájek [19] proposed to replace the quantitative reasoning in form of linear inequalities with many-valued reasoning, namely Łukasiewicz logic, in such formalism on the upper level to obtain a fuzzy probability logic for formal reasoning under uncertainty. The graded modality "probably", which can be used to model belief of an agent understood as a kind of subjective probability, is interpreted as a finitely-additive probability on a Boolean algebra of events with values in the real unit interval. Consequently, a class of modal logics for dealing with virtually any uncertainty measure has been covered by the formalism in [7]. In this paper, we aim at extending the framework to encompass reasoning with inconsistent probability information.

We look at an agent who considers a set of issues, has access to (multiple) sources providing positive and negative information on the issues in form of non-standard probabilities, and builds beliefs based on information aggregated from these sources. From plethora of possible scenarios we single out two case studies that we use to illustrate the different concepts at stake.

Example 1 (Aggregating heterogeneous data). A company launching a new car model needs to decide its selling price and its advertising strategy. Hence, its data analysts must study the reports on the sells of the previous products launched by the company and the success or failure of the advertisement campaigns. This study relies on factual information such as "during the year 2015, the company sold n items of product Y", but also on statement based on statistical analyses such as "the advertisement broadcasted in June 2016 increased the sells of product Y among the 20–30 years old of 30%". The second statement is based on aggregated information about the buyers that might be partial and partly false. Plus, the company has access to statistical studies about the population on increase or decrease in expenses for cars.

Example 2 (How to lead an investigation). An investigator needs to know if one of the suspects was present at the crime scene. She collects information from various sources: CCTV camera recordings, ATM logs, witnesses' statements, etc. No information of this kind is absolutely precise, and typically different sources of information contradict each other. Sources provide information of a probabilistic nature: camera recordings are imprecise due to light conditions, witnesses are not absolutely sure what they have seen. Moreover, the pieces of evidence confirming investigator's hypothesis that the suspect was present at the place of crime (that is, the positive information) are different from, and somewhat independent of, those rejecting it (that is, the negative information): there is a CCTV camera closed to the crime scene vs. ATM in a supermarket in a different city. For example, a lack of evidence supporting the suspect was present at the crime scene does not yield a proof she was not there. In the end, the investigator has to aggregate the available information and form beliefs about what likely happened.

In many scenarios we can adapt *aggregation strategies* that have been introduced on classical probabilities: a company that has access to a huge amount of heterogeneous data from various sources and uses software capable of analyzing these data. In this case it makes sense to consider aggregation methods that require a substantial computational power. A natural strategy here is to evaluate sources with respect to their reliability and aggregate them by taking their weighted average. Another kind of agent is an investigator of a criminal case who builds her opinion on the guilt of a suspect based on different pieces of evidence. We assume that all the sources are equally reliable and the investigator is very cautious and does not want to draw conclusions hastily. Hence, she relies on statements as little as all her sources agree on them, and the aggregation she uses returns the minimum of the positive and the minimum of the negative probabilities provided by the sources. If on the other hand the investigator considers all the sources being perfectly reliable, she accepts every piece of evidence and builds her belief using the aggregation maximazing both probabilities.

In what follows, we will propose two-layer modal logics of belief of a single agent, belief that is grounded on probabilistic information provided (positive and negative information independently) by multiple sources. The underlying logic of facts or events is chosen to be BD, the upper logic varies between BD and logics derived from Łukasiewicz logic and based on product or bilattice algebras, to systematically account for positive and negative information independently (and thus incompleteness and conflict) on both levels.

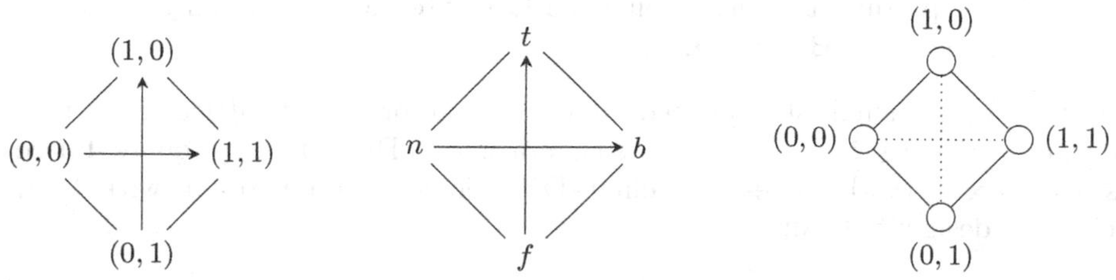

Fig. 1. The product bilattice $2 \odot 2$ (left), which is isomorphic to Dunn-Belnap square **4** (middle), and its continuous probabilistic extension (right). Negation flips the values along the horizontal line.

2 Preliminaries

We will first introduce algebraic structures involved as algebras of truth-values in the resulting two-layer logics of belief presented in Sect. 3, where we also motivate their choice (namely bilattices of Examples 3, 4, and 6, and the product algebra of Example 5). Then we briefly describe the Belnap-Dunn logic, and explain the approach to probability based on Belnap-Dunn logic.

2.1 Some Bilattices and MV Algebras

A *bilattice* is an algebra $\mathbf{B} = (B, \wedge, \vee, \sqcap, \sqcup, \neg)$ such that the reducts $(B, \wedge, \vee)$ and $(B, \sqcap, \sqcup)$ are both lattices and the negation $\neg$ is a unary operation satisfying that for every $a, b \in B$,

$$\text{if } a \leq_t b \text{ then } \neg b \leq_t \neg a, \qquad \text{if } a \leq_k b \text{ then } \neg a \leq_k \neg b, \qquad a = \neg\neg a,$$

with $\leq_t$ (resp. $\leq_k$) the order on $(B, \wedge, \vee)$ (resp. $(B, \sqcap, \sqcup)$) called the truth (resp. knowledge or information) order. A bilattice is *interlaced* if each one of the four operations $\wedge$, $\vee$, $\sqcap$, $\sqcup$ is monotone w.r.t. both orders $\leq_t$ and $\leq_k$. Bilattices, as well as interlaced bilattices, form a variety.

Given an arbitrary lattice $\mathbf{L} = (L, \wedge_L, \vee_L)$, we can construct the *product bilattice* $\mathbf{L} \odot \mathbf{L} = (L \times L, \wedge, \vee, \sqcap, \sqcup, \neg)$ as follows: for all $(a_1, a_2), (b_1, b_2) \in L \times L$,

$$\begin{aligned}
(a_1, a_2) \leq_t (b_1, b_2) \ &\textit{iff} \ \ a_1 \leq b_1 \textit{ and } b_2 \leq a_1 \\
\neg(a_1, a_2) &:= (a_2, a_1) \\
(a_1, a_2) \wedge (b_1, b_2) &:= (a_1 \wedge_L b_1, a_2 \vee_L b_2) \\
(a_1, a_2) \vee (b_1, b_2) &:= (a_1 \vee_L b_1, a_2 \wedge_L b_2) \\
(a_1, a_2) \sqcap (b_1, b_2) &:= (a_1 \wedge_L b_1, a_2 \wedge_L b_2) \\
(a_1, a_2) \sqcup (b_1, b_2) &:= (a_1 \vee_L b_1, a_2 \vee_L b_2)
\end{aligned}$$

$\mathbf{L} \odot \mathbf{L}$ is always an interlaced bilattice, and any interlaced bilattice can be represented as a product billatice: a bilattice $\mathbf{B}$ is interlaced if and only if there is a lattice $\mathbf{L}$ such that $\mathbf{B} \cong \mathbf{L} \odot \mathbf{L}$ [2].

Example 3. The smallest interlaced bilattice is the product bilattice of the two-element lattice $\mathbf{2} \odot \mathbf{2}$ (Fig. 1 left). It is isomorphic to Dunn-Belnap square $\mathbf{4}$ used as a matrix of truth values for Belnap-Dunn logic (Fig. 1 middle), with $\{t, b\}$ being the designated values.

Example 4. A probabilistic extension of Dunn-Belnap square (Fig. 1 right) can be seen as based on the product bilattice $\mathbf{L}_{[0,1]} \odot \mathbf{L}_{[0,1]}$, where $\mathbf{L}_{[0,1]} = ([0,1], \min, \max)$.

A *residuated lattice* is an algebra $\mathbb{L} = (L, \wedge_L, \vee_L, \cdot, \backslash, /)$, where the reduct $(L, \wedge_L, \vee_L)$ is a lattice, $(L, \cdot)$ is a semi-group (i.e. the operation $\cdot$ is associative) and the residuation properties hold: for all $a, b, c \in L$:

$$a \cdot b \leq c \quad \text{iff} \quad b \leq a \backslash c \quad \text{iff} \quad a \leq c/b.$$

Example 5. 1. $[0,1]_{Ł} = ([0,1], \wedge, \vee, \&_{Ł}, \to_{Ł})$, the standard algebra of Łukasiewicz logic, is a residuated lattice, an MV algebra[2], and it generates the variety of MV algebras. (As $\&_{Ł}$ is commutative, the two implications coincide.) For all $a, b \in [0,1]$, we define a negation $\sim_{Ł} a := a \to_{Ł} 0 := 1 - a$, and the standard operations

$$a \wedge b := \min\{a, b\}, \qquad a \&_{Ł} b := \max\{0, a + b - 1\},$$
$$a \vee b := \max\{a, b\}, \qquad a \to_{Ł} b := \min\{1, 1 - a + b)\}.$$

2. $[0,1]^{op}_{Ł} = ([0,1]^{op}, \vee, \wedge, \oplus_{Ł}, \ominus_{Ł})$ arises turning the standard algebra upside down, and is isomorphic to the original one. Here, we have $\sim_{Ł} a := 1 \ominus_{Ł} a$,

$$a \oplus_{Ł} b \approx \sim a \to_{Ł} b = \min\{1, a + b\} \quad a \ominus_{Ł} b \approx \sim(a \to_{Ł} b) = \max\{0, a - b\}.$$

3. Finally, we will consider the product MV algebra $[0,1]_{Ł} \times [0,1]^{op}_{Ł} = ([0,1] \times [0,1]^{op}, \wedge, \vee, \&, \to)$ with operations defined pointwise, $\sim(a_1, a_2) := a \to (0,1) = (\sim a_1, \sim a_2)$, and:

$$(a_1, a_2) \& (b_1, b_2) := (a_1 \&_{Ł} b_1, a_2 \oplus_{Ł} b_2)$$
$$(a_1, a_2) \to (b_1, b_2) := (a_1 \to_{Ł} b_1, b_2 \ominus_{Ł} a_2) = (a_1 \to_{Ł} b_1, \sim a_2 \&_{Ł} b_2).$$

As both the projections are surjective homomorphisms of MV algebras, this algebra also generates the variety of MV algebras.

Given a residuated lattice $\mathbf{L} = (L, \wedge_L, \vee_L, \cdot, \backslash, /)$ the *product residuated bilattice* [22] $\mathbf{L} \odot \mathbf{L} = (L \times L, \wedge, \vee, \sqcap, \sqcup, \supset, \subset, \neg)$ is defined as follows: the reduct $(L \times L, \wedge, \vee, \sqcap, \sqcup)$ is the product bilattice $(L, \wedge_L, \vee_L) \odot (L, \wedge_L, \vee_L)$ and, for all $(a_1, a_2), (b_1, b_2) \in L \times L$,

$$(a_1, a_2) \supset (b_1, b_2) := (a_1 \backslash b_1, b_2 \cdot a_1), \quad (a_1, a_2) \subset (b_1, b_2) := (a_1 / b_1, b_1 \cdot a_2).$$

One can then define the following operations: for all $a, b \in L \times L$,

$$a \to b := (a \supset b) \wedge (\neg a \subset \neg b), \quad a \leftarrow b := \neg a \to \neg b, \quad a * b := \neg(b \to \neg a).$$

For any product residuated bilattice, the structure $(L \times L, \wedge, \vee, *, \to, \leftarrow, \neg)$ is a residuated bilattice endowed with an involutive negation. If $\cdot$ is commutative (associative), so is $*$.

Example 6. The product residuated bilattice arising from the standard MV algebra is the structure $[0,1]_{Ł} \odot [0,1]_{Ł} = ([0,1] \times [0,1], \wedge, \vee, \sqcap, \sqcup, \supset, \neg, (0,0))$ where:

$$(a_1, a_2) * (b_1, b_2) := (a_1 \&_{Ł} b_1, (a_1 \to_{Ł} b_2) \wedge (b_1 \to_{Ł} a_2))$$
$$(a_1, a_2) \to (b_1, b_2) := ((a_1 \to_{Ł} b_1) \wedge (b_2 \to_{Ł} a_2), a_1 \&_{Ł} b_2),$$

and $(1,1)$ acts as the unit of the $*$: $(1,1) * a = a * (1,1) = a$.[3] We define

[2] For more on Łukasiewicz logic and MV algebras (in particular finite standard completeness w.r.t. $[0,1]_{Ł}$) see e.g. [12].

[3] Definitions of $\to, *$ match those used in [10] for interval based fuzzy logics, via a transformation given by $(x_1, x_2) \mapsto (x_1, 1 - x_2)$ (symmetry across the $(0, 0.5)(1, 0.5)$ line).

$$\begin{aligned} {\sim}a &:= (a \supset (0,0)) \sqcup \neg(\neg a \supset (0,0)) = ({\sim}_{\text{L}} a_1, {\sim}_{\text{L}} a_2) \\ a \oplus b &:= ({\sim}a \supset b) \sqcup \neg({\sim}\neg a \supset \neg b) \ = (a_1 \oplus_{\text{L}} b_1, a_2 \oplus_{\text{L}} b_2) \\ a \ominus b &:= {\sim}(a \supset b) \sqcap \neg{\sim}(\neg a \supset \neg b) \ = (a_1 \ominus_{\text{L}} b_1, a_2 \ominus_{\text{L}} b_2). \end{aligned}$$

From [22], we know that the (isomorphic copies of) product residuated bilattices obtained from MV algebras form a variety, and its axiomatization can be obtained by translating the one of MV algebras (in the language of residuated lattices)[4].

2.2 Belnap-Dunn Logic

Belnap-Dunn four-valued logic BD, in the propositional language $\mathcal{L}_{\mathsf{BD}}$ built from a (countable) set Prop of propositional variables using connectives $\{\wedge, \vee, \neg\}$, evaluates formulas to Belnap-Dunn square – the (de Morgan) lattice **4** built over an extended set of truth values $\{t, f, b, n\}$ (Fig. 1, middle).

The consequence relation of logic BD is given, based on the logical matrix $(\mathbf{4}, F)$ with $F = \{t, b\}$ being the designated values, as

$$\Gamma \models_{\mathsf{BD}} \varphi \ iff \ \forall e \ (e[\Gamma] \subseteq F \rightarrow e(\varphi) \in F).$$

A frame semantics can also be given for BD, in two ways. Belnap-Dunn *four-valued model* is a tuple $\langle W, \mathbf{4}, e\rangle$ where W is a set of states and e is a valuation of atomic formulas $e : \texttt{Prop} \times W \rightarrow \mathbf{4}$. The valuation is extended to formulas of $\mathcal{L}_{\mathsf{BD}}$ using the algebraic operations on **4** in the expected way.

Following Dunn's approach [13], we adopt a *double valuation model* $M = \langle W, \Vdash^+, \Vdash^-\rangle$, giving the positive and negative support of atomic formulas in the states, extending in the following way:

$$\begin{array}{lll} s \Vdash^+ \varphi \vee \psi & \text{iff} & s \Vdash^+ \varphi \text{ or } s \Vdash^+ \psi, \\ s \Vdash^- \varphi \vee \psi & \text{iff} & s \Vdash^- \varphi \text{ and } s \Vdash^- \psi, \\ s \Vdash^+ \neg\varphi & \text{iff} & s \Vdash^- \varphi \end{array} \qquad \begin{array}{lll} s \Vdash^+ \varphi \wedge \psi & \text{iff} & s \Vdash^+ \varphi \text{ and } s \Vdash^+ \psi, \\ s \Vdash^- \varphi \wedge \psi & \text{iff} & s \Vdash^- \varphi \text{ or } s \Vdash^- \psi. \\ s \Vdash^- \neg\varphi & \text{iff} & s \Vdash^+ \varphi \end{array}$$

It can be seen as locally evaluating formulas in the product bilattice $2 \odot 2$ (Fig. 1 left), and thus in **4** (Fig. 1, middle), connecting it with the four-valued frame semantics above. BD is completely axiomatized using the following axioms and rules:

$$\begin{array}{llll} \varphi \wedge \psi \vdash \varphi & \varphi \wedge \psi \vdash \psi & \varphi \vdash \psi \vee \varphi & \varphi \vdash \varphi \vee \psi \\ \varphi \vdash \neg\neg\varphi & \neg\neg\varphi \vdash \varphi & \multicolumn{2}{l}{\varphi \wedge (\psi \vee \chi) \vdash (\varphi \wedge \psi) \vee (\varphi \wedge \chi)} \\ \dfrac{\varphi \vdash \psi, \psi \vdash \chi}{\varphi \vdash \chi} & \dfrac{\varphi \vdash \psi, \varphi \vdash \chi}{\varphi \vdash \psi \wedge \chi} & \dfrac{\varphi \vdash \chi, \psi \vdash \chi}{\varphi \vee \psi \vdash \chi} & \dfrac{\varphi \vdash \psi}{\neg\psi \vdash \neg\varphi} \end{array}$$

[4] [22] hints at the correspondence between subvarieties of residuated lattices and residuated bilattices being categorial. This would mean that the mentioned variety is in fact generated by the product bilattice of the standard MV algebra. One could then use the translation from [22] to obtain axiomatics of the logic introduced at the end of Subsect. 3.1.

It is known to be (strongly) complete w.r.t. the algebraic and the double valuation (or 4-valued) frame semantics. BD is also known to be *locally finite*.[5]

We will use BD in the two-layer formalism mainly to capture the underlying information states on which sources of probabilistic information are based.

2.3 Non-standard Probabilities

The idea of independence of positive and negative information naturally generalizes to probabilistic extensions of BD logic as follows. A probabilistic Belnap-Dunn (BD) model [24] is a double valuation BD model extended with a classical probability measure on the power set of states $P(W)$ generated by a mass function on the set of states W.[6] The positive and negative probabilities of a formula are defined as (classical) measures of its positive and negative extensions:

$$p^+(\varphi) := \sum_{s \Vdash^+ \varphi} m(s) \qquad \text{and} \qquad p^-(\varphi) := \sum_{s \Vdash^- \varphi} m(s).$$

The probabilities satisfy the following axioms (see [24, Lemma 1]):

(A1) normalization $0 \leq p(\varphi) \leq 1$
(A2) monotonicity if $\varphi \vdash_{\mathsf{BD}} \psi$ then $p^+(\varphi) \leq p^+(\psi)$ and $p^-(\psi) \leq p^-(\varphi)$
(A3) import-export $p(\varphi \wedge \psi) + p(\varphi \vee \psi) = p(\varphi) + p(\psi)$.

These axioms are weaker than classical Kolmogorovian ones. In particular, axiom A3 can be derived from Kolmogorovian axioms of additivity and normalization, but additivity is strictly stronger and cannot be derived from A1-A3 [7]. As $p(\neg\varphi) \neq 1 - p(\varphi)$ in general, this account of probability admits positive probability of classical contradictions and thus allows for a non-trivial treatment of classically inconsistent information. When defined as above, the positive and negative probabilities are mutually definable via negation as $p^-(\varphi) = p^+(\neg\varphi)$. It has been shown in [24, Theorem 4] that any non-standard probability assignment (i.e., positive and negative probability satisfying the four axioms) arises from a classical probability measure on a BD double-valuation model as described above.

We can diagrammatically represent non-standard probabilities on a continuous extension of Belnap-Dunn square (Fig. 1, right), which we can see as a product bilattice $\mathbf{L}_{[0,1]} \odot \mathbf{L}_{[0,1]}$. For example, the point $(0, 0)$ corresponds to no information being provided (neither φ nor $\neg\varphi$ is supported by any state with positive measure in the underlying model), while $(1, 1)$ is the point of maximally conflicting information (both φ and $\neg\varphi$ are "certain" - supported by every state with positive measure). The left-hand triangle $(1, 0), (0, 0), (0, 1)$ corresponds to

[5] It means there are only finitely many (up to inter-derivability) formulas in a fixed finite set of propositional variables. It affects the completeness of the logic in Subsect. 3.1. More on BD and its properties can be found e.g. in the thesis [25].
[6] The probability of a set $X \subseteq W$ is defined as the sum of masses of its elements.
[7] Considering just the inequality $p(\varphi \vee \psi) \geq p(\varphi) + p(\psi) - p(\varphi \wedge \psi)$ in place of A3, we obtain belief functions on (finite) distributive lattices [20,28].

the cases of incomplete information, the right-hand triangle $(1,0),(1,1),(0,1)$ corresponds to the cases of conflicting information. The vertical dashed line corresponds to the "classical" probabilities when positive and negative support sum up to 1. The horizontal line represents situations where we have as much information supporting φ as contradicting it.

Example 7 (Consulting a panel). The company assembles a panel to which they ask whether a word describes the car well or not. That is, they ask how much they agree with the statements: "the car has property ϕ (e.g. being a family car)?" and "the car does not have property ϕ?" If humans were classical agents, every person would answer with a probability p that belongs to the vertical line of the probabilistic extension of the Belnap-Dunn square. However, experience has shown that often people don't reason classically [1]. When a person answers $(p^+(\phi), p^-(\phi))$, if $p^+(\phi) + p^-(\phi) > 1$, then she is conflicted about whether the property ϕ describes the car, if $p^+(\phi) + p^-(\phi) < 1$, then there might be some uncertainty on how to judge whether the car has property ϕ.

2.4 Aggregating Probabilities

We model an agent that considers a set of topics listed by the atomic variables in $\texttt{Prop}$, has access to sources giving information within the framework of non-standard probabilities (which we will call simply probabilities) and builds beliefs based on these sources using a so-called *aggregation strategy.* We focus on cases where the agent has no prior beliefs about the topics at stake. Depending on the context, the aggregation strategy should satisfy different properties.

A *source* s is a probability assignment over the set of formulas $s : \mathcal{L}_{\mathsf{BD}} \to [0,1] \times [0,1]$. In particular, we will later identify a source with a mass function on the BD states of a double-valuation model. An *aggregation strategy* $\texttt{Agg}$ is a function that takes in input a set of sources $\mathcal{S} = \{s_i\}_{i \in I}$ and returns a map $\texttt{Agg}_{\mathcal{S}} : \mathcal{L}_{\mathsf{BD}} \to [0,1] \times [0,1]$. For every $\varphi \in \mathcal{L}_{\mathsf{BD}}$, we denote $\texttt{Agg}_{\mathcal{S}}(\varphi)^+$ (resp. $\texttt{Agg}_{\mathcal{S}}(\varphi)^-$) the positive (resp. negative) support assigned to φ.

$\texttt{Agg}$ is *monotone* if $\varphi \vdash \psi$ implies $\texttt{Agg}_{\mathcal{S}}(\varphi) \leq \texttt{Agg}_{\mathcal{S}}(\psi)$ for all $\varphi, \psi \in \mathcal{L}_{\mathsf{BD}}$ and for every $\mathcal{S}$. $\texttt{Agg}$ is *$\neg$-compatible* if $\texttt{Agg}_{\mathcal{S}}(\varphi)^- = \texttt{Agg}_{\mathcal{S}}(\neg\varphi)^+$ for every $\varphi \in \mathcal{L}_{\mathsf{BD}}$ and for every $\mathcal{S}$. $\texttt{Agg}$ *preserves probabilities* if $\texttt{Agg}_{\mathcal{S}}$ is a probability for every $\mathcal{S}$.

Many aggregation strategies have been introduced on classical probabilities. Some of them, such as the (weighted) average, straightforwardly generalize to non-standard probabilities. In the following, we present aggregation strategies for our two case studies.

Weighted Average. In Example 1, a company has access to a huge amount of heterogeneous data from various sources and to software to analyse these data. A natural proposal is to grade every source s_i with respect to its reliability w_i and to take the *weighted average* of the probabilities. The aggregation is then the map $\mathrm{WA} : \mathcal{L}_{\mathsf{BD}} \to [0,1] \times [0,1]$ such that, for every $\varphi \in \mathcal{L}_{\mathsf{BD}}$,

$$\mathrm{WA}^+(\varphi) := \frac{\sum_{1 \leq i \leq n} w_i \cdot p_i^+(\varphi)}{\sum_{1 \leq i \leq n} w_i} \qquad \text{and} \qquad \mathrm{WA}^-(\varphi) := \frac{\sum_{1 \leq i \leq n} w_i \cdot p_i^-(\varphi)}{\sum_{1 \leq i \leq n} w_i}.$$

One can easily prove that WA preserves probabilities, it is monotone, and $\neg$-compatible. This aggregation strategy is however not feasible when modelling human reasoning.

A Very Cautious Investigator. In Example 2, an investigator builds her opinion on the suspect based on different sources. We assume all the sources are equally reliable and the investigator does not want to draw conclusions hastily. Hence, she relies only on statements all her sources agree on. The aggregation is then the map Min : $\mathcal{L}_{\mathsf{BD}} \to [0,1] \times [0,1]$ such that

$$\mathrm{Min}(\varphi) := \sqcap_{1 \le i \le n} p_i(\varphi) = \left(\min_{1 \le i \le n} p_i^+(\varphi), \min_{1 \le i \le n} p_i^-(\varphi) \right).$$

Reasoning with Trusted Sources. Staying in Example 2, we now assume all the sources are perfectly reliable. Hence, the investigator builds her belief on every statement supported by at least one source. The aggregation is then the map Max : $\mathcal{L}_{\mathsf{BD}} \to [0,1] \times [0,1]$ such that

$$\mathrm{Max}(\varphi) := \sqcup_{1 \le i \le n} p_i(\varphi) = \left(\max_{1 \le i \le n} p_i^+(\varphi), \max_{1 \le i \le n} p_i^-(\varphi) \right).$$

Here, one has high chances of reaching contradiction. In a scientific analyses, if one gets experiments or information that is contradictory, there are two options. Either the information is incorrect or there is a mistake in the interpretation of the data. Here, if the sources are 100% reliable, reaching a contradiction state will simply indicate to our investigator that there is a flaw in her analysis of the problem and she needs to change perspective to resolve the conflict.

The two latter aggregation strategies are monotone and $\neg$-compatible, and they in general do not preserve probabilities.

3 Two-Layer Logics

To make a clear distinction between the level of events or facts, information on which the agent bases her beliefs, and the level of reasoning about her beliefs, we use a *two-layer* logical framework. The formalism originated with [15,19], and was further developed in [3,7] into an abstract algebraic framework with a general theory of syntax, semantics and completeness (we will employ this framework to derive completeness of the logics we define).

Syntax $(\mathcal{L}_e, \mathcal{M}, \mathcal{L}_u)$ of a two layer logic $\mathcal{L}$ consists of a lower language $\mathcal{L}_e$ of events or facts (we denote formulas of $\mathcal{L}_e$ by $\varphi, \psi, \ldots$), an upper language $\mathcal{L}_u$ (we denote formulas of $\mathcal{L}_u$ by $\alpha, \beta, \ldots$), and a set of unary modalities $\mathcal{M}$ which can only be applied to a non-modal formula of $\mathcal{L}_e$, forming a modal atomic formula of $\mathcal{L}_u$ (in particular, no nesting of modalities can occur).

Semantics of a two layer logic $\mathcal{L}$ is, in the abstract approach of [7], based on *frames* of the form $F = (W, E, U, \langle \mu^{\heartsuit} \rangle_{\heartsuit \in \mathcal{M}})$, where W is a set of states, E is a local algebra of evaluation of the lower language $\mathcal{L}_e$ within the states[8], U is an upper-level algebra interpreting the modal formulas, and for each modality its semantics is given by a map $\mu^{\heartsuit} : \prod_{s \in W} E \to U$, returning a value in the upper-level algebra for a tuple of values from the lower algebra (assigned to an argument formula within the states). We write algebras, but often we need to use matrices to evaluate formulas, i.e. algebras with a set of designated values. Such a frame is called E-based and U-measured. A model is a frame equipped with valuations of $\mathcal{L}_e$ in E (the values of atomic modal formulas are then computed by μ, and values of modal formulas are computed in U in an expected way). A non-modal formula φ is valid in a model iff it is assigned a designated value in E by all the states, a modal formula α is valid in a model iff its value is designated in U. A consequence relation is defined via preserving validity in every model. It is of the sorted form $\Psi, \Gamma \models \xi$ where $\Psi \subseteq \mathcal{L}_e, \Gamma \subseteq \mathcal{L}_u, \xi \in \mathcal{L}_e \cup \mathcal{L}_u$.

The resulting logic as an axiomatic system $L = (L_e, M, L_u)$ consists of an axiomatics of the lower logic L_e, modal rules (i.e. rules with non-modal premises and modal conclusion) and modal axioms (modal rules with zero premises) M, and an axiomatics of the upper logic L_u. Proofs can be defined in the expected way. We can see that $\Psi, \Gamma \vdash \varphi$ iff $\Psi \vdash_{L_e} \varphi$, and $\Psi, \Gamma \vdash \alpha$ iff $\Psi_{MR}, \Gamma \vdash_{L_u} \alpha$, where Ψ_{MR} consists of conclusions of modal rules whose premises are derivable from Ψ in L_e (for more detail see [3, Proposition 3]).

3.1 Logic of Probabilistic Belief

In scenarios like that of Example 1, it is reasonable to represent agents beliefs as probabilities. In such two-layer logics, the bottom layer is that of events or facts, represented by BD-information states. A source provides probabilistic information given as a mass function on the states, multiple sources are to be aggregated with an aggregation strategy preserving probabilities. The modality is that of probabilistic belief. For the upper-layer – the logic of thus formed beliefs – we propose two logics derived from Łukasiewicz logic. The main reason to choose Łukasiewicz logic as a starting point is that it can express the probability axioms, and contains a well-behaved (continuous) implication. We however also aim at a formalism that allows us to separate the positive and negative dimensions of information or support also on the level of beliefs (just like BD does on the lower level). This motivates the use of product or bilattice algebras (those of Examples 5 and 6) on the upper level.

I. An extension of Łukasiewicz logic with bilattice negation. Consider the product of the standard algebra of Łukasiewicz logic $[0,1]_{\text{Ł}} = ([0,1], \wedge, \vee, \&_{\text{Ł}}, \rightarrow_{\text{Ł}})$ with the algebra $[0,1]_{\text{Ł}}^{op} = ([0,1]^{op}, \vee, \wedge, \oplus_{\text{Ł}}, \ominus_{\text{Ł}})$, as introduced in Example 5(3.), with only $(1,0)$ as the designated value. The logic of this product algebra (understood as the set of theorems - formulas always evaluated at $(1,0)$ - or as a consequence relation preserving the value $(1,0)$) is Łukasiewicz logic Ł. It can be axiomatized

8 For this paper, we always consider the lower algebras be the same for all states. But different algebras can be later used when modelling heterogeneous information.

in the (complete) language $\{\to, \sim\}$ by axioms of weakening, suffixing, commutativity of disjunction, and contraposition, and the rule of Modus Ponens (see the axioms below). To be able to operate the pairs of values as a positive and negative support of formulas, we extend the signature of the algebra with the bilattice negation $\neg(a_1, a_2) = (a_2, a_1)$, and extend the language to $\{\to, \sim, \neg\}$ (notice in particular, that $\oplus$ and $\ominus$ can be defined as in Example 5). We obtain the following axioms and rules, and denote the resulting consequence relation $\vdash_{Ł(\neg)}$:

$$\begin{array}{cc} \alpha \to (\beta \to \alpha) & \neg\neg\alpha \leftrightarrow \alpha \\ (\alpha \to \beta) \to ((\beta \to \gamma) \to (\alpha \to \gamma)) & \neg{\sim}\alpha \leftrightarrow {\sim}\neg\alpha \\ ((\alpha \to \beta) \to \beta) \to ((\beta \to \alpha) \to \alpha) & ({\sim}\neg\alpha \to {\sim}\neg\beta) \leftrightarrow {\sim}\neg(\alpha \to \beta) \\ ({\sim}\beta \to {\sim}\alpha) \to (\alpha \to \beta) & \alpha, \alpha \to \beta / \beta \quad \alpha / {\sim}\neg\alpha \end{array}$$

The $\neg$ negations can be pushed to the atomic formulas, and we can thus consider formulas up to provable equivalence in a *negation normal form (nnf)*, i.e. formulas built using $\{\to, \sim\}$ from *literals* of the form $p, \neg p$. It is easy to see, because we have $\neg{\sim}\alpha \leftrightarrow {\sim}\neg\alpha$ and $\neg(\alpha \to \beta) \leftrightarrow {\sim}{\sim}\neg(\alpha \to \beta) \leftrightarrow {\sim}({\sim}\neg\alpha \to {\sim}\neg\beta)$ provable. A procedure can be defined which turns each α into $\alpha^\neg$ in nnf, so that we can prove, by induction, that $({\sim}\alpha)^\neg \leftrightarrow {\sim}\alpha^\neg$ and $(\alpha \to \beta)^\neg \leftrightarrow {\sim}({\sim}\alpha^\neg \to {\sim}\beta^\neg)$. We denote $\boxdot\Gamma := {\sim}\neg\Gamma \cup \Gamma$.

Lemma 1. *For any finite set of formulas Γ, α in a nnf,*

$$\Gamma \vdash_{Ł(\neg)} \alpha \text{ iff for some finite } \Delta : \boxdot\Gamma, \Delta \vdash_Ł \alpha,$$

where Δ contains instances of $\neg$-axioms.

Proof. The right-left direction is almost trivial: Ł is a subsystem of Ł($\neg$), and all the axioms in Δ are provable in Ł($\neg$), and, thanks to the ${\sim}\neg$-rule, $\Gamma \vdash_{Ł(\neg)} \boxdot\gamma$ for each $\gamma \in \Gamma$.

For the other direction, we proceed in a few steps. First, we denote by $\vdash_{Ł(\neg)^-}$ provability in Ł($\neg$) *without* the ${\sim}\neg$-rule. By routine induction on proofs (and using that ${\sim}\neg$ distributes from/to implications and negations), we can see that

$$\Gamma \vdash_{Ł(\neg)} \alpha \text{ iff } \boxdot\Gamma \vdash_{Ł(\neg)^-} \alpha.$$

Then we can list all the instances of $\neg$-axioms in the proof in Δ, and obtain:

$$\boxdot\Gamma \vdash_{Ł(\neg)^-} \alpha \text{ iff } \boxdot\Gamma, \Delta \vdash_Ł \alpha.$$

First, note that we can list in Δ all instances of $\neg$-axioms for all subformulas of Γ, α as well and still keep the Lemma valid. This will come handy in the following proof. Second, we stress that in the final proof $\boxdot\Gamma, \Delta \vdash_Ł \alpha$ in Ł, we still use language of Ł($\neg$), where formulas starting with $\neg$ are seen from the point of view of Ł as atomic. □

Lemma 1 provides a translation of provability in Ł(¬) to provability in Ł and allows us to observe that the extension of Ł by ¬ is conservative. Now, using finite completeness of Ł, we can see that Ł(¬) is finitely strongly complete w.r.t. $[0,1]_{Ł} \times [0,1]_{Ł}^{op}$:

Lemma 2 (Finite strong standard completeness of Ł(¬)). *For a* finite *set of formulas* Γ,

$$\Gamma \vdash_{Ł(\neg)} \alpha \;\; \textit{iff} \;\; \forall e : \mathcal{L} \to [0,1]_{Ł} \times [0,1]_{Ł}^{op} \; (e[\Gamma] \subseteq \{(1,0)\} \to e(\alpha) = (1,0)).$$

Proof. The left-right direction is soundness, and consists of checking that the axioms are valid and the rules sound. We only do some cases:

First the $\sim\neg$-rule: assume that e is given and $e(\alpha) = (1,0)$. Then $e(\sim\neg\alpha) = \sim\neg(1,0) = \sim(0,1) = (1,0)$.

Next, for any e, $e(\sim\neg(\alpha \to \beta)) = \sim\neg(e(\alpha) \to e(\beta)) = \sim\neg(e(\alpha)_1 \to_Ł e(\beta)_1, \sim_Ł(e(\beta)_2 \to_Ł e(\alpha)_2)) = ((e(\beta)_2 \to_Ł e(\alpha)_2), \sim_Ł(e(\alpha)_1 \to_Ł e(\beta)_1))$,

and, $e(\sim\neg\alpha \to \sim\neg\beta) = \sim\neg e(\alpha) \to \sim\neg e(\beta) = (\sim_Ł e(\alpha)_2, \sim_Ł e(\alpha)_1) \to (\sim_Ł e(\beta)_2, \sim_Ł e(\beta)_1) = (\sim_Ł e(\alpha)_2 \to_Ł \sim_Ł e(\beta)_2, e(\alpha)_1 \&_Ł \sim_Ł e(\beta)_1) = ((e(\beta)_2 \to_Ł e(\alpha)_2), \sim_Ł(e(\alpha)_1 \to_Ł e(\beta)_1))$.

Last, for any e, $e(\neg\sim\alpha) = \neg\sim e(\alpha) = (\sim_Ł e(\alpha)_2, \sim_Ł e(\alpha)_1) = \sim\neg e(\alpha) = e(\sim\neg\alpha)$.

For the other direction, let us assume that $\Gamma \nvdash_{Ł(\neg)} \alpha$. Then for some finite Δ containing instances of $\neg$-axioms (in particular those for subformulas of Γ, α), we have $\boxdot\Gamma, \Delta \nvdash_Ł \alpha$. Because Ł is finitely standard complete, there is an evaluation e : At $\to [0,1]_Ł$ sending all formulas in $\boxdot\Gamma, \Delta$ to 1, while $e(\alpha) < 1$. Here, At contains literals from Γ, α of the form $p, \neg p$, and atoms and formulas of the form $\neg\delta$ from $\boxdot\Gamma, \Delta$. We define e' : $\texttt{Prop} \to [0,1]_Ł \times [0,1]_Ł^{op}$ by $e'(p) = (e(p), e(\neg p))$. We can then prove, by routine induction, that for each formula $e'(\beta) = (e(\beta), e(\beta^\neg))$. We use the fact that $e[\Delta] \subseteq \{1\}$, and Δ contains all instances of $\neg$-axioms for all subformulas of Γ, α.

We now immediately see that $e'(\alpha) < (1,0)$, because $e(\alpha) < 1$. To prove that indeed $e'[\Gamma] \subseteq \{(1,0)\}$, we use the fact that $e[\boxdot\Gamma] \subseteq \{1\}$: as for all $\gamma \in \Gamma$, $e(\sim\neg\gamma) = 1$, $e(\neg\gamma) = e(\gamma^\neg) = 0$. For the latter, we again need to use the fact that $e[\Delta] \subseteq \{1\}$, and Δ contains all instances of $\neg$-axioms for all subformulas of Γ, as they prove, by means of Ł, that $\neg\gamma \leftrightarrow \gamma^\neg$, and e has to respect that. Now we conclude, that for all $\gamma \in \Gamma$, $e'(\gamma) = (e(\gamma), e(\gamma^\neg)) = (1,0)$. □

We can now put together the two-layer syntax of the first two-layer logic to be

- $\mathcal{L}_e = \{\wedge, \vee, \neg\}$ language of BD,
- $\mathcal{M} = \{B\}$ a belief modality,
- $\mathcal{L}_u = \{\to, \sim, \neg\}$ language of Ł(¬).

The intended models can be described as follows: the lower layer is a double-valuation model of BD $(W, \Vdash^+, \Vdash^-)$ (a set of states W, and the two support relations, which in fact can be seen as arising from an evaluation of formulas of BD locally in the states in the product bilattice $2 \odot 2$, which is isomorphic to

4, as noted in Subsect. 2.2). A source is given by a mass function on the states $m_i : W \to [0,1]$, we assume there are n sources, and each source comes with a weight $w_i \in [0,1]$. For a non-modal formula $\varphi \in \mathcal{L}_e$, we obtain the value $||B\varphi|| \in [0,1]_{\text{Ł}} \times [0,1]_{\text{Ł}}^{op}$ as a pair of its positive and negative probabilities as follows. First, for each source m_i, we have $(\sum_{v \Vdash^+ \varphi} m_i(v), \sum_{v \Vdash^- \varphi} m_i(v)) = (p_i^+(\varphi), p_i^-(\varphi))$. Now, applying the weighted average aggregation strategy we obtain

$$||B\varphi|| = \left(\frac{\sum_{1 \le i \le n} w_i \cdot p_i^+(\varphi)}{\sum_{1 \le i \le n} w_i}, \frac{\sum_{1 \le i \le n} w_i \cdot p_i^-(\varphi)}{\sum_{1 \le i \le n} w_i}\right).$$

The modal part M of the two-layer logic consists of two axioms and a rule reflecting directly the axioms of probabilities listed in Subsect. 2.3:[9]

$$B(\varphi \vee \psi) \leftrightarrow (B\varphi \ominus B(\varphi \wedge \psi)) \oplus B\psi \quad B\neg\varphi \leftrightarrow \neg B\varphi$$
$$\varphi \vdash_{\mathsf{BD}} \psi / \vdash_{\text{Ł}(\neg)} B\varphi \to B\psi$$

The resulting logic is $(\mathsf{BD}, M, \text{Ł}(\neg))$. As BD is locally finite and strongly complete w.r.t. **4**, and $\text{Ł}(\neg)$ is finitely strongly complete w.r.t. $[0,1]_{\text{Ł}} \times [0,1]_{\text{Ł}}^{op}$, we can apply [7, Theorems 1 and 2] directly to obtain finite strong completeness (soundness of the modal axioms and rules is easy to see). But first, we need to observe that the frames as we have described them can be seen within the framework of [7]:

The frames, seen in the format of [7], are $F = (W, \mathbf{4}, [0,1]_{\text{Ł}} \times [0,1]_{\text{Ł}}^{op}, \mu^B)$, formulas of $\mathcal{L}_e$ are evaluated locally in the states of W using **4**, as in the four-valued models for BD (which we can see as equivalent to the double-valuation models). The interpretation of modalities μ^B is computed as follows. A source is given by a mass function on the states $m : W \to [0,1]$. Each source comes with a weight $w_i \in [0,1]$. Given $\mathbf{e} \in \prod_{v \in W} \mathbf{4}$, we obtain, for each source m_i, first the following sums of weights over states: $(\sum_{\mathbf{e}_v \in \{t,b\}} m_i(v), \sum_{\mathbf{e}_v \in \{f,b\}} m_i(v)) = (p_i^+(\mathbf{e}), p_i^-(\mathbf{e}))$. The assignment μ^B now computes the weighted average of those as follows:

$$\mu^B(\mathbf{e}) = \text{WA}(\mathbf{e}) = \left(\frac{\sum_{1 \le i \le n} w_i \cdot p_i^+(\mathbf{e})}{\sum_{1 \le i \le n} w_i}, \frac{\sum_{1 \le i \le n} w_i \cdot p_i^-(\mathbf{e})}{\sum_{1 \le i \le n} w_i}\right).$$

Thus, for a non-modal formula $\varphi \in \mathcal{L}_e$, applying μ^B to the tuple of its values in the states (which we denote by $||\phi||$), we obtain the value of $B\varphi$ as $||B\varphi|| \in [0,1]_{\text{Ł}} \times [0,1]_{\text{Ł}}^{op}$ as a pair of its positive and negative probabilities as follows: First, for each source we have[10]

$$\left(\sum_{v \Vdash^+ \varphi} m_i(v), \sum_{v \Vdash^- \varphi} m_i(v)\right) = (p_i^+(\varphi), p_i^-(\varphi)).$$

[9] Considering just the right-left implication in the first axiom, we can express belief functions.

[10] The value of φ in v being among $\{t, b\}$ means it is positively supported in v, i.e. $v \Vdash^+ \varphi$. Similarly $\{f, b\}$ means negative support.

Now, applying the weighted average aggregation we obtain

$$||B\varphi|| = \mu^B(||\phi||) = \mathrm{WA}(||\phi||) = \left(\frac{\sum_{1\leq i\leq n} w_i \cdot p_i^+(\varphi)}{\sum_{1\leq i\leq n} w_i}, \frac{\sum_{1\leq i\leq n} w_i \cdot p_i^-(\varphi)}{\sum_{1\leq i\leq n} w_i}\right).$$

We can now conclude the completeness as follows:

Corollary 1. $(BD, M, Ł(\neg))$ *is finitely strongly complete w.r.t.* **4** *based,* $[0,1]_Ł \times [0,1]_Ł^{op}$*-measured frames validating* M.

In such frames, μ^B interprets B as a probability: For a frame to validate the axioms in M means they are sent to $(1,0)$, by an evaluation in $[0,1]_{\mathrm{Ł}} \times [0,1]_{\mathrm{Ł}}^{op}$ induced by μ^B over the lower state valuations (which determines values of modal atomic formulas). An equivalence $\alpha \leftrightarrow \beta$ is evaluated at $(1,0)$ iff the values of α and β are equal. $B(\varphi)^M = \mu^B(\varphi^M) = (p^+(\varphi), p^-(\varphi))$. Therefore, the first two axioms say that

$$p^+(\varphi \vee \psi) = (p^+(\varphi) - p^+(\varphi \wedge \psi)) + p^+(\psi) \textit{ and } p^+(\neg\varphi) = \neg p^-(\varphi)$$
$$p^-(\varphi \vee \psi) = (p^-(\varphi) - p^-(\varphi \wedge \psi)) + p^-(\psi) \textit{ and } p^-(\neg\varphi) = \neg p^+(\varphi).$$

Similarly, the fact that the frame validates the rule say that p^+ (p^-) are monotone (antitone) w.r.t. $\varphi \vdash_{\mathsf{BD}} \psi$. Analogous observation holds for the case the upper logic is the bilattice one.

From [24, Theorem 4], we know that it is the induced probability function of exactly one mass function on the BD canonical model, which in fact yields completeness w.r.t. the intended frames described above (with a single source).

II. A bilattice Łukasiewicz logic. Alternatively, if we wish to use full expressivity of a bilattice language, we can take in the upper layer $\mathcal{L}_u = \{\wedge, \vee, \sqcap, \sqcup, \supset, \neg, 0\}$ to be the language of the *product residuated bilattice* $[0,1]_{\mathrm{Ł}} \odot [0,1]_{\mathrm{Ł}} = ([0,1] \times [0,1], \wedge, \vee, \sqcap, \sqcup, \supset, \neg, (0,0))$, defined in the spirit of [22] in Example 6. We evaluate formulas of the upper logic in the matrix $([0,1]_{\mathrm{Ł}} \odot [0,1]_{\mathrm{Ł}}, F)$ with $F = \{(1,a) \mid a \in [0,1]\}$ as the designated values, so that we send 0 to $(0,0)$. The constants and connectives $\top, \bot, 1, *, \rightarrow, \sim, \oplus, \ominus$ are definable as follows:

$$\begin{array}{ll} {\sim}\alpha := (\alpha \supset 0) \sqcup \neg(\neg\alpha \supset 0) & \top := 0 \supset 0 \quad \bot := \neg\top \quad 1 := {\sim}0 \\ \alpha \rightarrow \beta := (\alpha \supset \beta) \wedge (\neg\beta \supset \neg\alpha) & \alpha \oplus \beta := ({\sim}\alpha \supset \beta) \sqcup \neg({\sim}\neg\alpha \supset \neg\beta) \\ \alpha * \beta := \neg(\beta \rightarrow \neg\alpha) & \alpha \ominus \beta := {\sim}(\alpha \supset \beta) \sqcup \neg{\sim}(\neg\alpha \supset \neg\beta) \end{array}$$

For an evaluation e, it holds that $e(\alpha \rightarrow \beta) \in F$ iff $e(\alpha \rightarrow \beta) \geq_t (1,1)$ iff $e(\alpha) \leq_t e(\beta)$. The upper logic L_u as a consequence relation is defined to be

$$\Gamma \models_{\mathrm{Ł}\odot\mathrm{Ł}} \alpha \text{ iff } \forall e(e[\Gamma] \subseteq F \rightarrow e(\alpha) \in F).$$

The intended frames now use $[0,1]_{\mathrm{Ł}} \odot [0,1]_{\mathrm{Ł}}$ as the upper algebra, otherwise semantics of atomic modal formulas is computed (from multiple sources) as in the previous logic. We also obtain literally the same modal axioms M as above. Only here, apart from a very generic completeness w.r.t. **4** based frames, where the upper algebra is an algebra (in fact the Lindenbaum-Tarski algebra) of the upper logic, we cannot provide a better insight at the moment and leave axiomatization of L_u, and completeness w.r.t $[0,1]_{\text{Ł}} \odot [0,1]_{\text{Ł}}$-measured frames to further investigations (cf. footnote 4).

3.2 Logic of Monotone Coherent Belief

The simplest logic we propose to deal with scenarios like the one of Example 2 is of the form $(\mathsf{BD}, M, \mathsf{BD})$. Both lower and upper languages are the language of BD, $\mathcal{M}$ consists of a single belief modality B. The intended frames are based on double-valuation semantics of BD as before, only now we evaluate formulas of the upper logic in the bilattice $\mathbf{L}_{[0,1]} \odot \mathbf{L}_{[0,1]}$ on Fig. 1 (right). A source is given by a mass function on the states $m_i : W \to [0,1]$, we again assume there are n sources. For a non-modal formula φ, we obtain the value $||B\varphi|| \in \mathbf{L}_{[0,1]} \odot \mathbf{L}_{[0,1]}$ as follows. First, for each source m_i, we have $(\sum_{v \Vdash^+ \varphi} m_i(v), \sum_{v \Vdash^- \varphi} m_i(v)) = (p_i^+(\varphi), p_i^-(\varphi))$. Now, applying the Min aggregation strategy we obtain

$$||B\varphi|| = \left(\min_{1 \le i \le n} p_i^+(\varphi), \min_{1 \le i \le n} p_i^-(\varphi) \right).$$

Similarly, we may use the Max aggregation strategy when reasoning with trusted sources. As before, we can see the frames inside the framework of [7] to derive completeness: frames are of the form $F = (W, \mathbf{4}, \mathbf{L}_{[0,1]} \odot \mathbf{L}_{[0,1]}, \mu^B)$ where $\mu^B : \prod_{v \in W} \mathbf{4} \to \mathbf{L}_{[0,1]} \odot \mathbf{L}_{[0,1]}$ computes the Min (Max) aggregation of the probabilities given by the individual sources. In general this aggregation strategy does not yield a probability, but it is monotone and $\neg$-compatible. This motivates considering logic $(\mathsf{BD}, M, \mathsf{BD})$, where the modal part M consists of the following two axioms and a rule

$$B\neg\varphi \dashv\vdash_{\mathsf{BD}_u} \neg B\varphi \qquad \varphi \vdash_{\mathsf{BD}_e} \psi / B\varphi \vdash_{\mathsf{BD}_u} B\psi.$$

As BD is strongly complete w.r.t. both **4** and $\mathbf{L}_{[0,1]} \odot \mathbf{L}_{[0,1]}$[11], we can apply [7, Theorem 1] to conclude that $(\mathsf{BD}, M, \mathsf{BD})$ is strongly complete w.r.t. **4**-based $\mathbf{L}_{[0,1]} \odot \mathbf{L}_{[0,1]}$-measured frames validating M. In such frames, μ^B interprets B as a monotone and $\neg$-compatible assignment (not necessarily a probability). We cannot in general see it as coming from a measure, or a set of measures[12], on the lower states (to recover sources), and connect it with the intended semantics.

One could however replace the upper language with the full bilattice language, consider modalities indexed by sources, and express the Min (Max) aggregations explicitly using $\sqcap, \sqcup$ connectives.

---

[11] Because it has $(2 \odot 2, \{(1,0),(1,1)\})$ as a sub-matrix: the obvious embedding is a *strict* homomorphism of de Morgan matrices - it preserves and reflects the filters.

[12] It is not hard to provide an example of such assignment which cannot be obtained by Min (Max) aggregation of probabilities.

4 Conclusion and Further Directions

We have proposed two-layer logics of belief based on potentially inconsistent probabilistic information coming from multiple sources. The framework keeps positive and negative aspect of information (support, evidence, belief) separate, though inter-linked, in both layers of the semantics, and thus allows for reasoning with inconsistencies, in contrast to getting rid of them. Doing so, we believe we have laid groundwork to a modular framework to model reasoning with inconsistent probabilistic information.

We see our contribution in the following: to see how Belnap-Dunn's logic BD (on the lower layer, and behind the non-standard probabilities) can be combined with many-valued reasoning on the upper layer provides a novel example of two-layer logics for reasoning under uncertainty. The only examples considered so far used either classical logic [15], or quantitative reasoning in form of linear inequalities on the upper layer [28]. The logic $Ł(\neg)$, extending Łukasiewicz logic with bi-lattice negation, we introduced in Subsect. 3.1 and proved its finite strong standard completeness, is to our best knowledge new and might be of independent interest. (The same can be said about the bi-lattice Łukasiewicz logic, which however remains to be axiomatized and its completeness studied.)

The project is subject to ongoing work. Apart from investigating further the logics proposed in this paper, we are pursuing the following research directions:

In the continuation of [16] that generalises Dempster-Shafer theory [27] to finite lattices, we are currently working on adapting the theory to the BD-based setting, and putting it in context of existing literature on belief functions. This would allow us to consider Dempster-Shafer combination rule as another aggregation strategy.

To cover cases when a source does not give an opinion about each formula of the language, we need to account for sources providing partial probability maps. Also cases where sources provide heterogeneous information need to be included.

An important direction to move further is to capture dynamics of information and belief given by updates on the level of sources, and to generalize the framework to the multi agent setting involving group modalities and dynamics of belief. Specifically, forming group belief, like common and distributed belief, will involve communication and sharing or pooling of sources. It might call for a use of various upper-layer languages, among those we see the ones with additional (nestable) modalities inside the upper logic to account for reflected, higher-order beliefs, in contrast to the beliefs grounded directly in the sources.

References

1. Aerts, D., Sozzo, S., Veloz, T.: New fundamental evidence of non-classical structure in the combination of natural concepts. Philos. Trans. R. Soc. A **374** (2016)
2. Avron, A.: The structure of interlaced bilattices. Math. Struct. Comput. Sci. **6**(3), 287–299 (1996)
3. Baldi, P., Cintula, P., Noguera, C.: On two-layered modal logics for uncertainty (2020, manuscript)

4. Baltag, A., Bezhanishvili, N., Özgün, A., Smets, S.: Justified belief and the topology of evidence. In: Väänänen, J., Hirvonen, Å., de Queiroz, R. (eds.) WoLLIC 2016. LNCS, vol. 9803, pp. 83–103. Springer, Heidelberg (2016). https://doi.org/10.1007/978-3-662-52921-8_6
5. Belnap, N.D.: How a computer should think. New Essays on Belnap-Dunn Logic. SL, vol. 418, pp. 35–53. Springer, Cham (2019). https://doi.org/10.1007/978-3-030-31136-0_4
6. Bílková, M., Majer, O., Peliš, M.: Epistemic logics for sceptical agents. J. Logic Comput. **26**(6), 1815–1841 (2015)
7. Cintula, P., Noguera, C.: Modal logics of uncertainty with two-layer syntax: a general completeness theorem. In: Kohlenbach, U., Barceló, P., de Queiroz, R. (eds.) WoLLIC 2014. LNCS, vol. 8652, pp. 124–136. Springer, Heidelberg (2014). https://doi.org/10.1007/978-3-662-44145-9_9
8. Codd, E.F.: Understanding relations (installment #7). FDT - Bull. ACM SIGMOD **7**(3), 23–28 (1975)
9. Console, M., Guagliardo, P., Libkin, L.: Propositional and predicate logics of incomplete information. In: Proceedings of KR 2018, Tempe, Arizona, pp. 592–601. AAAI Press (2018)
10. Cornelis, C., Deschrijver, G., Kerre, E.E.: Advances and challenges in interval-valued fuzzy logic. Fuzzy Sets Syst. **157**, 622–627 (2006)
11. Dempster, A.P.: A generalization of Bayesian inference. J. Roy. Stat. Soc.: Ser. B (Methodol.) **30**(2), 205–232 (1968)
12. Di Nola, A., Leustean, I.: Łukasiewicz logic and MV-algebras. In: Cintula, P., Hajek, P., Noguera, C. (eds.) Handbook of Mathematical Fuzzy Logic, vol. 2. College Publications (2011)
13. Dunn, J.M.: Intuitive semantics for first-degree entailments and 'coupled trees'. Philos. Stud. **29**(3), 149–168 (1976)
14. Dunn, J.M.: Contradictory information: too much of a good thing. J. Philos. Logic **39**, 425–452 (2010)
15. Fagin, R., Halpern, J.Y., Megiddo, N.: A logic for reasoning about probabilities. Inf. Comput. **87**, 78–128 (1990)
16. Frittella, S., Manoorkar, K., Palmigiano, A., Tzimoulis, A., Wijnberg, N.: Toward a Dempster-Shafer theory of concepts. Int. J. Approx. Reason. **125**, 14–25 (2020)
17. Ginsberg, M.: Multivalued logics: a uniform approach to reasoning in AI. Comput. Intell. **4**, 256–316 (1988)
18. Grahne, G., Moallemi, A., Onet, A.: Intuitionistic data exchange. In: 9th Alberto Mendelzon International Workshop on Foundations of Data Management (2015)
19. Hájek, P.: Metamathematics of Fuzzy Logic, Trends in Logic, vol. 4. Kluwer (1998)
20. Halpern, J.: Reasoning About Uncertainty. MIT Press, Cambridge (2005)
21. Hamblin, C.L.: The modal 'probably'. Mind **68**, 234–240 (1959)
22. Jansana, R., Rivieccio, U.: Residuated bilattices. Soft. Comput. **16**(3), 493–504 (2012)
23. Kleene, S.C.: Introduction to Metamathematics. North-Holland, Amsterdam (1952)
24. Klein, D., Majer, O., Raffie-Rad, S.: Probabilities with gaps and gluts. http://arxiv.org/abs/2003.07408, submitted
25. Přenosil, A.: Reasoning with inconsistent information. Ph.D. thesis, Charles University, Prague (2018)
26. Rivieccio, U.: An algebraic study of bilattice-based logics. Ph.D. thesis, University of Barcelona - University of Genoa (2010)

27. Shafer, G.: A Mathematical Theory of Evidence. Princeton University Press, Princeton (1976)
28. Zhou, C.: Belief functions on distributive lattices. Artif. Intell. **201**, 1–31 (2013)

Parameterized Complexity of Dynamic Belief Updates

Thomas Bolander[1] and Arnaud Lequen[2(✉)]

[1] DTU Compute, Technical University of Denmark, Kongens Lyngby, Denmark
tobo@dtu.dk
[2] Univ Rennes, ENS Rennes, Bruz, France
arnaud.lequen@ens-rennes.fr

Abstract. Dynamic Belief Update (DBU) is a model checking problem in Dynamic Epistemic Logic (DEL) concerning the effect of applying a number of epistemic actions on an initial epistemic model. It can also be considered as a plan verification problem in epistemic planning. The problem is known to be PSPACE-hard. To better understand the source of complexity of the problem, previous research has investigated the complexity of 128 parameterized versions of the problem with parameters such as number of agents and size of actions. The complexity of many parameter combinations has been determined, but previous research left a few combinations as open problems. In this paper, we solve most of the remaining open problems by proving all of them to be fixed-parameter intractable. Only two parameter combinations are still left as open problem for future research.

Keywords: Parameterized complexity · Model checking · Dynamic Epistemic Logic · Plan verification

1 Introduction

In the fields of psychology, ecology, economy, and various areas of computer science like automated planning and distributed systems, the need often arises to model multi-agent systems and reason about the knowledge of the involved agents. Indeed, situations where multiple human or artificial agents interact with their environment, and have to update their knowledge accordingly, are ubiquitous. Dynamic Epistemic Logic (DEL) is a well-suited framework to model such situations, as it is a family of modal logics that allow not only to reason about (higher-order) knowledge, but also to represent how such knowledge is dynamically updated through the occurrence of events. Unfortunately, many decision problems associated with DEL are provably hard [7,12]. Despite that, in real-life situations humans manage to reason fairly effectively about the knowledge of themselves and other agents (at least to modest depths of reasoning). Moreover, certain tasks involving DEL can be carried out fairly easily [12].

In this paper, we study the Dynamic Belief Update (DBU) problem, which boils down to verifying whether an epistemic formula holds in a model after a

M. A. Martins and I. Sedlár (Eds.): DaLí 2020, LNCS 12569, pp. 87–102, 2020.
https://doi.org/10.1007/978-3-030-65840-3_6

series of epistemic updates, *i.e.*, whether a certain epistemic fact holds after a sequence of (epistemic) events have occurred in an initial (epistemic) situation. The events can also be thought of as actions executed by agents, and hence DBU can equivalently be thought of as a plan verification problem in an epistemic setting. We extend the efforts of van de Pol *et al.* [12] to identify which aspects of DBU make it intractable. Of the set of sub-problems of DBU identified by van de Pol *et al.*, we manage to settle the tractability question of most problems previously left open, leaving only two undecided.

In Sect. 2, we present the DEL framework of this paper, and after recalling notions of parameterized complexity, we present DBU and its parameters. In Sect. 3, we prove our new fixed-parameter intractability results of DBU.

2 Background

2.1 Dynamic Epistemic Logic

Dynamic Epistemic Logic (DEL) is a modal logic focused on reasoning about knowledge, which can be revised according to the evolution of the situation [7]. In this paper, we use a variant of DEL that allows multi-pointed epistemic models and has propositional postconditions [3]. While various other variants of DEL exist, we present here a simple version, that can be readily extended into a version of DEL with more general preconditions, postconditions, or frame conditions. As we only present intractability results, our work still holds for more complex versions of DEL.

The language $\mathcal{L}_K(P, \mathcal{A})$ of multi-agent epistemic logic is defined as follows, where p ranges over a finite set of propositional variables P, and i over a finite set of agents $\mathcal{A}$:

$$\varphi := \top \mid p \mid \neg\varphi \mid \varphi \wedge \varphi \mid K_i\varphi,$$

The intended meaning of $K_i\varphi$ is "agent i knows φ". We will often use the abbreviated notation $\hat{K}_i\varphi = \neg K_i \neg\varphi$, which reads "agent i considers φ possible". Other symbols such as $\vee$ and $\rightarrow$ can be defined by abbreviation as usual. The semantic of the language is defined through *epistemic models* (Kripke models).

Definition 1. (Pointed Epistemic Model) *A* pointed epistemic model *for the language $\mathcal{L}_K(P, \mathcal{A})$ is a pair $(\mathcal{M}, W_d)$ where $\mathcal{M} = (W, R, V)$ and:*

- *W is a finite, non-empty set of worlds*
- *$W_d \subseteq W$ is the non-empty set of the* designated worlds
- *$R : \mathcal{A} \rightarrow 2^{W \times W}$ is a function assigning an equivalence relation R_i to every agent i, called the* indistinguishability relation *for agent i*
- *$V : P \rightarrow 2^W$ is a valuation function that assigns to every propositional variable the set of worlds in which it is true*

Definition 2. (Truth in a pointed epistemic model) *Let $(\mathcal{M}, W_d)$ be a pointed epistemic model, where $\mathcal{M} = (W, R, V)$, and let $\varphi \in \mathcal{L}_K(P, \mathcal{A})$, and $w \in W$. The truth conditions for φ are the standard propositional ones plus:*

$$(\mathcal{M}, \{w\}) \models K_i\varphi \quad \textit{iff} \quad \textit{for all } w' \textit{ s.t. } R_i(w, w'),\ (\mathcal{M}, \{w'\}) \models \varphi$$
$$(\mathcal{M}, W_d) \models \varphi \quad \textit{iff} \quad \textit{for all } w \in W_d,\ (\mathcal{M}, \{w\}) \models \varphi$$

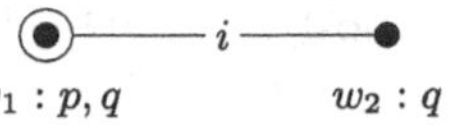

Fig. 1. A pointed epistemic model $(\mathcal{M}, \{w_1\})$ for $\mathcal{L}_K(\{p,q\},\{i\})$ with $\mathcal{M} = (W, R, V)$, $W = \{w_1, w_2\}$, $R_i = \{(w_1,w_1),(w_1,w_2),(w_2,w_1),(w_2,w_2)\}$ and $V(p) = \{w_1\}$, $V(q) = \{w_1, w_2\}$. Reflexive edges are generally omitted.

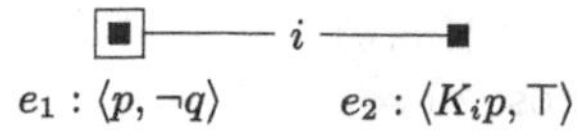

Fig. 2. A pointed event model $(\mathcal{E}, \{e_1\})$ for $\mathcal{L}_K(\{p,q\},\{i\})$ with $\mathcal{E} = (E, Q, \mathsf{pre}, \mathsf{post})$, $E = \{e_1, e_2\}$, $Q_i = \{(e_1,e_1),(e_1,e_2),(e_2,e_1),(e_2,e_2)\}$, $\mathsf{pre}(e_1) = p$, $\mathsf{pre}(e_2) = K_i p$, $\mathsf{post}(e_1) = \neg q$ and $\mathsf{post}(e_2) = \top$.

Example 1. Figure 1 shows an epistemic model where agent i can not make the distinction between worlds w_1 and w_2. Thus, it does not know whether p is true or not, as it holds in the "actual" world w_1, but not in w_2. As such, $(\mathcal{M}, \{w_1\}) \not\models K_i p$, although $(\mathcal{M}, \{w_1\}) \models p$. As q is true in both worlds, $(\mathcal{M}, \{w_1\}) \models K_i q$.

Event models, defined next, represent changes to the situation, which lead agents to update their knowledge.

Definition 3. (Pointed Event Model) *A* pointed event model *for* $\mathcal{L}_K(P, \mathcal{A})$ *is a pair* $(\mathcal{E}, E_d)$ *where* $\mathcal{E}$ *is a tuple* $\mathcal{E} = (E, Q, \mathsf{pre}, \mathsf{post})$, *such that*

- E *is a non-empty finite set of* events
- $E_d \subseteq E$ *is a non-empty set of* designated events
- $Q : \mathcal{A} \to 2^{E \times E}$ *is a function assigning an equivalence relation* Q_i *to every agent* i, *called the* indistinguishability relation *for agent* i
- $\mathsf{pre} : E \to \mathcal{L}_K(P, \mathcal{A})$ *is a function assigning to each event a precondition*
- $\mathsf{post} : E \to \mathcal{L}_K(P, \mathcal{A})$ *is a function assigning to each event a postcondition, which is a conjunction of literals (propositional variables and their negations, including* $\top$*)*

One could also define a precondition as a formula of the language $\mathcal{L}_{DK}(P, \mathcal{A})$, which extends $\mathcal{L}_K(P, \mathcal{A})$ with the modality $[\mathcal{E}', E'_d]\varphi$, where $(\mathcal{E}', E'_d)$ is a pointed event model and φ a formula of $\mathcal{L}_{DK}(P, \mathcal{A})$. Intuitively, this new modality means that, after the (applicable) events of $(\mathcal{E}', E'_d)$ occurred, φ is true. In this paper, we do not consider this modality, even though our results would still apply, as we only show intractability results.

When no confusion can arise, we will use the abbreviated notation $\mathcal{M}$ for pointed epistemic models $(\mathcal{M}, W_d)$, and similarly for pointed event models. Epistemic models can be updated with the application of event models through *product updates*, defined as follows.

Definition 4. *The product update of the (pointed) epistemic model* $(\mathcal{M}, W_d)$ *with the (pointed) event model* $(\mathcal{E}, E_d)$ *is the (pointed) epistemic model* $(\mathcal{M}, W_d) \otimes (\mathcal{E}, E_d) = (\mathcal{M}', W'_d)$, *such that* $\mathcal{M}' = (W', R', V')$ *and*

- $W' = \{(w, e) \in W \times E \mid \mathcal{M}, w \models \mathsf{pre}(e)\}$
- $R'_i = \{((w, e), (v, f)) \in W' \times W' \mid R_i(w, v)$ *and* $Q_i(e, f)\}$

- $V'(p) = (\{(w,e) \in W' \mid \mathcal{M}, w \models p\} \cup \{(w,e) \in W' \mid \mathsf{post}(e) \models p\}) - \{(w,e) \in W' \mid \mathsf{post}(e) \models \neg p\}$
- $W'_d = \{(w,e) \in W' \mid w \in W_d \textit{ and } e \in E_d\}$

Example 2. Figure 2 shows an event model where event e_1 or e_2 can occur, and agent i cannot distinguish which event actually happens. Event e_1 can only occur in worlds where p is true, and updates them by making q false. Event e_2 can only occur in worlds where agent i knows p, and does not change the truth value of any variable. If we take the product update $(\mathcal{M}, \{w_1\}) \otimes (\mathcal{E}, \{e_1\})$ of the epistemic model of Fig. 1 with the event model of Fig. 2, we get a model containing only a single world satisfying $p \wedge \neg q$: the only world satisfying any of the event preconditions is w_1 and it only satisfies the precondition of e_1. So only the world-event pair (w_1, e_1) "survives" the product update, and the postcondition of e_1 enforces q to become false (but otherwise preserves the truth-values from w_1).

2.2 Parameterized Complexity

In this section, we recall some notions of parameterized complexity. Parameterized complexity is a branch of complexity theory whose aim is to offer a finer-grained analysis of a computational problem, taking into account some characteristics of each instance. It studies *parameterized problems*, which resemble classical decision problems. Given an alphabet Σ, a parameterized problem L is a subset of $\Sigma^* \times \mathbb{N}$. Given an instance $\langle x, k \rangle$ of L, we call x the *main part* and k the *parameter*. The parameter k is a metric that gauges one dimension of x. For instance, if our problem is to model-check formulas of $\mathcal{L}_K(P, \mathcal{A})$, then x consists of a formula ϕ and a model $\mathcal{M}$, while k can e.g. be the modal depth of ϕ or the number of agents mentioned in ϕ and $\mathcal{M}$.

In classical complexity theory, the class of tractable problems is P. The corresponding class in parameterized complexity theory is the class of *fixed-parameter tractable* problems, which is denoted FPT. It encompasses all parameterized problems that can be solved by an *fpt-algorithm*, defined as follows.

Definition 5. (Fpt-algorithm) *Let L be a parameterized problem. An algorithm* $\mathbb{A}$ *is an* fpt-algorithm *for problem L if it solves L, and there exists a computable function* $f : \mathbb{N} \to \mathbb{N}$ *and a polynomial* $\mathcal{P}$*, such that the running time of* $\mathbb{A}$ *on any instance* $\langle x, k \rangle \in L$ *is at most*

$$f(k) \cdot \mathcal{P}(|x|)$$

For instance, the problem SAT is notoriously intractable [6]. However, its parameterized variant p-SAT, where p is the number of propositional variables, is fixed-parameter tractable. Indeed, checking all 2^{p} assignments of the p variables against a formula φ can be done in time $2^{\mathsf{p}} \cdot \mathcal{P}(|\varphi|)$, for some polynomial $\mathcal{P}$. Intuitively, this means that a set of instances of SAT, where all formulas have a number of variables bounded by some constant p, forms a tractable problem.

Proving that a parameterized problem is not fixed-parameter tractable can be done through *fpt-reductions*, defined next. They can be seen as the parameterized complexity counterpart of classical polynomial-time reductions, and are useful for proving membership and hardness results for parameterized problems.

Definition 6. (Fpt-reduction) *Let L and L' be two parameterized problems. An* fpt-reduction *from L to L' is a mapping $R : L \longrightarrow L'$ such that:*

- *$\langle x, k\rangle \in L$ iff $\langle x', k'\rangle = R(\langle x, k\rangle) \in L'$.*
- *R is computable by an fpt-algorithm,* i.e., *there is a computable function f and a polynomial $\mathcal{P}$ such that $R(\langle x, k\rangle)$ can be computed in time $f(k) \cdot \mathcal{P}(|x|)$.*
- *There exists a polynomial g such that, if $\langle x, k\rangle \in L$ and $\langle x', k'\rangle = R(\langle x, k\rangle) \in L'$, then $k' \leq g(k)$.*

When there exists an fpt-reduction from L to L', we write $L \leq_{fpt} L'$.

It follows from the way fpt-reductions are defined that FPT is closed by fpt-reduction. More specifically, suppose $L \leq_{fpt} L'$. Then if L' belongs to FPT, then so does L. Hence, to prove that a problem L' is not fixed-parameter tractable, it suffices to find an fpt-reduction to L' from a problem L known to be not fixed-parameter tractable (we call such problems *fixed-parameter intractable*). In this paper, we consider two complexity classes that are deemed fixed-parameter intractable, namely W[1] and para-NP [8]. W[1] is the class of problems that can be fpt-reduced to k-W2SAT, which is the problem where, given a 2CNF formula φ and a parameter k, one has to decide if there exists a valuation satisfying φ in which at most k variables are true. Para-NP is the class of parameterized problems that can be solved by a nondeterministic fpt-algorithm. Para-NP-hard problems are deemed fixed-parameter intractable, as W[1] $\subseteq$ para-NP [9].

In the remaining of this paper, we will allow problems to have multiple parameters. If a problem L has a set of parameters $\{\mathsf{k}_1, \ldots, \mathsf{k}_n\}$, then its instance are of the form $\langle x, \mathsf{k}_1 + \cdots + \mathsf{k}_n\rangle$. A problem L with parameters $\{\mathsf{k}_1, \ldots, \mathsf{k}_n\}$ is often denoted $\{\mathsf{k}_1, \ldots, \mathsf{k}_n\}$-$L$. When adding further parameters to a parameterized problem, we of course make it more constrained. That is, for any problem L and parameter sets X and Y, the problem $(X \cup Y)$-L is at least as constrained as X-L. Hence the following is easily proved.

Proposition 1. *Let X and Y be sets of parameters of a decision problem L. Then $(X \cup Y)$-$L \leq_{fpt} X$-L.*

2.3 Dynamic Belief Update

The decision problem considered in this paper is presented in Fig. 3, following van de Pol *et al.* [12]. It is the problem of checking whether a certain epistemic formula is true after having updated an initial epistemic situation (epistemic model)

Dynamic Belief Update (DBU)
Input: An epistemic model $(\mathcal{M}, W_d)$ on $\mathcal{L}_K(P, \mathcal{A})$;
A series of event models $(\mathcal{E}_1, E_1), \ldots, (\mathcal{E}_u, E_u)$ on $\mathcal{L}_K(P, \mathcal{A})$;
A goal formula $\varphi_g \in \mathcal{L}_K(P, \mathcal{A})$.
Output: *Yes* if $(\mathcal{M}, W_d) \otimes (\mathcal{E}_1, E_1) \otimes \cdots \otimes (\mathcal{E}_u, E_u) \models \varphi_g$
No otherwise

Fig. 3. The decision problem DBU considered in this paper

Table 1. Parameters for DBU

Param.	Description	Param.	Description
a	Number of agents	o	Goal formula's modal depth
c	Max. length of event preconditions	p	Number of prop. variables
e	Max. no. of events per event model	u	Number of event models
f	Length of goal formula		

with a sequence of epistemic actions (event models).[1] So it is about the complexity of keeping track of "who knows what" when observing a sequence of actions taking place, where these actions can both change ontic facts and what the different agents know. Such problems occur e.g. in the coordinated attack problem, the consecutive number puzzle, the muddy children puzzle, board games like Hanabi and Clue and the false-belief tasks studied in cognitive psychology [1,2,4]. We can also think of the problem as the plan verification problem in epistemic planning [3]: Given an initial state (epistemic model), a sequence of actions (event models) and a goal formula, does the action sequence achieve the goal from the initial state?

DBU is PSPACE-complete, as proven by van de Pol *et al.* [12]. Their paper proposes various parameters as an attempt to identify the mechanisms that make DBU hard. Those parameters are given in Table 1, and any combination of those form a parameterized version of DBU. This leads us to the class of problems of the form X-DBU, where X is a subset of the 7 parameters. For instance, {a, c, p}-DBU is the dynamic belief update problem where the parameters are the number of agents, the length of the preconditions and the number of propositional variables. There are $2^7 = 128$ problems of this form. Prior to our work, the (fixed-parameter) tractability or intractability of 114 of them was already known [12]. We show intractability results for an additional 12 problems, thus leaving only 2 (closely related) problems unsettled. Table 2 summarizes the known results, including the new ones of this paper. It only mentions

[1] A better name would probably be "Dynamic Knowledge Update" as we are here only considering models where the underlying accessibility relations are equivalence relations (*i.e.*, S5). However, since all our results are intractability results, these still hold if we generalise to arbitrary accessibility relations, including ones representing beliefs.

Table 2. Complexity results for the most general parameterized variants of DBU, from which all other results for our set of parameters can be immediately deduced. Results on the left table originate from [12], while results on the right table constitute the original contributions of this paper.

Param. for DBU	Complexity
{a, c, f, o, u}	W[1]-hard
{a, f, o, p, u}	W[1]-hard
{e, u}	FPT

Earlier known results [12]

Param. for DBU	Complexity
{a, c, e, f, o, p}	para-NP-hard
{c, f, o, p, u}	W[1]-hard
{a, c, o, p, u}	W[1]-hard

New results of this paper

the strongest ones, as all other results can be immediately deduced from them through Proposition 1, and the observation that, for any set of parameters X of DBU, $(X \cup \{\mathsf{f}\})$-DBU $\leq_{fpt}$ $(X \cup \{\mathsf{f}, \mathsf{o}\})$-DBU (if we constrain the length of the goal formula, we are also constraining its modal depth).

It can be hard to keep track of 128 different versions of the same problem. However, many are obviously interdependent in the sense that the (in)tractability of one immediately implies the (in)tractability of the other, e.g. through Proposition 1. To keep track of dependency and which problems are still open, we developed a small script, which can be found at https://github.com/arnaudlequen/dbuproblemfinder. The script allowed us to find the open problems that would solve most other open problems, and keeping track of the remaining open problems as we gradually settled more cases.

3 Complexity Results

Theorem 1. *{a, c, e, f, o, p}-DBU is fixed-parameter intractable (more precisely, para-NP-hard). In other words, the Dynamic Belief Update problem is intractable even when restricting the number of propositional variables and agents (p,a), the maximum number of events in event models (e), the maximum length of event preconditions (c), and the length and modal depth of the goal formula (f,o).*

Proof. In this proof, we build an fpt-reduction from an NP-hard problem to an instance of {a, c, e, f, o, p}-DBU with fixed values of a, c, e, f, o and p, thus proving para-NP-hardness of the latter (since the NP-hard problem doesn't have any parameter, the reduction is also a regular polynomial reduction). The construction used in the proof is an adaptation of the proof of Theorem 19 of Bolander *et al.* [3]. The general idea is to simulate, through an instance of DBU, the execution of a fixed nondeterministic Turing machine M that solves a given NP-hard problem (any NP-hard problem will do). We begin by encoding the initial configuration of the machine (*i.e.*, its tape, the position of its head and its internal state) into the initial epistemic model. Then, we build a series of event model updates, such that the epistemic model after n product updates contains the representation of every configuration of M that can be reached in exactly

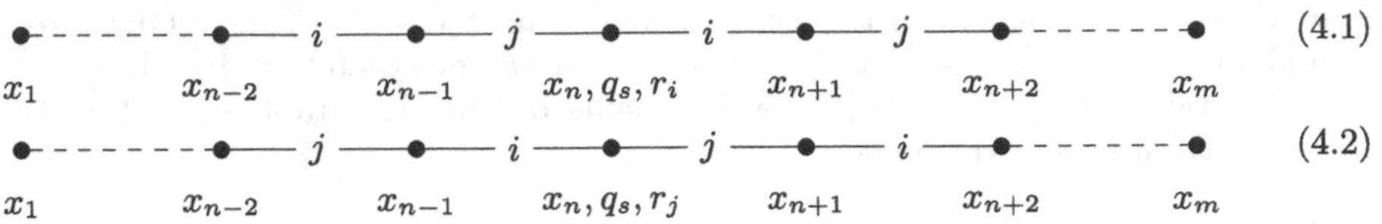

Fig. 4. Two information cells for agent k, both representing the ID $x_1 \cdots x_{n-1} q_s x_n \cdots x_m$ of the Turing machine $M = (\mathcal{S}, \Gamma, q_0, \delta, q_f)$, where $x_i \in \Gamma$ and $q_s \in \mathcal{S}$. This ID represents the configuration of M where the word on the tape is $x_1 \cdots x_m$, where M is in state q_s, and the head is at the nth symbol x_n of the word on the tape. Recall that $R_k = R_i \cup R_j$ and $R_g = W \times W$ is implicitly assumed, where W is the set of all worlds.

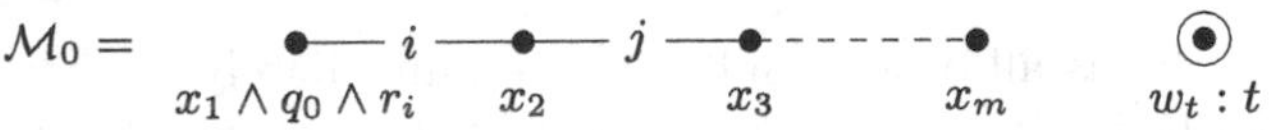

Fig. 5. The initial epistemic model $\mathcal{M}_0$ for the Turing machine M with input word $\omega = x_1 \cdots x_m$. It consists of the represented ID of the initial configuration of M plus an additional designated world w_t only accessible from the other worlds by the R_g relation (recall that $R_k = R_i \cup R_j$ and $R_g = W \times W$ is implicitly assumed).

n transitions (computation steps). Finally, we build a goal formula that checks whether an accepting configuration was encountered in the process or not. Thus, the DBU instance is positive if and only if M accepts the word in the input.

Let $M = (\mathcal{S}, \Gamma, q_0, \delta, q_f)$ be any nondeterministic Turing machine that solves an NP-hard problem in polynomial time, with states $\mathcal{S} = \{q_0, q_1, \ldots, q_f\}$, where q_0 is the only initial state, q_f is the only accepting state, Γ is the set of tape symbols including the blank symbol $\#$ and δ is the transition function [11].

The DBU instance we build has agents $\mathcal{A} = \{i, j, k, g\}$ and propositional variables $P = \Gamma \cup \mathcal{S} \cup \{r_i, r_j, t\}$. Information cells for agent k (*i.e.*, sets $W_k \subseteq W$ of maximum size that are closed under R_k) are used to encode configurations of M, and agents i and j are used to distinguish the right and the left of each cell of the tape that we encode. We will in all epistemic models enforce $R_k = R_i \cup R_j$ by having $R_k = R_i \cup R_j$ in the initial model, and $Q_k = Q_i \cup Q_j$ in all event models. We will similarly enforce R_g to be the universal relation—*i.e.*, make any two worlds indistinguishable—by making all pairs of worlds in the initial model indistinguishable, and by making all pairs of events of all event models indistinguishable. For simplicity, the R_k and R_g indistinguishability relations will not be explicitly drawn. Furthermore, the reflexive and transitive closure of all indistinguishability relations drawn is implicitly assumed.

A configuration of the machine can be represented by an Instantaneous Description (ID) [11]. Following Bolander *et al.* [3], we represent IDs by epistemic models as illustrated in Fig. 4. This pair of information cells for agent k offers two unique representations of an ID [3], and we call *represented ID* an information cell for k that has the form of either (4.1) or (4.2). Each world represents one cell of the tape of the machine, and is marked with a propositional variable

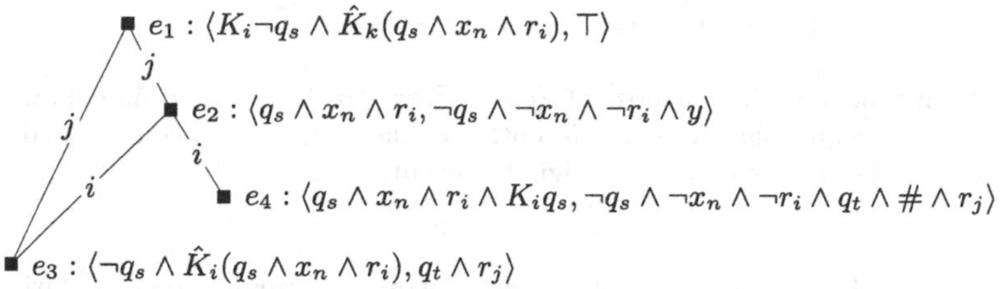

Fig. 6. The transition component τ_l^i, for a transition l of the form $\delta(q_s, x_n) = (q_t, y, R)$, where $x_n \neq y$.

representing the symbol in the cell. One world is marked with two additional propositions: one for the current state of the machine (q_s), as well as either r_i or r_j. This world represents the current position of the head and is called the *current world.* The propositions r_i and r_j are used to distinguish between the right and the left of the current cell. If r_i (resp. r_j) is true, then the cell at the right of the current one is reachable through an i-edge (resp. j-edge).

We proceed to show how to build the initial epistemic model and event models. Suppose that in its initial configuration, M is in state q_0 and with the word $\omega = x_1 \cdots x_m$ on its tape. Then the initial epistemic model $\mathcal{M}_0$ is the represented ID of the initial configuration of M, as shown in Fig. 5. In addition to that, we add a designated world w_t only labeled by the prop. variable t. Its purpose is to make sure the model doesn't end up being empty, which could otherwise happen if at some point no transition can be applied to any ID.

The next step consists in building the series of event models, which are all copies of a single model $\mathcal{E}_{trans}$. The aim of $\mathcal{E}_{trans}$ is to simulate one step of M, by applying all applicable transitions to each represented ID of the previous epistemic model. The event model mainly consists in a disjoint union of several sub-event models, that we call *transition components*, whose purpose is to attempt to apply a transition of the Turing machine M to a represented ID.

For each transition l, *i.e.*, each element of the transition function δ, we construct an i-transition component τ_l^i and a j-transition component τ_l^j. We construct these transition components such that given an ID s and valid transition l for s, applying τ_l^i (resp. τ_l^j) to the represented ID of s, of the form (4.1) (resp. (4.2)), will result in the represented ID of the successor of s after l was applied. Applying to an ID s a transition component whose form does not match the represented ID of s, or whose transition is not applicable to s, will yield no worlds.

Figure 6 shows an example of an i-transition component. The j-transition component can be obtained by swapping i and j everywhere. Other transitions, such as $\delta(q_s, x_n) = (q_t, y, L)$ or transitions satisfying $x_n = y$, can be handled similarly. Let us try to explain the intuition behind this construction. It is very similar to the construction of Bolander *et al.* [3]. Event e_1 makes sure that, after the update, worlds that represent cells of the tape that are unaffected by the transition are left unchanged. It copies into the updated model every world of

■ $e_f : \langle q_f, \top \rangle$ ▣ $e_t : \langle t, \top \rangle$

Fig. 7. Event model σ. The purpose of e_f is to carry to the updated model any world marked with q_f, as it means that an accepting configuration has been reached. Event e_t copies the world w_t, as the only designated event.

the represented ID, except the world representing the current head position and the one at its right. Event e_2 copies the current world, noted w, but removes the propositional variables that mark the head of the machine. It also updates the tape symbol. If the cell on the right of the current position of the head is not blank, then there exists a world w' on the right of the current world w, *i.e.*, such that $R_i(w, w')$. Event e_3 adds on w' the propositional variables that make it the current world of the updated model. It updates as well the current state of the machine, from q_s to q_t. If the cell on the right of the current position of the head is blank, then no world is on the right of the current world. Event e_4 creates it with a blank symbol, and sets it to be the current world of the updated model. Applying the i-transition component of Fig. 6 to a represented ID s of the form (4.2) results in no world. Indeed, in s, the current world is instead labeled by r_j, and thus, no world verifies r_i. Therefore, no event has its precondition satisfied, as each of the four events $e_1, \ldots, e_4$ has a precondition requiring r_i to hold in at least one world. Similarly, if the transition is not applicable to the ID represented by s, then the current world of s is labeled by $q'_s \neq q_s$ and/or $x'_n \neq x_n$, and thus does not satisfy $q_s \wedge x_n$. And as before, each of the four events $e_1, \ldots, e_4$ has a precondition requiring $q_s \wedge x_n$ to hold in at least one world.

In order to build $\mathcal{E}_{trans}$, we need to introduce another component σ, which consists of two events, e_f and e_t. Those events, as depicted in Fig. 7, carry to the updated model the information that will eventually allow the goal formula to check whether the instance is positive or not. Building $\mathcal{E}_{trans}$ is then straightforward. In addition to σ, it consists in the disjoint union of the i- and j-transition components τ_l^i and τ_l^j associated to every transition l of M. Recall again that we implicitly assume to also add a g-edge between any pair of events. Applying $\mathcal{E}_{trans}$ to an epistemic model that contains the representations of all IDs reachable in n transitions results in a model containing the representations of all IDs reachable in $n+1$ transitions. If the model contained any world where q_f was true, then in the updated model, there is also a world where q_f if true.

By assumption, there exists a polynomial $\mathcal{P}$ such that, for any word ω', M accepts ω' iff M accepts it in at most $\mathcal{P}(|\omega'|)$ steps. Then, for our given input ω, we only need to simulate $\mathcal{P}(|\omega|)$ steps of M, and thus create a series of $\mathcal{P}(|\omega|)$ product updates of $\mathcal{M}_0$ with the event model $\mathcal{E}_{trans}$. In the final model, the only designated world is w_t, which is linked by a g-edge to every other remaining world. The goal formula $\hat{K}_g q_f$ must thus be true in the final model iff a world verifying q_f has been reach after some initial sequence of product updates, *i.e.*, if M can reach an accepting state in at most $\mathcal{P}(|\omega|)$ steps. Thus, M accepts input ω iff the instance of DBU with initial state $\mathcal{M}_0$, with $\mathcal{P}(|\omega|)$ copies of the event model $\mathcal{E}_{trans}$ and with goal formula $\hat{K}_g q_f$ is positive. We have now fpt-reduced the problem "Does M accept input ω?", where M is fixed and ω is the input, to the problem {a, c, e, f, o, p}-DBU. We comply with the conditions of Definition 6: we respectively satisfy the second and third conditions as the reduction is polynomial, and all parameters of {a, c, e, f, o, p}-DBU are constants, by construction. In particular, p and e are constants as they only depend on M, which is fixed and not part of the input. Finally, as M solves an NP-hard problem, {a, c, e, f, o, p}-DBU is para-NP-hard.

Corollary 1. *{a, c, p}-DBU, {a, c, p, e}-DBU and {a, c, p, f}-DBU are all fixed-parameter intractable.*

The corollary is by Proposition 1. In addition to settling those four open problems, Theorem 1 shows a stronger result, which is that all parameterized versions of DBU that do not have u as a parameter are fixed-parameter intractable. This settles in itself the fixed-parameter intractability of 64 problems, out of the 128 total. It also constitutes an alternative proof of the intractability of three different problems shown separately by van de Pol *et al.* [12], which are {a, c, e, f, o}-DBU, {c, e, f, o, p}-DBU and {a, e, f, o, p}-DBU.

We now prove fixed-parameter intractability of two further problems that were left open by van de Pol *et al.* [12]: {c, f, o, p, u}-DBU and {a, c, p, u}-DBU. We here show that both are fixed-parameter intractable, which implies the fixed-parameter intractability of {c, f, p, u}-DBU and {a, c, p}-DBU. Our proofs of both theorems are adaptations of the fixed-parameter intractability proof of {c, o, p, u}-DBU by van de Pol *et al.* [12]. In addition to strengthening their construction to be able to generalize their intractability results, we also simplify their construction in a few places. The general point is to show W[1]-hardness by a reduction from the earlier mentioned W[1]-complete problem k-W2SAT: Given a 2CNF input formula φ and a parameter k, decide whether there exists a valuation satisfying φ in which at most k variables are true.

In the following we assume the variables of φ are named $x_1, \ldots, x_m$. The general trick in constructing an fpt-reduction from k-W2SAT to a parameterized DBU problem is as follows. First we define epistemic (sub)models that can be used to encode propositional valuations over $\{x_1, \ldots, x_m\}$. We call these *valuation gadgets* and use $\mathcal{M}_v$ to denote the valuation gadget encoding the valuation v. The initial model of the DBU instance is then the model $\mathcal{M}_0$ where 0 denotes the valuation with $0(x_i) = 0$ for all i (the valuation that sets every variable false). We then construct an event model that can take any set of valuation gadgets and for each gadget $\mathcal{M}_v$ it constructs m new gadgets $\mathcal{M}_{v[x_1 \mapsto 1]}, \ldots, \mathcal{M}_{v[x_m \mapsto 1]}$ (where $v[x \mapsto t]$ is the mapping that is as v except $v(x) = t$). After updating k times with this event model, we are guaranteed to have gadgets representing all valuations where at most k variables are true. If we have no bound on f, we can now directly use the goal formula of the DBU instance to check that there exists a gadget making φ true. This is what we do for the intractability proof of {a, c, p, u}-DBU. If we have a bound on f, as in the intractability proof of {c, f, o, p, u}-DBU, we need to perform product updates with additional event models that mark the gadgets making φ true.

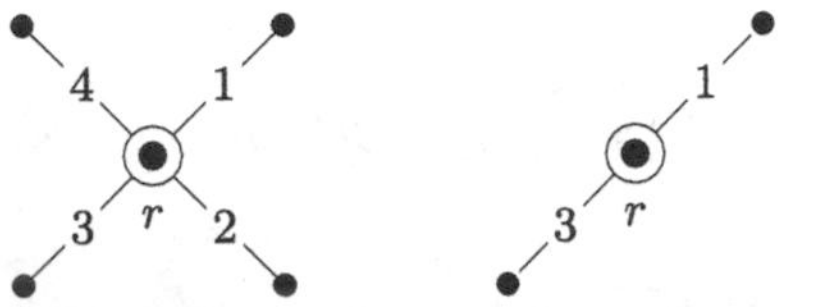

Fig. 8. Left: A valuation gadget for $m = 4$ representing the valuation 0 in which all x_i, $i = 1, \dots, m$, are false. Right: The gadget for the valuation where x_2 and x_4 are true (since the outgoing 2- and 4-edges have been deleted).

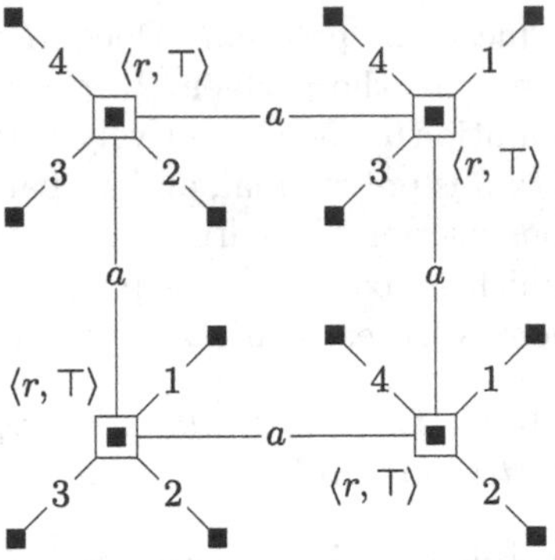

Fig. 9. The pointed event model $\mathcal{E}$ for $m = 4$. The unlabelled events are implicitly labelled $\langle \top, \top \rangle$.

Theorem 2. *{c, f, o, p, u}-DBU is fixed-parameter intractable (W[1]-hard). In other words, the Dynamic Belief Update problem is intractable even when restricting the number of propositional variables (p), the number of event models (u), the maximum length of event preconditions (c), and the length and modal depth of the goal formula (f,o).*

Proof. The main contribution of this proof over the proof of the fixed-parameter intractability of {c, o, p, u}-DBU by van de Pol *et al.* [12] is the construction of an additional event model ($\mathcal{E}_\varphi$) that allow us to only consider a goal formula of fixed length (while still preserving the fixed bound on the event preconditions). Let φ and k be given (an instance of k-W2SAT), where φ has variables $var(\phi) = \{x_1, \dots, x_m\}$. We will now create an instance of DBU that can decide the k-W2SAT instance, *i.e.*, whether there exists a valuation satisfying ϕ and setting at most k variables true. The DBU instance will be using agents $\mathcal{A} = \{1, \dots, m, a, b\}$. For each valuation v over $var(\varphi)$, we define the gadget $\mathcal{M}_v$ as the star-shaped model with a single root world satisfying proposition r, and for each x_i with $v(x_i) = 0$ it has an outgoing i-edge to a unique world satisfying no propositions. The construction is illustrated for $m = 4$ in Fig. 8. Now consider the event model $\mathcal{E}$ illustrated for $m = 4$ in Fig. 9. The events with no label are implicitly labelled $\langle \top, \top \rangle$, *i.e.*, they are events that preserve any world to which they are applied. The events labelled $\langle r, \top \rangle$ only apply to the roots of gadgets. When $\mathcal{E}$ is applied to a gadget $\mathcal{M}_v$, it creates m copies of the gadget, where in the first gadget x_1 is made true (by removing the outgoing 1-edge), in the second x_2 is made true (by removing the outgoing 2-edge), etc. These gadgets are furthermore connected by a-edges via their root worlds. When this event model is applied k times to the initial gadget model $\mathcal{M}_0$, we achieve a model with m^{k} gadgets connected by a-edges via their root worlds. Each gadget is obtained by starting with the initial gadget representing the valuation 0, and then making at most k variables true by consecutively removing k edges from the gadget model. Since we might attempt to remove the same edge multiple times, this construction gives us a representation of all valuations where at most k variables are true (except the valuation 0 that can be checked separately). Hence the final model $\mathcal{M}_0 \otimes \mathcal{E}^{\mathsf{k}}$ contains a gadget for each valuation with at most k variables set true (except the valuation 0).

Note that a clause $(\neg)x_i \vee (\neg)x_j$ is true in a valuation v iff the formula $(\neg)K_i r \vee (\neg)K_j r$ is true at the root of the gadget $\mathcal{M}_v$. We now construct an additional event model $\mathcal{E}_\varphi$ as follows. It has a single designated event labelled $\langle r, \top\rangle$. For each clause $(\neg)x_i \vee (\neg)x_j$ of φ, it has an additional event labelled $\langle r \wedge \neg((\neg)K_i r \vee (\neg)K_j r), f\rangle$, where f is a new propositional variable denoting "failure". All events of $\mathcal{E}_\varphi$ are connected by b-edges. Each event with postcondition f checks whether a particular clause of φ is false in the gadget to which it is applied. If it is, a b-accessible world satisfying f is created. When $\mathcal{E}_\varphi$ is applied to a valuation gadget, it will hence preserve the root (due to the event $\langle r, \top\rangle$), and additionally it will add a b-accessible f-world for each unsatisfied clause. If there are no unsatisfied clauses, it will only preserve the root. Hence, if we apply $\mathcal{E}_\varphi$ to the model $\mathcal{M}_0 \otimes \mathcal{E}^{\mathsf{k}}$ containing gadgets for all the relevant valuations, the resulting model $\mathcal{M}_0 \otimes \mathcal{E}^{\mathsf{k}} \otimes \mathcal{E}_\varphi$ will contain an r-world with no b-accessible f-worlds iff φ is true in one of the valuations. Hence, we can check whether φ is true in one of the relevant valuations by checking the goal formula $\varphi_g := \hat{K}_a(r \wedge K_b \neg f)$ in the model $\mathcal{M}_0 \otimes \mathcal{E}^{\mathsf{k}} \otimes \mathcal{E}_\varphi$.

To sum up, given a k-W2SAT instance φ with parameter k, we reduce it to the DBU instance with initial model $\mathcal{M}_0$, with k copies of the event model $\mathcal{E}$ followed by the event model $\mathcal{E}_\varphi$ and with goal formula φ_g. We now only have to verify that the reduction is an fpt-reduction from k-W2SAT to $\{\mathsf{c}, \mathsf{f}, \mathsf{o}, \mathsf{p}, \mathsf{u}\}$-DBU. Building the epistemic model $\mathcal{M}_0$ and the k copies of the event model $\mathcal{E}$ is clearly polynomial in m and k and hence in the input size of the k-W2SAT instance. Building $\mathcal{E}_\varphi$ is polynomial in the formula φ and hence also in the input size of the k-W2SAT instance. Finally, the goal formula has a fixed length. This shows that the reduction is computable by an fpt-algorithm. We then only need to show that the parameters of the translated $\{\mathsf{c}, \mathsf{f}, \mathsf{o}, \mathsf{p}, \mathsf{u}\}$-DBU instance can be bound by a computable function in k. The parameters $\mathsf{c}, \mathsf{f}, \mathsf{o}, \mathsf{p}$ all have a fixed value independent of the k-W2SAT instance, and u is $\mathsf{k}+1$. So the parameters are clearly bound by a computable function in k, and the proof is complete.

Theorem 3. *$\{a, c, o, p, u\}$-DBU is fixed-parameter intractable (W[1]-hard).*

Proof. The main contribution of this proof over the proof of the fixed-parameter intractability of $\{\mathsf{c}, \mathsf{o}, \mathsf{p}, \mathsf{u}\}$-DBU by van de Pol *et al.* [12] is that we show how to create gadgets that encode the truth value of the different variables via worlds at different depths of the model rather than via different agents. This is necessary since we have a as a parameter, so we need to put a bound on the number

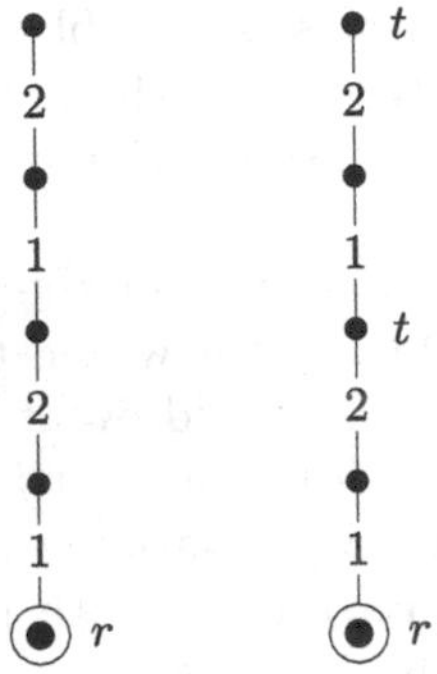

Fig. 10. Left: A valuation gadget for $m = 4$ representing the valuation 0 in which all x_i, $i = 1, \ldots, m$, are false. Right: The gadget for the valuation where x_2 and x_4 are true (since the worlds in distance 2 and 4 from the root have label t).

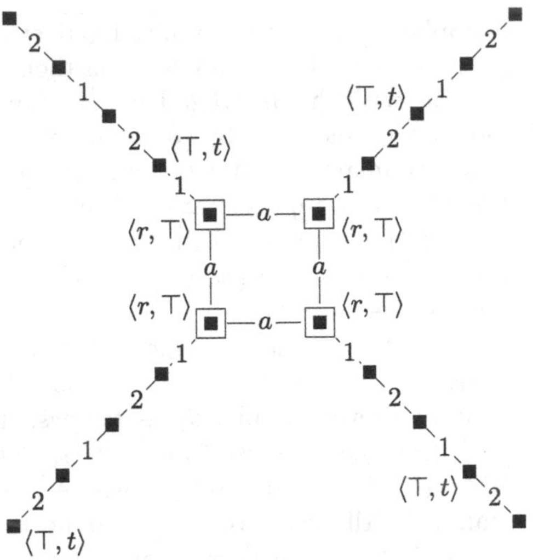

Fig. 11. The pointed event model $\mathcal{E}$ for $m = 4$. The unlabelled events are implicitly labelled $\langle \top, \top \rangle$.

of agents. When referring to worlds at different depths of a model, and with no bound on the depth of a model, we usually also need preconditions of unbounded length. But our construction shows that it is possible to still do with only preconditions of bounded length. In our proof, in order to encode a valuation, we use chains of worlds linked by alternating agents. This trick, central to our proof, resembles a trick used by de Haan and van de Pol [10]. The main difference is that they encode the truth-value of a single variable as a chain, and create as many chains as there are true propositional variables in the encoded valuation, whereas we encode an entire valuation in a single chain.

Essentially, the structure of this proof is as the previous, except we need a different type of gadgets. Let φ and k be given with $var(\varphi) = \{x_1, \ldots, x_m\}$. Let $\mathcal{A} = \{1, 2, a\}$. For each valuation v, we define the gadget $\mathcal{M}_v$ as an alternating $1, 2$-chain of worlds with a root world satisfying r, and where the world at distance i from the root makes t true iff $v(x_i) = 1$. The construction is illustrated for $m = 4$ in Fig. 10. Now consider the event model $\mathcal{E}$ illustrated for $m = 4$ in Fig. 11. As in the previous proof, when this event model is applied to a gadget $\mathcal{M}_v$, it creates m copies of the gadget, where in the first gadget x_1 is made true (by adding t to the world at distance 1 from the root), in the second x_2 is made true (by adding t to the world at distance 2 from the root), etc. As before, these gadgets will be connected by a-edges via their root worlds. Also as before, when this event model is applied k times to the initial gadget model $\mathcal{M}_0$, we achieve a model with m^{k} gadgets containing at least one gadget for each valuation making at most k variables true (again except the valuation 0 that can be treated separately). The only essential difference is that instead of making use of agents to encode the truth value of the different variables, we use the depth of the event model. This means we can use a as a parameter in our reduction (the number of agents is fixed independently of the input).

Let $\psi_1 := \hat{K}_1 t$, $\psi_2 := \hat{K}_1 \hat{K}_2 t$, $\psi_3 := \hat{K}_1 \hat{K}_2 \hat{K}_1 t$, etc. Then note that φ is true in the valuation v iff the formula $\varphi[\psi_i/x_i]$ is true in the root of the gadget $\mathcal{M}_v$. Hence, to check whether φ is true in a valuation making at most k variables true, we can check whether the formula $\varphi_g := \hat{K}_a \varphi[\psi_i/x_i]$ is true in $\mathcal{M}_0 \otimes \mathcal{E}^{\mathsf{k}}$. To sum up, given a k-W2SAT instance φ with parameter k, we reduce it to the DBU instance with initial model $\mathcal{M}_0$, with k copies of the event model $\mathcal{E}$ and with goal formula φ_g. Building $\mathcal{M}_0$ and the k copies of $\mathcal{E}$ is polynomial in m and k, and building φ_g is polynomial in m and the length of φ. Hence the DBU instance can be computed in polynomial time in the size of the k-W2SAT instance, and is hence computable by an fpt-algorithm. We then only need to show that the parameters of the translated $\{\mathsf{a}, \mathsf{c}, \mathsf{o}, \mathsf{p}, \mathsf{u}\}$-DBU instance can be bound by a computable function in k. This trivially holds, as the parameters a, c, o, p all have fixed value independent of the k-W2SAT instance, and u is k.

4 Discussion and Future Work

We managed to solve most of the open tractability problems for the dynamic belief update problem. In all cases, our results were negative, *i.e.*, we proved fixed-parameter intractability. When entering the new results into our previously mentioned tool, we get that tractability of the following parameter combinations is still open: $\{\mathsf{a}, \mathsf{c}, \mathsf{f}, \mathsf{p}, \mathsf{u}\}$ and $\{\mathsf{a}, \mathsf{c}, \mathsf{f}, \mathsf{o}, \mathsf{p}, \mathsf{u}\}$.

The *short Turing machine acceptance problem* (STMA) is the acceptance problem of single-tape nondeterministic Turing machines with bound k on the number of computation steps. It is a parameterized problem with parameter k known to be W[1]-complete, *i.e.*, fixed-parameter intractable [5]. The proof of Theorem 1 gives us a construction allowing us to encode an instance of STMA as a DBU instance. Since the parameter k is the number of computation steps, which translates into the parameter u in the DBU instance, we can do an fpt-reduction from STMA to $\{\mathsf{a}, \mathsf{c}, \mathsf{f}, \mathsf{o}, \mathsf{u}\}$-DBU, *i.e.*, we can replace e, p by u in the fixed-parameter intractability result of Theorem 1. We have to drop the parameters e and p as their sizes depend on the alphabet of the Turing machine. This reduction then immediately gives W[1]-hardness of $\{\mathsf{a}, \mathsf{c}, \mathsf{f}, \mathsf{o}, \mathsf{u}\}$-DBU. This result was already established by van de Pol *et al.* [12], but with our Turing machine construction in Theorem 1, we get this additional result essentially for free.

In the proof of Theorem 2, we introduced the trick of checking each clause of the 2CNF formula with a single event model, hence allowing us to put a bound on the length of the goal formula. One might be tempted to try out the same trick in the proof of Theorem 3, however that would blow up the length and modal depth of the preconditions, since we need a formula of modal depth i to check whether x_i is true in a valuation gadget. If we found a way to preserve the bound on c, we would achieve a proof of the fixed-parameter intractability of $\{\mathsf{a}, \mathsf{c}, \mathsf{f}, \mathsf{o}, \mathsf{p}, \mathsf{u}\}$-DBU.

As future work, we hope to extend our results to epistemic planning, i.e, the problem of plan *synthesis* rather than plan *verification* as considered here, and we would at the same time consider additional relevant parameters.

Acknowledgement. The authors would like to thank the anonymous reviewers for their meticulous reading of our paper, as well as for their numerous and valuable suggestions that helped improve this manuscript.

References

1. Baral, C., Bolander, T., van Ditmarsch, H., McIlrath, S.: Epistemic planning (dagstuhl seminar 17231). In: Dagstuhl Reports, vol. 7. Schloss Dagstuhl-Leibniz-Zentrum fuer Informatik (2017)
2. Bolander, T.: Seeing is believing: formalising false-belief tasks in dynamic epistemic logic. In: van Ditmarsch, H., Sandu, G. (eds.) Jaakko Hintikka on Knowledge and Game-Theoretical Semantics. OCL, vol. 12, pp. 207–236. Springer, Cham (2018). https://doi.org/10.1007/978-3-319-62864-6_8
3. Bolander, T., Andersen, M.: Epistemic planning for single- and multi-agent systems. J. Appl. Non-classical Logics - JANCL **21**, 9–34 (2011). https://doi.org/10.3166/jancl.21.9-34
4. Bolander, T., Charrier, T., Pinchinat, S., Schwarzentruber, F.: DEL-based epistemic planning: decidability and complexity. Artificial Intelligence (2020, to appear). https://doi.org/10.1016/j.artint.2020.103304. http://www.sciencedirect.com/science/article/pii/S0004370219301146
5. Cesati, M.: The turing way to parameterized complexity. J. Comput. Syst. Sci. **67**, 654–685 (2003). https://doi.org/10.1016/S0022-0000(03)00073-4
6. Cook, S.A.: The complexity of theorem-proving procedures. In: Proceedings of the Third Annual ACM Symposium on Theory of Computing, STOC 1971, pp. 151–158. Association for Computing Machinery, New York (1971). https://doi.org/10.1145/800157.805047
7. van Ditmarsch, H., van der Hoek, W., Kooi, B.: Dynamic Epistemic Logic, 1st edn. Springer, Heidelberg (2007). https://doi.org/10.1007/978-1-4020-5839-4
8. Downey, R.G., Fellows, M.R.: Fundamentals of Parameterized Complexity. Springer, Heidelberg (2013). https://doi.org/10.1007/978-1-4471-5559-1
9. Flum, J., Grohe, M.: Parameterized Complexity Theory. Texts in Theoretical Computer Science. An EATCS Series. Springer, Heidelberg (2006). https://doi.org/10.1007/3-540-29953-X
10. de Haan, R., van de Pol, I.: On the computational complexity of model checking for dynamic epistemic logic with s5 models. arXiv abs/1805.09880 (2018)
11. Hopcroft, J.E., Motwani, R., Ullman, J.D.: Introduction to Automata Theory, Languages, and Computation, 3rd edn. Addison-Wesley Longman Publishing Co. Inc., Boston (2006)
12. van de Pol, I., van Rooij, I., Szymanik, J.: Parameterized complexity of theory of mind reasoning in dynamic epistemic logic. J. Logic Lang. Inform. **27**(3), 255–294 (2018). https://doi.org/10.1007/s10849-018-9268-4

Default Modal Systems as Algebraic Updates

Valentin Cassano[1,2,3(✉)], Raul Fervari[1,2], Carlos Areces[1,2], and Pablo F. Castro[1,3]

[1] Consejo Nacional de Investigaciones Científicas y Técnicas, Buenos Aires, Argentina
[2] Universidad Nacional de Córdoba, Córdoba, Argentina
vcassano@famaf.unc.edu.ar
[3] Universidad Nacional de Río Cuarto, Río Cuarto, Argentina

Abstract. Default Logic refers to a family of formalisms designed to carry out non-monotonic reasoning over a monotonic logic (in general, Classical First-Order or Propositional Logic). Traditionally, default logics have been defined and dealt with via syntactic consequence relations. Here, we introduce a family of default logics defined over modal logics. First, we present these default logics syntactically. Then, we elaborate on an algebraic counterpart. We do the latter by extending the notion of a modal algebra to acommodate for the main elements of default logics: defaults and extensions. Our algebraic treatment of default logics concludes with an algebraic completeness result. To our knowledge, our approach is novel, and it lays the groundwork for studying default logics from a dynamic logic perspective.

1 Introduction

Default Logic refers to a family of non-monotonic formalisms tailored to reasoning with incomplete knowledge, and to dealing with contradictory information. The main features of a default logic DL are defaults and extensions. Defaults are used as a tool to handle reasoning from incomplete knowledge. In turn, extensions are a mechanism for reasoning in the presence of contradictory information (via consistent alternatives). Intuitively, defaults can be seen as defeasible rules of inference, i.e., rules of inference whose conclusions are subject to annulment; whereas extensions can be understood as sets of formulas closed under the application of defaults.

The history of Default Logic traces back to Reiter's seminal work [21]. Since then, many variants of Reiter's original ideas have been proposed – with each variant giving rise to a different default logic (see [2] for a comprehensive summary). For the most part, these variants have focused their attention on what is meant by an extension. In particular, the emphasis has been on how different interactions between defaults, and the rules of inference of the underlying proof calculus,[1] concoct different notions of an extension satisfying one or more

[1] Typically the underlying proof calculi is one for Classical First-Order Logic (FOL) (see, e.g., [21]) or for Classical Propositional Logic (CPL) (see, e.g., [6,17,19,22]).

M. A. Martins and I. Sedlár (Eds.): DaLí 2020, LNCS 12569, pp. 103–119, 2020.
https://doi.org/10.1007/978-3-030-65840-3_7

properties of interest. This treatment of extensions carries with it the definition and analysis of a default logic from a syntactic perspective. The other side of the coin is missing. In studying a logic (of any kind), we also wish to address it from a semantic perspective via a model theory and/or a class of algebras. This yields interesting completeness results, interpolation properties, bisimulations, etc. This semantic perspective on default logics is mostly absent, making it difficult to investigate their logical properties using standard semantic tools.

Our Work. Following the tradition in Default Logic, we start with a formulation of default logics over modal logics via deducibility (i.e., syntactical consequence in the proof calculus). We rely on the notion of global deducibility for modal logics [10]. Our formulation of a default logic is parametric, and can be instantiated with any modal system from K to $\mathsf{S5}$ extended with the universal modality [4].

For each default modal logic, we make explicit how defaults interact with the rules of inference of the underlying proof calculus by integrating the use of the former into the notion of deducibility of the latter. In addition, we show how we can parametrically define for each default modal system an algebraic counterpart. We do this by extending modal algebras to accommodate for defaults and extensions. Modal algebras are Boolean algebras with additional operators for modalities, and they make up the algebraic counterpart of modal systems [12,28].

The algebraic treatment of defaults and extensions is done as follows. We carry out a Lindenbaum-Tarski construction that acts as an algebraic canonical model for a set of permisses. We enrich this construction with an operator to deal with defaults. This operator can be thought of as "updating" the Lindenbaum-Tarski algebra w.r.t. the application of a default. The result of the update is the algebraic counterpart of an extension. On this basis we prove an algebraic completeness result.

Related Work. Our treatment of defaults and extensions enables us to think of default logics as algebraic "model changing" logics; in the sense of, e.g., public announcement logic [20].

In our case, a model update corresponds to the application of a default (a sort of inference step). The idea of updating a model dynamically to represent syntactic steps of inference can be found in several places in the literature on dynamic logics. For instance, the problem of logical omniscience in epistemic logic (see, e.g., [26]) has been thought of as a property to be achieved after the application of a dynamic operation. In [1,7,16,23], omniscience is achieved by updating models containing sets of formulas. In [15,25] the updates are performed over awareness relational models. Dynamics of evidence are presented in [24,27] over neighbourhood models. Finally, dynamic modalities allowing to achieve introspective states over Kripke models are introduced in [8,9].

Closer to our work is the algebraic treatment of public announcements introduced in [18]. Therein, the algebraic submodel relation induced by the announcement of a formula ψ is represented by taking the quotient algebra modulo an equivalence relation given by ψ. We show that the application of a default δ can be captured in a similar way, i.e., by taking the quotient algebra modulo the equivalence relation given by the conclusion of δ.

Motivation. Our choice of defining default logics over modal logics is not arbitrary. Modal logics provide a wide spectrum of logics which are more expressive than CPL, with better computational properties than FOL. Moreover, these logics have a well-developed algebraic theory in terms of modal algebras. In our constructions we exploit the combination of these two features. As we will see, defaults are better modeled by means of a global consequence relation, which will be captured by the use of the universal modality. While not pursued on here, building default logics on modal logics is also interesting if one has applications of the developed formalism in mind. This is particularly true in the setting of description logics – wherein it is possible to think of defaults as a way of capturing exceptions to a taxonomy of concepts modeled in a knowledge base (see [3]).

Main Contributions. We provide a syntactic and algebraic treatment of default logics built over modal logics and study their properties. Syntactically, our construction of a default modal system is parametric on a modal system and a set of defaults. We make precise how defaults interact with the rules of inference of the underlying modal system. Algebraically, we address defaults and extensions via modal algebras. This enables us to obtain an algebraic completeness result. Moreover, it enables us the use of standard algebraic tools to study metalogical properties of default modal systems. We view this work as a first step towards an algebraization of default logic, and towards a better understanding of default systems from a logical perspective. Finally, the algebraic construction for default logics over modal logics lays the groundwork to study default systems from a dynamic logic perspective.

Structure of the Article. Section 2 covers background material. Section 3 contains our main results. Section 3.1 introduces default modal systems. Section 3.2 presents default deducibility. Section 4 provides our algebraic characterization of defaults and extensions, and a completeness theorem. In Sect. 4 we discuss default modal systems from a dynamic logic perspective. In Sect. 5 we offer some final remarks.

2 Background

2.1 Boolean Algebra in a Nutshell

We introduce some definitions and notation for Boolean algebras (see, e.g., [13] for details).

Definition 1. *A* Boolean Algebra *(BA) is a structure* $\mathbf{A} = \langle A, *, -, 1\rangle$ *satisfying a well-known set of equations.* A *is also denoted as* $|\mathbf{A}|$. *Occasionally, we consider operations* $+$ *and* 0 *defined as* $a + b = -(-a * -b)$, *and* $0 = -1$.

Definition 2. *Every BA* $\mathbf{A}$ *brings in a partial order* $\preceq_{\mathbf{A}}$ *defined as* $x \preceq_{\mathbf{A}} y$ *iff* $x = x * y$ *(sometimes we omit the subindex* $\mathbf{A}$ *and write just* $\preceq$*). We write* $\uparrow X = \{y \mid \text{there is } x \in X \text{ s.t. } x \preceq y\}$. *A filter is a non-empty subset* $F \subseteq |\mathbf{A}|$ *s.t.:* $F = \uparrow F$ *and for all* $x, y \in F$, $(x * y) \in F$. *A filter is principal if it is of the form* $\uparrow\{a\}$ *for* $a \in |\mathbf{A}|$. *A filter* F *is* proper *if* $0 \notin F$.

2.2 Modal Systems

We begin by making precise the set Form of well formed formulas we work with.

Definition 3. *Let* $\mathsf{Prop} = \{p_i \mid i \in \mathbb{N}\}$ *be a denumerable set of* proposition symbols*; the set* Form *of well formed formulas (wffs, or simply formulas) is determined by the grammar*

$$\varphi, \psi ::= p_i \mid \top \mid \neg\varphi \mid \varphi \wedge \psi \mid \Box\varphi \mid [\mathsf{u}]\varphi.$$

We use $\bot$, $\varphi \vee \psi$, $\varphi \to \psi$, $\varphi \leftrightarrow \psi$, $\Diamond\varphi$ *and* $\langle\mathsf{u}\rangle\varphi$ *as abbreviations defined in the usual way.*

The set Form can be seen as an enrichment of the basic modal language with the universal modality $[\mathsf{u}]$. We use the universal modality as a technical tool to internalize a global consequence relation.

A modal system is determined by a subset of Form, called axioms, and the rules of inference in Definition 4.

Definition 4. *The set of* rules of inference *of a modal system consists of*

$$\frac{\varphi \quad \varphi \to \psi}{\psi}\ (\mathsf{mp}) \qquad\qquad \frac{\varphi}{[\mathsf{u}]\varphi}\ (\mathsf{u}).$$

The modal system $\mathsf{K}^{[\mathsf{u}]}$ is determined by the axioms in Definition 5.

Definition 5. *The* axioms *of* $\mathsf{K}^{[\mathsf{u}]}$ *is the smallest set of formulas which contains all instances of* propositional tautologies *and the* schemas*:*

1. $\Box(\varphi \to \psi) \to (\Box\varphi \to \Box\psi)$;
2. $[\mathsf{u}](\varphi \to \psi) \to ([\mathsf{u}]\varphi \to [\mathsf{u}]\psi)$;
3. $[\mathsf{u}]\varphi \to \varphi$;
4. $\varphi \to [\mathsf{u}]\langle\mathsf{u}\rangle\varphi$;
5. $[\mathsf{u}]\varphi \to [\mathsf{u}][\mathsf{u}]\varphi$;
6. $[\mathsf{u}]\varphi \to \Box\varphi$.

We take $\mathsf{K}^{[\mathsf{u}]}$ as our basic modal system. The rest of the modal systems we consider are constructed by enlarging the set of axioms of $\mathsf{K}^{[\mathsf{u}]}$ with (all instances of) any of the schemas below, or any combination thereof, as additional axioms.

$$(4)\ \Box\varphi \to \Box\Box\varphi \quad (5)\ \Diamond\varphi \to \Box\Diamond\varphi \quad (\mathrm{B})\ \varphi \to \Box\Diamond\varphi \quad (\mathrm{D})\ \Box\varphi \to \Diamond\varphi \quad (\mathrm{T})\ \Box\varphi \to \varphi$$

E.g., the system $\mathsf{D}^{[\mathsf{u}]}$ is obtained by adding to the axioms of $\mathsf{K}^{[\mathsf{u}]}$ all instances of the schema D as further axioms. Similarly, the systems $\mathsf{S4}^{[\mathsf{u}]}$ and $\mathsf{S5}^{[\mathsf{u}]}$ are obtained by adding the schemas T and 4, and T and 5, respectively.

For each modal system M, we define a consequence relation $\vdash_{\mathsf{M}}$ between sets of formulas and formulas. This relation is made precise in Definition 6.

Definition 6. *Let* M *be a modal system; an* M-deduction of φ from Φ *is a finite sequence* $\psi_1 \ldots \psi_n$ *of formulas such that* $\psi_n = \varphi$*, and for each* $k < n$ *at least one of the following conditions hold:*

1. ψ_k *is an axiom of* M*;*
2. ψ_k *is a premiss, i.e.,* $\psi_k \in \Phi$*;*
3. ψ_k *is obtained from two earlier formulas using* mp*, i.e., there are* $i, j < k$ *s.t.* $\psi_j = \psi_i \to \psi_k$*;*
4. ψ_k *is obtained from an earlier formula using* u*, i.e., there is* $j < k$ *s.t.* $\psi_k = \boxed{u}\psi_j$*.*

We write $\Phi \vdash_{\mathsf{M}} \varphi$ *iff there is an* M*-deduction of* φ *from* Φ*. The relation* $\vdash_{\mathsf{M}}$ *is commonly referred to as* global consequence.

If there is no need to distinguish between modal systems, we simply speak of a relation $\vdash$ and of a deduction.

We end this section by taking note of the following properties of $\vdash_{\mathsf{M}}$. Notice that the first item refers to the *necessitation* property in modal logics, whereas the second item refers to a version of the *deduction theorem.*

Proposition 1. *The following properties hold:*

1. *If* $\vdash_{\mathsf{M}} \varphi$*, then,* $\vdash_{\mathsf{M}} \Box\varphi$*.*
2. *If* $\Phi \cup \{\varphi\} \vdash_{\mathsf{M}} \psi$*, then,* $\Phi \vdash_{\mathsf{M}} \boxed{u}\varphi \to \psi$*.*

2.3 Algebraizing Modal Systems

We present the semantics of a modal system from an algebraic perspective. Following [28], and borrowing ideas and results from [12,14], we associate with any modal system M a suitable class of algebras in a way such that the properties of M are in correspondence to the properties of this class.

For the case of the modal systems we consider we will use $\boxed{u}$-modal algebras. We use this algebraic treatment of modal systems to perform default reasoning from a semantic point of view. This algebraic treatment is also instrumental to viewing default reasoning as a logic of *updates* over algebras. But this is us getting ahead of ourselves. For now, we focus on introducing some basic concepts and results regarding $\boxed{u}$-modal algebras.

Definition 7. *The* formula algebra *corresponding to the set* Form *of formulas is the structure* $\mathbf{F} = \langle \mathsf{Form}, \wedge, \neg, \top, \Box, \boxed{u} \rangle$ *where:* $\neg$, $\Box$, $\boxed{u}$ *are unary functions on* Form*, and* $\wedge$ *is a binary function on* Form*, such that* $\neg$ *applied to* $\varphi \in \mathsf{Form}$ *returns* $\neg\varphi \in \mathsf{Form}$*,* $\Box$ *applied to* $\varphi \in \mathsf{Form}$ *returns* $\Box\varphi \in \mathsf{Form}$*,* $\boxed{u}$ *applied to* $\varphi \in \mathsf{Form}$ *returns* $\boxed{u}\varphi \in \mathsf{Form}$*, and* $\wedge$ *applied to* $\varphi, \psi \in \mathsf{Form}$ *returns* $\varphi \wedge \psi \in \mathsf{Form}$.

Just as Boolean algebras (as interpretation structures) and filters (as the semantic counterpart of deducibility) are fundamental for the algebraization of Classical Propositional Logic, $\boxed{u}$-modal algebras and *open filters* are fundamental for the algebraization of modal systems.

Definition 8. *A* $\boxed{\sqcup}$-modal algebra *is a structure* $\mathbf{M} = \langle B, *, -, 1, f^{\Box}, f^{\boxed{\sqcup}} \rangle$ *where:* $\langle B, *, -, 1 \rangle$ *is a Boolean algebra; and* $f^{\Box}$ *and* $f^{\boxed{\sqcup}}$ *are unary functions on* B *satisfying the following equations*

$$
\begin{array}{rcl}
f^{\Box}(1) = 1 & \qquad & f^{\boxed{\sqcup}}(b_1) \preccurlyeq b_1 \\
f^{\Box}(b_1 * b_2) = f^{\Box}(b_1) * f^{\Box}(b_2) & & f^{\boxed{\sqcup}}(b_1) \preccurlyeq f^{\boxed{\sqcup}}(-f^{\boxed{\sqcup}}(-b_1)) \\
f^{\boxed{\sqcup}}(1) = 1 & & f^{\boxed{\sqcup}}(b_1) \preccurlyeq f^{\boxed{\sqcup}} f^{\boxed{\sqcup}}(b_1) \\
f^{\boxed{\sqcup}}(b_1 * b_2) = f^{\boxed{\sqcup}}(b_1) * f^{\boxed{\sqcup}}(b_2) & & f^{\boxed{\sqcup}}(b_1) \preccurlyeq f^{\Box}(b_1).
\end{array}
$$

An open filter is a subset $F \subseteq B$ *such that* F *is a filter in* $\langle B, *, -, 1 \rangle$*, and for all* $b \in F$, $f^{\boxed{\sqcup}}(b) \in F$.

Definition 9. *An* interpretation *of the formula algebra* $\mathbf{F}$ *on a* $\boxed{\sqcup}$*-modal algebra* $\mathbf{M} = \langle B, *, -, 0, f^{\Box}, f^{\boxed{\sqcup}} \rangle$*, a.k.a. an interpretation on* $\mathbf{M}$*, is a homomorphism* $v : \mathbf{F} \to \mathbf{M}$ *such that:*

$$
\begin{array}{lll}
v(\top) = 1 \qquad & v(\neg\varphi) = -v(\varphi) \qquad & v(\Box\varphi) = f^{\Box}(v(\varphi)) \\
 & v(\varphi \wedge \psi) = v(\varphi) * v(\psi) & v(\boxed{\sqcup}\varphi) = f^{\boxed{\sqcup}}(v(\varphi)).
\end{array}
$$

Proposition 2. *Every interpretation* v *on* $\mathbf{M}$ *is uniquely determined by an assignment* $v_0 : \mathsf{Prop} \to |\mathbf{M}|$.

Definition 10. *Let* $\mathbf{M}$ *be a* $\boxed{\sqcup}$*-modal algebra; we define:*

1. *an* equation *is a member of* Form^2*; we write an equation* (φ, ψ) *as* $\varphi \approx \psi$*;*
2. *an equation* $\varphi \approx \psi$ *is* valid under an interpretation v on $\mathbf{M}$ *iff* $v(\varphi) = v(\psi)$*; we write* $\mathbf{M}, v \vDash \varphi \approx \psi$ *if* $\varphi \approx \psi$ *is valid under* v*;*
3. *an equation* $\varphi \approx \psi$ *is* valid in $\mathbf{M}$ *iff* $\mathbf{M}, v \vDash \varphi \approx \psi$ *for all interpretations* v *on* $\mathbf{M}$*; we write* $\mathbf{M} \vDash \varphi \approx \psi$ *if* $\varphi \approx \psi$ *is valid in* v.

We are now in a position to connect $\boxed{\sqcup}$-modal algebras and modal systems.

Proposition 3. *Let* M *be a modal system; the relation* $\cong^{\Phi}_{\mathsf{M}}$ *defined as:* $\varphi \cong^{\Phi}_{\mathsf{M}} \psi$ *iff* $\Phi \vdash_{\mathsf{M}} \varphi \leftrightarrow \psi$ *yields a congruence on* $\mathbf{F}$.

Definition 11. *Let* M *be a modal system; the* M-Lindenbaum-Tarski algebra *of a set* Φ *of wffs is the structure* $\mathbf{L}^{\Phi}_{\mathsf{M}} = \langle \mathsf{Form}/_{\cong^{\Phi}_{\mathsf{M}}}, *_{\cong^{\Phi}_{\mathsf{M}}}, -_{\cong^{\Phi}_{\mathsf{M}}}, 1_{\cong^{\Phi}_{\mathsf{M}}}, f^{\Box}_{\cong^{\Phi}_{\mathsf{M}}}, f^{\boxed{\sqcup}}_{\cong^{\Phi}_{\mathsf{M}}} \rangle$ *where:* $\mathsf{Form}/_{\cong^{\Phi}_{\mathsf{M}}} = \{ [\varphi]_{\cong^{\Phi}_{\mathsf{M}}} \mid \varphi \in \mathsf{Form} \}$*; and*

$$
\begin{array}{lll}
1_{\cong^{\Phi}_{\mathsf{M}}} = [\top]_{\cong^{\Phi}_{\mathsf{M}}} \qquad & -_{\cong^{\Phi}_{\mathsf{M}}}([\varphi]_{\cong^{\Phi}_{\mathsf{M}}}) = [\neg\varphi]_{\cong^{\Phi}_{\mathsf{M}}} \qquad & f^{\Box}_{\cong^{\Phi}_{\mathsf{M}}}([\varphi]_{\cong^{\Phi}_{\mathsf{M}}}) = [\Box\varphi]_{\cong^{\Phi}_{\mathsf{M}}} \\
 & [\varphi]_{\cong^{\Phi}_{\mathsf{M}}} *_{\cong^{\Phi}_{\mathsf{M}}} [\psi]_{\cong^{\Phi}_{\mathsf{M}}} = [\varphi \wedge \psi]_{\cong^{\Phi}_{\mathsf{M}}} & f^{\boxed{\sqcup}}_{\cong^{\Phi}_{\mathsf{M}}}([\varphi]_{\cong^{\Phi}_{\mathsf{M}}}) = [\boxed{\sqcup}\varphi]_{\cong^{\Phi}_{\mathsf{M}}}.
\end{array}
$$

The canonical interpretation v *on* $\mathbf{L}^{\Phi}_{\mathsf{M}}$ *is defined as* $v(\varphi) = [\varphi]_{\cong^{\Phi}_{\mathsf{M}}}$.

Proposition 4. *Every* M*-Lindenbaum-Tarski algebra is a* $\boxed{\sqcup}$*-modal algebra.*

Theorem 1. *For every modal system* M, $\Phi \vdash_{\mathsf{M}} \varphi$ *iff* $\mathbf{L}^{\Phi}_{\mathsf{M}} \vDash \varphi \approx \top$.

The algebraic completeness of a modal system M w.r.t. a corresponding subclass of $\boxed{\mathrm{u}}$-modal algebras is obtained as a corollary of Theorem 1. In other words, an M-Lindenbaum-Tarski $\boxed{\mathrm{u}}$-modal algebra acts as an 'algebraic canonical model' for a set of formulas in the modal system M, i.e., they provide a witness for $\Phi \nvdash_{\mathsf{M}} \varphi$. We make full use of M-Lindenbaum-Tarski $\boxed{\mathrm{u}}$-modal algebras in Sect. 3.3.

3 Default Modal Logic

In this section we integrate the elements of Default Logic, defaults and extensions, into modal systems. This integration yields what we call a default modal system. For each default modal system, we introduce an associated notion of default consequence and show how defaults interact with the rules of the Hilbert-style notion of deduction for the underlying modal system. Moreover, we present how a default modal system can be viewed from an algebraic perspective, and prove a completeness result using algebraic tools. Later on, we discuss how the algebraic treatment of default modal systems can be seen as an update operation on algebraic structures. This opens up the door to thinking about default systems from a dynamic logic perspective (akin to public announcements).

3.1 Default Modal Systems

The main elements of Default Logic, i.e., defaults and extensions, are given in Definitions 12 and 13, respectively. These definitions are adapted from [21]. For the rest of this section we assume that M is an arbitrary but fixed modal system.

Definition 12. *A default is a triple* (π, ρ, χ) *of formulas written as* $\pi : \rho \,/\, \chi$. *The formulas* π, ρ, *and* χ, *are called prerequisite, justification, and consequent.*

Definition 13. *Let* Φ *be a set of formulas and* Δ *a set of defaults. Let* $\mathsf{E}^{\Phi}_{\Delta\mathsf{M}}$ *be a function s.t. for all sets of formulas* Ψ, $\mathsf{E}^{\Phi}_{\Delta\mathsf{M}}(\Psi)$ *is the* $\subseteq$*-smallest set of formulas which satisfies:*

(a) $\Phi \subseteq \mathsf{E}^{\Phi}_{\Delta\mathsf{M}}(\Psi)$;
(b) $\mathsf{E}^{\Phi}_{\Delta\mathsf{M}}(\Psi) = \{\psi \mid \mathsf{E}^{\Phi}_{\Delta\mathsf{M}}(\Psi) \vdash_{\mathsf{M}} \psi\}$;
(c) for all $\pi : \rho \,/\, \chi \in \Delta$, *if* $\pi \in \mathsf{E}^{\Phi}_{\Delta\mathsf{M}}(\Psi)$ *and* $\neg\rho \notin \Psi$, *then,* $\chi \in \mathsf{E}^{\Phi}_{\Delta\mathsf{M}}(\Psi)$.

A set $\mathrm{E} \subseteq \mathsf{Form}$ *is an* M-extension *of* Φ *under* Δ *iff it is a fixed point of* $\mathsf{E}^{\Phi}_{\Delta}$, *i.e., iff* $\mathrm{E} = \mathsf{E}^{\Phi}_{\Delta}(\mathrm{E})$. *We write* $\mathscr{E}^{\Phi}_{\Delta\mathsf{M}}$ *for the set of all* M*-extensions of* Φ *under* Δ.

Intuitively, an M-extension can be thought of as a set of formulas which contains Φ, is closed under $\vdash_{\mathsf{M}}$, and is saturated under the application of the defaults in Δ. When it can be clearly understood from the context, we will drop the prefix M and refer to an M-extension as an extension.

In the literature on Default Logic, defaults are intuitively understood as defeasible rules of inference, i.e., rules of inference whose conclusions are subject to annulment, or rules which allow us to "jump" to conclusions. In turn, extensions are intuitively understood as sets of formulas closed under the application of defaults. The next two examples illustrate two properties of extensions: multiplicity and absence of extensions.

Example 1. Let $\Phi = \{\Diamond p\}$ and $\Delta = \{\Diamond p : \Diamond\neg p \mathbin{/} \Diamond\neg p, \Diamond p : \Box p \mathbin{/} \Box p\}$; the set $\mathscr{E}^{\Phi}_{\Delta\mathsf{M}}$ of extensions of Φ under Δ consists of exactly two extensions: (1) the set $\mathrm{E}_1 = \{\varphi \mid \{\Diamond p, \Diamond\neg p\} \vdash_{\mathsf{M}} \varphi\}$; and (2) the set $\mathrm{E}_2 = \{\varphi \mid \{\Diamond p, \Box p\} \vdash_{\mathsf{M}} \varphi\}$.

Each of the extensions in Example 1 corresponds to the application of each default in Δ. Once one default has been applied, the application of the other one is blocked. This example illustrates how to handle contradictory information.

Example 2. Let $\Phi = \{\Diamond p\}$ and $\Delta = \{\Diamond p : \Diamond q \mathbin{/} \Box\neg q\}$; the set $\mathscr{E}^{\Phi}_{\Delta\mathsf{M}}$ of extensions of Φ under Δ is empty, i.e., $\mathscr{E}^{\Phi}_{\Delta\mathsf{M}} = \emptyset$, i.e., there are no extensions of Φ under Δ.

Example 2 highlights a subtletly in thinking of extensions as being constructed by the successive application of defaults: applying a default may result in its own annulment. To make this point clear, w.l.o.g., notice that plausible candidates for extensions are: the set $\mathrm{E}_1 = \{\varphi \mid \{\Diamond p\} \vdash_{\mathsf{M}} \varphi\}$ (i.e., not applying the default); or the set $\mathrm{E}_2 = \{\varphi \mid \{\Diamond p, \Box\neg q\} \vdash_{\mathsf{M}} \varphi\}$ (i.e., result of applying the default to E_1).Neither of these sets is a fixed point of $\mathsf{E}^{\Phi}_{\Delta}$, i.e., $\mathsf{E}^{\Phi}_{\Delta}(\mathrm{E}_1) = \mathrm{E}_2$ and $\mathsf{E}^{\Phi}_{\Delta}(\mathrm{E}_2) = \mathrm{E}_1$. This results in $\mathscr{E}^{\Phi}_{\Delta\mathsf{M}} = \emptyset$.

We are now in a position to define what we mean by a default modal system. This definition arises as a natural construction over a modal system M.

Definition 14. *A default modal system is a tuple* $\Delta\mathsf{M} = \langle\Delta, \mathsf{M}\rangle$ *where* Δ *is a set of defaults and* M *is a modal system.*

In analogy with the case in modal systems, we associate with each default modal system $\Delta\mathsf{M}$ a relation $\Vdash\!\sim_{\Delta\mathsf{M}}$ between sets of formulas and formulas. This relation is based on the relation $\vdash_{\mathsf{M}}$ and it can be understood as its default version. This is made clear in Definition 15.

Definition 15. *Let* $\Delta\mathsf{M}$ *be a default modal system; define*

$$\Phi \Vdash\!\sim_{\Delta\mathsf{M}} \varphi \quad \textit{iff} \quad \varphi \in \mathrm{E} \textit{ for some } \mathrm{E} \in \mathscr{E}^{\Phi}_{\Delta\mathsf{M}}.$$

We use $\Vdash\!\sim_{\Delta\mathsf{M}} \varphi$ as a shorthand for $\emptyset \Vdash\!\sim_{\Delta\mathsf{M}} \varphi$. The relation $\Vdash\!\sim_{\Delta\mathsf{M}}$ is called *credulous* in the literature on Default Logic, because the existence of just one extension is enough to grant the inference (see [2]). The principle of *monotonicity* fails for $\Vdash\!\sim_{\Delta\mathsf{M}}$. In other words: it is not necessarily the case that if $\Phi \Vdash\!\sim_{\Delta\mathsf{M}} \varphi$, then $\Phi \cup \Psi \Vdash\!\sim_{\Delta\mathsf{M}} \varphi$ (for an arbitrary Ψ).

Building the relation $\Vdash\!\sim_{\Delta\mathsf{M}}$ on the underlying relation $\vdash_{\mathsf{M}}$ raises the question of which properties of $\vdash_{\mathsf{M}}$ are preserved at the level of $\Vdash\!\sim_{\Delta\mathsf{M}}$. Definition 16 sets a basis on which to start answering this question.

Definition 16. *The relation* $\Vdash\!\sim_{\Delta\mathsf{M}}$ *interprets* $\vdash_{\mathsf{M}}$ *iff if* $\Phi \vdash_{\mathsf{M}} \varphi$ *then* $\Phi \Vdash\!\sim_{\Delta\mathsf{M}} \varphi$.

Interpretability seems to be a natural requirement on $\Vdash\!\sim_{\Delta\mathsf{M}}$. However, as established in Example 2 (which shows that sometimes extensions do not exist) this property fails to hold in general. To overcome this problem we can go down two possible paths: (i) modify Definition 13 to guarantee the existence of extensions; or (ii) single out defaults for which extensions are guaranteed to exist. Among the most popular modifications of Definition 13 which guarantee the existence of extensions we have: *justified* extensions (see [17]); and *constrained* extensions (see [6]). For option (ii), we have the set of *well-behaved*[2] defaults as a very large and natural set which guarantees the existence of extensions (see [21]). Going down path (i) overburdens the definition of an extension with additional machinery which departs from the purposes of our work here. For this reason, we choose to go down path (ii); i.e., we restrict ourselves to well-behaved defaults. Interestingly, the notions of extensions, justified extensions, and constrained extensions, coincide for well-behaved defaults (see [5,11]).

Definition 17. *A default $\pi : \rho \,/\, \chi$ is well-behaved, written π/χ, iff $\rho = \chi$. A set of defaults Δ is well-behaved iff all defaults in Δ are well-behaved. A default modal system $\Delta\mathsf{M}$ is well-behaved iff Δ is well-behaved.*

Proposition 5. *Let $\Delta\mathsf{M}$ be a default modal system; if $\Delta\mathsf{M}$ is well-behaved, then, $\Vdash\!\sim_{\Delta\mathsf{M}}$ interprets $\vdash_{\mathsf{M}}$.*

We conclude this section by drawing attention to an interesting point regarding necessitation in default modal systems in Proposition 6 (cf. item 1 in Proposition 1).

Proposition 6. *If $\Vdash\!\sim_{\Delta\mathsf{M}} \varphi$, then $\Vdash\!\sim_{\Delta\mathsf{M}} \Box\varphi$.*

Proof. Suppose that $\Vdash\!\sim_{\Delta\mathsf{M}} \varphi$; by definition, there is an M-extension $\mathrm{E} \in \mathscr{E}^{\Phi}_{\Delta\mathsf{M}}$ s.t. $\mathrm{E} \vdash_{\mathsf{M}} \varphi$. It follows that $\mathrm{E} \vdash_{\mathsf{M}} \Box\varphi$. Thus, $\Vdash\!\sim_{\Delta\mathsf{M}} \Box\varphi$.

The analogous to item 2 in Proposition 1, a form of the deduction theorem, i.e., if $\Phi \cup \{\varphi\} \Vdash\!\sim_{\Delta\mathsf{M}} \psi$, then, $\Phi \Vdash\!\sim_{\Delta\mathsf{M}} \boxdot\varphi \to \psi$ fails to hold for an arbitrary $\Delta\mathsf{M}$ (even with the presense of $\boxdot$).

3.2 Deducibility in Default Modal Systems

We formulate a notion of $\Delta\mathsf{M}$-deduction for an arbitrary but fixed well-behaved default modal system $\Delta\mathsf{M}$. This notion of a $\Delta\mathsf{M}$-deduction extends that of an M-deduction by incorporating defaults in a natural way.

Definition 18. *A $\Delta\mathsf{M}$-deduction of φ from Φ is a finite sequence $\psi_1 \ldots \psi_n$ of formulas s.t. $\psi_n = \varphi$, and for each $k < n$ at least one of the following conditions hold:*

[2] In the literature on Default Logic well-behaved defaults are called normal. We avoid using this terminology here to avoid any confusion with normality in Modal Logic.

1. ψ_k *is an axiom of* M*;*
2. ψ_k *is a premiss, i.e.,* $\psi_k \in \Phi$*;*
3. ψ_k *is obtained from two earlier formulas using* mp*, i.e., there are* $i, j < k$ *s.t.* $\psi_j = \psi_i \to \psi_k$*;*
4. ψ_k *is obtained from an earlier formula using* u*, i.e., there is* $j < k$ *s.t.* $\psi_k = \boxed{u}\psi_j$*.*
5. ψ_k *is obtained from an earlier formula using* Δ*-detachment, i.e., there is* $j < k$ *s.t.* $\psi_j/\psi_k \in \Delta$*;*

A ΔM*-deduction is* credulous *whenever:*

$$(\Phi \cup \{\, \psi_i \mid 1 \leq i \leq n \,\}) \vdash_{\mathsf{M}} \bot \quad \textit{iff} \quad \Phi \vdash_{\mathsf{M}} \bot. \tag{1}$$

We define $\Phi \mathrel{|\!\sim}_{\Delta\mathsf{M}} \varphi$ *iff there is a credulous* ΔM*-deduction of* φ *from* Φ*.*

The notion of a credulous ΔM-deduction extends the notion of M-deduction with a rule of default detachment and the condition of being credulous. The rule of default detachment shows how defaults interact with the rules of the underlying proof system. The condition of being credulous in Eq. (1) captures the fact that defaults cannot be a source of inconsistency. Intuitively, a credulous ΔM-deduction of φ from Φ internalizes the construction of (part of) an extension containing φ together with the M-deduction which witnesses this containment. This is made precise in the following result.

Theorem 2. $\Phi \mathrel{|\!\sim}_{\Delta\mathsf{M}} \varphi$ *iff* $\Phi \mathrel{|\!|\!\sim}_{\Delta\mathsf{M}} \varphi$*.*

3.3 Towards an Algebraic Treatment of Default Modal Systems

We turn now our attention to a characterization of defaults and extensions by means of Lindenbaum-Tarski $\boxed{u}$-modal algebras. This algebraic treatment of defaults and extensions reveals how default modal systems may be thought of as updates on $\boxed{u}$-modal algebras. For the rest of this section, we assume that ΔM is an arbitrary but fixed well-behaved default modal system. We use $\mathfrak{L}$ to indicate the class of Lindenbaum-Tarski $\boxed{u}$-modal algebras of M, i.e., $\mathfrak{L} = \{\, \mathbf{L}^{\Phi}_{\mathsf{M}} \mid \Phi \subseteq \mathsf{Form} \,\}$. We drop the sub-index M and use Φ instead of $\cong^{\Phi}_{\mathsf{M}}$ as a way of further simplifying the notation. We construct this section around the following definition.

Definition 19. *Let* $\delta = \pi/\chi \in \Delta$*; the function* $\hat{\delta} : \mathfrak{L} \to \mathfrak{L}$ *is defined as:*

$$\hat{\delta}(\mathbf{L}^{\Phi}) = \begin{cases} \mathbf{L}^{\Phi \cup \{\chi\}} & \textit{if } [\pi]_{\Phi} = 1_{\Phi} \textit{ and } 0_{\Phi} \notin \uparrow\{[\boxed{u}\chi]_{\Phi}\} \quad \text{(2a)} \\ \mathbf{L}^{\Phi} & \textit{otherwise.} \quad \text{(2b)} \end{cases}$$

Definition 19 is the algebraic counterpart of the application of a default w.r.t. a set of sentences. More precisely, $\delta = \pi/\chi$ is applicable w.r.t. a set Φ satisfying $\Phi = \{\varphi \mid \Phi \vdash \varphi\}$ if: (a) $\pi \in \Phi$; and (b) $\Phi \cup \{\chi\} \nvdash \bot$. Applying the default

δ results in $\{\varphi \mid \Phi \cup \{\chi\} \vdash \varphi\}$. On the algebraic side, we capture the application of a default as a transformation between Lindenbaum-Tarski $\boxed{\sqcup}$-modal algebras. More precisely, consider the Lindenbaum-Tarski $\boxed{\sqcup}$-modal algebra for Φ, i.e., $\mathbf{L}^{\Phi}$. The condition (a) of applicability of $\delta = \pi/\chi$ w.r.t. $\mathbf{L}^{\Phi}$ is captured in (2a) as $[\pi]_{\Phi} = 1_{\Phi}$; and the condition (b) of applicability is captured in (2a) as $0_{\Phi} \notin \uparrow\{[\boxed{\sqcup}\chi]_{\Phi}\}$. In other words, the equivalence class of 1_{Φ} captures the deducibility of π from Φ, i.e., $\pi \in \Phi$, alt., $\Phi \vdash \pi$. In turn, the condition of *being proper* on the (open) filter generated by $[\boxed{\sqcup}\chi]_{\Phi}$ captures the consistency of χ w.r.t. Φ, i.e., $\Phi \cup \{\chi\} \nvdash \bot$. Notice that if the default is applicable, the return value of $\hat{\delta}$ incorporates χ to $\mathbf{L}^{\Phi}$, i.e., it results in $\mathbf{L}^{\Phi\cup\{\chi\}}$. Otherwise, $\hat{\delta}$ has no effect on $\mathbf{L}^{\Phi}$. When seen in this light, the operator $\hat{\delta}$ performs an *update* reflecting the application of δ on its input. The situation with $\hat{\delta}$ is similar to the case in dynamic logics such as Public Announcement Logic [20] (in particular, in relation to the approach proposed in [18]). We retake this discussion in Sect. 4.

Having dealt with defaults we turn our attention to extensions. For well-behaved defaults, extensions can be seen as being constructed in a step-wise fashion applying defaults one at a time. From a syntactic perspective, this construction of an extension starts with a closed set Φ, and applies the defaults $\delta \in \Delta$ one by one until we obtain a closed set of formulas that is saturated under the application of defaults. From the perspective of Lindenbaum-Tarski $\boxed{\sqcup}$-modal algebras we obtain the following.

Proposition 7. *Each function $\hat{\delta}$ induces a function $\bar{\delta} : |\mathbf{L}| \to |\hat{\delta}(\mathbf{L})|$ defined as: $\bar{\delta}([\varphi]_{\Phi}) = [\varphi]_{\Phi\cup\{\chi\}}$ if Eq. (2a) holds; or $\bar{\delta}([\varphi]_{\Phi}) = [\varphi]_{\Phi}$ if Eq. (2b) holds. The function $\bar{\delta}$ is a homomorphism from $\mathbf{L}$ to $\hat{\delta}(\mathbf{L})$.*

Proof. That $\bar{\delta}$ is a function is trivial. The proof that $\bar{\delta}$ is a homomorphism is by cases. If Eq. (2b) holds, then, the result is obtained immediately. Otherwise:

$$\bar{\delta}(f_{\Phi}^{\Box}([\varphi]_{\Phi})) = \bar{\delta}([\Box\varphi]_{\Phi}) = [\Box\varphi]_{\Phi\cup\{\chi\}} = f_{\Phi\cup\{\chi\}}^{\Box}([\varphi]_{\Phi\cup\{\chi\}}) = f_{\Phi\cup\{\chi\}}^{\Box}(\bar{\delta}([\varphi]_{\Phi})).$$

The remaining cases are similar.

The following are some immediate properties of default operators.

Definition 20. *Let $\mathbf{L}_1, \mathbf{L}_2 \in \mathfrak{L}$; we write $\mathbf{L}_1 \leq \mathbf{L}_2$ iff there is a homomorphism $h : \mathbf{L}_1 \to \mathbf{L}_2$; and $\mathbf{L}_1 < \mathbf{L}_2$ iff $\mathbf{L}_1 \leq \mathbf{L}_2$ and $\mathbf{L}_1$, $\mathbf{L}_2$ are not isomorphic.*

Proposition 8. *Every $\hat{\delta}$ is extensive and idempotent, i.e., it satisfies $\mathbf{L} \leq \hat{\delta}(\mathbf{L})$ and $\hat{\delta}(\mathbf{L}) = \hat{\delta}(\hat{\delta}(\mathbf{L}))$, resp. An arbitrary $\hat{\delta}$ needs not satisfy monotonicity, i.e., there are $\delta = \pi/\chi$ s.t. $\mathbf{L}_1 \leq \mathbf{L}_2$ and $\hat{\delta}(\mathbf{L}_1) \nleq \hat{\delta}(\mathbf{L}_2)$.*

Proof. Extensivity follows from Proposition 7. Idempotence is proven by cases. If Eq. (2b) holds, then, the result is obtained immediately. Otherwise, Eq. (2a) holds. In this case, $\hat{\delta}(\mathbf{L}^{\Phi}) = \mathbf{L}^{\Phi\cup\{\chi\}}$. Trivially, $\hat{\delta}(\mathbf{L}^{\Phi\cup\{\chi\}}) = \mathbf{L}^{\Phi\cup\{\chi\}}$. For a counter-example to monotonicity consider $\mathbf{L}_{\mathsf{K}\boxed{\sqcup}}^{\emptyset}$ and $\mathbf{L}_{\mathsf{K}\boxed{\sqcup}}^{\{\Box p\}}$, and $\delta = \top/\Diamond\neg p$.

The set Δ of defaults leads naturally to a set $\{\hat{\delta} : \mathfrak{L} \to \mathfrak{L} \mid \delta \in \Delta\}$. Each $\hat{\delta}$ in this set can be seen as "taking a step" in the construction of the algebraic counterpart of an extension. To carry out this construction, we would need to compose such steps. This leads to the formulation of Definition 21.

Definition 21. *The default monoid associated to* $\Delta\mathsf{M}$ *is the monoid* $\mathbf{D}^*$ *freely generated by* $\{\hat{\delta} \mid \delta \in \Delta\}$, *i.e.,* $\mathbf{D}^* = \langle \mathrm{D}, -;-, \mathrm{id}\rangle$ *where:*

1. D *is the* $\subseteq$*-smallest set s.t.:* $\{\hat{\delta} : \mathfrak{L} \to \mathfrak{L} \mid \delta \in \Delta\} \subseteq \mathrm{D}$; $\mathrm{id} : \mathfrak{L} \to \mathfrak{L} \in \mathrm{D}$; *and if* $\{d_1 : \mathfrak{L} \to \mathfrak{L}, d_2 : \mathfrak{L} \to \mathfrak{L}\} \subseteq \mathrm{D}$, *then* $(d_1;d_2) : \mathfrak{L} \to \mathfrak{L} \in \mathrm{D}$;
2. id *and* $-;-$ *satisfy:* $\mathrm{id}(\mathbf{L}) = \mathbf{L}$; *and* $(d_1;d_2)(\mathbf{L}) = d_2(d_1(\mathbf{L}))$.

Proposition 9. *Every* $d \in |\mathbf{D}^*|$ *is either: the identity, i.e.,* $d = \mathrm{id}$; *or a composition of the form* $d = (\hat{\delta}_1;\ldots;\hat{\delta}_n)$, *where* $\delta_i \in \Delta$.

We define $\overline{\mathrm{id}}([\varphi]_\Phi) = [\varphi]_\Phi$; and $\overline{(\hat{\delta}_1;\ldots;\hat{\delta}_n)} = (\bar{\delta}_1;\ldots;\bar{\delta}_n)$.

Definition 22. *Let* $\mathbf{L}$ *be a Lindenbaum-Tarski* $\boxdot$*-modal algebra in* $\mathfrak{L}$, *and* v *be an assignment on* $\mathbf{L}$; *for an equation* $\varphi \approx \psi$, *define:*

$$\mathbf{D}^*, \mathbf{L}, v \mathrel{|\!\approx} \varphi \approx \psi \quad \textit{iff} \quad d(\mathbf{L}), (v;\bar{d}) \models \varphi \approx \psi \textit{ for some } d \in |\mathbf{D}^*|.$$

We write $\mathbf{D}^*, \mathbf{L} \mathrel{|\!\approx} \varphi \approx \psi$ *iff* $\mathbf{D}^*, \mathbf{L}, v \mathrel{|\!\approx} \varphi \approx \psi$ *for all assignments* v.

Intuitively, the Lindenbaum-Tarski $\boxdot$-modal algebra $d(\mathbf{L})$ in Definition 22 is the algebraic counterpart of the concept of an extension. This is made clear in Theorem 3.

Theorem 3. $\Phi \mathrel{|\!\sim} \varphi$ *iff* $\mathbf{D}^*, \mathbf{L}^\Phi \mathrel{|\!\approx} \varphi \approx \top$.

Proof. The interesting part is the right-to-left implication: if $\mathbf{D}^*, \mathbf{L}^\Phi \mathrel{|\!\approx} \varphi \approx \top$, then, $\Phi \mathrel{|\!\sim} \varphi$. We prove the contrapositive: if $\Phi \not\mathrel{|\!\sim} \varphi$, then, $\mathbf{D}^*, \mathbf{L}^\Phi \not\mathrel{|\!\approx} \varphi \approx \top$. Let $\Phi \not\mathrel{|\!\sim} \varphi$, the proof is concluded if for all $d \in |\mathbf{D}^*|$, $d(\mathbf{L}^\Phi) \not\models \varphi \approx \top$. We continue by induction on d. Let $d = \mathrm{id}$; we must have $\mathrm{id}(\mathbf{L}^\Phi) \not\models \varphi \approx \top$; otherwise we would obtain $\Phi \vdash \varphi$ (from Theorem 1); and so that $\Phi \mathrel{|\!\sim} \varphi$ (which contradicts our assumption). For the next case, let $d = \hat{\delta}$ for $\delta = \pi/\chi \in \Delta$; either Eq. (2b) holds or Eq. (2a) holds. If Eq. (2b) holds, $\hat{\delta}$ behaves like id (and we are back to the previous case). If Eq. (2a) holds, $\hat{\delta}(\mathbf{L}^\Phi) = \mathbf{L}^{\Phi \cup \{\chi\}}$. Assuming (i) $\mathbf{L}^{\Phi \cup \{\chi\}} \models \varphi \approx \top$ leads to a contradiction. More precisely, if Eq. (2a) holds, from Theorem 1, we obtain $\Phi \vdash \pi$ and $\Phi \cup \{\chi\} \not\vdash \bot$. From (i) and Theorem 1, we obtain $\Phi \cup \{\chi\} \vdash \varphi$. If we place the M-deduction of π from Φ in front of the M-deduction of φ from $\Phi \cup \{\chi\}$, we obtain $\Phi \mathrel{|\!\sim} \varphi$. This yields the contradiction. For the inductive step, let $d = (\hat{\delta}_1;\ldots;\hat{\delta}_n;\hat{\delta}_{(n+1)})$. Suppose that $(\hat{\delta}_1;\ldots;\hat{\delta}_n)(\mathbf{L}^\Phi) = \mathbf{L}^{\Phi'}$. From the inductive hypothesis, we obtain $\mathbf{L}^{\Phi'} \not\models \varphi \approx \top$. Assuming that $\hat{\delta}_{(n+1)}(\mathbf{L}^{\Phi'}) \models \varphi \approx \psi$ leads to a contradiction using the same argument as in (i).

We conclude this section by taking some steps beyond dealing with defaults and extensions in the context of Lindenbaum-Tarski $\boxdot$-modal algebras. In particular, we show how some of the constructions used in Sect. 3.3 can be extended to a more abstract setting via suitable congruences.

Definition 23. *Let $\mathbf{L}^{\Phi}$ be a Lindenbaum-Tarski $\boxed{u}$-modal algebra and χ a formula; define $[\varphi_1]_{\Phi} \equiv_{\chi} [\varphi_2]_{\Phi}$ iff $[\varphi_1]_{\Phi} *_{\Phi} [\boxed{u}\chi]_{\Phi} = [\varphi_2]_{\Phi} *_{\Phi} [\boxed{u}\chi]_{\Phi}$.*

Definition 23 is a step towards treating the application of default as a device for obtaining a $\boxed{u}$-modal algebra $\mathbf{M}$ updated by the element $[\chi]_{\Phi}$ in $\mathbf{L}^{\Phi}$. The updated $\boxed{u}$-modal algebra $\mathbf{M}$ is meant to be obtained as a quotient algebra modulo the congruence $\equiv_{\chi}$. Proposition 10 shows that $\equiv_{\chi}$ indeed is a congruence.

Proposition 10. *The relation $\equiv_{\chi}$ is a congruence on $\mathbf{L}^{\Phi}$.*

Proof. That $\equiv_{\chi}$ is an equivalence relation is immediate. To improve notation we drop the subscript $_{\Phi}$. We need to show that: if $[\varphi_1] \equiv_{\chi} [\varphi_2]$ and $[\varphi_3] \equiv_{\chi} [\varphi_4]$, then, $[\varphi_1] * [\varphi_3] \equiv_{\chi} [\varphi_2] * [\varphi_4]$; $-[\varphi_1] \equiv_{\chi} -[\varphi_2]$; $f^{\Box}([\varphi_1]) \equiv_{\chi} f^{\Box}([\varphi_2])$; and $f^{\boxed{u}}([\varphi_1]) \equiv_{\chi} f^{\boxed{u}}([\varphi_2])$. The proof continues by cases (we only show the cases $f^{\Box}$ and $f^{\boxed{u}}$, the rest are routine):

$$\begin{aligned} & f^{\Box}([\varphi_1]) * [\boxed{u}\chi] \\ & \geq f^{\Box}([\varphi_1] * [\boxed{u}\chi]) * [\boxed{u}\chi] \\ & = f^{\Box}([\varphi_2] * [\boxed{u}\chi]) * [\boxed{u}\chi] \\ & = f^{\Box}([\varphi_2]) * (f^{\Box}([\boxed{u}\chi]) * [\boxed{u}\chi]) \\ & \geq f^{\Box}([\varphi_2]) * [\boxed{u}\chi] \end{aligned}$$

$$\begin{aligned} & f^{\boxed{u}}([\varphi_1]) * [\boxed{u}\chi] \\ & = f^{\boxed{u}}([\varphi_1]) * [\boxed{u}\boxed{u}\chi] \\ & = f^{\boxed{u}}([\varphi_1]) * f^{\boxed{u}}([\boxed{u}\chi]) \\ & = f^{\boxed{u}}([\varphi_1] * [\boxed{u}\chi]) \\ & = f^{\boxed{u}}([\varphi_2] * [\boxed{u}\chi]) \\ & = f^{\boxed{u}}([\varphi_2]) * f^{\boxed{u}}([\boxed{u}\chi]) \\ & = f^{\boxed{u}}([\varphi_2]) * [\boxed{u}\boxed{u}\chi] \\ & = f^{\boxed{u}}([\varphi_2]) * [\boxed{u}\chi]. \end{aligned}$$

Proposition 11. *The quotient algebra $\mathbf{L}^{\Phi}/_{\equiv_{\chi}}$ is isomorphic to $\mathbf{L}^{\Phi\cup\{\chi\}}$.*

Proof (sketch).
Observe that $\Phi \cup \{\chi\} \vdash (\varphi_1 \leftrightarrow \varphi_2)$ iff $\Phi \vdash (\varphi_1 \wedge \boxed{u}\chi \leftrightarrow \varphi_2 \wedge \boxed{u}\chi)$. The isomorphism between $\mathbf{L}^{\Phi}/_{\equiv_{\chi}}$ and $\mathbf{L}^{\Phi\cup\{\chi\}}$ is given by mappings ι_1 and ι_2 defined as: $\iota_1([[\varphi]_{\Phi}]_{\equiv_{\chi}}) = [\varphi]_{\Phi\cup\{\chi\}}$; and $\iota_2([\varphi]_{\Phi\cup\{\chi\}}) = [[\varphi]_{\Phi}]_{\equiv_{\chi}}$.

The isomorphism in Proposition 11 shows that the relation $\equiv_{\chi}$ yields the "correct" congruence if the application of a default is to be seen as an update on a $\boxed{u}$-modal algebra. Moreover, it is possible to define a function $\varepsilon : \mathbf{L}^{\Phi}/_{\equiv_{\chi}} \to \mathbf{L}^{\Phi}$ defined by $\varepsilon([[\varphi]_{\Phi}]_{\equiv_{\chi}}) = [\varphi]_{\Phi} *_{\Phi} [\chi]_{\Phi}$. The image of ε is also isomorphic to $\mathbf{L}^{\Phi\cup\{\chi\}}$. The results discussed in this paragraph open a pathway on how to lift the constructions in Definitions 19 and 21 to the setting of arbitrary $\boxed{u}$-modal algebras.

4 On Defaults as Model Updates

We are now in a position to establish a connection between our algebraic approach for default modal systems and the algebraic treatment of Public Announcement Logic (PAL) in [18]. To set up context for discussion, we briefly introduce some basic notions of PAL (see, e.g., [20] for details). As a modal logic, PAL extends the modal logic S5 (seen as the logic of knowledge) with a new modality $\langle !\psi \rangle$ of announcement. Intuitively, a formula $\langle !\psi \rangle \varphi$ states that after the truthful announcement of ψ, φ holds. Model theoretically, the interpretation of announcing ψ relativizes the model in which ψ is announced to the submodel in which ψ holds. The formula φ is then evaluated on the relativized model. It is important to remark that the announcement of ψ must be truthful: it occurs only if ψ is true. Otherwise, the announcement fails and $\langle !\psi \rangle \varphi$ evaluates to false.

There are some interesting similarities between announcements in PAL and defaults. From an algebraic perspective, an announcement may be understood as a homomorphism between the modal algebra in which the announcement occurs and the modal algebra corresponding to the submodel in which the announced formula holds. The algebraic machinery introduced in Sect. 3.3 sets the basis for thinking about the application of defaults as a logic of updates between particular modal algebras (Lindenbaum-Tarski $\boxed{\mathrm{u}}$-modal algebras). In other words, we may construe the algebraic semantics of a default as an update from the Lindenbaum-Tarski $\boxed{\mathrm{u}}$-modal algebra in which the default is considered, and the one updated with the consequent of the default (if the default is applicable). Notice that a default update takes place only if the prerequisite of the default is provable and its justification does not yield an inconsistency. The situation here is similar to the case of announcements, where the update takes place only if the formula being announced is true. In both cases, that of an announcement and that of the algebraic application of a default, the update is captured by a homomorphism from the original modal algebra to an updated modal algebra (obtained as a quotient construction). There is, however, subtle difference between announcements and defaults: if the announcement of ψ is not truthful the whole formula $\langle !\psi \rangle \varphi$ amounts to a falsity; whereas if the prerequisite of a default is not provable, or its justification is inconsistent in the modal algebra, the application of the default has no effect.

The similarities between announcements in PAL and defaults are even more apparent when contrasted with the proposal presented in [18]. This proposal exploits the duality between models and algebras in order to algebraize PAL. In particular, in [18], a formula ψ is interpreted as an element b in an S5 modal algebra $\mathbf{M} = \langle B, *, -, f^{\Box} \rangle$. The result of announcing this formula is a modal algebra constructed as a quotient modulo a congruence $\equiv_b$ defined as $b_1 \equiv_b b_2$ iff $b_1 * b = b_2 * b$. This congruence bears a close resemblance to the one we presented in Sect. 3.3. The main difference between this congruence and ours rests on the fact that the former is presented in the setting of S5, whereas ours is presented in a setting where global modal consequence is taken as the basis on which to build default modal systems. This said, the approach in [18] is more abstract than ours; since it considers arbitrary modal algebras and not just Lindenbaum-Tarski modal algebras.

The discussion above offers only some first steps in understanding the relationship between defaults and updates: both in terms of a full algebraization of default modal systems, and in terms of establishing a tight connection with logics of updates. In working towards a full algebraization of default modal systems, we would like to interpret the application of a default over arbitrary modal algebras, and not only as an update over Lindenbaum-Tarski $\boxed{u}$-modal algebras. In this regard, the main challenge is how to generalize the way in which we capture the application of one default to the application of a sequence of defaults needed to build an extension. Moreover, it would also be interesting to know whether it is possible to develop a class of algebraic structures for default modal systems parallel to the class of modal algebras for modal systems. This would require an internalization of defaults as algebraic operators. In turn, in what refers to establishing a tight connection with logics of updates, it would be interesting to be able to prove a reduction result between a default modal system and a logic of announcement (or establishing a difference in expressive power between one and the other). In this case, the challenge is deciding on an adequate logic of announcement and in finding whether it is possible to faithfully translate the application of a default as a form of update in this logic. Finally, upon defining the semantics of defaults as updates, we would like to study defaults as dynamic epistemic operators. In particular, we would like to explore whether defaults can be used to represent some novel form of communication in a multi-agent setting.

5 Final Remarks

We presented a family of default logics built over modal logics and studied some properties.

First, we presented default logics syntactically as a default modal system. For each default modal system we formulated a notion of default deducibility to make explicit how defaults interact with the rules of the underlying proof calculus. Then, we offered an algebraic treatment of defaults and extensions. The algebraic treatment enabled us to obtain an algebraic completeness result. To our knowledge, this is the first work addressing default logic algebraically.

Moreover, we discussed a connection between default modal systems and modal logics with updates. In particular, our algebraic treatment of defaults is inspired by the ideas introduced in [18] for PAL. We believe that considering default modal systems as logics of updates is an interesting pathway to the study of the meta-logical properties of such systems from a semantic perspective.

Acknowledgment. We would like to thank the anonymous reviewers for their helpful comments and suggestions. This work is supported by projects ANPCyT-PICTs-2017-1130 and 2016-0215, Stic-AmSud 20-STIC-03 “DyLo-MPC”, Secyt-UNC, GRFT Mincyt-Cba, and by the Laboratoire International Associé SINFIN.

References

1. Ågotnes, T., Alechina, N.: The dynamics of syntactic knowledge. J. Log. Comput. **17**(1), 83–116 (2007)

2. Antoniou, G., Wang, K.: Default logic. In: Gabbay, D., Woods, J. (eds.) The Many Valued and Nonmonotonic Turn in Logic. Handbook of the History of Logic, North-Holland, vol. 8, pp. 517–555 (2007)
3. Baader, F., Hollunder, B.: Embedding defaults into terminological knowledge representation formalisms. In: Nebel, B., Rich, C., Swartout, W. (eds.) 3rd International Conference on Principles of Knowledge Representation and Reasoning (KR 1992), pp. 306–317. Morgan Kaufmann (1992)
4. Blackburn, P., de Rijke, M., Venema, Y. (eds.): Modal Logic. Cambridge University Press, Cambridge (2002)
5. Cassano, V., Fervari, R., Areces, C., Castro, P.F.: Interpolation and beth definability in default logics. In: Calimeri, F., Leone, N., Manna, M. (eds.) JELIA 2019. LNCS (LNAI), vol. 11468, pp. 675–691. Springer, Cham (2019). https://doi.org/10.1007/978-3-030-19570-0_44
6. Delgrande, J., Schaub, T., Jackson, W.: Alternative approaches to default logic. Artif. Intell. **70**(1–2), 167–237 (1994)
7. Duc, H.N.: Reasoning about rational, but not logically omniscient, agents. J. Log. Comput. **7**(5), 633–648 (1997)
8. Fervari, R., Velázquez-Quesada, F.R.: Dynamic epistemic logics of introspection. In: Madeira, A., Benevides, M. (eds.) DALI 2017. LNCS, vol. 10669, pp. 82–97. Springer, Cham (2018). https://doi.org/10.1007/978-3-319-73579-5_6
9. Fervari, R., Velázquez-Quesada, F.R.: Introspection as an action in relational models. J. Log. Algebraic Methods Program. **108**, 1–23 (2019)
10. Fitting, M.: Modal proof theory. In: Blackburn, P., van Benthem, J., Wolter, F. (eds.) Handbook of Modal Logic, pages 85–138. Elsevier (2007)
11. Froidevaux, C., Mengin, J.: Default logics: a unified view. Computat. Intell. **10**, 331–369 (1994)
12. Gabbay, D., Kurucz, A., Wolter, F., Zakharyaschev, M.: Many-Dimensional Modal Logics: Theory and Applications. Elsevier, Amsterdam (2003)
13. Givant, S., Halmos, P.: Introduction to Boolean Algebras. Undergraduate Texts in Mathematics. Springer, Heidelberg (2009). https://doi.org/10.1007/978-0-387-68436-9
14. Goranko, V., Passy, S.: Using the universal modality: gains and questions. J. Log. Comput. **2**(1), 5–30 (1992)
15. Grossi, D., Velázquez-Quesada, F.R.: Syntactic awareness in logical dynamics. Synthese **192**(12), 4071–4105 (2015). https://doi.org/10.1007/s11229-015-0733-1
16. Jago, M.: Epistemic logic for rule-based agents. J. Log. Lang. Inform. **18**(1), 131–158 (2009)
17. Łukaszewicz, W.: Considerations on default logic: an alternative approach. Comput. Intell. **4**, 1–16 (1988)
18. Ma, M.: Mathematics of public announcements. In: van Ditmarsch, H., Lang, J., Ju, S. (eds.) LORI 2011. LNCS (LNAI), vol. 6953, pp. 193–205. Springer, Heidelberg (2011). https://doi.org/10.1007/978-3-642-24130-7_14
19. Mikitiuk, A., Truszczynski, M.: Constrained and rational default logics. In: Proceedings of IJCAI 1995, pp. 1509–1517 (1995)
20. Plaza, J.: Logics of public communications. Synthese **158**(2), 165–179 (2007)
21. Reiter, R.: A logic for default reasoning. AI **13**(1–2), 81–132 (1980)
22. Schaub, T.: On constrained default theories. In: 11th European Conference on Artificial Intelligence (ECAI 1992), pp. 304–308 (1992)
23. Solaki, A.: Steps out of logical omniscience. Master's thesis, Institute for Logic, Language and Computation, Amsterdam (2017). MoL-2017-12

24. van Benthem, J., Pacuit, E.: Dynamic logics of evidence-based beliefs. Stud. Log. **99**(1), 61–92 (2011)
25. van Benthem, J., Velázquez-Quesada, F.R.: The dynamics of awareness. Synthese (Knowl. Rational. Action) **177**(Supplement 1), 5–27 (2010)
26. Vardi, M.Y.: On epistemic logic and logical omniscience. In: Proceedings of TARK, pp. 293–305. Morgan Kaufmann (1986)
27. Velázquez-Quesada, F.R.: Explicit and implicit knowledge in neighbourhood models. In: Grossi, D., Roy, O., Huang, H. (eds.) LORI 2013. LNCS, vol. 8196, pp. 239–252. Springer, Heidelberg (2013). https://doi.org/10.1007/978-3-642-40948-6_19
28. Venema, Y.: Algebras and general frames. In: Blackburn et al. [4], pp. 263–333

Expressivity of Some Versions of APAL

Hans van Ditmarsch[1(✉)], Mo Liu[1], Louwe B. Kuijer[2], and Igor Sedlár[3]

[1] CNRS, LORIA, University of Lorraine, Nancy, France
{hans.van-ditmarsch,mo.liu}@loria.fr
[2] University of Liverpool, Liverpool, UK
l.b.kuijer@gmail.com
[3] Institute of Computer Science, Czech Academy of Sciences, Prague, Czech Republic
sedlar@cs.cas.cz

Abstract. Arbitrary public announcement logic (APAL) is a logic of change of knowledge with modalities representing quantification over announcements. We present two rather different versions of APAL wherein this quantification is restricted to formulas only containing a subset of all propositional variables: FSAPAL and SCAPAL; and another version quantifying over all announcements implied by or implying a given formula: IPAL. We then determine the relative expressivity of these logics and APAL. The IPAL quantifier promises to provide a novel perspective on substructural implication as dynamic consequence.

Keywords: Dynamic epistemic logic · Expressivity · Modal logic

1 Introduction

The modal logic of knowledge was originally proposed to give a relational semantics for the perceived properties of knowledge, such as that what you know is true, and that you know what you know, and to contrast this with the properties of other epistemic notions such as belief [26]. Already in [26] the analysis of paradoxical phenomena that you cannot be informed of factual ignorance while 'losing' that ignorance, so-called Moorean phenomena [28], played an important role. On the heels of the logic of (single agent) knowledge came the multi-agent logics of knowledge, wherein similar phenomena are not so paradoxical: there is no issue with my knowledge of your ignorance. This led on the one hand to the development of group epistemic notions such as common knowledge [6,27] and distributed knowledge [25], topics that we will bypass in this contribution. On the other hand this led to increased interest in the analysis of multiple agents informing each other of their ignorance and knowledge, often inspired by logic puzzles [27,29]. This culminated in Plaza's public announcement logic (PAL) [30], wherein such informative actions became full members of the logical language besides the knowledge modalities; parallel developments of dynamic but not epistemic logics of information change are [11,21].

PAL contains a dynamic operator representing the consequences of information change that is similarly observed by all agents, so-called public (and

M. A. Martins and I. Sedlár (Eds.): DaLí 2020, LNCS 12569, pp. 120–136, 2020.
https://doi.org/10.1007/978-3-030-65840-3_8

truthful) announcement. We let $[\psi]\varphi$ stand for 'after truthful public announcement of ψ, φ (is true). Every PAL formula is equivalent to a formula without public announcements, so that PAL is as expressive as epistemic logic EL (a.k.a. the logic S5) [30].

From PAL there were various directions for further generalization. One could consider public announcements in the presence of group epistemic operators such as common knowledge, or non-public information change such as private or secret announcements to some agents while other agents do not or only partially observe that. Both were simultaneously realized in action model logic [9]; parallel, now lesser known, developments are [24].

A different direction of generalizing PAL is to consider quantifying over announcements. Arbitrary public announcement logic APAL was proposed in [7] and contains a construct $[!]\varphi$ standing for 'after any truthful public announcement, φ (is true)', i.e., for all ψ, $[\psi]\varphi$. In order to avoid circularity, the APAL quantifier is only over announcements not containing $[!]$ modalities. There is an infinitary (not RE) axiomatization for the logic [8], where an open question remains whether there is a finitary (RE) axiomatization. APAL is undecidable [22], and the complexity of model checking is PSPACE-complete [1]. There are versions of APAL with finitary axiomatizations or decidable satisfiability problems [10,16,17], or that model aspects of agency [1,2,23]. APAL is more expressive than PAL [7]. The relative expressivity of versions of APAL is rather intricate, and most relevant in view of potential applications. For example, group announcement logic GAL and APAL are incomparable in expressivity [23], and in GAL we can formalize goal reachability in finite two-principal security protocols [1].

In this contribution we investigate some novel versions of APAL. If we quantify over announcements only using atoms in *subsets* $Q \subseteq P$ we obtain the logic SAPAL, and if these subsets are required to be *finite* we get FSAPAL. If we quantify over announcements only using atoms occurring in the formula under the *scope* of the quantifier, we obtain the logic SCAPAL. If we quantify over announcements *implying* a given formula ψ or *implied by* a given formula ψ and if such ψ may also contain quantifiers we obtain logic QIPAL and if they are not allowed to contain quantifiers we obtain IPAL.

Our investigations are motivated by the search for 'tameable' versions of APAL, which would be useful in view of applications. The different kinds of taming we have in mind are, first and foremost, decidability, and also finitary (RE) axiomatizations and lower model checking complexity. Unfortunately we do not expect any of the investigated logics to be decidable or to have a finitary axiomatization. We did not consider whether model checking complexity is below that of APAL (PSPACE-complete). Our expressivity results, the principal focus of our contribution, can be seen as sanity checks that might point towards likely application areas (similarly as for GAL, as observed above). Concerning applications, when modelling dynamics of a multi-agent system it seems often the case that the vocabulary is finite. In particular, that only a finite number of atomic propositions are considered relevant for each given subtask of a problem to solve, where this vocabulary might vary between interdependent subtasks. In such cases, the logics SAPAL and even more FSAPAL (SAPAL for finite subsets of atoms), and also SCAPAL, might be more suitable modelling tools than 'generic' APAL. Note that there is a strong, but not well-known, relation between quantification over public announcements and epistemic planning [15]. In the latter, we wish to satisfy some epistemic goal φ by finding a sequence of actions, that could be public announcements, successively transforming multi-agent models for the system until ultimately leading to a model satisfying goal φ. In the former, we wish to satisfy $\Diamond\varphi$ (for 'there is an announcement, or a sequence of announcements, after which φ') by finding a sequence of announcements (successively transforming multi-agent models) after which φ. In both, undecidability can only be tamed by restricting what can be announced; for epistemic planning, this is e.g. discussed in [4]. For the logics IPAL and QIPAL we are additionally motivated by substructural logic, and how the quantifier there can be seen as the condition for a substructural implication, as will be discussed in some detail in our contribution.

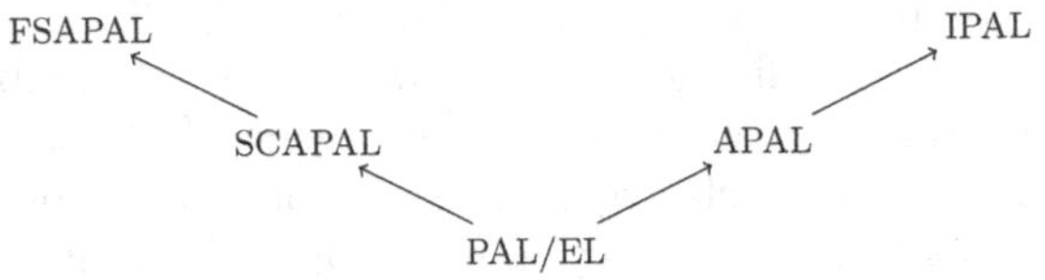

Fig. 1. Expressivity hierarchy of logics presented in this work. An arrow means larger expressivity. Assume transitivity. Absence of an arrow means incomparability.

In Sect. 2 we introduce their syntax and semantics, in Sect. 3 we prove some modal properties of these quantifiers. Section 4 determines the expressivity hierarchy for the reported logics. This section contains our main results. They are depicted in Fig. 1. Let $\prec$ mean '(strictly) less expressive' and $\asymp$ 'incomparable', then the results are that PAL is less expressive than any of the logics with quantifiers, and that SCAPAL $\prec$ FSAPAL, APAL $\asymp$ SCAPAL, APAL $\asymp$ FSAPAL, IPAL $\asymp$ SCAPAL, IPAL $\asymp$ FSAPAL, and APAL $\prec$ IPAL (proof omitted for lack of space and therefore called a conjecture). The complete axiomatizations and the undecidability of satisfiability of our APAL versions all promise to be the same as for APAL. We conclude with Sect. 5 reinterpreting dynamic consequence in the IPAL setting.

2 Syntax and Semantics: SAPAL, SCAPAL, QIPAL

Throughout this contribution, let a countable set P of propositional atoms and a finite set A of agents be given.

Definition 1 (Language). *The logical language $\mathcal{L}$ is defined inductively as:*

$$\varphi ::= \top \mid p \mid \neg\varphi \mid (\varphi \wedge \varphi) \mid K_a\varphi \mid [\varphi]\varphi \mid [!]\varphi \mid [Q]\varphi \mid [\subseteq]\varphi \mid [\varphi^{\downarrow}]\varphi \mid [\varphi^{\uparrow}]\varphi$$

where $p \in P$, $a \in A$, *and* $Q \subseteq P$. *The propositional sublanguage is* $\mathcal{L}_{PL}$, *with additionally the modalities* K_a *we get the* epistemic formulas $\mathcal{L}_{EL}$, *with additionally the construct* $[\varphi]\varphi$ *it is* $\mathcal{L}_{PAL}$, *and adding one of the* quantifiers $[!]$, $[Q]$, $[\subseteq]$, $[\varphi^{\downarrow}]\psi$ *and* $[\varphi^{\uparrow}]\psi$ *we obtain, respectively,* $\mathcal{L}_{APAL}$, $\mathcal{L}_{SAPAL}$ *and* $\mathcal{L}_{SCAPAL}$, $\mathcal{L}_{QIPAL^{\downarrow}}$ *and* $\mathcal{L}_{QIPAL^{\uparrow}}$. *Adding both* $[\varphi^{\downarrow}]\psi$ *and* $[\varphi^{\uparrow}]\psi$ *we obtain* $\mathcal{L}_{QIPAL}$, *and if the* φ *in* $[\varphi^{\downarrow}]\psi$ *and* $[\varphi^{\uparrow}]\psi$ *is restricted to* $\mathcal{L}_{PAL}$, *we get* $\mathcal{L}_{IPAL}$. *If the* Q *in* $[Q]\varphi$ *are (always)* finite *we get* $\mathcal{L}_{FSAPAL}$.

The meaning of all constructs will be explained after defining the semantics. The dual modalities for $[!]$, $[Q]$, $[\subseteq]$, $[\varphi^{\downarrow}]$, and $[\varphi^{\uparrow}]$ are, respectively, $\langle ! \rangle$, $\langle Q \rangle$, $\langle \subseteq \rangle$, $\langle \varphi^{\downarrow} \rangle$, and $\langle \varphi^{\uparrow} \rangle$. Instead of $\varphi \in \mathcal{L}_X$ we also say that φ *is an* X *formula.* For any language $\mathcal{L}$, $\mathcal{L}|Q$ is the sublanguage only containing atoms in $Q \subseteq P$. Given $\varphi \in \mathcal{L}$, $P(\varphi)$ denotes the set of atoms occurring in φ. For $[\{p_1, \ldots, p_n\}]\varphi$ we may write $[p_1 \ldots p_n]\varphi$. The *modal depth* $d(\varphi)$ of a formula is the maximum stack of epistemic modalities; it is defined as: $d(\bot) = d(p) = 0$, $d(\varphi \wedge \psi) = \max\{d(\varphi), d(\psi)\}$, $d(K_a\varphi) = d(\varphi) + 1$, $d([\varphi]\psi) = d([\varphi^{\downarrow}]\psi) = d([\varphi^{\uparrow}]\psi) = d(\varphi) + d(\psi)$, and $d([!]\varphi) = d([\subseteq]\varphi) = d([Q]\varphi) = d(\neg\varphi) = d(\varphi)$.

Definition 2 (Structures). *An* epistemic model *(or* model*) is a triple* $M = (S, \sim, V)$ *where* S *is a domain of states,* $\sim$ *is a set of binary relations* $\sim_a \subseteq S \times S$ *that are all equivalence relations, and* $V : P \to \mathcal{P}(S)$ *maps each atom* $p \in P$ *to its denotation* $V(p)$.

Given a model M, we may refer to its domain, relations, and valuation as S^M, $\sim_a^M$, and V^M respectively, and we also refer to the domain of M as $\mathcal{D}(M)$. Bisimulation to compare models will be defined later. A model N is a *submodel* of M, notation $N \subseteq M$, if $S^N \subseteq S^M$, for all $a \in A$, $\sim_a^N = \sim_a^M \cap (S^N \times S^N)$, and for all $p \in P$, $V^N(p) = V^M(p) \cap S^N$.

Definition 3 (Semantics). *Given model* $M = (S, \sim, V)$, $s \in S$ *and* $\varphi \in \mathcal{L}$ *we inductively define* $M, s \models \varphi$ *(*φ *is true in state* s *of model* M*) as:*

$$
\begin{array}{lll}
M, s \models p & \textit{iff} & s \in V(p) \\
M, s \models \neg\varphi & \textit{iff} & M, s \not\models \varphi \\
M, s \models \varphi \wedge \psi & \textit{iff} & M, s \models \varphi \textit{ and } M, s \models \psi \\
M, s \models K_a\varphi & \textit{iff} & \textit{for all } t \in S,\ s \sim_a t \textit{ implies } M, t \models \varphi \\
M, s \models [\psi]\varphi & \textit{iff} & M, s \models \psi \textit{ implies } M|\psi, s \models \varphi \\
M, s \models [!]\varphi & \textit{iff} & \textit{for any } \psi \in \mathcal{L}_{PAL} : M, s \models [\psi]\varphi \\
M, s \models [Q]\varphi & \textit{iff} & \textit{for any } \psi \in \mathcal{L}_{PAL}|Q\ : M, s \models [\psi]\varphi \\
M, s \models [\subseteq]\varphi & \textit{iff} & \textit{for any } \psi \in \mathcal{L}_{PAL}|P(\varphi) : M, s \models [\psi]\varphi \\
M, s \models [\chi^{\downarrow}]\varphi & \textit{iff} & \textit{for any } \psi \in \mathcal{L}_{PAL} \textit{ implying } \chi : M, s \models [\psi]\varphi \\
M, s \models [\chi^{\uparrow}]\varphi & \textit{iff} & \textit{for any } \psi \in \mathcal{L}_{PAL} \textit{ implied by } \chi : M, s \models [\psi]\varphi
\end{array}
$$

where $M|\varphi = (S', \sim', V')$ *is such that* $S' = [\![\varphi]\!]_M = \{s \in S \mid M, s \models \varphi\}$, $\sim'_a = \sim_a \cap ([\![\varphi]\!]_M \times [\![\varphi]\!]_M)$, *and* $V'(p) = V(p) \cap [\![\varphi]\!]_M$.

A formula φ is valid on model M, *notation* $M \models \varphi$, *iff for all* $s \in S$, $M, s \models \varphi$, *and* φ is valid, *notation* $\models \varphi$, *iff* φ *is valid on all models* M. *A formula* φ *is a* distinguishing formula *of a subset* $S' \subseteq S$ *of* M *(or* S' *is* definable *by* φ*) if for all* $t \in S'$, $M, t \models \varphi$ *and for all* $t \notin S'$, $M, t \not\models \varphi$.

In the dual existential reading of the semantics of the quantifiers, the ψ in 'there is a $\psi \in \mathcal{L}_{PAL}$' is the *witness* of the quantifier. In the semantics of the last two, 'ψ implies χ' means $\models \psi \rightarrow \chi$ and 'ψ is implied by χ' means $\models \chi \rightarrow \psi$.

PAL and APAL. *Public announcement logic* PAL and *arbitrary public announcement logic* APAL were already introduced.

SAPAL and FSAPAL. The logic with construct $[Q]\varphi$, for 'after any announcement only containing atoms in $Q \subseteq P$', is called SAPAL, for APAL with quantification over formulas restricted to *subsets* of variables. If those subsets are required to be *finite* we get FSAPAL.

SCAPAL. The logic with construct $[\subseteq]\varphi$, for 'after any announcement only containing atoms occurring in φ', is called SCAPAL (where φ is the formula under the *scope* of the quantifier $[\subseteq]$).

QIPAL. The logic with constructs $[\psi^{\downarrow}]\varphi$ and $[\psi^{\uparrow}]\varphi$ is called QIPAL; where $[\psi^{\downarrow}]\varphi$ stands for 'after every announcement implying ψ, φ is true', and $[\psi^{\uparrow}]\varphi$ stands for 'after every announcement implied by ψ, φ is true'. In QIPAL we can reason over restrictions of a given model M that are submodels of $M|\psi$, or over restrictions that contain $M|\psi$ as a submodel.

Bisimulation. We define several notions of bisimulation between models and obtain some elementary invariance results for our logics. They will be used much in the expressivity Sect. 4.

Definition 4 (Bisimulation). *Let M and N be epistemic models. A non-empty relation $Z \subseteq S^M \times S^N$ is a* bisimulation *between M and N if for all Zst, $p \in P$ and $a \in A$:*
*— **atoms**: $s \in V^M(p)$ iff $t \in V^N(p)$.*
*— **forth**: if $s \sim_a^M s'$, then there is a $t' \in S^N$ such that $t \sim_a^N t'$ and $Zs't'$.*
*— **back**: if $t \sim_a^N t'$, then there is a $s' \in S^M$ such that $s \sim_a^M s'$ and $Zs't'$.*
If there exists a bisimulation Z between M and N we write $M \leftrightarroweq N$ (or $Z : M \leftrightarroweq N$, to indicate the relation), and if it contains pair (s,t), we write $(M,s) \leftrightarroweq (N,t)$. If the **atoms** *clause is only satisfied for atoms $Q \subseteq P$, we write $M \leftrightarroweq^Q N$ and Z is called a Q-*bisimulation *or a (Q-)*restricted bisimulation.

Definition 5 (Bounded bisimulation). *Let M and N be epistemic models. For $n \in \mathbb{N}$ we define a sequence $Z^0 \supseteq \cdots \supseteq Z^n$ of relations on $S^M \times S^N$.*
A non-empty relation Z^0 is a 0-bisimulation if for all Z^0st and $p \in P$:
*— **atoms**: $s \in V^M(p)$ iff $t \in V^N(p)$.*
A non-empty relation Z^{n+1} is an $(n+1)$-bisimulation if for all $Z^{n+1}st$, $a \in A$:
*— $(n+1)$-**forth**: if $s \sim_a^M s'$, then there is a $t' \in S^N$ s.t. $t \sim_a^N t'$ and $Z^n s't'$.*
*— $(n+1)$-**back**: if $t \sim_a^N t'$, then there is a $s' \in S^M$ s.t. $s \sim_a^M s'$ and $Z^n s't'$.*
If there exists a n-bisimulation Z^n between M and N we write $M \leftrightarroweq^n N$. (We also combine the notations $\leftrightarroweq^Q$ and $\leftrightarroweq^n$ in the obvious way, writing $\leftrightarroweq^{Q,n}$.)

Given pointed models (M,s) and (N,t) and a logic L with language $\mathcal{L}_L$, $(M,s) \equiv_L (N,t)$ (for '(M,s) and (N,t) are modally equivalent') denotes: for all $\varphi \in \mathcal{L}_L$, $M, s \models \varphi$ iff $N, t \models \varphi$. Given $Q \subseteq P$ and $n \in \mathbb{N}$, annotations $\equiv_L^n$ and $\equiv_L^Q$ restrict the evaluated formulas $\varphi \in \mathcal{L}_L$ to those of modal depth $d(\varphi) \leq n$ and (resp.) to $\varphi \in \mathcal{L}_L|Q$. APAL is invariant for bisimilarity, but not for restricted bisimilarity or bounded bisimilarity: $(M, s) \leftrightarrows (N, t)$ implies $(M, s) \equiv_{APAL} (N, t)$, whereas $(M, s) \leftrightarrows^n (N, t)$ may not imply $(M, s) \equiv_{APAL}^n (N, t)$, and $(M, s) \leftrightarrows^Q (N, t)$ may not imply $(M, s) \equiv_{APAL}^Q (N, t)$ [7,18]. This is because the APAL modality [!] implicitly quantifies over formulas of arbitrarily large modal depth and over infinitely many atoms. All logics we consider in this paper are invariant for bisimilarity.

Lemma 1. *For any L considered,* $(M, s) \leftrightarrows (N, t)$ *implies* $(M, s) \equiv_L (N, t)$.

Proof. For L = EL, PAL, this is known from the literature [14] for EL, and for PAL because EL and PAL are equally expressive [30]. For the other logics, let us for example consider SAPAL; the proof for all remaining logics is similar. By induction on the structure of φ we show that

For all $\varphi \in \mathcal{L}_{SAPAL}$ and for all pointed models (M, s), (N, t):
$(M, s) \leftrightarrows (N, t)$ implies $M, s \models \varphi$ iff $N, t \models \varphi$.

All inductive cases are elementary except 'public announcement' and 'quantifier'.

Case Quantifier
$M, s \models [Q]\psi$, iff $M, s \models [\varphi]\psi$ for all $\varphi \in \mathcal{L}_{PAL}|Q$, iff $M, s \models \varphi$ implies $M|\varphi, s \models \psi$ for all $\varphi \in \mathcal{L}_{PAL}|Q$, iff (*) $\boldsymbol{N, t \models \varphi}$ implies $M|\varphi, s \models \psi$ for all $\varphi \in \mathcal{L}_{PAL}|Q$, iff (**) $N, t \models \varphi$ implies $\boldsymbol{N|\varphi, t \models \psi}$ for all $\varphi \in \mathcal{L}_{PAL}|Q$, iff $N, t \models [\varphi]\psi$ for all $\varphi \in \mathcal{L}_{PAL}|Q$, iff $N, t \models [Q]\psi$.

(*): By bisimulation invariance of PAL, we obtain $M, s \models \varphi$ iff $N, t \models \varphi$.

(**): Let $Z : (M, s) \leftrightarrows (N, t)$. Define Z' beween $M|\varphi$ and $N|\varphi$ as follows: $Z'uv$ iff (Zuv and $M, u \models \varphi$). By bisimulation invariance for $\varphi \in \mathcal{L}_{PAL}$ it follows that also $N, v \models \varphi$, so that Z' is indeed a relation between $M|\varphi$ and $N|\varphi$. We now show that $Z' : (M|\varphi, s) \leftrightarrows (N|\varphi, t)$. The clause **atoms** is obviously satisfied. Concerning **forth** for some agent a, take any pair (v, v') such that $Z'vv'$ and let u in the domain of $M|\varphi$ be such that $v \sim_a u$. As u is in the domain of $M|\varphi$, $M, u \models \varphi$. From $Z'vv'$ follows Zvv'. As $v \sim_a u$ in $M|\varphi$, also $v \sim_a u$ in M. From Zvv', $v \sim_a u$ in M, and **forth** (for Z) it follows that there is u' in the domain of N such that Zuu' and $v' \sim_a u'$. From Zuu', $M, u \models \varphi$, and bisimulation invariance for $\varphi \in \mathcal{L}_{PAL}$ it follows that $N, u' \models \varphi$, i.e., u' is also in the domain of $N|\varphi$. From Zuu', $M, u \models \varphi$, and the fact the u' is in the domain of $M|\varphi$ it follows that $Z'uu'$, as required. This proves **forth**. The step **back** is shown similarly. Note that in particular $Z'st$. This therefore establishes that $Z' : (M|\varphi, s) \leftrightarrows (N|\varphi, t)$, so that by definition $(M|\varphi, s) \leftrightarrows (N|\varphi, t)$. By induction for ψ it now follows that $M|\varphi, s \models \psi$ iff $N|\varphi, t \models \psi$, as desired.

Case Public Announcement
The case public announcement, wherein we show that $M, s \models [\varphi]\psi$ iff $N, t \models [\varphi]\psi$, is shown fairly similarly to the case quantifier, except that in step $(*)$ we do not use bisimulation invariance for $\varphi \in \mathcal{L}_{PAL}$ but we use the inductive hypothesis for $\varphi \in \mathcal{L}_{SAPAL}$, and similarly on two occasions in step $(**)$.

Corollary 1.
Let $\varphi \in \mathcal{L}_L$ *and* $M, s \models \varphi$. *Then* $(M, s) \leftrightarroweq (N, t)$ *implies* $(M|\varphi, s) \leftrightarroweq (N|\varphi, t)$.

For bounded bisimilarity this only holds for L = EL, PAL (a special case of [14], and given that PAL is as expressive as EL). As we use this result virtually identically for the inductive case announcement in subsequent proofs in the expressivity section, we give its full proof.

Lemma 2. *Let* $n \in \mathbb{N}$ *and* $\varphi \in \mathcal{L}_{PAL}$ *with* $d(\varphi) = k \leq n$, *models* (M, s) *and* (N, t), *and* $M, s \models \varphi$ *be given. If* $(M, s) \leftrightarroweq^n (N, t)$, *then* $(M|\varphi, s) \leftrightarroweq^{n-k} (N|\varphi, t)$.

Proof. Let $Z^0 \supseteq \cdots \supseteq Z^n$ be such that $Z^0 : (M, s) \leftrightarroweq^0 (N, t)$, ..., $Z^n : (M, s) \leftrightarroweq^n (N, t)$. For all $i = 0, \ldots, n-k$, let $Z^i_\varphi : \mathcal{D}(M) \to \mathcal{D}(N)$ be defined as: $Z^i_\varphi st$ iff $Z^{i+k} st$ and $M, s \models \varphi$. As $d(\varphi) \leq n$, from n-bisimulation invariance for PAL and $M, s \models \varphi$ also follows that $N, t \models \varphi$.

By natural induction on $n - k$ we show that $Z^n : (M, s) \leftrightarroweq^n (N, t)$ implies $Z^{n-k}_\varphi : (M|\varphi, s) \leftrightarroweq^{n-k} (N|\varphi, t)$, from which the required follows.

Case $n - k = 0$. We show **atoms**. We have that $Z^0_\varphi st$ iff $Z^k st$, where the latter follows from $Z^k \supseteq Z^n$ and $Z^n st$. Therefore, $Z^0_\varphi : (M|\varphi, s) \leftrightarroweq^0 (N|\varphi, t)$.

Case $n - k > 0$. We show $(n - k)$-**forth**. Let $s \sim_a s'$ and $M, s' \models \varphi$, i.e., $s \sim_a s'$ in $M|\varphi$. From $Z^n : (M, s) \leftrightarroweq^n (N, t)$ and $s \sim_a s'$ follows that there is a $t' \sim_a t$ such that $Z^{n-1} : (M, s') \leftrightarroweq^{n-1} (N, t')$. As $n - k = n - d(\varphi) > 0$, $d(\varphi) < n$, so $d(\varphi) \leq n - 1$. From $Z^{n-1} : (M, s') \leftrightarroweq^{n-1} (N, t')$, $M, s' \models \varphi$ and $d(\varphi) \leq n - 1$ it follows by bisimulation invariance that $N, t' \models \varphi$. Therefore t' is in the domain of $N|\varphi$. By induction, from $Z^{n-1} : (M, s') \leftrightarroweq^{n-1} (N, t')$ it follows that $Z^{n-k-1}_\varphi : (M|\varphi, s') \leftrightarroweq^{n-k-1} (N|\varphi, t')$. Therefore, t' satisfies the requirement for $(n - k)$-**forth** for relation Z^{n-k}_φ.

The clause $(n - k)$-**back** is shown similarly.

Proposition 1. $(M, s) \leftrightarroweq^Q (N, t)$ *implies* $(M, s) \equiv^Q_{SAPAL} (N, t)$ *and implies* $(M, s) \equiv^Q_{SCAPAL} (N, t)$.

Proof. The proof is by induction on formulas true in (M, s). The crucial case quantifier is satisfied because (let $R \subseteq Q$): $M, s \models [R]\varphi$, iff $M, s \models [\psi]\varphi$ for all $\psi \in \mathcal{L}_{PAL}|R$, iff for all $\psi \in \mathcal{L}_{PAL}|R$, $M, s \models \psi$ implies $M|\psi, s \models \varphi$, iff (induction, Cor. 1) for all $\psi \in \mathcal{L}_{PAL}|R$, $N, s \models \psi$ implies $N|\psi, s \models \varphi$, iff $(\ldots)$ $N, s \models [R]\varphi$.

The proof for SCAPAL is similar.

3 Modal Properties of the Quantifiers

We continue by discussing some peculiarities of the semantics, where we focus on modal properties of the quantifiers. We recall that APAL satisfies: $[!]\varphi \to \varphi$ (T), $[!]\varphi \to [!][!]\varphi$ (4), $\langle ! \rangle [!]\varphi \to [!]\langle ! \rangle\varphi$ (CR), and $[!]\langle ! \rangle\varphi \to \langle ! \rangle [!]\varphi$ (MK) [7,18].

3.1 SAPAL and FSAPAL

The logic SAPAL generalizes APAL, as $[P]\varphi$ is equivalent to $[!]\varphi$. We also considered FSAPAL where $Q \subseteq P$ in $[Q]\varphi$ is required to be finite.

Proposition 2. *SAPAL-valid are* $[Q]\varphi \to \varphi$ *(T) and* $[Q \cup R]\varphi \to [Q][R]\varphi$ *(4)*

Proof. The validity of $[Q]\varphi \to \varphi$ follows from the validity of $[\top]\varphi \leftrightarrow \varphi$. Just as for APAL, $[Q \cup R]\varphi \to [Q][R]\varphi$ is valid because two announcements can be made into one announcement, as in the PAL validity $[\psi][\chi]\varphi \leftrightarrow [\psi \wedge [\psi]\chi]\varphi$, and because $P(\psi \wedge [\psi]\chi) \subseteq Q \cup R$ if $P(\psi) \subseteq Q$ and $P(\chi) \subseteq R$.

Concerning $\langle Q\rangle[R]\varphi \to [Q]\langle R\rangle\varphi$ (CR) and $[Q]\langle R\rangle\varphi \to \langle Q\rangle[R]\varphi$ (MK) the first is invalid in SAPAL (counterexample omitted) and we do not know whether the second one is valid, but this seems unlikely. The proof of their APAL validity consists in first announcing the value of all variables occurring in the formula φ, and then using that φ is true in the subsequent model restriction iff it is valid on that restriction. This announcement cannot be made if $Q \cup R \subset P(\varphi)$.

3.2 SCAPAL

The SCAPAL quantifier does not distribute over conjunction: $[\subseteq]\varphi \wedge [\subseteq]\psi$ is not equivalent to $[\subseteq](\varphi \wedge \psi)$. This is easily demonstrated by an example.

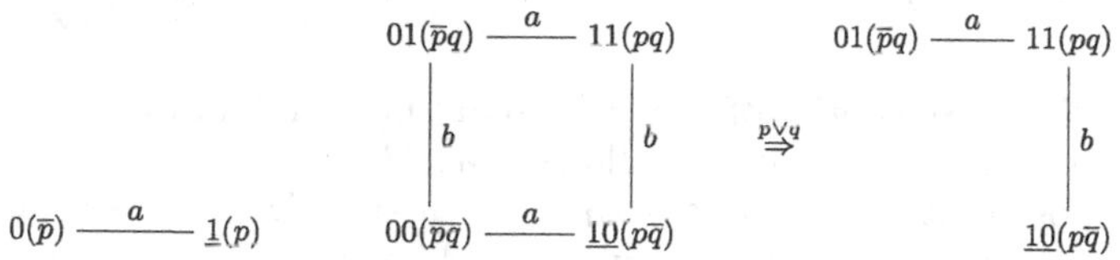

Fig. 2. Model $(N, 1)$ on the left, $(M, 10)$ in the middle, $(M|(p \vee q), 10)$ on the right.

Example 1. Consider model $(M, 10)$ in Fig. 2 ($p\bar{q}$: p is true and q is false). Then:

$$M, 10 \not\models [\subseteq]((K_a p \to K_b K_a p) \wedge \neg q)$$
$$M, 10 \models [\subseteq](K_a p \to K_b K_a p)$$
$$M, 10 \models [\subseteq]\neg q$$

The first is false because, as depicted:

$$M, 10 \models \langle p \vee q\rangle(K_a p \wedge \neg K_b K_a p), \text{ so}$$
$$M, 10 \models \langle p \vee q\rangle((K_a p \wedge \neg K_b K_a p) \vee q), \text{ and therefore}$$
$$M, 10 \models \langle\subseteq\rangle((K_a p \wedge \neg K_b K_a p) \vee q), \text{ which is equivalent to}$$
$$M, 10 \not\models [\subseteq]((K_a p \to K_b K_a p) \wedge \neg q).$$

The second is true because the only model restrictions containing 10 that we can obtain with formulas involving p are $\{10, 11\}$ and $\{10, 11, 00, 01\}$. The third is true because q is false in state 10.

Therefore, $[\subseteq]\varphi \wedge [\subseteq]\psi$ is not equivalent to $[\subseteq](\varphi \wedge \psi)$.

Proposition 3. *Valid in SCAPAL are:* $[\subseteq]\varphi \rightarrow \varphi$ *(T),* $[\subseteq]\varphi \rightarrow [\subseteq][\subseteq]\varphi$ *(F),* $[\subseteq]\langle\subseteq\rangle\varphi \rightarrow \langle\subseteq\rangle[\subseteq]\varphi$ *(MK) and* $\langle\subseteq\rangle[\subseteq]\varphi \rightarrow [\subseteq]\langle\subseteq\rangle\varphi$ *(CR).*

Proof. T and 4 are valid for the same reason as in SAPAL. For CR and MK we can now (unlike for SAPAL) use the same method as in APAL, as in any state of a model we can announce the value of all variables occurring in φ. A proof of CR is found in [18, Prop. 3.10] (for the similar logic APAL$^+$), which corrects the incorrect proof of CR for APAL in [7]). A proof of MK it is found in [7].

3.3 QIPAL and IPAL

We recall that in APAL the quantification is over $\varphi \in \mathcal{L}_{PAL}$. Fairly complex counterexamples demonstrate that $[!]\varphi \rightarrow [\psi]\varphi$ is invalid for certain $\psi \in \mathcal{L}_{APAL}$ containing quantifiers. Now in $[\psi^{\downarrow}]\varphi$, $\psi \in \mathcal{L}_{QIPAL}$ may also contain quantifiers. This makes the relation to $[!]$ unclear. In $\mathcal{L}_{IPAL}$, that ψ must be in $\mathcal{L}_{PAL}$ and the relation is clearer.

Proposition 4. *Let* $\psi \in \mathcal{L}_{PAL}$, $\chi \in \mathcal{L}_{IPAL}$ *and pointed model* (M, s) *be given. The following are equivalent:*

1. $M, s \models \langle\psi^{\downarrow}\rangle\chi$
2. *there is a* $\varphi \in \mathcal{L}_{PAL}$ *such that* $\models \varphi \rightarrow \psi$ *and* $M, s \models \langle\varphi\rangle\chi$,
3. *there is a* $\varphi \in \mathcal{L}_{PAL}$ *such that* $M \models \varphi \rightarrow \psi$ *and* $M, s \models \langle\varphi\rangle\chi$,
4. *there is a* $\varphi \in \mathcal{L}_{PAL}$ *such that* $M, s \models \langle\varphi \wedge \psi\rangle\chi$.

Proof.

$1 \Leftrightarrow 2$ This is the semantics of the $\langle\psi^{\downarrow}\rangle$ quantifier (in dual form).

$2 \Rightarrow 3$ From $\models \varphi \rightarrow \psi$ it trivially follows that $M \models \varphi \rightarrow \psi$.

$3 \Rightarrow 4$ Suppose that there is a $\varphi \in \mathcal{L}_{PAL}$ such that $M \models \varphi \rightarrow \psi$ and $M, s \models \langle\varphi\rangle\chi$. Because $M \models \varphi \rightarrow \psi$, we have $M \models \varphi \leftrightarrow (\varphi \wedge \psi)$, and therefore $M|\varphi = M|(\varphi \wedge \psi)$. From $M, s \models \langle\varphi\rangle\chi$ then follows that $M, s \models \langle\varphi\wedge\psi\rangle\chi$.

$4 \Rightarrow 2$ Suppose that there is a $\varphi \in \mathcal{L}_{PAL}$ such that $M, s \models \langle\varphi \wedge \psi\rangle\chi$. Let $\varphi' = \varphi \wedge \psi$, and note that $\varphi' \in \mathcal{L}_{PAL}$. We have $\models \varphi' \rightarrow \psi$ and $M, s \models \langle\varphi'\rangle\chi$.

The *positive formulas* $\mathcal{L}^{+}_{PAL}$ are the PAL-fragment $p \mid \neg p \mid \varphi \wedge \varphi \mid \varphi \vee \varphi \mid K_a\varphi \mid [\neg\varphi]\varphi$. The truth of positive formulas (corresponding to the universal fragment in first-order logic) is preserved after update [19].

Corollary 2. *Let* $\psi \in \mathcal{L}^{+}_{PAL}$. *Then* $\langle\psi^{\downarrow}\rangle\chi$ *is equivalent to* $\langle!\rangle\langle\psi\rangle\chi$.

Proof. Let $M, s \models \langle\psi^{\downarrow}\rangle\chi$. From Proposition 4.4. we obtain that there is $\varphi \in \mathcal{L}_{PAL}$ such that $M, s \models \langle\varphi \wedge \psi\rangle\chi$. As ψ is positive, from that we obtain $M, s \models \langle\varphi\rangle\langle\psi\rangle\chi$. By the definition of the APAL quantifier, it follows that $M, s \models \langle!\rangle\langle\psi\rangle\chi$.

Proposition 5. *Let* $\varphi \in \mathcal{L}_{IPAL}$. *Then* $[\top^{\downarrow}]\varphi$ *and* $[\bot^{\uparrow}]\varphi$ *are equivalent to* $[!]\varphi$.

Proof. Let model (M, s) and $\varphi \in \mathcal{L}_{QIPAL}$ be given. Then: $M, s \models [\top^{\downarrow}]\varphi$, iff $M, s \models [\psi]\varphi$ for all $\psi \in \mathcal{L}_{PAL}$ with $\models \psi \rightarrow \top$, iff $M, s \models [\psi]\varphi$ for all $\psi \in \mathcal{L}_{PAL}$, iff $M, s \models [!]\varphi$.

Similarly, $M, s \models [\bot^{\uparrow}]\varphi$, iff $M, s \models [\psi]\varphi$ for all $\psi \in \mathcal{L}_{PAL}$ with $\models \bot \rightarrow \psi$, iff $M, s \models [\psi]\varphi$ for all $\psi \in \mathcal{L}_{PAL}$, iff $M, s \models [!]\varphi$.

Proposition 6. *Valid in QIPAL are* $[\psi^{\uparrow}]\varphi \rightarrow \varphi$ *(T) and also* $[\psi^{\uparrow}]\varphi \rightarrow [\psi^{\uparrow}][\chi^{\uparrow}]\varphi$ *and* $[\psi^{\downarrow}]\varphi \rightarrow [\psi^{\downarrow}][\chi^{\downarrow}]\varphi$ *(4)*

Proof. All proofs are as in Prop. 2 and 3.

However, $[\psi^{\downarrow}]\varphi \rightarrow \varphi$ (T) is invalid. Whenever $M|\psi$ is a proper submodel of a given model M, the trivial announcement is not allowed. Also, $[\psi^{\uparrow}]\varphi \rightarrow [\chi^{\uparrow}][\psi^{\uparrow}]\varphi$ and $[\psi^{\downarrow}]\varphi \rightarrow [\chi^{\downarrow}][\psi^{\downarrow}]\varphi$ are invalid because of Moorean phenomena.

We envisage similar results for the more general QIPAL quantifier in future.

4 Expressivity

We now address the relative expressivity of APAL, FSAPAL and SCAPAL and IPAL. Given logics L and L' with languages $\mathcal{L}_L$ and $\mathcal{L}_{L'}$, L is at least as expressive as L', notation $L' \preceq L$, iff for $\varphi \in \mathcal{L}_L$ there is a $\varphi' \in \mathcal{L}_{L'}$ such that φ is equivalent to φ'. Logics L and L' are equally expressive iff $L \preceq L'$ and $L' \preceq L$, L is less expressive than L', notation $L \prec L'$, iff $L \preceq L'$ but $L' \not\preceq L$; L and L' are incomparable (in expressivity), notation $L \asymp L'$, iff $L \not\preceq L'$ and $L' \not\preceq L$.

4.1 APAL $\not\preceq$ FSAPAL and APAL $\not\preceq$ SCAPAL

We show that there is an APAL-formula that can distinguish two pointed models that cannot be distinguished by any FSAPAL-formula. We use that APAL, unlike FSAPAL, quantifies over arbitrarily many atoms. The proof is similar to the proof that APAL $\not\preceq$ PAL in [7].

Proposition 7. *APAL* $\not\preceq$ *FSAPAL and APAL* $\not\preceq$ *SCAPAL.*

Proof. Consider APAL formula $\langle ! \rangle (K_a p \wedge \neg K_b K_a p)$, and assume towards a contradiction that ψ is an equivalent FSAPAL formula. Let $q \notin P(\psi)$. Now consider models $(M, 10)$ and $(N, 1)$ in Fig. 2 (where the value of q in states 0 and 1 of N is irrelevant). These models are p-bisimilar. We now have that:

1. $M, 10 \models \langle ! \rangle (K_a p \wedge \neg K_b K_a p)$ (observe $M|(p \vee q)$ in Fig. 2)
2. $N, 1 \not\models \langle ! \rangle (K_a p \wedge \neg K_b K_a p)$
3. $M, 10 \models \psi$ iff $N, 1 \models \psi$ ($(M, 10) \leftrightarroweq^p (N, 1)$ implies $(M, 10) \equiv^p_{FSAPAL} (N, 1)$ by Proposition 1)

This is a contradiction. Therefore APAL $\not\preceq$ FSAPAL.

As Proposition 1 also applies to SCAPAL, this also proves that APAL $\not\preceq$ SCAPAL.

4.2 SCAPAL $\not\preceq$ APAL and FSAPAL $\not\preceq$ APAL

The proof is similar to that of the previous section, but more involved. We now show that the assumption that there is an APAL formula ψ equivalent to SCAPAL formula $\langle\subseteq\rangle(\neg q \wedge K_a p \wedge \neg K_b K_a p)$ leads to a contradiction. Prior to that we present models and lemmas used in the proof.

Consider models M_n and N_n as follows, where $n \in \mathbb{N}$ is odd. Model $M_n = (S, \sim, V)$ is such that (i) $S = [0, 2n-1]$, (ii) for any $i < n$, $2i \sim_b (2i+1)$ and, except for $i = 0$, $(2i-1) \sim_a 2i$ and also $(2n-1) \sim_a 0$, and (iii) for any $i < n$, variable p is true in states $2i$, variable q is only true in state n and variable r is always false. Model N_n is like model M_n except that variable r is only true in n and variable q is always false. Figure 3 depicts M_3 and N_3.

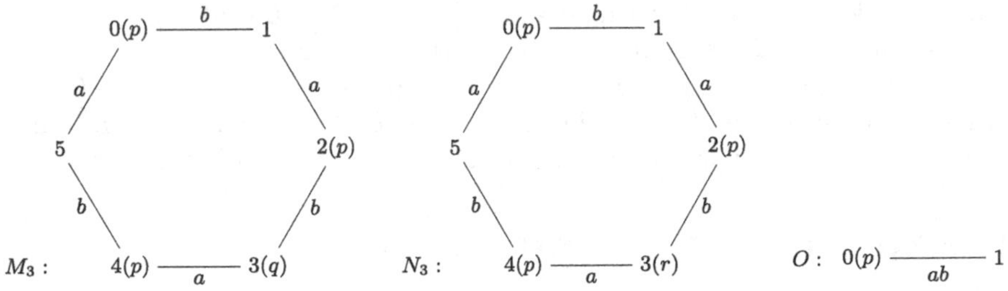

Fig. 3. The models M_3 and N_3

Lemma 3. *Let $M \subseteq M_n$, $N \subseteq N_n$, $i, j, k \in \mathbb{N}$, with $i \in \mathcal{D}(M)$ and $j \in \mathcal{D}(N)$. If $(M, i) \simeq^k (N, j)$, then for all $\chi \in \mathcal{L}_{PAL}$ such that $M, i \models \chi$ there is a $\chi' \in \mathcal{L}_{PAL}$ such that $N, j \models \chi'$ and $M|\chi \simeq^k N|\chi'$.*

Proof. All subsets of M_n and all subsets of N_n are distinguishable in $\mathcal{L}_{EL}$ (where we use that PAL is as expressive as EL), using the distance from the q-state respectively r-state.[1] Also, any proper submodel of M_n or N_n, where without loss of generality we only consider connected submodels containing the evaluation point, is a finite chain of alternating a-links and b-links of which all subsets are distinguishable, using that both edges of the chain are distinguishable: either a or b knows either p or $\neg p$ in one edge but not in the other edge, except for the singleton model that however is a trivial case.

Lemma 4. *Let $M \subseteq M_n$, $N \subseteq N_n$ and $i, j, k \in \mathbb{N}$, with $i \in \mathcal{D}(M)$ and $j \in \mathcal{D}(N)$. If $(M, i) \simeq^k (N, j)$, then $(M, i) \equiv^k_{APAL} (N, j)$.*

Proof. We show the equivalent formulation:

[1] For example, state 0 is M_3 is distinguished by $\hat{K}_b\hat{K}_a\hat{K}_b q \wedge \neg\hat{K}_a\hat{K}_b q$; 0 is the unique state where we can get with three steps but not with two.

For all $\varphi \in \mathcal{L}_{APAL}$, $M \subseteq M_n$, $N \subseteq N_n$ and $i, j, k \in \mathbb{N}$ with $i \in \mathcal{D}(M)$ and $j \in \mathcal{D}(N)$: if $(M, i) \simeq^k (N, j)$ and $d(\varphi) \leq k$, then $M, i \models \varphi$ iff $N, j \models \varphi$.

The proof is by induction on the structure of φ. The cases of interest are $K_b\varphi$, $[\psi]\varphi$, and $[!]\varphi$. As k-bisimilarity is a symmetric relation, it suffices to show only one direction of the equivalence.

Case $K_a\varphi$**:** Suppose $d(K_a\varphi) \leq k$. We have $M, i \models K_a\varphi$ iff for all $i' \sim_a i$, $M, i' \models \varphi$. As $(M, i) \simeq^n (N, j)$, for all $j' \sim_a j$ there is some $i' \sim_a i$ such that $(M, i') \simeq^{k-1} (N, j')$. As $d(K_a\varphi) \leq n$, $d(\varphi) \leq k - 1$. Therefore, by induction, $N, j' \models \varphi$. And therefore $N, j \models K_a\varphi$.

Case $[\psi]\varphi$**:** Suppose $d([\psi]\varphi) \leq k$, and $M, i \models [\psi]\varphi$. Let $d(\psi) = x$ and $d(\varphi) = y$, then $x + y = d(\psi) + d(\varphi) = d([\psi]\varphi) \leq k$. By definition, $M, i \models [\psi]\varphi$ iff $M, i \models \psi$ implies $M|\psi, i \models \varphi$. From $M, i \models \psi$, $(M, i) \simeq^k (N, j)$ and $d(\psi) = x \leq k$ and induction we obtain $N, j \models \psi$. From $(M, i) \simeq^k (N, j)$, $M, i \models \psi$, $d(\psi) = x \leq k - y$, a part identical to that of Lemma 2 except that where bisimulation invariance for PAL is used on $\psi \in \mathcal{L}_{PAL}$ we now use induction on $\psi \in \mathcal{L}_{APAL}$, we obtain that $(M|\psi, i) \simeq^y (N|\psi, j)$. From that, $M|\psi, i \models \varphi$, $d(\varphi) = y$ and induction we obtain $N|\psi, j \models \varphi$. Then, $N, j \models \psi$ implies $N|\psi, j \models \varphi$ is by definition $N, j \models [\psi]\varphi$.

Case $[!]\varphi$**:**
$M, i \models [!]\varphi$, iff
$M, i \models [\psi]\varphi$ for all $\psi \in \mathcal{L}_{PAL}$, iff
$M, i \models \psi$ implies $M|\psi, i \models \varphi$ for all $\psi \in \mathcal{L}_{PAL}$, iff (Lemma 3)
$N, j \models \psi'$ implies $N|\psi', i \models \varphi$ for all $\psi' \in \mathcal{L}_{PAL}$, iff
$N, j \models [\psi']\varphi$ for all $\psi' \in \mathcal{L}_{PAL}$, iff
$N, j \models [!]\varphi$.

Proposition 8. *SCAPAL* $\not\preceq$ *APAL.*

Proof. Consider $\mathcal{L}_{SCAPAL}$ formula $\varphi = \langle\subseteq\rangle(\neg q \wedge K_a p \wedge \neg K_b K_a p)$. Let ψ be the supposedly equivalent $\mathcal{L}_{APAL}$ formula. Take $n > d(\psi)$. We now show that:

1. $M_n, 0 \models \langle\subseteq\rangle(\neg q \wedge K_a p \wedge \neg K_b K_a p)$
2. $N_n, 0 \not\models \langle\subseteq\rangle(\neg q \wedge K_a p \wedge \neg K_b K_a p)$
3. $M_n, 0 \models \psi$ iff $N_n, 0 \models \psi$

These items are proved by the following arguments:

1. The state n is distinguished by formula q. This allows us to distinguish each finite subset of the domain, in the usual way, in $\mathcal{L}_{EL}$ (note that there is no mirror symmetry along the 0—n 'diameter' of the circular models M_n and N_n). Thus there is a formula $\eta \in \mathcal{L}_{EL}|q$ that distinguishes the set of states $\{0, 1\}$. We now have that:

$$\begin{array}{l} M_n, 0 \models \eta \\ M_n|\eta, 0 \models \neg q \wedge K_a p \wedge \neg K_b K_a p \\ M_n, 0 \models \langle\eta\rangle(\neg q \wedge K_a p \wedge \neg K_b K_a p) \\ M_n, 0 \models \langle\subseteq\rangle(\neg q \wedge K_a p \wedge \neg K_b K_a p) \end{array}$$

2. On the other hand, $N_n, 0 \not\models \langle\subseteq\rangle(\neg q \wedge K_a p \wedge \neg K_b K_a p)$. This is because we cannot use that r is only true in n, as $r \notin P(\neg q \wedge K_a p \wedge \neg K_b K_a p)$, and because $(N_n, 0) \simeq^{pq} (O, 0)$. Clearly $O, 0 \not\models \langle\subseteq\rangle(\neg q \wedge K_a p \wedge \neg K_b K_a p)$.
3. However, $M_n, 0 \models \psi$ iff $N_n, 0 \models \psi$. This follows from Lemma 4, as $n > d(\psi)$ and $(M_n, 0) \leftrightarroweq^{d(\psi)} (N_n, 0)$.

Proposition 9. *FSAPAL* $\not\preceq$ *APAL.*

Proof. As Proposition 8, but we now take FSAPAL formula $\langle q\rangle(\neg q \wedge K_a p \wedge \neg K_b K_a p)$ instead of SCAPAL formula $\langle\subseteq\rangle(\neg q \wedge K_a p \wedge \neg K_b K_a p)$.

As $[!]\varphi$ is equivalent to $[P]\varphi$ we rather trivially have that APAL $\preceq$ SAPAL, so that with Proposition 9 and its consequence SAPAL $\not\preceq$ APAL we immediately obtain:

Corollary 3. *APAL* $\prec$ *SAPAL.*

4.3 SCAPAL $\prec$ FSAPAL

Proposition 10. *SCAPAL* $\preceq$ *FSAPAL.*

Proof. It is trivial that SCAPAL $\preceq$ FSAPAL, since $\models [\subseteq]\varphi \leftrightarrow [P(\varphi)]\varphi$. Formally, we inductively define a translation function f from SCAPAL to FSAPAL by

$$\begin{array}{lll} f(p) = p & f(\varphi \vee \psi) = f(\varphi) \vee f(\psi) & f([\varphi]\psi) = [f(\varphi)]f(\psi) \\ f(\neg\varphi) = \neg f(\varphi) & f(K_a\varphi) = K_a f(\varphi) & f([\subseteq]\varphi) = [P(\varphi)]f(\varphi) \end{array}$$

In the final line we could equivalently have written $f([\subseteq]\varphi) = [P(f(\varphi))]f(\varphi)$, as f does not affect the set of atoms that occur in a formula. We then have $\models \varphi \leftrightarrow f(\varphi)$ (which is shown by induction), and therefore SCAPAL $\preceq$ FSAPAL.

We now show SCAPAL $\prec$ FSAPAL. In the proof we use models $M_{-n,n}$ and $N_{-n,n}$ similar to M_n and N_n used in the previous subsection. They are depicted in Fig. 4 for $n = 3$, compare to Fig. 3. (Imagine 'cutting open' M_3 and N_3 at the q resp. r state, and remove r as we can now use the distinguishing power of p on the edges of the chain.) Similarly to Lemma 4, we first show a Lemma 5.

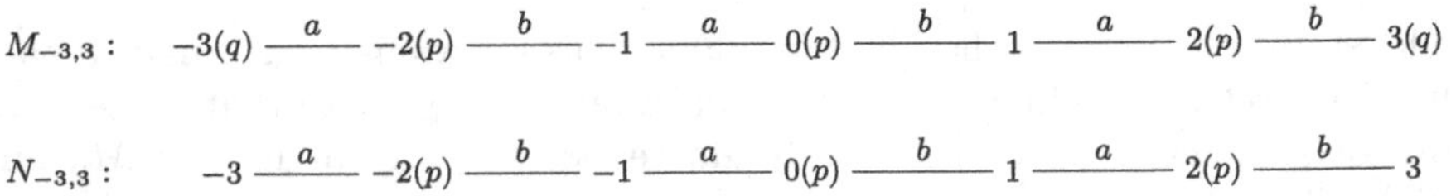

Fig. 4. The models $M_{-3,3}$ and $N_{-3,3}$

Lemma 5. *Let* $M \subseteq M_{-n,n}$, $N \subseteq N_{-n,n}$ *and* $i, j, k \in \mathbb{N}$, *with* $i \in \mathcal{D}(M)$ *and* $j \in \mathcal{D}(N)$. *If* $(M, i) \simeq^k (N, j)$, *then* $(M, i) \equiv^k_{SCAPAL} (N, j)$.

Proof. We show by formula induction that $M, i \models \varphi$ iff $N, j \models \varphi$ for any $\varphi \in \mathcal{L}_{SCAPAL}$ with $d(\varphi) \leq k$. Cases $K_a\psi$ and $[\chi]\psi$ are the same. The case quantifier $[\subseteq]\psi$ is different and shown as follows.

First, suppose that $q \notin P(\psi)$. Then from $(M, i) \leftrightarrows^{P(\psi)} (N, j)$ and Lemma 1 it directly follows that $M, i \models [\subseteq]\psi$ iff $N, j \models [\subseteq]\psi$.

Next, suppose that $q \in P(\psi)$; w.l.o.g. we may also assume that $p \in P(\psi)$. By assumption, $(M, i) \leftrightarrows^k (N, j)$. Just as for Lemma 3, every $M' \subseteq M$ is definable in M by a formula in $\mathcal{L}_{PAL}|pq$, and every $N' \subseteq N$ is definable in N by a formula in $\mathcal{L}_{PAL}|pq$. It follows that for every $\chi \in \mathcal{L}_{PAL}|pq$ with $M, i \models \chi$ there is a $\xi \in \mathcal{L}_{PAL}|pq$ such that $(M|\chi, i) \leftrightarrows^k (N|\xi, j)$, and vice versa. Therefore, $M, i \models [\subseteq]\psi$ iff $N, j \models [\subseteq]\psi$.

Proposition 11. *SCAPAL* $\prec$ *FSAPAL.*

Proof. We proceed as usual, however, with distinguishing FSAPAL formula $\langle q \rangle(K_a p \wedge \neg K_b K_a p)$. Let ψ be the supposedly equivalent $\mathcal{L}_{SCAPAL}$ formula. Take $n > d(\psi)$. Then:

1. $M_{-n,n}, 0 \models \langle q \rangle(K_a p \wedge \neg K_b K_a p)$
2. $N_{-n,n}, 0 \not\models \langle q \rangle(K_a p \wedge \neg K_b K_a p)$ (obvious)
3. $M_{-n,n}, 0 \models \psi$ iff $N_{-n,n}, 0 \models \psi$ (use $(M_{-n,n}, 0) \leftrightarrows^{d(\psi)} (N_{-n,n}, 0)$ & Lemma 5)

4.4 IPAL

Proposition 12. *APAL* $\preceq$ *IPAL.*

Proof. This follows from Prop. 5 that $[\top^{\downarrow}]\varphi$ is equivalent to $[!]\varphi$.

We also obtained strictness, by a rather involved proof that is omitted from the submission for space constraints and therefore called a conjecture.

Conjecture 1. *APAL* $\prec$ *IPAL.*

The relative expressivity between IPAL and FSAPAL/SCAPAL mirrors the results already obtained between APAL and FSAPAL/SCAPAL.

Proposition 13. *IPAL* $\asymp$ *FSAPAL and IPAL* $\asymp$ *SCAPAL.*

Proof. FSAPAL $\not\preceq$ IPAL and SCAPAL $\not\preceq$ IPAL are shown as FSAPAL $\not\preceq$ APAL (Proposition 9) and SCAPAL $\not\preceq$ APAL (Proposition 8), except that in the inductive case for the quantifier of the proof of Lemma 4 we do not consider all witnesses ψ for the quantifier $\langle ! \rangle$ but only those that imply the given χ in $\langle \chi^{\downarrow} \rangle$ or that are implied by the given χ in $\langle \chi^{\downarrow} \rangle$.

From APAL $\preceq$ IPAL, APAL $\not\preceq$ FSAPAL and APAL $\not\preceq$ SCAPAL (Prop. 7), we immediately obtain IPAL $\not\preceq$ FSAPAL and IPAL $\not\preceq$ SCAPAL.

5 Substructural Implication, PAL and IPAL

The satisfaction clause for IPAL announcements $[\varphi^{\downarrow}]\psi$ is loosely inspired by the satisfaction clause for substructural implication $\varphi \Rightarrow \psi$ in the relational semantics for substructural logics [32,33] and the informational interpretation of the semantics. Relational models for substructural logics comprise a set of states S and a *ternary* accessibility relation R on S. The substructural implication is a box-like binary modal operator with the following satisfaction clause:

$$x \Vdash \varphi \Rightarrow \psi \iff (\forall y, z \in S)(Rxyz \;\&\; y \Vdash \varphi \implies z \Vdash \psi)$$

Dunn and Restall point out that "perhaps the best reading [of $Rxyz$] is to say that the combination of the pieces of information x and y (not necessarily the union) is a piece of information in z" [20, p. 67]. Restall adds that "a body of information warrants $\varphi \Rightarrow \psi$ if and only if whenever you *update* that information with new information which warrants φ, the resulting (perhaps new) body of information warrants ψ" [31, p. 362] (notation adjusted).

On the informational reading, substructural implication clearly resembles an information update operator. It is therefore natural to inquire into the similarities and differences between substructural implication and epistemic update operators such as public announcements. Similarities between substructural logic and information update have been noted before. Van Benthem [12,13] observes that various *dynamic consequence relations*, arising from defining consequence in terms of the effects of successive updates (such that $\varphi \Rightarrow \psi$ roughly corresponds to $[\varphi]\psi$), lack most of the standard structural properties. Aucher [3,5] observes that dynamic epistemic logic can be seen as a two-sorted substructural logic and that the product update is a special case of the ternary accessibility relation.

Differences between substructural logics and PAL are plentiful. For example, the former are closed under substitution and the latter contains Boolean negation and conservatively extends classical propositional logic. The aspect of substructural implication that directly influenced our formulation of the IPAL$^{\downarrow}$ announcement is that *multiple bodies of information y supporting φ* are taken into account when evaluating $\varphi \Rightarrow \psi$. This aspect is easily incorporated in PAL by requiring that, in evaluating "after announcing φ, ψ is the case" in (M, s), we have to look at multiple submodels N of M containing s such that φ is satisfied in *all* states in N. This is precisely what the satisfaction clause for $[\varphi^{\downarrow}]\psi$ requires. This new $[\varphi^{\downarrow}]$ operator has interesting properties that we wish to explore later. For example, Proposition 6 established $[\psi^{\downarrow}]\varphi \rightarrow [\psi^{\downarrow}][\chi^{\downarrow}]\varphi$ which translates into the substructural property of *right weakening* 'from $\psi \Rightarrow \varphi$ infer $\psi, \chi \Rightarrow \varphi$'; whereas 'van Benthem' dynamic consequence does not satisfy right weakening.

6 Conclusions and Further Research

We investigated the expressivity of the logics FSAPAL, SCAPAL and IPAL. Let us finally also observe that their axiomatizations promise to be very similar to that of APAL, and we also expect these logics still to have undecidable satisfiability problems. The use of the IPAL quantification $[\varphi^{\downarrow}]\psi$ to model substructural implication $\varphi \Rrightarrow \psi$ clearly needs further research.

Acknowledgements. We thank the reviewers for their comments. Hans van Ditmarsch is also affiliated to IMSc, Chennai, India, as a research associate.

References

1. Ågotnes, T., Balbiani, P., van Ditmarsch, H., Seban, P.: Group announcement logic. J. Appl. Logic **8**, 62–81 (2010)
2. Ågotnes, T., van Ditmarsch, H., French, T.: The undecidability of quantified announcements. Studia Logica **104**(4), 597–640 (2016)
3. Aucher, G.: Dynamic epistemic logic as a substructural logic. In: Baltag, A., Smets, S. (eds.) Johan van Benthem on Logic and Information Dynamics. OCL, vol. 5, pp. 855–880. Springer, Cham (2014). https://doi.org/10.1007/978-3-319-06025-5_33
4. Aucher, G., Bolander, T.: Undecidability in epistemic planning. In: Rossi, F. (ed.) Proceedings of 23rd IJCAI, pp. 27–33 (2013)
5. Aucher, G.: Dynamic epistemic logic in update logic. J. Logic Comput. **26**(6), 1913–1960 (2016)
6. Aumann, R.: Agreeing to disagree. Ann. Stat. **4**(6), 1236–1239 (1976)
7. Balbiani, P., Baltag, A., van Ditmarsch, H., Herzig, A., Hoshi, T., Lima, T.D.: 'Knowable' as 'known after an announcement'. Rev. Symbolic Logic **1**(3), 305–334 (2008)
8. Balbiani, P., van Ditmarsch, H.: A simple proof of the completeness of APAL. Stud. Logic **8**(1), 65–78 (2015)
9. Baltag, A., Moss, L., Solecki, S.: The logic of public announcements, common knowledge, and private suspicions. In: Proceedings of 7th TARK, pp. 43–56. Morgan Kaufmann (1998)
10. Baltag, A., Özgün, A., Vargas Sandoval, A.L.: APAL with memory is better. In: Moss, L.S., de Queiroz, R., Martinez, M. (eds.) WoLLIC 2018. LNCS, vol. 10944, pp. 106–129. Springer, Heidelberg (2018). https://doi.org/10.1007/978-3-662-57669-4_6
11. van Benthem, J.: Semantic parallels in natural language and computation. In: Logic Colloquium '87. North-Holland, Amsterdam (1989)
12. van Benthem, J.: Structural properties of dynamic reasoning. In: Peregrin, J. (ed.) Meaning: The Dynamic Turn, pp. 15–31. Elsevier, Amsterdam (2003)
13. van Benthem, J.: Logical dynamics meets logical pluralism? Austr. J. Logic **6**, 182–209 (2008)
14. Blackburn, P., de Rijke, M., Venema, Y.: Modal Logic. Cambridge University Press, Cambridge (2001)
15. Bolander, T., Andersen, M.: Epistemic planning for single and multi-agent systems. J. Appl. Non-classical Logics **21**(1), 9–34 (2011)
16. Charrier, T., Schwarzentruber, F.: Arbitrary public announcement logic with mental programs. In: Proceedings of AAMAS, pp. 1471–1479. ACM (2015)
17. van Ditmarsch, H., French, T.: Quantifying over Boolean announcements (2018). https://arxiv.org/abs/1712.05310
18. van Ditmarsch, H., French, T., Hales, J.: Positive announcements. Studia Logica (2020). https://doi.org/10.1007/s11225-020-09922-1, https://arxiv.org/abs/1803.01696

19. van Ditmarsch, H., Kooi, B.: The secret of my success. Synthese **151**, 201–232 (2006)
20. Dunn, J.M., Restall, G.: Relevance logic. In: Gabbay, D.M., Guenthner, F. (eds.) Handbook of Philosophical Logic, 2nd edn., vol. 6, pp. 1–128. Kluwer (2002)
21. van Emde Boas, P., Groenendijk, J., Stokhof, M.: The Conway paradox: its solution in an epistemic framework. Truth Interpretation and Information, pp. 159–182. Foris Publications, Dordrecht (1984)
22. French, T., van Ditmarsch, H.: Undecidability for arbitrary public announcement logic. In: Advances in Modal Logic 7, pp. 23–42. College Publications (2008)
23. Galimullin, R.: Coalition announcements. Ph.D. thesis, University of Nottingham, UK (2019)
24. Gerbrandy, J., Groeneveld, W.: Reasoning about information change. J. Logic Lang. Inf. **6**, 147–169 (1997)
25. Hilpinen, R.: Remarks on personal and impersonal knowledge. Can. J. Philos. **7**, 1–9 (1977)
26. Hintikka, J.: Knowledge and Belief. Cornell University Press (1962)
27. McCarthy, J.: Formalization of two puzzles involving knowledge. In: Lifschitz, V. (ed.) Formalizing Common Sense: Papers by John McCarthy. Ablex Publishing Corporation, Norwood (1990)
28. Moore, G.: A reply to my critics. In: Schilpp, P. (ed.) The Philosophy of G.E. Moore, pp. 535–677. Northwestern University, Evanston (1942)
29. Moses, Y., Dolev, D., Halpern, J.: Cheating husbands and other stories: a case study in knowledge, action, and communication. Distrib. Comput. **1**(3), 167–176 (1986)
30. Plaza, J.: Logics of public communications. In: Proceedings of the 4th ISMIS, pp. 201–216. Oak Ridge National Laboratory (1989)
31. Restall, G.: Relevant and substructural logics. In: Gabbay, D., Woods, J. (eds.) Handbook of the History of Logic, vol. 7, pp. 289–398. Elsevier (2006)
32. Restall, G.: An Introduction to Substrucutral Logics. Routledge, London (2000)
33. Routley, R., Meyer, R.K.: Semantics of entailment. In: Leblanc, H. (ed.) Truth, Syntax and Modality, pp. 194–243. North Holland, Amsterdam (1973)

Constructive Dynamic Logic of Relation Changers

Ryo Hatano[1(✉)] and Katsuhiko Sano[2]

[1] Tokyo University of Science, 2641 Yamazaki, Noda, Chiba, Japan
r-hatano@rs.tus.ac.jp
[2] Hokkaido University, Nishi 7 Chome, Kita 10 Jo, Kita-ku, Sapporo, Hokkaido, Japan
v-sano@let.hokudai.ac.jp

Abstract. This paper proposes an intuitionistic generalization of van Benthem and Liu's dynamic logic of relation changers, where relation changers are dynamic operators which rewrite each agent's accessibility relation. We employ Nishimura's Kripke semantics for a constructive propositional dynamic logic to define the semantics of relation changers. A sound and complete axiomatization of the constructive dynamic logic of relation changers is provided. Moreover, we follow Hatano et al.'s approach to provide a different semantics for dynamic logic of relation changers, where relation changers are regarded as bounded morphisms. This alternative semantics leads us to a semantic completeness proof of the axiomatization for the original semantics, which does not require a reduction strategy based on recursion axioms.

Keywords: Dynamic epistemic logic · Relation changers · Bounded morphisms · Complete axiomatization · Intuitionistic Logic

1 Introduction

Dynamic epistemic logic [7] is a family of expansions of a modal logic (in particular, epistemic logic) by dynamic operators, which often represent the knowledge change of an intelligent agent. In a standard setting, the agent's knowledge is defined in terms of a relational structure called Kripke model, and his/her knowledge change (or update) is defined as a *model transformation* triggered by a dynamic operator in dynamic epistemic logic. Although a well-known example of dynamic epistemic logic is a public announcement logic (**PAL**) [9,19], this

We would like to thank anonymous reviewers for their helpful comments and suggestions on our manuscript. Both authors were partially supported by JSPS Core-to-Core Program (A. Advanced Research Networks). The work of the second author was also partially supported by JSPS KAKENHI Grant-in-Aid for Scientific Research (C) Grant Number 19K12113 and JSPS KAKENHI Grant-in-Aid for Scientific Research (B) Grant Number 17H02258.

M. A. Martins and I. Sedlár (Eds.): DaLí 2020, LNCS 12569, pp. 137–154, 2020.
https://doi.org/10.1007/978-3-030-65840-3_9

paper focuses on dynamic logic of relation changers (**DLRC**) proposed by van Benthem and Liu [4,15].

The logic **DLRC** is an expansion of an iteration-free propositional dynamic logic [8] with a dynamic operator [r], called a *relation changer*, which updates each atomic program by a new program. As is well-known, propositional dynamic logic (**PDL**) is an expansion of modal logic that allows us to represent structured actions of programs by program constructors. In **PDL**, each atomic program a is regarded as a (primitive) computer program in information systems, and it is interpreted as a binary relation R_a. Intuitively, wR_av means that state v is reachable from state w by executing atomic program a. In **DLRC**, such an atomic program is regarded as representing knowledge (or, belief or preference) of an agent and relation changers rewrite each agent's atomic program by a new (possibly compounded) program of the iteration-free propositional dynamic logic. Examples of relation changers include a public update [4,9,13,15], an introspective announcement [7, p.58] or an eliminative command [29], a suggestion [4,15] and a radical upgrade [4,15].

Although there are several studies [4,11,12,15] on **DLRC**, all of them are based on the *classical logic*. Hence, the main purpose of this paper is to provide an *intuitionistic (or constructive) generalization* of the dynamic logic of relation changers. As far as the authors know, an intuitionistic generalization of **DLRC** has never been proposed, and the research area of *non-classical generalization* of **DLRC** has room for further investigation. This is in contrast to the study of non-classical generalizations of the public announcement logic and the logic of epistemic actions and knowledge, e.g., in [1,2,16]. In an intuitionistic generalization of **DLRC**, we regard an atomic program as an agent's (constructive) knowledge (or we restrict the agent to use only constructive inference). That is, an agent might have to deduce consequences from partial information about their world, e.g., he/she is not allowed to use the law of excluded middle for deriving possible consequences.

In a Kripke model of the (classical) propositional dynamic logic, it is assumed that a state has the *complete* information, i.e., for any formula A, A is true or $\neg A$ is true there (the law of excluded middle holds). That is, it is not allowed that neither A nor $\neg A$ holds at some state. This implies that we are allowed to use the truth of arbitrary formulas (or statement) at arbitrary states instantly in all programs (cf. [27, p.5]). In order to relax this assumption, it is desirable to have a non-classical generalization of the propositional dynamic logic that restricts us to deduce consequences of *partial information* about information systems (cf. [27]). Constructive variants of **PDL** were proposed since Leivant [14] and Nishimura [18].[1] Then, many non-classical dynamic logics for a wide-range of applications have been proposed, e.g., paraconsistent four-valued propositional dynamic logic [21], substructural propositional dynamic logic [22] and construc-

[1] As a part of the study to show the Craig interpolation theorem for **PDL**, Leivant mentioned a proof system of "simplified" constructive **PDL** which is based on logical connectives $\rightarrow$, $\neg$ and $[\alpha]$ and program constructors of **PDL**. We owe this point to Malvin Gattinger.

tive concurrent dynamic logic [27]. To define the semantics of our intuitionistic generalization of **DLRC**, this paper employs Nishimura [18]'s Kripke semantics for a constructive **PDL** where we focus on an iteration-free fragment for the sake of simplicity.

Our main contribution consists of providing a sound and complete axiomatization of an intuitionistic generalization of **DLRC** and establishing the completeness of the axiomatization with and without a reduction strategy by recursion axioms. Let us comment on the completeness proof without a reduction strategy (cf. [3,25,26]). We follow Hatano et al.'s approach [11] (the core semantic idea is: "relation changers are bounded morphisms") to provide an alternative semantics for an intuitionistic generalization of **DLRC**. This alternative semantics leads us to a *direct* proof of a semantic completeness of the axiomatization for the original semantics, which does not require the reduction strategy.

The rest of the paper is organized as follows. Section 2 provides background of **DLRC**. Section 3 proposes our intuitionistic generalization of **DLRC** and presents a Hilbert-style axiomatization of the logic based on the iteration-free constructive **PDL**. Section 4 shows the semantic completeness of our axiomatization by the well-known reduction strategy (cf. [7]). Section 5 proposes an alternative semantics for our intuitionistic generalization of **DLRC** and provides a direct proof of the semantic completeness of our axiomatization, which implies we can still keep the semantic idea of "relation changers are bounded morphisms" [11] in the intuitionistic setting. Finally, Section 6 concludes this paper with further remarks.

2 Dynamic Logic of Relation Changers

2.1 Syntax and Kripke Semantics

Let $\mathsf{PROP} = \{ p, q, \dots \}$ be a countably infinite set of *propositional variables* and $\mathsf{AP} = \{ a, b, \dots \}$ a finite set of *atomic programs*. Let us denote by $\mathcal{L}$ the syntax of the iteration-free propositional dynamic logic. We define the set $\mathsf{FORM}_{\mathcal{L}}$ of all formulas of the syntax $\mathcal{L}$ and the set $\mathsf{PR}_{\mathcal{L}}$ of all programs of the syntax $\mathcal{L}$ simultaneously by:

$$\mathsf{FORM}_{\mathcal{L}} \ni A ::= p \mid \bot \mid A \wedge A \mid A \vee A \mid A \to A \mid [\alpha]A,$$
$$\mathsf{PR}_{\mathcal{L}} \ni \alpha ::= a \mid \alpha \cup \alpha \mid \alpha ; \alpha \mid ?A.$$

where $p \in \mathsf{PROP}$ and $a \in \mathsf{AP}$. We add the relation changer $[\mathsf{r}]$ to our syntax $\mathcal{L}$ to define the expanded syntax $\mathcal{L}^{+}$. We define the sets $\mathsf{FORM}_{\mathcal{L}^+}$, $\mathsf{PR}_{\mathcal{L}^+}$ and $\mathsf{RC}_{\mathcal{L}^+}$ of all formulas, programs and relation changers, respectively, by simultaneous induction as follows.

$$\mathsf{FORM}_{\mathcal{L}^+} \ni A ::= p \mid \bot \mid A \wedge A \mid A \vee A \mid A \to A \mid [\alpha]A \mid [\mathsf{r}]A,$$
$$\mathsf{PR}_{\mathcal{L}^+} \ni \alpha ::= a \mid \alpha \cup \alpha \mid \alpha ; \alpha \mid ?A,$$
$$\mathsf{RC}_{\mathcal{L}^+} \ni \mathsf{r} ::= (a := \alpha)_{a \in \mathsf{AP}}.$$

We can regard a relation changer $\mathsf{r} = (a := \alpha_a)_{a \in \mathsf{AP}}$ (which rewrites each atomic program a with a (new possibly compounded) program α_a) as a function from AP

to $\mathsf{PR}_{\mathcal{L}^+}$, so we may use the notation $\mathsf{r}(a)$ to mean α_a. We also define the following abbreviations: $\neg A := A \to \bot$, $\top := \neg\bot$, $A \leftrightarrow B := (A \to B) \wedge (B \to A)$. Let Γ and Δ be sets of formulas and $\Box \in \{[\alpha], [\mathsf{r}]\}$. We define $\Box^{-1}\Gamma := \{A \mid \Box A \in \Gamma\}$ and $\Box\Gamma := \{\Box A \mid A \in \Gamma\}$, where it is remarked that $\Box^{-1}\Gamma \subseteq \Delta$ iff $\Gamma \subseteq \Box\Delta$.

We follow the standard reading of formulas involving programs from [10]. We read a formula $[\alpha]A$ as "after executing α, it is necessary that A," a program $\alpha \cup \beta$ "choose either α or β non-deterministically and execute the chosen one," a program $\alpha;\beta$ "execute α, then execute β" and a program $?A$ "test A, proceed if A is true, fail otherwise," respectively. A formula of the form $[\mathsf{r}]A$ stands for "after changing an accessibility relation for each program a by α_a, A holds" when $\mathsf{r} = (a := \alpha_a)_{a \in \mathsf{AP}}$.

Let us move to Kripke semantics. A *Kripke model* $\mathfrak{M}$ is a tuple $(W, (R_a)_{a\in\mathsf{AP}}, V)$ if W is a non-empty set of *possible worlds* (or *states*), $R_a \subseteq W \times W$ is an *accessibility relation* ($a \in \mathsf{AP}$), and V is a *valuation* from PROP to the powerset of W. For $(w, v) \in R_a$, we also use the infix notation wR_av. We define the *satisfaction relation* $\mathfrak{M}, w \models A$ and the *interpretation* $wR_\alpha v$ *of programs* α by simultaneous induction, as usual, except:

$$
\begin{array}{ll}
\mathfrak{M}, w \models [\alpha]A & \text{iff for all } v \in W (wR_\alpha v \text{ implies } \mathfrak{M}, v \models A),\\
wR_{\alpha\cup\beta}v & \text{iff } wR_\alpha v \text{ or } wR_\beta v,\\
wR_{\alpha;\beta}v & \text{iff for some } u \in W (wR_\alpha u \text{ and } uR_\beta v),\\
wR_{?A}v & \text{iff } w = v \text{ and } \mathfrak{M}, v \models A,\\
\mathfrak{M}, w \models [\mathsf{r}]A & \text{iff } \mathfrak{M}^{\mathsf{r}}, w \models A,
\end{array}
$$

where $\mathfrak{M}^{\mathsf{r}} = (W, (R^{\mathsf{r}}_a)_{a\in\mathsf{AP}}, V)$ and R^{r}_a is defined by:

$$R^{\mathsf{r}}_a := R_{\mathsf{r}(a)} = R_{\alpha_a} \text{ if } \mathsf{r} = (a := \alpha_a)_{a\in\mathsf{AP}}.$$

Intuitively, a relation changer r only updates (or rewrites) an accessibility relation R_a of $\mathfrak{M}$ by a (new) program $\mathsf{r}(a)$ ($= \alpha_a$). We define the *truth set* $[\![A]\!]_{\mathfrak{M}}$ of a formula A in a model $\mathfrak{M}$ by $[\![A]\!]_{\mathfrak{M}} := \{w \in W \mid \mathfrak{M}, w \models A\}$. When the underlying model $\mathfrak{M}$ is clear from the context, we simply write $[\![A]\!]$ instead of writing $[\![A]\!]_{\mathfrak{M}}$. We say that A is *valid on a model* $\mathfrak{M}$ (notation: $\mathfrak{M} \models A$) if $[\![A]\!]_{\mathfrak{M}} = W$ or $\mathfrak{M}, w \models A$ for all possible worlds $w \in W$.

By the notion of programs of iteration-free propositional dynamic logic, we can define many types of dynamic operators that only update accessibility relation of a given model. For example, a *link-cutting public update* operator [4,9,13,15] is defined as follows: $\mathsf{r}_{\dagger A} = (a := (?A; a; ?A) \cup (?\neg A; a; ?\neg A))_{a\in\mathsf{AP}}$. Intuitively, this relation changer eliminates all links between A-worlds and non-A worlds from a given model. In the following example, let us demonstrate a relation changer of *an introspective announcement* [7] (or an *eliminative command* which captures the acts of commanding in the context of deontic logic proposed by Yamada [29]).

Example 1. For the sake of simplicity, let us fix $\mathsf{AP} = \{a\}$ and consider a model $\mathfrak{M} = (W, R_a, V)$ where $W = \{w, v\}, R_a = W \times W, V(p) = \{v\}$ (see the left-hand-side of Fig. 1). Then, a relation changer $\mathsf{r}_{!p} = (a := a; ?p)$ amounts to an introspective announcement (eliminative command) with respect to p (cf. [7, 29]), i.e., $\mathsf{r}_{!p}$ eliminates all links of an accessibility relation of a to *not* p-worlds. If we update the model $\mathfrak{M}$ by this relation changer, the updated accessibility relation becomes $R_a^{\mathsf{r}_{!p}} = \{ (w, v), (v, v) \}$ (see the right-hand-side of Fig. 1). Let us also consider a relation changer $\mathsf{r}_{!(p \vee \neg p)} = (a := a; ?(p \vee \neg p))$ of introspective announcement with respect to $p \vee \neg p$. Since $p \vee \neg p$ holds at every world in the model, $\mathsf{r}_{!(p\vee\neg p)}$ does not update anything in the model, i.e., R_a is the same as $R_a^{\mathsf{r}_{!(p\vee\neg p)}}$ in $\mathfrak{M}^{\mathsf{r}_{!(p\vee\neg p)}}$.

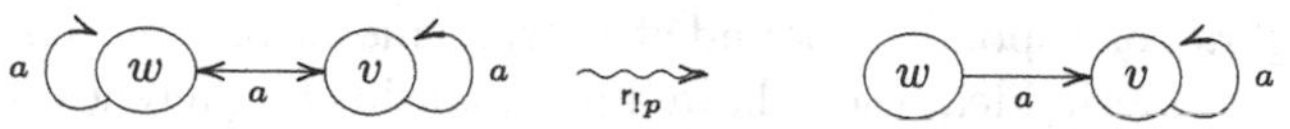

Fig. 1. Model update by introspective announcement $\mathsf{r}_{!p}$

2.2 Hilbert-style Axiomatization

Table 1 provides a Hilbert system **HDLRC** of dynamic logic of relation changers. Let us denote by $\mathbf{HPDL}^-$ a Hilbert system consisting of axioms and rules of propositional logic and additional axioms and rules of the iteration-free propositional dynamic logic in Table 1. To define **HDLRC**, we add the set of six recursion axioms together with the necessitation rule for $[\mathsf{r}]$ to the axiomatization $\mathbf{HPDL}^-$. These recursion axioms allow us to reduce the semantic completeness of **HDLRC** to that of the iteration-free propositional dynamic logic.

Table 1. Hilbert-style Axiomatizations $\mathbf{HPDL}^-$ and **HDLRC**

Axioms and Rules for Classical Logic	
(**Taut**) All instances of propositional tautologies	
(**MP**) From A and $A \to B$, infer B	
Additional Axioms and Rules for $\mathbf{HPDL}^-$	
($\mathbf{K}_{[\alpha]}$) $[\alpha](A \to B) \to ([\alpha]A \to [\alpha]B)$	($[\cup]$) $[\alpha \cup \beta]A \leftrightarrow [\alpha]A \wedge [\beta]A$
($[;]$) $[\alpha; \beta]A \leftrightarrow [\alpha][\beta]A$	($[?]$) $[?B]A \leftrightarrow (B \to A)$
($\mathbf{Nec}_{[\alpha]}$) From A, infer $[\alpha]A$	
Additional Axioms and Rules to $\mathbf{HPDL}^-$ for **HDLRC**	
($[\mathsf{r}]$**at**) $[\mathsf{r}]p \leftrightarrow p$	($[\mathsf{r}]\bot$) $[\mathsf{r}]\bot \leftrightarrow \bot$
($[\mathsf{r}]\wedge$) $[\mathsf{r}](A \wedge B) \leftrightarrow ([\mathsf{r}]A \wedge [\mathsf{r}]B)$	($[\mathsf{r}]\vee$) $[\mathsf{r}](A \vee B) \leftrightarrow ([\mathsf{r}]A \vee [\mathsf{r}]B)$
($[\mathsf{r}] \to$) $[\mathsf{r}](A \to B) \leftrightarrow ([\mathsf{r}]A \to [\mathsf{r}]B)$	($[\mathsf{r}][a]$) $[\mathsf{r}][a]A \leftrightarrow [\mathsf{r}(a)][\mathsf{r}]A$
($\mathbf{Nec}_{[\mathsf{r}]}$) From A, infer $[\mathsf{r}]A$	

Fact 1 **([4,15]).** For any formula A, A is valid in all models iff $\vdash_{\mathbf{HDLRC}} A$.

The proof in [4,15] of Fact 1 employed a reduction strategy based on recursion axioms. To be more specific, we start rewriting one of the innermost occurrences of $[\mathsf{r}]$ (this is called the *inside-out strategy*) to reduce the semantic completeness of **HDLRC** to Hilbert system $\mathbf{HPDL}^{-}$ of the iteration-free propositional dynamic logic. In contrast, Hatano et al. [11] provided an alternative proof of the semantic completeness of **HDLRC** which does not employ such a reduction strategy. Following the same spirit as in [3,26] for the public announcement logic, they provided an alternative semantics for **DLRC**, where the key idea is that relation changers correspond to bounded morphisms in one big Kripke model. Based on this semantic idea, they showed a semantic completeness of **HDLRC** for the alternative semantics by the canonical model construction, which in turn implies the semantic completeness of **HDLRC** for the original semantics. The alternative semantics has an advantage over the original Kripke semantics in that it reveals the "meaning" of recursion axioms as bounded morphisms.

3 Constructive Dynamic Logic of Relation Changers

This section extends the idea of relation changers to Nishimura's constructive propositional dynamic logic [18]. To define an intuitionistic generalization of **DLRC**, we employ exactly the same syntax $\mathcal{L}^{+}$ as the one provided in Section 2.1. In what follows, let us denote by **CDLRC** our intuitionistic generalization of **DLRC**.

Let $\leqslant$ be a *preorder* on a non-empty set W. We say that $X \subseteq W$ is *$\leqslant$-closed* (or *monotone*) if X is closed under taking $\leqslant$-successors, i.e., $w \leqslant v$ and $w \in X$ jointly imply $v \in X$, for any $w, v \in W$. Given a preorder $(W, \leqslant)$, a binary relation $R \subseteq W \times W$ is *stable* if it satisfies $\leqslant; R \subseteq R$ where ; is the relational composition. [2] An *intuitionistic* (Kripke) *model* is a tuple $(W, \leqslant, (R_a)_{a \in \mathsf{AP}}, V)$ if W is a non-empty set of possible worlds, $\leqslant$ is a preorder on W, $R_a \subseteq W \times W$ is a *stable relation* ($a \in \mathsf{AP}$), and V is a valuation from PROP to the set of all $\leqslant$-closed sets on W.

Given any intuitionistic model $\mathfrak{M} = (W, \leqslant, (R_a)_{a \in \mathsf{AP}}, V)$ and any possible worlds $w, v \in W$, we define the *satisfaction relation* $\mathfrak{M}, w \models A$ and the *interpretation of $wR_{\alpha}v$ of programs α* by simultaneous induction as follows:

[2] We may follow [28] to require that R satisfies $\leqslant; R; \leqslant \subseteq R$, which is equivalent to $\leqslant; R; \leqslant = R$. It is noted that this is a stronger condition than Nishimura [18]'s one. But, this is not a crucial difference.

$\mathfrak{M}, w \models p$ iff $w \in V(p)$,
$\mathfrak{M}, w \not\models \bot$,
$\mathfrak{M}, w \models A \wedge B$ iff $\mathfrak{M}, w \models A$ and $\mathfrak{M}, w \models B$,
$\mathfrak{M}, w \models A \vee B$ iff $\mathfrak{M}, w \models A$ or $\mathfrak{M}, w \models B$,
$\mathfrak{M}, w \models A \to B$ iff for all $v \in W(w \leqslant v$ and $\mathfrak{M}, v \models A$ imply $\mathfrak{M}, v \models B)$,
$\mathfrak{M}, w \models [\alpha]A$ iff for all $v \in W(wR_\alpha v$ implies $\mathfrak{M}, v \models A)$,
$wR_{\alpha\cup\beta}v$ iff $wR_\alpha v$ or $wR_\beta v$,
$wR_{\alpha;\beta}v$ iff for some $u \in W(wR_\alpha u$ and $uR_\beta v)$,
$wR_{?A}v$ iff $w \leqslant v$ and $\mathfrak{M}, v \models A$,
$\mathfrak{M}, w \models [\mathsf{r}]A$ iff $\mathfrak{M}^{\mathsf{r}}, w \models A$,

where $\mathfrak{M}^{\mathsf{r}} = (W, \leqslant, (R^{\mathsf{r}}_a)_{a\in\mathsf{AP}}, V)$ and R^{r}_a is defined as:

$$R^{\mathsf{r}}_a := R_{\mathsf{r}(a)} = R_{\alpha_a} \text{when } \mathsf{r} = (a := \alpha_a)_{a\in\mathsf{AP}}.$$

It is noted that the above interpretation of $R_{?A}$ is originally proposed by [18] and this is a key to obtain the monotonicity of a formula (if we replace $w \leqslant v$ with $w = v$ in the interpretation of $R_{?A}$, we lose the monotonicity, see [5]). We also use the similar definition of the *truth set* and the *validity* as provided in Section 2.1. A formula A is said to be *valid in a class* $\mathbb{M}$ *of models* if $\mathfrak{M} \models A$ for all $\mathfrak{M} \in \mathbb{M}$. We denote *the class of all models* by $\mathbb{M}_{\text{all}}$.

Proposition 2. *Given any intuitionistic model* $\mathfrak{M} = (W, \leqslant, (R_a)_{a\in\mathsf{AP}}, V)$, *any formula* A *and any program* α, (i) $[\![A]\!]_{\mathfrak{M}}$ *is* $\leqslant$*-closed and* (ii) R_α *is stable, i.e.,* $\leqslant; R_\alpha \subseteq R_\alpha$.

Example 2. Let us consider $\mathsf{AP} = \{a\}$ and an intuitionistic model $\mathfrak{M} = (W, \leqslant, R_a, V)$ where $W = \{w, v\}$, $\leqslant = \{(w,w), (v,v), (w,v)\}$, $R_a = W \times W$, $V(p) = \{v\}$, as depicted in the left-hand-side of Fig. 2 where the dotted arrow from w to v indicates the link of the preorder from w to v and the reflexive links of the preorder for w and v are omitted from the figure. For this model, one can easily check that R_a is stable and $V(p)$ is $\leqslant$-closed. Since the law of excluded middle $p \vee \neg p$ does not hold at w in $\mathfrak{M}$, $\mathfrak{M}, w \not\models [a](p \vee \neg p)$. Now, let us consider an intuitionistic model update by relation changers $\mathsf{r}_{!p}$ and $\mathsf{r}_{!(p\vee\neg p)}$. If we update the model $\mathfrak{M}$ by the relation changer $\mathsf{r}_{!p}$, then we get a new model $\mathfrak{M}^{\mathsf{r}_{!p}} = (W, \leqslant, (R^{\mathsf{r}_{!p}}_a)_{a\in\mathsf{AP}}, V)$ and $R^{\mathsf{r}_{!p}}_a = \{(w,v), (v,v)\}$ (see the right-hand-side of Fig. 2) where $\mathfrak{M}^{\mathsf{r}_{!p}}, w \models [a](p \vee \neg p)$ holds. It is noted that $\mathfrak{M}^{\mathsf{r}_{!(p\vee\neg p)}}$ and $\mathfrak{M}^{\mathsf{r}_{!p}}$ are the same.

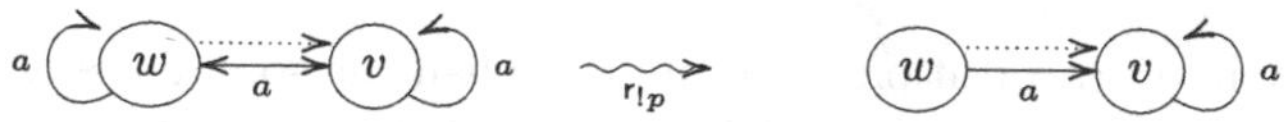

Fig. 2. Intuitionistic model update by introspective announcement $\mathsf{r}_{!p}$

Given a set $\Gamma \cup \{A\}$ of formulas in $\mathsf{FORM}_{\mathcal{L}^+}$, we say that A is a *semantic consequence* of Γ (notation: $\Gamma \models A$) if, for any intuitionistic model $\mathfrak{M}$ and any

$w \in W$, whenever $\mathfrak{M}, w \models B$ for all $B \in \Gamma$, $\mathfrak{M}, w \models A$ holds. If Γ is an empty set, we simply write $\models A$ instead of $\emptyset \models A$.

Let us move to proof theory. While Nishimura [18] provided a sequent calculus for the constructive propositional dynamic logic (with the Kleene star), this paper proposes a Hilbert system for the iteration-free constructive propositional dynamic logic. Table 2 provides Hilbert-style axiomatization **HCDLRC** of our intuitionistic generalization **CDLRC** of dynamic logic of relation changers. We also denote by $\mathbf{HCPDL}^-$ a Hilbert system consisting of axioms and rules of intuitionistic logic and additional axioms and rules of the iteration-free constructive propositional dynamic logic in Table 2. Similarly to the definition of **HDLRC**, we add the set of six recursion axioms together with the necessitation rule for $[\mathsf{r}]$ to the axiomatization $\mathbf{HCPDL}^-$ to define **HCDLRC**. The notion of theorem for these systems is defined as usual.

Given a finite set Γ of formulas, we write the conjunction of all formulas in Γ as $\bigwedge \Gamma$ where $\bigwedge \emptyset := \top$. Given a set $\Gamma \cup \{A\}$ of formulas in $\mathsf{FORM}_{\mathcal{L}^+}$, we say that A is *provable* from Γ in **HCDLRC** (notation: $\Gamma \vdash_{\mathbf{HCDLRC}} A$) if there exists a finite set $\Gamma' \subseteq \Gamma$ such that $\bigwedge \Gamma' \to A$ is a theorem of **HCDLRC**. The notion of provability for $\mathbf{HCPDL}^-$ is also similarly defined.

Table 2. Hilbert-style Axiomatizations $\mathbf{HCPDL}^-$ and **HCDLRC**

Axioms and Rules for Intuitionistic Logic			
(**k**)	$A \to (B \to A)$	($\wedge$**e**$_1$)	$(A \wedge B) \to A$
(**s**)	$(A \to (B \to C)) \to ((A \to B) \to (A \to C))$	($\wedge$**e**$_2$)	$(A \wedge B) \to B$
($\vee$**i**$_1$)	$A \to (A \vee B)$	($\wedge$**i**)	$A \to (B \to (A \wedge B))$
($\vee$**i**$_2$)	$B \to (A \vee B)$	($\bot$)	$\bot \to A$
($\vee$**e**)	$(A \to C) \to ((B \to C) \to ((A \vee B) \to C))$	(**MP**)	From A and $A \to B$, infer B
Additional Axioms and Rules for $\mathbf{HCPDL}^-$			
($\mathbf{K}_{[\alpha]}$)	$[\alpha](A \to B) \to ([\alpha]A \to [\alpha]B)$	($[\cup]$)	$[\alpha \cup \beta]A \leftrightarrow [\alpha]A \wedge [\beta]A$
($[;]$)	$[\alpha;\beta]A \leftrightarrow [\alpha][\beta]A$	($[?]$)	$[?B]A \leftrightarrow (B \to A)$
($\mathbf{Nec}_{[\alpha]}$)	From A, infer $[\alpha]A$		
Additional Axioms and Rules to $\mathbf{HCPDL}^-$ for **HCDLRC**			
($[\mathsf{r}]$**at**)	$[\mathsf{r}]p \leftrightarrow p$	($[\mathsf{r}]\bot$)	$[\mathsf{r}]\bot \leftrightarrow \bot$
($[\mathsf{r}]\wedge$)	$[\mathsf{r}](A \wedge B) \leftrightarrow ([\mathsf{r}]A \wedge [\mathsf{r}]B)$	($[\mathsf{r}]\vee$)	$[\mathsf{r}](A \vee B) \leftrightarrow ([\mathsf{r}]A \vee [\mathsf{r}]B)$
($[\mathsf{r}] \to$)	$[\mathsf{r}](A \to B) \leftrightarrow ([\mathsf{r}]A \to [\mathsf{r}]B)$	($[\mathsf{r}][a]$)	$[\mathsf{r}][a]A \leftrightarrow [\mathsf{r}(a)][\mathsf{r}]A$
($\mathbf{Nec}_{[\mathsf{r}]}$)	From A, infer $[\mathsf{r}]A$		

With the help of Proposition 2, we can establish the soundness of **HCDLRC** (and $\mathbf{HCPDL}^-$) for the standard Kripke semantics.

Proposition 3. (i) *If* $\vdash_{\mathbf{HCPDL}^-} A$, *then* $\mathbb{M}_{\mathrm{all}} \models A$, *for any formula* A. (ii) *If* $\vdash_{\mathbf{HCDLRC}} A$, *then* $\mathbb{M}_{\mathrm{all}} \models A$, *for any formula* A.

Proof. We only show the validity of the axiom of ($[?]$). It suffices to show that $\mathfrak{M}, w \models [?B]A$ iff $\mathfrak{M}, w \models B \to A$ for every $w \in W$. This is shown by: $\mathfrak{M}, w \models$

$[?B]A$ iff for all $v \in W$ ($wR_{?B}v$ implies $\mathfrak{M}, v \models A$) iff for all $v \in W$ ($w \leqslant v$ and $\mathfrak{M}, v \models B$ jointly imply $\mathfrak{M}, v \models A$) iff $\mathfrak{M}, w \models B \rightarrow A$. □

4 Completeness of Constructive Dynamic Logic of Relation Changers with Recursion Strategy

Since Nishimura [18] considered the constructive propositional dynamic logic with the Kleene star, his completeness proof of the sequent calculus is finitary, i.e., he used Fischer-Ladner closure in the intuitionistic setting. In this section, however, we first establish the semantic completeness of HCPDL^- by the canonical model construction. Second, we show the *relative* semantic completeness of HCDLRC to HCPDL^- with the help of the recursion axioms.

4.1 Completeness of HCPDL^- by Canonical Model Construction

Definition 4. Given a finite set Γ of formulas, we write the disjunction of all formulas in Γ as $\bigvee \Gamma$ where $\bigvee \emptyset := \bot$. Let (Γ, Δ) be a pair of sets of formulas in $\mathsf{FORM}_{\mathcal{L}}$. We say that (Γ, Δ) *is provable* (in HCPDL^-) if $\Gamma \vdash_{\mathsf{HCPDL}^-} \bigvee \Delta'$ for some finite $\Delta' \subseteq \Delta$ and that (Γ, Δ) *is unprovable* (in HCPDL^-) if it is not provable. We say that (Γ, Δ) *is complete* if $\Gamma \cup \Delta = \mathsf{FORM}_{\mathcal{L}}$.

Lemma 5. *Let (Γ, Δ) be a complete and unprovable pair.*

(i) $\Gamma \vdash_{\mathsf{HCPDL}^-} A$ iff $A \in \Gamma$.
(ii) *If* $\{A, A \rightarrow B\} \subseteq \Gamma$ *then* $B \in \Gamma$.
(iii) $\bot \notin \Gamma$.
(iv) $A \wedge B \in \Gamma$ iff $A \in \Gamma$ *and* $B \in \Gamma$.
(v) $A \vee B \in \Gamma$ iff $A \in \Gamma$ *or* $B \in \Gamma$.
(vi) $[\alpha \cup \beta]A \in \Gamma$ iff $\{[\alpha]A, [\beta]A\} \subseteq \Gamma$.
(vii) $[\alpha; \beta]A \in \Gamma$ iff $[\alpha][\beta]A \in \Gamma$.
(viii) $[?B]A \in \Gamma$ iff $B \rightarrow A \in \Gamma$.

Lemma 6. *Given any unprovable pair (Γ, Δ) of formulas in $\mathsf{FORM}_{\mathcal{L}}$, there exists a complete and unprovable pair (Γ^+, Δ^+) such that $\Gamma \subseteq \Gamma^+$ and $\Delta \subseteq \Delta^+$.*

Definition 7. The canonical model $\mathfrak{M}^c = (W^c, \leqslant^c, (R^c_a)_{a \in \mathsf{AP}}, V^c)$ is defined as:

- $W^c := \{(\Gamma, \Delta) \mid (\Gamma, \Delta)$ is a complete and unprovable pair$\}$,
- $(\Gamma_1, \Delta_1) \leqslant^c (\Gamma_2, \Delta_2)$ iff $\Gamma_1 \subseteq \Gamma_2$,
- $(\Gamma_1, \Delta_1) R^c_a (\Gamma_2, \Delta_2)$ iff $[a]^{-1}\Gamma_1 \subseteq \Gamma_2$, i.e., $\{A \mid [a]A \in \Gamma_1\} \subseteq \Gamma_2$.
- $(\Gamma, \Delta) \in V^c(p)$ iff $p \in \Gamma$.

Lemma 8. *The canonical model $\mathfrak{M}^c$ is an intuitionistic model.*

Lemma 9. *Let (Γ, Δ) be any complete and unprovable pair.*

(i) *If $A \rightarrow B \notin \Gamma$, then a pair $(\{A\} \cup \Gamma, \{B\})$ is unprovable.*
(ii) *If $[\alpha]A \notin \Gamma$, then a pair $([\alpha]^{-1}\Gamma, \{A\})$ is unprovable.*
(iii) *Let (Γ', Δ') be a complete and unprovable pair such that $[\alpha_1; \alpha_2]^{-1}\Gamma \subseteq \Gamma'$. Then, a pair $([\alpha_1]^{-1}\Gamma, [\alpha_2]\Delta') = (\{B \mid [\alpha_1]B \in \Gamma\}, \{[\alpha_2]B \mid B \in \Delta'\})$ is unprovable.*

Lemma 10 (Truth Lemma). *Let A be a formula, α a program, (Γ, Δ) and (Γ', Δ') complete and unprovable pairs. Then, the following equivalences hold:*

(i) $A \in \Gamma$ iff $\mathfrak{M}^c, (\Gamma, \Delta) \models A$,
(ii) $(\Gamma, \Delta) R^c_\alpha (\Gamma', \Delta')$ iff $[\alpha]^{-1}\Gamma \subseteq \Gamma'$, *i.e.*, $\{ B \in \mathsf{FORM}_\mathcal{L} \mid [\alpha]B \in \Gamma \} \subseteq \Gamma'$.

Proof. By simultaneous induction on a formula A and a program α. Most of the cases can be shown by Lemma 5. The cases where A is of the form $B \to C$ and the form $[\alpha]B$ in (i), and α is of the form $\beta_1; \beta_2$ in (ii) can be shown by Lemmas 6 and 9. In what follows, we prove the case when α is of the form $?A$ in (ii). We show that $(\Gamma, \Delta) R^c_{?A} (\Gamma', \Delta')$ iff for all $B \in \mathsf{FORM}_\mathcal{L}$ ($[?A]B \in \Gamma$ implies $B \in \Gamma'$). Since the left-to-right direction is straightforward by Lemma 5 (viii), we only show the right-to-left direction. Suppose that $[?A]B \in \Gamma$ implies $B \in \Gamma'$ for all $B \in \mathsf{FORM}_\mathcal{L}$. Our goal is to show $(\Gamma, \Delta) R^c_{?A} (\Gamma', \Delta')$, i.e., $(\Gamma, \Delta) \leqslant^c (\Gamma', \Delta')$ and $\mathfrak{M}^c, (\Gamma', \Delta') \models A$. To show $(\Gamma, \Delta) \leqslant^c (\Gamma', \Delta')$, fix any formula $C \in \Gamma$. Our goal is to show $C \in \Gamma'$. Since $C \in \Gamma$, we get $A \to C \in \Gamma$ hence $[?A]C \in \Gamma$ by axiom ([?]). By our supposition, we conclude $C \in \Gamma'$. Next, in order to show $\mathfrak{M}^c, (\Gamma', \Delta') \models A$, it suffices to show $A \in \Gamma'$ by induction hypothesis. We deduce from $\vdash_{\mathbf{HCPDL}^-} A \to A$ that $A \to A \in \Gamma$, which implies $[?A]A \in \Gamma$ holds by axiom ([?]). By this and our supposition, we obtain $A \in \Gamma'$, as desired. □

Theorem 1. *Given any set $\Gamma \cup \{ A \} \subseteq \mathsf{FORM}_\mathcal{L}$, $\Gamma \models A$ implies $\Gamma \vdash_{\mathbf{HCPDL}^-} A$.*

Proof. By the contrapositive implication. Suppose that $\Gamma \nvdash_{\mathbf{HCPDL}^-} A$, which implies $(\Gamma, \{ A \})$ is unprovable. By Lemma 6, we can get a complete and unprovable pair (Γ^+, Δ^+) such that $\Gamma \subseteq \Gamma^+$ and $\{ A \} \subseteq \Delta^+$. By $A \in \Delta^+$ and the unprovability of (Γ^+, Δ^+), it is noted that $A \notin \Gamma^+$. It follows from Lemma 10 that $\mathfrak{M}^c, (\Gamma^+, \Delta^+) \models B$ for all $B \in \Gamma^+ \supseteq \Gamma$ and that $\mathfrak{M}^c, (\Gamma^+, \Delta^+) \not\models A$. Therefore, we conclude $\Gamma \not\models A$, because $\mathfrak{M}^c$ is an intuitionistic model by Lemma 8. □

4.2 Relative Completeness of HCDLRC to HCPDL$^-$ by Recursion Axioms

Now, we have the semantic completeness of **HCPDL**$^-$. In what follows of this section, we proceed to show the semantic completeness of **HCDLRC**.

Definition 11. The *translation* $t : \mathsf{FORM}_{\mathcal{L}^+} \to \mathsf{FORM}_\mathcal{L}$ is defined by:

$$
\begin{array}{rlrl}
t(p) &= p, & t([\mathsf{r}]p) &= p,\\
t(\bot) &= \bot, & t([\mathsf{r}]\bot) &= \bot,\\
t(A \wedge B) &= t(A) \wedge t(B), & t([\mathsf{r}](A \wedge B)) &= t([\mathsf{r}]A) \wedge t([\mathsf{r}]B),\\
t(A \vee B) &= t(A) \vee t(B), & t([\mathsf{r}](A \vee B)) &= t([\mathsf{r}]A) \vee t([\mathsf{r}]B),\\
t(A \to B) &= t(A) \to t(B), & t([\mathsf{r}](A \to B)) &= t([\mathsf{r}]A) \to t([\mathsf{r}]B),\\
t([a]A) &= [a]t(A), & t([\mathsf{r}][a]A) &= [\mathsf{r}(a)]t([\mathsf{r}]A),\\
t([\alpha \cup \beta]A) &= t([\alpha]A) \wedge t([\beta]A), & t([\mathsf{r}][\alpha \cup \beta]A) &= t([\mathsf{r}][\alpha]A) \wedge t([\mathsf{r}][\alpha]B),\\
t([\alpha; \beta]A) &= t([\alpha][\beta]A), & t([\mathsf{r}][\alpha; \beta]A) &= t([\mathsf{r}][\alpha][\beta]A),\\
t([?B]A) &= t(B) \to t(A), & t([\mathsf{r}][?B]A) &= t([\mathsf{r}]B) \to t([\mathsf{r}]A),\\
 & & t([\mathsf{r}][\mathsf{r}']A) &= t([\mathsf{r}]t([\mathsf{r}']A)).
\end{array}
$$

The definition of this translation reflects the idea of 'inside-out' strategy, i.e., we start rewriting a formula from one of the innermost occurrences of [r].

Lemma 12. *For any formula A, $\vdash_{\mathbf{HCDLRC}} A \leftrightarrow t(A)$.*

Theorem 2. *Given any set $\Gamma \cup \{A\} \subseteq \mathsf{Form}_{\mathcal{L}+}$, $\Gamma \models A$ implies $\Gamma \vdash_{\mathbf{HCDLRC}} A$.*

Proof. Similarly to the proof of Fact 1, we can reduce the strong completeness of **HCDLRC** to that of **HCPDL**$^-$. Suppose that $\Gamma \models A$. By Propositions 3 and Lemma 12, $B \leftrightarrow t(B)$ is valid in all models, for any formula $B \in \Gamma \cup \{A\}$. It follows that $t[\Gamma] \models t(A)$. Since **HCPDL**$^-$ is strongly complete (Theorem 1), $t[\Gamma] \vdash_{\mathbf{HCPDL}^-} t(A)$. This implies that $t[\Gamma] \vdash_{\mathbf{HCDLRC}} t(A)$ because **HCDLRC** is an axiomatic extension of **HCPDL**$^-$. Finally, again by Lemma 12, we obtain $\Gamma \vdash_{\mathbf{HCDLRC}} A$, as desired. □

5 Completeness of Constructive Dynamic Logic of Relation Changers without Recursion Strategy

In what follows, we present a direct proof of the semantic completeness of **HCDLRC** for the standard semantics. To achieve the goal, we provide **CDLRC** with an alternative semantics and connect it with the standard semantics via the notion of bounded morphism (or p-morphism), which was originally proposed by [23]. It is remarked that our semantics for [r] in the extended semantics below is similar to the semantics of the next time operator ◯ over intuitionistic logic in [6].

5.1 Bounded Morphisms and Extended Models

Definition 13 (Bounded Morphism). Given any (standard) intuitionistic models $\mathfrak{M} = (W, \leqslant, (R_a)_{a \in \mathsf{AP}}, V)$ and $\mathfrak{M}' = (W', \leqslant', (R'_a)_{a \in \mathsf{AP}}, V')$, a mapping $f : W \to W'$ is a *bounded morphism* (notation: $f : \mathfrak{M} \twoheadrightarrow \mathfrak{M}'$) if it enjoys the following properties:

(Atom) $w \in V(p)$ iff $f(w) \in V'(p)$, for any $w \in W$ ($p \in \mathsf{PROP}$).
(Forth) If $wR_a v$, then $f(w)R'_a f(v)$, for any $w, v \in W$ ($a \in \mathsf{AP}$).
(Back) If $f(w)R'_a v'$, then there exists some $v \in W$ such that $wR_a v$ and $f(v) = v'$, for any $w \in W$ and $v' \in W'$ ($a \in \mathsf{AP}$).
($\leqslant$-Forth) If $w \leqslant v$, then $f(w) \leqslant' f(v)$, for any $w, v \in W$.
($\leqslant$-Back) If $f(w) \leqslant' v'$, then there exists some $v \in W$ such that $w \leqslant v$ and $f(v) = v'$, for any $w \in W$ and $v' \in W'$.

Proposition 14. *Given any intuitionistic models $\mathfrak{M} = (W, \leqslant, (R_a)_{a \in \mathsf{AP}}, V)$ and $\mathfrak{M}' = (W', \leqslant', (R'_a)_{a \in \mathsf{AP}}, V')$, a bounded morphism $f : \mathfrak{M} \twoheadrightarrow \mathfrak{M}'$, any formula $A \in \mathsf{FORM}_{\mathcal{L}+}$ and any program $\alpha \in \mathsf{PR}_{\mathcal{L}+}$, the following hold:*

(i) $\mathfrak{M}, w \models A$ iff $\mathfrak{M}', f(w) \models A$, *for any $w \in W$.*
(ii) *If $wR_\alpha v$, then $f(w)R'_\alpha f(v)$, for any $w, v \in W$.*

(iii) *If* $f(w)R'_{\alpha}v'$, *then there exists some* $v \in W$ *such that* $wR_{\alpha}v$ *and* $f(v) = v'$, *for any* $w \in W$ *and* $v' \in W'$.
f *is also a bounded morphism from* $\mathfrak{M}^{\mathsf{r}}$ *to* $(\mathfrak{M}')^{\mathsf{r}}$.

Definition 15. (Extended Model and Extended Semantics). An *extended intuitionistic model* $\mathfrak{M}$ is a tuple $(W, \leqslant, (R_a)_{a \in \mathsf{AP}}, (f_{\mathsf{r}})_{\mathsf{r} \in \mathsf{RC}}, V)$ where $(W, \leqslant, (R_a)_{a \in \mathsf{AP}}, V)$ is a standard intuitionistic model for **CDLRC** (notation: $\mathfrak{M}^{-}$), and $f_{\mathsf{r}} : W \to W$ is a function for relation changer r such that $w \leqslant v$ implies $f_{\mathsf{r}}(w) \leqslant f_{\mathsf{r}}(v)$ for any $w, v \in W$, i.e., f_{r} satisfies ($\leqslant$-**Forth**) condition.

Given any extended intuitionistic model $\mathfrak{M} = (W, \leqslant, (R_a)_{a \in \mathsf{AP}}, (f_{\mathsf{r}})_{\mathsf{r} \in \mathsf{RC}}, V)$ and any possible worlds $w, v \in W$, the *extended satisfaction relation* $\mathfrak{M}, w \Vdash A$ and the *extended interpretation* $w\|\alpha\|v$ *of programs* are defined by simultaneous induction, as follows:

$$
\begin{array}{ll}
\mathfrak{M}, w \Vdash p & \text{iff } w \in V(p), \\
\mathfrak{M}, w \nVdash \bot, & \\
\mathfrak{M}, w \Vdash A \wedge B & \text{iff } \mathfrak{M}, w \Vdash A \text{ and } \mathfrak{M}, w \Vdash B, \\
\mathfrak{M}, w \Vdash A \vee B & \text{iff } \mathfrak{M}, w \Vdash A \text{ or } \mathfrak{M}, w \Vdash B, \\
\mathfrak{M}, w \Vdash A \to B & \text{iff for all } v \in W (w \leqslant v \text{ and } \mathfrak{M}, v \Vdash A \text{ imply } \mathfrak{M}, v \Vdash B), \\
\mathfrak{M}, w \Vdash [\alpha]A & \text{iff for all } v \in W (w\|\alpha\|v \text{ implies } \mathfrak{M}, v \Vdash A), \\
w\|a\|v & \text{iff } wR_a v, \\
w\|\alpha \cup \beta\|v & \text{iff } w\|\alpha\|v \text{ or } w\|\beta\|v, \\
w\|\alpha ; \beta\|v & \text{iff for some } u \in W (w\|\alpha\|u \text{ and } u\|\beta\|v), \\
w\|?A\|v & \text{iff } w \leqslant v \text{ and } \mathfrak{M}, v \Vdash A, \\
\mathfrak{M}, w \Vdash [\mathsf{r}]A & \text{iff } \mathfrak{M}, f_{\mathsf{r}}(w) \Vdash A.
\end{array}
$$

We define the *truth set* $\|A\|_{\mathfrak{M}}$ *of a formula* A *in an extended intuitionistic model* $\mathfrak{M}$ by $\|A\|_{\mathfrak{M}} := \{ w \in W \mid \mathfrak{M}, w \Vdash A \}$. Given a class $\mathbb{X}$ of extended intuitionistic models, we say that a formula A is *valid in* $\mathbb{X}$ *with respect to the extended semantics* (notation: $\mathbb{X} \Vdash A$) if $\mathfrak{M}, w \Vdash A$ for any extended intuitionistic models $\mathfrak{M} \in \mathbb{X}$ and any possible worlds $w \in W$.

It is remarked that an essential difference between the extended semantics and the standard semantics in Sect. 3 is merely the clause for relation changer r.

Example 3. Let $\mathsf{AP} = \{ a \}$. Here, we demonstrate a *partial description* of an extended intuitionistic model $\mathfrak{N}$ where two models $\mathfrak{M}$ and $\mathfrak{M}^{\mathsf{r}_{!p}}$ of Example 2 are embedded. In Fig. 3, the dotted arrow from w (or w') to v (or v', respectively) indicates the link of the preorder from w to v and the double arrows from w to w' and v to v' indicate the links for the relation changer $\mathsf{r}_{!p}$ of the introspective announcement $!p$. One can also check that $\mathfrak{N}, w \nVdash [a](p \vee \neg p)$ by $\mathfrak{N}, w \nVdash p \vee \neg p$ and $wR_a w$, and verify that $\mathfrak{N}, w \Vdash [\mathsf{r}_{!p}][a](p \vee \neg p)$, since $\mathfrak{N}, v' \Vdash p \vee \neg p$ and v' is the unique $\|\mathsf{r}_{!p}(a)\|$-successor of $w' = f_{\mathsf{r}_{!p}}(w)$.

Proposition 16. *Given any extended intuitionistic model* $\mathfrak{M}$, *any formula* A *and any program* α, (i) $\|A\|_{\mathfrak{M}}$ *is* $\leqslant$*-closed, and* (ii) $\|\alpha\|$ *is stable, i.e.,* $\leqslant ; \|\alpha\| \subseteq \|\alpha\|$.

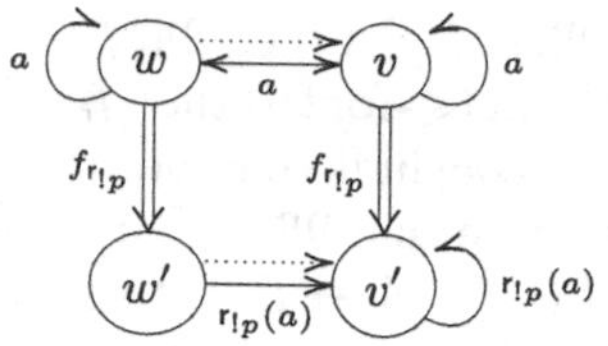

Fig. 3. Partial description of a function $f_{\mathsf{r}_{!p}}$ by introspective announcement $\mathsf{r}_{!p}$

Proof. It suffices to check that $\|[\mathsf{r}]B\|$ is $\leqslant$-closed. Fix any $w, v \in W$ such that $w \leqslant v$ and $\mathfrak{M}, w \Vdash [\mathsf{r}]B$ hence $\mathfrak{M}, f_{\mathsf{r}}(w) \Vdash B$. Since f_{r} satisfies ($\leqslant$-**forth**) condition, $w \leqslant v$ implies $f_{\mathsf{r}}(w) \leqslant f_{\mathsf{r}}(v)$. By induction hypothesis, we conclude that $\mathfrak{M}, f_{\mathsf{r}}(v) \Vdash B$ hence $\mathfrak{M}, v \Vdash [\mathsf{r}]B$. □

Definition 17. An extended intuitionistic model $\mathfrak{M} = (W, \leqslant, (R_a)_{a \in \mathsf{AP}}, (f_{\mathsf{r}})_{\mathsf{r} \in \mathsf{RC}}, V)$ is r-*normal* if the following properties hold:

(r-**Atom**) $w \in V(p)$ iff $f_{\mathsf{r}}(w) \in V(p)$, for any $w \in W$ ($p \in \mathsf{PROP}$).
(r-**Forth**) If $w \|\mathsf{r}(a)\| v$, then $f_{\mathsf{r}}(w) R_a f_{\mathsf{r}}(v)$, for any $w, v \in W$ ($a \in \mathsf{AP}$).
(r-**Back**) If $f_{\mathsf{r}}(w) R_a v$, then there exists some $u \in W$ such that $w \|\mathsf{r}(a)\| u$ and $f_{\mathsf{r}}(u) = v$, for any $w, v \in W$ ($a \in \mathsf{AP}$).
($\leqslant$-**Back**) If $f_{\mathsf{r}}(w) \leqslant v$, then there exists some $u \in W$ such that $w \leqslant u$ and $f_{\mathsf{r}}(u) = v$, for any $w, v \in W$.

We say that an extended intuitionistic model is *normal* if it is r-normal for any $\mathsf{r} \in \mathsf{RC}$. We define $\mathbb{NX}_{\mathsf{all}}$ to be the class of all normal extended intuitionistic models.

Recall that a function f_{r} satisfies ($\leqslant$-**Forth**) condition. Hence, the four conditions (r-**Atom**), (r-**Forth**), (r-**Back**) and ($\leqslant$ -**Back**) for the function f_{r} are equivalent to the condition that f_{r} is a bounded morphism from a model $(W, \leqslant, (\|\mathsf{r}(a)\|)_{a \in \mathsf{AP}}, V)$ to a model $(W, \leqslant, (R_a)_{a \in \mathsf{AP}}, V)$. This observation implies the following lemma.

Lemma 18. *Let* $\mathfrak{M} = (W, \leqslant, (R_a)_{a \in \mathsf{AP}}, (f_{\mathsf{r}})_{\mathsf{r} \in \mathsf{RC}}, V)$ *be any normal extended intuitionistic model. Then, all mappings* $f_{\mathsf{r}} : W \to W$ *are bounded morphisms from* $(W, \leqslant, (\|\mathsf{r}(a)\|)_{a \in \mathsf{AP}}, V)$ *to* $\mathfrak{M}^-$ iff *the extended model* $(W, \leqslant, (R_a)_{a \in \mathsf{AP}}, (f_{\mathsf{r}})_{\mathsf{r} \in \mathsf{RC}}, V)$ *is normal, where recall that* $\mathfrak{M}^- := (W, \leqslant, (R_a)_{a \in \mathsf{AP}}, V)$.

Lemma 19. *For any formula* A, $\vdash_{\mathbf{HCDLRC}} A$ *implies* $\mathbb{NX}_{\mathsf{all}} \Vdash A$.

Proof. It suffices to check the validity of the axioms for $[\mathsf{r}]$. The axioms ($[\mathsf{r}]\bot$), ($[\mathsf{r}]\wedge$), and ($[\mathsf{r}]\vee$) are easily shown to be valid, since f_{r} is a function. It is easy to see that ($[\mathsf{r}]$**at**) is valid in all normal extended models by (r-**Atom**) condition.

The validity of ($[\mathsf{r}] \to$) is shown by ($\leqslant$-**Forth**) and ($\leqslant$-**Back**). Let us see the detail. It suffices to show that $\mathfrak{M}, w \Vdash [\mathsf{r}](A \to B)$ iff $\mathfrak{M}, w \Vdash [\mathsf{r}]A \to [\mathsf{r}]B$ for all $w \in W$. First, we establish the left-to-right direction. Suppose that $\mathfrak{M}, w \Vdash [\mathsf{r}](A \to B)$, i.e., $\mathfrak{M}, f_{\mathsf{r}}(w) \Vdash A \to B$. To show that $\mathfrak{M}, w \Vdash [\mathsf{r}]A \to [\mathsf{r}]B$, let us fix any v such that $w \leqslant v$ and $\mathfrak{M}, v \Vdash [\mathsf{r}]A$, i.e., $\mathfrak{M}, f_{\mathsf{r}}(v) \Vdash A$. Our goal is to show that $\mathfrak{M}, f_{\mathsf{r}}(v) \Vdash B$. It follows from (**$\leqslant$-forth**) that $f_{\mathsf{r}}(w) \leqslant f_{\mathsf{r}}(v)$. By $\mathfrak{M}, f_{\mathsf{r}}(v) \Vdash A$ and $\mathfrak{M}, f_{\mathsf{r}}(w) \Vdash A \to B$, we can conclude that $\mathfrak{M}, f_{\mathsf{r}}(v) \Vdash B$. Second, we establish the right-to-left direction. Suppose that $\mathfrak{M}, w \Vdash [\mathsf{r}]A \to [\mathsf{r}]B$. Our goal is to show $\mathfrak{M}, w \Vdash [\mathsf{r}](A \to B)$, i.e., $\mathfrak{M}, f_{\mathsf{r}}(w) \Vdash A \to B$. Let us fix any v such that $f_{\mathsf{r}}(w) \leqslant v$ and $\mathfrak{M}, v \Vdash A$. By (**$\leqslant$-back**), there exists a state $u \in W$ such that $f_{\mathsf{r}}(u) = v$ and $w \leqslant u$. It follows that $\mathfrak{M}, f_{\mathsf{r}}(u) \Vdash A$ hence $\mathfrak{M}, u \Vdash [\mathsf{r}]A$. By $w \leqslant u$ and our supposition, we get $\mathfrak{M}, u \Vdash [\mathsf{r}]B$, i.e., $\mathfrak{M}, v \Vdash B$ by $f_{\mathsf{r}}(u) = v$.

The validity of ($[\mathsf{r}][a]$) can be checked with the help of (**r-Forth**) and (**r-Back**) as follows. It suffices to show that $\mathfrak{M}, w \Vdash [\mathsf{r}][a]A$ iff $\mathfrak{M}, w \Vdash [\mathsf{r}(a)][\mathsf{r}]A$ for all $w \in W$. First, we show the left-to-right direction. Suppose that $\mathfrak{M}, w \Vdash [\mathsf{r}][a]A$, i.e., $\mathfrak{M}, f_{\mathsf{r}}(w) \Vdash [a]A$. To show that $\mathfrak{M}, w \Vdash [\mathsf{r}(a)][\mathsf{r}]A$, let us fix any $u \in W$ such that $w \|\mathsf{r}(a)\| u$. Our goal is to show that $\mathfrak{M}, f_{\mathsf{r}}(u) \Vdash A$. It follows from (**r-Forth**) that $f_{\mathsf{r}}(w) R_a f_{\mathsf{r}}(u)$. Since $f_{\mathsf{r}}(w) R_a f_{\mathsf{r}}(u)$ holds, we obtain $\mathfrak{M}, f_{\mathsf{r}}(u) \Vdash A$ by our initial supposition. Second, we show the right-to-left direction. Suppose that $\mathfrak{M}, w \Vdash [\mathsf{r}(a)][\mathsf{r}]A$. Our goal is to show $\mathfrak{M}, w \Vdash [\mathsf{r}][a]A$, i.e., $\mathfrak{M}, f_{\mathsf{r}}(w) \Vdash [a]A$. Let us fix any $v \in W$ such that $f_{\mathsf{r}}(w) R_a v$. Our goal is to show $\mathfrak{M}, v \Vdash A$. By (**r-Back**), there exists a state $u \in W$ such that $w \|\mathsf{r}(a)\| u$ and $f_{\mathsf{r}}(u) = v$. Then, it follows from $\mathfrak{M}, w \Vdash [\mathsf{r}(a)][\mathsf{r}]A$ that $\mathfrak{M}, f_{\mathsf{r}}(u) \Vdash A$, which implies $\mathfrak{M}, v \Vdash A$. □

The following theorem connects the extended semantics with the original semantics. Moreover, this theorem is a key component of a semantic completeness proof of the axiomatization **HCDLRC** for the original semantics without the reduction strategy.

Theorem 3. *Given any formula A, any program α and any normal extended intuitionistic model $\mathfrak{M}$,* (i) $\mathfrak{M}, w \Vdash A$ iff $\mathfrak{M}^-, w \models A$, *and* (ii) $\|\alpha\| = R_\alpha$.

Proof. By simultaneous induction on α and A. It suffices to check the case where A is of the form $[\mathsf{r}]B$. We proceed as follows: $\mathfrak{M}, w \Vdash [\mathsf{r}]B$ iff $\mathfrak{M}, f_{\mathsf{r}}(w) \Vdash B$ iff $\mathfrak{M}^-, f_{\mathsf{r}}(w) \models B$ (by induction hypothesis) iff $(\mathfrak{M}^-)^{\mathsf{r}}, w \models B$ (by Proposition 14, Lemma 18 and induction hypothesis) iff $\mathfrak{M}^-, w \models [\mathsf{r}]B$, as required. □

Definition 20. Given a set $\Gamma \cup \{A\}$ of formulas in $\mathsf{FORM}_{\mathcal{L}^+}$, we say that A is a *semantic consequence* of Γ with respect to a class $\mathbb{X}$ of extended intuitionistic models (notation: $\Gamma \Vdash_{\mathbb{X}} A$) if, for every extended model $\mathfrak{M}$ in $\mathbb{X}$ and state w in M, when $\mathfrak{M}, w \Vdash B$ for all $B \in \Gamma$, $\mathfrak{M}, w \Vdash A$ holds.

By Theorem 3, we can obtain the following corollary.

Corollary 1. *For any formula set $\Gamma \cup \{A\}$, $\Gamma \models A$ implies $\Gamma \Vdash_{\mathbb{NX}_{\mathrm{all}}} A$.*

5.2 Completeness of HCDLRC via Extended Canonical Model

To show the semantic completeness of **HCDLRC** by the canonical model construction, we employ the similar definitions of the *provability* (in **HCDLRC**) and the *completeness for a pair (Γ, Δ) of formulas* in $\mathsf{FORM}_{\mathcal{L}^+}$, as we did in Sect. 4.1.

Lemma 21. *Given any unprovable pair* (Γ, Δ) *of formulas in* $\mathsf{FORM}_{\mathcal{L}^+}$, *there exists a complete and unprovable pair* (Γ^+, Δ^+) *such that* $\Gamma \subseteq \Gamma^+$ *and* $\Delta \subseteq \Delta^+$.

Definition 22. Define $\mathfrak{M}^c := (W^c, \leqslant^c, (R^c_a)_{a \in \mathsf{AP}}, (f^c_{\mathsf{r}})_{\mathsf{r} \in \mathsf{RC}}, V^c)$ as the *extended canonical intuitionistic model* by

- $W^c := \{ (\Gamma, \Delta) \mid (\Gamma, \Delta) \text{ is a complete and unprovable pair} \}$,
- $(\Gamma_1, \Delta_1) \leqslant^c (\Gamma_2, \Delta_2)$ iff $\Gamma_1 \subseteq \Gamma_2$,
- $(\Gamma_1, \Delta_1) R^c_a (\Gamma_2, \Delta_2)$ iff $[a]^{-1}\Gamma_1 \subseteq \Gamma_2$.
- $f^c_{\mathsf{r}}(\Gamma_1, \Delta_1) = ([\mathsf{r}]^{-1}\Gamma_1, [\mathsf{r}]^{-1}\Delta_1)$.
- $(\Gamma, \Delta) \in V^c(p)$ iff $p \in \Gamma$.

Lemma 23. *The map* f^c_{r} *of the extended canonical intuitionistic model is a function and it satisfies the* ($\leqslant$**-Forth**) *condition. Moreover, the extended canonical intuitionistic model* $\mathfrak{M}^c$ *is an intuitionistic model.*

Proof. Let (Γ, Δ) be a complete and unprovable pair. First, we show that $([\mathsf{r}]^{-1}\Gamma, [\mathsf{r}]^{-1}\Delta)$ is also a complete and unprovable pair. This implies that f^c_{r} is a function. Since the completeness of the pair is easy to establish, we focus on the unprovability of $([\mathsf{r}]^{-1}\Gamma, [\mathsf{r}]^{-1}\Delta)$. Suppose not. There exists finite families $(A_i)_{i \in I}$ and $(B_j)_{j \in J}$ such that $[\mathsf{r}]A_i \in \Gamma$ and $[\mathsf{r}]B_j \in \Delta$ and $\vdash \bigwedge_{i \in I} A_i \to \bigvee_{j \in J} B_j$. By the necessitation law of $[\mathsf{r}]$, we get $\vdash [\mathsf{r}](\bigwedge_{i \in I} A_i \to \bigvee_{j \in J} B_j)$. It follows from the axioms for $[\mathsf{r}]$, we have $\vdash \bigwedge_{i \in I}[\mathsf{r}]A_i \to \bigvee_{j \in J}[\mathsf{r}]B_j$, which implies a contradiction with the unprovability of (Γ, Δ). Therefore, $([\mathsf{r}]^{-1}\Gamma, [\mathsf{r}]^{-1}\Delta)$ is unprovable. As for the forth condition of $\leqslant^c$, suppose that $(\Gamma, \Delta) \leqslant^c (\Gamma', \Delta')$, i.e., $\Gamma \subseteq \Gamma'$. In order to show $f^c_{\mathsf{r}}(\Gamma, \Delta) \leqslant^c f^c_{\mathsf{r}}(\Gamma', \Delta')$, it suffices to establish $[\mathsf{r}]^{-1}\Gamma \subseteq [\mathsf{r}]^{-1}\Gamma'$. Fix any formula B such that $[\mathsf{r}]B \in \Gamma$. Since $\Gamma \subseteq \Gamma'$, we obtain $[\mathsf{r}]B \in \Gamma'$ hence $B \in [\mathsf{r}]^{-1}\Gamma'$. □

Lemma 24 (Truth lemma for $\Vdash$). *Let* $A \in \mathsf{FORM}_{\mathcal{L}^+}$, $\alpha \in \mathsf{PR}_{\mathcal{L}^+}$, $(\Gamma, \Delta), (\Gamma', \Delta') \in W^c$. *Then, the following equivalences hold:* (i) $A \in \Gamma$ iff $\mathfrak{M}^c, (\Gamma, \Delta) \Vdash A$; (ii) $(\Gamma, \Delta) \|\alpha\| (\Gamma', \Delta')$ iff $[\alpha]^{-1}\Gamma \subseteq \Gamma'$.

Proof. It suffices for us to check the case where A is of the form $[\mathsf{r}]B$. We need to establish the equivalence $[\mathsf{r}]B \in \Gamma$ iff $\mathfrak{M}^c, f^c_{\mathsf{r}}((\Gamma, \Delta)) \Vdash B$. By induction hypothesis, this is trivial, since $[\mathsf{r}]B \in \Gamma$ iff $B \in [\mathsf{r}]^{-1}\Gamma$. □

Lemma 25. *Let* (Γ_1, Δ_1) *and* (Γ'_2, Δ'_2) *be any complete and unprovable pairs.*

(i) *If* $f^c_{\mathsf{r}}(\Gamma_1, \Delta_1) R^c_a (\Gamma'_2, \Delta'_2)$, *then* $([\mathsf{r}(a)]^{-1}\Gamma_1 \cup [\mathsf{r}]\Gamma'_2, [\mathsf{r}]\Delta'_2)$ *is unprovable.*
(ii) *If* $f^c_{\mathsf{r}}(\Gamma_1, \Delta_1) \leqslant^c (\Gamma'_2, \Delta'_2)$, *then* $(\Gamma_1 \cup [\mathsf{r}]\Gamma'_2, [\mathsf{r}]\Delta'_2)$ *is unprovable.*

Proof. We prove (i) alone because we can prove (ii) similarly to the proof of (i). Suppose that $f^c_{\mathsf{r}}(\Gamma_1, \Delta_1) R^c_a (\Gamma'_2, \Delta'_2)$, i.e., $[a]^{-1}([\mathsf{r}]^{-1}\Gamma_1) \subseteq \Gamma'_2$. It follows that $\{ B \mid [\mathsf{r}][a]B \in \Gamma_1 \} \subseteq \Gamma'_2$. Assume for contradiction that $([\mathsf{r}(a)]^{-1}\Gamma_1 \cup [\mathsf{r}]\Gamma'_2, [\mathsf{r}]\Delta'_2)$ is provable in HCDLRC. Thus, there exists finite families $(A_i)_{i \in I}$, $(B_j)_{j \in J}$ and $(C_k)_{k \in K}$ of formulas such that $\vdash (\bigwedge_{i \in I} A_i \wedge \bigwedge_{j \in J}[\mathsf{r}]B_j) \to \bigvee_{k \in K}[\mathsf{r}]C_k$, $[\mathsf{r}(a)]A_i \in \Gamma_1$, $B_j \in \Gamma'_2$, and $C_k \in \Delta'_2$. It follows from the axioms for $[\mathsf{r}]$ that

$\vdash \bigwedge_{i \in I} A_i \to [\mathsf{r}](\bigwedge_{j \in J} B_j \to \bigvee_{k \in K} C_k)$. By the necessitation law for $[\mathsf{r}(a)]$ and the axiom $\mathbf{K}_{[a]}$, we have $\vdash (\bigwedge_{i \in I}[\mathsf{r}(a)]A_i) \to [\mathsf{r}(a)][\mathsf{r}](\bigwedge_{j \in J} B_j \to \bigvee_{k \in K} C_k)$. By $[\mathsf{r}(a)]A_i \in \Gamma_1$ for all indices $i \in I$, we have $\bigwedge_{i \in I}[\mathsf{r}(a)]A_i \in \Gamma_1$. It follows that $[\mathsf{r}(a)][\mathsf{r}](\bigwedge_{j \in J} B_j \to \bigvee_{k \in K} C_k) \in \Gamma_1$ hence $[\mathsf{r}][a](\bigwedge_{j \in J} B_j \to \bigvee_{k \in K} C_k) \in \Gamma_1$ by the axiom $([\mathsf{r}][a])$. By the initial supposition, we get $\bigwedge_{j \in J} B_j \to \bigvee_{k \in K} C_k \in \Gamma_2'$. Since $B_j \in \Gamma_2'$ $(j \in J)$ and $C_k \in \Delta_2'$ $(k \in K)$, we can conclude that (Γ_2', Δ_2') is provable in **HCDLRC**. We get the desired contradiction. □

Lemma 26. *The extended canonical intuitionistic model* $\mathfrak{M}^c$ *is normal.*

Proof. Since the space is limited, we show that $\mathfrak{M}^c$ satisfies the conditions of (**r-Forth**), (**r-Back**) and (**⩽-Back**).

(**r-Forth**) Suppose that $(\Gamma_1, \Delta_1)\|\mathsf{r}(a)\|(\Gamma_2, \Delta_2)$, i.e., $[\mathsf{r}(a)]B \in \Gamma_1$ implies $B \in \Gamma_2$ for all $B \in \mathsf{FORM}_{\mathcal{L}^+}$. Our goal is to show $f_{\mathsf{r}}((\Gamma_1, \Delta_1))R_a^c f_{\mathsf{r}}((\Gamma_2, \Delta_2))$, i.e., $([\mathsf{r}]^{-1}\Gamma_1, [\mathsf{r}]^{-1}\Delta_1)R_a^c([\mathsf{r}]^{-1}\Gamma_2, [\mathsf{r}]^{-1}\Delta_2)$. Thus, fix any formula A such that $[a]A \in [\mathsf{r}]^{-1}\Gamma_1$ hence $[\mathsf{r}][a] \in \Gamma_1$. Our goal is to show that $A \in [\mathsf{r}]^{-1}\Gamma_2$. It follows from the axiom $([\mathsf{r}][a])$ that $[\mathsf{r}(a)][\mathsf{r}]A \in \Gamma_1$. By the initial supposition, this implies that $[\mathsf{r}]A \in \Gamma_2$, which implies our goal.

(**r-Back**) Suppose that $f_{\mathsf{r}}^c(\Gamma_1, \Delta_1)R_a^c(\Gamma_2', \Delta_2')$. This implies $[a]^{-1}([\mathsf{r}]^{-1}\Gamma_1) \subseteq \Gamma_2'$, i.e., $\{ B \mid [\mathsf{r}][a]B \in \Gamma_1 \} \subseteq \Gamma_2'$. Our goal is to find some $(\Gamma_2, \Delta_2) \in W^c$ such that $(\Gamma_1, \Delta_1)\|\mathsf{r}(a)\|(\Gamma_2, \Delta_2)$ and $f_{\mathsf{r}}^c(\Gamma_2, \Delta_2) = (\Gamma_2', \Delta_2')$, or equivalently, to find some pair $(\Gamma_2, \Delta_2) \in W^c$ such that $[r(a)]\Gamma_1 \cup [\mathsf{r}]\Gamma_2' \subseteq \Gamma_2$ and $[\mathsf{r}]\Delta_2' \subseteq \Delta_2$. By Lemmas 21 and 25 (i), we can find such a pair. □

(**⩽-Back**) Suppose that $f_{\mathsf{r}}^c(\Gamma_1, \Delta_1) \leqslant^c (\Gamma_2', \Delta_2')$. This implies $[\mathsf{r}]^{-1}\Gamma_1 \subseteq \Gamma_2'$. Our goal is to find a $(\Gamma_2, \Delta_2) \in W^c$ such that Our goal is to find a $(\Gamma_2, \Delta_2) \in W^c$ such that $(\Gamma_1, \Delta_1) \leqslant^c (\Gamma_2, \Delta_2)$ and $f_{\mathsf{r}}^c(\Gamma_2, \Delta_2) = (\Gamma_2', \Delta_2')$, or equivalently, a pair $(\Gamma_2, \Delta_2) \in W^c$ such that $\Gamma_1 \cup [\mathsf{r}]\Gamma_2' \subseteq \Gamma_2$ and $[\mathsf{r}]\Delta_2' \subseteq \Delta_2$. By Lemmas 21 and 25(i), we can find such a pair.

By Lemmas 21, 23, 24, and 26, we obtain the following.

Theorem 4. *For any formula set* $\Gamma \cup \{ A \}$, $\Gamma \Vdash_{\mathbb{NX}_{\mathrm{all}}} A$ *implies* $\Gamma \vdash_{\mathbf{HCDLRC}} A$.

By Theorem 4 and Corollary 1, we can provide an alternative proof of Theorem 2: $\Gamma \models A$ implies $\Gamma \vdash_{\mathbf{HCDLRC}} A$, for any set $\Gamma \cup \{ A \}$ of formulas. This finishes establishing the strong completeness of **HCDLRC** without the reduction strategy.

6 Conclusion

Let us explain possible directions of further research. First of all, let us comment on the decidability of $\mathbf{CPDL}^-$. Since it is easy to see that our Hilbert system $\mathsf{H}\mathbf{CPDL}^-$ and the iteration-free fragment of Nishimura's sequent calculus for **CPDL** [18] are equipollent, Nishimura's argument for the semantic completeness of **CPDL** with respect to the finite models implies the finite model property of $\mathbf{CPDL}^-$ hence the decidability of $\mathbf{CPDL}^-$. The second direction is on a proof theory of **CDLRC**. While Hatano et al. [11,12] defined a labelled sequent calculus for the classical **DLRC**, Nishimura [18] provided non-labelled sequent calculus for constructive propositional dynamic logic (with the Kleene star), which is not cut-free. But, if we drop the Kleene star from the calculus, we may obtain a cut-free calculus of $\mathbf{CPDL}^{-}$, which is the iteration-free fragment of Nishimura's sequent calculus for **CPDL** [18]. It would be interesting to consider *non-labelled* sequent calculus for **CDLRC**. This may also be a proof-theoretic basis for considering a substructural generalization of **CDLRC**. The third direction is to add the backward *diamond* for each atomic program a to talk about backtracking. While Nishimura [17] considered the converse operator $-$ for program α, he kept the syntax simpler for the constructive propositional dynamic logic [18]. We may follow the idea of bi-intuitionistic stable tense logic by [20,24] to realize this direction. The fourth direction is to consider the strong completeness proof of the other non-classical dynamic epistemic logics (e.g., in [1,2,16]) without reduction strategy. For example, an intuitionistic public announcement logic proposed in [2,16] is a promising candidate.

References

1. Bakhtiari, Z., van Ditmarsch, H., Rivieccio, U.: Bilattice logic of epistemic actions and knowledge. Ann. Pure Appl. Logic **171**(6), 102790 (2020)
2. Balbiani, P., Galmiche, D.: About intuitionistic public announcement logic. In: Advances in Modal Logic, vol. 11, pp. 97–116. College Publications, London (2016)
3. van Benthem, J.: Man Muss Immer Umkehren!, Tributes, vol. 7, pp. 53–66. College Publications, London (2008)
4. van Benthem, J., Liu, F.: Dynamic logic of preference upgrade. J. Appl. Non-Classical Logics **17**(2), 157–182 (2007)
5. Degen, J., Werner, J.: Towards intuitionistic dynamic logic. Logic Logical Philos. **15**(4), 305–324 (2006)
6. Diéguez, M., Fernández-Duque, D.: An intuitionistic axiomatization of 'eventually'. In: Advances in Modal Logic, vol. 12, pp. 199–218. College Publications, London (2018)
7. van Ditmarsch, H., van der Hoek, W., Kooi, B.P.: Dynamic Epistemic Logic, vol. 337. Springer, Heidelberg (2007). https://doi.org/10.1007/978-1-4020-5839-4
8. Fischer, M.J., Ladner, R.E.: Propositional dynamic logic of regular programs. Comput. Syst. Sci. **18**(2), 194–211 (1979)
9. Gerbrandy, J., Groeneveld, W.: Reasoning about information change. J. Logic Lang. Inf. **6**(2), 147–169 (1997)
10. Harel, D., Kozen, D., Tiuryn, J.: Dynamic Logic. MIT Press, Cambridge (2000)
11. Hatano, R., Sano, K.: Recapturing dynamic logic of relation changers via bounded morphisms. Studia Logica (2020). https://doi.org/10.1007/s11225-020-09902-5
12. Hatano, R., Sano, K., Tojo, S.: Cut free labelled sequent calculus for dynamic logic of relation changers. In: Yang, S.C.-M., Lee, K.Y., Ono, H. (eds.) Philosophical Logic: Current Trends in Asia. LASLL, pp. 153–180. Springer, Singapore (2017). https://doi.org/10.1007/978-981-10-6355-8_8
13. Kooi, B.: Expressivity and completeness for public update logics via reduction axioms. J. Appl. Non-Classical Logics **17**(2), 231–253 (2007)

14. Leivant, D.: Proof theoretic methodology for propositional dynamic logic. In: Díaz, J., Ramos, I. (eds.) ICFPC 1981. LNCS, vol. 107, pp. 356–373. Springer, Heidelberg (1981). https://doi.org/10.1007/3-540-10699-5_111
15. Liu, F.: Reasoning About Preference Dynamics, vol. 354. Springer, Heidelberg (2011). https://doi.org/10.1007/978-94-007-1344-4
16. Ma, M., Palmigiano, A., Sadrzadeh, M.: Algebraic semantics and model completeness for intuitionistic public announcement logic. Ann. Pure Appl. Logic **165**(4), 963–995 (2014)
17. Nishimura, H.: Sequential method in propositional dynamic logic. Acta Informatica **12**(4), 377–400 (1979)
18. Nishimura, H.: Semantical analysis of constructive PDL. Publ. Res. Inst. Math. Sci. Kyoto Univ. **18**(2), 847–858 (1982)
19. Plaza, J.: Logics of public communications. In: Emrich, M.L., Pfeifer, M.S., Hadzikadic, M., Ras, Z.W. (eds.) Proceedings of the 4th International Symposium on Methodologies for Intelligent Systems, pp. 201–216 (1989)
20. Sano, K., Stell, J.: Strong completeness and the finite model property for bi-intuitionistic stable tense logics. Electron. Proc. Theoret. Comput. Sci. **243**, 105–121 (2017)
21. Sedlár, I.: Propositional dynamic logic with Belnapian truth values. In: Advances in Modal Logic, vol. 11, pp. 503–519. College Publications, London (2016)
22. Sedlár, I.: Substructural propositional dynamic logics. In: Iemhoff, R., Moortgat, M., de Queiroz, R. (eds.) Logic, Language, Information, and Computation, pp. 594–609. Springer, Heidelberg (2019). https://doi.org/10.1007/978-3-662-59533-6_36
23. Segerberg, K.: An Essay in Classical Modal Logic, Filosofiska Studier, vol. 13. University of Uppsala (1971)
24. Stell, J.G., Schmidt, R.A., Rydeheard, D.: A bi-intuitionistic modal logic: foundations and automation. J. Logical Algebraic Methods Program. **85**(4), 500–519 (2016)
25. Wang, Y., Aucher, G.: An alternative axiomatization of DEL and its applications. In: Proceedings of the Twenty-Third IJCAI International Joint Conference in Artificial Intelligence, pp. 1139–1146 (2013)
26. Wang, Y., Cao, Q.: On axiomatizations of public announcement logic. Synthese **190**(1), 103–134 (2013)
27. Wijesekera, D., Nerode, A.: Tableaux for constructive concurrent dynamic logic. Ann. Pure Appl. Logic **135**(1), 1–72 (2005)
28. Wolter, F., Zakharyaschev, M.: Intuitionistic modal logic. In: Cantini, A., Casari, E., Minari, P. (eds.) Logic and Foundations of Mathematics, pp. 227–238. Springer, Netherlands (1999). https://doi.org/10.1007/978-94-017-2109-7_17
29. Yamada, T.: Acts of commanding and changing obligations. In: Inoue, K., Satoh, K., Toni, F. (eds.) CLIMA 2006. LNCS (LNAI), vol. 4371, pp. 1–19. Springer, Heidelberg (2007). https://doi.org/10.1007/978-3-540-69619-3_1

Complexity of Commutative Infinitary Action Logic

Stepan Kuznetsov(✉)

Steklov Mathematical Institute of RAS, Moscow, Russia
sk@mi-ras.ru

Abstract. We consider commutative infinitary action logic, that is, the equational theory of commutative *-continuous action lattices, and show that its derivability problem is Π_1^0-complete. Thus, we obtain a commutative version of Π_1^0-completeness for non-commutative infinitary action logic by Buszkowski and Palka (2007). The proof of the upper bound is more or less the same as Palka's argument. For the lower bound, we encode non-terminating behaviour of two-counter Minsky machines.

Keywords: Complexity · Infinitary action logic · Commutative action lattices

1 Introduction

Action logic is the equational theory (algebraic logic) for action lattices, that is, Kleene lattices with residuals. The concept of action lattice, introduced by Pratt [17] and Kozen [8], combines several algebraic structures: a partially ordered monoid with residuals ("multiplicative structure"), a lattice ("additive structure") sharing the same partial order, and Kleene star. (Pratt introduced the notion of action algebra, which bears only a semi-lattice structure with join, but not meet. Action lattices are due to Kozen.)

Definition 1. *An action lattice is a structure* $\langle A; \preceq, \cdot, \mathbf{0}, \mathbf{1}, \multimap, \circ\!-, \vee, \wedge, {}^* \rangle$*, where:*

1. $\preceq$ *is a partial order on* A*;*
2. $\mathbf{0}$ *is the smallest element for* $\preceq$*, that is,* $\mathbf{0} \preceq a$ *for any* $a \in A$*;*
3. $\langle \mathcal{A}; \cdot, \mathbf{1} \rangle$ *is a monoid;*
4. $\multimap$ *and* $\circ\!-$ *are residuals of the product* $(\cdot)$ *w.r.t.* $\preceq$*, that is:*

$$b \preceq a \multimap c \iff a \cdot b \preceq c \iff a \preceq c \circ\!- b;$$

5. $\langle \mathcal{A}; \preceq, \vee, \wedge \rangle$ *is a lattice;*
6. *for each* $a \in A$*,* $a^* = \min_{\preceq} \{ b \mid \mathbf{1} \preceq b \text{ and } a \cdot b \preceq b \}$*.*

An important subclass of action lattices is formed by **-continuous* action lattices.

M. A. Martins and I. Sedlár (Eds.): DaLí 2020, LNCS 12569, pp. 155–169, 2020.
https://doi.org/10.1007/978-3-030-65840-3_10

Definition 2. *Action lattice $\mathcal{A}$ is *-continuous, if for any $a \in A$ we have $a^* = \sup_{\preceq}\{a^n \mid n \geq 0\}$, where $a^n = a \cdot \ldots \cdot a$ (n times) and $a^0 = \mathbf{1}$.*

Interesting examples of action lattices are mostly *-continuous; non-*-continuous action lattices also exist, but are constructed artificially.

The equational theory for the class of action lattices or its subclass (*e.g.*, the class of *-continuous action lattices) is the set of all statements of the form $A \preceq B$, where A and B are formulae (terms) built from variables and constants $\mathbf{0}$ and $\mathbf{1}$ using action lattice operations, which are true in any action lattice from the given class under any valuation of variables. More precisely, the previous sentence defines the *in*equational theory, but in the presence of lattice operations it is equivalent to the equational one: $A \preceq B$ can be equivalently represented as $A \vee B = B$.

In a different terminology, equational theories of classes of action lattices are seen as algebraic logics. These logics are substructural, extending the multiplicative-additive ("full") Lambek calculus [6,13], which is a non-commutative intuitionstic variant of Girard's linear logic [4].

The equational theory of all action lattices is called action logic and denoted by **ACT**. For the subclass of *-continuous action lattices, the equational theory is *infinitary action logic* $\mathbf{ACT}_\omega$, introduced by Buszkowski and Palka [2,3,16].

The interest to such a weak language—only (in)equations—is motivated by complexity considerations. Namely, for the next more expressible language, the language of Horn theories, the corresponding theory of the class of *-continuous action lattices is already Π_1^1-complete [9], that is, has a non-arithmetical complexity level. In contrast, $\mathbf{ACT}_\omega$ is Π_1^0-complete, as shown by Buszkowski and Palka [2,16]. For the general case, **ACT** is Σ_1^0-complete [10,11], which is already the maximal possible complexity: iteration in action lattices in general allows a finite axiomatization, unlike the *-continuous situation, which requires infinitary mechanisms.

Kleene algebras and their extensions are used in computer science for reasoning about program correctness. In particular, elements of an action lattice are intended to represent *types of actions* performed by a computing system (say, transitions in a finite automaton). Multiplication corresponds to composition of actions, Kleene star is iteration (perform an action several times, maybe zero). Residuals represent *conditional* types of actions. An action of type $a \multimap b$, being preceded by an action of type a, gives an action of type b. Dually, $b \multimapinv a$ is the type of actions which require to be followed by an action of type a to achieve b.

The monoid operation (multiplication) in action lattices is in general non-commutative, since so is, in general, composition of actions. However, in his original paper Pratt designates the subclass of commutative action algebras:

> "A *commutative* action algebra is an action algebra satisfying $ab = ba$. Whereas action logic in general is neutral as to whether ab combines a and b sequentially or concurrently, commutative action logic in effect commits to concurrency". [17]

Later on, however, commutative action algebras (lattices) were not studied systematically. Concurrent computations are usually treated using a more flexible approach, using a specific parallel execution connective, $\|$, in the framework of concurrent Kleene algebras, CKA [5], and its extensions. In particular, the author is not aware of a study of equational theories (algebraic logics) for commutative action lattices.

In this paper, we focus on *-continuous commutative action lattices and their equational theory, which we denote by $\mathbf{CommACT}_\omega$. The general, non-*-continuous case is left for further research. For $\mathbf{CommACT}_\omega$, we present (Sect. 2) an infinitary cut-free sequent calculus and using this calculus prove an upper Π_1^0 complexity bound. This is a commutative adaptation of Palka's reasoning on the non-commutative $\mathbf{ACT}_\omega$. Next (Sect. 3), we establish the commutative counter-part of Buszkowski's [2] lower complexity bound, which is also Π_1^0. Thus, in short, the result of our paper can be formulated as follows:

$$\mathbf{CommACT}_\omega \text{ is } \Pi_1^0\text{-complete.}$$

The present work is based, on one side, on the work of Palka [16] and, on the other side, on the work of Lincoln et al. [14]. Palka's approach is used for constructing a cut-free infinitary sequent calculus for $\mathbf{CommACT}_\omega$ and proving the Π_1^0 lower complexity bound. These proofs basically copy Palka's ones; commutativity does not add anything significantly new here.

In contrast, for proving Π_1^0-hardness (lower bound) we could not have used Buszkowski's argument [2], since it uses a reduction from the totality problem for context-free grammars, which is intrinsically non-commutative. Instead, we use an encoding of two-counter Minsky machines, which are commutative-friendly. The encoding of Minsky instructions and configurations is taken from the work of Lincoln et al. [14], with minor modifications.

The principal difference from [14], however, is the usage of Kleene star to model *non-halting* behaviour of Minsky machines (while Lincoln et al. use the exponential modality of linear logic for modelling halting computations). This gives Π_1^0-hardness for $\mathbf{CommACT}_\omega$, dual to Σ_1^0-hardness of propositional linear logic [14]. Also, in succedents of our sequents we now have to represent an *arbitrary* configuration of the Minsky machine being encoded, as opposed to representing only the *final* configuration in [14]. This is also implemented using Kleene star.

2 Proof Theory for $\mathbf{CommACT}_\omega$

We present an infinitary sequent calculus for $\mathbf{CommACT}_\omega$, which is a commutative version of Palka's system for $\mathbf{ACT}_\omega$. Formulae of $\mathbf{CommACT}_\omega$ are built from a countable set of variables $\mathrm{Var} = \{p, q, r, \dots\}$ and constant $\mathbf{1}$ using four binary connectives, $\multimap$, $\cdot$, $\vee$, and $\wedge$, and one unary connective, *. (Due to commutativity, $B \mathbin{\circ\!\!-} A$ is always equivalent to $A \multimap B$, so we have only one residual here.) Sequents are expressions of the form $\Gamma \vdash A$, where Γ is a multiset of formulae (that is, the number of occurrences matters, while the order does not) and A is a formula. In our notations, capital Greek letters denote multisets of formulae and capital Latin letters denote formulae.

Axioms and inference rules of $\mathbf{CommACT}_\omega$ are as follows:

$$\frac{}{A \vdash A}\ Id \qquad \frac{}{\Gamma, \mathbf{0} \vdash C}\ \mathbf{0}L \qquad \frac{\Gamma \vdash C}{\Gamma, \mathbf{1} \vdash C}\ \mathbf{1}L \qquad \frac{}{\vdash \mathbf{1}}\ \mathbf{1}R$$

$$\frac{\Pi \vdash A \quad \Gamma, B \vdash C}{\Gamma, \Pi, A \multimap B \vdash C} \multimap L \qquad \frac{A, \Pi \vdash B}{\Pi \vdash A \multimap B} \multimap R$$

$$\frac{\Gamma, A, B \vdash C}{\Gamma, A \cdot B \vdash C} \cdot L \qquad \frac{\Pi \vdash A \quad \Delta \vdash B}{\Pi, \Delta \vdash A \cdot B} \cdot R$$

$$\frac{\Gamma, A \vdash C \quad \Gamma, B \vdash C}{\Gamma, A \vee B \vdash C} \vee L \qquad \frac{\Pi \vdash A}{\Pi \vdash A \vee B} \vee R \qquad \frac{\Pi \vdash B}{\Pi \vdash A \vee B} \vee R$$

$$\frac{\Gamma, A \vdash C}{\Gamma, A \wedge B \vdash C} \wedge L \qquad \frac{\Gamma, B \vdash C}{\Gamma, A \wedge B \vdash C} \wedge L \qquad \frac{\Pi \vdash A \quad \Pi \vdash B}{\Pi \vdash A \wedge B} \wedge R$$

$$\frac{\left(\Gamma, A^n \vdash C\right)_{n=0}^{\infty}}{\Gamma, A^* \vdash C} *L \qquad \frac{\Pi_1 \vdash A \quad \dots \quad \Pi_n \vdash A}{\Pi_1, \dots, \Pi_n \vdash A^*} *R,\ n \geq 0$$

$$\frac{\Pi \vdash A \quad \Gamma, A \vdash C}{\Gamma, \Pi \vdash C}\ Cut$$

The set of derivable sequents (theorems) is the smallest set which includes all instances of axioms and which is closed under inference rules. Thus, derivation trees in $\mathbf{CommACT}_\omega$ may have infinite branching (at instances of $*L$, which is an ω-rule), but are required to be well-founded (infinite paths are forbidden).

Let us formulate several properties of $\mathbf{CommACT}_\omega$ and give proof sketches, following Palka [16], but in the commutative setting. The proofs are essentially the same as Palka's ones; we give their sketches here in order to make this paper logically self-contained.

The sequents of $\mathbf{CommACT}_\omega$ presented above enjoy a natural algebraic interpretation on commutative action lattices. Namely, given an action lattice $\mathcal{A}$, we intepret variables as arbitrary elements of $\mathcal{A}$, by a valuation function $v \colon \mathrm{Var} \to \mathcal{A}$, and then propagate this interpretation to formulae. Let us denote the interpretation of formula A under valuation v by $\bar{v}(A)$. A sequent of the form $A_1, \dots, A_n \vdash B$ ($n \geq 1$) is true under this interpretation if $\bar{v}(A_1) \cdot \ldots \cdot \bar{v}(A_n) \preceq \bar{v}(B)$ (due to commutativity of $\cdot$, the order of A_i's does not matter). For $n = 0$, the sequent $\vdash B$ is declared true if $\mathbf{1} \preceq \bar{v}(B)$. A soundness-and-completeness theorem holds:

Theorem 1. *A sequent is derivable in* $\mathbf{CommACT}_\omega$ *if and only if it is true in all commutative *-continuous action lattices under all valuations of variables.*

Proof. The "only if" part (soundness) is proved by (transfinite) induction on the structure of derivation. For the "if" part (completeness), we use the standard Lindenbaum – Tarski canonical model construction. □

Thus, **CommACT**$_\omega$ is indeed an axiomatization for the equational theory of commutative *-continuous action lattices.

In order to facilitate induction on derivation in the infinitary setting, we define the *depth* of a derivable sequent in the following way. For an ordinal α, let us define the set S_α by transfinite recursion:

$$S_0 = \varnothing;$$
$$S_{\alpha+1} = \{\Gamma \vdash A \mid \Gamma \vdash A \text{ is derivable by one rule application from } S_\alpha\};$$
$$S_\lambda = \bigcup_{\alpha<\lambda} S_\alpha \text{ for } \lambda \in \mathrm{Lim}.$$

(In particular, S_1 is the set of all axioms of **CommACT**$_\omega$.) For a derivable sequent $\Gamma \vdash A$ let $d(\Gamma \vdash A) = \min\{\alpha \mid (\Gamma \vdash A) \in S_\alpha\}$ be its depth.

The complexity of a formula A is defined as the total number of subformula occurrences in it.

Theorem 2. *The calculus* **CommACT**$_\omega$ *enjoys cut elimination, that is, any derivable sequent can be derived without using Cut.*

Proof. First we eliminate one cut on the bottom of a derivation, that is, show that if $\Pi \vdash A$ and $\Gamma, A \vdash C$ are cut-free derivable, then so is $\Gamma, \Pi \vdash C$. This is established by triple induction on the following parameters: (1) complexity of A; (2) depth of $\Pi \vdash A$; (3) depth of $\Gamma, \Pi \vdash C$. See [16, Theorem 3.1] for details.

Next, let a sequent $\Gamma \vdash B$ be derivable using cuts. Let $d(\Gamma \vdash B)$ be its depth, counted for the calculus with cut as an official rule. Let us show that $\Gamma \vdash B$ is cut-free derivable by induction on $\alpha = d(\Gamma \vdash B)$. Notice that α is not a limit ordinal: otherwise, $(\Gamma \vdash B) \in S_\beta$ for some $\beta < \alpha$. Also $\alpha \neq 0$. Thus, $\alpha = \beta + 1$. The sequent $\Gamma \vdash B$ is immediately derivable, by one rule application, from a set of sequents from S_β, that is, of smaller depth. By the induction hypothesis, these sequents are cut-free derivable. Now consider the rule which was used to derive $\Gamma \vdash B$. If it is not cut, then $\Gamma \vdash B$ is also cut-free derivable. If it is cut, we apply the reasoning from the beginning of this proof and establish cut-free derivability of $\Gamma \vdash B$. □

In order to prove that **CommACT**$_\omega$ belongs to the Π_1^0 complexity class, we use Palka's *-elimination technique. For each sequent, we define its *n-th approximation.* Informally, we replace each negative occurrence of A^* with $A^{\leq n} = \mathbf{1} \vee A \vee A^2 \vee \ldots \vee A^n$. The n-th approximation of a sequent $A_1, \ldots, A_m \vdash B$ is defined as $N_n(A_1), \ldots, N_n(A_m) \vdash P_n(B)$, where mappings N_n and P_n are defined by joint recursion:

$$N_n(\alpha) = P_n(\alpha) = \alpha,\ \alpha \in \mathrm{Var} \cup \{\mathbf{0}, \mathbf{1}\}$$
$$N_n(A \multimap B) = P_n(A) \multimap N_n(B) \qquad P_n(A \multimap B) = N_n(A) \multimap P_n(B)$$
$$N_n(A \cdot B) = N_n(A) \cdot N_n(B) \qquad P_n(A \cdot B) = P_n(A) \cdot P_n(B)$$
$$N_n(A \vee B) = N_n(A) \vee N_n(B) \qquad P_n(A \vee B) = P_n(A) \vee P_n(B)$$
$$N_n(A \wedge B) = N_n(A) \wedge N_n(B) \qquad P_n(A \wedge B) = P_n(A) \wedge P_n(B)$$
$$N_n(A^*) = \mathbf{1} \vee N_n(A) \vee (N_n(A))^2 \vee \ldots \vee (N_n(A))^n$$
$$P_n(A^*) = (P_n(A))^*$$

(In Palka's notation, N and P are inverted.)

The *-elimination theorem, resembling Palka's [16] Theorem 5.1, is now formulated as follows:

Theorem 3. *A sequent is derivable in* $\mathbf{CommACT}_\omega$ *if and only if its n-th approximation is derivable in* $\mathbf{CommACT}_\omega$ *for any n.*

Proof. The "only if" part is easier. We establish by induction that $A \vdash P_n(A)$ and $N_n(A) \vdash A$ are derivable for any A: see [16, Lemma 4.3] for $\mathbf{ACT}_\omega$; commutativity does not alter this part of the prove. Next, we apply cut several times:

$$\frac{N_n(A_1) \vdash A_1 \quad \ldots \quad N_n(A_m) \vdash A_m \quad A_1, \ldots, A_m \vdash B \quad B \vdash P_n(B)}{N_n(A_1), \ldots, N_n(A_m) \vdash P_n(B)}$$

For the "if" part, a specific induction parameter is introduced. This parameter is called the *rank* of a formula and is represented by a sequence of natural numbers. These sequences are formally infinite, but include only zeroes starting from some point. For a sequent $\Gamma \vdash A$ its rank $\rho(\Gamma \vdash A)$ is the sequence $(c_0, c_1, c_2, \ldots)$, where c_i is the number of subformulae of complexity i in $\Gamma \vdash A$.

The order on ranks is anti-lexicographical: $(c_0, c_1, c_2, \ldots) \prec (c'_0, c'_1, c'_2, \ldots)$, if there exists a natural number i such that $c_i < c'_i$ and for any $j > i$ we have $c_j = c'_j$. In any rank $(c_0, c_1, c_2, \ldots)$ of a sequent there exists such a k_0 that $c_k = 0$ for all $k > k_0$ (k_0 is the maximal complexity of a subformula in $\Gamma \vdash A$). Hence, any two ranks are comparable. Moreover, the order on ranks is well-founded. Thus, we can perform induction on ranks.

The rules of $\mathbf{CommACT}_\omega$ enjoy the following property: each premise has a smaller rank than the conclusion. In particular, this holds for $*L$: despite A is copied n times, its complexity is smaller, than that of A^*. Thus, when going from conclusion to premise, we reduce some c_i by one and increase c_{i-1} (where i is the complexity of A^*). The rank gets reduced.

Now we prove the "if" part by contraposition. Suppose a sequent $\Pi \vdash B$ is not derivable in $\mathbf{CommACT}_\omega$. We shall prove that for some n the n-th approximation of this sequent is also not derivable. We proceed by induction on $\rho(\Pi \vdash B)$. Consider two cases.

Case 1: one of the formulae in Π is of the form A^*. Then $\Pi = \Pi', A^*$ and for some m the sequent $\Pi', A^m \vdash B$ is not derivable (otherwise $\Pi \vdash B$ would be derivable by $*L$). Since $\rho(\Pi', A^m \vdash B) \prec \rho(\Pi', A^* \vdash B)$, we can apply the induction hypothesis and conclude that for some k the sequent $N_k(\Pi'), (N_k(A))^m \vdash P_k(B)$ is not derivable. Here $N_k(\Pi')$, for $\Pi' = C_1, \ldots, C_s$, is defined as $N_k(C_1), \ldots, N_k(C_s)$.

Now take $n = \max\{m, k\}$. We claim that $N_n(\Pi'), N_n(A^*) \vdash P_n(B)$ is not derivable. This is indeed the case, because otherwise we could derive the sequent $N_k(\Pi'), (N_k(A))^m \vdash P_k(B)$ using cut. The sequents used in cut are $N_k(C_j) \vdash N_n(C_j)$, for each C_j in Π', $(N_k(A))^m \vdash N_n(A)^*$, and $P_n(B) \vdash P_k(B)$, which are derivable (see [16, Lemma 4.4]).

Case 2: no formula of Π is of the form A^*. Thus, our sequent cannot be derived using (immediately) the $*L$ rule. All other rules are finitary, and there is only a finite number of possible applications of these rules (for example, for $\multimap L$ there is a finite number of possible splittings of the context to Γ and Π). For each of these possible rule applications, at least one of its premises should be non-derivable (otherwise we derive the original sequent $\Pi \vdash B$).

The premises have smaller ranks than $\Pi \vdash B$, so we can apply the induction hypothesis. This gives, for each premise, non-derivability of its k-th approximation for some k. Let n be the maximum of these k's. Increasing k keeps each approximation non-derivable, and we get non-derivability of the n-th approximation of the original sequent. □

The *-elimination technique yields the upper complexity bound:

Theorem 4. *The derivability problem in* **CommACT**$_\omega$ *belongs to the* Π_1^0 *complexity class.*

Proof. By Theorem 3, derivability of a sequent is reduced to derivability of all its n-th approximations. Each n-th approximation, in its turn, is a sequent without negative occurrences of *, that is, its derivation in **CommACT**$_\omega$ is always finite (does not use $*L$). For such sequents, the derivability problem is decidable by exhausting proof search, since all rules, except $*L$, reduce the complexity of the sequent (when looking upwards). The "$\forall n$" quantifier yields Π_1^0. □

3 Π_1^0-hardness of CommACT$_\omega$

In this section we prove Π_1^0-hardness for **CommACT**$_\omega$ by reducing the *non-halting* problem for deterministic two-counter Minsky machines [15] to derivability in **CommACT**$_\omega$. The halting problem for such machines is equivalent to that for Turing machines [15, Theorem Ia] and therefore Σ_1^0-complete. The dual problem of non-halting is Π_1^0-complete.

Our approach is in a sense dual to the undecidability proof for (commutative) propositional linear logic by Lincoln et al. [14]. Unlike Turing machines or semi-Thue systems, Minsky machines keep only integers in their memory. Thus, Minsky machine configurations can be encoded by formulae of a commutative substructural logic (see below). For linear logic, Lincoln et al. [14] use a reduction from the halting problem of Minsky machines to derivability in linear logic. They use the exponential modality, $!A$, which is expanded to A^n, for *some* n, using the contraction rule. This encodes termination of Minsky computation after n steps. Here A encodes the instruction set of our Minsky machine. Dually, we use A^*, which is expanded using the ω-rule, $*L$, to an infinite series of sequents with A^n for *any* n. This corresponds to an infinite run of the Minsky machine: it can perform arbitrarily many steps.

Notice that, as in [14], we essentially use commutativity. It is needed to deliver the instruction to the correct place in the formula encoding the machine configuration. In the non-commutative setting, this is a separate issue, and Buszkowski's Π_1^0-hardness proof for $\mathbf{ACT}_\omega$ [2] uses an indirect reduction from non-halting of Turing machines, via totality for context-free grammars.

A Minsky machine $\mathcal{M}$ has two registers (counters), denoted by a and b, and a finite memory represented by a finite set of states Q. Each register keeps a natural number (possibly zero), thus, a configuration of $\mathcal{M}$ is represented by a triple of the form $\langle q, a, b\rangle$, where $q \in Q$ and $a, b \in \mathbb{N}$.

Instructions of $\mathcal{M}$ are of the following forms (here $r \in \{\mathsf{a}, \mathsf{b}\}$, $p, q, q_0, q_1 \in Q$):

$\text{INC}(p, r, q)$	being in state p, increase register r by 1 and move to state q;
$\text{JZDEC}(p, r, q_0, q_1)$	being in state p, check whether the value of r is 0: if yes, move to state q_0, if no, decrease r by 1 and move to state q_1.

The machine $\mathcal{M}$ is required to be deterministic, that is, enjoy only one possible way of execution. This means that for any $p \in Q$ there is no more than one instruction with this p as the first parameter.

In $\mathbf{CommACT}_\omega$, configurations of $\mathcal{M}$ are encoded as follows. Let $\{\mathsf{a}, \mathsf{b}\} \cup Q \subset \mathrm{Var}$ and encode configuration $\langle q, a, b\rangle$ as

$$\underbrace{\mathsf{a}, \ldots, \mathsf{a}}_{a \text{ times}}, \underbrace{\mathsf{b}, \ldots, \mathsf{b}}_{b \text{ times}}, q.$$

This encoding will appear in antecedents of $\mathbf{CommACT}_\omega$ sequents, thus, it is considered as a multiset. This keeps the numbers of a's and b's, which is crucial for representing Minsky configurations.

Each instruction I is encoded by a specific $\mathbf{CommACT}_\omega$ formula A_I. For INC, the encoding is straightforward:

$$A_{\text{INC}(p,r,q)} = p \multimap (q \cdot r).$$

For JZDEC, the encoding is more involved. We introduce two extra variables, z_{a} and z_{b}, and encode $\text{JZDEC}(p, r, q_0, q_1)$ by the following formula:

$$A_{\text{JZDEC}(p,r,q_0,q_1)} = ((p \cdot r) \multimap q_1) \wedge (p \multimap (q_0 \vee z_r)).$$

Moreover, we introduce two extra formulae, $N_{\mathsf{a}} = z_{\mathsf{a}} \multimap z_{\mathsf{a}}$ and $N_{\mathsf{b}} = z_{\mathsf{b}} \multimap z_{\mathsf{b}}$.

Let us first explain the informal idea behind this encoding. In our derivations, formulae of the form A_I are going to appear in left-hand sides of sequents (along with the code of the configuration), instantiated using Kleene star. For INC, when the formula $A_{\mathrm{INC}(p,r,q)}$ gets introduced by $\multimap L$, we replace p with $q \cdot r$ (looking from bottom to top). This corresponds to changing the state from p to q and increasing register r.

For JZDEC, we use additive connectives, $\wedge$ and $\vee$. Being in the negative position (in the left-hand side of the sequent), $\wedge$ implements *choice* and $\vee$ implements *branching* (parallel computations). In JZDEC, the choice is as follows. If there is at least one copy of variable r (*i.e.*, the value of register r is not zero), we can choose $(p \cdot r) \multimap q_1$ which changes the state from p to q_1 and decreases r. We could also choose $p \multimap (q_0 \vee z_r)$, for the zero case. This operation continues the main execution thread by changing to state q_0, but also forks a new thread with a "state" z_r. This new thread is designed to check whether r is actually zero. Since the thread was forked in the middle of the execution, say, after k steps, it still has to perform $(n - k)$ steps of execution. They get replaced by dummy instructions, encoded by $N_r = z_r \multimap z_r$.

The set of instructions (including "dummies") is encoded by the formula

$$E = N_{\mathsf{a}} \wedge N_{\mathsf{b}} \wedge \bigwedge_I A_I,$$

which is going to be copied using Kleene star.

The key feature of our encoding is the right-hand side of the sequent, which is going to be

$$D = (\mathsf{a}^* \cdot \mathsf{b}^* \cdot \bigvee_{q \in Q} q) \vee (\mathsf{b}^* \cdot z_{\mathsf{a}}) \vee (\mathsf{a}^* \cdot z_{\mathsf{b}}).$$

This formula represents constraints on the configuration after performing n steps of computation. For the main execution thread, it just says that it should reach a correctly encoded configuration of the form $\langle q, a, b \rangle$, $q \in Q$. For zero-checking thread, with "state" z_r, D enforces register r to be zero.

The encoding lemma, for a given finite number of steps, is as follows:

Lemma 1. *Minsky machine $\mathcal{M}$ can perform n steps of execution starting from configuration $\langle q_S, 0, 0 \rangle$ if and only if the sequent $E^n, q_S \vdash D$ is derivable in* **CommACT**$_\omega$.

This lemma immediately yields the necessary reduction:

Theorem 5. *Deterministic Minsky machine $\mathcal{M}$ runs forever if and only if the sequent $E^*, q_S \vdash D$ is derivable in* **CommACT**$_\omega$. *Therefore,* **CommACT**$_\omega$ *is Π_1^0-hard.*

Indeed, $E^*, q_S \vdash D$ is derivable from $\left(E^n, q_S \vdash D\right)_{n=0}^{\infty}$ by $*L$, and the opposite implication is by cut with $E^n \vdash E^*$.

Proof (of Lemma 1). The **"only if"** part, from computation to derivation, is easier. We prove the following statement by induction on k: if $\mathcal{M}$ can perform k steps starting from configuration $\langle p, a, b \rangle$, then $E^k, \mathsf{a}^a, \mathsf{b}^b, p \vdash D$ is derivable. The base case is $k = 0$. In this case we derive the necessary sequent $\mathsf{a}^a, \mathsf{b}^b, p \vdash D$ by $\vee R$ (twice) from $\mathsf{a}^a, \mathsf{b}^b, p \vdash \mathsf{a}^* \cdot \mathsf{b}^* \cdot \bigvee_{q \in Q} q$. The latter is derived using $*R$, $\vee R$, and $\cdot R$.

For the induction step, consider the first $\mathcal{M}$ instruction executed. If it is $\mathrm{INC}(p, \mathsf{a}, q)$, we perform the following derivation:

$$\dfrac{\dfrac{p \vdash p \qquad \dfrac{E^{k-1}, \mathsf{a}^{a+1}, \mathsf{b}^b, q \vdash D}{E^{k-1}, \mathsf{a}^a, \mathsf{b}^b, q \cdot \mathsf{a} \vdash D}\ {\cdot L}}{E^{k-1}, A_{\mathrm{INC}(p,\mathsf{a},q)}, \mathsf{a}^a, \mathsf{b}^b, p \vdash D}\ {\multimap L}\ (A_{\mathrm{INC}(p,\mathsf{a},q)} = p \multimap (q \cdot \mathsf{a}))}{E^k, \mathsf{a}^a, \mathsf{b}^b, p \vdash D}\ \wedge L \text{ several times}$$

The topmost sequent $E^{k-1}, \mathsf{a}^{a+1}, \mathsf{b}^b, q \vdash D$ is derivable by inductive hypothesis, since $\mathcal{M}$ can perform $k - 1$ execution steps starting from the next configuration $\langle q, a + 1, b \rangle$. The case of $\mathrm{INC}(p, \mathsf{b}, q)$ is considered similarly.

For $\mathrm{JZDEC}(p, \mathsf{a}, q_0, q_1)$, we consider two cases. If $a \neq 0$, then the derivation is similar to the one for INC:

$$\dfrac{\dfrac{\dfrac{\dfrac{p \vdash p \quad \mathsf{a} \vdash \mathsf{a}}{p, \mathsf{a} \vdash p \cdot \mathsf{a}}\ {\cdot R} \qquad E^{k-1}, \mathsf{a}^{a-1}, \mathsf{b}^b, q_1 \vdash D}{E^{k-1}, (p \cdot \mathsf{a}) \multimap q_1, \mathsf{a}^a, \mathsf{b}^b, p \vdash D}\ {\multimap L}}{E^{k-1}, A_{\mathrm{JZDEC}(p,\mathsf{a},q_0,q_1)}, \mathsf{a}^a, \mathsf{b}^b, p \vdash D}\ \wedge L}{E^k, \mathsf{a}^a, \mathsf{b}^b, p \vdash D}\ \wedge L \text{ several times}$$

Here $E^{k-1}, \mathsf{a}^{a-1}, \mathsf{b}^b, q_1 \vdash D$ is derivable by the induction hypothesis.

The interesting part is the zero test. Let $a = 0$ and perform the following derivation:

$$\dfrac{\dfrac{\dfrac{p \vdash p \qquad \dfrac{E^{k-1}, \mathsf{b}^b, q_0 \vdash D \quad E^{k-1}, \mathsf{b}^b, z_\mathsf{a} \vdash D}{E^{k-1}, q_0 \vee z_\mathsf{a}, \mathsf{b}^b \vdash D}\ \vee L}{E^{k-1}, p \multimap (q_0 \vee z_\mathsf{a}), \mathsf{b}^b, p \vdash D}\ {\multimap L}}{E^{k-1}, A_{\mathrm{JZDEC}(p,\mathsf{a},q_0,q_1)}, \mathsf{b}^b, p \vdash D}\ \wedge L}{E^k, \mathsf{b}^b, p \vdash D}\ \wedge L \text{ several times}$$

On the left branch, we have $E^{k-1}, \mathsf{b}^b, q_0 \vdash D$, which is derivable by the induction hypothesis: $\langle q_0, 0, b \rangle$ is the successor for $\langle p, 0, b \rangle$ after applying $\mathrm{JZDEC}(p, \mathsf{a}, q_0, q_1)$.

The sequent on the right branch, $E^{k-1}, \mathsf{b}^b, z_\mathsf{a} \vdash D$, can be derived using $\wedge L$ and $\vee R$ from $(z_\mathsf{a} \multimap z_\mathsf{a})^{k-1}, \mathsf{b}^b, z_\mathsf{a} \vdash \mathsf{b}^* \cdot z_\mathsf{a}$. Indeed, E is a conjunction which includes $N_\mathsf{a} = z_\mathsf{a} \multimap z_\mathsf{a}$, and D is a disjunction which includes $\mathsf{b}^* \cdot z_\mathsf{a}$. The latter sequent, $(z_\mathsf{a} \multimap z_\mathsf{a})^{k-1}, \mathsf{b}^b, z_\mathsf{a} \vdash \mathsf{b}^* \cdot z_\mathsf{a}$, is derivable.

The case of $\mathrm{JZDEC}(p, \mathsf{b}, q_0, q_1)$ is similar.

For the **"if"** part (from derivation to computation), we are going to perform an analysis of cut-free derivations and establish the following statements by induction on the natural parameter k:

1. if $E^k, \mathsf{a}^a, \mathsf{b}^b, z_\mathsf{a} \vdash D$ is derivable, then $a = 0$;
2. if $E^k, \mathsf{a}^a, \mathsf{b}^b, z_\mathsf{b} \vdash D$ is derivable, then $b = 0$;
3. if $E^k, \mathsf{a}^a, \mathsf{b}^b, p \vdash D$ is derivable, then $\mathcal{M}$ can perform k steps of computation starting from configuration $\langle p, a, b \rangle$.

Let us first perform some transformations of derivations. These transformations are closely related to *focusing* [1,7] of linear logic derivations. Notice that sequents in our statements do not include negative occurrences of Kleene star, so their derivations are finite. The only rules which can be used in cut-free derivations of the sequents in these statements are: $\wedge L$, $\vee L$, $\multimap L$, $\cdot L$; $\vee R$, $\cdot R$, $*R$.

We formulate our **first claim:** if a sequent is derivable using this set of rules, then this sequent enjoys a (cut-free) derivation in which no right rule ($\vee R$, $\cdot R$, or $*R$) appears below a left rule ($\wedge L$, $\vee L$, $\multimap L$, $\cdot L$).

Indeed, each right rule in this list is exchangeable upwards with each of the left rules. We show exchanging of $\cdot R$ and $\vee L$. In this case,

$$\dfrac{\dfrac{\Pi', E, \Pi'' \vdash A \quad \Pi', F, \Pi'' \vdash A}{\Pi', E \vee F, \Pi'' \vdash A}\,\vee L \qquad \Delta \vdash B}{\Pi', E \vee F, \Pi'', \Delta \vdash A \cdot B}\,\cdot R$$

transforms into

$$\dfrac{\dfrac{\Pi', E, \Pi'' \vdash A \quad \Delta \vdash B}{\Pi', E, \Pi'', \Delta \vdash A \cdot B}\,\cdot R \qquad \dfrac{\Pi', F, \Pi'' \vdash A \quad \Delta \vdash B}{\Pi', F, \Pi'', \Delta \vdash A \cdot B}\,\cdot R}{\Pi', E \vee F, \Pi'', \Delta \vdash A \cdot B}\,\vee L$$

Transformations in possible cases are similar. In order to proceed by induction, let us consider the following parameter. By an *incorrect pair* of rule applications let us denote a pair of applications of a left rule and a right rule, where the right rule appears below the left one. Now let use consider each path from the goal sequent to an axiom leaf of the derivation tree, and calculate the number of incorrect pairs on such a path. Next, take the maximum of these numbers. Proceed by induction on this parameter: take the path on which this maximum is achieved, take an incorrect pair in which the right rule appears immediately below the left one. Perform the necessary transformation. The parameter gets reduced. Our first claim is justified.

Next, we perform the following *disbalancing transformations:* if the left premise of $\multimap L$ were derived using a left rule, then this rule can be moved downwards. For $\wedge L$ and $\cdot L$, the transformation is as follows:

$$\dfrac{\dfrac{\widetilde{\Pi} \vdash A}{\Pi \vdash A} \quad \Gamma, B \vdash C}{\Gamma, \Pi, A \multimap B \vdash C}\,\multimap L \quad \rightsquigarrow \quad \dfrac{\dfrac{\widetilde{\Pi} \vdash A \quad \Gamma, B \vdash C}{\Gamma, \widetilde{\Pi}, A \multimap B \vdash C}\,\multimap L}{\Gamma, \Pi, A \multimap B \vdash C}$$

For $\vee L$,

$$\dfrac{\dfrac{\Pi', E, \Pi'' \vdash A \quad \Pi', F, \Pi'' \vdash A}{\Pi', E \vee F, \Pi'' \vdash A}\,\vee L \qquad \Gamma, B \vdash C}{\Gamma, \Pi', E \vee F, \Pi'', A \multimap B \vdash C}\,\multimap L$$

gets transformed into

$$\dfrac{\dfrac{\Gamma, \Pi', E \vdash A \quad \Gamma, B \vdash C}{\Gamma, \Pi', E, \Pi'', A \multimap B \vdash C} \multimap L \qquad \dfrac{\Gamma, \Pi', F \vdash A \quad \Gamma, B \vdash C}{\Gamma, \Pi', F, \Pi'', A \multimap B \vdash C} \multimap L}{\Gamma, \Pi', E \vee F, \Pi'', A \multimap B \vdash C} \vee L$$

For another instance of $\multimap L$, we have

$$\dfrac{\dfrac{\Phi \vdash E \quad \Pi, F \vdash A}{\Pi, \Phi, E \multimap F \vdash A} \multimap L \qquad \Gamma, B \vdash C}{\Gamma, \Pi, \Phi, E \multimap F, A \multimap B \vdash C} \multimap L$$

which transforms into

$$\dfrac{\Phi \vdash E \quad \dfrac{\Pi, F \vdash A \quad \Gamma, B \vdash C}{\Gamma, \Pi, F, A \multimap B \vdash C} \multimap L}{\Gamma, \Pi, \Phi, E \multimap F, A \multimap B \vdash C} \multimap L$$

Now we are ready to prove our **second claim:** if our sequent is derivable, it enjoys a derivation in which each left premise of $\multimap L$ is derived using only right rules.

Again, let us consider paths from the goal sequent to axiom leaves, and at each path let us calculate the number of incorrect pairs of rule applications, in which a left rule is used in a derivation of the left premise of $\multimap L$. The maximum of these numbers over all paths is our induction parameter, and it gets reduced by applying an appropriate transformation.

Let us call a derivation which satisfies our second claim a *disbalanced* one.

Now let us notice that in our antecedents formulae of the form $A \multimap B$ have either $A = p$ or $A = p \cdot r$. In a disbalanced derivation, the left premise of $\multimap L$ trivializes to an axiom or an axiom-like sequent of the form $p, r \vdash p \cdot r$.

Finally, applications of $\wedge L$ can be moved upwards and applied immediately below the left rule which introduces one of the conjuncts **(claim 3)**. Rules $\vee L$ and $\cdot L$ are invertible, so they can always be applied immediately (as low as possible), which is denoted by **claim 4.**

Having said that, let us analyze the derivation of $E^k, \mathsf{a}^a, \mathsf{b}^b, z_\mathsf{a} \vdash D$ (statement 1). The lowermost rule applications are a series of $\wedge L$ decomposing one of the E's. Immediately above, by claim 3, we have to decompose the chosen conjunct using $\multimap L$. Thanks to disbalancing, the left premise of $\multimap L$ is an axiom, and it should be $z_\mathsf{a} \vdash z_\mathsf{a}$. Thus, the conjunct chosen from E is $z_\mathsf{a} \multimap z_\mathsf{a}$. Now the right premise of $\multimap L$ is $E^{k-1}, \mathsf{a}^a, \mathsf{b}^b, z_\mathsf{a} \vdash D$. Decreasing k to zero, we show derivability of $\mathsf{a}^a, \mathsf{b}^b, z_\mathsf{a} \vdash D$. Now we have to apply $\vee R$ to decompose D, and the only way is to choose $\mathsf{b}^* \cdot z_\mathsf{a}$, getting $\mathsf{a}^a, \mathsf{b}^b, z_\mathsf{a} \vdash \mathsf{b}^* \cdot z_\mathsf{a}$. Since there are no right occurrences of a, there should be no left ones, that is, $a = 0$.

Statement 2 is established similarly.

Now let us establish the main statement 3. Again, we decompose one of the E's. Now we cannot choose $z_\mathsf{a} \multimap z_\mathsf{a}$ or $z_\mathsf{b} \multimap z_\mathsf{b}$, since there is no z_a or z_b freely available in the left-hand side. Thus, we choose A_I for some instruction I.

If $I = \text{INC}(p, r, q)$, then applying $\multimap L$ (in a disbalanced derivation) replaces p with $q \cdot r$. Since $\cdot L$ is invertible, we apply it immediately and get q, r. This corresponds exactly to application of $\text{INC}(p, r, q)$: the state is verified to be p and changed to q, register r is increased by 1. In the right premise of $\multimap L$ we now have E^{k-1}, and proceed further by induction on k.

If $I = \text{JZDEC}(p, r, q_0, q_1)$, we have one more choice to make: $(p \cdot r) \multimap q_1$ or $p \multimap (q_0 \vee z_r)$. The first choice is available only if the value of register r is non-zero, and in this case applying a disbalanced $\multimap L$ does the correct step: changes p to q and decreases the number of r's by 1. Now consider the second option. Let $r = \mathsf{a}$ (the b case is similar). Applying $\multimap L$ replaces p with $q_0 \vee z_{\mathsf{a}}$. We apply $\vee L$ immediately (claim 4) and get derivability of the following two sequents:

$$E^{k-1}, \mathsf{a}^a, \mathsf{b}^b, q_0 \vdash D;$$
$$E^{k-1}, \mathsf{a}^a, \mathsf{b}^b, z_{\mathsf{a}} \vdash D.$$

Derivability of the second sequent ensures the zero-condition, $a = 0$, by statement 1. Thus, applying JZDEC from $\langle p, a, b\rangle$ to $\langle q_0, a, b\rangle$ (that is, from $\langle p, 0, b\rangle$ to $\langle q_0, 0, b\rangle$) is legal. Using the first sequent, we proceed forward by induction on k.

Finally, if $k = 0$, then we have nothing to prove: any machine, starting from any configuration, can perform zero steps (do nothing).

Statement 3 immediately yields the "if" direction in Lemma 1. □

4 Concluding Remarks

In this paper, we have established Π_1^0-completeness of infinitary commutative action logic, $\mathbf{CommACT}_\omega$, that is, the equational theory of commutative *-continuous action lattices. This result is a commutative counterpart of results by Buszkowski and Palka [2,16]. The upper bound is proved in the same way as Palka's result. For the lower bound (Π_1^0-hardness), in contrast, we had to use a different encoding, using Minsky machines. This encoding is more straightforward, than the one Buszkowski used, as it directly encodes Minsky infinite computations as infinitary derivations in $\mathbf{CommACT}_\omega$.

This paper only begins the study of action lattices in the commutative situation. There are many questions are left for further research, below we formulate some of them.

1. We have commutative action logic **CommACT**, a weaker system with induction (Pratt-style) axioms instead of the ω-rule. Our conjecture is that this system is Σ_1^0-complete, as its non-commutative counterpart [10,11]. It is also interesting what subclass of infinite Minsky computations can be simulated in **CommACT**. Such computations are likely to include circular (looping) ones, but maybe some more.
2. The complexity question for $\mathbf{CommACT}_\omega$ without additive connectives ($\wedge$ and $\vee$) is open. Notice that additives are crucial for encoding the JZDEC instruction; in [14], there is no JZDEC, but there are parallel computations, also simulated using $\vee$.

3. It is an open question whether the same complexity results hold for the variant of $\mathbf{CommACT}_\omega$ with distributivity of $\vee$ over $\wedge$ added.
4. The complexity of the Horn theory for commutative action lattices or even commutative Kleene algebras is, to the best of the author's knowledge, unknown. Comparing with Kozen's result for non-commutative Kleene algebras [9], we conjecture Π_1^1-completeness, while the proof should again use Minsky machines instead of Turing ones.
5. It is also interesting to look at the non-associative, but commutative, version of infinitary action logic. In the non-associative case, it is problematic to define iteration, and it gets replaced with so-called *iterative division,* that is, compound connectives of the form $A^* \multimap B$ and $B \multimapinv A^*$. The interesting phenomenon here is that the corresponding non-commutative system happens to be algorithmically decidable, at least with the distributivity axiom added [18]. On the other hand, as shown in [12], in the associative case iterative division is sufficient for Π_1^0-hardness.

Financial Support. The work was supported by the Russian Science Foundation, in cooperation with the Austrian Science Fund, under grant RSF–FWF 20-41-05002.

Acknowledgments. The author is grateful to the participants of the DaLí 2020 online meeting for fruitful discussions, especially on directions of further research. Being a Young Russian Mathematics award winner, the author thanks the jury of the competition and sponsors of the award for this high honour.

References

1. Andreoli, J.-M.: Logic programming with focusing proofs in linear logic. J. Logic Comput. **2**(3), 297–347 (1992)
2. Buszkowski, W.: On action logic: equational theories of action algebras. J. Logic Comput. **17**(1), 199–217 (2007)
3. Buszkowski, W., Palka, E.: Infinitary action logic: complexity, models and grammars. Stud. Logica. **89**(1), 1–18 (2008)
4. Girard, J.-Y.: Linear logic. Theor. Comput. Sci. **50**(1), 1–101 (1987)
5. Hoare, T., Möller, B., Struth, G., Wehrman, I.: Concurrent Kleene algebra and its foundations. J. Logic Algebr. Meth. Progr. **80**, 266–296 (2011)
6. Kanazawa, M.: The Lambek calculus enriched with additional connectives. J. Logic Lang. Inform. **1**(2), 141–171 (1992)
7. Kanovich, M., Kuznetsov, S., Nigam, V., Scedrov, A.: A logical framework with commutative and non-commutative subexponentials. In: Galmiche, D., Schulz, S., Sebastiani, R. (eds.) IJCAR 2018. LNCS (LNAI), vol. 10900, pp. 228–245. Springer, Cham (2018). https://doi.org/10.1007/978-3-319-94205-6_16
8. Kozen, D.: On action algebras. In: van Eijck, J., Visser, A. (eds.) Logic and Information Flow, pp. 78–88. MIT Press (1994)
9. Kozen, D.: On the complexity of reasoning in Kleene algebra. Inform. Comput. **179**(2), 152–162 (2002)
10. Kuznetsov, S.: The logic of action lattices is undecidable. In: 34th Annual ACM/IEEE Symposium on Logic in Computer Science (LICS 2019). IEEE (2019)

11. Kuznetsov, S.: Action logic is undecidable. arXiv preprint 1912.11273 (2019). https://arxiv.org/abs/1912.11273
12. Kuznetsov, S.L., Ryzhkova, N.S.: A restricted fragment of the Lambek calculus with iteration and intersection operations. Algebra Logic **59**(2), 129–146 (2020)
13. Lambek, J.: The mathematics of sentence structure. Amer. Math. Monthly **65**, 154–170 (1958)
14. Lincoln, P., Mitchell, J., Scedrov, A., Shankar, N.: Decision problems for propositional linear logic. Ann. Pure Appl. Logic **56**(1–3), 239–311 (1992)
15. Minsky, M.L.: Recursive unsolvability of Post's problem of "Tag" and other topics in theory of turing machines. Ann. Math. **74**(3), 437–455 (1961)
16. Palka, E.: An infinitary sequent system for the equational theory of *-continuous action lattices. Fundam. Inform. **78**(2), 295–309 (2007)
17. Pratt, V.: Action logic and pure induction. In: van Eijck, J. (ed.) JELIA 1990. LNCS, vol. 478, pp. 97–120. Springer, Heidelberg (1991). https://doi.org/10.1007/BFb0018436
18. Sedlár, I.: Iterative division in the distributive full non-associative Lambek calculus. In: Soares Barbosa, L., Baltag, A. (eds.) DALI 2019. LNCS, vol. 12005, pp. 141–154. Springer, Cham (2020). https://doi.org/10.1007/978-3-030-38808-9_9

Grounding Awareness on Belief Bases

Emiliano Lorini[1](✉) and Pengfei Song[1,2]

[1] IRIT-CNRS, Toulouse University, Toulouse, France
Emiliano.Lorini@irit.fr

[2] Department of Philosophy, Institute of Logic and Cognition, Sun Yat-Sen University, Guangzhou, China

Abstract. We introduce a multi-agent logic of explicit, implicit belief and awareness with a semantics using belief bases. The novelty of our approach is that an agent's awareness is not a primitive but is directly computed from the agent's belief base. We prove soundness and completeness of the logic relative to the belief base semantics. Furthermore, we provide a polynomial embedding of the logic of propositional awareness into it.

1 Introduction

The notion of awareness was introduced in the area of epistemic logic by Fagin & Halpern (F&H) [4] to cope with the problem of *logical omniscience* [10]. Their approach is *syntactic* to the extent that they associate a subset of formulas to each agent at each state, indicating the formulas the agent is aware of. Following the idea suggested by Levesque [11], F&H make the distinction between *explicit belief* and *implicit belief*, where explicit belief is defined to be implicit belief *plus* awareness.

There is another tradition in the formalization of awareness, initiated by Modica & Rustichini [15,16] and Heifetz et al. [8,9]. They support a *semantic* approach by letting possible worlds be associated with a subset of all propositional variables being defined. Hence, an agent is aware of a formula if and only if, every atomic proposition occurring in the formula is defined at every epistemically accessible state for the agent. Such a notion of awareness is often called *propositional awareness* in opposition to the notion of *general awareness*, according to which an agent can be "primitively" aware not only of atomic propositions but also of complex formulas. Halpern [5] proves an equivalence result between the syntactic approach and the semantic approach to propositional awareness in a single-agent setting. Moreover, Halpern & Rêgo [6] present an analogous equivalence result for multi-agent awareness structures. van Ditmarsch et al. [3] give a novel notion called *speculative knowledge*, which is also built on propositional awareness.

The concept of explicit belief, which is central in the logic of awareness, is closely related to the concept of *belief base* [7,14,17,18]. The latter plays an important role in the AGM approach to belief revision [1] and, more generally, in

M. A. Martins and I. Sedlár (Eds.): DaLí 2020, LNCS 12569, pp. 170–186, 2020.
https://doi.org/10.1007/978-3-030-65840-3_11

the area of knowledge representation and reasoning (KR). Recently, in [12,13] we defined a formal semantics for multi-agent epistemic logic exploiting belief bases which clearly distinguishes explicit from implicit belief. Specifically, according to this semantics, an agent explicitly believes that a certain fact α is true if α is a piece of information included in the agent's belief base. On the contrary, the agent implicitly believes that α, if α is derivable from the agent's belief base. A logic of explicit and implicit belief, called Logic of Doxastic Attitudes (LDA), was defined on the top of this semantics.

In this paper, we extend the semantics introduced in [12] and the corresponding logic LDA with propositional awareness. We call LDAA the resulting logic. The novelty of our approach lies in the fact that the notion of awareness is not primitive but is directly computed from the notion of belief base. In particular, for an agent to be aware of a proposition p, p has to be included in the agent's vocabulary, that is to say, there should exist a formula in the agent's belief base which contains p. From this perspective, we offer a minimalistic logic approach to explicit, implicit belief and awareness in which only the former concept is primitive, while the other two concepts are defined from it.

The paper is organized as follows. In Sect. 2, we present the language of our logic of explicit, implicit belief and awareness. In Sect. 3, we first present the belief base semantics with respect to which the language is interpreted. Then, we introduce two alternative semantics which are closer in spirit to the standard semantics for epistemic logic based on multi-relational Kripke structures. We show that the three semantics are all equivalent with respect to the language under consideration. Section 4 is devoted to axiomatic results for our logic, while in Sect. 5 we explore the connection between our logic and Halpern's logic of propositional awareness (LPA) [5], by providing a satisfiability-preserving embedding of the latter into the former. Finally, in Sect. 6 we conclude.

2 Language

This section presents the language of the Logic of Doxastic Attitudes with Awareness (LDAA) to represent explicit beliefs, implicit beliefs, and awareness. It extends the language in [12] by the awareness modality. Let $Atm = \{p, q, ...\}$ be a countably infinite set of atomic propositions and let $Agt = \{1, ..., n\}$ be a finite set of agents. The language is given by the two levels in the following definition.

Definition 1. *The language $\mathcal{L}_0(Atm, Agt)$ is defined as follows:*

$$\alpha ::= p \mid \neg\alpha \mid \alpha_1 \wedge \alpha_2 \mid \triangle_i\alpha \mid \bigcirc_i\alpha$$

where p ranges over Atm and i ranges over Agt. The language $\mathcal{L}_{\mathsf{LDAA}}(Atm, Agt)$ extends $\mathcal{L}_0(Atm, Agt)$ by implicit belief operators and is defined as follows:

$$\varphi ::= \alpha \mid \neg\varphi \mid \varphi_1 \wedge \varphi_2 \mid \Box_i\varphi \mid \bigcirc_i\varphi$$

where i ranges over Agt.

When it is unambiguous from the context, we write $\mathcal{L}_0$ instead of $\mathcal{L}_0(Atm, Agt)$ and $\mathcal{L}_{\mathsf{LDAA}}$ instead of $\mathcal{L}_{\mathsf{LDAA}}(Atm, Agt)$. The other Boolean connectives $\vee$, $\rightarrow$, $\leftrightarrow$, $\top$ and $\bot$ are defined from $\neg$ and $\wedge$ in the standard way. The formula $\triangle_i \alpha$ is read "agent i explicitly believes that α is true". The formula $\bigcirc_i \alpha$ is read "agent i is aware of α". The $\triangle_i$-operator can be iterated, which means that the language contains expressions for higher-order explicit beliefs, such as $\triangle_i \triangle_j \alpha$, which is read "agent i explicitly believes that agent j explicitly believes that α is true". The iteration is possibly a mix of explicit belief and awareness, such as $\triangle_i \bigcirc_j \alpha$, which is read "agent i explicitly believes that agent j is aware of α".

And the formula $\Box_i \varphi$ is read "agent i implicitly believes that φ is true". The dual operator $\Diamond_i$ is defined as follows:

$$\Diamond_i \varphi := \neg \Box_i \neg \varphi,$$

where $\Diamond_i \varphi$ is read "φ is consistent with agent i's explicit beliefs".

Note that the modality $\bigcirc_i$ appears at both levels of the language, but the modality $\triangle_i$ only appears at the first level. As a result, we can have awareness operators in the scope of explicit belief operators, but not implicit belief operators. Moreover, both explicit belief operator and implicit belief operator are allowed inside the awareness operator. It is for the reason that, the concept of *propositional awareness* allows awareness of any formula that is constituted by atomic propositions that the agent is aware of.

Since we represent a propositional notion of awareness, i.e., being aware of a formula is equivalent to being aware of every atomic proposition occurring in it, we need the following inductive definition to represent the set of atomic propositions occurring in a formula φ, denoted by $Atm(\varphi)$:

- $Atm(p) := \{p\}$,
- $Atm(\neg\varphi) := Atm(\varphi)$,
- $Atm(\varphi_1 \wedge \varphi_2) := Atm(\varphi_1) \cup Atm(\varphi_2)$,
- $Atm(X_i \varphi) := Atm(\varphi)$, for $X \in \{\triangle, \bigcirc, \Box\}$.

Let $Y \subseteq \mathcal{L}_{\mathsf{LDAA}}$ be finite, we define $Atm(Y) := \bigcup_{\varphi \in Y} Atm(\varphi)$.

3 Semantics

In this section, we present three families of formal semantics for $\mathcal{L}_{\mathsf{LDAA}}$. The first semantics exploits belief bases. An agent's set of doxastic alternatives and awareness set are not primitive but computed from them. The second semantics is a Kripke-style semantics, in which we require each agent's set of doxastic alternatives to be equal to the set of worlds in which his explicit beliefs are true, and the agent's awareness set to be equal to the set of of atomic propositions occurring in his explicit beliefs. The third semantics relaxes these requirements, so that an agent's set of doxastic alternatives is included in the set of worlds in which the agent's explicit beliefs are true, and the set of atomic propositions occurring in an agent's explicit beliefs is a subset of the agent's awareness set.

3.1 Multi-agent Belief-Awareness Base Semantics

Let us start with the definition of belief-awareness base.

Definition 2. *A multi-agent belief-awareness base is a tuple* $BA = (B_1, ..., B_n, A_1, ..., A_n, V)$ *where,*

- $B_i \subseteq \mathcal{L}_0$ *is agent* i*'s belief base for any* $i \in Agt$,
- $A_i = Atm(B_i)$ *is agent* i*'s awareness set for any* $i \in Agt$,
- $V \subseteq Atm$ *is the actual state.*

The set of all multi-agent belief-awareness bases is denoted by **BA**. With the definition of multi-agent belief-awareness bases, we have the following interpretations for $\mathcal{L}_0$.

Definition 3. *For any* $BA = (B_1, ..., B_n, A_1, ..., A_n, V) \in \mathbf{BA}$:

- $BA \models p$ *iff* $p \in V$,
- $BA \models \neg\alpha$ *iff* $BA \not\models \alpha$,
- $BA \models \alpha_1 \wedge \alpha_2$ *iff* $BA \models \alpha_1$ *and* $BA \models \alpha_2$,
- $BA \models \triangle_i\alpha$ *iff* $\alpha \in B_i$,
- $BA \models \bigcirc_i\alpha$ *iff* $Atm(\alpha) \subseteq A_i$.[1]

By the interpretation, our awareness is propositional, i.e., being aware of a formula is equivalent to being aware of every atomic proposition occurring in the formula. Such a notion of awareness is different with the notion of general awareness according to which an agent can be aware of $p \wedge q$ without being aware of $p \vee q$.

The following definition introduces the concept of multi-agent belief-awareness model.

Definition 4. *A multi-agent belief-awareness model* (MABA) *is a pair* (BA, Cxt), *where* $BA \in \mathbf{BA}$ *and* $Cxt \subseteq \mathbf{BA}$.

Cxt is the agents' context or common ground [19]. It corresponds to the body of information that the agents share and that they use to make inferences from their explicit beliefs. Following [12], in the following definition we compute the agents' doxastically accessibility relations from their belief bases.

Definition 5. *For any* $i \in Agt$, $\mathcal{R}_i$ *is the binary relation on* **BA** *such that for any* $BA = (B_1, ..., B_n, A_1, ..., A_n, V), BA' = (B'_1, ..., B'_n, A'_1, ..., A'_n, V') \in \mathbf{BA}$,

$$(BA, BA') \in \mathcal{R}_i \text{ if and only if } \forall\alpha \in B_i \text{ , } BA' \models \alpha.$$

[1] Note that the awareness component of Definition 2 seems unnecessary, as we could interpret it equivalenty by postulating "$BA \models \bigcirc_i\alpha$ iff $Atm(\alpha) \subseteq Atm(B_i)$". We keep it for the reason that it has counterparts in NDAM semantics and quasi-NDAM semantics hereinafter. In quasi-NDAM semantics, an agent's awareness set is supposed to be a superset of the set of atomic propositions occurring in the agent's belief set.

With the accessibility relation defined, we have the following definition of interpretations for formulas in $\mathcal{L}_{\mathsf{LDAA}}$. The boolean case is defined in the usual way and omitted.

Definition 6. *Let* (BA, Cxt) *be a* MABA *with* $BA = (B_1, ..., B_n, A_1, ..., A_n, V)$. *Then,*

- $(BA, Cxt) \models \alpha$ *iff* $BA \models \alpha$,
- $(BA, Cxt) \models \Box_i \varphi$ *iff* $\forall BA' \in Cxt$, *if* $(BA, BA') \in \mathcal{R}_i$ *then* $(BA', Cxt) \models \varphi$,
- $(BA, Cxt) \models \bigcirc_i \varphi$ *iff* $Atm(\varphi) \subseteq A_i$.

The following two definitions specify two interesting properties of MABAs.

Definition 7. *The* MABA (BA, Cxt) *satisfies global consistency (GC) if and only if, for any* $i \in Agt$ *and for any* $BA' \in (\{BA\} \cup Cxt)$, *there exists* $BA'' \in Cxt$ *such that* $(BA', BA'') \in \mathcal{R}_i$.

Definition 8. *The* MABA (BA, Cxt) *satisfies belief correctness (BC) if and only if* $BA \in Cxt$ *and, for any* $i \in Agt$ *and for any* $BA' \in Cxt$, $(BA', BA') \in \mathcal{R}_i$.

For $\mathrm{X} \subseteq \{\mathrm{GC}, \mathrm{BC}\}$, $\mathbf{MABA}_{\mathrm{X}}$ is the class of MABAs satisfying all the conditions in X. $\mathbf{MABA}_{\emptyset}$ is the class of all MABAs, and we write **MABA** instead of $\mathbf{MABA}_{\emptyset}$. It is easy to see that $\mathbf{MABA}_{\{\mathrm{GC},\mathrm{BC}\}} = \mathbf{MABA}_{\{\mathrm{BC}\}}$.

Let $\varphi \in \mathcal{L}_{\mathsf{LDAA}}$, we say that φ is valid for the class $\mathbf{MABA}_{\mathrm{X}}$ if and only if, for every $(BA, Cxt) \in \mathbf{MABA}_{\mathrm{X}}$ we have $(BA, Cxt) \models \varphi$. We say that φ is satisfiable of the class $\mathbf{MABA}_{\mathrm{X}}$ if and only if $\neg\varphi$ is not valid for the class $\mathbf{MABA}_{\mathrm{X}}$

3.2 Notional Model Semantics

In this section we introduce an alternative Kripke-style semantics for the language $\mathcal{L}_{\mathsf{LDAA}}$ based on notional doxastic-awareness model which extend notional doxastic models defined in [12,13] by awareness functions.

Definition 9. *A notional doxastic-awareness model* (NDAM) *is a tuple* $\mathcal{M} = (\mathsf{W}, \mathsf{D}, \mathsf{A}, \mathsf{N}, \mathsf{V})$ *where,*

- W *is a non-empty set of worlds,*
- D: $Agt \times W \longrightarrow 2^{\mathcal{L}_0}$ *is a doxastic function,*
- A: $Agt \times W \longrightarrow 2^{Atm}$ *is an awareness function,*
- N: $Agt \times W \longrightarrow 2^{\mathsf{W}}$ *is a notional function,*
- V: $Atm \longrightarrow 2^{\mathsf{W}}$ *is a valuation function.*

and such that, given the following inductive definition of the semantic interpretation of formulas in $\mathcal{L}_{\mathsf{LDAA}}$:

- $(\mathcal{M}, w) \models p$ *iff* $w \in \mathsf{V}(p)$,
- $(\mathcal{M}, w) \models \neg\varphi$ *iff* $(\mathcal{M}, w) \not\models \varphi$,
- $(\mathcal{M}, w) \models \varphi \wedge \psi$ *iff* $(\mathcal{M}, w) \models \varphi$ *and* $(\mathcal{M}, w) \models \psi$,

- $(\mathcal{M}, w) \models \triangle_i \alpha$ *iff* $\alpha \in \mathsf{D}(i, w)$,
- $(\mathcal{M}, w) \models \Box_i \varphi$ *iff* $\forall u \in \mathsf{N}(i, w)$, $(\mathcal{M}, u) \models \varphi$,
- $(\mathcal{M}, w) \models \bigcirc_i \varphi$ *iff* $Atm(\varphi) \subseteq \mathsf{A}(i, w)$.

it satisfies the following conditions (C1) and (C2), for all $i \in Agt$ *and for all* $w \in \mathsf{W}$*:*

(C1) $\mathsf{A}(i, w) = Atm(\mathsf{D}(i, w))$,
(C2) $\mathsf{N}(i, w) = \bigcap_{\alpha \in \mathsf{D}(i,w)} ||\alpha||_M$, *where* $||\alpha||_M = \{u \in \mathsf{W} \mid (\mathcal{M}, u) \models \alpha\}$.

The following definitions specify global consistency (GC) and belief correctness (BC) for notional models.

Definition 10. *The* NDAM $\mathcal{M} = (\mathsf{W}, \mathsf{D}, \mathsf{A}, \mathsf{N}, \mathsf{V})$ *satisfies global consistency if and only if, for any* $i \in Agt$ *and for any* $w \in \mathsf{W}$, $\mathsf{N}(i, w) \neq \emptyset$.

Definition 11. *The* NDAM $\mathcal{M} = (\mathsf{W}, \mathsf{D}, \mathsf{A}, \mathsf{N}, \mathsf{V})$ *satisfies belief correctness if and only if, for any* $i \in Agt$ *and for any* $w \in \mathsf{W}$, $w \in \mathsf{N}(i, w)$.

For any $\mathrm{X} \subseteq \{\mathrm{GC}, \mathrm{BC}\}$, $\mathbf{NDAM}_{\mathrm{X}}$ is the class of NDAMs satisfying the conditions in X. $\mathbf{NDAM}_{\emptyset}$ is the class of all NDAMs, and we write **NDAM** instead of $\mathbf{NDAM}_{\emptyset}$. Analogously to MABAs, we have $\mathbf{NDAM}_{\{\mathrm{GC},\mathrm{BC}\}} = \mathbf{NDAM}_{\{\mathrm{BC}\}}$. A NDAM $\mathcal{M} = (\mathsf{W}, \mathsf{D}, \mathsf{A}, \mathsf{N}, \mathsf{V})$ is finite if and only if W, $\mathsf{D}(i, w)$, and $\mathsf{V}^{\leftarrow}(w)$ are finite sets for any $i \in Agt$ and any $w \in \mathsf{W}$, where $\mathsf{V}^{\leftarrow}(w) = \{p \in Atm \mid w \in \mathsf{V}(p)\}$. As $A(i, w) = Atm(\mathsf{D}(i, w))$, it follows that, if a NDAM $\mathcal{M}$ is finite, $A(i, w)$ is also a finite set for any $i \in Agt$ and any $w \in \mathsf{W}$. We use finite-$\mathbf{NDAM}_{\mathrm{X}}$ to denote the class of finite NDAMs satisfying the conditions in X.

Let $\varphi \in \mathcal{L}_{\mathsf{LDAA}}$, we say that φ is valid for the class $\mathbf{NDAM}_{\mathrm{X}}$ if and only if, for every $\mathcal{M} = (\mathsf{W}, \mathsf{D}, \mathsf{A}, \mathsf{N}, \mathsf{V}) \in \mathbf{NDAM}_{\mathrm{X}}$ and for every $w \in \mathsf{W}$, we have $(\mathcal{M}, w) \models \varphi$. We say that φ is satisfiable for the class $\mathbf{NDAM}_{\mathrm{X}}$ if and only if $\neg\varphi$ is not valid for the class $\mathbf{NDAM}_{\mathrm{X}}$.

3.3 Quasi-model Semantics

This section provides an alternative semantics for the language $\mathcal{L}_{\mathsf{LDAA}}$ based on a more general class of models, called quasi-notional doxastic-awareness models (quasi-NDAMs) in which the restrictions on the notional and awareness function are weakened.

Definition 12. *A quasi-notional doxastic-awareness model (quasi-NDAM) is a tuple* $\mathcal{M} = (\mathsf{W}, \mathsf{D}, \mathsf{A}, \mathsf{N}, \mathsf{V})$ *where* $\mathsf{W}, \mathsf{D}, \mathsf{A}, \mathsf{N}$ *and* V *are as in Definition 9 except that Condition C1 and C2 are replaced by the following weaker conditions, for all* $i \in Agt$ *and for all* $w \in \mathsf{W}$*:*

(C1)* $\mathsf{A}(i, w) \supseteq Atm(\mathsf{D}(i, w))$,
(C2)* $\mathsf{N}(i, w) \subseteq \bigcap_{\alpha \in \mathsf{D}(i,w)} ||\alpha||_M$.

As for NDAMs, for any $X \subseteq \{GC, BC\}$, $\mathbf{QNDAM}_X$ is the class of quasi-NDAMs satisfying the conditions in X. $\mathbf{QNDAM}_\emptyset$ is the class of all quasi-NDAMs, and we write **QNDAM** instead of $\mathbf{QNDAM}_\emptyset$. As for MABAs and NDAMs, we have $\mathbf{QNDAM}_{\{GC,BC\}} = \mathbf{QNDAM}_{\{BC\}}$. A quasi-NDAM $\mathcal{M} = (\mathsf{W}, \mathsf{D}, \mathsf{A}, \mathsf{N}, \mathsf{V})$ is finite if W, $\mathsf{D}(i, w)$, $\mathsf{A}(i, w)$ and $\mathsf{V}^{\leftarrow}(w)$ are finite sets for any $i \in Agt$ and any $w \in \mathsf{W}$. We use finite-$\mathbf{QNDAM}_X$ to denote the class of finite quasi-NDAMs satisfying the conditions in X. Validity and satisfiability of formulas for a class $\mathbf{QNDAM}_X$ are defined in the usual way.

3.4 Equivalence Results

In this section, we present equivalence results between the five different semantics for $\mathcal{L}_{\mathsf{LDAA}}$ we presented above (i.e., **MABA**, **NDAM**, finite-**NDAM**, **QNDAM**, and finite-**QNDAM**).

Equivalence Between Quasi-NDAMs and Finite Quasi-NDAMs
First of all, we consider the relationship between **QNDAM** and finite-**QNDAM**. Let us define a filtrated model for the proof.

Let $\mathcal{M} = (\mathsf{W}, \mathsf{D}, \mathsf{A}, \mathsf{N}, \mathsf{V})$ be a (possibly infinite) quasi-NDAM and let $\Sigma \subseteq \mathcal{L}_{\mathsf{LDAA}}$ be an arbitrary finite set of formulas which is closed under subformulas. The equivalence relation $\equiv_\Sigma$ on W is defined as follows:

$$\equiv_\Sigma = \{(w, v) \in \mathsf{W} \times \mathsf{W} : \forall \varphi \in \Sigma, (\mathcal{M}, w) \models \varphi \text{ iff } (\mathcal{M}, v) \models \varphi\}.$$

Let $[w]_\Sigma$ be the equivalence class of the world w generated by the relation $\equiv_\Sigma$. The model $\mathcal{M}_\Sigma = (\mathsf{W}_\Sigma, \mathsf{D}_\Sigma, \mathsf{A}_\Sigma, \mathsf{N}_\Sigma, \mathsf{V}_\Sigma)$ is the filtration of $\mathcal{M}$ under Σ where,

- $\mathsf{W}_\Sigma = \{[w]_\Sigma \mid w \in \mathsf{W}\}$,
- for any $i \in Agt$ and for any $[w]_\Sigma \in \mathsf{W}_\Sigma$, $\mathsf{D}_\Sigma(i, [w]_\Sigma) = (\bigcap_{w \in [w]_\Sigma} \mathsf{D}(i, w)) \cap \Sigma$,
- for any $i \in Agt$ and for any $[w]_\Sigma \in \mathsf{W}_\Sigma$, $\mathsf{A}_\Sigma(i, [w]_\Sigma) = (\bigcap_{w \in [w]_\Sigma} \mathsf{A}(i, w)) \cap \Sigma$,
- for any $i \in Agt$ and for any $[w]_\Sigma \in \mathsf{W}_\Sigma$, $\mathsf{N}_\Sigma(i, [w]_\Sigma) = \{[u]_\Sigma \in \mathsf{W}_\Sigma \mid \exists w \in [w]_\Sigma, \exists u \in [u]_\Sigma$ such that $u \in \mathsf{N}(i, w)\}$,
- for any $p \in Atm$, $\mathsf{V}_\Sigma(p) = \{[w]_\Sigma \mid (\mathcal{M}, w) \models p\}$ if $p \in Atm(\Sigma)$, $\mathsf{V}_\Sigma(p) = \emptyset$ otherwise.

We have the following filtration lemma showing that the filtrated model is semantically equivalent with the original model with respect to Σ.

Lemma 1. *Let $\varphi \in \Sigma$ and let $w \in \mathsf{W}$. Then, $(\mathcal{M}, w) \models \varphi$ if and only if $(\mathcal{M}_\Sigma, [w]_\Sigma) \models \varphi$.*

Proof. The proof is by induction on the structure of φ. For the cases other than $\varphi = \bigcirc_i \psi$, the proof is identical with that of Lemma 4 in the appendix of [12]. So we only need to prove the case when $\varphi = \bigcirc_i \psi$.

($\Rightarrow$) Suppose $(\mathcal{M}, w) \models \bigcirc_i \psi$ with $\bigcirc_i \psi \in \Sigma$. Thus, $Atm(\psi) \subseteq \mathsf{A}(i, w)$. Hence, by the definition of $\mathsf{A}_\Sigma(i, [w]_\Sigma)$ and the fact that Σ is closed under subformulas, we have $Atm(\psi) \subseteq \mathsf{A}_\Sigma(i, [w]_\Sigma)$. It follows that $(\mathcal{M}_\Sigma, [w]_\Sigma) \models \bigcirc_i \psi$.

($\Leftarrow$) For the other direction, suppose $(\mathcal{M}_\Sigma, [w]_\Sigma) \models \bigcirc_i \psi$ with $\bigcirc_i \psi \in \Sigma$. Thus, $Atm(\psi) \subseteq \mathsf{A}_\Sigma(i, [w]_\Sigma)$. Hence, by the definition of $\mathsf{A}_\Sigma(i, [w]_\Sigma)$, $Atm(\psi) \subseteq \mathsf{A}(i, w)$. □

The following proposition highlights that $\mathcal{M}_\Sigma$ is finite and preserves the properties of $\mathcal{M}$.

Proposition 1. *$\mathcal{M}_\Sigma = (\mathsf{W}_\Sigma, \mathsf{D}_\Sigma, \mathsf{A}_\Sigma, \mathsf{N}_\Sigma, \mathsf{V}_\Sigma)$ is a finite* quasi-**NDAM**. *Moreover, for any* $\mathrm{X} \in \{\mathrm{GC}, \mathrm{BC}\}$, *if $\mathcal{M}$ satisfies* X, *then $\mathcal{M}_\Sigma$ also satisfies it.*

Proof. By the proof of Proposition 12 in the appendix of [12], we have that, $\mathcal{M}_\Sigma$ is finite and satisfies Condition (C2*) in Definition 12, and that, for any $\mathrm{X} \in \{\mathrm{GC}, \mathrm{BC}\}$, if $\mathcal{M}$ satisfies X, then $\mathcal{M}_\Sigma$ also satisfies it. Here, we only need to prove that $\mathcal{M}$ satisfies Condition (C1*) in Definition 12. Suppose $\varphi \in \mathsf{D}_\Sigma(i, [w]_\Sigma)$, we need to prove that $Atm(\varphi) \subseteq \mathsf{A}_\Sigma(i, [w]_\Sigma)$. By the definition of $\mathsf{D}_\Sigma(i, [w]_\Sigma)$, we have $\varphi \in \mathsf{D}(i, w)$. By Condition (C1*), it follows that, $Atm(\varphi) \subseteq \mathsf{A}(i, w)$. By the definition of $\mathsf{A}_\Sigma(i, [w]_\Sigma)$ and the fact that Σ is closed under subformulas, we have $Atm(\varphi) \subseteq \mathsf{A}_\Sigma(i, [w]_\Sigma)$. As a result, $\mathsf{A}_\Sigma(i, [w]_\Sigma) \supseteq Atm(\varphi \in \mathsf{D}_\Sigma(i, [w]_\Sigma))$.□

The following lemma is a straighforward consequence of Lemma 1 and Proposition 1.

Lemma 2. *Let* $\mathrm{X} \in \{\mathrm{GC}, \mathrm{BC}\}$ *and* $\varphi \in \mathcal{L}_{\mathsf{LDAA}}$. *If φ is satisfiable for the class* $\mathbf{QNDAM}_\mathrm{X}$ *then φ is satisfiable for the class finite-*$\mathbf{QNDAM}_\mathrm{X}$.

Equivalence Between Finite NDAMs and Finite Quasi-NDAMs
Our next result concerns the equivalence between finite-**NDAM** and finite-**QNDAM**.

Lemma 3. *Let* $\mathrm{X} \in \{\mathrm{GC}, \mathrm{BC}\}$ *and* $\varphi \in \mathcal{L}_{\mathsf{LDAA}}$. *If φ is satisfiable for the class finite-*$\mathbf{QNDAM}_\mathrm{X}$, *then φ is satisfiable for the class finite-*$\mathbf{NDAM}_\mathrm{X}$.

Proof. We are going to build a finite NDAM from a finite quasi-NDAM without changing the satisfiability of φ. To accomplish this goal, two things are essential in the construction. Firstly, we enlarge each agent's belief base with an identifier proposition to make his set of doxastic alternatives smaller and coincide with his set of notional worlds. Secondly, we combine the identifier with some tautologies by conjunctions, so that the set of atomic propositions occurring in his belief base is equal to his awareness set.

Let $\mathcal{M} = (\mathsf{W}, \mathsf{D}, \mathsf{A}, \mathsf{N}, \mathsf{V})$ be a finite quasi-NDAM that satisfies φ, i.e., there exists $w \in \mathsf{W}$ such that $(\mathcal{M}, w) \models \varphi$. We define the set of all atomic propositions occurring in some belief base of some agent at some world in $\mathcal{M}$ as follows:

$$\mathcal{T}(\mathcal{M}) = \bigcup_{w \in \mathsf{W}, i \in Agt} Atm(\mathsf{D}(i, w)) \cup \bigcup_{w \in \mathsf{W}, i \in Agt} \mathsf{A}(i, w).$$

Since $\mathcal{M}$ is finite, $\mathcal{T}(\mathcal{M})$ is also finite.

We have the following injective function which assigns an identifier to each agent and each world in W.

$$f : Agt \times \mathsf{W} \longrightarrow Atm \backslash (\mathcal{T}(\mathcal{M}) \cup Atm(\varphi)).$$

As Atm is infinite while W, $\mathcal{T}(\mathcal{M})$ and $Atm(\varphi)$ are finite, such an injection exists.

We define a new model $\mathcal{M}' = (\mathsf{W}', \mathsf{D}', \mathsf{A}', \mathsf{N}', \mathsf{V}')$ with $\mathsf{W}' = \mathsf{W}$, $\mathsf{N}' = \mathsf{N}$ and where D', V' and A' are defined as follows:

- $\mathsf{A}'(i, w) = \mathsf{A}(i, w) \cup \{f(i, w)\}$ for every $i \in Agt$ and for every $w \in \mathsf{W}$,
- $\mathsf{D}'(i, w) = \mathsf{D}(i, w) \cup \{f(i, w) \wedge (\bigwedge_{p \in \mathsf{A}(i,w) \backslash Atm(\mathsf{D}(i,w))} (p \vee \neg p))\}$ for every $i \in Agt$ and for every $w \in \mathsf{W}$,
- for every $p \in Atm$,
  $\mathsf{V}'(p) = \mathsf{V}(p)$ if $p \in \mathcal{T}(\mathcal{M}) \cup Atm(\varphi)$,
  $\mathsf{V}'(p) = \mathsf{N}(i, w)$ if $p = f(i, w)$,
  $\mathsf{V}'(p) = \emptyset$ otherwise.

It is easy to verify that $\mathcal{M}'$ satisfies Condition (C1) and (C2) in Definition 9. Thus, $\mathcal{M}'$ is a finite NDAM.

The rest of the proof consists in checking that, for every $X \in \{\text{GC}, \text{BC}\}$, if $\mathcal{M}$ satisfies X then $\mathcal{M}'$ also satisfies X, which is straightforward, and that, $(\mathcal{M}, w) \models \varphi$ iff $(\mathcal{M}', w) \models \varphi$. We prove the latter by induction on the structure of φ.

The case $\varphi = p$ is immediate from the definition of V'. The boolean cases are straightforward.

Let us prove the case $\varphi = \triangle_i \alpha$.

($\Rightarrow$) Suppose $(\mathcal{M}, w) \models \triangle_i \alpha$. Then, we have $\alpha \in \mathsf{D}(i, w)$. Hence, by the definition of D', $\alpha \in \mathsf{D}'(i, w)$. Thus, $(\mathcal{M}', w) \models \triangle_i \alpha$.

($\Leftarrow$) Suppose $(\mathcal{M}', w) \models \triangle_i \alpha$. Then, we have $\alpha \in \mathsf{D}'(i, w)$. Since $f(i, w) \notin Atm(\triangle_i \alpha)$, by the definition of D', we have that,

$$\alpha \neq f(i, w) \wedge (\bigwedge_{p \in \mathsf{A}(i,w) \backslash Atm(\mathsf{D}(i,w))} (p \vee \neg p))$$

Thus, $\alpha \in \mathsf{D}(i, w)$ and, consequently, $(\mathcal{M}, w) \models \triangle_i \alpha$.

Then let us prove the case $\varphi_i = \bigcirc_i \psi$.

($\Rightarrow$) Suppose $(\mathcal{M}, w) \models \bigcirc_i \psi$. Then, we have $Atm(\psi) \subseteq \mathsf{A}(i, w)$. Hence, by the definition of A', $Atm(\psi) \subseteq \mathsf{A}'(i, w)$. Thus, $(\mathcal{M}', w) \models \bigcirc_i \psi$.

($\Leftarrow$) Suppose $(\mathcal{M}', w) \models \bigcirc_i \psi$. Then, we have $Atm(\psi) \subseteq \mathsf{A}'(i, w)$. The definition of A' ensures that $f(i, w) \notin Atm(\psi)$. Thus, $Atm(\psi) \subseteq \mathsf{A}(i, w)$ and, consequently, $(\mathcal{M}, w) \models \bigcirc_i \psi$.

At last, let us prove the case $\varphi = \Box_i \psi$. $(\mathcal{M}, w) \models \Box_i \psi$ means that $(\mathcal{M}, u) \models \psi$ for all $u \in \mathsf{N}(i, w)$, which is equivalent to $(\mathcal{M}', u) \models \psi$ for all $u \in \mathsf{N}'(i, w)$ by the induction hypothesis and the fact that $\mathsf{N}'(i, w) = \mathsf{N}(i, w)$. The latter means that $(\mathcal{M}', w) \models \Box_i \psi$.

Now we have that $(\mathcal{M}, w) \models \varphi$ iff $(\mathcal{M}', w) \models \varphi$. Then, if $\mathcal{M}$ satisfies φ, $\mathcal{M}'$ satisfies φ as well. □

Equivalence Between MABAs and NDAMs

The following lemma concerns the equivalence between **MABA** and **NDAM** (Fig. 1).

Lemma 4. *Let $\varphi \in \mathcal{L}_{\mathsf{LDAA}}$ and $\mathrm{X} \in \{\mathrm{GC}, \mathrm{BC}\}$. Then, φ is satisfiable for the class $\mathbf{MABA}_{\mathrm{X}}$ if and only if φ is satisfiable for the class $\mathbf{NDAM}_{\mathrm{X}}$.*

Proof. The proof is almost identical to that of Lemma 7 in the appendix of [12]. We leave it to the reader. □

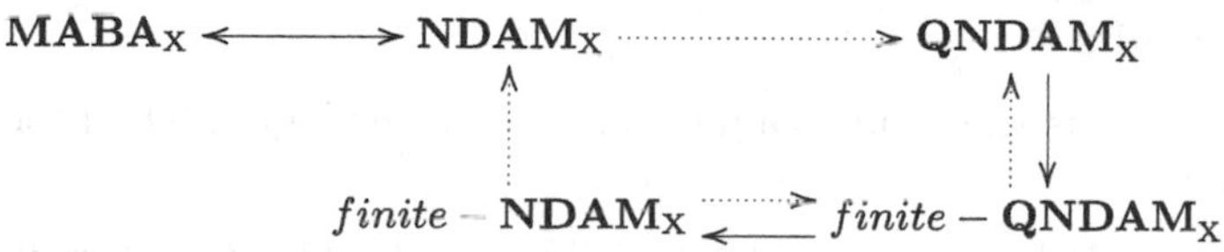

Fig. 1. Relations between semantics for the language $\mathcal{L}_{\mathsf{LDAA}}$. An arrow means that satisfiability relative to the first class of structures implies satisfiability relative to the second class of structures. Full arrows correspond to the results stated in Lemmas 2, 3 and 4. Dotted arrows denote relations that follow straightforwardly given the inclusion between classes of structures.

Theorem 1. *Let $\varphi \in \mathcal{L}_{\mathsf{LDAA}}$ and $\mathrm{X} \subseteq \{\mathrm{GC}, \mathrm{BC}\}$. Then, the following five statements are equivalent:*

- *φ is satisfiable for the class $\mathbf{MABA}_{\mathrm{X}}$,*
- *φ is satisfiable for the class $\mathbf{NDAM}_{\mathrm{X}}$,*
- *φ is satisfiable for the class $\mathbf{QNDAM}_{\mathrm{X}}$,*
- *φ is satisfiable for the class finite-$\mathbf{QNDAM}_{\mathrm{X}}$,*
- *φ is satisfiable for the class finite-$\mathbf{NDAM}_{\mathrm{X}}$.*

Proof. The theorem is a direct consequence of Lemmas 2, 3 and 4. □

4 Axiomatization

In this section, we define some variants of the LDAA logics and prove their soundness and completeness for their corresponding model classes.

We define the base logic LDAA to be the extension of classical propositional logic given by the following axioms and rule of inference:

$\mathrm{K}_{\Box}$. $(\Box_i \varphi \wedge \Box_i(\varphi \rightarrow \psi)) \rightarrow \Box_i \psi$
$\mathrm{Int}_{\triangle,\Box}$. $\triangle_i \alpha \rightarrow \Box_i \alpha$
$\mathrm{Int}_{\triangle,\bigcirc}$. $\triangle_i \alpha \rightarrow \bigcirc_i \alpha$

AGPP. $\bigcirc_i\varphi \leftrightarrow \bigwedge_{p\in Atm(\varphi)} \bigcirc_i p$
Nec$_\square$. From φ infer $\square_i\varphi$

For $X \subseteq \{D_\square, T_\square\}$, let LDAA_X be the extension of logic LDAA by every axiom in X, where:

$D_\square$. $\neg(\square_i\varphi \wedge \square_i\neg\varphi)$
$T_\square$. $\square_i\varphi \rightarrow \varphi$

We first prove completeness relative to the quasi-notional model semantics by using a canonical model argument. As usual, we have the following property for maximally consistent sets (MCSs).

Proposition 2. *Let Γ be a* MCS *for* LDAA_X. *Then:*

- *if* $\varphi, \varphi \rightarrow \psi \in \Gamma$ *then* $\psi \in \Gamma$,
- $\varphi \in \Gamma$ *or* $\neg\varphi \in \Gamma$,
- $\varphi \vee \psi \in \Gamma$ *iff* $\varphi \in \Gamma$ *or* $\psi \in \Gamma$.

The following is the Lindenbaum's lemma for our logics. The proof is standard, so we omit it.

Lemma 5. *Let Γ be a consistent set of formulas for* LDAA_X, *then there exists a MCS Γ' for* LDAA_X *such that* $\Gamma \subseteq \Gamma'$.

To prove completeness with respect to the class $\mathbf{QNDAM}_X$, we construct a canonical model as follows.

Definition 13. *Let* $X \subseteq \{D_\square, T_\square\}$. *Then, the canonical model for* LDAA_X *is the tuple* $\mathcal{M}^c = (\mathsf{W}^c, \mathsf{D}^c, \mathsf{A}^c, \mathsf{N}^c, \mathsf{V}^c)$ *such that:*

- W^c *is the set of maximally consistent sets (MCSs) for* LDAA_X,
- $\forall w \in \mathsf{W}^c$, $\forall i \in Agt$, *and* $\forall \alpha \in \mathcal{L}_0$, $\alpha \in \mathsf{D}^c(w,i)$ *iff* $\triangle_i\alpha \in w$,
- $\forall w \in \mathsf{W}^c$, $\forall i \in Agt$, *and* $\forall p \in Atm$, $p \in \mathsf{A}^c(w,i)$ *iff* $\bigcirc_i p \in w$,
- $\forall w, u \in \mathsf{W}^c$ *and* $\forall i \in Agt$, $u \in \mathsf{N}^c(i,w)$ *iff* $\forall \varphi \in \mathcal{L}_{\mathsf{LDAA}}$, *if* $\square_i\varphi \in w$ *then* $\varphi \in u$,
- $\forall w \in \mathsf{W}^c$ *and* $\forall p \in Atm$, $w \in \mathsf{V}^c(p)$ *iff* $p \in w$.

The following existence lemma is necessary for the proof of completeness. We omit its proof since it is completely standard.

Lemma 6. *Let $\varphi \in \mathcal{L}_{\mathsf{LDAA}}$ and let $w \in \mathsf{W}^c$. Then, if $\Diamond_i\varphi \in w$ then there exists $u \in \mathsf{N}^c(i,w)$ such that $\varphi \in u$.*

The following is the truth lemma for our logic.

Lemma 7. *Let $\varphi \in \mathcal{L}_{\mathsf{LDAA}}$ and let $w \in \mathsf{W}^c$. Then, $(\mathcal{M}^c, w) \models \varphi$ iff $\varphi \in w$.*

Proof. The proof is by induction on the structure of the formula φ. For the cases that φ is atomic, Boolean, or of the form $\square_i\psi$, the proof is standard by means of Proposition 2 and Lemma 6. The proof for the case $\varphi = \triangle_i\alpha$ goes as follows: $\triangle_i\alpha \in w$ iff $\alpha \in \mathsf{D}^c(i,w)$ iff $(\mathcal{M}^c, w) \models \triangle_i\alpha$.

For the case $\varphi = \bigcirc_i\psi$, by the axiom AGPP, $\bigcirc_i\psi \in w$ iff $\forall p \in Atm(\psi)$, $\bigcirc_i p \in w$. By the definition of the canonical model, the latter is equivalent to that, $\forall p \in Atm(\psi)$, $p \in \mathsf{A}^c(w,i)$. The latter is equivalent to $Atm(\psi) \subseteq \mathsf{A}^c(w,i)$, which means $(\mathcal{M}^c, w) \models \bigcirc_i\psi$ by our semantics. $\square$

We have to show that the canonical model satisfies the corresponding semantic properties if each axiom in $\mathrm{X} \subseteq \{\mathrm{D}_{\Box}, \mathrm{T}_{\Box}\}$ is valid in the model. Let us define the following correspondence function between axioms and semantic properties:

- $cf(\mathrm{D}_{\Box}) = \mathrm{GC}$
- $cf(\mathrm{T}_{\Box}) = \mathrm{BC}$

Proposition 3. *Let* $\mathrm{X} \subseteq \{\mathrm{D}_{\Box}, \mathrm{T}_{\Box}\}$. *If* $\mathcal{M}^c$ *is the canonical model for* $\mathsf{LDAA}_{\mathrm{X}}$, *then it belongs to the class* $\mathrm{QNDAM}_{\{cf(x) \,|\, x \in \mathrm{X}\}}$.

Proof. Firstly, we need to prove that $\mathcal{M}^c$ satisfies Condition (C1*) and (C2*) in Definition 12. For Condition (C1*), we have to prove that if $\alpha \in \mathsf{D}^c(i, w)$ then $Atm(\alpha) \subseteq \mathsf{A}^c(i, w)$. Suppose $\alpha \in \mathsf{D}^c(i, w)$. Thus, $\triangle_i \alpha \in w$. Hence, by the axiom $\mathrm{Int}_{\triangle,\bigcirc}$, $\bigcirc_i \alpha \in w$. By the axiom AGPP, it follows that, $\forall p \in Atm(\alpha)$, $\bigcirc_i p \in w$. Then, by the definition of $\mathcal{M}^c$, $\forall p \in Atm(\alpha)$, $p \in \mathsf{A}^c(i, w)$, which means $Atm(\alpha) \subseteq \mathsf{A}^c(i, w)$. For Condition (C2*), we have to prove that if $\alpha \in \mathsf{D}^c(i, w)$ then $\mathsf{N}^c(i, w) \subseteq ||\alpha||_{\mathcal{M}^c}$. Suppose $\alpha \in \mathsf{D}^c(i, w)$. Thus, $\triangle_i \alpha \in w$. Hence, by the axiom $\mathrm{Int}_{\triangle,\Box}$, $\Box_i \alpha \in w$. By the definition of $\mathcal{M}^c$, if follows that, $\forall u \in \mathsf{N}^c(i, w)$, $\alpha \in u$. Thus, by Lemma 7, we have that, $\forall u \in \mathsf{N}^c(i, w)$, $(\mathcal{M}^c, u) \models \alpha$. The latter means that $\mathsf{N}^c(i, w) \subseteq ||\alpha||_{\mathcal{M}^c}$.

It is easy to verify that $\mathcal{M}^c$ has the corresponding properties in $\{cf(x) \,|\, x \in \mathrm{X}\}$ using the standard proof. □

By Lemma 7 and Proposition 3, we are able to prove the following soundness and completeness theorem. Proving soundness is just a routine exercise.

Theorem 2. *Let* $\mathrm{X} \subseteq \{\mathrm{D}_{\Box}, \mathrm{T}_{\Box}\}$. *Then, the logic* $\mathsf{LDAA}_{\mathrm{X}}$ *is sound and complete for the class* $\mathbf{QNDAM}_{\{cf(x) \,|\, x \in \mathrm{X}\}}$.

The following is a corollary of Theorem 1 and Theorem 2.

Corollary 1. *Let* $\mathrm{X} \subseteq \{\mathrm{D}_{\Box}, \mathrm{T}_{\Box}\}$. *Then,*

- $\mathsf{LDAA}_{\mathrm{X}}$ *is sound and complete for the class* $\mathbf{NDAM}_{\{cf(x) \,|\, x \in \mathrm{X}\}}$, *and*
- $\mathsf{LDAA}_{\mathrm{X}}$ *is sound and complete for the class* $\mathbf{MABA}_{\{cf(x) \,|\, x \in \mathrm{X}\}}$.

5 Relationship with Logic of Propositional Awareness

In this section, we build a connection between LDAA and the logic of propositional awareness (LPA), where the latter, first introduced in [5], is a special case of the logic of general awareness (LGA) by Fagin & Halpern [4]. Specifically, we provide a polynomial, satisfiability preserving translation of LPA into LDAA. The language of LPA, denoted by $\mathcal{L}_{\mathsf{LPA}}$, is defined by the following grammar:

$$\varphi ::= p \,|\, \neg\varphi \,|\, \varphi_1 \wedge \varphi_2 \,|\, B_i\varphi \,|\, A_i\varphi \,|\, X_i\varphi$$

where p ranges over Atm and i ranges over Agt. At the semantics level, the logic of propositional awareness exploits awareness structures in which the awareness function is assumed to be propositional.

Definition 14. *A propositional awareness model* (PAM) *is a tuple* $\mathcal{M} = (\mathsf{S}, \mathsf{R}, \rho, \pi)$ *where:*

- S *is a non-empty set of states,*
- $\mathsf{R} : Agt \times \mathsf{S} \longrightarrow 2^{\mathsf{S}}$ *is a doxastic accessibility function,*
- $\rho : Agt \times \mathsf{S} \longrightarrow 2^{Atm}$ *is a propositional awareness function,*
- $\pi : Atm \longrightarrow 2^{\mathsf{S}}$ *is a valuation function.*

The class of propositional awareness models is denoted by **PAM**.

We have the following semantic interpretation of formulas in $\mathcal{L}_{\mathsf{LPA}}$ relative to pointed models.

Definition 15. *Given a* PAM $\mathcal{M}$ *and state* s *in* $\mathcal{M}$, *formulas in* $\mathcal{L}_{\mathsf{LPA}}$ *are interpreted relative to* $(\mathcal{M}, s)$ *as follows:*

- $(\mathcal{M}, s) \models p$ *iff* $s \in \pi(p)$,
- $(\mathcal{M}, s) \models \neg\varphi$ *iff* $(\mathcal{M}, s) \not\models \varphi$,
- $(\mathcal{M}, s) \models \varphi \wedge \psi$ *iff* $(\mathcal{M}, s) \models \varphi$ *and* $(\mathcal{M}, s) \models \psi$,
- $(\mathcal{M}, s) \models B_i\varphi$ *iff* $\forall t \in \mathsf{R}(i, s)$, $(\mathcal{M}, t) \models \varphi$,
- $(\mathcal{M}, s) \models A_i\varphi$ *iff* $Atm(\varphi) \subseteq \rho(i, s)$,
- $(\mathcal{M}, s) \models X_i\varphi$ *iff* $(\mathcal{M}, s) \models B_i\varphi$ *and* $(\mathcal{M}, s) \models A_i\varphi$.

We translate formulas of $\mathcal{L}_{\mathsf{LPA}}$ into formulas of $\mathcal{L}_{\mathsf{LDAA}}$ via the following translation function $tr : \mathcal{L}_{\mathsf{LPA}} \longrightarrow \mathcal{L}_{\mathsf{LDAA}}$ which is defined as follows:

- $tr(p) = p$ for $p \in Atm$
- $tr(\neg\varphi) = \neg tr(\varphi)$
- $tr(\varphi_1 \wedge \varphi_2) = tr(\varphi_1) \wedge tr(\varphi_2)$
- $tr(A_i\varphi) = \bigcirc_i tr(\varphi)$
- $tr(B_i\varphi) = \Box_i tr(\varphi)$
- $tr(X_i\varphi) = \bigcirc_i tr(\varphi) \wedge \Box_i tr(\varphi)$

The interesting aspect of the previous translation is that the LPA notion of explicit belief is mapped into the combination of implicit belief *plus* awareness in our logic LDAA, and not directly into the LDAA notion of explicit belief. This highlights that the two notions of explicit belief do not capture the same type of epistemic attitude. While the LDAA notion represents an agent's actual belief which is active and accessible in his working memory (we assume an agent's belief base to be a rough approximation of his working memory), the LPA notion is aimed at capturing the agent's beliefs that are built from his vocabulary and therefore understandable by him.[2]

As the following theorem highlights, the translation is satisfiability preserving.

[2] Note that if we defined the translation sending explicit beliefs of LPA into explicit beliefs of LDAA, satisfiability would be preserved only in the direction from LDAA to LPA. For the other direction, a formula of the form $X_iB_i\varphi$ in $\mathcal{L}_{\mathsf{LPA}}$ cannot be translated into $\mathcal{L}_{\mathsf{LDAA}}$ with this alternative translation.

Theorem 3. *Let $\varphi \in \mathcal{L}_{\mathsf{LPA}}$. Then, φ is satisfiable for the class* **PAM** *if and only if $tr(\varphi)$ is satisfiable for the class* **NDAM**.

Proof. We first prove a weaker result of the left-to-right direction, i.e., if φ is satisfiable for the class **PAM**, then $tr(\varphi)$ is satisfiable for the class **QNDAM**. Let $\mathcal{M} = (\mathsf{S}, \mathsf{R}, \rho, \pi)$ be a PAM and let $s \in \mathsf{S}$ such that $(\mathcal{M}, s) \models \varphi$. We build the corresponding $\mathcal{M}' = (\mathsf{W}, \mathsf{D}, \mathsf{A}, \mathsf{N}, \mathsf{V})$ as follows:

- $\mathsf{W} = \mathsf{S}$,
- $\forall i \in Agt$ and $\forall s \in \mathsf{S}$, $\mathsf{D}(i, s) = \{p \vee \neg p \mid (\mathcal{M}, s) \models A_i p\}$,
- $\forall i \in Agt$ and $\forall s \in \mathsf{S}$, $\mathsf{A}(i, s) = \rho(i, s)$,
- $\forall i \in Agt$ and $\forall s \in \mathsf{S}$, $\mathsf{N}(i, s) = \mathsf{R}(i, s)$,
- $\forall p \in Atm$, $\mathsf{V}(p) = \pi(p)$.

We prove that $\mathcal{M}'$ is a quasi-NDAM by showing that it satisfies Condition (C1*) and (C2*) in Definition 12.

For Condition (C1*), by the semantics of PAM and the definitions of $\mathsf{D}(i, s)$ and $\mathsf{A}(i, s)$, it is easy to show that, $Atm(\mathsf{D}(i, s)) = \mathsf{A}(i, s)$, which implies that, $Atm(\mathsf{D}(i, s)) \subseteq \mathsf{A}(i, s)$.

For Condition (C2*), by the definition of $\mathsf{D}(i, s)$, there are only tautologies in it. So we have that $\bigcap_{tr(\varphi) \in \mathsf{D}(i,w)} ||tr(\varphi)||_M = \mathsf{W}$. Then, clearly, Condition (C2*) is satisfied.

It is easy to verify that, for every $x \in \{\text{GC}, \text{BC}\}$, if $\mathcal{M}$ satisfies x then $\mathcal{M}'$ satisfies it as well.

By induction on the structure of φ, we prove that, $\forall s \in \mathsf{S}$, $(\mathcal{M}, s) \models \varphi$ iff $(\mathcal{M}', s) \models tr(\varphi)$.

For the case $\varphi = p$ and the boolean cases $\varphi = \neg\psi$ and $\varphi = \psi_1 \wedge \psi_2$, it is straightforward.

Now we consider the case $\varphi = A_i\psi$. Suppose $(\mathcal{M}, s) \models A_i\psi$. By the semantics of PAM, it is equivalent to $Atm(\psi) \subseteq \rho(i, s)$. By the definition of $\mathsf{A}(i, s)$ and the function tr, the latter is equivalent to $Atm(tr(\psi)) \subseteq \mathsf{A}(i, s)$. And in turn the latter means $(\mathcal{M}', s) \models \bigcirc_i tr(\psi)$. Then, by the definition of the function tr, the latter is equivalent to $(\mathcal{M}', s) \models tr(A_i\psi)$.

Let us consider the case $\varphi = B_i\psi$. Suppose $(\mathcal{M}, s) \models B_i\psi$. By the induction hypothesis, we have $||\psi||_{\mathcal{M}} = ||tr(\psi)||_{\mathcal{M}'}$. $(\mathcal{M}, s) \models B_i\psi$ means that $\mathsf{R}(i, s) \subseteq ||\psi||_{\mathcal{M}}$. By the definition of $\mathsf{N}(i, s)$ and the fact that $||\psi||_{\mathcal{M}} = ||tr(\psi)||_{\mathcal{M}'}$, the latter it equivalent to $\mathsf{N}(i, s) \subseteq ||tr(\psi)||_{\mathcal{M}'}$, which is equivalent to $(\mathcal{M}', s) \models \Box_i tr(\psi)$. The latter means $(\mathcal{M}', s) \models tr(B_i\psi)$ by the definition of the function tr.

Finally, let us consider the case $\varphi = X_i\psi$. Suppose $(\mathcal{M}, s) \models X_i\psi$. Given the fact that $X_i\psi$ is equivalent to $B_i\psi \wedge A_i\psi$, by the previous cases, it means that, $(\mathcal{M}', s) \models \Box_i tr(\psi) \wedge \bigcirc_i tr(\psi)$. By the function tr, the latter is equivalent to $(\mathcal{M}', s) \models trX_i\psi$.

Thus, we conclude that $(\mathcal{M}, s) \models \varphi$ iff $(\mathcal{M}', s) \models tr(\varphi)$ for all $s \in \mathsf{S}$. Then we have that, if φ is satisfiable for the class **PAM**, then $tr(\varphi)$ is satisfiable for the class **QNDAM**. By Theorem 1, it follows that, if φ is satisfiable for the class **PAM**, then $tr(\varphi)$ is satisfiable for the class **NDAM**.

Then we prove the right-to-left direction. Let $\mathcal{M} = (\mathsf{W}, \mathsf{D}, \mathsf{A}, \mathsf{N}, \mathsf{V})$ be a NDAM. We build the model $\mathcal{M}' = (\mathsf{S}, \mathsf{R}, \rho, \pi)$ as follows:

- $\mathsf{S} = \mathsf{W}$,
- $\forall i \in Agt$ and $\forall w \in \mathsf{W}$, $\mathsf{R}(i, w) = \mathsf{N}(i, w)$,
- $\forall i \in Agt$ and $\forall w \in \mathsf{W}$, $\rho(i, w) = \mathsf{A}(i, w)$,
- $\forall p \in Atm$, $\pi(p) = \mathsf{V}(p)$.

It is easy to show that $\mathcal{M}'$ is a PAM.

The next step is to prove that for all $w \in \mathsf{W}$, $(\mathcal{M}, w) \models tr(\varphi)$ iff $(\mathcal{M}', w) \models \varphi$.

The case $\varphi = p$ and the boolean cases are straightforward.

Let us consider the case $\varphi = A_i\psi$. Suppose $(\mathcal{M}, w) \models tr(A_i\psi)$. By the semantics of NDAM and the function tr, it is equivalent to $Atm(\psi) \subseteq \mathsf{A}(i, w)$. By the definition of $\rho(i, w)$, the latter is equivalent to $Atm(\psi) \subseteq \rho(i, w)$. Then by the semantics of PAM, the latter is equivalent to $(\mathcal{M}', w) \models A_i\psi$.

Let us consider the case $\varphi = B_i\psi$. Suppose $(\mathcal{M}, w) \models tr(B_i\psi)$. By the induction hypothesis, we have $||\psi||_{\mathcal{M}'} = ||tr(\psi)||_{\mathcal{M}}$. By the function tr, $(\mathcal{M}, w) \models tr(B_i\psi)$ means $(\mathcal{M}, w) \models \Box_i tr(\psi)$. By the semantics of NDAM, the latter is equivalent to $\mathsf{N}(i, w) \subseteq ||tr(\psi)||_{\mathcal{M}}$. By the definition of $\mathsf{R}(i, w)$ and the fact $||\psi||_{\mathcal{M}'} = ||tr(\psi)||_{\mathcal{M}}$, the latter is equivalent to $\mathsf{R}(i, w) \subseteq ||\psi||_{\mathcal{M}'}$, which is equivalent to $(\mathcal{M}', w) \models B_i\psi$

Finally, let us consider the case $\varphi = X_i\psi$. Suppose $(\mathcal{M}, w) \models tr(X_i\psi)$. Given the fact that $X_i\psi$ is equivalent to $B_i\psi \wedge A_i\psi$, by the previous cases, it is equivalent to $(\mathcal{M}', w) \models B_i\psi \wedge A_i\psi$, which in turn is equivalent to $(\mathcal{M}', w) \models X_i\psi$.

Thus, we conclude that $(\mathcal{M}, w) \models tr(\varphi)$ iff $(\mathcal{M}', w) \models \varphi$ for all $w \in \mathsf{W}$. Then we have that, if $tr(\varphi)$ is satisfiable for the class **NDAM**, then φ is satisfiable for the class **PAM**. $\square$

Theorem 3 shows that the translation of any satisfiable LPA-formula is satisfiable relative to NDAM models. This highlights that $\mathcal{L}_{\mathsf{LDAA}}$ is at least as expressive as the translated version $\mathcal{L}_{\mathsf{LPA}}$ with repect to the class **NDAM**. We do not know whether the other direction works as well. What we can affirm is that the formula $\neg\triangle_i(p \wedge p) \wedge \Box_i p \wedge \bigcirc_i p$ is satisfiable in the class **NDAM**, but it cannot be satisfied in the class **PAM**, if we translated $\triangle_i$, $\Box_i$, and $\bigcirc_i$ into X_i, B_i, and A_i, respectively. Again this shows that the LPA notion of explicit belief and the LDAA notion of explicit belief capture epistemic attitudes of different nature.

6 Conclusion

We have provided a novel investigation of propositional awareness and of its relationship with explicit and implicit belief. In our approach, explicit belief is the only primitive concept, and awareness and implicit belief are grounded on it. Specifically, an agent's awareness set and set of doxastic alternatives are directly computed from the agent's belief base. The main results of the paper are an axiomatics for our logic of awareness, explicit and implicit belief as well as a polynomial embedding of Halpern's logic of propositional awareness into our logic. Future work will be devoted to explore more properties of awareness typically discussed in the literature, such as beliefs of awareness and unawareness (also known as awareness/unawareness introspection), and the dynamic aspects of awareness and beliefs. We expect our approach to offer a new foundation for the dynamics of awareness, alternative to [2], in which awareness change is anchored in belief base change.

Acknowledgements. This work is supported by the major project of Key Research Institutes of Humanities and Social Sciences of Ministry of Education of China (No. 17JJD720008), and by the key project of National Social Science Foundation of China (No. 16AZX017). Support from the ANR-3IA Artificial and Natural Intelligence Toulouse Institute (ANITI) is also gratefully acknowledged.

References

1. Alchourrón, C.E., Gärdenfors, P., Makinson, D.: On the logic of theory change: partial meet contraction and revision functions. J. Symb. Logic. **50**(2), 510–530 (1985)
2. van Benthem, J., Velázquez-Quesada, F.R.: The dynamics of awareness. Synthese **177**, 5–27 (2010)
3. van Ditmarsch, H., French, T., Velázquez-Quesada, F., Wang, Y.: Implicit, explicit and speculative knowledge. Artif. Intell. **256**, 35–67 (2018)
4. Fagin, R., Halpern, J.: Belief, awareness, and limited reasoning. Artif. Intell. **34**(1), 39–76 (1988)
5. Halpern, J.: Alternative semantics for unawareness. Games Econ. Behav. **37**(2), 321–339 (2001)
6. Halpern, J., Rêgo, L.: Interactive unawareness revisited. Games Econ. Behav. **62**(1), 232–262 (2008)
7. Hansson, S.O.: Theory contraction and base contraction unified. J. Symb. Logic **58**(2), 602–625 (1993)
8. Heifetz, A., Meier, M., Schipper, B.: Interactive unawareness. J. Econ. Theory **130**, 78–94 (2006)
9. Heifetz, A., Meier, M., Schipper, B.: A canonical model for interactive unawareness. Games Econ. Behav. **62**, 304–324 (2008)
10. Hintikka, J.: Knowledge and Belief. Cornell University Press, Ithaca (1962)
11. Levesque, H.: A logic of implicit and explicit belief. In: Proceedings of AAAI 1984, pp. 198–220. AAAI Press (1984)
12. Lorini, E.: Rethinking epistemic logic with belief bases. Artif. Intell. **282**, 103233 (2020)
13. Lorini, E.: In Praise of belief bases: doing epistemic logic without possible worlds. In: Proceedings of AAAI 2018, pp. 1915–1922. AAAI Press (2018)
14. Makinson, D.: How to give it up: a survey of some formal aspects of the logic of theory change. Synthese **62**, 347–363 (1985)
15. Modica, S., Rustichini, A.: Awareness and partitional information structures. Theor. Decis. **37**, 107–124 (1994)
16. Modica, S., Rustichini, A.: Unawareness and partitional information structures. Games Econ. Behav. **27**, 265–298 (1999)
17. Nebel, B.: Syntax-based approaches to belief revision. In: Gärdenfors, P. (ed.) Belief Revision, pp. 52–88. Cambridge University Press (1992)

18. Rott, A.: Just because: taking belief bases seriously. In: Logic Colloquium 1998: Proceedings of the 1998 ASL European Summer Meeting. Lecture Notes in Logic, vol. 13, pp. 387–408. Association for Symbolic Logic (1998)
19. Stalnaker, R.: Common ground. Linguist. Philos. **25**(5–6), 701–721 (2002)

Ecumenical Modal Logic

Sonia Marin[1], Luiz Carlos Pereira[2], Elaine Pimentel[3](✉), and Emerson Sales[4]

[1] Department of Computer Science, University College London, London, UK
[2] Philosophy Department, PUC-Rio, Rio de Janeiro, Brazil
[3] Department of Mathematics, UFRN, Natal, Brazil
elaine.pimentel@gmail.com
[4] Graduate Program in Applied Mathematics and Statistics, UFRN, Natal, Brazil

Abstract. The discussion about how to put together Gentzen's systems for classical and intuitionistic logic in a single unified system is back in fashion. Indeed, recently Prawitz and others have been discussing the so called ecumenical Systems, where connectives from these logics can co-exist in peace. In Prawitz' system, the classical logician and the intuitionistic logician would share the universal quantifier, conjunction, negation, and the constant for the absurd, but they would each have their own existential quantifier, disjunction, and implication, with different meanings. Prawitz' main idea is that these different meanings are given by a semantical framework that can be accepted by both parties. In this work we extend Prawitz' ecumenical idea to alethic K-modalities.

1 Introduction

In [17] Dag Prawitz proposed a natural deduction system for what was later called *ecumenical logic* (EL), where classical and intuitionistic logic could coexist in peace. In this system, the classical logician and the intuitionistic logician would share the universal quantifier, conjunction, negation, and the constant for the absurd (*the neutral connectives*), but they would each have their own existential quantifier, disjunction, and implication, with different meanings. Prawitz' main idea is that these different meanings are given by a semantical framework that can be accepted by both parties. While proof-theoretical aspects were also considered, his work was more focused on investigating the philosophical significance of the fact that classical logic can be translated into intuitionistic logic.

Pursuing the idea of having a better understanding of ecumenical systems under the proof-theoretical point of view, in [15] an ecumenical sequent calculus (LEci) was proposed. This enabled not only the proof of some important proof theoretical properties (such as cut-elimination and invertibility of rules), but it also provided a better understanding of the ecumenical nature of consequence: it is intrinsically intuitionistic, being classical only in the presence of classical succedents.

This work was partially financed by CNPq and CAPES (Finance Code 001).

M. A. Martins and I. Sedlár (Eds.): DaLí 2020, LNCS 12569, pp. 187–204, 2020.
https://doi.org/10.1007/978-3-030-65840-3_12

Ecumenism in logic is interesting for different reasons, and we discuss some in Sect. 7. But maybe the most compelling argument for considering ecumenical systems is the analysis of mathematical theories and proofs. In fact, the possibility of having classical and intuitionistic reasoning in a single framework allows determining, for example, which parts of a proof can be done constructively, or which axioms in a theory can be restricted to its intuitionistic formulation. As a simple example, consider the following statement, where $x, y \in \mathbb{R}$:

$$\text{if } x + y = 16 \text{ then } x \geq 8 \text{ or } y \geq 8.$$

Of course, this could always be translated into a classical formula, but a finer analysis shows that the disjunction should definitely be classical, while the implication does not need to. That is, the statement should be translated as $(x + y = 16) \rightarrow_i x \geq 8 \vee_c y \geq 8$.

In this work, we propose lifting this discussion to modal logics, by presenting an extension of EL with the alethic modalities of *necessity* and *possibility*. There are many choices to be made and many relevant questions to be asked, *e.g.*: what is the ecumenical interpretation of ecumenical modalities? Should we add classical, intuitionistic, or neutral versions for modal connectives? What is really behind the difference between the classical and intuitionistic notions of truth?

We propose an answer for these questions in the light of Simpson's meta-logical interpretation of modalities [20] by embedding the expected semantical behavior of the modal operator into the ecumenical first order logic.

We start by highlighting the main proof theoretical aspects of LEci (Sect. 2). This is vital for understanding how the embedding mentioned above will mold the behavior of ecumenical modalities, since modal connectives are interpreted in first order logics using quantifiers. In Sect. 3 and 4, we justify our choices by following closely Simpson's script, with the difference that we prove meta-logical soundness and completeness using proof theoretical methods only. We then provide an axiomatic and semantical interpretation of ecumenical modalities in Sect. 5. This makes it possible to extend the discussion, in Sect. 6, to relational systems with the usual restrictions on the relation in the Kripke model. We end the paper with a discussion about logical ecumenism in general.

2 The System LEci

The language $\mathcal{L}$ used for ecumenical systems is described as follows. We will use a subscript c for the classical meaning and i for the intuitionistic, dropping such subscripts when formulae/connectives can have either meaning.

Classical and intuitionistic n-ary predicate symbols $(p_c, p_i, \ldots)$ co-exist in $\mathcal{L}$ but have different meanings. The neutral logical connectives $\{\bot, \neg, \wedge, \forall\}$ are common for classical and intuitionistic fragments, while $\{\rightarrow_i, \vee_i, \exists_i\}$ and $\{\rightarrow_c, \vee_c, \exists_c\}$ are restricted to intuitionistic and classical interpretations, respectively.

The sequent system LEci (depicted in Fig. 1) was presented in [15] as the sequent counterpart of Prawitz' natural deduction system. Observe that the

INITIAL AND STRUCTURAL RULES

$$\frac{}{A, \Gamma \Rightarrow A}\ \mathsf{init} \qquad \frac{\Gamma \Rightarrow \bot}{\Gamma \Rightarrow A}\ \mathsf{W}$$

PROPOSITIONAL RULES

$$\frac{A, B, \Gamma \Rightarrow C}{A \wedge B, \Gamma \Rightarrow C}\ \wedge L \quad \frac{\Gamma \Rightarrow A \quad \Gamma \Rightarrow B}{\Gamma \Rightarrow A \wedge B}\ \wedge R \quad \frac{A, \Gamma \Rightarrow C \quad B, \Gamma \Rightarrow C}{A \vee_i B, \Gamma \Rightarrow C}\ \vee_i L \quad \frac{\Gamma \Rightarrow A_j}{\Gamma \Rightarrow A_1 \vee_i A_2}\ \vee_i R_j$$

$$\frac{A, \Gamma \Rightarrow \bot \quad B, \Gamma \Rightarrow \bot}{A \vee_c B, \Gamma \Rightarrow \bot}\ \vee_c L \quad \frac{\Gamma, \neg A, \neg B \Rightarrow \bot}{\Gamma \Rightarrow A \vee_c B}\ \vee_c R \quad \frac{A \rightarrow_i B, \Gamma \Rightarrow A \quad B, \Gamma \Rightarrow C}{\Gamma, A \rightarrow_i B \Rightarrow C}\ \rightarrow_i L$$

$$\frac{\Gamma, A \Rightarrow B}{\Gamma \Rightarrow A \rightarrow_i B}\ \rightarrow_i R \quad \frac{A \rightarrow_c B, \Gamma \Rightarrow A \quad B, \Gamma \Rightarrow \bot}{A \rightarrow_c B, \Gamma \Rightarrow \bot}\ \rightarrow_c L \quad \frac{\Gamma, A, \neg B \Rightarrow \bot}{\Gamma \Rightarrow A \rightarrow_c B}\ \rightarrow_c R$$

$$\frac{\neg A, \Gamma \Rightarrow A}{\neg A, \Gamma \Rightarrow \bot}\ \neg L \quad \frac{\Gamma, A \Rightarrow \bot}{\Gamma \Rightarrow \neg A}\ \neg R \quad \frac{}{\bot, \Gamma \Rightarrow A}\ \bot L \quad \frac{p_i, \Gamma \Rightarrow \bot}{p_c, \Gamma \Rightarrow \bot}\ L_c \quad \frac{\Gamma, \neg p_i \Rightarrow \bot}{\Gamma \Rightarrow p_c}\ R_c$$

QUANTIFIERS

$$\frac{A[y/x], \forall x.A, \Gamma \Rightarrow C}{\forall x.A, \Gamma \Rightarrow C}\ \forall L \quad \frac{\Gamma \Rightarrow A[y/x]}{\Gamma \Rightarrow \forall x.A}\ \forall R$$

$$\frac{A[y/x], \Gamma \Rightarrow C}{\exists_i x.A, \Gamma \Rightarrow C}\ \exists_i L \quad \frac{\Gamma \Rightarrow A[y/x]}{\Gamma \Rightarrow \exists_i x.A}\ \exists_i R \quad \frac{A[y/x], \Gamma \Rightarrow \bot}{\exists_c x.A, \Gamma \Rightarrow \bot}\ \exists_c L \quad \frac{\Gamma, \forall x.\neg A \Rightarrow \bot}{\Gamma \Rightarrow \exists_c x.A}\ \exists_c R$$

Fig. 1. Ecumenical sequent system LEci. In rules $\forall R, \exists_i L, \exists_c L$, the eigenvariable y is fresh.

rules R_c and L_c describe the intended meaning of the predicate p_c, from the intuitionistic predicate p_i.

LEci has very interesting proof theoretical properties, together with a Kripke semantical interpretation, that allowed the proposal of a variety of ecumenical proof systems, such as multi-conclusion and nested sequent systems, as well as several fragments of such systems [15].

Denoting by $\vdash_{\mathsf{S}} A$ the fact that the formula A is a theorem in the proof system S, the following theorems are easily provable in LEci:

1. $\vdash_{\mathsf{LEci}} (A \rightarrow_c \bot) \leftrightarrow_i (A \rightarrow_i \bot) \leftrightarrow_i (\neg A)$;
2. $\vdash_{\mathsf{LEci}} (A \vee_c B) \leftrightarrow_i \neg(\neg A \wedge \neg B)$;
3. $\vdash_{\mathsf{LEci}} (A \rightarrow_c B) \leftrightarrow_i \neg(A \wedge \neg B)$;
4. $\vdash_{\mathsf{LEci}} (\exists_c x.A) \leftrightarrow_i \neg(\forall x.\neg A)$.

Note that (2) means that the ecumenical system defined in Fig. 1 does not distinguish between intuitionistic or classical negations, thus they can be called simply $\neg A$. We prefer to keep the negation operator in the language since the calculi presented in this work make heavy use of it.

Theorems (2) to (2) are of interest since they relate the classical and the neutral operators: the classical connectives can be defined using negation, conjunction, and the universal quantifier. On the other hand,

5. $\vdash_{\mathsf{LEci}} (A \rightarrow_i B) \rightarrow_i (A \rightarrow_c B)$ but $\nvdash_{\mathsf{LEci}} (A \rightarrow_c B) \rightarrow_i (A \rightarrow_i B)$ in general;
6. $\vdash_{\mathsf{LEci}} A \vee_c \neg A$ but $\nvdash_{\mathsf{LEci}} A \vee_i \neg A$ in general;
7. $\vdash_{\mathsf{LEci}} (\neg\neg A) \rightarrow_c A$ but $\nvdash_{\mathsf{LEci}} (\neg\neg A) \rightarrow_i A$ in general;
8. $\vdash_{\mathsf{LEci}} (A \wedge (A \rightarrow_i B)) \rightarrow_i B$ but $\nvdash_{\mathsf{LEci}} (A \wedge (A \rightarrow_c B)) \rightarrow_i B$ in general;
9. $\vdash_{\mathsf{LEci}} \forall x.A \rightarrow_i \neg\exists_c x.\neg A$ but $\nvdash_{\mathsf{LEci}} \neg\exists_c x.\neg A \rightarrow_i \forall x.A$ in general.

Observe that (2) and (2) reveal the asymmetry between definability of quantifiers: while the classical existential can be defined from the universal quantification, the other way around is not true, in general. This is closely related with the fact that, proving $\forall x.A$ from $\neg\exists_c x.\neg A$ depends on A being a classical formula. We will come back to this in Sect. 3.

On its turn, the following result states that logical consequence in LEci is intrinsically intuitionistic.

Proposition 1 ([15]). *$\Gamma \vdash B$ is provable in* LEci *iff* $\vdash_{\mathsf{LEci}} \bigwedge \Gamma \rightarrow_i B$.

To preserve the "classical behaviour", *i.e.*, to satisfy all the principles of classical logic *e.g. modus ponens* and the *classical reductio*, it is sufficient that the main operator of the formula be classical (see [14]). Thus, "hybrid" formulas, *i.e.*, formulas that contain classical and intuitionistic operators may have a classical behaviour. Formally,

Definition 1. *A formula B is called externally classical (denoted by B^c) if and only if B is $\bot$, a classical predicate letter, or its root operator is classical (that is: $\rightarrow_c, \vee_c, \exists_c$). A formula C is* classical *if it is built from classical atomic predicates using only the connectives: $\rightarrow_c, \vee_c, \exists_c, \neg, \wedge, \forall$, and the unit $\bot$.*

For externally classical formulas we can now prove the following theorems

10. $\vdash_{\mathsf{LEci}} (A \rightarrow_c B^c) \rightarrow_i (A \rightarrow_i B^c)$.
11. $\vdash_{\mathsf{LEci}} (A \wedge (A \rightarrow_c B^c)) \rightarrow_i B^c$.
12. $\vdash_{\mathsf{LEci}} \neg\neg B^c \rightarrow_i B^c$.
13. $\vdash_{\mathsf{LEci}} \neg\exists_c x.\neg B^c \rightarrow_i \forall x.B^c$.

Moreover, notice that all classical right rules as well as the right rules for the neutral connectives in LEci are invertible. Since invertible rules can be applied eagerly when proving a sequent, this entails that classical formulas can be eagerly decomposed. As a consequence, the ecumenical entailment, when restricted to classical succedents (antecedents having an unrestricted form), is classical.

Theorem 1 ([15]). *Let C be a classical formula and Γ be a multiset of ecumenical formulas. Then*

$$\vdash_{\mathsf{LEci}} \bigwedge \Gamma \rightarrow_c C \text{ iff } \vdash_{\mathsf{LEci}} \bigwedge \Gamma \rightarrow_i C.$$

This sums up well, proof theoretically, the *ecumenism* of Prawitz' original proposal.

3 Ecumenical Modalities

In this section we will propose an ecumenical view for alethic modalities. Since there are a number of choices to be made, we will construct our proposal step-by-step.

3.1 Normal Modal Logics

The language of *(propositional, normal) modal formulas* consists of a denumerable set $\mathcal{P}$ of propositional symbols and a set of propositional connectives enhanced with the unary *modal operators* $\Box$ and $\Diamond$ concerning necessity and possibility, respectively [3].

The semantics of modal logics is often determined by means of *Kripke models*. Here, we will follow the approach in [20], where a modal logic is characterized by the respective interpretation of the modal model in the meta-theory (called *meta-logical characterization*).

Formally, given a variable x, we recall the standard translation $[\cdot]_x$ from modal formulas into first-order formulas with at most one free variable, x, as follows: if p is atomic, then $[p]_x = p(x)$; $[\bot]_x = \bot$; for any binary connective $\star$, $[A \star B]_x = [A]_x \star [B]_x$; for the modal connectives

$$[\Box A]_x = \forall y(R(x,y) \rightarrow [A]_y) \quad [\Diamond A]_x = \exists y(R(x,y) \wedge [A]_y)$$

where $R(x,y)$ is a binary predicate.

Opening a parenthesis: such a translation has, as underlying justification, the interpretation of alethic modalities in a Kripke model $\mathcal{M} = (W, R, V)$:

$$\begin{array}{lll} \mathcal{M}, w \models \Box A & \text{iff} & \text{for all } v \text{ such that } wRv, \mathcal{M}, v \models A. \\ \mathcal{M}, w \models \Diamond A & \text{iff} & \text{there exists } v \text{ such that } wRv \text{ and } \mathcal{M}, v \models A. \end{array} \quad (1)$$

$R(x,y)$ then represents the *accessibility relation* R in a Kripke frame. This intuition can be made formal based on the one-to-one correspondence between classical/intuitionistic translations and Kripke modal models [20]. We close this parenthesis by noting that this justification is only motivational, aiming at introducing modalities. Models will be discussed formally in Sect. 5.1.

The object-modal logic OL is then characterized in the first-order meta-logic ML as

$$\vdash_{OL} A \quad \text{iff} \quad \vdash_{ML} \forall x.[A]_x$$

Hence, if ML is classical logic (CL), the former definition characterizes the classical modal logic K [3], while if it is intuitionistic logic (IL), then it characterizes the intuitionistic modal logic IK [20].

In this work, we will adopt EL as the meta-theory (given by the system LEci), hence characterizing what we will define as the ecumenical modal logic EK.

3.2 An Ecumenical View of Modalities

The language of *ecumenical modal formulas* consists of a denumerable set $\mathcal{P}$ of (ecumenical) propositional symbols and the set of ecumenical connectives enhanced with unary *ecumenical modal operators*. Unlike for the classical case, there is not a canonical definition of constructive or intuitionistic modal logics. Here we will mostly follow the approach in [20] for justifying our choices for the ecumenical interpretation for *possibility* and *necessity*.

The ecumenical translation $[\cdot]^e_x$ from propositional ecumenical formulas into LEci is defined in the same way as the modal translation $[\cdot]_x$ in the last section. For the case of modal connectives, observe that, due to Proposition 1, the interpretation of ecumenical consequence should be essentially *intuitionistic*. This implies that the box modality is a *neutral connective*. The diamond, on the other hand, has two possible interpretations: classical and intuitionistic, since its leading connective is an existential quantifier. Hence we should have the ecumenical modalities: $\Box, \Diamond_i, \Diamond_c$, determined by the translations

$$[\Box A]^e_x = \forall y(R(x,y) \to_i [A]^e_y)$$
$$[\Diamond_i A]^e_x = \exists_i y(R(x,y) \wedge [A]^e_y) \qquad [\Diamond_c A]^e_x = \exists_c y(R(x,y) \wedge [A]^e_y)$$

Observe that, due to the equivalence (2), we have

14. $\Diamond_c A \leftrightarrow_i \neg\Box\neg A$

On the other hand, $\Box$ and $\Diamond_i$ are not inter-definable due to (2). Finally, if A^c is externally classical, then

15. $\Box A^c \leftrightarrow_i \neg\Diamond_c\neg A^c$

This means that, when restricted to the classical fragment, $\Box$ and $\Diamond_c$ are duals. This reflects well the ecumenical nature of the defined modalities. We will denote by EK the ecumenical modal logic meta-logically characterized by LEci via $[\cdot]^e_x$.

4 A Labeled System for EK

The basic idea behind labeled proof systems for modal logic is to internalize elements of the associated Kripke semantics (namely, the worlds of a Kripke structure and the accessibility relation between them) into the syntax.

Labeled modal formulas are either *labeled formulas* of the form $x : A$ or *relational atoms* of the form xRy, where x, y range over a set of variables and A is a modal formula. *Labeled sequents* have the form $\Gamma \vdash x : A$, where Γ is a multiset containing labeled modal formulas. The labeled ecumenical system labEK is presented in Fig. 2.

We will denote by $[\Gamma \vdash x : A]$ the LEci sequent $[\Gamma] \Rightarrow [A]^e_x$ where $[\Gamma] = \{R(x,y) \mid xRy \in \Gamma\} \cup \{[B]^e_x \mid x : B \in \Gamma\}$. The following is a meta-logical soundness and completeness result.

Initial and structural rules

$$\frac{}{x:A,\Gamma\vdash x:A}\ \mathsf{init}\qquad \frac{\Gamma\vdash y:\bot}{\Gamma\vdash x:A}\ \mathsf{W}$$

Propositional rules

$$\frac{x:A,x:B,\Gamma\vdash z:C}{x:A\wedge B,\Gamma\vdash z:C}\ \wedge L\qquad \frac{\Gamma\vdash x:A\quad \Gamma\vdash x:B}{\Gamma\vdash x:A\wedge B}\ \wedge R$$

$$\frac{x:A,\Gamma\vdash z:C\quad x:B,\Gamma\vdash z:C}{x:A\vee_i B,\Gamma\vdash z:C}\ \vee_i L\qquad \frac{\Gamma\vdash x:A_j}{\Gamma\vdash x:A_1\vee_i A_2}\ \vee_i R_j$$

$$\frac{x:A,\Gamma\vdash x:\bot\quad x:B,\Gamma\vdash x:\bot}{x:A\vee_c B,\Gamma\vdash x:\bot}\ \vee_c L\qquad \frac{\Gamma,x:\neg A,x:\neg B\vdash x:\bot}{\Gamma\vdash x:A\vee_c B}\ \vee_c R$$

$$\frac{x:A\rightarrow_i B,\Gamma\vdash x:A\quad x:B,\Gamma\vdash z:C}{x:A\rightarrow_i B,\Gamma\vdash z:C}\ \rightarrow_i L\qquad \frac{x:A,\Gamma\vdash x:B}{\Gamma\vdash x:A\rightarrow_i B}\ \rightarrow_i R$$

$$\frac{x:A\rightarrow_c B,\Gamma\vdash x:A\quad x:B,\Gamma\vdash x:\bot}{x:A\rightarrow_c B,\Gamma\vdash x:\bot}\ \rightarrow_c L\qquad \frac{x:A,x:\neg B,\Gamma\vdash x:\bot}{\Gamma\vdash x:A\rightarrow_c B}\ \rightarrow_c R$$

$$\frac{x:\neg A,\Gamma\vdash x:A}{x:\neg A,\Gamma\vdash x:\bot}\ \neg L\qquad \frac{x:A,\Gamma\vdash x:\bot}{\Gamma\vdash x:\neg A}\ \neg R\qquad \frac{}{x:\bot,\Gamma\vdash z:C}\ \bot$$

$$\frac{\Gamma,x:P_i\vdash x:\bot}{\Gamma,x:P_c\vdash x:\bot}\ L_c\qquad \frac{\Gamma,x:\neg P_i\vdash x:\bot}{\Gamma\vdash x:P_c}\ R_c$$

Modal rules

$$\frac{xRy,y:A,x:\Box A,\Gamma\vdash z:C}{xRy,x:\Box A,\Gamma\vdash z:C}\ \Box L\qquad \frac{xRy,\Gamma\vdash y:A}{\Gamma\vdash x:\Box A}\ \Box R\qquad \frac{xRy,y:A,\Gamma\vdash z:C}{x:\Diamond_i A,\Gamma\vdash z:C}\ \Diamond_i L$$

$$\frac{xRy,\Gamma\vdash y:A}{xRy,\Gamma\vdash x:\Diamond_i A}\ \Diamond_i R\qquad \frac{xRy,y:A,\Gamma\vdash x:\bot}{x:\Diamond_c A,\Gamma\vdash x:\bot}\ \Diamond_c L\qquad \frac{x:\Box\neg A,\Gamma\vdash x:\bot}{\Gamma\vdash x:\Diamond_c A}\ \Diamond_c R$$

Fig. 2. Ecumenical modal system labEK. In rules $\Box R, \Diamond_i L, \Diamond_c L$, the eigenvariable y does not occur free in any formula of the conclusion.

Theorem 2. *The following are equivalent:*

1. $\Gamma\vdash x:A$ *is provable in* labEK.
2. $[\Gamma\vdash x:A]$ *is provable in* LEci.

Proof. We will consider the following translation between labEK rule applications and LEci derivations, where the translation for the propositional rules is the trivial one:

$$\frac{xRy,y:A,x:\Box A,\Gamma\vdash z:C}{xRy,x:\Box A,\Gamma\vdash z:C}\ \Box L\quad\rightsquigarrow$$

$$\frac{\dfrac{}{R(x,y),[\Box A]_x^e,R(x,y)\rightarrow_i [A]_y^e,[\Gamma]\Rightarrow R(x,y)}\quad [xRy,y:A,x:\Box A,\Gamma\vdash z:C]}{[xRy,x:\Box A,\Gamma\vdash z:C]}\ (\forall L,\rightarrow_i L)$$

$$\frac{xRy,\Gamma\vdash y:A}{\Gamma\vdash x:\Box A}\ \Box R\quad\rightsquigarrow\quad \frac{[xRy,\Gamma\vdash y:A]}{[\Gamma\vdash x:\Box A]}\ (\forall R,\rightarrow_i R)$$

$$\frac{xRy, y : A, \Gamma \vdash z : C}{x : \Diamond_i A, \Gamma \vdash z : C} \Diamond_i L \quad \rightsquigarrow \quad \frac{[xRy, y : A, \Gamma \vdash z : C]}{[x : \Diamond_i A, \Gamma \vdash z : C]} (\exists_i L, \wedge L)$$

$$\frac{xRy, y : A, \Gamma \vdash x : \bot}{x : \Diamond_c A, \Gamma \vdash x : \bot} \Diamond_c L \quad \rightsquigarrow \quad \frac{[xRy, y : A, \Gamma \vdash x : \bot]}{[x : \Diamond_c A, \Gamma \vdash x : \bot]} (\exists_c L, \wedge L)$$

$$\frac{xRy, \Gamma \vdash y : A}{xRy, \Gamma \vdash x : \Diamond_i A} \Diamond_i R \quad \rightsquigarrow \quad \frac{\overline{R(x,y), [\Gamma] \Rightarrow R(x,y)} \quad [xRy, \Gamma \vdash y : A]}{[xRy, \Gamma \vdash x : \Diamond_i A]} (\exists_i R, \wedge R)$$

$$\frac{x : \Box\neg A, \Gamma \vdash x : \bot}{\Gamma \vdash x : \Diamond_c A} \Diamond_c R \quad \rightsquigarrow \quad \frac{\forall y.\neg(R(x,y) \wedge [A]^e_y), [\Gamma] \Rightarrow \bot}{[\Gamma \vdash x : \Diamond_c A]} (\exists_c R)$$

(1) $\Rightarrow$ (2) is easily proved by induction on a proof of $\Gamma \vdash x : A$ in labEK, observing that $\vdash_{\mathsf{LEci}} \forall y.\neg(R(x,y) \wedge [A]^e_y) \leftrightarrow_i (\forall y.R(x,y) \rightarrow_i [\neg A]^e_y) = [\Box\neg A]^e_x$.

For proving (2) $\Rightarrow$ (1) observe that the rules $\rightarrow_i R, \wedge L, \wedge R$ are invertible in LEci and $\rightarrow_i L$ is semi-invertible on the right (*i.e.* if its conclusion is valid, so is its right premise). Hence, in the translated derivations in LEci *provability* is maintained from the end-sequent to the open leaves. This means that choosing a formula $[A]^e_x$ to work on is equivalent to performing all the steps of the translation given above, ending with translated sequents of smaller proofs. Therefore, any derivation of $[\Gamma \vdash x : A]$ in LEci can be transformed into a derivation of the same sequent where all the steps of the translation are actually performed. This is, in fact, one of the pillars of the *focusing* method [1,9]. In order to illustrate this, consider the derivation

$$\frac{\overset{\pi}{R(x,y), R(x,y) \rightarrow_i [A]^e_y, [\Box A]^e_x, [\Gamma] \Rightarrow [C]^e_z}}{R(x,y), [\Box A]^e_x, [\Gamma] \Rightarrow [C]^e_z} (\forall L)$$

where one decides to work on the formula $\forall y.(R(x,y) \rightarrow_i [A]^e_y) = [\Box A]^e_x$ obtaining a premise containing the formula $B = R(x,y) \rightarrow_i [A]^e_y$, with proof π. Since $\rightarrow_i L$ is semi-invertible on the right and the left premise is straightforwardly provable, then π can be substituted by the proof:

$$\frac{\overline{R(x,y), R(x,y) \rightarrow_i [A]^e_y, [\Box A]^e_x, [\Gamma] \Rightarrow R(x,y)} \quad \overset{\pi'}{R(x,y), [A]^e_y, [\Box A]^e_x, [\Gamma] \Rightarrow [C]^e_z}}{R(x,y), R(x,y) \rightarrow_i [A]^e_y, [\Box A]^e_x, [\Gamma] \Rightarrow [C]^e_z} \rightarrow_i L$$

where $\pi' = \pi$ if B is never principal in π, while π' is constructed from π by permuting down the application of the rule $\rightarrow_i L$ over B. Thus, by inductive hypothesis, $[xRy, y : A, x : \Box A, \Gamma \vdash z : C]$ is provable in labEK.

Finally, observe that, when restricted to the intuitionistic and neutral operators, labEK matches *exactly* Simpson's sequent system $\mathcal{L}_{\Box\Diamond}$ [20]. This implies that $\mathcal{L}_{\Box\Diamond}$ is trivially embedded into labEK. The analyticity of labEK is presented next.

4.1 Cut-Elimination for labEK

In face of Theorem 2 most of the proof theoretical properties of the system labEK can be inherited from LEci. It is not different for the property of cut-elimination. Hence we will only illustrate the process here.

The extension of the Ecumenical weight for formulas presented [14] to modalities is defined bellow.

Definition 2. *The Ecumenical weight* (ew) *of a formula in* $\mathcal{L}$ *is recursively defined as*

- $\mathsf{ew}(P_i) = \mathsf{ew}(\bot) = 0$;
- $\mathsf{ew}(A \star B) = \mathsf{ew}(A) + \mathsf{ew}(B) + 1$ *if* $\star \in \{\wedge, \rightarrow_i, \vee_i\}$;
- $\mathsf{ew}(\heartsuit A) = \mathsf{ew}(A) + 1$ *if* $\heartsuit \in \{\neg, \Diamond_i, \Box\}$;
- $\mathsf{ew}(A \circ B) = \mathsf{ew}(A) + \mathsf{ew}(B) + 4$ *if* $\circ \in \{\rightarrow_c, \vee_c\}$;
- $\mathsf{ew}(P_c) = 4$;
- $\mathsf{ew}(\Diamond_c A) = \mathsf{ew}(A) + 4$.

Intuitively, the Ecumenical weight measures the amount of extra information needed (the negations added) in order to define the classical connectives from the intuitionistic and neutral ones.

Theorem 3. *The rule*

$$\frac{\Gamma \vdash x : A \quad x : A, \Gamma \vdash z : C}{\Gamma \vdash z : C}\ \mathsf{cut}$$

is admissible in labEK.

Proof. The proof is by the usual Gentzen method. The principal cases either eliminate the top-most cut or substitute it for cuts over simpler ecumenical formulas, *e.g.*

$$\dfrac{\dfrac{\overset{\pi_1}{x : \Box\neg A, \Gamma \vdash x : \bot}}{\Gamma \vdash x : \Diamond_c A}\ \Diamond_c R \quad \dfrac{\overset{\pi_2}{xRy, y : A, \Gamma \vdash x : \bot}}{x : \Diamond_c A, \Gamma \vdash z : \bot}\ \Diamond_c L}{\Gamma \vdash z : \bot}\ \mathsf{cut} \ \rightsquigarrow$$

$$\dfrac{\dfrac{\dfrac{\overset{\pi_2}{xRy, y : A, \Gamma \vdash y : \bot}}{xRy, \Gamma \vdash y : \neg A}\ \neg R}{\Gamma \vdash x : \Box\neg A}\ \Box R \quad \overset{\pi_1}{x : \Box\neg A, \Gamma, \vdash z : \bot}}{\Gamma \vdash z : \bot}\ \mathsf{cut}$$

Observe that the label of bottom is irrelevant due to the weakening rule W (that we have suppressed). Hence the Ecumenical weight on the cut formula passes from $\mathsf{ew}(\Diamond_c x.A) = \mathsf{ew}(A) + 4$ to $\mathsf{ew}(\Box\neg A) = \mathsf{ew}(A) + 2$.

The non-principal cuts can be flipped up as usual, generating cuts with smaller cut-height.

5 Axiomatization and Semantics

Classical modal logic K is characterized as propositional classical logic, extended with the *necessitation rule* (presented in Hilbert style) $A/\Box A$ and the *distributivity axiom* $\mathsf{k}: \Box(A \rightarrow B) \rightarrow (\Box A \rightarrow \Box B)$. Intuitionistic modal logic should then consist of propositional intuitionistic logic plus necessitation and distributivity.

As it is well known [16,20], there are many variants of axiom k that induces classically, but not intuitionistically, equivalent systems. In fact, the following axioms classically follow from k and the De Morgan laws, but not in an intuitionistic setting

$$\mathsf{k}_1 : \Box(A \rightarrow B) \rightarrow (\Diamond A \rightarrow \Diamond B) \qquad \mathsf{k}_2 : \Diamond(A \vee B) \rightarrow (\Diamond A \vee \Diamond B)$$
$$\mathsf{k}_3 : (\Diamond A \rightarrow \Box B) \rightarrow \Box(A \rightarrow B) \qquad \mathsf{k}_4 : \Diamond\bot \rightarrow \bot$$

The combination of axiom k with axioms $\mathsf{k}_1 - \mathsf{k}_4$ characterizes intuitionistic modal logic IK [16]. And $\mathcal{L}_{\Box\Diamond}$ is sound and complete w.r.t. IK [20].

In the ecumenical setting, there are many more variants from k, depending on the classical or intuitionistic interpretation of the implication and diamond. Since $\mathcal{L}_{\Box\Diamond}$ is a sub-system of labEK, EK is *complete* w.r.t. the intuitionistic version of this set of axioms. *Soundness* will be established next.

For the sake of readability, we will abuse the notation and represent the connectives of IK/$\mathcal{L}_{\Box\Diamond}$ using the neutral/intuitionistic correspondents in EK/labEK.

Definition 3. *Let $[\![\cdot]\!]_{\mathsf{K}}$ be the following formula translation from* EK *to* IK

$$\begin{array}{llll}
[\![p_i]\!]_{\mathsf{K}} & = p_i & [\![p_c]\!]_{\mathsf{K}} & = \neg(\neg(p_i)) \\
[\![\bot]\!]_{\mathsf{K}} & = \bot & [\![\neg A]\!]_{\mathsf{K}} & = \neg[\![A]\!]_{\mathsf{K}} \\
[\![A \wedge B]\!]_{\mathsf{K}} & = [\![A]\!]_{\mathsf{K}} \wedge [\![B]\!]_{\mathsf{K}} & [\![A \vee_i B]\!]_{\mathsf{K}} & = [\![A]\!]_{\mathsf{K}} \vee_i [\![B]\!]_{\mathsf{K}} \\
[\![A \rightarrow_i B]\!]_{\mathsf{K}} & = [\![A]\!]_{\mathsf{K}} \rightarrow_i [\![B]\!]_{\mathsf{K}} & [\![A \vee_c B]\!]_{\mathsf{K}} & = \neg(\neg[\![A]\!]_{\mathsf{K}} \wedge \neg[\![B]\!]_{\mathsf{K}}) \\
[\![A \rightarrow_c B]\!]_{\mathsf{K}} & = \neg([\![A]\!]_{\mathsf{K}} \wedge \neg[\![B]\!]_{\mathsf{K}}) & [\![\Box A]\!]_{\mathsf{K}} & = \Box[\![A]\!]_{\mathsf{K}} \\
[\![\Diamond_i A]\!]_{\mathsf{K}} & = \Diamond_i[\![A]\!]_{\mathsf{K}} & [\![\Diamond_c A]\!]_{\mathsf{K}} & = \neg\Box\neg[\![A]\!]_{\mathsf{K}}
\end{array}$$

The translation $[\![\cdot]\!]$: labEK $\rightarrow \mathcal{L}_{\Box\Diamond}$ is defined as $[\![x : A]\!] = x : [\![A]\!]_{\mathsf{K}}$ and assumed identical on relational atoms.

Since the translations above preserve the double-negation interpretation of classical connectives into intuitionistic (modal) logic, the following holds.

Lemma 1. $\vdash_{\mathsf{labEK}} \Gamma \vdash x : A$ *iff* $\vdash_{\mathsf{labEK}} [\![\Gamma \vdash x : A]\!]$ *iff* $\vdash_{\mathcal{L}_{\Box\Diamond}} [\![\Gamma \vdash x : A]\!]$.

Hence we have that

Theorem 4. EK *is sound w.r.t. the intuitionistic version of axioms* $\mathsf{k} - \mathsf{k}_4$.

Remark 1. One could ask: what happens if we exchange the intuitionistic versions of the connectives with classical ones? For answering that, consider $\mathsf{k}_{\alpha\beta\gamma}$: $\Box(A \rightarrow_\alpha B) \rightarrow_\beta (\Box A \rightarrow_\gamma \Box B)$ with $\alpha, \beta, \gamma \in \{i, c\}$. Since $C \rightarrow_i D \Rightarrow C \rightarrow_c D$ in EK, $\mathsf{k}_{\alpha ii} \Rightarrow \mathsf{k}_{\alpha\beta\gamma}$ for any value of β, γ. Moreover, k_{cii} is not provable in EK. Hence, k_{iii} is the *minimal* version of k provable in EK. The same holds for all the other axioms.

5.1 Ecumenical Birelational Models

In [2], the negative translation was used to relate cut-elimination theorems for classical and intuitionistic logics. Since part of the argumentation was given semantically, a notion of Kripke semantics for classical logic was stated, via the respective semantics for intuitionistic logic and the double negation interpretation (see also [7]). In [14] a similar definition was given, but under the ecumenical approach, and it was extended to the first-order case in [15]. We will propose a birelational Kripke semantics for ecumenical modal logic, which is an extension of the proposal in [14] to modalities.

Definition 4. *A* birelational Kripke model *is a quadruple* $\mathcal{M} = (W, \leq, R, V)$ *where* (W, R, V) *is a Kripke model such that* W *is partially ordered with order* $\leq$*, the satisfaction function* $V : \langle W, \leq\rangle \to \langle 2^{\mathcal{P}}, \subseteq\rangle$ *is monotone and:*
F1. For all worlds w, v, v'*, if* wRv *and* $v \leq v'$*, there is a* w' *such that* $w \leq w'$ *and* $w'Rv'$*;*
F2. For all worlds w', w, v*, if* $w \leq w'$ *and* wRv*, there is a* v' *such that* $w'Rv'$ *and* $v \leq v'$*.*

An ecumenical modal Kripke model *is a birelational Kripke model such that truth of an ecumenical formula at a point* w *is the smallest relation* $\models_{\mathsf{E}}$ *satisfying*

$$\begin{array}{lll}
\mathcal{M}, w \models_{\mathsf{E}} p_i & \text{iff} & p_i \in V(w); \\
\mathcal{M}, w \models_{\mathsf{E}} A \wedge B & \text{iff} & \mathcal{M}, w \models_{\mathsf{E}} A \text{ and } \mathcal{M}, w \models_{\mathsf{E}} B; \\
\mathcal{M}, w \models_{\mathsf{E}} A \vee_i B & \text{iff} & \mathcal{M}, w \models_{\mathsf{E}} A \text{ or } \mathcal{M}, w \models_{\mathsf{E}} B; \\
\mathcal{M}, w \models_{\mathsf{E}} A \to_i B & \text{iff} & \text{for all } v \text{ such that } w \leq v, \mathcal{M}, v \models_{\mathsf{E}} A \text{ implies } \mathcal{M}, v \models_{\mathsf{E}} B; \\
\mathcal{M}, w \models_{\mathsf{E}} \neg A & \text{iff} & \text{for all } v \text{ such that } w \leq v, \mathcal{M}, v \not\models_{\mathsf{E}} A; \\
\mathcal{M}, w \models_{\mathsf{E}} \bot & & \text{never holds}; \\
\mathcal{M}, w \models_{\mathsf{E}} \Box A & \text{iff} & \text{for all } v, w' \text{ such that } w \leq w' \text{ and } w'Rv, \mathcal{M}, v \models_{\mathsf{E}} A. \\
\mathcal{M}, w \models_{\mathsf{E}} \Diamond_i A & \text{iff} & \text{there exists } v \text{ such that } wRv \text{ and } \mathcal{M}, v \models_{\mathsf{E}} A. \\
\mathcal{M}, w \models_{\mathsf{E}} p_c & \text{iff} & \mathcal{M}, w \models_{\mathsf{E}} \neg(\neg p_i); \\
\mathcal{M}, w \models_{\mathsf{E}} A \vee_c B & \text{iff} & \mathcal{M}, w \models_{\mathsf{E}} \neg(\neg A \wedge \neg B); \\
\mathcal{M}, w \models_{\mathsf{E}} A \to_c B & \text{iff} & \mathcal{M}, w \models_{\mathsf{E}} \neg(A \wedge \neg B). \\
\mathcal{M}, w \models_{\mathsf{E}} \Diamond_c A & \text{iff} & \mathcal{M}, w \models_{\mathsf{E}} \neg\Box\neg A.
\end{array}$$

Since, restricted to intuitionistic and neutral connectives, $\models_{\mathsf{E}}$ is the usual birelational interpretation $\models$ for IK (and, consequently, $\mathcal{L}_{\Box\Diamond}$ [20]), and since the classical connectives are interpreted via the neutral ones using the double-negation translation, an ecumenical modal Kripke model is nothing else than the standard birelational Kripke model for intuitionistic modal logic IK. Hence, in the face of Theorem 4, the following result is trivial.

Theorem 5. EK *is sound and complete w.r.t. the ecumenical modal Kripke semantics, that is,* $\vdash_{\mathsf{EK}} A$ *iff* $\models_{\mathsf{E}} A$*.*

6 Extensions

Depending on the application, several further modal logics can be defined as extensions of K by simply restricting the class of frames we consider. Many of

Table 1. Axioms and corresponding first-order conditions on R.

Axiom	Condition	First-Order (FO) Formula
$\mathsf{T}: \Box A \to A \wedge A \to \Diamond A$	Reflexivity	$\forall x.R(x,x)$
$4: \Box A \to \Box\Box A \wedge \Diamond\Diamond A \to \Diamond A$	Transitivity	$\forall x,y,z.(R(x,y) \wedge R(y,z)) \to R(x,z)$
$5: \Box A \to \Box\Diamond A \wedge \Diamond\Box A \to \Diamond A$	Euclideaness	$\forall x,y,z.(R(x,y) \wedge R(x,z)) \to R(y,z)$
$\mathsf{B}: A \to \Box\Diamond A \wedge \Diamond\Box A \to A$	Symmetry	$\forall x,y.R(x,y) \to R(y,x)$

$$\frac{xRx, \Gamma \vdash w : C}{\Gamma \vdash w : C}\ \mathsf{T} \qquad \frac{xRz, xRy, yRz, \Gamma \vdash w : C}{xRy, yRz, \Gamma \vdash w : C}\ 4$$
$$\frac{yRz, xRy, xRz, \Gamma \vdash w : C}{xRy, xRz, \Gamma \vdash w : C}\ 5 \qquad \frac{yRx, xRy, \Gamma \vdash w : C}{xRy, \Gamma \vdash w : C}\ \mathsf{B}$$

Fig. 3. Labeled sequent rules corresponding to axioms in Table 1.

the restrictions one can be interested in are definable as formulas of first-order logic, where the binary predicate $R(x,y)$ refers to the corresponding accessibility relation. Table 1 summarizes some of the most common logics, the corresponding frame property, together with the modal axiom capturing it in the intuitionistic framework [18].

We divide the problem of modal extensions in 3 parts: (i) transform the FO formulas in Table 1 into inference rules; (ii) prove that the axioms are theorems in the extended systems; and (iii) prove that the axioms actually enforce the respective condition. In this work, we will show (i) and (ii), and start the discussion of (iii) in the ecumenical setting.

The general problem of systematically extending standard proof-theoretical results obtained for pure logic to non-logical axioms has been focus of attention for quite some time now (see *e.g.* [4,6,13,20,22]). In [11], a systematic procedure for transforming a class of FO formulas (called *bipolars*) into rules for atoms was presented. This procedure involves polarization of formulas and focusing [1].

The main idea of this method is that assuming a FO clause as a theory is the same as applying a rule, determined by the shape of the formula, on its atomic subformulas. In order to illustrate the process, consider the formula $\forall x,y.R(x,y) \to_i R(y,x)$. Having it as a theory and working throughout it in LEci:

$$\dfrac{\dfrac{\Gamma \vdash R(x,y) \quad \Gamma, R(y,x) \vdash C}{\Gamma, R(x,y) \to_i R(y,x) \vdash C}\ \to_i L}{\Gamma, \forall x,y.R(x,y) \to_i R(y,x) \vdash C}\ \forall L$$

From that, there are two protocols: the *forward-chaining* insists that the left premise above is trivial, meaning that it is proved by the initial rule (hence $R(x,y) \in \Gamma$ and $R(y,x)$ is "produced" from it); and the *backward-chaining* insists that the right-most premise is trivial: that is, $R(y,x)$ and C are the same atomic formula. These protocols give rise to the rules, respectively

$$\frac{\Gamma, R(y,x) \vdash C}{\Gamma, R(x,y) \vdash C} \qquad \frac{\Gamma \vdash R(x,y)}{\Gamma \vdash R(y,x)}$$

The first one appears, *e.g.* in [20], while the second occurs in [22]. Adopting the forward-chaining protocol, the FO formulas in Table 1 are transformed into the rules in Fig. 3, hence fulfilling the goal (i). Observe that, as noted in Remark 1, we only need to consider the intuitionistic version of the FO formulas.

Regarding (ii), it is easy to see that the axioms listed in the first column of Table 1 are theorems in labEK extended with the respective rules. For example

$$\dfrac{\dfrac{\dfrac{\dfrac{\dfrac{}{xRx, x : A \vdash x : A}\ \mathsf{init}}{xRx, x : \Box A \vdash x : A}\ \Box L}{x : \Box A \vdash x : A}\ \mathsf{T}}{\vdash x : \Box A \to_i A}\ \to_i R \qquad \dfrac{\dfrac{\dfrac{\dfrac{}{xRx, x : A \vdash x : A}\ \mathsf{init}}{xRx, x : A \vdash x : \Diamond_i A}\ \Diamond_i R}{x : A \vdash \Diamond_i A}\ \mathsf{T}}{\vdash x : A \to_i \Diamond_i A}\ \to_i R}{\vdash x : (\Box A \to_i A) \wedge (A \to_i \Diamond_i A)}\ \wedge R$$

Finally, item (iii) remains: do such axioms indeed reflect the respective conditions in Fig. 3? We illustrate the complexity of the interaction of modal axioms and ecumenical connectives in the case of axiom T.

It is well known that, by itself, $\Box A \to_i A$ does not enforce reflexivity of an intuitionistic model [20,21]. In fact, the derivation above shows that, in frames having the reflexivity property, both $\Box A \to_i A$ and $A \to_i \Diamond_i A$ are provable. For the converse, since $\Box$ and $\Diamond_i$ are not inter-definable, we need to add $A \to_i \Diamond_i A$ in order to still be complete w.r.t. reflexive models. This is also true for any extension of EK by path axioms plus contrapositives w.r.t. their corresponding models. But beyond that it wouldn't be as clean cut, unless one adds the preorder relation into the mix as in [16]. This not mentioning the ecumenical nature of *atoms* [10]. In fact, in the ecumenical setting, the possibility of mixing intuitionistic and classical relational formulas and modalities can make this discussion even harder, and it is left for a future work.

Finally, since adding ecumenical axioms can deeply affect the resulting system, it should be studied carefully. For example, the modalities in EK are not inter-definable, but what would be the consequence of adding $\neg\Diamond_i\neg A \to_i \Box A$ as an extra axiom to labEK added with the rule T? The following derivation shows that the addition of this new axiom has a disastrous propositional consequence.

$$\dfrac{\dfrac{\dfrac{\dfrac{\dfrac{\dfrac{\dfrac{}{xRy, y : A, y : \neg(A \vee_i \neg A) \vdash y : A}\ \mathsf{init}}{xRy, y : A, y : \neg(A \vee_i \neg A) \vdash y : \bot}\ \neg L, \vee_i R1}{xRy, y : \neg(A \vee_i \neg A) \vdash x : \bot}\ \neg L, \vee_i R2, \neg R}{x : \Diamond_i \neg(A \vee_i \neg A) \vdash x : \bot}\ \Diamond_i L}{\vdash x : \neg\Diamond_i\neg(A \vee_i \neg A)}\ \neg R}{\vdash x : \Box(A \vee_i \neg A)}\ eq \qquad \dfrac{\dfrac{\dfrac{}{xRx, x : (A \vee_i \neg A) \vdash x : (A \vee_i \neg A)}\ \mathsf{init}}{xRx, x : \Box(A \vee_i \neg A) \vdash x : (A \vee_i \neg A)}\ \Box L}{x : \Box(A \vee_i \neg A) \vdash x : (A \vee_i \neg A)}\ \mathsf{T}}{\vdash x : (A \vee_i \neg A)}\ \mathsf{cut}$$

where *eq* represents the proof steps of the substitution of a boxed formula for its diamond version.[1] That is, if $\square$ and $\lozenge_i$ are inter-definable, then $A \vee_i \neg A$ is a theorem and intuitionistic KT collapses to a classical system!

7 Discussion and Conclusion

Some questions naturally arise with respect to ecumenical systems: what (really) are ecumenical systems? What are they good for? Why should anyone be interested in ecumenical systems? What is the real motivation behind the definition and development of ecumenical systems? Based on the specific case of the ecumenical system that puts classical logic and intuitionist logic coexisting in peace in the same codification, we would like to propose three possible motivations for the definition, study and development of ecumenical systems.

Philosophical Motivation. This was the motivation of Prawitz. Inferentialism, and in particular, logical inferentialism, is the semantical approach according to which the meaning of the logical constants can be specified by the rules that determine their correct use. According to Prawitz [17],

> *"Gentzen's introduction rules, taken as meaning constitutive of the logical constants of the language of predicate logic, agree, as is well known, with how intuitionistic mathematicians use the constants. On the one hand, the elimination rules stated by Gentzen become all justified when the constants are so understood because of there being reductions, originally introduced in the process of normalizing natural deductions, which applied to proofs terminating with an application of elimination rules give canonical proofs of the conclusion in question. On the other hand, no canonical proof of an arbitrarily chosen instance of the law of the excluded middle is known, nor any reduction that applied to a proof terminating with an application of the classical form of reduction ad absurdum gives a canonical proof of the conclusion."*

But what about the use classical mathematicians make of the logical constants? Again, according to Prawitz,

> *"What is then to be said about the negative thesis that no coherent meaning can be attached on the classical use of the logical constants? Gentzen's introduction rules are of course accepted also in classical reasoning, but some of them cannot be seen as introduction rules, that is they cannot serve as explanations of meaning. The classical understanding of disjunction is not such that $A \vee B$ may be rightly asserted only if it is possible to prove either A or B, and hence Gentzen's introduction rule for disjunction does not determine the meaning of classical disjunction."*

---

[1] We have presented a proof with cut for clarity, remember that labEK has the cut-elimination property (see Appendix 4.1).

As an alternative, in a recent paper [12] Murzi presents a different approach to the extension of inferentialism to classical logic. There are some natural (proof-theoretical) inferentialist requirements on admissible logical rules, such as harmony and separability (although harmonic, Prawitz' rules for the classical operators do not satisfy separability). According to Murzi, our usual logical practice does not seem to allow for an inferentialist account of classical logic (unlike what happens with respect to intuitionistic logic). Murzi proposes a new set of rules for classical logical operators based on: absurdity as a punctuation mark, and Higher-level rules [19]. This allows for a "pure" logical system, where negation is not used in premises.

Mathematical/Computational Motivation. (This was actually the original motivation for proposing ecumenical systems.) The first ecumenical system (as far as we know) was defined by Krauss in a technical report of the University of Kassel [8] (the text was never published in a journal). The paper is divided in two parts: in the first part, Krauss' ecumenical system is defined and some properties proved. In the second part, some theorems of basic algebraic number theory are revised in the light of this (ecumenical) system, where constructive proofs of some "familiar classical proofs" are given (like the proof of Dirichlet's Unit Theorem). The same motivation can be found in the final passages of the paper [5], where Dowek examines what would happen in the case of axiomatizations of mathematics. Dowek gives a simple example from Set Theory, and ends the paper with this very interesting remark:

> *"Which mathematical results have a classical formulation that can be proved from the axioms of constructive set theory or constructive type theory and which require a classical formulation of these axioms and a classical notion of entailment remains to be investigated."*

Logical Motivation. In a certain sense, the logical motivation naturally combines certain aspects of the philosophical motivation with certain aspects of the mathematical motivation. According to Prawitz, one can consider the so-called classical first order logic as *"an attempted codification of a fragment of inferences occurring in [our] actual deductive practice"*. Given that there exist different and even divergent attempts to codify our (informal) deductive practice, it is more than natural to ask about what relations are entertained between these codifications. Ecumenical systems may help us to have a better understanding of the relation between classical logic and intuitionistic logic. But one could say that, from a logical point of view, there's nothing new in the ecumenical proposal: Based on translations, the new classical operators could be easily introduced by "explicit definitions". Let us consider the following dialogue between a classical logician (CL) and an intuitionistic logician (IL), a dialogue that may arise as a consequence of the translations mentioned above:

- IL: if what you mean by $(A \vee B)$ is $\neg(\neg A \wedge \neg B)$, then I can accept the validity of $(A \vee \neg A)$!

- CL: but I do not mean $\neg(\neg A \wedge \neg\neg A)$ by $(A \vee \neg A)$. One must distinguish the excluded-middle from the principle of non-contradiction. When I say that Goldbach's conjecture is either true or false, I am not saying that it would be contradictory to assert that it is not true and that it is not the case that it is not true!
- IL: but you must realize that, at the end of the day, you just have one logical operator, the Sheffer stroke (or the Quine's dagger).
- CL: But this is not at all true! The fact that we can define one operator in terms of other operators does not imply that we don't have different operators! We do have 16 binary propositional operators (functions). It is also true that we can prove $\vdash (A \vee_c B) \leftrightarrow \neg(\neg A \wedge \neg B)$ in the ecumenical system, but this does not mean that we don't have three different operators, $\neg$, $\vee_c$ and $\wedge$.

Maybe we can resume the logical motivation in the following (very simple) sentence:

> Ecumenical systems constitute a new and promising instrument to study the nature of different (maybe divergent!) logics.

Now, what can we say about *modal* ecumenical systems? Regarding the **philosophical view**, in [15] we have used invertibility results in order to obtain a sequent system for Prawitz' ecumenical logic with a minimal occurrences of negations, moving then towards a "purer" ecumenical system. Nevertheless, negation still plays an important role on interpreting classical connectives. This is transferred to our definition of ecumenical modalities, where the classical possibility is interpreted using negation. We plan to investigate what would be the meaning of classical possibility without impure rules. For the **mathematical view**, our use of intuitionistic/classical/neutral connectives allows for a more chirurgical detection of the parts of a mathematical proof that are intrinsically intuitionistic, classical or independent. We now bring this discussion to modalities. There is an interesting aspect of this expansion, that would be the ecumenical interpretation of *relational formulas*, as noted in Sect. 6. Finally, concerning the **logical view**, it would be interesting to explore some relations between general results on translations and ecumenical systems.

We end the present text by noting that there is an obvious connection between the Ecumenical approach and Gödel-Gentzen's double-negation translations of classical logic into intuitionistic logic. This could lead to the erroneous conclusion that the ecumenical refinement of classical logic is *essentially* the same refinement produced by such translation. But, on a closer inspection, shows that this is not true! Indeed, classical mathematical practice does not require that every occurrence of $\vee$ in real mathematical proofs be replaced by its Gödel-Gentzen translation. For example, there is no reason to translate the occurrence of $\vee$ in the theorem $(A \rightarrow (A \vee B))$. Given that the Gödel-Gentzen translation function systematically and globally eliminates every occurrence of $\vee$ and $\exists$ from the language of classical logic, one may say that the ecumenical system reflects more faithfully the "local" necessary uses of classical reasoning.

That is, the ecumenical refinement "interpolates" the Gödel-Gentzen-translation function. And this is extended, in our work, to reasoning with modalities.

References

1. Andreoli, J.M.: Focussing and proof construction. Ann. Pure Appl. Logic **107**(1), 131–163 (2001)
2. Avigad, J.: Algebraic proofs of cut elimination. J. Log. Algebr. Program. **49**(1–2), 15–30 (2001)
3. Blackburn, P., Rijke, M.D., Venema, Y.: Modal Logic. Cambridge Tracts in Theoretical Computer Science, Cambridge University Press (2001)
4. Ciabattoni, A., Maffezioli, P., Spendier, L.: Hypersequent and labelled calculi for intermediate logics. In: Galmiche, D., Larchey-Wendling, D. (eds.) TABLEAUX 2013. LNCS (LNAI), vol. 8123, pp. 81–96. Springer, Heidelberg (2013). https://doi.org/10.1007/978-3-642-40537-2_9
5. Dowek, G.: On the definition of the classical connectives and quantifiers. Why is this a Proof? Festschrift for Luiz Carlos Pereira, vol. 27, pp. 228–238 (2016)
6. Dyckhoff, R., Negri, S.: Geometrisation of first-order logic. Bull. Symb. Logic **21**(2), 123–163 (2015). http://www.jstor.org/stable/24327109
7. Ilik, D., Lee, G., Herbelin, H.: Kripke models for classical logic. Ann. Pure Appl. Logic **161**(11), 1367–1378 (2010)
8. Krauss, P.: A constructive refinement of classical logic draft (1992)
9. Liang, C., Miller, D.: A focused approach to combining logics. Ann. Pure Appl. Logic **162**(9), 679–697 (2011)
10. Maffezioli, P., Naibo, A.: An intuitionistic logic for preference relations. Log. J. IGPL **27**(4), 434–450 (2019). https://doi.org/10.1093/jigpal/jzz013
11. Marin, S., Miller, D., Pimentel, E., Volpe, M.: From axioms to synthetic inference rules via focusing (2020. https://drive.google.com/file/d/1_gNtKjvmxyH7T7VwpUD0QZtXARei8t5K/view
12. Murzi, J.: Classical harmony and separability. Erkenntnis **85**, 391–415 (2020)
13. Negri, S., von Plato, J.: Cut elimination in the presence of axioms. Bull. Symb. Logic **4**(4), 418–435 (1998). http://www.math.ucla.edu/~asl/bsl/0404/0404-003.ps
14. Pereira, L.C., Rodriguez, R.O.: Normalization, soundness and completeness for the propositional fragment of Prawitz' ecumenical system. Revista Portuguesa de Filosofia **73**(3–3), 1153–1168 (2017)
15. Pimentel, E., Pereira, L.C., de Paiva, V.: An ecumenical notion of entailment (2020), https://doi.org/10.1007/s11229-019-02226-5. accepted to Synthese
16. Plotkin, G.D., Stirling, C.P.: A framework for intuitionistic modal logic. In: Halpern, J.Y. (ed.) 1st Conference on Theoretical Aspects of Reasoning About Knowledge. Morgan Kaufmann (1986)
17. Prawitz, D.: Classical versus intuitionistic logic. Why is this a Proof?, Festschrift for Luiz Carlos Pereira, vol. 27, pp. 15–32 (2015)
18. Sahlqvist, H.: Completeness and correspondence in first and second order semantics for modal logic. In: Kanger, N.H.S. (ed.) Proceedings of the Third Scandinavian Logic Symposium, pp. 110–143 (1975)
19. Schroeder-Heister, P.: The calculus of higher-level rules, propositional quantification, and the foundational approach to proof-theoretic harmony. Stud. Logica. **102**(6), 1185–1216 (2014)

20. Simpson, A.K.: The Proof Theory and Semantics of Intuitionistic Modal Logic. Ph.D. thesis, College of Science and Engineering, School of Informatics, University of Edinburgh (1994)
21. Straßburger, L.: Cut elimination in nested sequents for intuitionistic modal logics. Proc. FOSSACS **2013**, 209–224 (2013)
22. Viganò, L.: Labelled Non-Classical Logics. Kluwer Academic Publishers (2000)

Inquisitive Dynamic Epistemic Logic in a Non-classical Setting

Vít Punčochář(✉)

Institute of Computer Science, Czech Academy of Sciences,
Pod Vodárenskou věží 271/2, 182 07 Praha 8, Czech Republic
puncochar@cs.cas.cz

Abstract. This paper studies the operations of public announcement of statements and public utterance of questions in the context of substructutral inquisitive epistemic logic. It was shown elsewhere that the logical laws governing the modalities of knowing and entertaining from standard inquisitive epistemic logic generalize smoothly to substructural logics. In this paper we show that the situation is different with the reduction axioms that in the standard setting govern the modality of public announcement/utterance. The standard reduction axioms depend on some features of classical logic that are not preserved in substructural logics. Using an additional auxiliary modality, we show how to overcome this obstacle and formulate an alternative set of reduction axioms for the public announcement/utterance modality that can be used even in the context of our general non-classical setting.

Keywords: Dynamic logic · Epistemic logic · Inquisitive logic · Substructural logic · Public announcement · Reduction axioms

1 Introduction

Public announcement logic (PAL, see, e.g. [9]), as a particular form of dynamic epistemic logic, aims at capturing the logical structure of public communication and reasoning about agents, and their changing believes and knowledge. In other words, it is concerned with reasoning involving information about the dynamics of information accessible to other agents. Inquisitive dynamic epistemic logic (IDEL, see [3,4]) enriches PAL with the realm of questions. Agents are equipped not only with information states but also with issues and not only statements but also questions may be publicly announced/uttered.

The standard dynamic epistemic logic, as well as its inquisitive extension, are based on classical logic. The aim of this paper is to present a general semantic framework that can serve as a basis for non-classical inquisitive dynamic epistemic logics. It incorporates public announcement logic based on substructural logic but at the same time applies to a language involving questions.

The work on this paper was supported by grant no. 18-19162Y of the Czech Science Foundation.

M. A. Martins and I. Sedlár (Eds.): DaLí 2020, LNCS 12569, pp. 205–221, 2020.
https://doi.org/10.1007/978-3-030-65840-3_13

Our approach relies significantly on the static framework for substructural inquisitive epistemic logics developed in [5]. The main contribution of this paper is an extension of this particular framework with an extra layer that allows one to capture the dynamics of publicly announcing statements and raising issues. The resulting semantics can be seen as a generalization of the semantics of IDEL. However, we will see that the reduction axioms for the public announcement/utterance modality used in [4] to syntactically characterize IDEL are not valid in our more general setting. Our solution to this problem is that we add to the language an auxiliary modality for which simple and elegant reduction axioms can be formulated, and we will reduce the public announcement/utterance modality to this additional modality.

2 The Object Language

The object language we will work with involves atomic formulas and the following logical symbols: (a) standard logical symbols used in propositional substructural logics, namely the constant for contradiction ($\bot$), the constant for logical truth (t), negation ($\neg$), implication ($\rightarrow$), extensional conjunction ($\wedge$), intensional conjunction ($\otimes$), declarative disjunction ($\vee$); (b) a binary connective $\mathbin{\vee\!\!\!\vee}$ that is called inquisitive disjunction and that allows one to form disjunctive and polar (yes/no) questions so that $p \mathbin{\vee\!\!\!\vee} q$ amounts to the disjunctive question *whether p or q*, and $p \mathbin{\vee\!\!\!\vee} \neg p$ to the polar question *whether p* (see, e.g., [2]); (c) two epistemic modalities, I_a and E_a (where a represents an agent); (d) a dynamic public utterance modality $[\varphi]$;[1] (e) an auxiliary dynamic modality $\{\varphi\}$. We will also use equivalence as a defined symbol: $\varphi \leftrightarrow \psi =_{def} (\varphi \rightarrow \psi) \wedge (\psi \rightarrow \varphi)$. The resulting language will be called $\mathcal{L}_{SIDEL}$ (the language of *Substructural Inquisitive Dynamic Epistemic Logic*). It can be defined in the following compact way:

$$\varphi ::= p \mid \bot \mid \mathsf{t} \mid \neg\varphi \mid \varphi \rightarrow \varphi \mid \varphi \wedge \varphi \mid \varphi \otimes \varphi \mid \varphi \vee \varphi \mid \varphi \mathbin{\vee\!\!\!\vee} \varphi \mid I_a\varphi \mid E_a\varphi \mid [\varphi]\varphi \mid \{\varphi\}\varphi$$

The modality I_a is interpreted as meaning: *according to a's information.* This modality can be applied to statements as well as to questions. In particular, we have the following basic cases:[2]

[1] It is common to interpret the modality $[\varphi]$ as *public announcement of* φ. However, we will follow [4] in using the term "public utterance" instead of "public announcement". The reason is that φ may represent a question, e.g. the question *whether p or q*, and it seems that there is an intuitive difference between *announcing whether p or q* and *uttering whether p or q*. The former indicates that an answer to the question is uttered, while the latter means only that the question itself is uttered, which corresponds better to what the modality $[\varphi]$ is supposed to model.

[2] In the standard inquisitive epistemic logic, the letter K, instead of I, is used for this modality since it is interpreted as knowing that/whether. However, in our more general framework, we will not assume the specific features of knowledge, as for example factivity (the agent can know only what is true) so the letter I seems to be more appropriate.

The formula	Represents
$I_a p$	According to a's information, p holds
$I_a(p \vee\!\!\!\vee q)$	a's information resolves the question whether p or q

The modality E_a is called an entertaining modality. When applied to statements this modality is assumed to behave just like I_a but its behavior differs when it is applied to questions. This modality does not have a direct counterpart in natural language but its meaning can be illustrated as follows. Assume, for example, that an agent would like to have the information whether there are two or three apples on a table. We also say that this is the agent's *issue*. This presupposes that the agent already has the information that at least one of these numbers is correct and she wants to know which one it is. In that case we say that *the agent entertains the question whether there are two or three apples on the table* but also, for example, that *she entertains the question whether there is an even or odd number of apples on the table* because every information that resolves the former issue (two or three?), resolves also the latter one (even or odd?).

In the standard framework of inquisitive epistemic logic the entertaining modality serves mainly as a mean to define a more common wondering modality in this way: $W_a\varphi =_{df} E_a\varphi \wedge \neg I_a\varphi$. In our example, the agent for instance also entertains the question whether there are less or more than five apples on the table because every information that resolves her issue (two or three?) trivially resolves also this question (less or more than five?). However, the agent does not wonder whether there are less or more than five apples on the table because this question is already resolved by her information that there are either two or three apples on the table.

The formula	Represents
$E_a(p \vee\!\!\!\vee q)$	a entertains the question whether p or q
$W_a(p \vee\!\!\!\vee q)$	a wonders whether p or q

For a statement α the formula $[\varphi]\alpha$ means: *after a public utterance of* φ, α *would be established.* For example, assume that the agent a has the information that if there are not two apples on the table then there are three apples there, which is formalized as $I_a(\neg p \rightarrow q)$. Then it holds that after a public utterance that there are not two apples on the table, the agent will have the information that there are three apples there, which is formalized as $[\neg p]I_a q$. However, if $[\varphi]$ is applied to a question (e.g. a question of the form $\alpha \vee\!\!\!\vee \beta$) the result is typically again a question. For instance, $[\varphi](\alpha \vee\!\!\!\vee \beta)$ amounts to: *after a public utterance of* φ, *would* α *or* β *be established?* More concretely, in the example above, $[\neg p](I_a q \vee\!\!\!\vee \neg I_a q)$ would encode the following question: *after a public utterance that there are not two apples on the table, would the agent* a *have the information that there are three apples on the table?*

The modality $\{\varphi\}$ is auxiliary. It will help us to characterize syntactically the logic of $[\varphi]$. There is a subtle difference between $[\varphi]$ and $\{\varphi\}$ which will be clear after the semantics of these operators is introduced in Sect. 4.

3 Substructural Inquisitive Epistemic Logic

In this section, we will focus on the static fragment of $\mathcal{L}_{SIDEL}$ basically recapitulating the framework of [5]. The proofs of the results presented in this section are also worked out in [5]. The new contribution of this paper, which concerns the treatment of the dynamic modality $[\varphi]$ with the help of the modality $\{\varphi\}$, will be presented in the next section. The language $\mathcal{L}_{SIDEL}$ without the two dynamic modalities will be denoted as $\mathcal{L}_{SIEL}$.

Our semantics of $\mathcal{L}_{SIEL}$ is based on the idea of information states as points with respect to which formulas are evaluated. In standard semantic frameworks of epistemic logic, as well as in the standard inquisitive semantics, an information state is modeled as a set of possible worlds. Information states thus form a complete atomic Boolean algebra (the algebra of all sets of possible worlds). In our more general setting, more general algebraic structures will be employed and information states will be regarded as primitive entities characterized by their role within such structures.

In the semantics of standard inquisitive epistemic logic there is a crucial interplay between the layer of possible worlds and the layer of information states. In our generalization we need to have an analogue of these two layers. However, since we intend to base the framework on non-classical logics we will need to employ on the "lower layer" a notion that is more general than the notion of a possible world. Inspired by situation semantics [1], the generalized possible worlds will be called *situations*.

If we look just at the Boolean algebra of information states in the standard framework, possible worlds correspond to the atoms in the algebra, i.e. to the singleton states. From the lattice-theoretic point of view, a characteristic feature of singletons is that they are completely join-irreducible elements in the algebra of information state. This will be also the definitory feature of situations, the analogues of worlds in our general setting.

Moreover, in the standard setting, where information states are represented by sets of possible worlds, every information state can be viewed as union (i.e. set-theoretic join) of a set of singletons (i.e. completely join-irreducible states). We will need to preserve also this feature. So, in our framework, we will require that every information state can be expressed as the join of a set of situations (completely join-irreducible elements).

We will also need a formal notion of an issue. An issue will be represented by a set of information states that can be intuitively viewed as those states that resolve the issue. Like in the standard inquisitive semantics, we will require that such a set must be downward closed and nonempty. The former condition is motivated by interpreting $s \sqsubseteq t$ (where $\sqsubseteq$ is the lattice ordering) as saying that s is informationally stronger than t.[3] The latter condition is motivated by interpreting the bottom element of the lattice as the absolutely inconsistent state in which everything holds. A more detailed explanation of how particular

[3] In the standard setting $s \sqsubseteq t$ reduces to $s \subseteq t$. In that case, the set of worlds s is informationally stronger than t since it excludes more possibilities.

features of the framework are motivated is contained in [5]. Let us summarize the definition of situations and issues.

Definition 1. *Let* $L = \langle S, \sqsubseteq \rangle$ *be a complete lattice (of information states), where* $\bigsqcup X$ *denotes the join of* X *w.r.t.* $\sqsubseteq$*. An element* $s \in S$ *is called a situation in* L *iff it is completely join-irreducible, i.e.* $s = \bigsqcup X$ *only if* $s = t$*, for some* $t \in X$*. For any* $s \in S$*, the set of situations below* s*, i.e. the set* $\{i \in S \mid i \text{ is a situation such that } i \sqsubseteq s\}$ *will be denoted as* $Sit(s)$*. An issue in* L *is any nonempty downward closed subset of* S*.*

We will denote situations by the letters $i, j, \ldots$ and arbitrary states by $s, t, \ldots$

The models of our semantics also involve a *compatibility relation* C among states, a binary operation $\cdot$ representing *fusion* of two states, the *logical state* 1, and, for each agent, an *inquisitive state map* assigning to each situation an issue interpreted as the issue of the agent in the situation. A valuation will be a function that assigns to every atomic formula an information state.

Definition 2. *An abstract epistemic information model (AEI-model, for short) is a structure* $\mathcal{M} = \langle S, \sqsubseteq, C, \cdot, 1, \{\Sigma_a\}_{a \in \mathcal{A}}, V \rangle$ *such that (a)* $\langle S, \sqsubseteq \rangle$ *is a complete lattice; (b) every state from* S *is identical to the join of a set of situations, that is, for any* $s \in S$*,* $s = \bigsqcup Sit(s)$*; (c) 1 is a left-identity with respect to fusion, i.e.* $1 \cdot s = s$*; (d)* $\sqcap$ *and* $\cdot$ *distribute over arbitrary joins from both directions; (e)* C *is symmetric; (f)* $sC(\bigsqcup X)$ *iff there is* $t \in X$ *such that* sCt*; (g) for each agent* $a \in \mathcal{A}$*,* Σ_a *is a function assigning issues to situations and satisfying: if* i, j *are situations such that* $i \sqsubseteq j$ *then* $\Sigma_a(i) \subseteq \Sigma_a(j)$*; (h)* $V(p) \in S$*.*

In accordance with the standard framework of inquisitive epistemic logic we will denote the information state of the agent a in the situation i (in a given AEI-model $\mathcal{M}$) as $\sigma_a(i)$ and we define:

$$\sigma_a(i) = \bigsqcup \Sigma_a(i).$$

Note that each AEI-model is based on a complete lattice and so it is bounded and has the least element (the meet of all states). We will denote this special state as 0. This state will represent an absolutely inconsistent state that supports every piece of information (see Theorem 1(a)).

It might be useful to see in which sense AEI-models generalize structures that naturally arise from the standard Kripke models for epistemic logic. An epistemic Kripke model is a structure $\langle W, \{R_a\}_{a \in \mathcal{A}}, V \rangle$, where W is a nonempty set (of possible worlds); for each agent $a \in \mathcal{A}$, R_a is a binary (accessibility) relation on W such that $R_a(w)$ represents the information state of the agent a in the world w, i.e. the set of those worlds that are compatible with a's information in w; and V is a valuation function such that $V(p) \subseteq W$. We will not assume any special properties of the accessibility relations such as "factivity" ($w \in R_a(w)$).

Every Kripke model $\mathcal{K} = \langle W, \{R_a\}_{a \in \mathcal{A}}, V \rangle$ determines a particular AEI-model $\mathcal{M}_{\mathcal{K}} = \langle S, \sqsubseteq, C, \cdot, 1, \{\Sigma_a\}_{a \in \mathcal{A}}, V \rangle$, where $S = \mathcal{P}(W)$ (i.e. the power set of W); $\sqsubseteq$ is identical with $\subseteq$ (so that situations are singletons); sCt iff $s \cap t \neq \emptyset$;

$s \cdot t = s \cap t$; $1 = W$; and $s \in \Sigma_a(\{w\})$ iff $s \subseteq R_a(w)$. V is a valuation in $\mathcal{K}$ as well as in $\mathcal{M}_{\mathcal{K}}$. It can be easily verified that every structure $\mathcal{M}_{\mathcal{K}}$ that arises in this way from a Kripke model $\mathcal{K}$ satisfies all the conditions required in Definition 2 and thus is an example of an AEI-model.

Formulas of the language $\mathcal{L}_{SIDEL}$ are evaluated with respect to states of AEI-models. The support conditions fixing the semantic behaviour of the logical symbols from $\mathcal{L}_{SIEL}$ are defined as follows (the support conditions for the dynamic modalities from $\mathcal{L}_{SIDEL}$ will be defined in the next section):

- $\mathcal{M}, s \Vdash p$ iff $s \sqsubseteq V(p)$,
- $\mathcal{M}, s \Vdash \bot$ iff $s = 0$,
- $\mathcal{M}, s \Vdash \mathrm{t}$ iff $s \sqsubseteq 1$,
- $\mathcal{M}, s \Vdash \neg\varphi$ iff for any $t \in S$, if tCs then $\mathcal{M}, t \nVdash \varphi$,
- $\mathcal{M}, s \Vdash \varphi \rightarrow \psi$ iff for any $t \in S$, if $\mathcal{M}, t \Vdash \varphi$, then $\mathcal{M}, s \cdot t \Vdash \psi$,
- $\mathcal{M}, s \Vdash \varphi \wedge \psi$ iff $\mathcal{M}, s \Vdash \varphi$ and $\mathcal{M}, s \Vdash \psi$,
- $\mathcal{M}, s \Vdash \varphi \otimes \psi$ iff for some $t, u \in S$, $s \sqsubseteq t \cdot u$, $\mathcal{M}, t \Vdash \varphi$ and $\mathcal{M}, u \Vdash \psi$,
- $\mathcal{M}, s \Vdash \varphi \vee \psi$ iff for some $t, u \in S$, $s \sqsubseteq t \sqcup u$, $\mathcal{M}, t \Vdash \varphi$ and $\mathcal{M}, u \Vdash \psi$,
- $\mathcal{M}, s \Vdash \varphi \vee\!\!\!\vee \psi$ iff $\mathcal{M}, s \Vdash \varphi$ or $\mathcal{M}, s \Vdash \psi$,
- $\mathcal{M}, s \Vdash I_a\varphi$ iff for any $i \in Sit(s)$, $\mathcal{M}, \sigma_a(i) \Vdash \varphi$,
- $\mathcal{M}, s \Vdash E_a\varphi$ iff for any $i \in Sit(s)$ and for any $t \in \Sigma_a(i)$, $\mathcal{M}, t \Vdash \varphi$.

We say that φ is valid in $\mathcal{M}$ if φ is supported by the state 1 in $\mathcal{M}$. The set of states that support φ in $\mathcal{M}$ will be denoted as $||\varphi||_{\mathcal{M}}$ (where the subscript $\mathcal{M}$ will be usually omitted) and it will be called *the proposition expressed by φ in $\mathcal{M}$*. The logic of all AEI-models for the language $\mathcal{L}_{SIEL}$ will be called SIEL (Substructural Inquisitive Epistemic Logic). We say that φ is SIEL-valid if it is valid in every AEI-model. We say that two formulas are SIEL-equivalent if in all AEI-models they are supported by the same states.

In the particular cases of AEI-models generated by Kripke models the above support conditions are intimately related to standard truth conditions. Let us consider only the logical symbols $\neg, \rightarrow, \wedge, \vee, I_a$ with their standard truth conditions:

- $\mathcal{K}, w \vDash p$ iff $w \in V(p)$,
- $\mathcal{K}, w \vDash \neg\alpha$ iff $\mathcal{K}, w \nvDash \alpha$,
- $\mathcal{K}, w \vDash \alpha \wedge \beta$ iff $\mathcal{K}, w \vDash \alpha$ and $\mathcal{K}, w \vDash \beta$,
- $\mathcal{K}, w \vDash \alpha \vee \beta$ iff $\mathcal{K}, w \vDash \alpha$ or $\mathcal{K}, w \vDash \beta$,
- $\mathcal{K}, w \vDash \alpha \rightarrow \beta$ iff $\mathcal{K}, w \nvDash \alpha$ or $\mathcal{K}, w \vDash \beta$,
- $\mathcal{K}, w \vDash I_a\alpha$ iff for all $v \in R_a(w)$, $\mathcal{K}, v \vDash \alpha$.

Then the support conditions above correspond to truth conditions in the following sense. For any Kripke model $\mathcal{K}$, any $s \subseteq W$, and any formula α in the simplified language for which the truth conditions were just introduced, it holds that

$$\mathcal{M}_{\mathcal{K}}, s \Vdash \varphi \text{ iff } \mathcal{K}, w \vDash \varphi \text{ , for all } w \in s.$$

Let us continue with the description of the most important general features of our semantics. Note that an implication $\varphi \rightarrow \psi$ is valid in a model $\mathcal{M}$ iff for any state s in $\mathcal{M}$, if $\mathcal{M}, s \Vdash \varphi$ then $\mathcal{M}, s \Vdash \psi$. It is also useful to observe that at situations, the support conditions for the modalities I_a and E_a may be significantly simplified. Assume that i is a situation of a given AEI-model $\mathcal{M}$. Then it holds:

(a) $\mathcal{M}, i \Vdash I_a\varphi$ iff $\mathcal{M}, \sigma_a(i) \Vdash \varphi$,
(b) $\mathcal{M}, i \Vdash E_a\varphi$ iff for any $t \in \Sigma_a(i)$, $\mathcal{M}, t \Vdash \varphi$.

Let us define the set of *declarative* $\mathcal{L}_{SIEL}$-formulas as the smallest set containing all atomic formulas, $\perp$, t, containing all $\mathcal{L}_{SIEL}$-formulas of the form $I_a\varphi$, $E_a\varphi$ and closed under the connectives $\neg, \rightarrow, \wedge, \otimes, \vee$. Declarative formulas represent statements (note that even if φ represents a question, $I_a\varphi$ and $E_a\varphi$ are always statements). The following theorem expresses the most crucial features of the support relation.

Theorem 1. *In every AEI-model: (a) every $\mathcal{L}_{SIEL}$-formula is supported by the state* 0*; (b) the support of $\mathcal{L}_{SIEL}$-formulas is downward persistent, i.e., if a $\mathcal{L}_{SIEL}$-formula is supported by a state s and $t \sqsubseteq s$ then it is also supported by the state t; (c) the support of declarative $\mathcal{L}_{SIEL}$ formulas is closed under arbitrary joins, i.e., if a declarative $\mathcal{L}_{SIEL}$-formula is supported by each state $s \in X$, then it is also supported by the state $\bigsqcup X$.*

It follows from (a) and (b) of Theorem 1 that every $\mathcal{L}_{SIEL}$-formula expresses an issue. For any $\mathcal{L}_{SIEL}$-formula φ we define the informational content of φ, denoted as $info(\varphi)$, as follows:

$$info(\varphi) = \bigsqcup ||\varphi||.$$

If φ represents a question, $info(\varphi)$ captures the information presupposed by the question. (For example, the question *whether p or q* presupposes the information *that p or q*.) Now, the meaning of Theorem 1(c) can be interpreted as stating that declarative formulas express a special kind of issues, namely those issues that contain their own informational content ($info(\varphi) \in ||\varphi||$). Let us call the issues that are already resolved by their own presuppositions, i.e. that contain their own join, *declarative propositions.* Declarative propositions are semantic counterparts of statements.

Now, we can present a syntactic characterization of SIEL-validity. We say that an $\mathcal{L}_{SIEL}$-formula is SIEL-provable if it is provable in the axiomatic system formulated in Table 1.[4] The system is a basic substructural logic that can be characterized as non-associative, distributive Full Lambek Logic with a paraconsistent negation and with only one implication (of course the second implication $\leftarrow$ that is normally present in Full Lambek Logic could be easily added), and extended with inquisitive disjunction and the epistemic modalities I_a, E_a.[5]

Theorem 2. *For every $\mathcal{L}_{SIEL}$-formula φ, φ is* SIEL*-valid if and only if φ is* SIEL*-provable.*

[4] In [5], the logic generated by this system is called InqSE.
[5] It is discussed in detail in [5] why the distributivity axiom D1 is needed.

Table 1. Axiomatization of the substructural inquisitive epistemic logic SIEL

Non-modal axioms:

A1 $\varphi \to \varphi$	A2 $\bot \to \varphi$
A3 $(\varphi \wedge \psi) \to \varphi$	A4 $(\varphi \wedge \psi) \to \psi$
A5 $\varphi \to (\varphi \vee \psi)$	A6 $\psi \to (\varphi \vee \psi)$
A7 $(\varphi \vee \psi) \to (\psi \vee \varphi)$	A8 $(\alpha \vee \alpha) \to \alpha$ (for declarative α)
A9 $\varphi \to (\varphi \mathbin{\mathbb{V}} \psi)$	A10 $\psi \to (\varphi \mathbin{\mathbb{V}} \psi)$

Modal axioms:

ID $I_a(\varphi \mathbin{\mathbb{V}} \psi) \leftrightarrow (I_a\varphi \vee I_a\psi)$
IE $I_a\alpha \leftrightarrow E_a\alpha$ (for declarative α)

Distributive axioms:

D1 $(\varphi \wedge (\psi \vee \chi)) \to ((\varphi \wedge \psi) \vee (\varphi \wedge \chi))$
D2 $(\varphi \otimes (\psi \vee \chi)) \to ((\varphi \otimes \psi) \vee (\varphi \otimes \chi))$
D3 $(\varphi \wedge (\psi \mathbin{\mathbb{V}} \chi)) \to ((\varphi \wedge \psi) \mathbin{\mathbb{V}} (\varphi \wedge \chi))$
D4 $(\varphi \otimes (\psi \mathbin{\mathbb{V}} \chi)) \to ((\varphi \otimes \psi) \mathbin{\mathbb{V}} (\varphi \otimes \chi))$
D5 $(\varphi \vee (\psi \mathbin{\mathbb{V}} \chi)) \to ((\varphi \vee \psi) \mathbin{\mathbb{V}} (\varphi \vee \chi))$
D6 $(\alpha \to (\psi \mathbin{\mathbb{V}} \chi)) \to ((\alpha \to \psi) \mathbin{\mathbb{V}} (\alpha \to \chi))$ (for declarative α)

Non-modal rules:

R1 $\varphi, \varphi \to \psi / \psi$	R2 $\varphi \to \psi / (\psi \to \chi) \to (\varphi \to \chi)$
R3 $\chi \to \varphi, \chi \to \psi / \chi \to (\varphi \wedge \psi)$	R4 $\varphi \to \chi, \psi \to \vartheta / (\varphi \vee \psi) \to (\chi \vee \vartheta)$
R5 $\varphi \to (\psi \to \chi) / (\varphi \otimes \psi) \to \chi$	R6 $(\varphi \otimes \psi) \to \chi / \varphi \to (\psi \to \chi)$
R7 $\mathsf{t} \to \varphi / \varphi$	R8 $\varphi / \mathsf{t} \to \varphi$
R9 $\varphi \to \neg\psi / \psi \to \neg\varphi$	R10 $\varphi \to \chi, \psi \to \chi / (\varphi \mathbin{\mathbb{V}} \psi) \to \chi$

Modal rules:

MR1 $\varphi \to \psi / E_a\varphi \to E_a\psi$	MR2 $E_a\varphi \wedge E_a\psi / E_a(\varphi \wedge \psi)$
MR3 $\varphi \to \psi / I_a\varphi \to I_a\psi$	MR4 $I_a\varphi \wedge I_a\psi / I_a(\varphi \wedge \psi)$

The following two results express crucial features of SIEL-validity. The first one is a disjunctive normal form theorem.

Theorem 3. *For every $\mathcal{L}_{SIEL}$-formula φ there is a finite set of declarative $\mathcal{L}_{SIEL}$-formulas $\mathcal{R}(\varphi) = \{\alpha_1, \ldots, \alpha_n\}$ s.t. φ is* SIEL*-equivalent to $\alpha_1 \mathbin{\mathbb{V}} \ldots \mathbin{\mathbb{V}} \alpha_n$.*

Note that it follows from Theorem 3 that if an $\mathcal{L}_{SIEL}$-formula expresses a declarative proposition it must be SIEL-equivalent to a declarative $\mathcal{L}_{SIEL}$-formula. Another crucial feature of SIEL-validity is the disjunction property of the inquisitive disjunction.

Theorem 4. *The logic* SIEL *has the inquisitive disjunction property, that is,* $\varphi \mathbin{\vee\!\!\!\vee} \psi$ *is* SIEL*-valid only if* φ *or* ψ *is* SIEL*-valid.*

Theorem 3 shows that every question in the language corresponds to a disjunctive question. The set $\mathcal{R}(\varphi)$ can be seen as an exhaustive set of direct answers. Theorems 3 and 4 together imply that a question is SIEL-valid iff a direct answer to the question is SIEL-valid, i.e., iff the question can be resolved by logical means.

4 The Dynamics

The main goal of this paper is to extend the framework presented in the previous section with the semantics of the dynamic modality $[\varphi]$. Our treatment of the dynamic modality is motivated by the framework developed in [4]. As in [4], we will attempt to characterize the logical behaviour of this modality by reduction axioms. However, in the substructural setting, we will face some obstacles that are not present in the classical setting of [4]. To overcome these obstacles we will employ the auxiliary modality $\{\varphi\}$.

Take an arbitrary AEI-model $\mathcal{M} = \langle S, \sqsubseteq, C, \cdot, 1, \{\Sigma_a\}_{a\in\mathcal{A}}, V\rangle$. Given two nonempty sets of states X and Y in $\mathcal{M}$, one can define their fusion in the following way:

$$X \circ Y = \{u \in S \mid \text{for some } s \in X, t \in Y, u \sqsubseteq s \cdot t\}.$$

The result of this operation is always an issue. Assume that the support conditions for a $\mathcal{L}_{SIDEL}$-formula φ are already defined so that the set $||\varphi||$ of states supporting the formula in $\mathcal{M}$ is determined. We now assume that φ might be publicly uttered. Such a public utterance updates the issues of the agents. The updated model is defined as follows:

$$\mathcal{M}^{\varphi} = \langle S, \sqsubseteq, C, \cdot, 1, \{\Sigma_a^{\varphi}\}_{a\in\mathcal{A}}, V\rangle,$$

where for any situation i we have:

$$\Sigma_a^{\varphi}(i) = \Sigma_a(i) \circ ||\varphi||.$$

Later on, we will use the following proposition.

Proposition 1. *Let* $\mathcal{M}$ *be an AEI-model,* i *one of its situations, and* φ *any* $\mathcal{L}_{SIDEL}$*-formula. Then* $\bigsqcup \Sigma_a^{\varphi}(i) = \sigma_a(i) \cdot info(\varphi)$.

Proof. The following equations hold:

$$\begin{aligned}
&\sigma_a(i) \cdot info(\varphi) = \bigsqcup \Sigma_a(i) \cdot \bigsqcup ||\varphi|| = \\
&= \bigsqcup \{\bigsqcup \Sigma_a(i) \cdot t \mid t \in ||\varphi||\} = \\
&= \bigsqcup \{\bigsqcup \{s \cdot t \mid s \in \Sigma_a(i)\} \mid t \in ||\varphi||\} = \\
&= \bigsqcup \{s \cdot t \mid s \in \Sigma_a(i), t \in ||\varphi||\} = \\
&= \bigsqcup \{u \in S \mid \text{for some } s \in \Sigma_a(i), t \in ||\varphi||, u \sqsubseteq s \cdot t\} = \\
&= \bigsqcup (\Sigma_a(i) \circ ||\varphi||) = \bigsqcup \Sigma_a^{\varphi}(i).
\end{aligned}$$

A public utterance of φ modifies the point of evaluation as well as the issues of the agents so that the semantic clause for $[\varphi]$ can be specified as follows:

$$\mathcal{M}, s \vDash [\varphi]\psi \text{ iff } \mathcal{M}^{\varphi}, s \cdot info(\varphi) \vDash \psi.$$

This clause generalizes the semantics of the standard public announcement operator. To see this, take again any epistemic Kripke model $\mathcal{K} = \langle W, \{R_a\}_{a\in\mathcal{A}}, V\rangle$. Consider again the simplified language based on $\neg, \rightarrow, \wedge, \vee, I_a$, now also extended with the public announcement operator $[\alpha]$. An update of $\mathcal{K}$ by a formula α of this language can be defined as $\mathcal{K}^{\alpha} = \langle W, \{R_a^{\alpha}\}_{a\in\mathcal{A}}, V\rangle$, where

$$R_a^{\alpha}(w) = R_a(w) \cap info(\alpha).$$

In this equation, $info(\alpha)$ is just the set of all worlds in which α is true in $\mathcal{K}$. Given the correspondence between truth and support this is completely in accordance with the notation introduce above, for the set of all worlds in which α is true in $\mathcal{K}$ is identical to union of all states in $\mathcal{M}_{\mathcal{K}}$ that support α, i.e. to $\bigsqcup ||\alpha||$, which is exactly how we defined $info(\alpha)$.

The update of a Kripke model is usually defined so that also the set of worlds W and the valuation $V$are updated. But this is not an essential aspect of the semantics. One can easily obtain an equivalent semantics without updating these two components. Now consider the standard truth condition for public announcement:

$$\mathcal{K}, w \vDash [\alpha]\beta \text{ iff } \mathcal{K}, w \nvDash \alpha \text{ or } \mathcal{K}^{\alpha}, w \vDash \beta,$$

Now the corresponding support condition in $\mathcal{M}_{\mathcal{K}}$ is

$$\mathcal{M}_{\mathcal{K}}, s \Vdash [\alpha]\beta \text{ iff } \mathcal{M}_{\mathcal{K}}^{\alpha}, s \cap info(\alpha) \Vdash \beta.$$

Under this condition support by a state is still equivalent to truth in all the worlds of the state. Since fusion $\cdot$ and intersection coincide in $\mathcal{M}_{\mathcal{K}}$, this condition corresponds to our general condition for support of public utterance introduced above. This reasoning shows that our general semantics of public utterance can be viewed as a generalization of the standard semantics of public announcement.

The formula $\{\varphi\}\psi$ behaves like $[\varphi]\psi$ with the difference that the point of evaluation is not updated, only the issues of the agents are. The support condition for this modality is:

$$\mathcal{M}, s \vDash \{\varphi\}\psi \text{ iff } \mathcal{M}^{\varphi}, s \vDash \psi.$$

The logic of all AEI-models for the language $\mathcal{L}_{SIDEL}$ will be called SIDEL (Substructural Inquisitive Dynamic Epistemic Logic). We say that φ is SIDEL-valid if it is valid in every AEI-model. Our main goal is to provide an axiomatic characterization of SIDEL-validity. But first, it will be useful to formulate the following observation concerning AEI-models.

Proposition 2. *For states s, t, u, v of any AEI-model it holds:*

(a) $0 \cdot s = s \cdot 0 = 0$,
(b) if $s \sqsubseteq t$ *and* $u \sqsubseteq v$ *then* $s \cdot u \sqsubseteq t \cdot v$.

Proof. (a) It holds that $0 = \bigsqcup \emptyset$. So, $0 \cdot s = (\bigsqcup \emptyset) \cdot s = \bigsqcup \{x \cdot s \mid x \in \emptyset\} = \bigsqcup \emptyset = 0$. The case of $s \cdot 0$ is analogous.

(b) Assume $s \sqsubseteq t$ and $u \sqsubseteq v$. Then $(s \cdot u) \sqcup (t \cdot v) \sqsubseteq (s \cdot u) \sqcup (t \cdot u) \sqcup (s \cdot v) \sqcup (t \cdot v) = (s \sqcup t) \cdot (u \sqcup v) = t \cdot v$.

Let us define the set of *declarative* $\mathcal{L}_{SIDEL}$-formulas as the smallest set containing all atomic formulas, the constants $\perp$, t, containing all $\mathcal{L}_{SIDEL}$-formulas of the forms $I_a\varphi$, $E_a\varphi$, closed under the connectives $\neg, \rightarrow, \wedge, \otimes, \vee$, and closed under the application of any $[\varphi]$ and any $\{\varphi\}$, that is, if φ is any $\mathcal{L}_{SIDEL}$-formula and α a declarative $\mathcal{L}_{SIDEL}$-formula then $[\varphi]\alpha$ and $\{\varphi\}\alpha$ are declarative $\mathcal{L}_{SIDEL}$-formulas. From now on, we will use the letters $\varphi, \psi, \chi, \vartheta$ as variables for arbitrary $\mathcal{L}_{SIDEL}$-formulas, and α, β as variables for declarative $\mathcal{L}_{SIDEL}$-formulas. Now we can extend Theorem 1 to the language $\mathcal{L}_{SIDEL}$.

Theorem 5. *In every AEI-model: (a) every $\mathcal{L}_{SIDEL}$-formula is supported by the state 0; (b) the support of $\mathcal{L}_{SIDEL}$-formulas is downward persistent, i.e., if a $\mathcal{L}_{SIDEL}$-formula is supported by a state s and $t \sqsubseteq s$ then it is also supported by the state t; (c) the support of declarative $\mathcal{L}_{SIDEL}$-formulas is closed under arbitrary joins, i.e., if a declarative $\mathcal{L}_{SIDEL}$-formula is supported by each state $s \in X$, then it is supported also by the state $\bigsqcup X$.*

Proof. The theorem can be proved by induction. The inductive steps for the logical symbols from $\mathcal{L}_{SIEL}$ are as in the proof of Theorem 1. We need to go through the inductive steps concerning the dynamic modalities. The inductive steps for $\{\varphi\}$ are straightforward. We will consider only the steps for $[\varphi]$. Take an AEI-model $\mathcal{M}$ and assume that the claims (a)-(c) generally hold for some arbitrary $\mathcal{L}_{SIDEL}$-formulas φ, ψ, and some declarative $\mathcal{L}_{SIDEL}$-formula α.

(a) We assume that $\mathcal{M}^\varphi, 0 \Vdash \psi$. So, due to Proposition 2(a), we have also $\mathcal{M}^\varphi, 0 \cdot info(\varphi) \Vdash \psi$, i.e. $\mathcal{M}, 0 \Vdash [\varphi]\psi$.

(b) Assume that $\mathcal{M}, s \Vdash [\varphi]\psi$ and $t \sqsubseteq s$. The former assumption amounts to $\mathcal{M}^\varphi, s \cdot info(\varphi) \Vdash \psi$. The inductive assumption and monotonicity of fusion (Proposition 2(b)) imply $\mathcal{M}^\varphi, t \cdot info(\varphi) \vDash \psi$, and hence $\mathcal{M}, t \Vdash [\varphi]\psi$.

(c) Assume $\mathcal{M}, s \Vdash [\varphi]\alpha$, for every $s \in X$. That is, $\mathcal{M}^\varphi, s \cdot info(\varphi) \vDash \alpha$, for every $s \in X$, and thus it follows from the inductive assumption for α that $\mathcal{M}^\varphi, \bigsqcup_{s \in X}(s \cdot info(\varphi)) \vDash \alpha$. Due to distributivity of fusion over arbitrary joins, $\mathcal{M}^\varphi, (\bigsqcup X) \cdot info(\varphi) \vDash \alpha$, and hence $\mathcal{M}, \bigsqcup X \vDash [\varphi]\alpha$.

We will often use the following proposition that shows that the support condition for implication can be significantly simplified if the consequent of the implication is declarative.

Proposition 3. *For any state s of any AEI-model $\mathcal{M}$, any $\mathcal{L}_{SIDEL}$-formula φ, and any declarative $\mathcal{L}_{SIDEL}$-formula α:*

$$\mathcal{M}, s \Vdash \varphi \rightarrow \alpha \textit{ iff } \mathcal{M}, s \cdot info(\varphi) \Vdash \alpha.$$

Proof. First, assume $\mathcal{M}, s \Vdash \varphi \rightarrow \alpha$. That means that $\mathcal{M}, s \cdot t \Vdash \alpha$, for every $t \in ||\varphi||$. Since α is declarative, it follows from Theorem 5(c) that $\mathcal{M}, s \cdot info(\varphi) \Vdash \alpha$.

Second, assume $\mathcal{M}, s \cdot info(\varphi) \Vdash \alpha$. Take any t such that $\mathcal{M}, t \Vdash \varphi$. Then (by Proposition 2(b)) $s \cdot t \sqsubseteq s \cdot info(\varphi)$, and so (by Theorem 5(b)) $\mathcal{M}, s \cdot t \Vdash \alpha$. It follows that $\mathcal{M}, s \Vdash \varphi \rightarrow \alpha$.

In analogy to the standard public announcement logic PAL we would like to characterize the modality $[\varphi]$ by reduction axioms. However, here we have to face the problem that the standard reduction axioms rely on some features of classical logic that are not preserved in our substructural setting. In particular the standard reduction axioms for implication $([\varphi](\psi \rightarrow \chi) \leftrightarrow ([\varphi]\psi \rightarrow [\varphi]\chi))$ and negation $([\varphi]\neg\psi \leftrightarrow (\varphi \rightarrow \neg[\varphi]\psi))$, are not SIDEL-valid.

For example, as in PAL, $[p](q \rightarrow r)$ is SIDEL-equivalent to $p \rightarrow (q \rightarrow r)$, and $[p]q \rightarrow [p]r$ to $(p \rightarrow q) \rightarrow (p \rightarrow r)$. However, in contrast to classical logic on which PAL is based, $p \rightarrow (q \rightarrow r)$ is not SIDEL-equivalent to $(p \rightarrow q) \rightarrow (p \rightarrow r)$, so the equivalence of $[p](q \rightarrow r)$ and $[p]q \rightarrow [p]r$ fails.

To show how the equivalence between $p \rightarrow (q \rightarrow r)$ and $(p \rightarrow q) \rightarrow (p \rightarrow r)$ fails in our semantics consider the following artificial example of an AEI-model $\mathcal{M} = \langle S, \sqsubseteq, C, \cdot, 1, \{\Sigma_a\}_{a \in \mathcal{A}}, V \rangle$, where $S = \mathcal{P}(\omega)$, i.e. states are sets of natural numbers; $\sqsubseteq$ is the subset relation; C is empty; fusion is defined as follows: $s \cdot t = \{m+n \mid m \in s, n \in t\}$; $1 = \{0\}$; for any $a \in \mathcal{A}$ and any situation i , $\Sigma_a(i) = \{\emptyset\}$; and V is a valuation such that $V(p) = V(q) = \{1\}$, and $V(r) = \{2\}$. Then it can be shown that $\mathcal{M}$ is indeed an AEI-model. It holds that the state $\{0\}$ supports $p \rightarrow (q \rightarrow r)$. To show this we can use Proposition 3: $\mathcal{M}, \{0\} \Vdash p \rightarrow (q \rightarrow r)$ iff $\mathcal{M}, (\{0\} \cdot info(p)) \cdot info(q) \Vdash r$, iff $\mathcal{M}, (\{0\} \cdot \{1\}) \cdot \{1\} \Vdash r$ iff $\mathcal{M}, \{2\} \Vdash r$ which holds. Moreover, $\{0\}$ supports $p \rightarrow q$: $\mathcal{M}, \{0\} \Vdash p \rightarrow q$ iff $\mathcal{M}, \{1\} \Vdash q$, which also holds. But $\{0\}$ does not support $p \rightarrow r$: $\mathcal{M}, \{0\} \Vdash p \rightarrow r$ iff $\mathcal{M}, \{1\} \Vdash r$, which does not hold.

To show that $[\varphi]\neg\psi \leftrightarrow (\varphi \rightarrow \neg[\varphi]\psi)$ fails, we can consider the following simple instance: $[p]\neg q \leftrightarrow (p \rightarrow \neg[p]q)$. As in PAL, $[p]\neg q$ is SIDEL-equivalent to $p \rightarrow \neg q$ and $p \rightarrow \neg[p]q$ to $p \rightarrow \neg(p \rightarrow q)$. Of course, $p \rightarrow \neg q$ and $p \rightarrow \neg(p \rightarrow q)$ are equivalent in classical logic but they are not SIDEL-equivalent. To show a concrete counterexample, consider the AEI-model $\mathcal{M}$ introduced in the previous paragraph and modify the definition of the compatibility relation C: we now define sCt iff $0 \in s$ and $1 \in t$, or $1 \in s$ and $0 \in t$. Let us denote this modified structure as $\mathcal{N}$. It can be observed that $\mathcal{N}$ is indeed an AEI-model. Moreover, it can be shown that $\mathcal{N}, \{0\} \Vdash p \rightarrow \neg q$ but $\mathcal{N}, \{0\} \nVdash p \rightarrow \neg(p \rightarrow q)$.

To overcome the failure of standard reduction axioms, we will exploit the auxiliary modality $\{\varphi\}$. We will use axioms allowing to reduce $[\varphi]$ to $\{\varphi\}$ and further axioms allowing to eliminate $\{\varphi\}$. Moreover, we will need rules that will guarantee that provably equivalent formulas are universally replaceable. The whole system of the extra axioms and rules is formulated in Table 2.

We say that an $\mathcal{L}_{SIDEL}$-formula is SIDEL-provable if it is provable in the axiomatic system consisting of axioms and rules from Tables 1 and 2. We say that φ and ψ are SIDEL-provably equivalent if $\varphi \leftrightarrow \psi$ is SIDEL-provable. We will need to show that SIDEL-provably equivalent formulas are replaceable. Note

Table 2. Reduction axioms and rules of SIDEL

Reduction axioms for $[\varphi]$:

RA1 $[\varphi](\psi \vee\!\!\!\vee \chi) \leftrightarrow ([\varphi]\psi \vee\!\!\!\vee [\varphi]\chi)$
RA2 $[\varphi]\alpha \leftrightarrow (\varphi \rightarrow \{\varphi\}\alpha)$ (for declarative α)

Reduction axioms for $\{\varphi\}$:

RA3 $\{\varphi\}p \leftrightarrow p$
RA4 $\{\varphi\}\bot \leftrightarrow \bot$
RA5 $\{\varphi\}t \leftrightarrow t$
RA6 $\{\varphi\}\neg\psi \leftrightarrow \neg\{\varphi\}\psi$
RA7 $\{\varphi\}(\psi \rightarrow \chi) \leftrightarrow (\{\varphi\}\psi \rightarrow \{\varphi\}\chi)$
RA8 $\{\varphi\}(\psi \wedge \chi) \leftrightarrow (\{\varphi\}\psi \wedge \{\varphi\}\chi)$
RA9 $\{\varphi\}(\psi \otimes \chi) \leftrightarrow (\{\varphi\}\psi \otimes \{\varphi\}\chi)$
RA10 $\{\varphi\}(\psi \vee \chi) \leftrightarrow (\{\varphi\}\psi \vee \{\varphi\}\chi)$
RA11 $\{\varphi\}(\psi \vee\!\!\!\vee \chi) \leftrightarrow (\{\varphi\}\psi \vee\!\!\!\vee \{\varphi\}\chi)$
RA12 $\{\varphi\}E_a\psi \leftrightarrow E_a(\varphi \rightarrow \{\varphi\}\psi)$
RA13 $\{\varphi\}I_a\alpha \leftrightarrow I_a(\varphi \rightarrow \{\varphi\}\alpha)$ (for declarative α)

Monotonicity rules for dynamic modalities:

DR1 $\varphi \rightarrow \psi/[\chi]\varphi \rightarrow [\chi]\psi$ DR2 $\varphi \leftrightarrow \psi/[\varphi]\chi \leftrightarrow [\psi]\chi$
DR3 $\varphi \rightarrow \psi/\{\chi\}\varphi \rightarrow \{\chi\}\psi$ DR4 $\varphi \leftrightarrow \psi/\{\varphi\}\chi \leftrightarrow \{\psi\}\chi$

that an alternative formulation of the axiomatic system would be obtained by replacing the rules DR1-DR4 with a rule allowing directly the replacement of equivalents. Nevertheless, with the rules DR1-DR4 we can show that this rule is admissible in the system.

Theorem 6. *Assume that φ, ψ are SIDEL-provably equivalent $\mathcal{L}_{SIDEL}$-formulas. Assume that ϑ is a $\mathcal{L}_{SIDEL}$-formula containing φ as a subformula and $\vartheta[\psi/\varphi]$ is the result of replacing an occurrence of φ in ϑ with ψ. Then ϑ and $\vartheta[\psi/\varphi]$ are SIDEL-provably equivalent.*

Proof. It is necessary to show that every operator in the language preserves provable equivalences. For example, in the case of $\rightarrow$ that means that if $\varphi \leftrightarrow \psi$ is SIDEL-provable then, for any $\mathcal{L}_{SIDEL}$-formula χ, the formulas $(\varphi \rightarrow \chi) \leftrightarrow (\psi \rightarrow \chi)$ and $(\chi \rightarrow \varphi) \leftrightarrow (\chi \rightarrow \psi)$ are SIDEL-provable. All operators of the language $\mathcal{L}_{SIEL}$ have this property due to the axioms and rules from Table 1. For the dynamic operators this property says that if $\varphi \leftrightarrow \psi$ is SIDEL-provable then, for any $\mathcal{L}_{SIDEL}$-formula χ, $[\chi]\varphi \leftrightarrow [\chi]\psi$, $[\psi]\chi \leftrightarrow [\varphi]\chi$, $\{\chi\}\varphi \leftrightarrow \{\chi\}\psi$, and $\{\psi\}\chi \leftrightarrow \{\varphi\}\chi$ are SIDEL-provable. This is guaranteed by the rules DR1-DR4.

We will also need the disjunctive normal form theorem for SIDEL-provability.

Theorem 7. *For each $\mathcal{L}_{SIDEL}$-formula φ there is a finite set of declarative $\mathcal{L}_{SIDEL}$-formulas $\mathcal{R}(\varphi) = \{\alpha_1, \ldots, \alpha_n\}$ such that φ is* SIDEL*-provably equivalent to $\alpha_1 \vee\!\!\!\vee \ldots \vee\!\!\!\vee \alpha_n$.*

Proof. This can be proved, like Theorem 3, by induction on the complexity of φ. We have to add to the proof of Theorem 3 just the inductive steps for $[\varphi]$ and $\{\varphi\}$. But these steps can be obtained using the axioms RA1 and RA11.

Now we can show that the axioms from Table 2 allow us to eliminate the dynamic modalities.

Theorem 8. *For any $\mathcal{L}_{SIDEL}$-formula φ there is an $\mathcal{L}_{SIEL}$-formula φ^* such that φ and φ^* are* SIDEL*-provably equivalent.*

Proof. We will proceed in two steps. In the first step, we will find for any $\mathcal{L}_{SIDEL}$-formula φ an SIDEL-provably equivalent $\mathcal{L}_{SIDEL}$-formula φ° that does not contain any occurrence of the dynamic modality $[\psi]$ (for any ψ). In the second step, we will transform φ° into the SIDEL-provably equivalent $\mathcal{L}_{SIEL}$-formula φ^* by eliminating all occurrences of the modality $\{\psi\}$.

Take any subformula of φ that is of the form $[\psi]\chi$. According to Theorem 7 there are $\mathcal{L}_{SIEL}$-formulas $\alpha_1, \ldots, \alpha_n$ such that χ is SIDEL-provably equivalent to $\alpha_1 \vee\!\!\!\vee \ldots \vee\!\!\!\vee \alpha_n$. Hence, $[\psi]\chi$ must be SIDEL-provably equivalent to the following:

$[\psi](\alpha_1 \vee\!\!\!\vee \ldots \vee\!\!\!\vee \alpha_n)$ (Theorem 7),
$[\psi]\alpha_1 \vee\!\!\!\vee \ldots \vee\!\!\!\vee [\psi]\alpha_n$ (RA1),
$(\psi \rightarrow \{\psi\}\alpha_1) \vee\!\!\!\vee \ldots \vee\!\!\!\vee (\psi \rightarrow \{\psi\}\alpha_n)$ (RA2).

In this way we can, step by step, eliminate all occurrences of the modality $[\psi]$ from φ obtaining the formula φ°.

In the formula φ° we can recursively eliminate, using the axioms RA3-RA13, all occurrences of the modality $\{\psi\}$. By this elimination we obtain the $\mathcal{L}_{SIEL}$-formula φ^*. The only case that needs to be discussed is the case $\{\varphi\}I_a\psi$ with non-declarative ψ. Assume that ψ is SIDEL-provably equivalent to $\beta_1 \vee\!\!\!\vee \ldots \vee\!\!\!\vee \beta_m$, and thus $\{\varphi\}I_a\psi$ is SIDEL-provably equivalent to $\{\varphi\}I_a(\beta_1 \vee\!\!\!\vee \ldots \vee\!\!\!\vee \beta_m)$. The last formula is SIDEL-provably equivalent (due to the axiom ID from Table 1 and RA10 from Table 2) to $\{\varphi\}I_a\beta_1 \vee \ldots \vee \{\varphi\}I_a\beta_m$. Now we can apply RA13.

Let us illustrate the elimination with a simple example. Consider the formula $\varphi = [I_ap]I_b(q \vee\!\!\!\vee r)$. In this case the dynamic modality can be eliminated in the following steps:

1. $[I_ap]I_b(q \vee\!\!\!\vee r)$
2. $I_ap \rightarrow \{I_ap\}I_b(q \vee\!\!\!\vee r)$ (RA2, Table 2)
3. $I_ap \rightarrow \{I_ap\}(I_bq \vee I_br)$ (ID, Table 1)
4. $I_ap \rightarrow (\{I_ap\}I_bq \vee \{I_ap\}I_br)$ (RA10, Table 2)
5. $I_ap \rightarrow (I_b(I_ap \rightarrow \{I_ap\}q) \vee I_b(I_ap \rightarrow \{I_ap\}r))$ (RA13, Table 2)
6. $I_ap \rightarrow (I_b(I_ap \rightarrow q) \vee I_b(I_ap \rightarrow r))$ (RA3, Table 2)

The step 2 corresponds to φ° in the proof of Theorem 8 and the formula in the step 6 corresponds to φ^{*} that is already in the language $\mathcal{L}_{SIEL}$.
The following theorem shows that the system is sound with respect to our semantics.

Theorem 9. *All instances of axioms RA1-RA13 are* SIDEL*-valid. The rules DR1-DR4 preserve* SIDEL*-validity.*

Proof. We will discuss only some of the cases.

RA1: $\mathcal{M}, s \Vdash [\varphi](\psi \mathbin{\vee\!\!\!\vee} \chi)$ iff $\mathcal{M}^{\varphi}, s \cdot info(\varphi) \Vdash \psi \mathbin{\vee\!\!\!\vee} \chi$ iff $\mathcal{M}^{\varphi}, s \cdot info(\varphi) \Vdash \psi$ or $\mathcal{M}^{\varphi}, s \cdot info(\varphi) \Vdash \chi$ iff $\mathcal{M}, s \Vdash [\varphi]\psi$ or $\mathcal{M}, s \Vdash [\varphi]\chi$ iff $\mathcal{M}, s \Vdash [\varphi]\psi \mathbin{\vee\!\!\!\vee} [\varphi]\chi$.

RA2: $\mathcal{M}, s \Vdash [\varphi]\alpha$ iff $\mathcal{M}^{\varphi}, s \cdot info(\varphi) \Vdash \alpha$ iff $\mathcal{M}, s \cdot info(\varphi) \Vdash \{\varphi\}\alpha$ iff $\mathcal{M}, s \Vdash \varphi \to \{\varphi\}\alpha$.

RA3: $\mathcal{M}, s \Vdash \{\varphi\}p$ iff $\mathcal{M}^{\varphi}, s \Vdash p$ iff $\mathcal{M}, s \Vdash p$.

RA6: $\mathcal{M}, s \Vdash \{\varphi\}\neg\psi$ iff $\mathcal{M}^{\varphi}, s \Vdash \neg\psi$ iff for any t, if sCt then $\mathcal{M}^{\varphi}, t \nVdash \psi$ iff for any t, if sCt then $\mathcal{M}, t \nVdash \{\varphi\}\psi$ iff $\mathcal{M}, s \Vdash \neg\{\varphi\}\psi$.

RA7: $\mathcal{M}, s \Vdash \{\varphi\}(\psi \to \chi)$ iff $\mathcal{M}^{\varphi}, s \Vdash \psi \to \chi$ iff for any t, if $\mathcal{M}^{\varphi}, t \Vdash \psi$ then $\mathcal{M}^{\varphi}, s \cdot t \Vdash \chi$ iff for any t, if $\mathcal{M}, t \Vdash \{\varphi\}\psi$ then $\mathcal{M}, s \cdot t \Vdash \{\varphi\}\chi$ iff $\mathcal{M}, s \Vdash \{\varphi\}\psi \to \{\varphi\}\chi$.

RA12: $\mathcal{M}, s \Vdash \{\varphi\}E_a\psi$ iff $\mathcal{M}^{\varphi}, s \Vdash E_a\psi$ iff for any $i \in Sit(s)$, for any $t \in \Sigma_a(i) \circ ||\varphi||$, $\mathcal{M}^{\varphi}, t \Vdash \psi$ iff for any $i \in Sit(s)$, for any $t \in \Sigma_a(i) \circ ||\varphi||$, $\mathcal{M}, t \Vdash \{\varphi\}\psi$ iff for any $i \in Sit(s)$, for any $u \in \Sigma_a(i)$ and for any v, if $\mathcal{M}, v \Vdash \varphi$ then $\mathcal{M}, u \cdot v \Vdash \{\varphi\}\psi$ iff for any $i \in Sit(s)$, for any $u \in \Sigma_a(i)$, $\mathcal{M}, u \Vdash \varphi \to \{\varphi\}\psi$ iff $\mathcal{M}, s \Vdash E_a(\varphi \to \{\varphi\}\psi)$.

RA13: $\mathcal{M}, s \Vdash \{\varphi\}I_a\alpha$ iff $\mathcal{M}^{\varphi}, s \Vdash I_a\alpha$ iff for any $i \in Sit(s)$, $\mathcal{M}^{\varphi}, \bigsqcup \Sigma_a^{\varphi}(i) \Vdash \alpha$ iff for any $i \in Sit(s)$, $\mathcal{M}, \bigsqcup \Sigma_a^{\varphi}(i) \Vdash \{\varphi\}\alpha$ iff (using Proposition 1) for any $i \in Sit(s)$, $\mathcal{M}, \sigma_a(i) \cdot info(\varphi) \Vdash \{\varphi\}\alpha$ iff for any $i \in Sit(s)$, $\mathcal{M}, \sigma_a(i) \Vdash \varphi \to \{\varphi\}\alpha$ iff $\mathcal{M}, s \Vdash I_a(\varphi \to \{\varphi\}\alpha)$.

We have explained above that epistemic Kripke models determine particular AEI-models. Theorem 9 shows that the axioms and rules presented in Table 2 are sound with respect all AEI-models, and thus also with respect to those AEI-models that are determined by the Kripke models of the standard public announcement logic PAL. This means that if we take any formula α of the language of PAL (it can be a formula using only the operators $\neg, \to, \wedge, \vee, I_a, [\beta]$) then α is equivalent to α^{*} also in PAL. In other words, the procedure of eliminating the public utterance modality that we introduced in this paper and that is based on the axioms RA1-RA13 can be used also in the context of PAL, though it differs from the standardly used procedure based on the standard reduction axioms.

The following theorem provides a sound and complete syntactic characterization of SIDEL-validity through SIDEL-provability.

Theorem 10. *For every $\mathcal{L}_{SIDEL}$-formula φ, φ is* SIDEL*-valid if and only if φ is* SIDEL*-provable.*

Proof. Soundness, i.e. the right-to-left direction, is given by soundness of the SIEL-axioms and rules, and by Theorem 9. Completeness, i.e. the left-to-right direction, can be proved as follows: Assume that φ is SIDEL-valid. Due to Theorem 8, φ is SIDEL-provably equivalent to the $\mathcal{L}_{SIEL}$-formula φ^*. Due to soundness of the system, φ^* must be also SIDEL-valid. Since SIDEL is a conservative extension of SIEL, φ^* is SIEL-valid and hence SIEL-provable. It follows that φ^*, and thus also φ, is SIDEL-provable.

Our next application of the previous results shows that the logic SIDEL has the inquisitive disjunction property.

Theorem 11. *The logic* SIDEL *has the inquisitive disjunction property, that is,* $\varphi \mathbin{\backslash\!\!\!\vee} \psi$ *is* SIDEL*-valid only if* φ *or* ψ *is* SIDEL*-valid.*

Proof. Assume $\varphi \mathbin{\backslash\!\!\!\vee} \psi$ is SIDEL-valid. Then also $\varphi^* \mathbin{\backslash\!\!\!\vee} \psi^*$ is SIDEL-valid, and thus SIEL-valid. Since SIEL has the inquisitive disjunction property, φ^* or ψ^* is SIEL-valid. It follows that φ or ψ is SIDEL-valid.

5 Conclusion

To sum up, we have developed a logic SIDEL of public announcement of statements and public utterance of questions based on a basic substructural logic. We focused on one particular minimal logic but the framework is quite flexible and can be adapted easily to other substructural logics. It was shown in [6,7] how to obtain semantics for inquisitive versions of relevant logics, fuzzy logics and other substructural logics within the framework of information models. These logics could be further enriched with the epistemic modalities I_a, E_a and the dynamic modalities $[\varphi], \{\varphi\}$ using the same reduction axioms and the semantic approach elaborated in this paper.

The semantics of SIDEL can be viewed as a generalization of the semantics of the inquisitive dynamic epistemic logic IDEL developed in [4]. This observation implies that our reduction axioms are valid even in the context IDEL and hence also in the context of PAL since IDEL just extends PAL with the inquisitive dimension. In other words, the method of elimination of the dynamic modalities that we employed could be used also in IDEL and PAL in the sense that for any formula φ from the language of IDEL (or PAL), the corresponding formula φ^*, obtained by our reduction axioms from φ, is equivalent to φ not only in SIDEL but also in IDEL (or PAL).

On the other hand, as we showed above, in the context of SIDEL we cannot use the reduction axioms that are normally used for IDEL (or PAL). To be more concrete, IDEL uses the reduction axioms from Table 3. From these axioms only !Atom, $!\bot$, $!\wedge$, $!\mathbin{\backslash\!\!\!\vee}$, and $!I_a$ are SIDEL-valid. However, the axioms $!\!\rightarrow$ and $!E_a$ are invalid in SIDEL.

Table 3. Reduction axioms of IDEL used in [3]

!Atom	$[\varphi]p \leftrightarrow (\varphi \rightarrow p)$
$!\bot$	$[\varphi]\bot \leftrightarrow (\varphi \rightarrow \bot)$
$!\wedge$	$[\varphi](\psi \wedge \chi) \leftrightarrow ([\varphi]\psi \wedge [\varphi]\chi)$
$!\rightarrow$	$[\varphi](\psi \rightarrow \chi) \leftrightarrow ([\varphi]\psi \rightarrow [\varphi]\chi)$
$!\vee\!\!\!\vee$	$[\varphi](\psi \vee\!\!\!\vee \chi) \leftrightarrow ([\varphi]\psi \vee\!\!\!\vee [\varphi]\chi)$
$!E_a$	$[\varphi]E_a\psi \leftrightarrow (\varphi \rightarrow E_a(\varphi \rightarrow [\varphi]\psi))$
$!I_a$	$[\varphi]I_a\psi \leftrightarrow (\varphi \rightarrow I_a[\varphi]\psi)$

In future work we would like to explore whether our framework could be also seen as a generalization of Dynamic Logic of Questions developed in [8].

References

1. Barwise, J., Perry, J.: Situations and Attitudes. MIT Press, Cambridge (2019)
2. Ciardelli, I., Groenendijk, J., Roelofsen, F.: Inquisitive Semantics. Oxford University Press, Oxford (2019)
3. Ciardelli, I., Roelofsen, F.: Inquisitive dynamic epistemic logic. Synthese **192**(6), 1643–1687 (2015). https://doi.org/10.1007/s11229-014-0404-7
4. Ciardelli, I.: The dynamic logic of stating and asking: a study of inquisitive dynamic modalities. In: Baltag, A., Seligman, J., Yamada, T. (eds.) LORI 2017. LNCS, vol. 10455, pp. 240–255. Springer, Heidelberg (2017). https://doi.org/10.1007/978-3-662-55665-8_17
5. Punčochář, V., Sedlár, I.: Epistemic extensions of substructural inquisitive logics (Submitted manuscript)
6. Punčochář, V.: Substructural inquisitive logics. Rev. Symb. Logic **12**(2), 296–330 (2019)
7. Punčochář, V.: A relevant logic of questions. J. Philos. Logic **49**(5), 905–939 (2020). https://doi.org/10.1007/s10992-019-09541-9
8. van Benthem, J., Minică, Ş.: Toward a dynamic logic of questions. J. Philos. Logic **41**(4), 633–669 (2012)
9. van Ditmarsch, H., van der Hoek, W., Kooi, B.: Dynamic Epistemic Logic. Springer, Dordrecht (2007). https://doi.org/10.1007/978-1-4020-5839-4

Public Announcement Logic in HOL

Sebastian Reiche(✉) and Christoph Benzmüller(✉)

Freie Universität Berlin, Berlin, Germany
{sebastian.reiche,c.benzmueller}@fu-berlin.de

Abstract. A shallow semantical embedding for public announcement logic with relativized common knowledge is presented. This embedding enables the first-time automation of this logic with off-the-shelf theorem provers for classical higher-order logic. It is demonstrated (i) how meta-theoretical studies can be automated this way, and (ii) how non-trivial reasoning in the target logic (public announcement logic), required e.g., to obtain a convincing encoding and automation of the wise men puzzle, can be realized. Key to the presented semantical embedding—in contrast, e.g., to related work on the semantical embedding of normal modal logics—is that evaluation domains are modeled explicitly and treated as additional parameter in the encodings of the constituents of the embedded target logic, while they were previously implicitly shared between meta logic and target logic.

Keywords: Public announcement logic · Relativized common knowledge · Semantical embedding · Higher-order logic · Proof automation

1 Introduction

Previous work has studied the application of a universal (meta-)logical reasoning approach [4,5] for solving a prominent riddle in epistemic reasoning, known as the *wise men puzzle*, on the computer [5]. The solution presented there puts a particular emphasis on the adequate modeling of (ordinary) common knowledge and it also illustrates the elegance and the practical relevance of the shallow semantical embedding approach (in classical higher-order logic) [4], when being utilized within modern proof assistant systems such as Isabelle/HOL [20]. However, this work nevertheless falls short, since it did not convincingly address the interaction dynamics between the involved agents. To do so, we extend and adapt in this paper the universal (meta-)logical reasoning approach for "public announcement logic" and we demonstrate how it can be adapted to achieve a convincing encoding and automation of the wise men puzzle in Isabelle/HOL that also captures the interaction dynamics of the wise men puzzle scenario. In more general terms, we present the first automation of public announcement logic with relativized common knowledge, and we demonstrate that, and how, this logic can be seen and elegantly handled as a fragment of classical higher-order logic. Key to the presented extension of the shallow semantical embedding

M. A. Martins and I. Sedlár (Eds.): DaLí 2020, LNCS 12569, pp. 222–238, 2020.
https://doi.org/10.1007/978-3-030-65840-3_14

approach is that the evaluation domains of the embedded target logic (public announcement logic with relativized common knowledge) are no longer implicitly shared with the meta-logic (classical higher-order logic), but they are now explicitly modeled as an additional parameter in the encoding of the embedded logics constituents.

This paper is structured as follows: Sect. 2 briefly recaps classical higher-order logic (Church's type theory), and Sect. 3 sketches public announcement logic with relativized common knowledge. The main contributions of this paper are then presented in Sect. 4, where a shallow semantical embedding of public announcement logic in classical higher-order logic is studied. In Sect. 5 the newly acquired embedding is tested and applied to achieve an encoding and automation of the prominent wise men puzzle. Section 6 discusses related work and Sect. 7 concludes the paper.

2 Classical Higher-Order Logic

We briefly recap classical higher-order logic (HOL), respectively Church's *simple theory of types* [6,10], which is a logic defined on top of the simply typed lambda calculus. The presentation is partly adapted from Benzmüller [3]. For further information on the syntax and semantics of HOL we refer to [7].

Syntax of HOL. We start out with defining the set $\mathcal{T}$ of *simple types* by the following abstract grammar: $\alpha, \beta := o \mid i \mid (\alpha \rightarrow \beta)$. Type o denotes a bivalent set of truth values, containing *truth* and *falsehood*, and i denotes a non-empty set of individuals. Further base types are optional. $\rightarrow$ is the function type constructor, such that $(\alpha \rightarrow \beta) \in \mathcal{T}$ whenever $\alpha, \beta \in \mathcal{T}$. We may generally omit parentheses.

The *terms* of HOL are defined by the following abstract grammar:

$$s, t := p_\alpha \mid X_\alpha \mid (\lambda X_\alpha s_\beta)_{\alpha\rightarrow\beta} \mid (s_{\alpha\rightarrow\beta} t_\alpha)_\beta$$

where $\alpha, \beta, o \in \mathcal{T}$. The $p_\alpha \in C_\alpha$ are typed constants and the $X_\alpha \in V_\alpha$ are typed variables (distinct from the p_α). If $s_{\alpha\rightarrow\beta}$ and t_α are HOL terms of types $\alpha \rightarrow \beta$ and α, respectively, then $(s_{\alpha\rightarrow\beta} t_\alpha)_\beta$, called *application*, is an HOL term of type β. If $X_\alpha \in V_\alpha$ is a typed variable symbol and s_β is an HOL term of type β, then $(\lambda X_\alpha s_\beta)_{\alpha\rightarrow\beta}$, called *abstraction*, is an HOL term of type $\alpha \rightarrow \beta$. The type of each term is given as a subscript. We call terms of type o *formulas*. As *primitive logical connectives* we choose $\neg_{o\rightarrow o}$, $\vee_{o\rightarrow o\rightarrow o}$, $=_{\alpha\rightarrow\alpha\rightarrow\alpha}$ and $\Pi_{(\alpha\rightarrow o)\rightarrow o}$. Other logical connectives can be introduced as abbreviations; e.g. $\longrightarrow_{o\rightarrow o\rightarrow o} = \lambda X_o \lambda Y_o \neg X \vee Y$.

Semantics of HOL. A *frame* $\mathcal{D}$ for HOL is a collection $\{\mathcal{D}_\alpha\}_{\alpha\in\mathcal{T}}$ of nonempty sets $\mathcal{D}_\alpha$, such that $\mathcal{D}_o = \{T, F\}$ (for true and false). $\mathcal{D}_i$ is chosen freely and $\mathcal{D}_{\alpha\rightarrow\beta}$ are collections of functions mapping $\mathcal{D}_\alpha$ into $\mathcal{D}_\beta$.

A *model* for HOL is a tuple $\mathcal{M} = \langle \mathcal{D}, I \rangle$, where $\mathcal{D}$ is a frame, and I is a family of typed interpretation functions mapping constant symbols $p_\alpha \in C_\alpha$ to appropriate elements of $\mathcal{D}_\alpha$, called the *denotation* of p_α. The logical connectives $\neg, \vee, \Pi$ and $=$ are always given their expected standard denotations:

$$\begin{array}{lll} I(\neg_{o\to o}) & = not \in \mathcal{D}_{o\to o} & \text{s.t. } not(\text{T}) = \text{F and } not(\text{F}) = \text{T} \\ I(\vee_{o\to o\to o}) & = or \in \mathcal{D}_{o\to o\to o} & \text{s.t. } or(\text{a,b}) = \text{T iff (a = T or b = T)} \\ I(=_{\alpha\to\alpha\to o}) & = id \in \mathcal{D}_{\alpha\to\alpha\to o} & \text{s.t. for all a,b} \in \mathcal{D}_\alpha,\ id(\text{a,b}) = \text{T} \\ & & \quad \text{iff a is identical to b.} \\ I(\Pi_{(\alpha\to o)\to o}) & = all \in \mathcal{D}_{(\alpha\to o)\to o} & \text{s.t. for all } s \in \mathcal{D}_{\alpha\to o},\ all(\text{s}) = \text{T} \\ & & \quad \text{iff s(a) = T for all a} \in \mathcal{D}_\alpha \end{array}$$

A *variable assignment* g maps variables X_α to elements in $\mathcal{D}_\alpha$. $g[d/W]$ denotes the assignment that is identical to g, except for variable W, which is now mapped to d.

The *denotation* $[\![s_\alpha]\!]^{M,g}$ of an HOL term s_α on a model $\mathcal{M} = \langle \mathcal{D}, I \rangle$ under assignment g is an element $d \in \mathcal{D}_\alpha$ defined in the following way:

$$\begin{array}{ll} [\![p_\alpha]\!]^{\mathcal{M},g} & = I(p_\alpha) \\ [\![X_\alpha]\!]^{\mathcal{M},g} & = g(X_\alpha) \\ [\![(s_{\alpha\to\beta}t_\alpha)_\beta]\!]^{\mathcal{M},g} & = [\![s_{\alpha\to\beta}]\!]^{\mathcal{M},g}([\![t_\alpha]\!]^{\mathcal{M},g}) \\ [\![(\lambda X_\alpha s_\beta)_{\alpha\to\beta}]\!]^{\mathcal{M},g} & = \text{the function } f \text{ from } \mathcal{D}_\alpha \text{ to } \mathcal{D}_\beta \\ & \quad \text{s.t. } f(d) = [\![s_\beta]\!]^{\mathcal{M},g[d/X_\alpha]} \text{ for all } d \in \mathcal{D}_\alpha \end{array}$$

In a *standard model* a domain $\mathcal{D}_{\alpha\to\beta}$ is defined as the set of all total functions from $\mathcal{D}_\alpha$ to $\mathcal{D}_\beta$: $\mathcal{D}_{\alpha\to\beta} = \{f \mid f : \mathcal{D}_\alpha \to \mathcal{D}_\beta\}$. In a *Henkin model* (or general model) [14] function spaces are not necessarily required to be the full set of functions: $\mathcal{D}_{\alpha\to\beta} \subseteq \{f \mid f : \mathcal{D}_\alpha \to \mathcal{D}_\beta\}$. However, we require that the valuation function remains total, so that every term denotes.

A HOL formula s_o is *valid in an Henkin model $\mathcal{M}$ under assignment g* if and only if $[\![s_o]\!]^{\mathcal{M},g} = T$; also denoted by $\mathcal{M}, g \models^{\texttt{HOL}} s_o$. A HOL formula s_o is called *valid in* $\mathcal{M}$, denoted by $\mathcal{M} \models^{\texttt{HOL}} s_o$, iff $\mathcal{M}, g \models^{\texttt{HOL}} s_o$ for all assignments g. Moreover, a formula s_o is called *valid*, denoted by $\models^{\texttt{HOL}} s_o$, if and only if s_o is valid in all Henkin models $\mathcal{M}$.

Due to Gödel [13] a sound and complete mechanization of HOL with standard semantics cannot be achieved. For HOL with Henkin semantics sound and complete calculi exist; cf. e.g. [7,8] and the references therein.

Each standard model is obviously also a Henkin model. Consequently, when a HOL formula is Henkin-valid, it is also valid in all standard models.

3 Public Announcement Logic

The most important concepts and definitions of a public announcement logic (PAL) with relativized common knowledge are depicted. For more details we refer to [16,23].

Before exploring these definitions some general descriptions of the modeling approach might be worthwhile. We use a graph-theoretical structure, called *epistemic models*, to represent knowledge. Epistemic models describe situations in terms of possible worlds. A world represents one possibility about how the current situation can be. Each agent is assumed to entertain a number of these possibilities. Knowledge is described using an accessibility relation between worlds, rather than directly representing the agent's information.

Let $\mathcal{A}$ be a set of agents and $\mathcal{P}$ a set of atomic propositions. Atomic propositions are intended to describe ground facts. We use a set W to denote possible worlds and a valuation function $V : \mathcal{P} \to \wp(W)$ that assigns a set of worlds to each atomic proposition. Vice versa, we may identify each world with the set of propositions that are validated in them.

Definition 1 (Epistemic Model). *Let $\mathcal{A}$ be a (finite) set of agents and $\mathcal{P}$ a (finite or countable) set of atomic propositions. An Epistemic Model is a triple $\mathcal{M} = \langle W, \{R_i\}_{i\in\mathcal{A}}, V\rangle$ where $W \neq \emptyset$, $R_i \subseteq W \times W$ is an accessibility relation (for each $i \in \mathcal{A}$), and $V : \mathcal{P} \to \wp(W)$ is a valuation function ($\wp(W)$ is the powerset of W).*

Information of agent i at world w can now be defined as: $R_i(w) = \{v \in W \mid wR_iv\}$. Having a separate (accessibility) relation for each agent enables them to have their own viewpoints.

Next, we introduce the syntax of our base epistemic logic as the set of sentences generated by the following grammar (where $p \in \mathcal{P}$ and $i \in \mathcal{A}$):

$$\varphi, \psi := p \mid \neg\varphi \mid \varphi \vee \psi \mid K_i\varphi$$

We also introduce the abbreviations $\varphi \wedge \psi := \neg(\neg\varphi \vee \neg\psi)$ and $\varphi \to \psi := \neg\varphi \vee \psi$.

Definition 2 (Truth at world w). *Given an epistemic model $\mathcal{M} = \langle W, \{R_i\}_{i\in\mathcal{A}}, V\rangle$. For each $w \in W, \varphi$* is true at world *w, denoted $\mathcal{M}, w \models \varphi$, is defined inductively as follows:*

$$\begin{array}{ll} \mathcal{M}, w \models p & \textit{iff } w \in V(p) \\ \mathcal{M}, w \models \neg\varphi & \textit{iff } \mathcal{M}, w \not\models \varphi \\ \mathcal{M}, w \models \varphi \vee \psi & \textit{iff } \mathcal{M}, w \models \varphi \textit{ or } \mathcal{M}, w \models \psi \\ \mathcal{M}, w \models K_i\varphi & \textit{iff for all } v \in W, \textit{ if } wR_iv \textit{ then } \mathcal{M}, v \models \varphi \end{array}$$

The formula $K_i\varphi$ expresses that "Agent i knows φ". This describes knowledge as an all-or-nothing definition. If we postulate that agent i knows φ, we say that φ is true throughout all worlds in agents i's range of considerations.

Satisfiabilty of a formula φ for a model $\mathcal{M} = \langle W, \{R_i\}_{i\in\mathcal{A}}, V\rangle$ and a world $w \in W$ is expressed by writing that $\mathcal{M}, w \models \varphi$. We define $V^{\mathcal{M}}(\varphi) = \{w \in W \mid \mathcal{M}, w \models \varphi\}$. Formula φ is *valid* if and only if for all $\mathcal{M}$ and for all worlds w we have $\mathcal{M}, w \models \varphi$.

Our modal logic above (corresponding to the normal modal logic K) is not yet sufficiently suited to encode epistemic reasoning. Therefore, additional conditions (reflexivity, transitivity and euclideaness) are imposed on the accessibility relations. This can e.g. be achieved by postulating the following principles, resp. axiom schemata (in a Hilbert-style proof system).

	Assumption	Formula	Property
T	*Truth*	$K_i\varphi \rightarrow \varphi$	Reflexive
4	*Positive Introspection*	$K_i\varphi \rightarrow K_iK_i\varphi$	Transitive
5	*Negative Introspection*	$\neg K_i \rightarrow K_i\neg K_i\varphi$	Euclidean

We add public announcements [18] to our logic. The objective is to formulate an operation that transforms the epistemic model such that all agents *find out that φ is true*. This is achieved by taking the model $\mathcal{M}$ and discarding all worlds in which φ is false. Afterwards all agents will only consider worlds in which φ is true. Because of the *publicity* of the announcement all agents are aware of the fact that all other agents know that φ holds true afterwards.

Definition 3 (Public Announcement). *Suppose that $\mathcal{M} = \langle W, \{R_i\}_{i\in\mathcal{A}}, V\rangle$ is an epistemic model and φ is a formula (in the language of our base logic). After all the agents find out that φ is true (i.e., φ is publicly announced), the resulting model is $\mathcal{M}^{!\varphi} = \langle W^{!\varphi}, \{R_i^{!\varphi}\}_{i\in\mathcal{A}}, V^{!\varphi}\rangle$ where $W^{!\varphi} = \{w \in W \mid \mathcal{M}, w \models \varphi\}$, $R_i^{!\varphi} = R_i \cap (W^{!\varphi} \times W^{!\varphi})$ for all $i \in \mathcal{A}$, and $V^{!\varphi}(p) = V(p) \cap W^{!\varphi}$ for all $p \in \mathcal{P}$.*

To say that "ψ is true after the announcement of φ" is represented as $[!\varphi]\psi$. Truth for this new operator is defined as:

$$\mathcal{M}, w \models [!\varphi]\psi \text{ iff } \mathcal{M}, w \not\models \varphi \text{ or } \mathcal{M}^{!\varphi}, w \models \psi$$

We conclude this section with the introduction of notions for group knowledge.

Mutual knowledge, often stated as *everyone knows*, describes knowledge that each member of the group holds. Usually, it is defined for a group of agents $G \subseteq \mathcal{A}$ as $E_G\varphi := \bigwedge_{i\in G} K_i\varphi$. Equivalently, a new relation can be introduced to express mutual knowledge with the knowledge operator.

Definition 4 (Mutual Knowledge). *Let $G \subseteq \mathcal{A}$ be a group of agents. Let $R_G = \bigcup_{i\in G} R_i$. The truth clause for mutual knowledge is:*

$$\mathcal{M}, w \models E_G\psi \text{ iff for all } v \in W, \text{ if } wR_Gv \text{ then } \mathcal{M}, v \models \psi$$

Still, there is a distinction to make between *everyone knows* φ and *it is common knowledge that* φ. A statement p is common knowledge when all agents know p, know that they all know p, know that they all know that they all know p, and so ad infinitum. Relativized common knowledge was introduced by van Benthem, van Eijck and Kooi [22] as a variant of common knowledge for dynamic epistemic logics. As the name suggests knowledge update is then treated as a *relativization*.

Definition 5 (Relativized Common Knowledge). *Let $G \subseteq \mathcal{A}$ be a group of agents. Let $R_G = \bigcup_{i\in G} R_i$. The truth clause for relativized common knowledge is:*

$$\mathcal{M}, w \models \mathcal{C}_G(\varphi|\psi) \text{ iff for all } v \in W, \text{ if } w(R_G^\varphi)^+v \text{ then } \mathcal{M}, v \models \psi$$

where $R_G^\varphi = R_G \cap (W \times V^{\mathcal{M}}(\varphi))$, and $(R_G^\varphi)^+$ denotes the transitive closure of R_G^φ.

Intuitively, $\mathcal{C}_G(\varphi|\psi)$ expresses, that after φ is announced, ψ becomes common knowledge in the group. This means, that every path from w, that is accessible using the agent's relations through worlds in which φ is true, must end in a world in which ψ is true. Ordinary common knowledge of φ can be abbreviated as $\mathcal{C}_G(\top|\varphi)$, where $\top$ denotes an arbitrary tautology.

In the remainder we use PAL to refer to the depicted logic consisting of modal logic K, extended by the principles T45, public announcement and relativized common knowledge.

4 Modeling PAL as a Fragment of HOL

A shallow semantical embedding (SSE) of a target logic into HOL provides a translation between the two logics in such a way that the former logic is identified and characterized as a proper fragment of the latter.[1] Once such an SSE is obtained, all that is needed to prove (or refute) conjectures in the target logic is to provide the SSE, encoded in an input file, to the HOL prover in addition to the encoded conjecture. We can then use the HOL prover as-is, without making any changes to its source code, and use it to solve problems in our target logic.

4.1 Shallow Semantical Embedding

To define an SSE for target logic PAL we lift the type of propositions in order to explicitly encode their dependency on possible worlds; this is analogous to prior work [4,5]. In order to capture the model-changing behavior of PAL we additionally introduce world domains (sets of worlds) as parameters/arguments in the encoding. The rationale thereby is to be able to suitably constrain, and recursively pass-on, these domains after each model changing action.

PAL formulas are thus identified in our semantical embedding with certain HOL terms (predicates) of type $(i \rightarrow o) \rightarrow i \rightarrow o$. They can be applied to terms of type $i \rightarrow o$, which are assumed to denote evaluation domains, and subsequently to terms of type i, which are assumed to denote possible worlds. That is, the HOL type i is identified with a (non-empty) set of worlds, and the type $i \rightarrow o$, abbreviated by σ, is identified with a set of sets of worlds, i.e., a set of evaluation domains. Type $(i \rightarrow o) \rightarrow i \rightarrow o$ is abbreviated as τ, and type α is an abbreviation for $i \rightarrow i \rightarrow o$, the type of accessibility relations between worlds.

For each propositional symbol p^i of PAL, the corresponding HOL signature is assumed to contain a corresponding constant symbol p^i_σ, which is (rigidly) denoting the set of all those worlds in which p^i holds. We call the p^i_σ *σ-type-lifted propositions.* Moreover, for $k = 1, \ldots, |\mathcal{A}|$ the HOL signature is assumed to contain the constant symbols $r^1_\alpha, \ldots, r^{|\mathcal{A}|}_\alpha$. Without loss of generality, we assume that besides those constants symbols and the primitive logical connectives of HOL, no other constant symbols are given in the signature of HOL.

[1] The SSE technique is not be confused with higher-order abstract syntax [17].

As a simplifying assumption in this ongoing work (which has a particular focus on an automation of the Wise Men Puzzle in PAL) we continue with choosing $|\mathcal{A}| = 3$. (A generalization for arbitrary $\mathcal{A}$ is straightforward).

The mapping $\lfloor\cdot\rfloor$ translates a formula φ of PAL into a term $\lfloor\varphi\rfloor$ of HOL of type τ. The mapping is defined recursively:

$$\begin{aligned}
\lfloor p^j \rfloor &= ({}^{A}(p^j_\sigma))_\tau \\
\lfloor \neg\varphi \rfloor &= \neg_{\tau\to\tau} \lfloor\varphi\rfloor \\
\lfloor \varphi \vee \psi \rfloor &= \vee_{\tau\to\tau\to\tau} \lfloor\varphi\rfloor \lfloor\psi\rfloor \\
\lfloor K\ \mathrm{r}^k\ \varphi \rfloor &= K_{\alpha\to\tau\to\tau}\ \mathrm{r}^k_\alpha\ \lfloor\varphi\rfloor \\
\lfloor [!\varphi]\psi \rfloor &= [!\cdot\,]\cdot_{\tau\to\tau\to\tau} \lfloor\varphi\rfloor \lfloor\psi\rfloor \\
\lfloor \mathcal{C}(\varphi|\psi) \rfloor &= \mathcal{C}(\cdot|\cdot)_{\tau\to\tau\to\tau} \lfloor\varphi\rfloor \lfloor\psi\rfloor
\end{aligned}$$

Operator ${}^{A}(\cdot)$, which evaluates atomic formulas, is defined as follows:

$${}^{A}\cdot_{\sigma\to\tau} = \lambda A_\sigma \lambda D_\sigma \lambda X_i (D\ X \wedge A\ X)$$

As a first argument it accepts a σ-type-lifted proposition A_σ, which are rigidly interpreted. As a second argument it accepts an evaluation domain D_σ, that is, an arbitrary subset of the domain associated with type σ. And as a third argument it accepts a current world. It then checks whether (i) the current world is a member of evaluation domain D_σ and (ii) whether the σ-type-lifted proposition A_σ holds in the current world.

The other logical connectives of PAL, except for $[!\cdot\,]\cdot_{\tau\to\tau\to\tau}$, are now defined in a way so that they simply pass-on the evaluation domains as parameters to the atomic-level. Only $[!\cdot\,]\cdot_{\tau\to\tau\to\tau}$ is modifying, in fact, constraining, the evaluation domain it passes on, and it does this in the expected way (cf. Definition 3):

$$\begin{aligned}
\neg_{\tau\to\tau} &= \lambda A_\tau \lambda D_\sigma \lambda X_i \neg(A\ D\ X) \\
\vee_{\tau\to\tau\to\tau} &= \lambda A_\tau \lambda B_\tau \lambda D_\sigma \lambda X_i (A\ D\ X \vee B\ D\ X) \\
\mathrm{K}_{\alpha\to\tau\to\tau} &= \lambda R_\alpha \lambda A_\tau \lambda D_\sigma \lambda X_i \forall Y_i ((D\ Y\ \wedge\ R\ X\ Y) \longrightarrow A\ D\ Y) \\
[!\cdot\,]\cdot_{\tau\to\tau\to\tau} &= \lambda A_\tau \lambda B_\tau \lambda D_\sigma \lambda X_i (\neg(A\ D\ X) \vee (B\ (\lambda Y_i\ D\ Y\ \wedge\ A\ D\ Y)\ X))
\end{aligned}$$

To model $\mathcal{C}(\cdot|\cdot)_{\tau\to\tau\to\tau}$ we reuse the following operations on relations; cf. [4,5].

$$\begin{aligned}
\mathtt{transitive}_{\alpha\to o} &= \lambda R_\alpha \forall X_i \forall Y_i \forall Z_i (\neg(R\ X\ Y\ \wedge\ R\ Y\ Z) \vee R\ X\ Z) \\
\mathtt{intersection}_{\alpha\to\alpha\to\alpha} &= \lambda R_\alpha \lambda Q_\alpha \lambda X_i \lambda Y_i (R\ X\ Y\ \wedge\ Q\ X\ Y) \\
\mathtt{union}_{\alpha\to\alpha\to\alpha} &= \lambda R_\alpha \lambda Q_\alpha \lambda X_i \lambda Y_i (R\ X\ Y\ \vee\ Q\ X\ Y) \\
\mathtt{sub}_{\alpha\to\alpha\to o} &= \lambda R_\alpha \lambda Q_\alpha \forall X_i \forall Y_i (\neg R\ X\ Y\ \vee\ Q\ X\ Y) \\
\mathtt{tc}_{\alpha\to\alpha} &= \lambda R_\alpha \lambda X_i \lambda Y_i \forall Q_\alpha \\
&\quad (\neg\mathtt{transitive}\ Q\ \vee\ (\neg\mathtt{sub}\ R\ Q\ \vee\ Q\ X\ Y))
\end{aligned}$$

Additionally, EVR is defined as the union of three agents r^1, r^2 and r^3 of type α. EVR can then be used as a relation, e.g., for the knowledge operator to describe mutual knowledge of the three agents. But most importantly, we need this relation in order to encode relativized common knowledge.

$$\texttt{EVR}_\alpha = \texttt{union}(\texttt{union}\ r^1\ r^2)\ r^3$$

We want to remark that a general higher-order definition for the union of a set of relations could alternatively be introduced first and then be applied to our concrete set of relations R consisting of r^1, r^2 and r^3. Nothing prevents us from generalizing the notion of mutual knowledge this way to an arbitrary group of agents R, and to consider R as a further parameter in e.g. the definition of $\mathcal{C}(\cdot|\cdot)_{\tau\to\tau\to\tau}$. However, in our first experiments as presented in this paper, which are primarily intended to study the practical feasibility of the embedding approach for PAL, we have still avoided this final generalization step. The operator $\mathcal{C}(\cdot|\cdot)_{\tau\to\tau\to\tau}$ thus abbreviates the following HOL term:

$$\begin{aligned}\mathcal{C}(\cdot|\cdot)_{\tau\to\tau\to\tau} = {} & \lambda A_\tau \lambda B_\tau \lambda D_\sigma \lambda X_i \forall Y_i \\ & (\texttt{tc}(\texttt{intersection}\ \texttt{EVR}\ (\lambda U_i \lambda V_i (D\ V\ \wedge\ A\ D\ V)))\ X\ Y \\ & \longrightarrow\ B\ D\ Y)\end{aligned}$$

Analyzing the truth of a PAL formula φ, represented by the HOL term $\lfloor\varphi\rfloor$, in a particular domain d, represented by the term D_σ, and a world s, represented by the term S_i, corresponds to evaluating the application $(\lfloor\varphi\rfloor\ D_\sigma\ S_i)$. φ is thus generally valid if and only if for all D_σ and all S_i we have $D\ S \to \lfloor\varphi\rfloor D\ S$.

The validity function, therefore, is defined as follows:

$$\texttt{vld}_{\tau\to o} = \lambda A_\tau \forall D_\sigma \forall S_i (D\ S\ \longrightarrow\ A\ D\ S).$$

The necessity to quantify over all possible domains in this definition will be further illustrated below.

4.2 Encoding into Isabelle/HOL

What follows is a description of the concrete encoding of the presented SSE of PAL in HOL within the higher-order proof assistant Isabelle/HOL.[2]

All necessary types can be modeled in a straightforward way. We declare `i` to denote possible worlds and then introduce type aliases for σ, τ and α. Type `bool` represents (the bivalent set of) truth values.

```
typedecl i
type_synonym σ = "i⇒bool"
type_synonym τ = "σ⇒i⇒bool"
type_synonym α = "i⇒i⇒bool"
```

[2] The full sources of our encoding can be found at http://logikey.org in subfolder `Public-Announcement-Logic`, resp. at https://github.com/cbenzmueller/LogiKEy/tree/master/Public-Announcement-Logic.

The agents are declared mutually distinct accessibility relations and the group of agents is denoted by predicate $\mathcal{A}$. In order to obtain $\mathcal{S}5$ (KT45) properties, we declare respective conditions on the accessibility relations in the group of agents $\mathcal{A}$. Various Isabelle/HOL encodings from [4,5] are reused here (without mentioning due to space restrictions), including the encoding of transitive closure.

```
consts a::"α" b::"α" c::"α"
abbreviation "𝒜 x ≡ x = a ∨ x = b ∨ x = c"
axiomatization where
  alldifferent: "¬(a = b) ∧ ¬(a = c) ∧ ¬(b = c)" and
  agents_S5: "∀i.𝒜 i ⟶ (reflexive i ∧ transitive i ∧ euclidean i)"
abbreviation EVR :: "α" ("EVR")
  where "EVR ≡ union_rel (union_rel a b) c"
```

To distinguish between HOL connectives (e.g. $\neg$) and the lifted PAL connectives (e.g. $\boldsymbol{\neg}_{\tau\to\tau}$) we make use of bold face fonts, see for example the definition $\boldsymbol{\neg}_{\tau\to\tau} \equiv \lambda\varphi_\tau.\lambda W_\sigma.\lambda w_i.\neg\varphi$ W w below. Each of the lifted unary and binary connectives of PAL accepts arguments of type τ, i.e. lifted PAL formulas, and returns such a lifted PAL formula.

A special case, as discussed before, is the new operator for atomic propositions ${}^{A}(\cdot)$. When evaluating σ-type lifted atomic propositions p we need to check if p is true in the given world w, but we also need to check whether the given world w is still part of our evaluation domain W that has been recursively passed-on. Operator ${}^{A}(\cdot)$ is thus of type "$\sigma \Rightarrow \tau$".

```
abbreviation patom :: "σ ⇒ τ" ("ᴬ_")
  where "ᴬp ≡ λW w. W w ∧ p w"
abbreviation ptop :: "τ" ("⊤")
  where "⊤ ≡ λW w. True"
abbreviation pneg :: "τ⇒τ" ("¬")
  where "¬φ ≡ λW w. ¬(φ W w)"
abbreviation pand :: "τ⇒τ⇒τ" ("∧")
  where "φ ∧ ψ ≡ λW w. (φ W w) ∧ (ψ W w)"
abbreviation por :: "τ⇒τ⇒τ" ("∨")
  where "φ ∨ ψ ≡ λW w. (φ W w) ∨ (ψ W w)"
abbreviation pimp :: "τ⇒τ⇒τ" ("→")
  where "φ → ψ ≡ λW w. (φ W w) ⟶ (ψ W w)"
abbreviation pequ :: "τ⇒τ⇒τ" ("↔")
  where "φ ↔ ψ ≡ λW w. (φ W w) ⟷ (ψ W w)"
```

In the definition of the knowledge operator K, we have to make sure to add a domain check in the implication.

```
abbreviation pknow :: "τ⇒τ⇒τ" ("K_ _")
  where "K r φ ≡ λW w.∀v. (W v ∧ r w v)⟶(φ W v)"
```

Two additional abbreviations are introduced to improve readability. A more concise way to state knowledge and an additional operator for mutual knowledge, in which the EVR relation gets used.

```
abbreviation agtknows :: "τ⇒τ⇒τ" ("K_ _")
  where "K_r φ ≡ K r φ"
```

```
abbreviation evrknows :: "τ⇒τ" ("E𝒜 _")
   where "E𝒜 φ ≡ K EVR φ"
```

We finally see the change of the evaluation domain in action, when introducing the public announcement operator. We already inserted domain checks in the definition of the operators K and $^{A}(\cdot)$. Now, we need to constrain the domain after each public announcement. So far the evaluation domain, modeled by W, got passed-on through all lifted operators without any change. In the public announcement operator, however, we modify the evaluation domain W into (λz. W z ∧ φ W z) (i.e., the set of all worlds z in W, such that φ holds for W and z), which is then recursively passed-on. The public announcement operator is thus defined as:

```
abbreviation ppal :: "τ⇒τ⇒τ" ("[!_]_")
   where "[!φ]ψ ≡ λW w. ¬(φ W w) ∨ (ψ (λz. W z ∧ φ W z) w)"
```

The following embedding of relativized common knowledge is a straightforward encoding of the semantic properties and definitions as proposed in Definition 5.

```
abbreviation prck :: "τ⇒τ⇒ τ" ("C⦇_|_⦈")
   where "C⦇φ|ψ⦈" ≡ λW w.∀v.
       (tc (intersection_rel EVR (λu v. W v ∧ φ W w)) w v) ⟶ (ψ W v)"
```

As described earlier we can abbreviate ordinary common knowledge as $\mathcal{C}_G(\top|\varphi)$:

```
abbreviation pcmn :: "τ⇒τ" ("C𝒜 _") where "C𝒜 φ ≡ C⦇⊤|φ⦈"
```

Finally an embedding for the notion of validity is needed. Generally, for a type-lifted formula φ to be valid, the application of φ has to hold true for all worlds w. In the context of PAL the evaluation domains also have to be incorporated in the definition. Originally we were tempted to define PAL validity in such that we start with a "full evaluation domain", a domain that evaluates to True for all possible worlds and gets restricted, whenever necessary after an announcement. Such a validity definition would look like this:

```
abbreviation tvalid::"τ⇒bool" ("⌊_⌋ᵀ") where "⌊_⌋ᵀ ≡ ∀w. φ (λx. True) w"
```

But this leads to undesired behavior, which we can easily see when using our reasoning tools to study e.g. the validity of an often proposed schematic axiom of PAL, *Announcement Necessitation*: *from* ψ, *infer* $[!\varphi]\psi$. If we check for a counterexample in Isabelle/HOL, the model finder Nitpick reports the following:

```
lemma necessitation: assumes "⌊ψ⌋ᵀ" shows "⌊[!φ]ψ⌋ᵀ" nitpick oops
```

```
Nitpick found a counterexample for card i = 2:
Free variables:
φ = (λx. _)
    (((λx. _)(i1 := True, i2 := True), i1) := False,
     ((λx. _)(i1 := True, i2 := True), i2) := True,
     ((λx. _)(i1 := True, i2 := False), i1) := False,
     ((λx. _)(i1 := True, i2 := False), i2) := False,
     ((λx. _)(i1 := False, i2 := True), i1) := False,
```

```
    ((λx. _)(i1 := False, i2 := True), i2) := False,
    ((λx. _)(i1 := False, i2 := False), i1) := False,
    ((λx. _)(i1 := False, i2 := False), i2) := False)
ψ = (λx. _)
   (((λx. _)(i1 := True, i2 := True), i1) := True,
    ((λx. _)(i1 := True, i2 := True), i2) := True,
    ((λx. _)(i1 := True, i2 := False), i1) := False,
    ((λx. _)(i1 := True, i2 := False), i2) := False,
    ((λx. _)(i1 := False, i2 := True), i1) := False,
    ((λx. _)(i1 := False, i2 := True), i2) := False,
    ((λx. _)(i1 := False, i2 := False), i1) := False,
    ((λx. _)(i1 := False, i2 := False), i2) := False)
Skolem constant:
   ??.tvalid.w = i2
```

The valid function needs instead to be defined such that it checks validity not only for all worlds, but for all domains and worlds. Otherwise, the observed but undesired value flipping may occur.

```
abbreviation pvalid :: "τ⇒bool" ("⌊_⌋")
  where "⌊_⌋ ≡ ∀W.∀w. W w ⟶ φ W w "
```

All here introduced definitions are hidden from the user, who can construct formulas in PAL and prove these using the newly embedded operators.

5 Experiments

5.1 Proving Axioms and Rules of Inference of PAL in HOL

The presented SSE of PAL is able to prove the following axioms and rules of inference as presented for PAL in [2, see also Appendix F]:

System K	
–	All substitutions instances of propositional tautologies
Axiom K	$K_i(\varphi \to \psi) \to (K_i\varphi \to K_i\psi)$
Modus ponens	From φ and $\varphi \to \psi$ infer ψ
Necessitation	From φ infer $K_i\varphi$
System $\mathcal{S}5$	
Axiom T	$K_i\varphi \to \varphi$
Axiom 4	$K_i\varphi \to K_iK_i\varphi$
Axiom 5	$\neg K_i\varphi \to K_i\neg K_i\varphi$
Reduction Axioms	
Atomic Permanence	$[!\varphi]p \leftrightarrow (\varphi \to p)$
Conjunction	$[!\varphi](\psi \wedge \chi) \leftrightarrow ([!\varphi]\psi \wedge [!\varphi]\chi)$
Partial Functionality	$[!\varphi]\neg\psi \leftrightarrow (\varphi \to \neg[!\varphi]\psi)$
Action-Knowledge	$[!\varphi]K_i\psi \leftrightarrow (\varphi \to K_i(\varphi \to K_i(\varphi \to [!\varphi]\psi)))$
–	$[!\varphi]\mathcal{C}(\chi\|\psi) \leftrightarrow (\varphi \to \mathcal{C}(\varphi \wedge [!\varphi]\chi\|[!\varphi]\psi))$

Axiom schemes for RCK	
$\mathcal{C}$-normality	$\mathcal{C}(\chi\vert(\varphi \to \psi)) \to (\mathcal{C}(\chi\vert\varphi) \to \mathcal{C}(\chi\vert\psi))$
Mix axiom	$\mathcal{C}(\psi\vert\varphi) \leftrightarrow E(\psi \to (\varphi \wedge \mathcal{C}(\psi\vert\varphi)))$
Induction axiom	$(E(\psi \to \varphi) \wedge \mathcal{C}(\psi\vert\varphi \to E(\psi \to \varphi))) \to \mathcal{C}(\psi\vert\varphi)$
Rules of Inference	
Announcement Nec.	from φ, infer $[!\psi]\varphi$
RKC Necessitation	from φ, infer $\mathcal{C}(\psi\vert\varphi)$

Only for the mix- and induction axiom (schemata) for relativized common knowledge is one direction, respectively, not automatically provable yet. Structural induction is required and a proof still needs to be provided by hand.

```
(*System K*)
lemma tautologies: "⌊⊤⌋" by auto
lemma axiom_K: "𝒜 i ⟹ ⌊(Kᵢ (φ → ψ)) → ((Kᵢ φ) → (Kᵢ ψ))⌋" by auto
lemma modusponens: assumes 1: "⌊φ → ψ⌋" and 2: "⌊φ⌋" shows "⌊ψ⌋"
  using 1 2 by auto
lemma necessitation: assumes 1: "⌊φ⌋" shows "𝒜 i ⟹ ⌊Kᵢ φ⌋"
  using 1 by auto
(*More axiom systems*)
lemma axiom_T: "𝒜 i ⟹ ⌊(Kᵢ φ) → φ)⌋"
  using group_S5 reflexive_def by auto
lemma axiom_4: "𝒜 i ⟹ ⌊(Kᵢ φ) → (Kᵢ (Kᵢ φ))⌋"
  by (meson group_S5 transitive_def)
lemma axiom_5: "𝒜 i ⟹ ⌊(¬Kᵢ φ) → (Kᵢ (¬Kᵢ φ))⌋
  by (meson euclidean_def group_S5)
(*Reduction Axioms*)
lemma atomic_permanence: "⌊([!φ]ᴬp) → (φ →ᴬ p)⌋ by auto
lemma conjunction: "⌊([!φ](ψ ∧ χ)) ↔ (([!φ]ψ) ∧ ([!φ]χ))⌋ by auto
lemma partial_functionality: "⌊([!φ]¬ψ) ↔ (φ → (¬[!φ]ψ))⌋ by auto
lemma action_knowledge: "𝒜 i ⟹ ⌊([!φ](Kᵢ ψ)) ↔ (φ → (Kᵢ (φ → (([!φ]ψ))))⌋
  by auto
lemma "⌊([!φ]C⦇ψ|χ⦈) ↔ (φ → C⦇φ ∧[! φ]χ|[!φ]ψ⦈)⌋
  by (smt intersection_rel_def sub_rel_def tc_def transitive_def)
(*Axiom schemes for RCK*)
lemma C_normality: "⌊(C⦇χ|φ → ψ⦈) → (C⦇χ|φ ⦈ → C⦇χ|ψ⦈)⌋
  unfolding Defs by blast
lemma mix_axiom1: "⌊C⦇χ|φ ⦈ → (E𝒜(χ → (φ ∧ C⦇χ|ψ⦈)))⌋
  unfolding Defs by metis
lemma mix_axiom2: "⌊(E𝒜 (χ → (φ ∧ C⦇χ|ψ⦈))) → C⦇χ|φ⦈⌋
  unfolding Defs sledgehammer (*timeout*)
lemma induction_axiom1: "⌊(E𝒜 (χ → φ)) ∧ C⦇χ|φ → (E𝒜 (χ → φ))⦈) → C⦇χ|φ⦈⌋
  unfolding Defs sledgehammer (*timeout*)
lemma induction_axiom2: "⌊C⦇χ|φ ⦈ → (E𝒜 (χ → φ)) ∧ C⦇χ|φ → (E𝒜 (χ → φ))⦈)⌋
  unfolding Defs by smt
```

```
(*Rules of Inference*)
lemma announcement_nec: assumes 1: "⌊φ⌋" shows "⌊[!ψ]φ⌋" using 1 by auto
lemma rkc_necessitation: assumes 1: "⌊φ⌋" shows "⌊C⦇χ|φ⦈⌋"
 using 1 by (metis intersection_rel_def sub_rel_def tc_def transitive_def)
```

5.2 Exploring Failures of Uniform Substitution

The following principles are examples of sentences that are *valid* for eternal sentences p, but not *schematically valid* [15].

1. $p \rightarrow \neg[!p](\neg p)$
```
lemma "⌊^Ap → ¬[!^Ap](¬^Ap)⌋ by simp
lemma "⌊φ → ¬[!φ](¬φ)⌋ nitpick oops (*countermodel found*)
```
2. $p \rightarrow \neg[!p](\neg K_i p)$
```
lemma "⌊^Ap → ¬[!^Ap](¬K_a ^Ap)⌋ by simp
lemma "⌊φ → ¬[!φ](¬K_a φ)⌋ nitpick oops (*countermodel found*)
```
3. $p \rightarrow \neg[!p](p \wedge \neg K_i p)$
```
lemma "⌊^Ap → ¬[!^Ap](^Ap ∧¬ K_a ^Ap)⌋ by simp
lemma "⌊φ → ¬[!φ](φ ∧ ¬K_a φ)⌋ nitpick oops (*countermodel found*)
```
4. $(p \wedge \neg K_i p) \rightarrow \neg[!p \wedge \neg K_i p](p \wedge \neg K_i p)$
```
lemma "⌊(^Ap ∧ ¬K_a ^Ap) → ¬[!^Ap ∧ ¬K_a ^Ap](^Ap ∧ ¬K_a ^Ap)⌋ by blast
lemma "⌊(φ ∧ ¬K_a φ) → ¬[!φ ∧ ¬K_a φ](φ ∧ ¬K_a φ)⌋ nitpick oops (*ctm. fd.*)
```
5. $K_i p \rightarrow \neg[!p](\neg K_i p)$
```
lemma "⌊(K_a ^Ap) → ¬[!^Ap](¬K_a ^Ap)⌋ using group_S5 reflexive_def by auto
lemma "⌊(K_a φ) → ¬[!φ](¬K_a φ)⌋ nitpick oops (*countermodel found*)
```
6. $K_i p \rightarrow \neg[!p](p \wedge \neg K_i p)$
```
lemma "⌊(K_a ^Ap) → ¬[!^Ap](^Ap ∧ ¬K_a ^Ap)⌋ using group_S5 reflexive_def by auto
lemma "⌊(K_a φ) → ¬[!φ](φ ∧ ¬K_a φ)⌋ nitpick oops (*countermodel found*)
```

5.3 Example Application: The Wise Men Puzzle

The Wise Men puzzle is a interesting riddle in epistemic reasoning. It is well suited to demonstrate epistemic actions in a multi-agent scenario. Baldoni [1] gave a formulation for this, which later got embedded into Isabelle/HOL by Benzmüller [4,5]. In the following implementation these results will be used as a stepping stone.

First the riddle is recited, and then we go into detail on how the uncertainties of all three agents change. The reader is invited to try to solve the riddle on her own before continuing with the analysis.

> *Once upon a time, a king wanted to find the wisest out of his three wisest men. He arranged them in a circle and told them that he would put a white or a black spot on their foreheads and that one of the three spots would*

certainly be white. The three wise men could see and hear each other but, of course, they could not see their faces reflected anywhere. The king, then, asked each of them [sequentially] to find out the color of his own spot. After a while, the wisest correctly answered that his spot was white.

The already existing encoding by Benzmüller puts a particular emphasis on the adequate modeling of common knowledge. Here, this solution will be enhanced by the public announcement operator. Consequently, common knowledge will not be statically stated after each iteration, but a dynamic approach is used for this.

Before we can evaluate the knowledge of the first wise man we need to formulate the initial circumstances and background knowledge. Let a, b and c be the wise men. It is common knowledge, that each wise man can see the foreheads of the other wise men. The only doubt a wise man has, is whether he has a white spot on his own forehead or not. Additionally, it is common knowledge that at least one of the three wise men has a white spot on his forehead. The rules of the riddle are embedded as follows:[3]

```
consts ws :: "α ⇒ σ"
axiomatization where
  (* Common knowledge: at least one of a, b and c has a white spot *)
  WM1: "⌊C𝒜 (ᴬws a ∨ ᴬws b ∨ ᴬws c)⌋"
  (* Common knowledge: if x has not a white spot then y know this *)
  WM2ab: "⌊C𝒜 (¬(ᴬws a) → Kb(¬(ᴬws a)))⌋"
  WM2ac: "⌊C𝒜 (¬(ᴬws a) → Kc(¬(ᴬws a)))⌋"
  WM2ba: "⌊C𝒜 (¬(ᴬws b) → Ka(¬(ᴬws b)))⌋"
  WM2bc: "⌊C𝒜 (¬(ᴬws b) → Kc(¬(ᴬws b)))⌋"
  WM2ca: "⌊C𝒜 (¬(ᴬws c) → Ka(¬(ᴬws c)))⌋"
  WM2cb: "⌊C𝒜 (¬(ᴬws c) → Kb(¬(ᴬws c)))⌋"
```

Now the king asks *a* whether he knows if he has a white spot or not. Assume that *a* publicly answers that he does not. This is a public announcement of the form: $\neg(\mathrm{K_a}(^{\mathtt{A}}\mathtt{ws\ a})) \vee (\mathrm{K_a}\neg(^{\mathtt{A}}\mathtt{ws\ a}))$. Again, a wise man gets asked by the king whether he knows if he has a white spot or not. Now its *b*'s turn and assume that *b* also announces that he does not know whether he has a white spot on his forehead.[4]

When asked, *c* is able to give the right answer, namely that he has a white spot on his forehead. We can prove this automatically in Isabelle/HOL:

```
theorem whitespot_c:
 "⌊[!¬((Ka(ᴬws a)) ∨ (Ka(¬(ᴬws a)))]([!¬((Kb(ᴬws b)) ∨ (Kb(¬(ᴬws b)))](Kc(ᴬws c)))⌋"
  using WM1 WM2ba WM2ca WM2cb group_S5
  unfolding reflexive_def intersection_rel_def
    union_rel_def sub_rel_def tc_def
  by smt
```

[3] One might also add axioms of the form $\lfloor \mathtt{C}_{\mathcal{A}}\ (^{\mathtt{A}}\mathtt{ws\ x}) \rightarrow \mathrm{K_y}(^{\mathtt{A}}\mathtt{ws\ x})\rfloor$" for $\mathtt{x}, \mathtt{y} \in \mathcal{A}$. This is not necessary as we will see in the proof found using Isabelle/HOL.

[4] The case where neither *a* nor *b* can correctly infer the color of their forehead when being asked by the king is the most challenging case; we only discuss this one here.

6 Comparison with Related Work

In related work [21], van Benthem, van Eijck and colleagues have studied a *"faithful representation of DEL [dynamic epistemic logic] models as so-called knowledge structures that allow for symbolic model checking"*. The authors show that such an approach enables efficient and effective reasoning in epistemic scenarios with state-of-the-art Binary Decision Diagram (BDD) reasoning technology, outperforming other existing methods [25,26] to automate DEL reasoning. Further related work [24] demonstrates how dynamic epistemic terms can be formalized in temporal epistemic terms to apply the model checkers MCK [11] or MCMAS [19]. Our approach differs in various respects, including:

External vs. internal representation transformation: Instead of writing external (e.g. Haskell-)code to realize the required conversions from DEL into Boolean representations, we work with logic-internal conversions into HOL, provided in form of a set of equations stated in HOL itself (thereby heavily exploiting the virtues of λ-abstraction and λ-conversion). Our encoding is concise (only about 50 lines in Isabelle/HOL) and human readable.

Meta-logical reasoning: Since our conversion "code" is provided within the (meta-)logic environment itself, the conversion becomes better controllable and even amenable to formal verification. Moreover, as we have also demonstrated in this paper, meta-logical studies about the embedded logics and their embedding in HOL are well-supported in our approach.

Scalability beyond propositional reasoning: Real world applications often require differentiation between entities/individuals, their properties and functions defined on them, and quantification over entities, or even properties and functions, supports generic statements that are not supported in propositional DEL. The shallow semantical embedding approach, in contrast, very naturally scales for first-order and higher-order extensions of the embedded logics; for more details on this we refer to [4,5] and the references therein.

Reuse of automated theorem proving and model finding technology: Both approaches reuse state-of-the-art automated reasoning technology. In our case this includes world-leading first-order and higher-order theorem provers and model finders already integrated with Isabelle/HOL [9]. These tools in turn internally collaborate with latest SMT and SAT solving technology. The burden to organize and orchestrate the technical communication with and between these tools is taken away from us by reuse of respective solutions as already provided in Isabelle/HOL (and recursively also within the integrated theorem provers). Well established and robustly supported language formats (e.g. TPTP syntax, http://www.tptp.org) are reused in these nested transformations. These cascades of already supported logic transformations are one reason why our embedding approach readily scales for automating reasoning beyond just propositional DEL.

We are convinced, as evidenced by the above discussion, that our approach is particularly well suited for the exploration and rapid prototyping of new logics (and logic combinations) and their embeddings in HOL, and for the study of their meta-logical properties, in particular, when it comes to first-order and higher-order extensions of DEL. At the same time we share with the related work by van Benthem, van Eijck and colleagues a deep interest in practical (object-level) applications, and therefore practical reasoning performance is obviously also of high relevance. In this regard, however, we naturally assume a performance loss in comparison to hand-crafted, specialist solutions. Previous studies in the context of first-order modal logic theorem proving nevertheless have shown that this is not always the case [12]. Future work therefore includes the conduction of comparative performance studies in which the work presented in this paper is compared with the existing alternative approaches.

7 Conclusion

A shallow semantical embedding of public announcement logic with relativized common knowledge in classical higher-order logic has been presented, and our implementation of this embedding in Isabelle/HOL delivers results as expected. In particular, we have shown how model-changing behaviour can be adequately and elegantly addressed in our embedding approach. With reference to uniform substitution, we saw that our embedding enables the study of meta-logical properties of public announcement logic, and object-level reasoning has been demonstrated by a first time automation of the wise men puzzle encoded in public announcement logic with a relativized common knowledge operator.

Further work includes the provision of proofs for the faithfulness of the presented embedding; this should be analogous to prior work, see e.g. [3].

Acknowledgments. We thank David Streit, David Fuenmayor, Arvid Becker and the anonymous reviewers for useful comments, suggestions and feedback to this work.

References

1. Baldoni, M.: Normal multimodal logics: automatic deduction and logic programming extension. Ph.D. thesis, Università degli Studi di Torino, Dipartimento di Informatica (1998)
2. Baltag, A., Renne, B.: Dynamic epistemic logic. In: Zalta, E.N. (ed.) The Stanford Encyclopedia of Philosophy. Metaphysics Research Lab, Stanford University, winter 2016 edition (2016)
3. Benzmüller, C.: Cut-elimination for quantified conditional logic. J. Philos. Logic **46**(3), 333–353 (2017). https://doi.org/10.1007/s10992-016-9403-0
4. Benzmüller, C.: Universal (meta-) logical reasoning: recent successes. Sci. Comput. Program. **172**, 48–62 (2019)
5. Benzmüller, C.: Universal (meta-) logical reasoning: the wise men puzzle (Isabelle/HOL Dataset). Data Brief **24**(103823), 1–5 (2019)
6. Benzmüller, C., Andrews, P.: Church's type theory. In: Zalta, E.N. (ed.) The Stanford Encyclopedia of Philosophy, (in pdf version). Metaphysics Research Lab, Stanford University, summer 2019 edition, pp. 1–62 (2019)

7. Benzmüller, C., Brown, C., Kohlhase, M.: Higher-order semantics and extensionality. J. Symb. Logic **69**(4), 1027–1088 (2004)
8. Benzmüller, C., Miller, D.: Automation of higher-order logic. In: Gabbay, D.M., Siekmann, J.H., Woods, J. (eds.) Handbook of the History of Logic. Computational Logic, vol. 9, pp. 215–254. Elsevier, North Holland (2014)
9. Blanchette, J., Böhme, S., Paulson, L.: Extending sledgehammer with SMT solvers. J. Autom. Reason. **51**, 116–130 (2011)
10. Church, A.: A formulation of the simple theory of types. J. Symb. Logic **5**(2), 56–68 (1940)
11. Gammie, P., van der Meyden, R.: MCK: model checking the logic of knowledge. In: Alur, R., Peled, D.A. (eds.) CAV 2004. LNCS, vol. 3114, pp. 479–483. Springer, Heidelberg (2004). https://doi.org/10.1007/978-3-540-27813-9_41
12. Gleißner, T., Steen, A., Benzmüller, C.: Theorem provers for every normal modal logic. In: Eiter, T., Sands, D. (eds.) LPAR-21. 21st International Conference on Logic for Programming, Artificial Intelligence and Reasoning, volume 46 of EPiC Series in Computing, pp. 14–30. EasyChair, Maun (2017)
13. Gödel, K.: Über formal unentscheidbare Sätze der Principia Mathematica und verwandter Systeme I. Monatshefte für Mathematik und Physik **38**(1), 173–198 (1931). https://doi.org/10.1007/BF01700692
14. Henkin, L.: Completeness in the theory of types. J. Symb. Logic **15**(2), 81–91 (1950)
15. Holliday, W.H., Hoshi, T., Icard, T.F.: Information dynamics and uniform substitution. Synthese **190**(1), 31–55 (2013). https://doi.org/10.1007/s11229-013-0278-0
16. Pacuit, E.: Dynamic epistemic logic i: modeling knowledge and belief. Philos. Comp. **8**(9), 798–814 (2013)
17. Pfenning, F., Elliott, C.: Higher-order abstract syntax. In: Proceedings of the ACM SIGPLAN 1988 Conference on Programming Language Design and Implementation (PLDI), Atlanta, Georgia, USA, 22–24 June 1988, pp. 199–208. ACM (1988)
18. Plaza, J.: Logics of public communications. In: Proceedings of the 4th International Symposium on Methodologies for Intelligent Systems (1989)
19. Raimondi, F., Lomuscio, A.: Verification of multiagent systems via ordered binary decision diagrams: an algorithm and its implementation. In: Proceedings of the Third International Joint Conference on Autonomous Agents and Multiagent Systems, AAMAS 2004, pp. 630–637. IEEE (2004)
20. Tobias Nipkow, M.W., Paulson, L.C.: Isabelle/HOL: A Proof Assistant for Higher-Order Logic. Springer, Heidelberg (2002). https://doi.org/10.1007/3-540-45949-9
21. van Benthem, J., van Eijck, J., Gattinger, M., Su, K.: Symbolic model checking for dynamic epistemic logic - S5 and beyond. J. Log. Comp. **28**(2), 367–402 (2018)
22. van Benthem, J., van Eijck, J., Kooi, B.: Logics of communication and change. Inf. Comput. **204**(11), 1620–1662 (2006)
23. van Ditmarsch, H., Halpern, J.Y., van Der Hoek, W., Kooi, B.: An introduction to logics of knowledge and belief. In: Handbook of Epistemic Logic, pp. 1–51 (2015)
24. van Ditmarsch, H., van der Hoek, W., van der Meyden, R., Ruan, J.: Model checking Russian cards. ENTCS **149**(2), 105–123 (2006)
25. van Eijck, J.: Demo-a demo of epistemic modelling. In: Interactive Logic. Selected Papers from the 7th Augustus de Morgan Workshop, London (2007). http://homepages.cwi.nl/~jve/papers/07/pdfs/DEMO_IL.pdf
26. van Eijck, J.: Demo-s5. Technical report, CWI (2014). http://homepages.cwi.nl/~jve/software/demo_s5

Bounded Multi-agent Reasoning: Actualizing Distributed Knowledge

Anthia Solaki(✉)

ILLC, University of Amsterdam, Amsterdam, The Netherlands
a.solaki2@uva.nl

Abstract. The idealizations resulting from the use of Kripke semantics in Epistemic Logic are inherited by formalizations of group epistemic notions. For example, *distributed knowledge* (DK) is often taken to reflect the potential knowledge of a group: what agents *would* know if they had unbounded means of communication and deductive ability. However, this does not specify whether/how this potential can be actualized, especially since real people are not unbounded reasoners. Inspired by experiments on group reasoning, we identify two dimensions of actualizing DK: communication and inference. We build a dynamic framework with effortful actions accounting for both, combining *impossible-worlds semantics* and *action models*, and we provide a method for extracting a sound and complete axiomatization.

1 Introduction

Epistemic Logic (EL), seen as a normal modal logic (usually S5), has been used in the study of multi-agent systems, modelling not only the individual knowledge of each agent, but also collective epistemic notions. For example, a group is said to have *common knowledge* (CK) of ϕ whenever everybody knows that everybody knows (ad infinitum) that ϕ, and *distributed knowledge* (DK) of ϕ whenever agents can deduce ϕ by pooling their knowledge together. With the tools of *Dynamic Epistemic Logic* (DEL), we can further capture the communicative actions giving rise to them, e.g. actions actualizing DK and converting it into CK.

However, EL is often criticized on grounds of idealization: its predictions are practically unattainable by real agents. This has implications for collective notions. It can well be that members of a group do not know all logical consequences of their knowledge (e.g. because of memory overload) or do not take all necessary communicative actions (e.g. because of time pressure). The same constraints apply to higher-order reasoning as agents cannot ascribe knowledge to others to an infinite modal depth. Group reasoning is a dynamic, mixed task that requires actions of both inference and communication. These are not always affordable by human agents, given their cognitive limitations. Therefore, the evolution of reasoning is bounded by agents' resources. Even from a normative viewpoint, it makes sense to study what can be *feasibly* asked of them.

M. A. Martins and I. Sedlár (Eds.): DaLí 2020, LNCS 12569, pp. 239–258, 2020.
https://doi.org/10.1007/978-3-030-65840-3_15

This is corroborated by empirical findings. In deductive reasoning tasks people often have trouble applying certain inference rules. Perhaps the best known task is the *Wason selection task* [34]:

> Four cards are given to the participants. Each card has a number on one side and a letter on the other. The visible sides of the cards read A, K, 4, and 7. The participants are asked which cards need to be turned to check whether the following holds: *if a card has a vowel on one side, it has an even number on the other.*

Individuals do notoriously bad in the task, although it involves just applications of Modus Ponens and Modus Tollens. This has given rise to theories in psychology of reasoning, explaining the asymmetry between the cognitive difficulty of different inferences [24,28]. Other findings study the difficulty of reasoning about others [32]. Group variants of deductive tasks similarly reveal limits in group reasoning. Nonetheless, they also allow us to track which actions underlie successful performance and the effort they require. Its distribution among members often yields better performance compared to the individual case [21,30].

In light of this, we can revisit group epistemic notions from the perspective of non-ideal agents. Using DEL, we can specify the intertwined effortful actions (communicative and inferential) that refine group knowledge, in accord with empirical facts. Revisiting DK is a first step because of the implicit flavour underlying its understanding as what *would* be known, *if* the agents were to pool their knowledge and deduce information on its basis. In revisiting DK, we need to specify (i) which actions may "actualize" it, i.e. turn it into (explicit) mutual knowledge of the group, and (ii) to what extent these can be undertaken, given that agents are bounded.

The first type of actions is *communicative actions*. Subtleties underpinning the understanding of DK as the outcome of some (unlimited) communication among group members have been discussed in [18,29,36]. The latter consider the formula $p \wedge \neg K_{a_1} p$: p is true but a_1 does not know it. The formula $D_G(p \wedge \neg K_{a_1} p)$, where G is a group including a_1, is consistent in extensions of EL with D_G operators standing for DK. Yet no communication could render this mutual knowledge of G. The problem lies in that the formula is evaluated in a model that does not explicitly encode the effect of information pooling taking place. The operation introduced by the authors to fill this gap is called *resolution* and it is similar to operations in [6,11].

Since our goal is to do justice to non-ideal agents, we should further account for the extent to which resolution can be undertaken. This has implications for the second type of actions too, namely *inferential actions*. There is more than pooling information together that occurs in group deliberations, but unlike communication, the deductive reasoning of group members is usually neglected in multi-agent EL, whereby agents automatically know all consequences of their knowledge. As with communication, we want to encode explicitly the inferential actions of group members, and the extent to which these can be undertaken.

Outline. In Sect. 2, we present our framework accounting for how agents actualize DK under resource-bounds, using a novel combination of *impossible-worlds semantics* [12] and *action models* [5]. We illustrate its workings in Sect. 3 and provide a method for the extraction of a sound and complete axiomatization in Sect. 4.

2 The Framework

2.1 Syntax

The logical language of our framework extends that of standard multi-agent epistemic logics. Given a non-empty set of agents Ag, it includes:

- i Quantitative comparisons between terms that are introduced to capture cognitive costs of actions (communicative, inferential) with the cognitive capacities of agents.
- ii Operators D_G, standing for the *distributed knowledge* of group $G \subseteq Ag$.
- iii Operators A_j, where $j \in Ag$, that indicate the inference rules that agent j has acknowledged as truth-preserving (similar to [16,31,35]).
- iv Operators $\langle R_G \rangle$, standing for *resolution* of group G, i.e. actions of communication through which members pool their knowledge together (in the spirit of operations appearing in [6,11,36]).
- v Operators of the form $\langle C, e \rangle$, where e is an *event* in *action model* C designed to capture applications of inference rules in a multi-agent setting.

In order to define the language formally we need the following two prerequisites. Given the propositional language $\mathcal{L}_P$ based on a set of atoms P:

Definition 2.1 (Rule). *An inference rule* ρ *is of the form* $\{\phi_1, \dots, \phi_n\} \rightsquigarrow \psi$ *where* $\phi_1, \dots, \phi_n, \psi \in \mathcal{L}_P$.

Inference rules should be read as *whenever every formula in* $\{\phi_1, \dots, \phi_n\}$ *is true, so is* ψ (as in [31, Chapter 2]). We use $pr(\rho)$ and $con(\rho)$ to abbreviate, respectively, the set of premises and the conclusion of ρ. The set of rules is denoted by $\mathcal{L}_R$.

Definition 2.2 (Terms). *The set of terms* T *is defined as* $T := \{c_\rho \mid \rho \in \mathcal{L}_R\} \cup \{c_G \mid G \subseteq Ag\} \cup \{cp_j \mid j \in Ag\}$. *It contains elements for (i) the cognitive costs of rule applications (of the form* c_ρ*), (ii) cognitive costs of resolution among members of groups (of the form* c_G*), (iii) cognitive capacities of agents (of the form* cp_j*).*

Definition 2.3 (Language). *With the above in place, language* $\mathcal{L}$ *is given by:*

$$\phi ::= p \mid z_1 s_1 + \ldots + z_n s_n \geq z \mid \neg\phi \mid \phi \wedge \psi \mid A_j\rho \mid D_G\phi \mid \langle R_G\rangle\phi \mid \langle C, e\rangle\phi$$

where $p \in P$, $z_1, \dots, z_n \in \mathbb{Z}$, $z \in \mathbb{Z}^r$, $s_1, \dots, s_n \in T$, $\rho \in \mathcal{L}_R$. *The dynamic operators are,* $\langle R_G \rangle$ *for resolution, and* $\langle C, e \rangle$*, where* C *is an action model and* e *an* *event of C. We will specify the effect of dynamic operators later when presenting the semantics; for now they should be thought as operators for communication and inference respectively.*[1]

Examples of Formulas. The formula $(cp_j \geq c_\rho) \wedge A_j\rho$ says that (i) the cognitive capacity of agent j (to which the term cp_j corresponds) is greater or equal than the cognitive cost of a rule ρ (to which the term c_ρ corresponds), and (ii) the agent j has acknowledged rule ρ as truth-preserving. Individual knowledge of an agent j is defined in terms of DK as $K_j := D_{\{j\}}$. A formula like $\langle C, e\rangle K_j\phi$ says that after the event e of the action model C takes place, the agent j knows that ϕ.

2.2 Resource-Sensitive Epistemic Models

In order to interpret these formulas, we define a resource-sensitive epistemic model and suitable model updates, induced by actions of resolution and inference, corresponding to the effect of our dynamic operators $\langle R_G\rangle$ and $\langle C, e\rangle$.

Our models supplement Kripke models with *impossible worlds* and cognitive components. Impossible worlds, unlike possible ones, are not closed under logical consequence, to do justice to the fallibility of agents as real people might entertain some inconsistent/incomplete scenarios. Yet by taking reasoning steps, to the extent they can cognitively afford them, they can gradually eliminate some of them. To start with, we impose *Minimal Consistency*: we rule out explicit contradictions, in line with the literature on *Minimal Rationality* [14].

For the other components, we first need to parameterize our models by *Res*, denoting the set of resources (*time*, *memory*, *attention* etc.) we want to consider. Then $r := |Res|$ is the number of these resources. Another parameter concerns the cognitive effort of the agents w.r.t. each resource. The *cost function* $c : \mathcal{L}_R \cup \mathcal{P}(Ag) \rightarrow \mathbb{N}^r$ assigns a *cognitive cost* to (i) each inference rule, (ii) each group, w.r.t. each resource. That is, cost is a vector (as in [2]), used to indicate the units consumed per resource for actions of inference and resolution. We use the notation c_k, $k = 1, \ldots, r$ to refer to the value of the k-th element of the vector and we assume that the first resource, hence the first element of the vector, concerns *time*. Concrete assignments of costs rely on empirical research. This is because the cognitive difficulty of reasoning tasks is often explained in

[1] The choice of number r is discussed in the next subsection. Formulas involving $\vee, \rightarrow, \leq, =, -$ can be defined in terms of the rest. This is why formulas like $cp_j \geq c_\rho$ or $cp_j \geq c_G$ are well-formed in this language.

terms of the number and the kind of the rules that have to be applied, also considering the different response times of people in different inferences [28] and memory constraints [15].[2]

With the above fixed, we introduce *cognitive capacity* to the model to capture the agents' available power w.r.t. each resource. As resources are depleted while reasoning evolves, capacity will not remain constant, but it may change as a result of actions of inference or resolution, that require effort by agents uncovering new information. This is because cognitive capacity w.r.t. certain resources, like memory, is correlated with deductive reasoning performance [7]. Overall:

Definition 2.4 (Resource-sensitive model (RSM)). *Given parameters* Res *and* c*, a RSM is a tuple* $M := \langle W^P, W^I, \{\sim_j\}_{j\in Ag}, V_P, V_I, R, \{cp_j\}_{j\in Ag}\rangle$ *where:*

- W^P *and* W^I *are sets of possible and impossible worlds, respectively.*
- *Each* $\sim_j$ *is an epistemic accessibility relation imposed on* $W := W^P \cup W^I$*, that is, a binary relation on* W*.*
- $V_P : W^P \to \mathcal{P}(P)$ *is a valuation function assigning to each possible world, the propositional atoms that are true there.*
- $V_I : W^I \to \mathcal{P}(\mathcal{L})$ *is a valuation function assigning to each impossible world, the formulas (atomic or complex) that are true there.*
- $R : W \times Ag \to \mathcal{P}(\mathcal{L}_R)$ *is a function that assigns to each pair of a world and an agent the rules that the agent has acknowledged there.*
- $cp_j \in \mathbb{Z}^r$ *stands for the cognitive capacity of each agent, i.e. what* j *can afford w.r.t. each resource. As a convention, we will consider that time is always a resource and the first component of the vector of* cp_j *refers to it.*

Each RSM comes parameterized by Res and c, yet we will not explicitly write them down as components of the model. This is to serve simplicity of notation but also to emphasize that these, unlike cp, are not meant to be modified in the aftermath of our actions.

Model Conditions. To fulfill *Minimal Consistency* we ask: $\{\phi, \neg\phi\} \not\subseteq V_I(w)$, for any $w \in W^I$ and $\phi \in \mathcal{L}$. To ensure that acknowledged inference rules are truth-preserving, we impose *Soundness of inference rules*: for $w \in W^P, j \in Ag$: $\rho \in R(w, j)$ implies $M, w \models tr(\rho)$ where $tr(\rho) := \bigwedge_{\phi\in pr(\rho)} \phi \to con(\rho)$.[3]

[2] Notice that different schools (e.g. *Mental Logic* [28], *Mental Models* [24]) point at different "measures" for the difficulty of deductive tasks; still, the very observation that not all inferences require equal effort is uncontroversial. Since this debate is not settled in the empirical realm, we have not committed to any view on cost assignments. Instead, we focus on providing the machinery to embed such features in formal logical modelling.

[3] We focus on truth-preserving rules because we accept the factivity of knowledge. Besides, this is one of the features distinguishing knowledge from belief, according to most theories of knowledge. However, notice that other notions, like belief, could be developed through non-truth-preserving inferences as well.

It is common in EL to ask that epistemic relations are reflexive, symmetric and transitive, properties that correspond to properties of knowledge: factivity, positive and negative introspection. In what follows, we will impose reflexivity (and thus factivity); still, we abstain from assuming unlimited introspection, thus from asking that relations are symmetric and transitive. In the context of resource-bounded agents, it is reasonable to extend considerations of non-ideal performance to higher-order reasoning as well.

Before we proceed to model updates, we define the truth clauses for the static fragment, i.e. $\mathcal{L}$ without $\langle R_G \rangle$ and $\langle C, e \rangle$ operators. To do that, we first need to interpret the terms in T. The intuition is that those of the form c_ρ and c_G correspond to the cognitive costs of rules and group resolution (respectively), and those of the form cp_j to the cognitive capacities of agents. This is why cp_j is used both as a model component and as a term of the language. The use can be understood from the context. Notice that our intended reading of $\geq$ is that $s \geq t$ iff *every* k-th component of s is greater or equal than the k-th component of t.

Definition 2.5 (Interpretation of terms). *Given a model M, the terms of T are interpreted as follows:* $c_\rho^M = c(\rho)$, $c_G^M = c(G)$ *and* $cp_j^M = cp_j$.

Definition 2.6 (Static truth clauses). *Take* $\sim_G := \bigcap_{j \in G} \sim_j$, *for* $G \subseteq Ag$.

$$
\begin{array}{lll}
 & M,w \models p & \textit{iff } p \in V_P(w) \\
 & M,w \models z_1 s_1 + \ldots + z_n s_n \geq z & \textit{iff } z_1 s_1^M + \ldots + z_n s_n^M \geq z \\
\textit{For } w \in W^P: & M,w \models \neg\phi & \textit{iff } M,w \not\models \phi \\
 & M,w \models \phi \wedge \psi & \textit{iff } M,w \models \phi \textit{ and } M,w \models \psi \\
 & M,w \models A_j \rho & \textit{iff } \rho \in R(w,j) \\
 & M,w \models D_G \phi & \textit{iff } M,u \models \phi \textit{ for all } u : w \sim_G u \\
\textit{For } w \in W^I: & M,w \models \phi & \textit{iff } \phi \in V_I(w)
\end{array}
$$

In impossible worlds, formulas are evaluated directly (i.e. not recursively) by the valuation function. Notice that the clause for D_G is given through the intersection of relations of G members (as in DEL), but it now quantifies over possible *and* impossible worlds, hence leaving room for deductively imperfect agents and groups. A formula is said to be *valid in a model* iff it is true at all possible worlds.

2.3 Resolution

We use resolution as the action that captures how information is pooled by group members, thereby enhancing the group's knowledge. As in [36], resolution is understood as publicly known private communication among members.[4] The resolution of group G induces a model update such that an epistemic relation

[4] There are alternative understandings compatible with our framework, e.g. generalizations where agents share all they know with different sets of agents [6]. This might allow to break down the effect of resolution into the incremental sharing actions of the members and study their possibly asymmetrical contribution in actualizing DK. This is left for future work.

for a member of G is the intersection of relations of the members of G, and it remains intact for the rest. Moreover resolution might come at a cost. It can be that "pooling" is effortless, e.g. because information is shared within the group for "free". However, it can be that adopting a piece of private information through a publicly known action requires effort, e.g. because the group is too big.[5] One way to formally account for this effort is as follows: resolution incurs a non-zero cost on cognitive capacity for members of G, but also a cost w.r.t. *time* (and only time) for agents outside G (as time passes while G deliberates). The model update of resolution is below:

Definition 2.7 (Resolution). *Given RSM* $M = \langle W^P, W^I, \sim_j, V_P, V_I, R, cp_j\rangle$, *the resolution of group* G *produces a new RSM* $M_G := \langle W^P, W^I, \sim'_j, V_P, V_I, R, cp'_j\rangle$ *where:*

$$\sim'_j = \begin{cases} \bigcap_{i \in G} \sim_i, & \text{if } j \in G \\ \sim_j, & \text{otherwise} \end{cases} \qquad cp'_j = \begin{cases} cp_j - c(G), & \text{for } j \in G \\ cp_j - (c_1(G), \ldots, 0), & \text{otherwise} \end{cases}$$

The conditions of RSMs are preserved by this definition. Resolution formulas are interpreted as follows. For $w \in W$:

$$M, w \models \langle R_G \rangle \phi \text{ iff } M, w \models (cp_i \geq c_G) \text{ for all } i \in G \text{ and } M_G, w \models \phi$$

i.e. the "precondition" of resolving knowledge among the group G is that the action is cognitively affordable to everyone in the group.

2.4 Inference

Action Models. Action models are used in DEL to represent complex informational actions [5]. They usually include (i) a set of events E, (ii) a binary relation $\approx_j$ on E for each agent, representing her uncertainty regarding events taking place, (iii) a *precondition function pre* assigning a formula to each event, to indicate what is required for the event to occur. A common example is *(semi-) private announcements*, whereby only some agents find out something while the rest do not. In this attempt, we design novel action models to represent the inferential steps of agents in a multi-agent context. For example, the events in our action models can represent rule applications. They will too contain relations $\approx_j$ and a precondition function $pre : E \to \mathcal{L}$. However, we need additional components to capture the effect of inferential actions on RSMs, since the latter also have additional components compared to plain Kripke models. More specifically:

- a second type of precondition $pre\_imp : E \to \mathcal{P}(\mathcal{L})$ that indicates which formulas should be represented by the impossible worlds entertained by the agent(s) acting in an event e. The rough idea is to impose a "measure" on the impossibilities they may entertain in order to qualify for a rule-application.

[5] It has been argued that there are two different kinds of such informational events, "implicit" and "explicit" [9,10]. This fits well with distinctions in the philosophical and linguistic literature [8] between *bare seeing* ("naked infinitives") and *seeing-that*, which additionally implies epistemic awareness of the fact described.

■ a *postcondition* function $pos : Ag \times \mathcal{P}(\mathcal{L}) \times E \rightarrow \mathcal{P}(\mathcal{L})$ that will allow us to capture the effect of each event on the valuation of impossible worlds.

■ a *cognitive capacity postcondition*, of the form $pos\_cp : Ag \times \mathbb{Z}^r \rightarrow \mathbb{Z}^r$, that will allow us to capture the effect of actions on cognitive capacities of agents.

■ for notational convenience, a *label* function assigning to each event which rule, if any, is applied and who the "actors" are. For example, if event e_1 stands for an application of ρ only by agent a_1, its label is $(\rho, \{a_1\})$ indicating that the applied rule is ρ and its actor is a_1. If the event represents that nothing happens, its label is $(\emptyset, \emptyset)$: no inferential step occurs and (naturally) no one undertakes it. The label function is of the form $lab : E \rightarrow (\mathcal{L}_R \cup \{\emptyset\}) \times \mathcal{P}(Ag)$.

Definition 2.8 (Action model for inference). *An action model C is a tuple $\langle E, \approx_j, pre, pre\_imp, pos, pos\_cp, lab\rangle$, with the components as above.*

Consider the group selection task; Modus Ponens is applied by all agents, as evinced by the reported dialogues of participants, e.g. in [21, p. 237], [30, p. 15–17]. We capture this type of inferential action with the action model below:

Inference by all (C_{ALL}). This action model captures that *all* agents perform the same reasoning step, the application of a rule ρ, e.g. a Modus Ponens instance. It comprises one event e_1, and clearly $lab(e_1) = \{\rho, Ag\}$. The precondition is that everybody knows the premises of ρ, has it available and has enough cognitive capacity to apply it. The precondition of impossibility is such that impossible worlds should at least represent the premises of ρ. The postcondition is used to show that agents can add the conclusion in their epistemic state through this rule-application, while the postcondition on capacity reduces it by the cost of ρ (Fig. 1).

$$pre(e_1) = \bigwedge_{j \in Ag} \bigwedge_{\phi \in pr(\rho)} K_j\phi \wedge \bigwedge_{j \in Ag} A_j\rho \wedge \bigwedge_{j \in Ag} (cp_j \geq c_\rho) \quad pos(j, X, e_1) = X \cup \{con(\rho)\}$$

$$pre\_imp(e_1) = pr(\rho) \quad pos\_cp(j, n) = n - c(\rho)$$

Fig. 1. The action model for an inference of ρ performed by all.

But back to the group selection task: not all agents apply Modus Tollens. In many groups, only one member applies it and figures out that 7 should be turned [21, p. 238, 241]. In [30, p. 18–20], some dyads succeed because there is a member with background in logic who has the rule available and affordable and thus applies it. This is captured by another type of action model:

Inference by some (C_{SOME}). It is not uncommon that only *some* agents ($G \subset Ag$) perform a rule unbeknownst to agents in $Ag \setminus G$ who do not. For simplicity, we design the action model in the case where *one* agent applies a rule ρ, but the design can be generalized to other subsets of Ag. The action model comprises two events, e_1 to represent the application of the rule by a (hence, $lab(e_1) = (\rho, \{a\})$)

and e_0 to represent that nothing happens (hence, $lab(e_0) = (\emptyset, \emptyset)$). The latter is needed to capture that agents other than a are uncertain about the content of their peer's action (the rule-application). The precondition for e_1 is that a knows the premises of the rule, has the rule available and has enough cognitive capacity to apply it. For e_0 it is just $\top$, as nothing happens. The precondition of impossibility in e_1 is such that impossible worlds should at least represent the premises of the rule ρ, while for e_0 it is the empty set. The postcondition will be used to show that the actor can add the conclusion of ρ in her epistemic state, while nothing changes for the other agents. The cognitive postcondition is such that only the cognitive capacity of the actor is reduced by the cognitive cost of applying ρ, while for the non-actors only time is consumed (Fig. 2).

$$pre(e) = \begin{cases} \bigwedge_{\phi \in pr(\rho)} K_a\phi \wedge A_a\rho \wedge (cp_a \geq c_\rho), \text{ if } e = e_1 \\ \top, \text{ if } e = e_0 \end{cases}$$

$$pre\_imp(e) = \begin{cases} pr(\rho) \text{ if } e = e_1 \\ \emptyset, \text{ if } e = e_0 \end{cases}$$

$$pos(j, X, e) = \begin{cases} X \cup \{con(\rho)\}, \text{if } j = a, e = e_1 \\ X, \text{ otherwise} \end{cases}$$

$$pos\_cp(j, n) = \begin{cases} n - c(\rho), \text{ if } j = a \\ n - (c_1(\rho), \ldots, 0), \text{ otherwise} \end{cases}$$

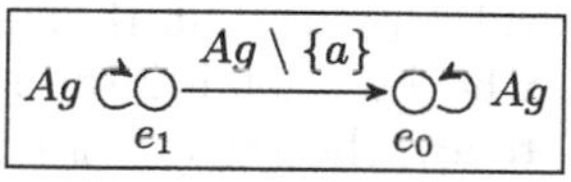

Fig. 2. The action model for an inference of ρ performed by a unbeknownst to the rest.

Product Models. We now define *product models*, i.e. the model updates induced by the inferential actions. Our RSMs have additional components compared to simple Kripke models, like the set of impossible worlds and the cognitive capacity, which should be also modified according to the effect of the actions. Roughly, impossible worlds entertained by actors of inference rules can be eliminated – if their inconsistency is uncovered by applying the rule – or become enriched because, through rule applications, actors come to know the conclusion of the rule. Moreover, cognitive capacities of agents are reduced by the suitable cost. We will describe the model transformations by actions of inference, i.e. the product models, component by component. First we need certain abbreviations:

Abbreviations. Given a RSM M and a world w in W^P we take:

$$[\sim_j (w)] := \{u \in W^I \mid w \sim_j u\} \qquad [\sim (w)]_G = \bigcup_{j \in G} [\sim_j (w)] \qquad [\sim]_G = \bigcup_{u \in W^P} [\sim (u)]_G$$

These abbreviations capture, respectively, which impossible worlds are accessible from w for agent j, for group G, and the ones overall entertained by G. Given a model M and a rule ρ we also need an abbreviation to talk about impossible worlds that *will* become inadmissible, given Minimal Consistency, once ρ is applied: $[MC]^{\rho} := \{w \in W^I \mid \neg con(\rho) \in V_I(w)$ or $con(\rho) = \neg\phi$, for some $\phi \in V_I(w)\}$. Next, given a model M and an action model C: $[MC]^e = \begin{cases} [MC]^{\rho} \cap [\sim]_{lab_2(e)}, & \text{if } lab_1(e) = \rho \\ \emptyset, & \text{otherwise} \end{cases}$.

This allows us to talk about the impossible worlds that will be uncovered as inadmissible by an occurrence of e. For example, if the event represents a ρ-application, then this set of worlds will contain those worlds susceptible to Minimal Consistency that are also entertained by the actors (those who do apply the rule).[6] The components of the product model are then built as follows:

- the new set $(W^P)'$ consists of pairs of possible worlds and events, such that the world satisfies the precondition of the event.
- the new set $(W^I)'$ consists of pairs of impossible worlds and events, such that the world satisfies the precondition of impossibility and it is not ruled out by Minimal Consistency. That is, if an event e represents a rule-application, the impossible worlds which are paired with it are the ones that survive the rule-application. If an impossible world lies in the epistemic state of an actor who by applying the rule unveils that she initially entertained an inconsistency, then that world will not give rise to such a pair.
- The valuation V'_P is simply V_P restricted to the surviving possible worlds.
- The valuation V'_I is given as follows with the help of the postcondition function: if the pair $(w, e) \in (W^I)'$ lies in the epistemic state of an actor, who applies ρ, then its valuation is extended by the conclusion of ρ: the agent came to know the conclusion via the rule-application. Otherwise, the valuation should not be extended, since the epistemic states of non-acting agents should not change: *they* do not come to know the conclusion.
- R' is simply R restricted to the surviving worlds.
- The new cognitive capacity is given through the capacity postcondition. That is, the capacities of non-actors remain unchanged as they did not make any cognitive effort, with the exception of time (which is consumed anyway). However, actors' capacity is reduced by the cost of the rule-application.

Definition 2.9 (Product model). *Let M be a RSM and C an action model. The product model $M \otimes C$ is a tuple $\langle (W^P)', (W^I)', \sim'_j, V'_P, V'_I, R', cp'_j \rangle$ where:*

$$
\begin{array}{ll}
(W^P)' & = \{(w,e) \in W^P \times E \mid M, w \models pre(e)\} \\
(W^I)' & = \{(w,e) \in W^I \times E \mid pre\_imp(e) \subseteq V_I(w) \text{ and } w \notin [MC]^e\} \\
(w,e) \sim'_j (w',e') & \text{iff } w \sim_j w' \text{ and } e \approx_j e') \\
V'_P(w,e) & = V_P(w), \text{ for } (w,e) \in (W^P)' \\
V'_I(w,e) & = \begin{cases} pos(j, V_I(w), e) \text{ with } j \in lab_2(e), \text{ if } w \in \bigcup_{(u,x) \in (W^P)'} [\sim (u)]_{lab_2(e)} \\ pos(j, V_I(w), e), \text{ with } j \notin lab_2(e), \text{ otherwise} \end{cases} \text{ for } (w,e) \in (W^I)' \\
R'((w,e),j) & = R(w,j), \text{ for } (w,e) \in W' \text{ where } W' = (W^P)' \cup (W^I)' \\
cp'_j & = pos\_cp(j, cp_j)
\end{array}
$$

[6] For example, if an impossible world w represents $p, p \rightarrow q, \neg q$ and is entertained by all agents, and event e_1 represents the application of $MP = \{p, p \rightarrow q\} \rightsquigarrow q$, then w will be contained in $[MC]^{e_1}$. This world will become inadmissible by an e_1 occurrence, because its inconsistency is uncovered by the application of the rule.

Then the semantic interpretation for operators $\langle C, e\rangle$ is given below. For $w \in W$:

$$M, w \models \langle C, e\rangle\phi \text{ iff } M, w \models pre(e) \text{ and } M \otimes C, (w, e) \models \phi$$

3 Discussion

We now see these constructions in action and discuss features of the framework.

*Example 3.1 (**Dyad selection task**).* For this variant of the task, we focus on two agents, each knowing the visible side of *one* card. The first (a_1) sees the letter card A, and the second (a_2) sees the number card 7.[7]

Language. Denote "card 1 has a vowel" with v_1 and "card 1 has an even number" with e_1. Likewise, v_2 (respectively, e_2) stand for "card 2 has a vowel (even number)". Abbreviate the formulas $v_i \to e_i$ for $i = 1, 2$ with *COND*. Also, $MP := \{v_1 \to e_1, v_1\} \rightsquigarrow e_1$ and $MT := \{v_2 \to e_2, \neg e_2\} \rightsquigarrow \neg v_2$.

Initial Model. The model representing that a_1 knows the content of the letter card and a_2 knows that of the number card is Fig. 3 (left). The formulas of *COND* are true throughout all worlds. Since agents are fallible, at the beginning they only know what they see (the visible sides) – they have not immediately put their observations together nor have they inferred immediately what lies in the back of the cards. The impossible (incomplete) worlds representing the combinations of letter and number on the first and the second card are:

- w_2: the first card depicts a vowel and the second card an even number.
- w_3: the first card depicts a vowel and the second card an odd number.
- w_4: the first card depicts a consonant and the second card an even number.
- w_5: the first card depicts a consonant and the second card an odd number.

We draw these worlds as rectangles and write down all formulas true there, to distinguish them from the real (possible) world (w_1), where we write the atoms that are true there, namely v_1, e_1 (thus $\neg e_2, \neg v_2$ are also true as possible worlds are maximal consistent alternatives). The epistemic relations represent the uncertainty of agents w.r.t. the card they have not seen. There are also reflexive and transitive arrows, not drawn for simplicity. Moreover, for $Res = \{time, memory\}$, take $cp(a_1) = (6, 6), cp(a_2) = (6, 4)$. Both agents have acknowledged MP, but only a_1 has acknowledged MT. Finally, $c(MP) = (1, 2)$, $c(MT) = (3, 2)$ as MT is provably more difficult than MP, and $c(G) = (1, 1)$, for the cost of resolution of $G = \{a_1, a_2\}$.

[7] The framework can also be applied to the *Shadow-Box experiment* [23], investigating the synthesis of disparate points of view. For example, [1] sees learning as a social process of belief revision of interacting agents and draws connections between the Shadow-Box and variants of selection tasks whereby agents have access to different part of the world (set of cards).

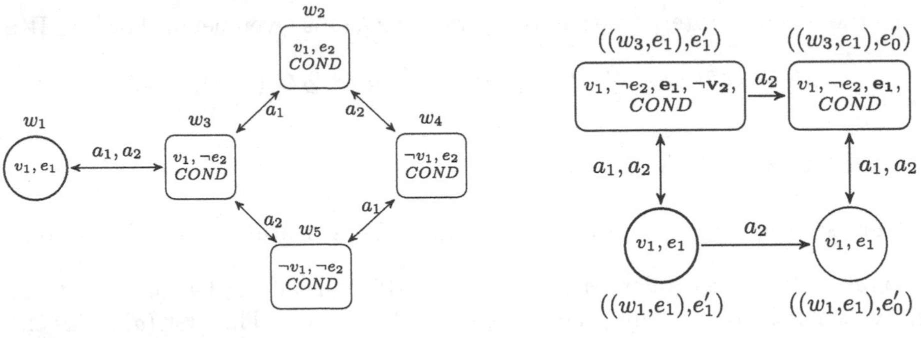

Fig. 3. The initial model M and the updated pointed model $(M_{fin}, ((w_1, e_1), e_1'))$

Actions. Afterwards, both agents share their observations. This is captured via resolution. This can be undertaken because $cp(a_i) \geq c(G)$, for $i = 1, 2$. However, it reduces capacities to $(5, 5)$ and $(5, 3)$ respectively. Then, all agents apply MP (captured by an action model C_1), since they both have the rule available and affordable, in accord with the experimental dialogues [21,30]. Their capacities become $(4, 3)$ and $(4, 1)$. However, only a_1 applies MT, having the rule available and affordable. This is in accord with the dialogues and captured by an action model C_2. Her capacity becomes $(1, 1)$, while a_2's becomes $(1, 1)$ too.

Final Model. The final pointed model is depicted in Fig. 3. We have $M_{fin} := (M_G \otimes C_1) \otimes C_2$, resulting from a resolution update (M_G) and then from product updates with C_1 amd C_2. As a result, $M_{fin}, ((w_1.e_1).e_1') \models K_{a_1} e_1 \wedge K_{a_1} \neg v_2 \wedge K_{a_2} e_1 \wedge \neg K_{a_2} \neg v_2$, so $M, w_1 \models \langle R_G \rangle \langle C_1, e_1 \rangle \langle C_2, e_1' \rangle (K_{a_1} e_1 \wedge K_{a_1} \neg v_2 \wedge K_{a_2} e_1 \wedge \neg K_{a_2} \neg v_2)$.

Further Development. After another resolution round, a_2 will also come to know $\neg v_2$, since she can afford *that* action (pooling information a_1 derived earlier). This corresponds naturally to the dialogues in [21, p. 238–240] and [30, p. 16, 19], where the member who figures out that 7 should be turned shares the newly deduced information. Notice that a_2 could use resolution, but not MT; at the end, she did not have to apply MT herself, because her teammate did so, and all she had to do is communicate with her. Had the group not shared their information they would not have reported the correct solution; had a_2 reasoned alone, her resources would not have allowed her to reach the solution. This illustrates one way in which reasoning in groups facilitates performance in tasks that are more challenging on the individual level.

Our framework models the crucial interplay of resolution and inference, also evident in tasks like the *Shadow-Box experiment* or interdisciplinary research itself. One member might provide input information and another the means (e.g. a proof strategy) to reach a result that would not have been reached if members worked alone. Scientific quests largely depend on gathering suitable information and deriving more on its basis to actualize scientific potential. However, this process is effortful; resolving and deducing comes with a cognitive cost.

We present some validities and invalidities, as further basis of discussion. The full-fledged proofs for all theorems that follow are omitted for brevity.

Theorem 3.1 (Some validities). $\models D_G\langle R_G\rangle\phi \leftrightarrow \langle R_G\rangle E_G\phi$ *where* $E_G := \bigwedge_{j\in G} K_j$

$$\models \bigwedge_{j\in Ag}\bigwedge_{\phi\in pr(\rho)} K_j\phi \wedge \bigwedge_{j\in Ag} A_j\rho \wedge \bigwedge_{j\in Ag}(cp_j \geq c_\rho) \rightarrow \langle C_{ALL}, e_1\rangle E_{Ag}con(\rho) \text{ where } lab_1(e_1) = \rho$$

$$\models \bigwedge_{\phi\in pr(\phi)} D_G\langle R_G\rangle\phi \wedge A_j\rho \wedge (cp_j \geq c_G + c_\rho) \rightarrow \langle R_G\rangle\langle C_{SOME}, e_1\rangle K_j con(\rho) \text{ where } j \in G, lab_1(e_1) = \rho, j \in lab_2(e_1)$$

$$\models \bigwedge_{\phi\in pr(\phi)} D_{Ag}\langle R_{Ag}\rangle\phi \wedge \bigwedge_{j\in Ag} A_j\rho \wedge \bigwedge_{j\in Ag}(cp_j \geq c_{Ag} + c_\rho) \rightarrow \langle R_{Ag}\rangle\langle C_{ALL}, e_1\rangle E_{Ag}con(\rho) \text{ where } lab_1(e_1) = \rho$$

The first validity pertains to the effect of resolution on the understanding of DK (as in [36]) showing that after a group resolves their knowledge, ϕ is known by its members. The second captures the effect of actions of inference. The agents do not immediately know all logical consequences of their knowledge: they have to undertake effortful reasoning steps. The other validities encapsulate the interplay of communication and inference: once members resolve their knowledge and come to know the premises, then those who apply the rule, come to know the conclusion as well. Contrary to these, we escape features of idealized agents:

Theorem 3.2 (Some invalidities).

$$\not\models D_G\phi \rightarrow \langle R_G\rangle E_G\phi \qquad \not\models D_G\langle R_G\rangle\phi \rightarrow \langle R_G\rangle E_G E_G\phi \qquad \not\models \bigwedge_{\phi\in pr(\rho)} D_G\phi \rightarrow D_G con(\rho)$$

$$\not\models \bigwedge_{\phi\in pr(\rho)} K_j\phi \wedge (cp_j \geq c_\rho) \wedge A_j\rho \rightarrow \langle C_{SOME}, e_1\rangle K_j con(\rho) \text{ where } \rho = lab_1(e_1) \text{ and } j \not\in lab_2(e_1)$$

The first invalidity unveils the problem behind the traditional understanding of DK (recall Sect. 1) and it is also identified in [36]. The second invalidity shows that higher orders of knowledge require additional reasoning steps that might not follow from attaining mutual knowledge alone. This departs from literature viewing actualizations of DK as CK, because our attempt focuses on *resource-boundedness*: higher-order knowledge, and hence CK, need extra effort that should not be taken for granted. The third invalidity shows that DK is not logically closed, therefore actualizing knowledge of logical consequences is not trivial. The fourth invalidity shows that non-acting agents might not come to know logical consequences, even if some of their peers do. This might need yet another round of resolution, exemplifying the continuous and resource-consuming interplay of communication and inference that takes place in reality when non-ideal groups deliberate.

The theorems illustrate how DK is actualized by non-ideal agents. The use of impossible worlds as "witnesses" of agents' fallibility did not result in a trivialized system where anything goes, due to the dynamics: agents come to know more via resolution and inference, provided that they can. Specifying these steps, monitoring their interplay and the effort they require allows us to track to which extent a group realizes its potential, instead of pre-setting an arbitrary bound.

This provides the "bridge" between the implicit notion of DK and the explicit knowledge real groups can achieve.

Related Work. Comparisons with related work concern: (a) the inferential aspect of knowledge, (b) the communicative aspect of actualizing group potential.

Consider aspect (a): this approach contributes to impossible-worlds semantics used against omniscience [27] by adding *dynamics* that avoid the extreme of trivial logics. Other approaches discern implicit (omniscient) and explicit (omniscience-free) attitudes through a syntactic "filter" (like an *awareness function* [17]). However, forms of the problem may persist and it not clear how resource-boundedness could fit in this picture. Closer to our view are [13,16,31,35], yet our elaborate specification of reasoning processes is important in bridging logic with empirical facts, because these usually pertain to the difficulty of *individual* inference rules [14,24,28]. This also discerns our framework from others with multiple, non-ideal agents [3,4] that too study the effect of communication and inference in multi-agent settings.

Consider aspect (b): [6,36] propose actions following the observation in [11]: it takes more than communication of formulas expressible in the standard languages to actualize DK. Our resolution action is based on [36]'s, and is similar to a special case of [6]'s *tell-all-you-know* actions, and to [11]'s *communication core*. While this wider variety of actions is compatible with the framework,[8] our dynamics is tailored to bounded agents, explaining how far group reasoning can go. It is precisely this difference in scope that justifies our divergence from studying actualizations of DK as CK. It would also be interesting to connect this resource-sensitive attempt and another generalization of operations for pooling information given in [26]: the authors provide an epistemic modality relative to structured communication scenarios as an alternative to distributed knowledge.

Overall, our approach addresses the problem of logical omniscience, in a multi-agent context and in agreement with experimental results and philosophical proposals (e.g. towards a *theory of feasible inferences* [14]). Departing from this well-known problem, this approach demarcates the communicative and inferential actions underlying whether and how DK is actualized. As [10] argues, information goes hand in hand with the processes that create, modify, and convey it; this analysis naturally applies to deliberating groups, and importantly, to resource-bounded ones.

4 Reduction and Axiomatization

In this section, we reduce RSMs to possible-worlds structures with syntactic functions, resembling awareness structures [17]. A reduction from impossible worlds to syntactic structures follows the converse direction to [33], showing how various

[8] Their model transformations could be captured as in the aforementioned attempts (epistemic relation-wise), accompanied by the incurrence of a cost to those receiving the information.

structures, like awareness ones, can be reduced to impossible-worlds models validating precisely the same formulas (given a fixed background language). Besides, the division of responses to logical omniscience into syntactic and semantic ones is common in the literature. Syntactic approaches are claimed to lack the elegance of semantic (impossible-worlds) ones, yet the latter's semantic rules do not adequately capture intuitions about knowledge formation [17]. Our framework is a semantic one, using impossible worlds to do justice to multiple non-ideal agents but nonetheless preserves explanatory power since agents can engage in knowledge-refining actions. While the model and its actions accommodate these intuitions, the reduction is instrumental in providing a sound and complete logic, as it allows for the use of standard DEL techniques. In this way, we wish to harvest both the benefits of impossible-worlds semantics and the more convenient technical treatment of syntactic approaches.

An outline of the reduction is as follows. First, we focus on the static part and we show that the effect of impossible worlds in the interpretation of D_G can be captured in a possible-worlds model, provided that suitable syntactic functions are introduced. Second, we obtain a sound and complete static axiomatization, through modal logic techniques. Third, we move to the dynamics. We explain why the common DEL procedure of giving *reduction axioms* is not straightforward but also how this issue can still be overcome.

4.1 Reduction and Static Axiomatization

Reduced (Static) Language. We fix an appropriate language $\mathcal{L}_{red}$ as the "common ground" to show that the reduction is successful, i.e. the same formulas are valid under the original and the reduced models. Take $\sim_G (w) := \{u \in W \mid w \sim_G u\}$, which denotes the set the truth clause for D_G quantifies over. Auxiliary operators (L_{D_G}, I_{D_G}) are then introduced to the static fragment of $\mathcal{L}$ to discern (syntactically) the effect of quantifying over (im)possible worlds in D_G-interpretations. Their semantic interpretations are given below. For $w \in W^P$:

$$M, w \models L_{D_G}\phi \text{ iff } M, u \models \phi \text{ for all } u \in W^P \cap \sim_G (w)$$
$$M, w \models I_{D_G}\phi \text{ iff } M, u \models \phi \text{ for all } u \in W^I \cap \sim_G (w)$$

These essentially help us break down the D_G operator. We also use $\bot$ as an auxiliary element of $\mathcal{L}_{red}$, that is never true in any world.

Building the Reduced Model. Towards interpreting the auxiliary operators I_{D_G} in a reduced model, we construct *awareness-like functions*:

- $\mathrm{I}_{D_G} : W^P \to \mathcal{P}(\mathcal{L})$ such that $\mathrm{I}_{D_G}(w) = \bigcap_{v \in W^I \cap \sim_G(w)} V_I(v)$. Intuitively, I_{D_G} takes a possible world and yields the set of formulas true at all impossible worlds in its quantification set (the set of worlds D_G quantifies over).

Definition 4.1 (Awareness-like structure (ALS)). *Given* $M = \langle W^P, W^I, \sim_j, V_P, V_I, R, cp_j \rangle$, *its ALS (reduced model) is* $\mathbf{M} := \langle \mathrm{W}, \sim_j^r, \mathrm{V}, \mathrm{R}, cp_j, \mathrm{I}_{D_G} \rangle$ *with:*

$$\mathrm{W} = W^P \quad w{\sim}^r_j u \textit{ iff } w \sim_j u, \textit{ for } w, u \in \mathrm{W} \quad \mathrm{V}(w) = V_P(w) \textit{ for } w \in \mathrm{W}$$
$$\mathrm{R}(w, j) = R(w, j) \textit{ for } w \in \mathrm{W} \quad cp_j \textit{ is as in the original} \quad \mathrm{I}_{D_G} \textit{ as explained before}$$

The clauses based on ALSs are such that the I_{D_G}-operators are interpreted via the awareness-like functions. Due to the construction of awareness-like functions, *Minimal Consistency* is inherited by the reduced model: for no $w \in \mathrm{W}$, $G \subseteq Ag$, is it the case that $\{\phi, \neg\phi\} \subseteq \mathrm{I}_{D_G}(w)$. *Soundness of inference rules* is also clearly preserved. Moreover, take ${\sim}^r_j(w) := \{u \in \mathrm{W} \mid w{\sim}^r_j u\}$ now based on the new ordering ${\sim}^r_j$. The interpretation of terms is as in the original, since the values of capacities and costs are unchanged. The semantic clauses, based on $\mathbf{M}$, are standard for the boolean connectives. The remaining:

$\mathbf{M}, w \models p$ iff $p \in \mathrm{V}(w)$

$\mathbf{M}, w \models z_1 s_1 + \ldots + z_n s_n \geq z$ iff $z_1 s_1^{\mathbf{M}} + \ldots + z_n s_n^{\mathbf{M}} \geq z$

$\mathbf{M}, w \models A_j \rho$ iff $\rho \in \mathrm{R}(w, j)$

$\mathbf{M}, w \models L_{D_G}\phi$ iff $\mathbf{M}, u \models \phi$ for all $u \in \bigcap_{j \in G} {\sim}^r_j(w)$

$\mathbf{M}, w \models I_{D_G}\phi$ iff $\phi \in \mathrm{I}_{D_G}(w)$

$\mathbf{M}, w \models D_G\phi$ iff $\mathbf{M}, w \models L_{D_G}\phi$ and $\mathbf{M}, w \models I_{D_G}\phi$

We now show that the definition of the ALSs indeed fulfills its purpose:

Theorem 4.1 (Reduction). *Given a RSM M, let* $\mathbf{M}$ *be its ALS. Then* $\mathbf{M}$ *is a reduction of M, i.e. for any $w \in W^P$ and formula $\phi \in \mathcal{L}_{red}$: $M, w \models \phi$ iff* $\mathbf{M}, w \models \phi$.

Proof. The proof goes by induction on the complexity of ϕ.

Based on this, we provide the static axiomatization:

Definition 4.2 (Static axiomatization). *Λ is axiomatized by Table 1 and the rules Modus Ponens, Necessitation$_{D_G}$ (from ϕ, infer $L_{D_G}\phi$).*

Table 1. The static axiomatization

PC	All instances of classical propositional tautologies
Ineq	All instances of valid formulas about linear inequalities
D-Distribution	$L_{D_G}(\phi \to \psi) \to (L_{D_G}\phi \to L_{D_G}\psi)$
D-factivity	$L_{D_G}\phi \to \phi$
D-Monotonicity	$L_{D_G}\phi \to L_{D_B}\phi$, if $G \subseteq B$
	$I_{D_G}\phi \to I_{D_B}\phi$, if $G \subseteq B$
Minimal Consistency	$I_{D_G}\bot \vee (\neg(I_{D_G}\phi \wedge I_{D_G}\neg\phi))$
Soundness of inference rules	$A_j\rho \to tr(\rho)$
Reducing D_G	$D_G\phi \leftrightarrow L_{D_G}\phi \wedge I_{D_G}\phi$

Ineq, described in [19], is introduced to account for the linear inequalities. The axioms for L_{D_G} mimic the behaviour of D_G-involving axioms in the standard logics with DK [18,20,22] only now using the auxiliary operator quantifying over the possible worlds alone. *Soundness of inference rules* and *Minimal Consistency* take care of the respective model conditions. Finally, the last axiom reduces D_G in terms of the corresponding auxiliary operators.

Theorem 4.2 (Λ soundness/completeness). *Λ is sound and complete w.r.t. ALSs.*

Proof. Soundness follows from the validity of axioms. Completeness follows [22, p. 65], as the crucial difference (auxiliary operators interpreted through syntactic functions) is accommodated from the construction of a suitable canonical model.

4.2 Dynamic Axiomatization

Moving to the dynamic part, consider a RSM M and its reduced ALS $\mathbf{M}$. If an update, either of resolution or inference, takes place, then we get an updated M' and thus an updated ALS $\mathbf{M}'$ corresponding to it. We observe that $\mathbf{M}'$ is such that an updated awareness-like function I'_{D_G} is given in terms of I_{D_G}, i.e the awareness-like function in $\mathbf{M}$. That is, the new values are set expressions of the original ones. We present the updated functions below.[9]

After resolution of G: $\mathrm{I}'_{D_B}(w) = \bigcap_{u \in (W^I) \cap \sim'_B(w)} V_I(u) = \begin{cases} \mathrm{I}_{D_{G \cup B}}(w), \text{ if } G \cap B \neq \emptyset \\ \mathrm{I}_{D_B}(w), \text{ if } G \cap B = \emptyset \end{cases}$

After C_{ALL}: $\mathrm{I}'_{D_G}(w, e_1) = \bigcap_{(w',e') \in (W^I)' \cap \sim'_G(w,e_1)} V'_I(w', e') = \begin{cases} \mathrm{I}_{D_G}(w) \cup \{con(\rho)\}, \text{ if } (W^I)' \neq \emptyset \\ \mathrm{I}_{D_G}(w) \cup \overline{\mathrm{I}_{D_G}(w)}, \text{ if } (W^I)' = \emptyset \end{cases}$

After C_{SOME}, we have the cases below regarding e_1 and e_0:

$$\mathrm{I}'_{D_G}(w, e_1) = \begin{cases} \mathrm{I}_{D_G}(w), \text{ if } (W^I)' \cap \sim'_G (w, e_1) \neq \emptyset \text{ and } a \notin G \\ \mathrm{I}_{D_G}(w) \cup \{con(\rho)\}, \text{ if } (W^I)' \cap \sim'_G (w, e_1) \neq \emptyset \text{ and } a \in G \\ \mathrm{I}_{D_G}(w) \cup \overline{\mathrm{I}_{D_G}(w)}, \text{ if } (W^I)' \cap \sim'_G (w, e_1) = \emptyset \end{cases} \quad \mathrm{I}'_{D_G}(w, e_0) = \mathrm{I}_{D_G}(w)$$

In DEL, it is common to provide *reduction axioms* for the dynamic operators, in our case, for $\langle R_G \rangle$ and $\langle C, e \rangle$. However, reducing dynamic formulas involving the auxiliary operator I_{D_G} (thus D_G too) cannot be straightforwardly obtained because the new sets obtained through the update of I_{D_G} cannot be described by means of the static language alone. Similar problems are encountered in [31, Chapter 5]; in that single-agent framework, there are syntactic functions which are expanded after certain actions. The focus is on actions that give rise to syntactic functions which are structured expressions of the original ones, in turn treatable with a specific static language. We follow a similar procedure, tailored to *our* syntactic functions I_{D_G}. This is because, as shown above, the updated values are too given in terms of the original ones, reflecting the refinement induced by each action. Just to sketch the idea, as in [31], we extend the static language, essentially re-expressing the auxiliary operators as set-expression operators, and provide reduction axioms that yield a full sound and complete axiomatization.

For reasons of brevity, we cannot present the full-fledged procedure and the reduction axioms here. Some remarks to give a flavor of the more important reduction axioms: for inequalities, they reflect, with the help of abbreviations, the resource consumption each action induces; for L_G operators, they reflect that these operators behave as D_G does in standard DEL; for I_G, making crucial use of the set-expression operators, they reflect that the awareness-like functions are updated in a principled way: as *specific* set expressions of the original ones.

[9] We get these results using Definition 2.7, Definition 2.9, Definition 4.1.

5 Conclusions and Future Work

The EL modelling of unbounded agents has repercussions for group reasoning and DK is instrumental in illustrating this because it presupposes that agents can undertake unlimited actions of communication and inference. We looked into actualizations of DK under bounded resources, using RSMs and actions for communication and inference. The combination of impossible-worlds semantics and action models might be of independent interest given the former's use in areas beyond epistemic logic and the latter's popularity in the study of multi-agent dynamics. We furthermore showed that our models can be reduced to syntactic structures. In doing so, we confirmed a pattern observed in the omniscience literature and offered a useful detour for a sound and complete logic.

One direction for future work concerns non-ideal higher-order reasoning, and hence connections of DK and CK. As with deductive reasoning, we envisage the introduction of effortful steps for introspection and reasoning about other agents, and the use of experimental results showing that groups usually act on a large, but finite, degree of mutual knowledge as if they had CK. On another note, group reasoning, in this attempt, can be better than individual in ways that agree with the distribution of skills observed in [21,30] and the view that at the upper limit groups perform as their best member [25]. However, the former also emphasize the facilitative effect of dialogue in group performance, which may be captured via a combination of RSMs with dialogical/inquisitive models.

Acknowledgments. Thanks to the audience and reviewers of DaLí 2020 for their remarks, as well as to Sonja Smets and the members of the "Logic of Conceivability" seminar. Anthia Solaki is supported by the Dutch Organisation for Scientific Research ("PhDs in the Humanities", grant No. 322-20-018).

References

1. Addis, T., Gooding, D.: Learning as collective belief-revision: simulating reasoning about disparate phenomena. In: AISB Symposium, pp. 6–9 (1999)
2. Alechina, N., Logan, B., Nga, N.H., Rakib, A.: A logic for coalitions with bounded resources. In: IJCAI, pp. 659–664 (2009)
3. Alechina, N., Logan, B., Nguyen, H.N., Rakib, A.: Reasoning about other agents' beliefs under bounded resources. In: Meyer, J.-J.C., Broersen, J. (eds.) KRAMAS 2008. LNCS (LNAI), vol. 5605, pp. 1–15. Springer, Heidelberg (2009). https://doi.org/10.1007/978-3-642-05301-6_1
4. Balbiani, P., Fernández-Duque, D., Lorini, E.: The dynamics of epistemic attitudes in resource-bounded agents. Studia Logica **107**(3), 457–488 (2018). https://doi.org/10.1007/s11225-018-9798-4
5. Baltag, A., Renne, B.: Dynamic epistemic logic. In: Zalta, E.N. (ed.) The Stanford Encyclopedia of Philosophy, Metaphysics Research Lab. Stanford University (2016)
6. Baltag, A., Smets, S.: Learning what others know. In: LPAR, pp. 90–119 (2020)
7. Bara, B.G., Bucciarelli, M., Johnson-Laird, P.N.: Development of syllogistic reasoning. Am. J. Psychol. **108**(2), 157–193 (1995)
8. Barwise, J., Perry, J.: Situations and Attitudes. MIT Press, Cambridge (1983)

9. van Benthem, J.: Merging observation and access in dynamic epistemic logic. Stud. Logic **1**, 1–16 (2008)
10. van Benthem, J.: 'Tell it like it is': information flow in logic. J. Peking Univ. (Human. Soc. Sci. Ed.) **1**, 80–90 (2008)
11. van Benthem, J.: Logical Dynamics of Information and Interaction. CUP, Cambridge (2011)
12. Berto, F., Jago, M.: Impossible Worlds. Oxford University Press, Oxford (2019)
13. Bjerring, J.C., Skipper, M.: A dynamic solution to the problem of logical omniscience. J. Philos. Logic **48**, 501–521 (2018)
14. Cherniak, C.: Minimal Rationality. Bradford Book. MIT Press, Cambridge (1986)
15. Cowan, N.: The magical number 4 in short-term memory: a reconsideration of mental storage capacity. Behav. Brain Sci. **24**, 87–114 (2001). https://doi.org/10.1007/s10992-018-9473-2
16. Elgot-Drapkin, J., Kraus, S., Miller, M., Nirkhe, M., Perlis, D.: Active logics: a unified formal approach to episodic reasoning (1999)
17. Fagin, R., Halpern, J.Y.: Belief, awareness, and limited reasoning. Artif. Intell. **34**(1), 39–76 (1987)
18. Fagin, R., Halpern, J.Y., Moses, Y., Vardi, M.Y.: Reasoning About Knowledge. MIT Press, Cambridge (1995)
19. Fagin, R., Halpern, J.Y.: Reasoning about knowledge and probability. J. ACM **41**(2), 340–367 (1994)
20. Fagin, R., Halpern, J.Y., Vardi, M.Y.: What can machines know? On the properties of knowledge in distributed systems. J. ACM **39**(2), 328–376 (1992)
21. Geil, D.M.M.: Collaborative reasoning: evidence for collective rationality. Think. Reason. **4**(3), 231–248 (1998)
22. Gerbrandy, J.D., et al.: Bisimulations on planet Kripke. Inst. for Logic, Language and Computation, Univ. van Amsterdam (1999)
23. Gruber, H.: The cooperative synthesis of disparate points of view. Leg. Solomon Asch: Essays Cogn. Soc. Psychol. **1**, 143–158 (1990)
24. Johnson-Laird, P.N., Byrne, R.M., Schaeken, W.: Propositional reasoning by model. Psychol. Rev. **99**(3), 418–439 (1992)
25. Laughlin, P.R., Ellis, A.L.: Demonstrability and social combination processes on mathematical intellective tasks. J. Exp. Soc. Psychol. **22**(3), 177–189 (1986)
26. Punčochář, V., Sedlár, I.: Substructural logics for pooling information. In: Baltag, A., Seligman, J., Yamada, T. (eds.) LORI 2017. LNCS, vol. 10455, pp. 407–421. Springer, Heidelberg (2017). https://doi.org/10.1007/978-3-662-55665-8_28
27. Rantala, V.: Impossible worlds semantics and logical omniscience. Acta Philosophica Fennica **35**, 106–115 (1982)
28. Rips, L.J.: The Psychology of Proof: Deductive Reasoning in Human Thinking. MIT Press, Cambridge (1994)
29. Roelofsen, F.: Distributed knowledge. J. Appl. Non-Classical Log. **17**(2), 255–273 (2007)
30. Trognon, A., Batt, M., Laux, J.: Why is dialogical solving of a logical problem more effective than individual solving?: A formal and experimental study of an abstract version of Wason's task. Lang. Dialogue **1**(1), 44–78 (2011)
31. Velázquez-Quesada, F.R.: Small steps in dynamics of information. Ph.D. thesis, Universiteit van Amsterdam (2011)
32. Verbrugge, R.: Logic and social cognition. J. Philos. Logic **38**(6), 649–680 (2009). https://doi.org/10.1007/s10992-009-9115-9

33. Wansing, H.: A general possible worlds framework for reasoning about knowledge and belief. Stud. Logica **49**(4), 523–539 (1990). https://doi.org/10.1007/BF00370163
34. Wason, P.C.: Reasoning. In: Foss, B. (ed.) New Horizons in Psychology, pp. 135–151. Penguin Books, Harmondsworth (1966)
35. Ågotnes, T., Walicki, M.: Syntactic knowledge: a logic of reasoning, communication and cooperation. In: Proceedings of the Second European Workshop on Multi-Agent Systems (EUMAS), Barcelona, Spain (2004)
36. Ågotnes, T., Wáng, Y.N.: Resolving distributed knowledge. Artif. Intell. **252**, 1–21 (2017)

Simpler Completeness Proofs for Modal Logics with Intersection

Yì N. Wáng[1(✉)] and Thomas Ågotnes[2,3]

[1] Department of Philosophy (Zhuhai), Sun Yat-sen University, Zhuhai, China
ynw@xixilogic.org
[2] University of Bergen, Bergen, Norway
[3] Southwest University, Chongqing, China
Thomas.Agotnes@uib.no

Abstract. There has been a significant interest in modal logics with intersection, prominent examples including epistemic and doxastic logics with distributed knowledge, propositional dynamic logic with intersection, and description logics with concept intersection. Completeness proofs for such logics tend to be complicated, in particular on model classes such as S5 used, e.g., in standard epistemic logic, mainly due to the undefinability of intersection of modalities in standard modal logic. A standard proof method for the S5 case uses an "unraveling-folding" technique to achieve a treelike model to deal with the problem of undefinability. This method, however, is not easily adapted to other logics, due to its reliance on S5 in a number of steps. In this paper we demonstrate a simpler and more general proof technique by building a treelike canonical model directly, which avoids the complications in the processes of unraveling and folding. We illustrate the technique by showing completeness of the normal modal logics K, D, T, B, S4 and S5 extended with intersection modalities. Furthermore, these treelike canonical models are compatible with Fischer-Ladner-style closures, and we combine the methods to show the completeness of the mentioned logics further extended with transitive closure of union modalities known from PDL or epistemic logic. Some of these completeness results are new.

Keywords: Modal logic · Intersection modality · Transitive closure of union modality · Completeness · Epistemic logic · Distributed knowledge

1 Introduction

Intersection plays a role in several areas of modal logic, including epistemic logics with distributed knowledge [11,15], propositional dynamic logic with intersection of programs [13], description logics with concept intersection [3,4], and coalition logic [1]. It is well-known that relational intersection in Kripke models is not modally definable and that standard logics with intersection are not canonical (cf., e.g., [14]).

M. A. Martins and I. Sedlár (Eds.): DaLí 2020, LNCS 12569, pp. 259–276, 2020.
https://doi.org/10.1007/978-3-030-65840-3_16

A method for proving completeness for certain modal logics with intersection was developed in [11,12,14–16] for various (static) epistemic logics with distributed knowledge, and later explicated and extended in [17–19] as the *unraveling-folding method* which is applicable to various static or dynamic epistemic S5 logics with distributed knowledge with or without common knowledge.

Let us take a closer look at this technique for epistemic logic with distributed knowledge (S5D). It is known that the canonical S5 model built in the standard way is not a model for the classical axiomatization for this logic. This is because the accessibility relation R_G (where G is a set) that is (implicitly) used to interpret the intersection (distributed knowledge) modality is not necessarily the intersection of individual accessibility relations R_a ($a \in G$). In the canonical S5 model we can ensure that $R_G \subseteq \bigcap_{a \in G} R_a$, but not that $R_G \supseteq \bigcap_{a \in G} R_a$.

The unraveling-folding method is carried out in the following way. A *pre-model* is a standard S5 model where R_G is treated as a primitive relation for each group G. A *pseudo model* is a pre-model satisfying the following two constraints:

1. $R_{\{a\}} = R_a$ for every agent a, and
2. $R_G \subseteq \bigcap_{a \in G} R_a$ for every agent a and group G

A (proper) S5D model is then a pseudo model that satisfies also a third constraint:

3. $R_G \supseteq \bigcap_{a \in G} R_a$ for every agent a and group G

A canonical pseudo model can be truth-preservingly translated to a *treelike* pre-model using an *unraveling* technique, and then *folded* to an S5D model while also preserving the truth of all formulas (for details of the two processes see [18]). Completeness is achieved by first building a canonical pseudo model for a given consistent set Φ of formulas, and then translating it to an S5D model for Φ using the unraveling-folding method.

There are many subtleties not mentioned in this simplified overview, which in particular makes the method cumbersome to adapt to extensions of basic epistemic logic or to non-S5 based logics.

In this paper we demonstrate a simpler way to prove completeness for modal logics with intersection. Since we know that a treelike model typically works for such logics, the idea is to build a treelike model *directly* for a given consistent set of formulas. We call such a model a *standard model*. This eliminates having to deal with the details of the unraveling and folding processes, and dramatically simplifies proofs.

We illustrate the technique by building the standard model for each of the modal logics, K, D, T, B, S4 and S5, extended with intersection. We furthermore demonstrate that the method is useful by showing that it is compatible with finitary methods based on Fischer-Ladner-style closures, and introduce finitary standard models for the mentioned logics further extended with the transitive closure of the union, used in, e.g., PDL and epistemic logic (common knowledge), as well. Some of these completeness results have been stated in the literature before, often without proof.

The rest of the paper is structured as follows. In the next section we introduce basic definitions and conventions. In Sect. 3 we give a taste of the proof technique by demonstrating it on a well-known case: $\mathbf{S5}^{\cap}$ with intersection. The reader who wants to immediately see what the technique looks like can jump directly to that section. In Sect. 4 we systematically consider a class of well-known modal logics extended with intersection. For each of them we introduce an axiomatization and show its completeness. We then extend the logics, proofs and results further with a modality for the transitive closure of union in Sect. refsec:logiccd. We conclude in Sect. 6.

2 Preliminaries

In this paper we study modal logics over multi-modal languages with countably many standard unary modal operators: $\Box_0$, $\Box_1$, $\Box_2$, etc. On top of these we focus on two types of modal operators, each *indexed* by a finite nonempty set I of natural numbers:

- *Intersection modalities*, denoted $\cap_I$;
- *Transitive closure of union modalities*, henceforth referred to as *union*$^+$ *modalities* for brevity, denoted $\uplus_I$.

We mention some applications of these modalities below.

The languages are parameterized by a countably infinite set PR of propositions, and a countable set $\mathcal{I}$ of primitive types. A finite non-empty subset $I \subseteq \mathcal{I}$ is called an *Index*. We are interested in the following languages.

Definition 1 (languages).

$$
\begin{array}{ll}
(\mathcal{L}) & \varphi ::= p \mid \neg\varphi \mid (\varphi \rightarrow \varphi) \mid \Box_i\varphi \\
(\mathcal{L}^{\cap}) & \varphi ::= p \mid \neg\varphi \mid (\varphi \rightarrow \varphi) \mid \Box_i\varphi \mid \cap_I\varphi \\
(\mathcal{L}^{\cap\uplus}) & \varphi ::= p \mid \neg\varphi \mid (\varphi \rightarrow \varphi) \mid \Box_i\varphi \mid \cap_I\varphi \mid \uplus_I\varphi
\end{array}
$$

where $p \in$ PR, $i \in \mathcal{I}$ and I is an index. Boolean connectives are defined as usual.

A Kripke model M (over PR and $\mathcal{I}$) is a triple (S, R, V), where S is a nonempty set of states, $R : \mathcal{I} \rightarrow \wp(S \times S)$ assigns to every modality $\Box_i$ a binary relation R_i on S, and $V :$ PR $\rightarrow S$ is a valuation which associates with every propositional variable a set of states where it is true.

Definition 2 (satisfaction). *For a given formula α, the* truth *of it in, or its* satisfaction *by, a model $M = (S, R, V)$ with a designated state s, denoted $M, s \models \alpha$, is defined inductively as follows.*

$$
\begin{array}{lll}
M, s \models p & \textit{iff} & s \in V(p) \\
M, s \models \neg\varphi & \textit{iff} & \textit{not } (M, s) \models \varphi \\
M, s \models (\varphi \rightarrow \psi) & \textit{iff} & M, s \models \varphi \textit{ implies } M, s \models \psi \\
M, s \models \Box_i\varphi & \textit{iff} & \textit{for all } t \in S, \textit{ if } (s,t) \in R_i \textit{ then } M, t \models \varphi \\
M, s \models \cap_I\varphi & \textit{iff} & \textit{for all } t \in S, \textit{ if } (s,t) \in \bigcap_{i \in I} R_i \textit{ then } M, t \models \varphi \\
M, s \models \uplus_I\varphi & \textit{iff} & \textit{for all } t \in S, \textit{ if } (s,t) \in \biguplus_{i \in I} R_i \textit{ then } M, t \models \varphi
\end{array}
$$

where[1] $\biguplus_{i \in I} R_i$ *is the transitive closure of* $\bigcup_{i \in I} R_i$.

Thus, the *intersection* modalities are interpreted by taking the intersection, and the *union*$^+$ modalities by taking the transitive closure of the union.

Given a formula φ and a class $\mathscr{C}$ of models, we say φ is *valid* ($\models \varphi$) in $\mathscr{C}$ iff φ is true in all states in all models of $\mathscr{C}$. A formula φ is a *logical consequence* of a set of formulas Φ ($\Phi \models \varphi$) if φ is true in a given state in a given model whenever all formulas in Φ are. We are interested in certain classes of models, in particular those defined by well-known *frame conditions.* In this paper we are going to focus on some of the most well known frame conditions (see, e.g., [9]). These are *seriality, reflexivity, symmetry, transitivity* and *Euclidicity.* It is well known that these frame conditions are characterized by the formulas D ($\Box_i\varphi \to \neg\Box_i\neg\varphi$), T ($\Box_i\varphi \to \varphi$), B ($\neg\varphi \to \Box_i\neg\Box_i\varphi$), 4 ($\Box_i\varphi \to \Box_i\Box_i\varphi$) and 5 ($\neg\Box_i\varphi \to \Box_i\neg\Box_i\varphi$), respectively. With respect to different combinations of these frame conditions, normal modal logics K, D (also known as KD), ¡(also known as KT), B (also known as KTB), S4 (also known as KT4) and S5 (also known as KT5) based on the language $\mathcal{L}$ are well studied in the literature. We shall refer an "S5 model" to a Kripke model in which the binary relation is an equivalence relation, and likewise for a D, T, B or S4 model.

In this paper we will focus on the corresponding logics over the languages $\mathcal{L}^{\cap}$ and $\mathcal{L}^{\cap\uplus}$, and they will be named in a comprehensive way as follows:

$$\begin{array}{c} \mathrm{K}^{\cap},\ \mathrm{D}^{\cap},\ \mathrm{T}^{\cap},\ \mathrm{B}^{\cap},\ \mathrm{S4}^{\cap},\ \mathrm{S5}^{\cap}, \\ \mathrm{K}^{\cap\uplus}, \mathrm{D}^{\cap\uplus}, \mathrm{T}^{\cap\uplus}, \mathrm{B}^{\cap\uplus}, \mathrm{S4}^{\cap\uplus}, \mathrm{S5}^{\cap\uplus}. \end{array}$$

There are well known applications of these logics, for example are $\mathrm{S5}^{\cap}$ and $\mathrm{S5}^{\cap\uplus}$ (under the restriction that $\mathcal{I}$ is finite) well known as S5D (multi-agent S5 with distributed knowledge) and S5CD (multi-agent S5 with distributed and common knowledge) respectively in the area of epistemic logic. The logics $\mathrm{K}^{\cap}$ and $\mathrm{S4}^{\cap}$ are known as $\mathcal{ALC}(\cap)$ (i.e., $\mathcal{ALC}$ with role intersection) and $\mathcal{S}(\cap)$ (where $\mathcal{S}$ is $\mathcal{ALC}$ with role transitivity) respectively in the area of description logic [3,4].[2] The logic $\mathrm{K}^{\cap\uplus}$ is close to propositional dynamic logic with intersection (IPDL) [13] or the description logic $\mathcal{ALC}(\cap, \cup, *)$, and similarly, $\mathrm{S4}^{\cap\uplus}$ is close to $\mathcal{S}(\cap, \cup, *)$.[3]

[1] Although the symbol $\biguplus$ is sometimes used for disjoint union, we repurpose it here for transitive closure of the union.

[2] The subscript i of a unary modal operator $\Box_i$ typically stands for an agent in epistemic logic or a role in description logic. In epistemic logic, a finite number of agents is assumed, and the intersection modality (i.e., a distributed knowledge operator) is an arbitrary intersection over a finite domain. In description logic, the number of roles are typically unbounded, but the intersection is binary, which is in effect equivalent to finite intersection.

[3] There are two major differences however. First, the Kleene star in both logics are the reflexive-transitive closure, and we consider the transitive closure which is denoted by a "+" in the symbol $\uplus$. Second, $\uplus_I$ is a compound modality (union and then take the transitive closure), while in those logics the Kleene star is separated from the union, and as a result, the Kleene star applies to the intersection as well, which we do not consider here.

The minimal logic K can be axiomatized by the system **K** composed of the following axiom (schemes) and rules (where $\varphi, \psi \in \mathcal{L}$ and $i \in \mathcal{I}$):

(PC) all instances of all propositional tautologies
(MP) from $(\varphi \to \psi)$ and φ infer ψ
(K) $\Box_i(\varphi \to \psi) \to (\Box_i\varphi \to \Box_i\psi)$
(N) from φ infer $\Box_i\varphi$.

Axiomatizations for D, T, B , S4 and S5, which are named **D**, **T**, **B**, **S4** and **S5** respectively, can be obtained by adding characterization axioms to **K**. In more detail, $\mathbf{D} = \mathbf{K}\oplus$D, $\mathbf{T} = \mathbf{K}\oplus$T, $\mathbf{B} = \mathbf{T}\oplus$B, $\mathbf{S4} = \mathbf{T}\oplus$4 and $\mathbf{S5} = \mathbf{T}\oplus$5, where the symbol $\oplus$ means combining the axioms and rules of the two parts. Details can be found in standard modal logic textbooks (see, e.g., [8,9]). Given an axiomatization **L**, we use "$\vdash_{\mathbf{L}} \varphi$" to denote that φ is derivable in **L**, and when Φ is a set of formulas "$\Phi \vdash_{\mathbf{L}} \varphi$" means that $\vdash_{\mathbf{L}} (\psi_0 \wedge \cdots \wedge \psi_n) \to \varphi$ for some $\psi_0, \ldots, \psi_n \in \Phi$.

A logic extended with the intersection modality is typically axiomatized by adding axioms and rules to the corresponding logic without intersection. The axioms and rules to be added are in total called the *characterization of intersection*, and depends on which logic we are dealing with. Similarly we can define the *characterization of the transitive closure of union*, which can be made independent to the concrete logic (will be made clearer in Sect. 5).

Characterizations of intersection and transitive closure of union can be found in the literature for some of the logics, including $\mathrm{K}^{\cap}$, $\mathrm{T}^{\cap}$, $\mathrm{S4}^{\cap}$, $\mathrm{S5}^{\cap}$ and $\mathrm{S5}^{\cap\uplus}$ in epistemic logic (see [11,15,17]). For base logic S5, intersection in $\mathbf{S5}^{\cap}$ and $\mathbf{S5}^{\cap\uplus}$ is characterized by the following axioms and rules:

- (K$\cap$) $\cap_I(\varphi \to \psi) \to (\cap_I\varphi \to \cap_I\psi)$
- (D$\cap$) $\cap_I\varphi \to \neg \cap_I \neg\varphi$
- (T$\cap$) $\cap_I\varphi \to \varphi$
- (4$\cap$) $\cap_I\varphi \to \cap_I\cap_I\varphi$
- (B$\cap$) $\neg\varphi \to \cap_I\neg\cap_I\varphi$
- (5$\cap$) $\neg\cap_I\varphi \to \cap_I\neg\cap_I\varphi$
- (N$\cap$) from φ infer $\cap_I\varphi$
- ($\cap$1) $\Box_i\varphi \leftrightarrow \cap_{\{i\}}\varphi$
- ($\cap$2) $\cap_I\varphi \to \cap_J\varphi$, if $I \subseteq J$

Transitive closure of union in $\mathbf{S5}^{\cap\uplus}$ is characterized by the following:

- (K$\uplus$) $\uplus_I(\varphi \to \psi) \to (\uplus_I\varphi \to \uplus_I\psi)$
- (D$\uplus$) $\uplus_I\varphi \to \neg\uplus_I\neg\varphi$
- (T$\uplus$) $\uplus_I\varphi \to \varphi$
- (4$\uplus$) $\uplus_I\varphi \to \uplus_I\uplus_I\varphi$
- (B$\uplus$) $\neg\varphi \to \uplus_I\neg\uplus_I\varphi$
- (5$\uplus$) $\neg\uplus_I\varphi \to \uplus_I\neg\uplus_I\varphi$
- (N$\uplus$) from φ infer $\uplus_I\varphi$
- ($\uplus$1) $\uplus_I\varphi \to \Box_i(\varphi \wedge \uplus_I\varphi)$, if $i \in I$
- ($\uplus$2) from $\varphi \to \bigwedge_{i\in I} \Box_i(\varphi \wedge \psi)$ infer $\varphi \to \uplus_I\psi$

It is known that the axiomatization $\mathbf{S5}^{\cap} = \mathbf{S5} \oplus \{\mathrm{K}\cap, \mathrm{T}\cap, 5\cap, \cap 1, \cap 2\}$ is sound and complete[4] for the logic $\mathrm{S5}^{\cap}$, and $\mathbf{S5}^{\cap\uplus} = \mathbf{S5}^{\cap} \oplus \{\mathrm{K}\uplus, \uplus 1, \uplus 2\}$ is sound and complete[5] for the logic $\mathrm{S5}^{\cap\uplus}$ (see, e.g., [11]), in the case that $\mathcal{I}$ is finite. However, since the intersection and union$^+$ modalities are interpreted as operations over relations for standard box operators, their properties change in accordance with those for standard boxes. As a result, the characterization axioms and rules vary for weaker logics. We shall look into this in the following sections. First we define some basic terminology that will be useful.

Definition 3 (paths, (proper) initial segments, rest, tail). *Given a model $M = (S, R, V)$, a* path *of M is a finite nonempty sequence $\langle s_0, I_1, \ldots, I_n, s_n\rangle$ where: (i) $s_0, \ldots, s_n \in S$, (ii) $I_1, \ldots, I_n$ are indices, and (iii) for all $x = 1, \ldots, n$, $(s_{x-1}, s_x) \in \bigcap_{i \in I_x} R_i$.*

For paths $s = \langle s_0, I_1, \ldots, I_m, s_m\rangle$ and $t = \langle t_0, J_1, \ldots, J_n, t_n\rangle$ of a model,

- *We say that s is an* initial segment *of t, denoted $s \preceq t$, if $m \leq n$, $s_x = t_x$ for all $x = 0, \ldots, m$, and $I_y = J_y$ for all $y = 1, \ldots, m$, and then we say that t extends s with $\langle J_{m+1}, t_{m+1}, \ldots, J_n, t_n\rangle$;*
- *We say s is a* proper initial segment *of t, denoted $s \prec t$, if the former is an initial segment of the latter and $m < n$;*
- *We write* tail(s) *for s_m, and similarly* tail(t) *for t_n;*
- *When s is an initial segment of t, we write $t \setminus s$ to stand for the path $\langle t_m, J_{m+1}, \ldots, J_n, t_n\rangle$. Note that* tail$(s)$ *is kept in $t \setminus s$, and when $s = t$, we have $t \setminus s = \langle t_n\rangle$.*

Given a natural number i, a path $s = \langle s_0, I_1, \ldots, I_n, s_n\rangle$ is called:

- *An* i-path, *if i appears in all the indices of the path, i.e., $i \in \bigcap_{x=1}^{n} I_x$ (note that a path of length 1, such as $\langle s_0\rangle$, is trivially an i-path).*
- *An* I-path, *where I is an index, if $I \subseteq \bigcap_{x=1}^{n} I_x$.*

3 A Simple Completeness Proof for $\mathbf{S5}^{\cap}$

To illustrate the new technique we now give a proof, omitting some details, for the particular case of $\mathbf{S5}^{\cap}$, assuming familiarity with the canonical model method for classical modal logics. In the next section we demonstrate the generality of the technique and provide all details.

Let MCS be the set of all maximal $\mathbf{S5}^{\cap}$-consistent sets of $\mathcal{L}^{\cap}$-formulas. For a given index I, the *canonical relation* $\rhd_I$ is a binary relation on MCS, such that $\Phi \rhd_I \Psi$ iff for all φ, $\cap_I \varphi \in \Phi$ implies $\varphi \in \Psi$. It is easy to see that $\rhd_I$ is an equivalence relation. A *canonical path* is a sequence $\langle \Phi_0, I_1, \ldots, I_n, \Phi_n\rangle$ such that: (i) $\Phi_0, \ldots, \Phi_n \in$ MCS, (ii) $I_1, \ldots, I_n$ are indices, and (iii) for all $x = 1, \ldots, n$, $(s_{x-1}, s_x) \in \rhd_{I_x}$. We use similar terminology and notation for canonical paths as for paths in a model (Definition 3).

[4] D$\cap$, 4$\cap$, B$\cap$ and N$\cap$ are not needed in the sense that they are derivable.

[5] D$\uplus$, T$\uplus$, 4$\uplus$, B$\uplus$, 5$\uplus$ and N$\uplus$ are not needed in the sense that they are derivable.

Definition 4. *The* standard model *for* $\boldsymbol{S5}^{\cap}$ *is a tuple* $\mathsf{M} = (\mathsf{S}, \mathsf{R}, \mathsf{V})$ *such that:*

- S *is the set of all canonical paths;*
- *For all* $i \in \mathcal{I}$, $\mathsf{R}_i \subseteq \mathsf{S} \times \mathsf{S}$ *such that* $(s, t) \in \mathsf{R}_i$ *iff (i)* s *and* t *have a common initial segment* u*, and (ii) both* $s \setminus u$ *and* $t \setminus u$ *are* i*-paths.*
- *For any propositional variable* p, $\mathsf{V}(p) = \{s \in \mathsf{S} \mid p \in \mathsf{tail}(s)\}$.

Lemma 5. *The* standard model *for* $\boldsymbol{S5}^{\cap}$ *is an S5 model.*

Proof. An easy verification of the definition of the standard model.

Lemma 6 (truth). *For any* $\varphi \in \mathcal{L}^{\cap}$ *and a state* s *of* M, $\mathsf{M}, s \models \varphi$ *iff* $\varphi \in \mathsf{tail}(s)$.

Proof. By induction on φ. The atomic and Boolean cases are easy to show. Interesting cases are for the modalities $\Box_i$ ($i \in \mathcal{I}$) and $\cap_I$ (I is an index), the former following easily from the latter.

$$\begin{aligned} & \mathsf{M}, s \models \cap_I \psi \\ \Leftrightarrow\ & \text{for all } t, \text{ if } (s,t) \in \textstyle\bigcap_{i \in I} \mathsf{R}_i \text{ then } \mathsf{M}^{\mathrm{L}}, t \models \psi \\ \Leftrightarrow\ & \text{for all } t, \text{ if } (s,t) \in \textstyle\bigcap_{i \in I} \mathsf{R}_i \text{ then } \psi \in \mathsf{tail}(t) \Leftrightarrow\ \cap_I \psi \in \mathsf{tail}(s) \end{aligned}$$

where the last step needs an argument.

Suppose $\cap_I \psi \notin \mathsf{tail}(s)$, we get $\neg \cap_I \psi \in \mathsf{tail}(s)$. Let $\Phi^- = \{\neg\psi\} \cup \{\psi' \mid \cap_I \psi' \in \mathsf{tail}(s)\}$. We can show that Φ^- is $\mathbf{S5}^{\cap}$-consistent just as in a classical proof of the existence lemma. Use the Lindenbaum construction to extend Φ^- into $\Phi \in$ MCS. Since $\neg\psi \in \Phi$, $\psi \notin \Phi$. Let t be s extended with $\langle I, \Phi \rangle$. Clearly, $\psi \notin \mathsf{tail}(t)$ and $(s,t) \in \bigcap_{i \in I} \mathsf{R}_i$ (since $s\, \mathsf{R}_i\, t$ for all $i \in I$).

Suppose $\cap_I \psi \in \mathsf{tail}(s)$ and assume towards a contradiction that there is a state t such that $(s,t) \in \bigcap_{i \in I} \mathsf{R}_i$ and $\psi \notin \mathsf{tail}(t)$. By definition, s and t have a common initial segment u, and $s \setminus u$ and $t \setminus u$ are both I-paths. There are three cases: (i) $s \preceq t$, (ii) $t \preceq s$, and (iii) s and t fork (i.e., neither (i) or (ii)). Since $\rhd_I$ is an equivalence relation, in all cases it is easy to verify that $\mathsf{tail}(s) \rhd_I \mathsf{tail}(t)$.

Theorem 7. $\boldsymbol{S5}^{\cap}$ *is a strongly complete axiomatization of* $S5^{\cap}$.

4 Logics over $\mathcal{L}^{\cap}$

In this section we study the logics over the language $\mathcal{L}^{\cap}$, namely, $\mathrm{K}^{\cap}$, $\mathrm{D}^{\cap}$, $\mathrm{T}^{\cap}$, $\mathrm{B}^{\cap}$, $\mathrm{S4}^{\cap}$ and $\mathrm{S5}^{\cap}$, which means that in this section a "formula" stands for a formula of $\mathcal{L}^{\cap}$, and a "logic" without further explanation refers to one of the six. We shall provide a general method for proving completeness for these logics.

The axiomatization **L** we will provide for a logic L is an extension of the axiomatization for the corresponding logic without intersection, with the characterization of intersection. The characterization of intersection depends on the frame conditions. For a given class of models, the characterization of intersection is listed below:

$$
\begin{aligned}
\mathbf{Int(K)} &= \{\mathrm{K}\cap, \cap 1, \cap 2\}\\
\mathbf{Int(D)} &= \{\mathrm{K}\cap, \cap 1, \cap 2\}\\
\mathbf{Int(T)} &= \{\mathrm{K}\cap, \mathrm{T}\cap, \cap 1, \cap 2\}\\
\mathbf{Int(B)} &= \{\mathrm{K}\cap, \mathrm{T}\cap, \mathrm{B}\cap, \cap 1, \cap 2\}\\
\mathbf{Int(S4)} &= \{\mathrm{K}\cap, \mathrm{T}\cap, 4\cap, \cap 1, \cap 2\}\\
\mathbf{Int(S5)} &= \{\mathrm{K}\cap, \mathrm{T}\cap, 5\cap, \cap 1, \cap 2\},
\end{aligned}
$$

where **Int(K)** is the characterization of intersection for the class of all models, **Int(D)** for the class of all D models, **Int(T)** for the class of all T models, and so on. Note that D$\cap$ is not included in **Int(D)**: it is in fact invalid in $\mathrm{D}^{\cap}$ [2].

By adding the characterization of intersection to the axiomatization of a logic, we get an axiomatization for the corresponding logic over $\mathcal{L}^{\cap}$. To be precise, we list the axiomatizations as follows:

$$
\begin{aligned}
\mathbf{K}^{\cap} &= \mathbf{K} \oplus \mathbf{Int(K)}\\
\mathbf{D}^{\cap} &= \mathbf{D} \oplus \mathbf{Int(D)}\\
\mathbf{T}^{\cap} &= \mathbf{T} \oplus \mathbf{Int(T)}\\
\mathbf{B}^{\cap} &= \mathbf{B} \oplus \mathbf{Int(B)}\\
\mathbf{S4}^{\cap} &= \mathbf{S4} \oplus \mathbf{Int(S4)}\\
\mathbf{S5}^{\cap} &= \mathbf{S5} \oplus \mathbf{Int(S5)}.
\end{aligned}
$$

It is not hard to verify that all the above axiomatizations are sound in their corresponding logics, respectively.

Some of the above axiomatizations, in particular, $\mathbf{K}^{\cap}$, $\mathbf{T}^{\cap}$, $\mathbf{S4}^{\cap}$ and $\mathbf{S5}^{\cap}$, are given in [11]. An outline of a completeness proof is also found there, without details. Similarly, equivalent axiomatizations for some of the cases are also found in [5], with proof of completeness only for the $\mathbf{K}^{\cap}$ case. For logics extending $\mathbf{K}^{\cap}$ detailed proofs can be found for certain cases, such as the $\mathbf{S5}^{\cap}$ with only a single intersection modality for the set of all agents (which is assumed to be finite) [10]. A more general and detailed proof based on this technique for the S5 case can be found in [18] (still for the S5 case). The proof goes through an unraveling-folding procedure, mentioned in the introduction. Due to the subtleties in the unraveling and folding processes, it is difficult to apply this technique directly to new logics, as it has to be adapted from the beginning (for example, even the definition of a *path* depends on the underlying logic) through several steps all the way to the very end of the procedure.

We introduce a simpler method for proving completeness, that can easily be adapted to a range of different logics. This is a relatively straightforward variant of the canonical model method. For each of the logics L mentioned above, with corresponding axiomatization **L**, we show that **L** is a complete axiomatization of L, which is equivalent to finding an L model for every **L**-consistent set of formulas. The model we are going to build is called a *standard model.*

Let $\mathrm{MCS}^{\mathbf{L}}$ be the set of all maximal **L**-consistent sets of $\mathcal{L}^{\cap}$-formulas.[6] Given **L**, given an index I, we shall write $\rhd_I$ to stand for the binary relation on $\mathrm{MCS}^{\mathbf{L}}$, such that $\Phi \rhd_I \Psi$ iff for all φ, $\cap_I \varphi \in \Phi$ implies $\varphi \in \Psi$. This type of relations is

[6] We refer to a modal logic textbook, say [8], for a definition of a *(maximal) consistent set of formulas.*

typically used in the definition of a canonical model, and are sometimes called *canonical relations*. We easily get the following proposition.

Proposition 8. *For any index I, the canonical relation $\rhd_I$ on $MCS^{\boldsymbol{L}}$ is:*

1. *serial, if I is singleton and $\boldsymbol{L}$ is $\boldsymbol{D}^\cap$;*
2. *reflexive, if $\boldsymbol{L}$ is $\boldsymbol{T}^\cap$;*
3. *reflexive and symmetric, if $\boldsymbol{L}$ is $\boldsymbol{B}^\cap$;*
4. *reflexive and transitive, if $\boldsymbol{L}$ is $\boldsymbol{S4}^\cap$;*
5. *an equivalence relation, if $\boldsymbol{L}$ is $\boldsymbol{S5}^\cap$;*
6. *s.t. $\rhd_J \subseteq \rhd_I$, for any index $J \supseteq I$.*

Definition 9 (canonical paths). *Given an axiomatization $\boldsymbol{L}$, a* canonical path *for $\boldsymbol{L}$ is a sequence $\langle \Phi_0, I_1, \ldots, I_n, \Phi_n \rangle$ such that:*

(i) $\Phi_0, \ldots, \Phi_n \in MCS^{\boldsymbol{L}}$,
(ii) $I_1, \ldots, I_n$ *are indices, and*
(iii) for all $x = 1, \ldots, n$, $(\Phi_{x-1}, \Phi_x) \in \rhd_{I_x}$.

Initial segments, $\mathsf{tail}(s)$, *("canonical") i-paths, I-paths, and so on, are defined exactly like for paths in a model (Definition 3).*

The *standard models* we will define for these logics are a bit different from the canonical model for a standard modal logic. As mentioned existing proofs are based on transforming the canonical model to a treelike model. We will construct a treelike model directly: in the standard model for a logic L, a state will be a canonical path for **L**. However, the binary relations in a standard model is dependent on the concrete logic we focus on. We now first define these binary relations and then introduce the definition of a standard model.

Definition 10 (standard relations). *Given a logic L with its axiomatization $\boldsymbol{L}$, we define R^L as follows. For any $i \in \mathcal{I}$, R^L_i is the binary relation on the set of canonical paths for $\boldsymbol{L}$, called the* standard relation for i, *such that:*

- *When L is $K^\cap$ or $D^\cap$: for all canonical paths s and t for $\boldsymbol{L}$, $(s,t) \in \mathsf{R}^L_i$ iff t extends s with $\langle I, \Phi \rangle$ for some $I \ni i$ and $\Phi \in MCS^{\boldsymbol{L}}$;*
- *When L is $T^\cap$: for all canonical paths s and t for $\boldsymbol{T}^\cap$, $(s,t) \in \mathsf{R}^{T^\cap}_i$ iff $t = s$ or t extends s with $\langle I, \Phi \rangle$ for some $I \ni i$ and $\Phi \in MCS^{\boldsymbol{T}^\cap}$;*
- *When L is $B^\cap$: for all canonical paths s and t for $\boldsymbol{B}^\cap$, $(s,t) \in \mathsf{R}^{B^\cap}_i$ iff one of the following holds for some $I \ni i$ and $\Phi \in MCS^{\boldsymbol{B}^\cap}$:*
  (i) $t = s$
  (ii) s *extends* t *with* $\langle I, \Phi \rangle$
  (iii) t *extends* s *with* $\langle I, \Phi \rangle$;
- *When L is $S4^\cap$: for all canonical paths s and t for $\boldsymbol{S4}^\cap$, $(s,t) \in \mathsf{R}^{S4^\cap}_i$ iff s is an initial segment of t and $t \setminus s$ is a canonical i-path;*
- *When L is $S5^\cap$: for all canonical paths s and t for $\boldsymbol{S5}^\cap$, $(s,t) \in \mathsf{R}^{S5^\cap}_i$ iff*
  (i) s and t have a common initial segment u, and
  (ii) both $s \setminus u$ and $t \setminus u$ are canonical i-paths.

Definition 11 (standard models). *Given a logic L, the* standard model *for L is a tuple $\mathsf{M}^L = (\mathsf{S}, \mathsf{R}, \mathsf{V})$ such that:*

- S *is the set of all canonical paths for* $\boldsymbol{L}$*;*
- $\mathsf{R} = \mathsf{R}^L$*;*
- *For any propositional variable p,* $\mathsf{V}(p) = \{s \in \mathsf{S} \mid p \in \mathsf{tail}(s)\}$.

Lemma 12 (standardness). *The following hold:*

1. $\mathsf{M}^{K^\cap}$ *is a Kripke model;*
2. $\mathsf{M}^{D^\cap}$ *is a D model;*
3. $\mathsf{M}^{T^\cap}$ *is a T model;*
4. $\mathsf{M}^{B^\cap}$ *is a B model;*
5. $\mathsf{M}^{S4^\cap}$ *is an S4 model;*
6. $\mathsf{M}^{S5^\cap}$ *is an S5 model.*

Lemma 13 (existence). *For any logic L, state s of M^L, and index I, if $\cap_I \varphi \notin \mathsf{tail}(s)$ then there is a state t of M^L such that $(s,t) \in \bigcap_{i\in I} \mathsf{R}_i^L$ and $\varphi \notin \mathsf{tail}(t)$.*

Proof. Let s be a state of M^L and $\cap_I \varphi \notin \mathsf{tail}(s)$. So $\neg \cap_I \varphi \in \mathsf{tail}(s)$. Consider the set $\Phi^- = \{\neg\varphi\} \cup \{\psi \mid \cap_I \psi \in \mathsf{tail}(s)\}$. We can show Φ^- is $\mathbf{L}$ consistent just as in a classical proof of the existence lemma (see, e.g., [8]). We can then extend it into a maximal consistent set Φ of formulas using the Lindenbaum construction. Since $\neg\varphi \in \Phi$, $\varphi \notin \Phi$. Let t be s extended with $\langle I, \Phi\rangle$. By definition it is clear that $\varphi \notin \mathsf{tail}(t)$ and for all L, $(s,t) \in \bigcap_{i\in I} \mathsf{R}_i^\mathrm{L}$ (since $s\ \mathsf{R}_i^\mathrm{L}\ t$ for all $i \in I$).

Lemma 14 (truth). *Given a logic L, a formula φ, and a state s of M^L, it holds that: $\mathsf{M}^L, s \models \varphi$ if and only if $\varphi \in \mathsf{tail}(s)$.*

Proof. The proof is by induction on φ. The atomic case is by definition. Boolean cases are easy to show. Interesting cases are for the modalities $\Box_i$ $(i \in \mathcal{I})$ and $\cap_I$ (I is an index). We start with the case for $\cap_I \psi$.

$$
\begin{aligned}
& \mathsf{M}^\mathrm{L}, s \models \cap_I \psi \\
\Leftrightarrow\ & \text{for all } t, \text{ if } (s,t) \in \textstyle\bigcap_{i\in I} \mathsf{R}_i^\mathrm{L} \text{ then } \mathsf{M}^\mathrm{L}, t \models \psi \\
\Leftrightarrow\ & \text{for all } t, \text{ if } (s,t) \in \textstyle\bigcap_{i\in I} \mathsf{R}_i^\mathrm{L} \text{ then } \psi \in \mathsf{tail}(t) \\
\Rightarrow\ & \cap_I \psi \in \mathsf{tail}(s) && \text{(existence lemma)}
\end{aligned}
$$

For the converse of the last step, suppose $\cap_I \psi \in \mathsf{tail}(s)$ and assume towards a contradiction that there is a state t such that $(s,t) \in \bigcap_{i\in I} \mathsf{R}_i^\mathrm{L}$ and $\psi \notin \mathsf{tail}(t)$.

- If L is $\mathrm{K}^\cap$ or $\mathrm{D}^\cap$, it must be that t extends s with $\langle J, \Phi\rangle$ for $J \supseteq I$ and $\Phi \in \mathrm{MCS}^\mathbf{L}$. By definition $\mathsf{tail}(s) \rhd_J \mathsf{tail}(t)$, and by Proposition 8.6, we have $\mathsf{tail}(s) \rhd_I \mathsf{tail}(t)$. Therefore $\psi \in \mathsf{tail}(t)$, which leads to a contradiction.
- If L is $\mathrm{T}^\cap$, we face an extra case compared with the above, namely $s = t$. A contradiction can be reached by applying the axiom $\mathrm{T}\cap$.

- If L is $B^\cap$, then (i) $t = s$ or (ii) $s = \langle t, J, \Phi \rangle$ or (iii) $t = \langle s, J, \Phi \rangle$ where $J \supseteq I$ and $\Phi \in \mathrm{MCS}^{\mathbf{B}}$. Case (i) can be shown similarly to the case when L is $T^\cap$, and case (iii) to the case when L is $K^\cap$ or $D^\cap$. For case (ii), it is important to observe that $\rhd_I$ is symmetric (Proposition 8.3) and $\rhd_J \subseteq \rhd_I$ (Proposition 8.6).
- If L is $S4^\cap$, s must be an initial segment of t and $t \setminus s$ is an I-path. We get $\mathsf{tail}(s) \rhd_I \mathsf{tail}(t)$ by Proposition 8.6 and the reflexivity and transitivity of $\rhd_I$ (Proposition 8.4). Therefore $\psi \in \mathsf{tail}(t)$ which leads to a contradiction.
- If L is $S5^\cap$, s and t have a common initial segment u, and $s \setminus u$ and $t \setminus u$ are both I-paths. When one of s and t is an initial segment of the other, it can be shown like in the case when L is $S4^\cap$. The interesting case is when s and t really fork, in this case we can show both $\mathsf{tail}(s) \rhd_I \mathsf{tail}(u)$ and $\mathsf{tail}(u) \rhd_I \mathsf{tail}(t)$ by transitivity and symmetry of $\rhd_I$ (Proposition 8.5) and Proposition 8.6, so that $\mathsf{tail}(s) \rhd_I \mathsf{tail}(t)$. Then $\psi \in \mathsf{tail}(t)$, which leads to a contradiction.

Finally, the case for $\Box_i\psi$: $\mathsf{M}^{\mathrm{L}}, s \models \Box_i\psi \iff \mathsf{M}^{\mathrm{L}}, s \models \cap_{\{i\}}\psi$ (validity of $\cap$1) $\iff \cap_{\{i\}}\psi \in \mathsf{tail}(s)$ (special case of $\cap_I\psi$) $\iff \Box_i\psi \in \mathsf{tail}(s)$ (axiom $\cap$1).

Theorem 15 (strong completeness). *Given $L \in \{K^\cap, D^\cap, T^\cap, B^\cap, S4^\cap, S5^\cap\}$ and its axiomatization $\mathbf{L}$, for any $\Phi \subseteq \mathcal{L}^\cap$ and $\varphi \in \mathcal{L}^\cap$, if $\Phi \models \varphi$, then $\Phi \vdash_{\mathbf{L}} \varphi$.*

Proof. Suppose $\Phi \nvdash_{\mathbf{L}} \varphi$. It follows that $\Phi \cup \{\neg\varphi\}$ is **L** consistent. Extend it to be a maximal consistent set Ψ, then $\langle \Psi \rangle$ is a canonical path. By the truth lemma, for any formula ψ, we have $\mathsf{M}, \langle \Psi \rangle \models \psi$ iff $\psi \in \Psi$. It follows that Ψ is satisfiable, which leads to $\Phi \not\models \varphi$.

5 Logics over $\mathcal{L}^{\cap\uplus}$

In this section we study the logics with both the intersection and union$^+$ modalities. The language is set to be $\mathcal{L}^{\cap\uplus}$ in this section, and by a "logic" without further explanation we mean one of $K^{\cap\uplus}$, $D^{\cap\uplus}$, $T^{\cap\uplus}$, $B^{\cap\uplus}$, $S4^{\cap\uplus}$ or $S5^{\cap\uplus}$.

Compared with the characterization of intersection, that of transitive closure of union is more straightforward:

$$\mathbf{Un(K)} = \mathbf{Un(D)} = \mathbf{Un(T)} = \mathbf{Un(B)} = \mathbf{Un(S4)} = \mathbf{Un(S5)} = \{\mathrm{K}\uplus, \uplus 1, \uplus 2\}.$$

These axioms are not new, see, e.g., [11], although as far as we know they have not been studied in combination with D and B in the literature. For simplicity we write **Un** for this set of axioms. Additional validities for union$^+$ corresponding to specific frame conditions can be derived in specific logic systems. For instance, D$\uplus$ is a theorem of $\mathbf{D} \oplus \mathbf{Un}$.

By adding to the axiomatization of a logic over $\mathcal{L}^\cap$ the characterization of union$^+$, we get a sound axiomatization for the corresponding logic over $\mathcal{L}^{\cap\uplus}$. To be precise, we list the axiomatizations as follows:

$$\begin{aligned}
\mathbf{K}^{\cap\uplus} &= \mathbf{K}^{\cap} \oplus \mathbf{Un}\\
\mathbf{D}^{\cap\uplus} &= \mathbf{D}^{\cap} \oplus \mathbf{Un}\\
\mathbf{T}^{\cap\uplus} &= \mathbf{T}^{\cap} \oplus \mathbf{Un}\\
\mathbf{B}^{\cap\uplus} &= \mathbf{B}^{\cap} \oplus \mathbf{Un}\\
\mathbf{S4}^{\cap\uplus} &= \mathbf{S4}^{\cap} \oplus \mathbf{Un}\\
\mathbf{S5}^{\cap\uplus} &= \mathbf{S5}^{\cap} \oplus \mathbf{Un}.
\end{aligned}$$

It is well known that logics with both a basic modality and a modality for the transitive closure of the basic modality is not semantically *compact*; we will thus be concerned only with *weak* rather than *strong* completeness in this section. We will make extensive references to the names of logics and axiomatizations, and for simplicity we shall call a tuple $\sigma = (\mathrm{L}, \mathbf{L}, \alpha, \iota)$ a *signature*, when L is one of the logics $\mathrm{K}^{\cap\uplus}$, $\mathrm{D}^{\cap\uplus}$, $\mathrm{T}^{\cap\uplus}$, $\mathrm{B}^{\cap\uplus}$, $\mathrm{S4}^{\cap\uplus}$ and $\mathrm{S5}^{\cap\uplus}$, $\mathbf{L}$ is the corresponding axiomatization for L, α is a formula of $\mathcal{L}^{\cap\uplus}$, and ι is an index such that (i) $i \in \iota$ for every $\Box_i$ occurring in α, and (ii) every index occurring in α is a subset of ι.

Definition 16 (closure). *Given a signature $\sigma = (L, \mathbf{L}, \alpha, \iota)$, the σ-*closure*, denoted $cl(\sigma)$, is the minimal set of formulas satisfying the following conditions:*

1. *$\alpha \in cl(\sigma)$;*
2. *If $\varphi \in cl(\sigma)$, then all the subformulas of φ are also in $cl(\sigma)$;*
3. *If φ does not start with a negation symbol and $\varphi \in cl(\sigma)$, then $\neg\varphi \in cl(\sigma)$;*
4. *For any $i \in \iota$,*
   (i) If $\cap_{\{i\}}\varphi \in cl(\sigma)$ then $\Box_i\varphi \in cl(\sigma)$, and
   (ii) If $\Box_i\varphi \in cl(\sigma)$ then $\cap_{\{i\}}\varphi \in cl(\sigma)$;
5. *For indices I and J with $I \subset J \subseteq \iota$, if $\cap_I\varphi \in cl(\sigma)$ then $\cap_J\varphi \in cl(\sigma)$;*
6. *For indices $I, J \subseteq \iota$, if $\uplus_I\varphi \in cl(\sigma)$ and $I \cap J \neq \emptyset$ then $\cap_J\uplus_I\varphi \in cl(\sigma)$.*[7]

It is not hard to verify that $cl(\sigma)$ is finite and nonempty for any signature σ. Given $\sigma = (\mathrm{L}, \mathbf{L}, \alpha, \iota)$, a set of formulas is said to be *maximal* $\mathbf{L}$*-consistent in* $cl(\sigma)$, if it is (i) a subset of $cl(\sigma)$, (ii) $\mathbf{L}$-consistent and (iii) maximal in $cl(\sigma)$ (i.e., any proper superset which is a subset of $cl(\sigma)$ is inconsistent). We write MCS^{σ} for the set of all maximal $\mathbf{L}$-consistent sets of formulas in $cl(\sigma)$.

Now we adapt the canonical relations to the finitary case. Given a signature σ and an index I, we may try to define a canonical relation $\rhd_I$ to be a binary relation on MCS^{σ}, such that $\Phi \rhd_I \Psi$ iff for all φ, $\cap_I\varphi \in \Phi$ implies $\varphi \in \Psi$, like we did for the logics over $\mathcal{L}^{\cap}$. But there are subtleties here. For example, transitivity may be lost for $\mathrm{S4}^{\cap\uplus}$, if $\cap_I\varphi \in \Phi$ but $\cap_I\cap_I\varphi \notin \Phi$ in case the latter is not included in the closure. We introduce the formal definition below.

Definition 17 (finitary canonical relation). *For a signature $\sigma = (L, \mathbf{L}, \alpha, \iota)$ and an index $I \subseteq \iota$, the* canonical relation *$\rhd_I$ for σ is the binary relation on MCS^{σ}, such that the following hold for all $\Phi, \Psi \in MCS^{\sigma}$:*

[7] This is the place where the use of ι is essential to make sure that a closure is finite.

- *If L is* $K^{\cap\uplus}$, $D^{\cap\uplus}$ *or* $T^{\cap\uplus}$: $\Phi \rhd_I \Psi$ *iff* $\{\varphi \mid \cap_I\varphi \in \Phi\} \subseteq \Psi$;
- *If L is* $B^{\cap\uplus}$: $\Phi \rhd_I \Psi$ *iff* $\{\varphi \mid \cap_I\varphi \in \Phi\} \subseteq \Psi$ *and* $\{\varphi \mid \cap_I\varphi \in \Psi\} \subseteq \Phi$;
- *If L is* $S4^{\cap\uplus}$: $\Phi \rhd_I \Psi$ *iff* $\{\cap_I\varphi \mid \cap_I\varphi \in \Phi\} \subseteq \{\cap_I\varphi \mid \cap_I\varphi \in \Psi\}$;
- *If L is* $S5^{\cap\uplus}$: $\Phi \rhd_I \Psi$ *iff* $\{\cap_I\varphi \mid \cap_I\varphi \in \Psi\} = \{\cap_I\varphi \mid \cap_I\varphi \in \Psi\}$.

Note that for all the logics, from $\Phi \rhd_I \Psi$ we still get that $\cap_I\varphi \in \Phi$ implies $\varphi \in \Psi$, as the criteria above are at least not weaker. We get the following proposition that is similar to Proposition 8.

Proposition 18. *For any signature* $\sigma = (L, \mathbf{L}, \alpha, \iota)$ *and any index* $I \subseteq \iota$, *the canonical relation* $\rhd_I$ *for* σ *is:*

1. *Serial, if* I *is singleton and* $\mathbf{L}$ *is* $\boldsymbol{D}^{\cap\uplus}$;
2. *Reflexive, if* $\mathbf{L}$ *is* $\boldsymbol{T}^{\cap\uplus}$;
3. *Reflexive and symmetric, if* $\mathbf{L}$ *is* $\boldsymbol{B}^{\cap\uplus}$;
4. *Reflexive and transitive, if* $\mathbf{L}$ *is* $\boldsymbol{S4}^{\cap\uplus}$;
5. *An equivalence relation, if* $\mathbf{L}$ *is* $\boldsymbol{S5}^{\cap\uplus}$.
6. $\rhd_J \subseteq \rhd_I$, *for any index* J *such that* $I \subset J \subseteq \iota$.

Proof. For seriality when $I = \{i\}$: given $\Phi \in \text{MCS}^\sigma$ and a formula φ such that $\cap_{\{i\}}\varphi \in \Phi$, it suffices to show the existence of a $\Psi \in \text{MCS}^\sigma$ such that $\varphi \in \Psi$. This is easy, take φ and extend it to be $\mathbf{L}$-maximal in $cl(\sigma)$ (note that $\varphi \in cl(\sigma)$).

For reflexivity, we make use of the axiom T$\cap$ and the fact that $cl(\sigma)$ is closed under subformulas.

For the combinations of frame conditions for $\mathbf{B}^{\cap\uplus}$, $\mathbf{S4}^{\cap\uplus}$ and $\mathbf{S5}^{\cap\uplus}$, we can see that they are enforced by the definition of the canonical relation.

Definition 19 (finitary canonical paths). *Given a signature* $\sigma = (L, \mathbf{L}, \alpha, \iota)$, *a* canonical path *for* $\mathbf{L}$ *in* $cl(\sigma)$ *is a sequence* $\langle \Phi_0, I_1, \ldots, I_n, \Phi_n \rangle$ *such that:*

(i) $\Phi_0, \ldots, \Phi_n \in MCS^\sigma$,
(ii) $I_1, \ldots, I_n \subseteq \iota$ *are indices, and*
(iii) for all $x = 1, \ldots, n$, $(\Phi_{x-1}, \Phi_x) \in \rhd_{I_x}$.

Initial segments, tails of paths, ("canonical") i-paths, I-paths, and so on, are defined like for paths in a model (Definition 3).

Definition 20 (standard relation). *Given a signature* $\sigma = (L, \mathbf{L}, \alpha, \iota)$, *for any* $i \in \iota$, *the* standard relation R_i^σ *is the binary relation on the canonical paths for* $\mathbf{L}$ *in* $cl(\sigma)$, *such that:*

- *If L is* $K^{\cap\uplus}$ *or* $D^{\cap\uplus}$: *for all canonical paths s and t for* $\mathbf{L}$ *in* $cl(\sigma)$, $(s,t) \in \mathsf{R}_i^\sigma$ *iff t extends s with* $\langle I, \Phi \rangle$ *for* $\Phi \in MCS^\sigma$ *and some index I such that* $i \in I \subseteq \iota$;
- *If L is* $T^{\cap\uplus}$: *for all canonical paths s and t for* $\boldsymbol{T}^{\cap\uplus}$ *in* $cl(\sigma)$, $(s,t) \in \mathsf{R}_i^\sigma$ *iff* $t = s$ *or t extends s with* $\langle I, \Phi \rangle$ *for* $\Phi \in MCS^\sigma$ *and some index I s.t.* $i \in I \subseteq \iota$;
- *If L is* $B^{\cap\uplus}$: *for all canonical paths s and t for* $\boldsymbol{B}^{\cap\uplus}$ *in* $cl(\sigma)$, $(s,t) \in \mathsf{R}_i^\sigma$ *iff (i)* $t = s$ *or (ii)* $s = \langle t, I, \Phi \rangle$ *or (iii)* $t = \langle s, I, \Phi \rangle$ *for* $\Phi \in MCS^\sigma$ *and some index I such that* $i \in I \subseteq \iota$;

- *If L is $S4^{\cap\uplus}$: for all canonical paths s and t for $\boldsymbol{S4}^{\cap\uplus}$ in $cl(\sigma)$, $(s,t) \in \mathsf{R}_i^\sigma$ iff s is an initial segment of t and $t \setminus s$ is a canonical i-path;*
- *If L is $S5^{\cap\uplus}$: for all canonical paths s and t for $\boldsymbol{S5}^{\cap\uplus}$ in $cl(\sigma)$, $(s,t) \in \mathsf{R}_i^\sigma$ iff (i) s and t have a common initial segment u, and (ii) both $s \setminus u$ and $t \setminus u$ are canonical i-paths.*

Definition 21 (finitary standard models). *Given a signature $\sigma = (L, \boldsymbol{L}, \alpha, \iota)$, the* standard model *for σ is a tuple $\mathsf{M}^\sigma = (\mathsf{S}, \mathsf{R}, \mathsf{V})$ such that:*

- *S is the set of all canonical paths for $\boldsymbol{L}$ in $cl(\sigma)$.*
- *$\mathsf{R}_i = \mathsf{R}_i^\sigma$.*
- *For any propositional variable p, $\mathsf{V}(p) = \{s \in \mathsf{S} \mid p \in \mathsf{tail}(s)\}$.*

Lemma 22 (standardness). *For any signature $\sigma = (L, \boldsymbol{L}, \alpha, \iota)$,*

1. *M^σ is a Kripke model;*
2. *M^σ is a D model when $L = D^{\cap\uplus}$ and $\boldsymbol{L} = \boldsymbol{D}^{\cap\uplus}$;*
3. *M^σ is a T model when $L = T^{\cap\uplus}$ and $\boldsymbol{L} = \boldsymbol{T}^{\cap\uplus}$;*
4. *M^σ is a B model when $L = B^{\cap\uplus}$ and $\boldsymbol{L} = \boldsymbol{B}^{\cap\uplus}$;*
5. *M^σ is an $S4$ model when $L = S4^{\cap\uplus}$ and $\boldsymbol{L} = \boldsymbol{S4}^{\cap\uplus}$;*
6. *M^σ is an $S5$ model when $L = S5^{\cap\uplus}$ and $\boldsymbol{L} = \boldsymbol{S5}^{\cap\uplus}$.*

Lemma 23 (existence). *For any signature σ, any state s of M^σ, and any index $I \subseteq \iota$,*

1. *Given $\cap_I \varphi \in cl(\sigma)$, if $\cap_I \varphi \notin \mathsf{tail}(s)$, then there is a state t of M^σ such that $(s,t) \in \bigcap_{i \in I} \mathsf{R}_i^\sigma$ and $\varphi \notin \mathsf{tail}(t)$.*
2. *Given $\uplus_I \varphi \in cl(\sigma)$, if $\uplus_I \varphi \notin \mathsf{tail}(s)$, then there is a state t of M^σ such that $(s,t) \in \biguplus_{i \in I} \mathsf{R}_i^\sigma$ and $\varphi \notin \mathsf{tail}(t)$.*

Proof. Let $\sigma = (\mathrm{L}, \mathbf{L}, \alpha, \iota)$ and s be a state of M^σ.

(1) Let $\cap_I \varphi \notin \mathsf{tail}(s)$. So $\neg \cap_I \varphi \in \mathsf{tail}(s)$. Consider the set $\Phi^- = \{-\varphi\} \cup \{\psi \mid \cap_I \psi \in \mathsf{tail}(s)\}$ (where $-\varphi$ is ψ if $\varphi = \neg\psi$, and is $\neg\varphi$ if φ does not start with a negation symbol). Clearly $\Phi^- \subseteq cl(\sigma)$ and it is not hard to show that it is $\mathbf{L}$ consistent. We can then extend it into a maximal consistent set Φ of formulas in $cl(\sigma)$. Since $-\varphi \in \Phi$, $\varphi \notin \Phi$. Let t be s extended with $\langle I, \Phi \rangle$. By definition it is clear that $\varphi \notin \mathsf{tail}(t)$ and $(s,t) \in \bigcap_{i \in I} \mathsf{R}_i^\sigma$ (since $s\, \mathsf{R}_i^\sigma\, t$ for all $i \in I$).

(2) Let $\mathcal{P}$ be the property on the states of M^σ such that for any s, $s \in \mathcal{P}$ iff for any t, if $(s,t) \in \biguplus_{i \in I} \mathsf{R}_i^\sigma$ then $\varphi \in \mathsf{tail}(t)$. The equivalent condition is that for any state s_0 of M^σ, $s_0 \in \mathcal{P}$ iff $\varphi \in \mathsf{tail}(s_n)$ holds for any path $\langle s_0, \{i_0\}, \ldots, \{i_{n-1}\}, s_n \rangle$ of M^σ with $\{i_0, \ldots, i_{n-1}\} \subseteq I$. Let $\psi = \bigvee_{s \in \mathcal{P}} \widehat{\mathsf{tail}(s)}$ (where $\widehat{\mathsf{tail}(s)}$ is the conjunction of all formulas in $\mathsf{tail}(s)$). We get the following:

(a) For any $i \in I$, $\vdash_{\mathbf{L}} \psi \to \Box_i \varphi$. First observe that for every $s_0 \in \mathcal{P}$, any path $\langle s_0, \{i_0\}, \ldots, \{i_{n-1}\}, s_n \rangle$ as described above is such that $\varphi \in \mathsf{tail}(s_n)$. As a special case, for any state s_1, if $\langle s_0, \{i\}, s_1 \rangle$ is a path, namely $\mathsf{tail}(s_0) \rhd_{\{i\}} \mathsf{tail}(s_1)$, then $\varphi \in \mathsf{tail}(s_1)$. It follows that $\Box_i \varphi \in \mathsf{tail}(s_0)$ (for otherwise it violates the first clause; just treat $\Box_i$ to be $\cap_{\{i\}}$). This means that $\Box_i \varphi$ is a conjunct of every disjunct of ψ, and so $\vdash_{\mathbf{L}} \psi \to \Box_i \varphi$.

(b) For any $i \in I$, $\vdash_{\mathbf{L}} \psi \to \Box_i\psi$. Suppose towards a contradiction that $\psi \wedge \neg\Box_i\psi$ is consistent. There must be a disjunct of ψ, say $\widehat{\mathsf{tail}(t)}$ (with $t \in \mathcal{P}$), such that $\widehat{\mathsf{tail}(t)} \wedge \neg\Box_i\psi$ is consistent. By properties of MCS$^\sigma$ we have $\vdash_{\mathbf{L}} \bigvee\{\widehat{\Phi} \mid \Phi \in \text{MCS}^\sigma\}$ (similarly $\widehat{\Phi}$ is the conjunction of formulas in Φ). So there must be $\Phi \in \text{MCS}^\sigma \setminus \{\mathsf{tail}(s) \mid s \in \mathcal{P}\}$ such that $\widehat{\mathsf{tail}(t)} \wedge \neg\Box_i\neg\widehat{\Phi}$ is consistent. It follows that $\mathsf{tail}(t) \rhd_{\{i\}} \Phi$. The path u which extends t with $\langle\{i\},\Phi\rangle$ is such that $(t,u) \in \mathsf{R}^\sigma_{\{i\}}$. Since $t \in \mathcal{P}$, we have $u \in \mathcal{P}$ as well. However, this conflicts with the fact that $\Phi \notin \{\mathsf{tail}(s) \mid s \in \mathcal{P}\}$.

Now suppose $s \in \mathcal{P}$, and we must show $\uplus_I\varphi \in \mathsf{tail}(s)$. By (a) and (b), $\vdash_{\mathbf{L}} \psi \to \bigwedge_{i\in I}\Box_i(\psi \wedge \varphi)$, and then by $\uplus$2 we have $\vdash_{\mathbf{L}} \psi \to \uplus_I\varphi$. Let $\xi = \widehat{\mathsf{tail}(s)}$. It follows that $\vdash_{\mathbf{L}} \xi \to \psi$, as ξ is one of the disjuncts of ψ. We get $\vdash_{\mathbf{L}} \xi \to \uplus_I\varphi$, and so $\uplus_I\varphi \in \mathsf{tail}(s)$ for $\mathsf{tail}(s)$ is consistent.

Lemma 24 (truth). *Given a signature σ, a formula $\varphi \in cl(\sigma)$, and a state s of M^σ, it holds that: $\mathsf{M}^\sigma, s \models \varphi$ iff $\varphi \in \mathsf{tail}(s)$.*

Proof. The proof is by induction on φ. The atomic and Boolean cases are easy to show. The cases for the modalities $\Box_i$ ($i \in \mathcal{I}$) and $\cap_I$ (I is an index) are not much different from those of the proof of Lemma 14 (we need to be careful with the closure, however; just note that all the i's and I's used here are bounded by an ι). Here we detail the case for $\uplus_I\psi$.

$$\begin{aligned}
&\mathsf{M}^\sigma, s \models \uplus_I\psi \\
&\Leftrightarrow \text{for all } t, \text{ if } (s,t) \in \textstyle\biguplus_{i\in I} \mathsf{R}^\sigma_i \text{ then } \mathsf{M}^\sigma, t \models \psi \\
&\Leftrightarrow \text{for all } t, \text{ if } (s,t) \in \textstyle\biguplus_{i\in I} \mathsf{R}^\sigma_i \text{ then } \psi \in \mathsf{tail}(t) \\
&\Rightarrow \uplus_I\psi \in \mathsf{tail}(s) \qquad\qquad \text{(existence lemma)}
\end{aligned}$$

For the converse direction of the last step, suppose $\uplus_I\psi \in \mathsf{tail}(s)$ and towards a contradiction that there is a state t such that $(s,t) \in \biguplus_{i\in I} \mathsf{R}^\sigma_i$ and $\psi \notin \mathsf{tail}(t)$. So there is a path $\langle s_0, \{i_0\}, \ldots, \{i_{n-1}\}, s_n\rangle$ of M^σ such that $\{i_0,\ldots,i_{n-1}\} \subseteq I$, $s = s_0$ and $t = s_n$.

- If L is $\mathrm{K}^{\cap\uplus}$ or $\mathrm{D}^{\cap\uplus}$, it must be that t extends s with $\langle J_0, \Phi_1, \ldots, J_{n-1}, \Phi_n\rangle$ where $\psi \notin \Phi_n$ and for each x, $i_x \in J_x$ and $\Phi_x \in \text{MCS}^\sigma$. By definition $\mathsf{tail}(s_0) \rhd_{J_0} \Phi_1 \rhd_{J_1} \cdots \rhd_{J_{n-1}} \Phi_n$. By the axioms $\uplus$1, $\cap$1 and $\cap$2 we can get $\vdash_{\mathbf{L}} \uplus_I\psi \to \cap_{J_0}\uplus_I\psi$, and $\uplus_I\psi \in \Phi_1$ for $\cap_{J_0}\uplus_I\psi \in cl(\sigma)$. Doing this recursively, we get $\uplus_I\psi \in \Phi_n$ and so $\psi \in \Phi_n$ by T$\uplus$, which contradicts $\psi \notin \mathsf{tail}(t)$.
- If L is $\mathrm{T}^{\cap\uplus}$, we face an extra case compared with the above, namely $s = t$. A contradiction can be achieved by applying the axiom T$\uplus$.
- If L is $\mathrm{B}^{\cap\uplus}$, there are three cases: (i) $s_{x+1} = s_x$ or (ii) $s_x = \langle s_{x+1}, J, \Phi\rangle$ or (iii) $s_{x+1} = \langle s_x, J, \Phi\rangle$ where $J \supseteq I$ and $\Phi \in \text{MCS}^\sigma$. In all cases, by similar reasoning to the above (for case (ii) we use the symmetric condition for $\rhd_I$), we can show that $\psi \in \mathsf{tail}(s_{x+1})$ given $\uplus_I\psi \in \mathsf{tail}(s_x)$, and then reach a contradiction similarly.

- If L is $S4^{\cap\uplus}$, s_x $(0 \leq x < n)$ must be an initial segment of s_{x+1} and $s_{x+1} \setminus s_x$ is a finitary canonical i_x-path $(i_x \in I)$. By the axioms $\uplus1$ and $\cap1$, $\vdash_{\mathbf{S4}^{\cap\uplus}} \uplus_I \psi \rightarrow \cap_J \uplus_I \psi$ (for all $i_x \in J \subseteq \iota$). So we get $\cap_J \uplus_I \psi \in \mathsf{tail}(s_{x+1})$ (we use $T\uplus$ in the case when $s = t$). Recursively carrying this out, we get $\cap_J \uplus_I \psi \in \mathsf{tail}(t)$, and so $\psi \in \mathsf{tail}(t)$ which leads to a contradiction.
- If L is $S5^{\cap\uplus}$, then s_x and s_{x+1} have a common initial segment u, and $s_x \setminus u$ and $s_{x+1} \setminus u$ are both finitary canonical i_x-paths. Since $\vdash_{\mathbf{S5}^{\cap\uplus}} \uplus_I \psi \rightarrow \cap_J \uplus_I \psi$ (for all $i_x \in J \subseteq \iota$), $\cap_J \uplus_I \psi \in \mathsf{tail}(s_0)$, and by the definition of $\triangleright$, $\cap_J \uplus_I \psi \in \mathsf{tail}(s_x)$, so $\psi \in \mathsf{tail}(t)$ which leads to a contradiction as well.

Theorem 25 (weak completeness). *Let $\boldsymbol{L}$ be the corresponding axiomatization introduced for a logic $L \in \{K^{\cap\uplus}, D^{\cap\uplus}, T^{\cap\uplus}, B^{\cap\uplus}, S4^{\cap\uplus}, S5^{\cap\uplus}\}$. For any $\varphi \in \mathcal{L}^{\cap\uplus}$, if $\models \varphi$, then $\vdash_{\boldsymbol{L}} \varphi$.*

Proof. Suppose $\nvdash_{\mathbf{L}} \varphi$. It follows that $\{\neg\varphi\}$ is $\mathbf{L}$ consistent. Extend it to be a maximal consistent set Φ in $cl((\mathrm{L}, \mathbf{L}, \neg\varphi, \iota))$ with ι including $\{i \mid \Box_i \text{ occurs in } \varphi\}$ and all the indices occurring in φ, then $\langle\Phi\rangle$ is a canonical path for $\mathbf{L}$ in $cl((\mathrm{L}, \mathbf{L}, \neg\varphi, \iota))$. By the truth lemma, for any formula ψ in the closure, we have $\mathsf{M}^{(\mathrm{L}, \mathbf{L}, \neg\varphi, \iota)}, \langle\Phi\rangle \models \psi$ iff $\psi \in \Phi$. It follows that Φ is satisfiable, which leads to $\not\models \varphi$.

6 Discussion

We focused mainly on the completeness proof for the modal logics, K, D, T, B, S4 and S5, extended with intersection and with or without the transitive closure of union. For some of these logics proofs of completeness using the unraveling-folding technique exist in the literature, for some no or only partial proofs exist. We have to omit details here, but the method can also be directly applied to many other canonical multi-modal logics with the intersection modality, including popular systems of epistemic and doxastic logics such as S4.2, S4.3, S4.4 – we have in fact already applied successfully for the KD45 case.[8] By avoiding the model translation processes used in the unraveling-folding method and building a standard model directly, the proofs we present are dramatically simpler than those found in the literature for special cases. We believe that the readers who are familiar with the canonical model method for completeness proofs of modal logics will find the proofs very familiar and straightforward.

While our approach is inspired by simplifying the existing proof technique, the standard model we build is not identical to the model produced by the unraveling-folding processes: it is simpler because we do not have to use so-called reductions of paths. We emphasize, however, that the unraveling-folding method was still important for us to arrive at this proof technique: it explains why we take (finitary) canonical paths to be the states of the standard model. Further work that could be interesting is to show possible bisimilarity of the model we build to that by the unraveling-folding processes.

[8] In an extension of [2], to appear.

It is worth mentioning that our results are slightly more general than most existing proofs from the literature on distributed knowledge in that it allows a (countably) infinite set of boxes. This slightly complicates the proofs in the cases with transitive closure of the union, requiring the use of the σ signatures.

Finally, as mentioned the full language of PDL with intersection (IPDL) is more general than the languages we have considered here: it allows, e.g., transitive closure of intersections. While there are complete axiomatizations of IPDL with infinitary and/or unorthodox inference rules [7], and complete axiomatizations with finitary orthodox rules of iteration-free IPDL [6], finitary orthodox axiomatization of full IPDL is a long-standing open problem. Perhaps the technique presented in this paper could help shed some new light on that problem.

Acknowledgments. We thank the anonymous reviewers for very detailed and useful comments and suggestions. Yì N. Wáng acknowledges funding support by the National Social Science Foundation of China (Grant No. 16CZX048, 18ZDA290), and the Fundamental Research Funds for the Central Universities of China.

References

1. Ågotnes, T., Alechina, N.: Embedding coalition logic in the minimal normal multi-modal logic with intersection. In: Ju, S., Liu, H., Ono, H. (eds.) Modality, Semantics and Interpretations. LASLL, pp. 1–22. Springer, Heidelberg (2015). https://doi.org/10.1007/978-3-662-47197-5_1
2. Ågotnes, T., Wáng, Y.N.: Group belief. In: Dastani, M., Dong, H.,van der Torre, L. (eds.) Logic and Argumentation, pp. 3–21. Springer, Cham (2020)
3. Baader, F., Calvanese, D., McGuinness, D.L., Nardi, D., Patel-Schneider, P.F.: The Description Logic Handbook, 2nd edn. Cambridge University Press, Cambridge (2017)
4. Baader, F., Horrocks, I., Lutz, C., Sattler, U.: An Introduction to Description Logic. Cambridge University Press, Cambridge (2017)
5. Balbiani, P.: Axiomatization of logics based on Kripke models with relative accessibility relations. In: Orłowska, E. (ed.) Incomplete Information: Rough Set Analysis, pp. 553–578. Physica-Verlag HD, Heidelberg (1998). https://doi.org/10.1007/978-3-7908-1888-8_17
6. Balbiani, P.: Eliminating unorthodox derivation rules in an axiom system for iteration-free PDL with intersection. Fundamenta Informaticae **56**(3), 211–242 (2003)
7. Balbiani, P., Vakarelov, D.: PDL with intersection of programs: a complete axiomatization. J. Appl. Non-classical Logics **13**(3–4), 231–276 (2003)
8. Blackburn, P., de Rijke, M., Venema, Y.: Modal Logic. Cambridge University Press, Cambridge (2001)
9. Chellas, B.F.: Modal Logic: An Introduction. Cambridge University Press, Cambridge (1980)
10. Fagin, R., Halpern, J.Y., Vardi, M.Y.: What can machines know? On the properties of knowledge in distributed systems. J. ACM **39**(2), 328–376 (1992)
11. Fagin, R., Halpern, J.Y., Moses, Y., Vardi, M.Y.: Reasoning about Knowledge. The MIT Press, Cambridge (1995)

12. Halpern, J.Y., Moses, Y.: A guide to completeness and complexity for modal logics of knowledge and belief. Artif. Intell. **54**(3), 319–379 (1992)
13. Harel, D., Kozen, D., Tiuryn, J.: Dynamic Logic. The MIT Press, Cambridge (2000)
14. van der Hoek, W., Meyer, J.J.C.: Making some issues of implicit knowledge explicit. Int. J. Found. Comput. Sci. **3**(2), 193–224 (1992)
15. Meyer, J.J.C., van der Hoek, W.: Epistemic Logic for AI and Computer Science. Cambridge University Press, Cambridge (1995)
16. Sahlqvist, H.: Completeness and correspondence in the first and second order semantics for modal logic. In: Kanger, S. (ed.) Proceedings of the Third Scandinavian Logic Symposium, Studies in Logic and the Foundations of Mathematics, vol. 82, pp. 110–143. Elsevier (1975)
17. Wáng, Y.N.: Logical Dynamics of Group Knowledge and Subset Spaces. Ph.D. thesis, University of Bergen (2013)
18. Wáng, Y.N., Ågotnes, T.: Public announcement logic with distributed knowledge: expressivity, completeness and complexity. Synthese **190**, 135–162 (2013). https://doi.org/10.1007/s11229-012-0243-3
19. Wáng, Y.N., Ågotnes, T.: Relativized common knowledge for dynamic epistemic logic. J. Appl. Logic **13**(3), 370–393 (2015)

Arbitrary Propositional Network Announcement Logic

Zuojun Xiong[1(✉)] and Thomas Ågotnes[1,2(✉)]

[1] Institute of Logic and Intelligence, Southwest University, Chongqing, China
zuojunxiong@swu.edu.cn
[2] Department of Information Science and Media Studies, University of Bergen, Bergen, Norway
thomas.agotnes@infomedia.uib.no

Abstract. Modal logics for reasoning about interaction in social networks is an active area of research. In this paper we introduce modalities for quantifying over possible "tweets", i.e., simultaneous messages sent to all an agent's "followers", into an existing basic framework for reasoning about this type of network events. Modalities that quantify over informational events in general, and over agent announcements in particular, is also an active area in the study of the dynamics of knowledge and belief. We combine these two directions by interpreting such modalities in social networks. We study the resulting logic, and provide a sound and strongly complete (infinitary) axiomatisation.

1 Introduction

Modal logics for reasoning about interaction in social networks is currently an active area of research, existing work characterising events and phenomena such as general messaging [18], cascades and diffusion [7], structural balance [20], or group conformity [17], to name a few. At the same time modalities *quantifying* over informational events have been of considerable interest in the study of the dynamics of knowledge and belief; notable examples include Arbitrary Public Announcement Logic (APAL) [5], Group Announcement Logic (GAL) [1], Coalition Announcement Logic (CAL) [2,11], Refinement Modal Logic [8], Arbitrary Action Model Logic [13], Future Event Logic (FEL) [10].

In this paper we add a GAL-style modality $\langle a \rangle$ for each agent a to a minimal logic for reasoning about "tweeting" [21] in social networks. A formula of the form $\langle a \rangle \varphi$ means that a can send a "tweet", i.e., send a message simultaneously to all her friends, after which φ, typically an epistemic formula, will be true. This allows the expression of potentially interesting properties involving an agent's ability to make some belief state come about such as ($[a]$ is the dual):

- $\langle a \rangle (B_b p \wedge \neg B_c p)$: it is possible for a to make a tweet such that b learns p without c learning it;

M. A. Martins and I. Sedlár (Eds.): DaLí 2020, LNCS 12569, pp. 277–293, 2020.
https://doi.org/10.1007/978-3-030-65840-3_17

- $[a](B_b p \rightarrow B_b q)$: no matter what a tweets b will believe q only if she believes p;
- $[a]\neg\langle b\rangle B_c r$: no matter what a tweets there is nothing b can tweet that will make c believe r;
- $\bigvee_{a \in \mathsf{Agnt}}\langle a\rangle\varphi$, where Agnt is the set of all agents: there is a possible tweet (by someone) after which φ becomes true.

Like in the starting point, Propositional Network Announcement Logic (PNAL) [21], we use a relatively simple epistemic model. In particular, we only model purely propositional tweets (no tweets about others' knowledge or belief) and we don't model higher-order knowledge. On the other hand, we allow arbitrary belief states, not only S5 knowledge. As shown in [21] even with this simple model there are interesting and subtle issues, and this level of abstraction is useful to tease out the fundamental principles for reasoning about these types of network events.

We study logical properties in the form of potentially valid formulas, such as, e.g., Church-Rosser and McKinsey properties, of the resulting logic. The main result is a sound and complete axiomatisation. The logic is not semantically compact, and thus a strongly complete finitary axiomatisation does not exist. The axiomatisation we provide is a strongly complete infinitary system. The same situation as for most of the logics with modalities quantifying over events mentioned above, including APAL and GAL, at present time only infinitary complete axiomatisations are known[1].

The rest of the paper is organised as follows. In the next section we review the basics of PNAL, before we extend it with the new modalities in Sect. 3 where we also look at some of their logical properties and the issue of compactness. In Sect. 4 we define the infinitary system, and show that it is sound and strongly complete. We conclude in Sect. 5.

2 Propositional Network Announcement Logic

In this section we give a succinct presentation of propositional network announcement logic. For further details and discussion, see [21].

The logic is parameterised by a non-empty set Agnt of agents and a non-empty set Prop of propositional letters. We will assume that Prop is countably infinite. Let $\mathcal{L}_{\text{PROP}}$ be the language of propositional logic over Prop, i.e., formulas generated by the grammar:

$$\theta ::= p \mid \neg\theta \mid \theta \wedge \theta$$

where $p \in \mathsf{Prop}$.

[1] Finitary axiomatisations for both APAL and GAL have been published but later discovered to be unsound [15].

A *valuation* is a function $v : \mathsf{Prop} \to \{true, false\}$; Val denotes the set of all valuations and $[\![\theta]\!] = \{v \in \mathsf{Val} \mid v(\theta) = true\}$ is the set of valuations making θ true, where v is extended from propositional letters to all propositional formulas in the usual truth-functional way.

The language of *Propositional Network announcement Logic* (PNAL) is defined by the following grammar, where $a \in \mathsf{Agnt}$ and $\theta \in \mathcal{L}_{\text{PROP}}$.

$$\varphi ::= B_a\theta \mid \neg\varphi \mid \varphi \wedge \varphi \mid \langle a : \theta\rangle\varphi$$

The intended meaning of $B_a\theta$ is that agent a believes θ, while $\langle a : \theta\rangle\varphi$ means that a can tweet θ, after which φ is the case. Formulas of the form $B_a\theta$ are called *belief formulas*; expressions of the type θ are sometimes called *messages*. The usual derived propositional connectives are used, as well as $[a : \theta]$ for $\neg\langle a : \theta\rangle\neg$. Another useful notation will be $\vec{c}$ which we will use as a variable over expressions of the form $c_0 : \theta_0, \ldots, c_n : \theta_n$ $(n \geq 0)$, where each c_i is an agent and each $\theta_i \in \mathcal{L}_{\text{PROP}}$, representing a (possibly empty) sequence of tweets. Abusing notation, we write $\langle\vec{c}\rangle$ for the sequence $\langle c_0 : \theta_0\rangle\ldots\langle c_n : \theta_n\rangle$, and $[\vec{c}]$ for $\neg\langle\vec{c}\rangle\neg$. The *reversal* of $\vec{c}$, denoted $\overleftarrow{c}$, is the reverse sequence of tweets $c_n : \theta_n, \ldots, c_0 : \theta_0$.

A *propositional network announcement model*, henceforth just a *model*, over Agnt and Prop is a pair (F, ω), where the *following relation* F is a binary relation on Agnt and the *belief state function* ω: $\mathsf{Agnt} \to \text{pow}(\mathsf{Val})$ assigns each agent a (possibly empty) set of valuations. bFa means that b is a follower of a, i.e., will receive all messages a send. We write Fa for the set $\{b \mid bFa\}$ of followers of a.

The satisfaction relation between formulas φ and models (F, ω) is defined recursively as follows:

$F, \omega \models B_a\theta$	iff	$\omega(a) \subseteq [\![\theta]\!]$
$F, \omega \models \neg\varphi$	iff	$F, \omega \not\models \varphi$
$F, \omega \models \varphi \wedge \psi$	iff	$F, \omega \models \varphi$ and $F, \omega \models \psi$
$F, \omega \models \langle a : \theta\rangle\varphi$	iff	$F, \omega \models B_a\theta$ and $F, [Fa\uparrow\theta]\omega \models \varphi$

$$\text{where } [C \uparrow \theta]\omega(b) = \begin{cases} \omega(b) \cap [\![\theta]\!] & \text{if } b \in C \\ \omega(b) & \text{otherwise} \end{cases}$$

– the result of simultaneously updating all the agents in a set C with θ. We get that $F, \omega \models [a : \theta]\varphi$ iff $F, \omega \models B_a\theta$ implies that $F, [Fa \uparrow \theta]\omega \models \varphi$. This semantics assumes, like in public announcement logic, that tweets are *truthful* (they are actually believed to be true) and that agents are *credulous*.

We write $F, \omega \models \Gamma$, when Γ is a set of formulas, to mean that $F, \omega \models \varphi$ for all $\varphi \in \Gamma$. As usual we say that a formula φ is *valid* on a given class of models $\mathcal{M}$, $\models_{\mathcal{M}}\varphi$ or just $\models\varphi$ when $\mathcal{M}$ is the class of all models, iff it is satisfied by every model in that class, and that φ is a *logical consequence* of a set of formulas Γ wrt. $\mathcal{M}$, $\Gamma \models_{\mathcal{M}} \varphi$ or just $\Gamma \models \varphi$, if φ is satisfied by every model in the class that satisfies all the formulas in Γ.

A Hilbert-style proof system pNAL is defined in Fig. 1. For a (finitary) Hilbert-style proof system S, when Γ is a set of formulas and φ is a formula, $\Gamma \vdash_S \varphi$ denotes the fact that there is a finite set of formulas $\Delta = \{\delta_1, \ldots, \delta_k\} \subseteq \Gamma$ such that $\vdash_S \bigwedge_{1 \leq i \leq k} \delta_i \to \varphi$. A system S is *sound* wrt. a class of models $\mathcal{M}$ if $\Gamma \vdash_S \varphi$ implies that $\Gamma \models_{\mathcal{M}} \varphi$, and it is *strongly complete* if that implication holds in the other direction.

Theorem 1 (Theorem 3 in [21]). pNAL *is sound and strongly complete with respect to the class of all models.*

Taut	$\vdash \varphi$, when φ is a substitution instance of a propositional tautology
K$_B$	$\vdash B_a(\theta \to \chi) \to (B_a\theta \to B_a\chi)$
K:	$\vdash [a:\theta](\varphi \to \psi) \to ([a:\theta]\varphi \to [a:\theta]\psi)$
Nec$_B$	$\vdash B_a\theta$ whenever $\vdash_0 \theta$
Sinc	$\vdash [a:\theta]\varphi \leftrightarrow (B_a\theta \to \langle a:\theta\rangle\varphi)$
Cnsv	$\vdash B_b\chi \to [a:\theta]B_b\chi$
Rat	$\vdash \langle a:\theta\rangle B_b\chi \to B_b(\theta \to \chi)$
Foll	$\vdash \langle\vec{c}\rangle(\neg B_b\chi \wedge \langle a:\chi'\rangle B_b\chi) \to [\vec{e}][a:\theta]B_b\theta$
Null	$\vdash \varphi \leftrightarrow \langle a:\theta\rangle\varphi$ whenever $\vdash_0 \theta$
MP	if $\vdash \varphi \to \psi$ and $\vdash \varphi$ then $\vdash \psi$
Nec:	if $\vdash \varphi$ then $\vdash [a:\theta]\varphi$

Fig. 1. Axioms and rules of pNAL. φ, ψ are any formulas in the language of PNAL; $\theta, \theta_i, \chi, \chi' \in \mathcal{L}_{\text{PROP}}$. $\vdash_0$ denotes derivability in propositional logic.

3 Arbitrary Propositional Network Announcement Logic

The language $\mathcal{L}_{\text{APNAL}}$ of Arbitrary Propositional Network Announcement Logic (APNAL) extends the PNAL language with a modality $[a]$ for each agent a.

Definition 2. $\mathcal{L}_{\text{APNAL}}$ *is defined as follows, where* $\theta \in \mathcal{L}_{\text{PROP}}$ *and* $a \in \mathsf{Agnt}$*:*

$$\varphi ::= B_a\theta \mid \neg\varphi \mid \varphi \wedge \varphi \mid \langle a:\theta\rangle\varphi \mid [a]\varphi$$

We use derived connectives as for PNAL, in addition to $\langle a\rangle\varphi$ for $\neg[a]\neg\varphi$[2]. The models are the same as for PNAL (propositional network announcement models).

[2] We choose to take $[a]$ as primary instead of $\langle a\rangle$ only because it makes some proofs simpler.

Definition 3. *Satisfaction of a formula in a model* F, ω *is defined by*

$$F, \omega \models [a]\varphi \textit{ iff } F, \omega \models [a : \theta]\varphi \textit{ for all } \theta \in \mathcal{L}_{\text{PROP}}$$

in addition to the clauses for PNAL.

In other words, $[a]$ quantifies over all possible announcements a can truthfully make. We get that

$$F, \omega \models \langle a \rangle \varphi \text{ iff } F, \omega \models \langle a : \theta \rangle \varphi \text{ for some } \theta \in \mathcal{L}_{\text{PROP}}$$

Validity and logical consequence are defined as in the case of PNAL.

3.1 Logical Properties

The following validities follow immediately from the semantics.

Proposition 4. *Let* $a \in \mathsf{Agnt}$, *and* $\varphi, \psi \in \mathcal{L}_{\text{APNAL}}$. *We have*

1. $\models [a]\varphi \to \varphi$
2. $\models [a]\varphi \to [a : \theta]\varphi$
3. $\models [a]\varphi \to \langle a \rangle \varphi$
4. $\models [a]\neg\varphi \leftrightarrow \neg \langle a \rangle \varphi$
5. $\models [a](\varphi \wedge \psi) \leftrightarrow ([a]\varphi \wedge [a]\psi)$
6. $\models [a](\varphi \to \psi) \to ([a]\varphi \to [a]\psi)$
7. $\models [a][a]\varphi \leftrightarrow [a]\varphi$

Let us look at combinations of the two types of modalities. The following combinations are generally *not* valid. There are formulas φ such that:

- $\not\models [a:\theta][b]\varphi \to [b][a:\theta]\varphi$
- $\not\models [b][a:\theta]\varphi \to [a:\theta][b]\varphi$
- $\not\models [a:\theta]\langle b \rangle\varphi \to \langle b \rangle[a:\theta]\varphi$

A counterexample for each of these is shown in Fig. 2. Assume that $\theta = p$. For the first item, see Fig. 2a. Let $\varphi = \neg B_c p$, then $F_1, \omega_1 \not\models [a:p][b]\varphi \to [b][a:p]\varphi$. For the second, see Fig. 2b. Let $\varphi = \neg B_c q$, then $F_2, \omega_2 \not\models [b][a:p]\varphi \to [a:p][b]\varphi$. For the third, see Fig. 2b. Let $\varphi = B_c q$, then $F_2, \omega_2 \not\models [a:p]\langle b \rangle\varphi \to \langle b \rangle[a:p]\varphi$.

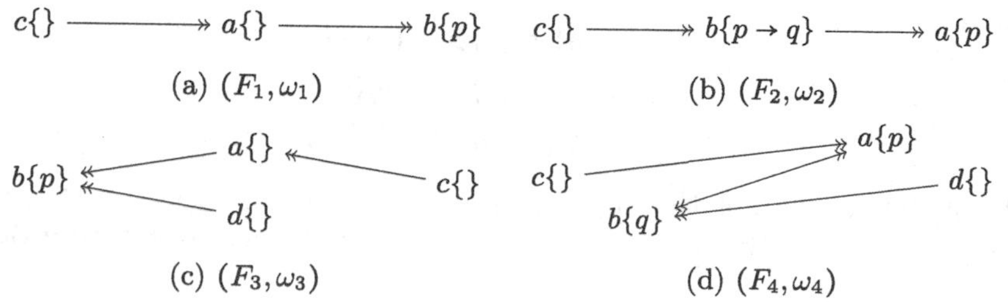

Fig. 2. Counterexamples for permutations, double-headed arrows stand for followership, e.g., cF_1a in (a). Brace brackets represent belief sets (implicitly closed under logical consequence).

The fourth combination, missing above, is a Church-Rosser like property. It is known that the explicit tweeting modalities satisfy the Church-Rosser property: the formula

$$\langle b:\chi\rangle[a:\theta]\varphi \rightarrow [a:\theta]\langle b:\chi\rangle\varphi$$

is valid [21, Pop. 11]. The fourth combination property is in fact valid:

Proposition 5 (Mixed-CR). *Let $a, b \in A$, $\theta \in \mathcal{L}_{\text{PROP}}$, and $\varphi \in \mathcal{L}_{\text{APNAL}}$. We have* $\models\langle b\rangle[a:\theta]\varphi \rightarrow [a:\theta]\langle b\rangle\varphi$.

Proof. Let $F, \omega \models \langle b\rangle[a:\theta]\varphi$. By semantics, for some $\delta \in \mathcal{L}_{\text{PROP}}$, $F, \omega \models \langle b:\delta\rangle [a:\theta]\varphi$. Thus (see above), $F, \omega \models [a:\theta]\langle b:\delta\rangle\varphi$. As we have $\models\langle b:\delta\rangle\varphi \rightarrow \langle b\rangle\varphi$ from Proposition 4, then for valuation $[Fa \uparrow \theta]\omega$, we get $F, [Fa \uparrow \theta]\omega \models \langle b:\delta\rangle\varphi \rightarrow \langle b\rangle\varphi$, that's $F, \omega \models [a:\theta](\langle b:\delta\rangle\varphi \rightarrow \langle b\rangle\varphi)$ by semantics, and $F, \omega \models [a:\theta]\langle b:\delta\rangle\varphi \rightarrow [a:\theta]\langle b\rangle\varphi$ by distribution of $[a:\theta]$. Then by MP, we get $F, \omega \models [a:\theta]\langle b\rangle\varphi$.

The mixed-CR property tells us that if a can make φ true by tweeting θ after b takes any action, then a will still preserve this ability after b tweets anything (take the contrapositive of the formula to get this reading). The arbitrary tweeting modalities satisfy a "pure" CR property as well:

Proposition 6 (CR). *Let $a, b \in A$, and $\varphi \in \mathcal{L}_{\text{APNAL}}$. We have* $\models \langle a\rangle[b]\varphi \rightarrow [b]\langle a\rangle\varphi$.

Proof. Let $F, \omega \models \langle a\rangle[b]\varphi$. $F, \omega \models \langle a:\theta\rangle[b]\varphi$ for some $\theta \in \mathcal{L}_{\text{PROP}}$, by the contraposition of mixed-CR, we get $F, \omega \models [b]\langle a:\theta\rangle\varphi$. As $\models \langle a:\theta\rangle\varphi \rightarrow \langle a\rangle\varphi$ from Proposition 4, then for any $\chi \in \mathcal{L}_{\text{PROP}}$, $\models [b:\chi](\langle a:\theta\rangle\varphi \rightarrow \langle a\rangle\varphi)$. By semantics, $\models [b](\langle a:\theta\rangle\varphi \rightarrow \langle a\rangle\varphi)$, then from Proposition 4, we get $\models [b]\langle a:\theta\rangle\varphi \rightarrow [b]\langle a\rangle\varphi$. Hence $F, \omega \models [b]\langle a\rangle\varphi$.

It's not hard to see that the McKinsey formula,

$$[a]\langle b\rangle\varphi \rightarrow \langle b\rangle[a]\varphi$$

is not valid. See Fig. 2c, let $\varphi = B_d p \wedge \neg B_c p$, then $F_3, \omega_3 \models [a]\langle b\rangle\varphi$, but $F_3, \omega_3 \not\models \langle b\rangle[a]\varphi$, as $F_3, \omega_3 \models [b]\langle a\rangle(\neg B_d p \vee B_c p)$. That's $\not\models [a]\langle b\rangle\varphi \rightarrow \langle b\rangle[a]\varphi$.

The following are non-validities involving combinations of diamonds.

$$\not\models \langle a\rangle\langle b\rangle\langle a\rangle\varphi \rightarrow \langle a\rangle\langle b\rangle\varphi$$
$$\not\models \langle a\rangle\langle b\rangle\langle a\rangle\varphi \rightarrow \langle b\rangle\langle a\rangle\varphi$$
$$\not\models \langle a\rangle\langle b\rangle\varphi \leftrightarrow \langle b\rangle\langle a\rangle\varphi$$

A counterexample for the first two is found in Fig. 2d. Let $\varphi = B_c q$, then we have $F_4, \omega_4 \models \langle a\rangle\langle b\rangle\langle a\rangle B_c q$ but $F_4, \omega_4 \not\models \langle a\rangle\langle b\rangle B_c q$. Therefore, $\not\models \langle a\rangle\langle b\rangle\langle a\rangle\varphi \rightarrow$

$\langle a\rangle\langle b\rangle\psi$. A counterexample for the third is found in Fig. 2a. Let $\varphi = B_c p$, we have $F_1, \omega_1 \vDash \langle b\rangle\langle a\rangle B_c p$ but $F_1, \omega_1 \nvDash \langle a\rangle\langle b\rangle B_c p$.

3.2 Non-compactness

Recall that a logic is (semantically) compact if it is the case that any set of formulas is satisfiable if and only if each of its finite subsets are. We now show that APNAL is not compact when there are at least two agents. Let $b \neq a$ and

$$\Delta = \{\neg B_b p, \langle a\rangle B_b p\} \cup \{B_a\theta \to B_b\theta \mid \theta \in \mathcal{L}_{\text{PROP}}\}.$$

We first argue that Δ is unsatisfiable. Assume otherwise: $F, \omega \vDash \varphi$ for any $\varphi \in \Delta$. From $F, \omega \vDash \langle a\rangle B_b p$, we know that there is a $\theta \in \mathcal{L}_{\text{PROP}}$ such that $F, \omega \vDash \langle a : \theta\rangle B_b p$, then $F, \omega \vDash B_a\theta$ and $F, [Fa \uparrow \theta]\omega \vDash B_b p$. Therefore $[Fa \uparrow \theta]\omega(b) \subseteq [\![p]\!]$. As $F, \omega \vDash \neg B_b p$, we have $\omega(b) \nsubseteq [\![p]\!]$, then we must have $[Fa \uparrow \theta]\omega(b) = \omega(b) \cap [\![\theta]\!] \subseteq [\![p]\!]$. But from $F, \omega \vDash B_a\theta \to B_b\theta$, and $F, \omega \vDash B_a\theta$, we get $F, \omega \vDash B_b\theta$, therefore $\omega(b) \subseteq [\![\theta]\!]$, and $\omega(b) \cap [\![\theta]\!] = \omega(b)$. Finally, we have $\omega(b) \subseteq [\![p]\!]$ and $\omega(b) \nsubseteq [\![p]\!]$ as a contradiction.

Now let Δ' be a finite subset of Δ. Let q be a propositional atom not occurring (anywhere) in Δ'. Let bFa and $\omega(b) = [\![q \to p]\!]$, and $\omega(a) = [\![q]\!]$. It is easy to see that we have that $F, \omega \vDash \Delta'$.

4 Proof System

In this section we will present a Hilbert-style proof system for APNAL, and show that it is sound and strongly complete. In the absence of compactness, our system is an *infinitary* proof system, allowing, unlike a standard finitary system, derivation rules that take infinitely many premises. A *proof* in such a system can be seen as a tree with possibly infinite width, but finite height. The standard meta logical proof technique for Hilbert systems of induction on the *length* of proofs thus can't be used directly. Instead, we abstract away from the notion of proof, and define the derivation relation $\vdash_\infty$ between sets of formulas and formulas directly and inductively, using base cases (for example axioms) and closure rules. We can then use induction over this definition in meta logical proofs. This is a standard technique for defining and dealing with infinitary Hilbert-style proof systems [4,14,16,19]. While we take inspiration from the completeness proof for APAL and make use of Goldblatt's necessitation forms in the formulation of our infinite derivation rule, the "theory" technique used in [6] for proving completeness of the infinitary system for APAL does not seem to be directly applicable to APNAL.

4.1 Axiomatisation and Soundness

In order to define a key (infinitary) derivation rule for the $[a]$ operator, we make use of a technique suggested by Goldblatt [12], and used in [6] for APAL, called *necessity forms*. The following is an adaption of necessity forms to APNAL.

Definition 7 (Necessity form). *Necessity forms are defined inductively as follows.*

- *$\#$ is a necessity form.*
- *If $\hat{\psi}$ is a necessity form and $\varphi \in \mathcal{L}_{\mathrm{APNAL}}$, then $\varphi \to \hat{\psi}$ is a necessity form.*
- *If $\hat{\psi}$ is a necessity form and $a \in \mathsf{Agnt}, \theta \in \mathcal{L}_{\mathrm{PROP}}$, then $[a:\theta]\hat{\psi}$ is a necessity form.*

We write $\mathcal{L}_{\mathrm{NEC}}$ to denote the set of all necessity forms. If $\hat{\varphi}$ is a necessity form and ψ a formula, then $\hat{\varphi}(\psi)$ is the formula obtained by substituting (the unique) $\#$ in $\hat{\varphi}$ with ψ.

We use Greek letters with a "hat" for general necessity forms, as in the definition. Note that any necessity form contains exactly one occurrence of the symbol $\#$. Also note that $\#$ cannot occur in the scope of a belief operator, $B_a\#$ is for example not a necessity form. The negation $\neg\hat{\varphi}$ of a necessity form $\hat{\varphi}$ is called a *possibility form*. Note that we have that $\psi' \to \hat{\psi}(\varphi)$ is equivalent to $(\psi' \to \hat{\psi})(\varphi)$; and that $[a:\theta]\hat{\psi}(\varphi)$ is equivalent to $([a:\theta]\hat{\psi})(\varphi)$. We will sometimes leave out the parentheses for simplicity.

Definition 8 (Axiomatization S^{∞}). *The derivation relation $\vdash_{S^{\infty}}$, written $\vdash_{\infty}$ for simplicity, between sets of $\mathcal{L}_{\mathrm{APNAL}}$-formulas and $\mathcal{L}_{\mathrm{APNAL}}$-formulas is the smallest relation satisfying the properties in Fig. 3 (lower part).*

([a]int)	$\langle a:\theta\rangle\varphi \to \langle a\rangle\varphi$	
(pnalAx)	all $\mathcal{L}_{\mathrm{APNAL}}$ instances of pNAL axiom schemas (upper part of Fig. 1)	
(Ax)	$\vdash_{\infty} \varphi$ where φ is an axiom	
(DiA)	$\{\hat{\varphi}([a:\theta]\psi) : \theta \in \mathcal{L}_{\mathrm{PROP}}\} \vdash_{\infty} \hat{\varphi}([a]\psi)$	(Derivation-Infinitary-Arbitrary)
(MP)	$\{\varphi, \varphi \to \psi\} \vdash_{\infty} \psi$	(Modus Ponens)
(Na)	$\vdash_{\infty} \varphi \Rightarrow\ \vdash_{\infty} [a]\varphi$	(Necessitation-Arbitrary)
(W)	$\Gamma \vdash_{\infty} \varphi \Rightarrow \Gamma \cup \Delta \vdash_{\infty} \varphi$	(Weakening)
(Cut)	$\Gamma \vdash_{\infty} \Delta\ \&\ \Gamma \cup \Delta \vdash_{\infty} \varphi \Rightarrow \Gamma \vdash_{\infty} \varphi$	(Cut)

Fig. 3. Axioms (upper part) and definition of the infinitary derivation relation $\vdash_{\infty}$ over the language $\mathcal{L}_{\mathrm{APNAL}}$ (lower part). $\vdash_{\infty} \varphi$ is shorthand for $\varnothing \vdash_{\infty} \varphi$. $\Gamma \vdash_{\infty} \Delta$ means that $\Gamma \vdash_{\infty} \varphi$ for each $\varphi \in \Delta$.

Soundness and completeness are defined as usual: S^{∞} is sound if $\Gamma \vdash_{\infty} \varphi$ implies that $\Gamma \models \varphi$, and strongly complete if $\Gamma \models \varphi$ implies that $\Gamma \vdash_{\infty} \varphi$, for φ and Γ.

The system can be viewed as consisting of three parts. The first is axioms and rules from pNAL (Nec: is derivable by using [a]int and **Na**). The second deals with the new $[a]$ modality; the axiom [a]int and the rules **DiA** and **Na**. The meaning of the [a]int axiom is obvious. The **Na** rule is a standard necessitation rule for the $[a]$ modalities. **DiA** is the only infinitary derivation rule. Intuitively it says that we can derive $[a]\psi$ if we have derived $[a:\theta]\psi$ for *any* θ, and, furthermore, that we can do that "anywhere" in a formula – more precisely anywhere a necessity form allows us to. Let us illustrate **DiA** with some examples.

C1: $\{[a:\theta]\varphi \mid \theta \in \mathcal{L}_{\text{PROP}}\} \vdash_\infty [a]\varphi$. We can infer that $[a]\varphi$, if we have that for any $\theta \in \mathcal{L}_{\text{PROP}}$, $[a:\theta]\varphi$.
C2: $\{\psi \rightarrow [a:\theta]\varphi \mid \theta \in \mathcal{L}_{\text{PROP}}\} \vdash_\infty \psi \rightarrow [a]\varphi$, which is actually derivable from C1.
C3: $\{[b:\chi][a:\theta]\varphi \mid \theta \in \mathcal{L}_{\text{PROP}}\} \vdash_\infty [b:\chi][a]\varphi$ illustrates why we need to define **DiA** rule based on necessity forms. It is easy to verify that C1 is implied by C3, but there are no general reduction axioms for nested modalities and the implication does not hold in the other direction. A general case of C3 can be given as follows:

$$\{\underbrace{[b_1:\chi_1]\cdots[a:\theta]\cdots[b_n:\chi_n]}_{\text{finite}}\varphi \mid \theta \in \mathcal{L}_{\text{PROP}}\} \vdash_\infty \underbrace{[b_1:\chi_1]\cdots[a]\cdots[b_n:\chi_n]}_{\text{only change } one \text{ modality}}\varphi.$$

The remaining rules, **W** and **Cut**, allow us to strengthen and weaken the set of premises, respectively. These are standard closure rules in inductive definition of the derivability relation for infinitary Hilbert-style systems (see, e.g., [4]).
In this inductive definition of $\vdash_\infty$, the base cases are **Ax**, **DiA** and **MP**, and the inductive cases are **Na**, **W** and **Cut**. We will now prove soundness.

Lemma 9. *For any formula φ and set of formulas Γ, if $\Gamma \vdash_\infty \varphi$ then $\Gamma \vDash \varphi$.*

Proof. The proof is by induction on the definition of the $\vdash_\infty$ relation.

Base cases. For **Ax**, $\Gamma = \varnothing$. That $\vDash\varphi$ holds for any instance φ of a pNAL axiom schema can be shown in exactly the same way as for pNAL (Theorem 1)[3]. Validity of the new axiom [a]int is straightforward. For **MP**, $\{\varphi, \varphi \rightarrow \psi\} \vDash \psi$ holds trivially. We show the **DiA** case below.

Inductive cases. For **Na**, we must show that if the induction hypothesis holds for $\vdash_\infty \varphi$, then it holds for $\vdash_\infty [a]\varphi$. Thus, assume that $\vDash\varphi$; we must show that $\vDash[a]\varphi$ – but that holds trivially. The cases for **W** and **Cut** are also trivial: for **W**, $\Gamma \vDash \varphi$ implies that $\Gamma \cup \Delta \vDash \varphi$, and for **Cut**, $\Gamma \vDash \Delta$ and $\Gamma \cup \Delta \vDash \varphi$ implies that $\Gamma \vDash \varphi$.

The interesting case is (the base case) **DiA**. We show that for any $\hat{\varphi}, a, \psi$,

$$\{\hat{\varphi}([a:\theta]\psi) \mid \theta \in \mathcal{L}_{\text{PROP}}\} \vDash \hat{\varphi}([a]\psi)$$

by induction on the complexity of the necessity form $\hat{\varphi}$. Let (F, ω) be an arbitrary model. we have the following cases:

- $\hat{\varphi} = \#$. We need show that $\{[a:\theta]\psi \mid \theta \in \mathcal{L}_{\text{PROP}}\} \vDash [a]\psi$. This follows immediately by definition of the semantics.
- $\hat{\varphi} = \varphi' \rightarrow \hat{\varphi''}$. Let $F, \omega \vDash (\varphi' \rightarrow \hat{\varphi''})([a:\theta]\psi)$ for all θ. We must show that $F, \omega \vDash (\varphi' \rightarrow \hat{\varphi''})([a]\psi)$. By definition of substitution, $(\varphi' \rightarrow \hat{\varphi''})([a:\theta]\psi) = \varphi' \rightarrow \hat{\varphi''}([a:\theta]\psi)$, and $(\varphi' \rightarrow \hat{\varphi''})([a]\psi) = \varphi' \rightarrow \hat{\varphi''}([a]\psi)$. Let $F, \omega \vDash \psi'$. Thus, $F, \omega \vDash \hat{\varphi''}([a:\theta]\psi)$ for all θ. By the induction hypothesis, $F, \omega \vDash \hat{\varphi''}([a]\psi)$. Thus, $F, \omega \vDash \psi' \rightarrow \hat{\varphi''}([a]\psi)$.

[3] While the axioms schemata are the same, the instances of the axioms are of course different, but validity can be shown in the same way.

– $\hat{\varphi} = [b:\chi]\hat{\varphi}'$. Let $F,\omega \models [b:\chi]\hat{\varphi}'([a:\theta]\psi)$ for all θ. We must show that $F,\omega \models [b:\chi]\hat{\varphi}'([a]\psi)$. If $F,\omega \not\models B_b\chi$ we are done. Assume that $F,\omega \models B_b\chi$. Thus we have that $F,[Fb\!\uparrow\!\chi]\omega \models \hat{\varphi}'([a:\theta]\psi)$ for any θ, and by the induction hypothesis we get that $F,[Fb\!\uparrow\!\chi]\omega \models \hat{\varphi}'([a]\psi)$, which again implies that $F,\omega \models [b:\chi](\hat{\varphi}'([a]\psi))$.

Lemma 10. *The statements in Fig. 4 all hold.*

(Mo)	$\Gamma \cup \{\varphi\} \vdash_\infty \varphi$	(Monotonicity)
(Imp)	$\Gamma \vdash_\infty \varphi \to \psi\ \&\ \Gamma \vdash_\infty \varphi \Rightarrow \Gamma \vdash_\infty \psi$	(Implication)
(RT)	$\Gamma \vdash_\infty \varphi \to \psi \Rightarrow \Gamma \cup \{\varphi\} \vdash_\infty \psi$	(Resolution Theorem)
(Ns)	$\vdash_\infty \varphi \Rightarrow \vdash_\infty [a:\theta]\varphi$	(Necessitation-Specific)
(Cond)	$\Gamma \cup \Delta \vdash_\infty \varphi \Rightarrow \Gamma \cup \{\psi \to \delta \mid \delta \in \Delta\} \vdash_\infty \psi \to \varphi$	(Conditionalization)
(DT)	$\Gamma \cup \{\psi\} \vdash_\infty \varphi \Rightarrow \Gamma \vdash_\infty \psi \to \varphi$	(Deduction Theorem)
(Raa)	$\Gamma \cup \{\varphi\} \vdash_\infty \bot \Rightarrow \Gamma \vdash_\infty \neg\varphi$	(Reductio ad absurdum)
(Con)	$\Gamma \vdash_\infty \varphi \wedge \psi \Rightarrow \Gamma \vdash_\infty \varphi\ \&\ \Gamma \vdash_\infty \psi$	(Conjunction)
(Eqv)	$\Gamma \vdash_\infty \varphi \leftrightarrow \psi \Rightarrow \Gamma \vdash_\infty \varphi \Leftrightarrow \Gamma \vdash_\infty \psi$	(Equivalence)

Fig. 4. Admissible rules in S^∞.

Proof. **Mo**, **Imp**, and **RT** are straightforward.

Ns: Let $\vdash_\infty \varphi$, then $\vdash_\infty [a]\varphi$ by **Na**. $\vdash_\infty [a]\varphi \to [a:\theta]\varphi$ by **Ax**, $\{[a]\varphi\} \vdash_\infty [a:\theta]\varphi$ by **RT**, then $\vdash_\infty [a:\theta]\varphi$ by **Cut**.

Cond: Infinitary induction on the derivation of $\Gamma \cup \Delta \vdash_\infty \varphi$. The base cases are **Ax**, **MP**, **DiA**, and inductive steps are **Na**, **W**, and **Cut**.

Ax: Let $\Gamma = \Delta = \varnothing$. We need show that $\vdash_\infty \psi \to \varphi$ when $\vdash_\infty \varphi$. Let $\vdash_\infty \varphi$, by **W**, $\{\varphi \to (\psi \to \varphi)\} \vdash_\infty \varphi$, and $\{\varphi, \varphi \to (\psi \to \varphi)\} \vdash_\infty \psi \to \varphi$ by **MP**, then by **Cut**, $\{\varphi \to (\psi \to \varphi)\} \vdash_\infty \psi \to \varphi$. By **Ax**, $\vdash_\infty \varphi \to (\psi \to \varphi)$, then by **Cut** again, we have $\vdash_\infty \psi \to \varphi$.

MP: Let $\Gamma \cup \Delta = \{\varphi', \varphi' \to \varphi\}$ and $\{\varphi', \varphi' \to \varphi\} \vdash_\infty \varphi$. We need show that

$$\Gamma \cup \{\psi \to \delta \mid \delta \in \Delta\} \vdash_\infty \psi \to \varphi.$$

There are four different possible combinations for Γ and Δ.

- $\Gamma = \{\varphi'\}$ and $\Delta = \{\varphi' \to \varphi\}$. We show that $\{\varphi', \psi \to (\varphi' \to \varphi)\} \vdash_\infty \psi \to \varphi$. By **Ax**, $\vdash_\infty (\psi \to (\varphi' \to \varphi)) \to (\varphi' \to (\psi \to \varphi))$, then $\{\varphi', \psi \to (\varphi' \to \varphi)\} \vdash_\infty \psi \to \varphi$, by apply **RT** twice.
- $\Gamma = \{\varphi' \to \varphi\}$ and $\Delta = \{\varphi'\}$. We show that $\{\varphi' \to \varphi, \psi \to \varphi'\} \vdash_\infty \psi \to \varphi$. By **Ax**, $\vdash_\infty (\psi \to \varphi') \to ((\varphi' \to \varphi) \to (\psi \to \varphi))$, then $\{\varphi' \to \varphi, \psi \to \varphi'\} \vdash_\infty \psi \to \varphi$ by apply **RT** twice.

- The other two combinations $\Gamma = \varnothing$, or $\Delta = \varnothing$ can be proved similarly.

DiA: Let $\varphi = \hat{\psi}([a]\xi)$ and $\Gamma \cup \Delta = \{\hat{\psi}([a:\theta]\xi) \mid \theta \in \mathcal{L}_{\text{PROP}}\}$. Then we have $\Gamma \cup \Delta \vdash_\infty \varphi$. For convenience, enumerate all $\theta \in \mathcal{L}_{\text{PROP}}$. Without loss of generality, fix a set Q such that

$$\Gamma = \{\hat{\psi}([a:\theta]\xi) \mid \theta \in Q\}, \text{ and } \Delta = \{\hat{\psi}([a:\theta]\xi) \mid \theta \in \mathcal{L}_{\text{PROP}} \backslash Q\}.$$

Let

$$\Gamma' = \{\psi \to \hat{\psi}([a:\theta]\xi) \mid \theta \in Q\},$$
$$\Delta' = \{\psi \to \hat{\psi}([a:\theta]\xi) \mid \theta \in \mathcal{L}_{\text{PROP}} \backslash Q\},$$

As for arbitrary $\theta \in \mathcal{L}_{\text{PROP}}$, $\psi \to \hat{\psi}([a:\theta]\xi)$ is a necessity form substituting # with $[a:\theta]\xi$, then $\Gamma' \cup \Delta' \vdash_\infty \varphi'$ by **DiA**, where $\varphi' = \psi \to \hat{\psi}([a]\xi) = \psi \to \varphi$. By **W**, $\Gamma \cup \Gamma' \cup \Delta' \vdash_\infty \varphi'$. For each $\theta \in Q$ and $\hat{\psi}([a:\theta]\xi) \in \Gamma$, by **Ax**, $\vdash_\infty \hat{\psi}([a:\theta]\xi) \to (\psi \to \hat{\psi}([a:\theta]\xi))$. Then $\Gamma \vdash_\infty \Gamma'$ by repeating **RT** for each $\theta \in Q$, therefore, $\Gamma \cup \Delta' \vdash_\infty \Gamma'$ by **W**. By **Cut**, $\Gamma \cup \Delta' \vdash_\infty \varphi'$, that's $\Gamma \cup \Delta' \vdash_\infty \psi \to \varphi$. Now by **W**, it follows $\Gamma \cup \Delta' \cup \{\psi \to \delta \mid \delta \in \Delta\} \vdash_\infty \psi \to \varphi$. Now for each formula in Δ, by **Mo**, $\Gamma \cup \{\psi \to \delta \mid \delta \in \Delta\} \vdash_\infty \Delta'$. Then by **Cut**, we have $\Gamma \cup \{\psi \to \delta \mid \delta \in \Delta\} \vdash_\infty \psi \to \varphi$ as the desired conclusion.

Na: $\Gamma = \Delta = \varnothing$. Let $\varphi = [a]\varphi'$, and $\vdash_\infty \varphi'$, we need prove that $\vdash_\infty \psi \to [a]\varphi'$. From $\vdash_\infty \varphi'$, by **Na**, $\vdash_\infty [a]\varphi'$, and $\vdash_\infty [a]\varphi' \to (\psi \to [a]\varphi')$ by **Ax**, then by **RT**, $\{[a]\varphi'\} \vdash_\infty \psi \to [a]\varphi'$, and by **Cut**, $\vdash_\infty \psi \to [a]\varphi'$.

W: Let $\Gamma' \cup \Delta' \vdash_\infty \varphi$ for some $\Gamma' \subseteq \Gamma$ and $\Delta' \subseteq \Delta$. By IH, we apply **Cond** to get $\Gamma' \cup \{\psi \to \delta \mid \delta \in \Delta'\} \vdash_\infty \psi \to \varphi$, that is $\Gamma \cup \{\psi \to \delta \mid \delta \in \Delta\} \vdash_\infty \psi \to \varphi$ by **W**.

Cut: Let $\Gamma \cup \Delta \vdash_\infty \Delta'$, and $\Gamma \cup \Delta \cup \Delta' \vdash_\infty \varphi$. Now for the first derivation, we apply IH for each $\delta' \in \Delta'$, $\Gamma \cup \{\psi \to \delta \mid \delta \in \Delta\} \vdash_\infty \psi \to \delta'$, that is $\Gamma \cup \{\psi \to \delta \mid \delta \in \Delta\} \vdash_\infty \{\psi \to \delta' \mid \delta' \in \Delta'\}$. For the second derivation, apply IH on φ, $\Gamma \cup \{\psi \to \delta \mid \delta \in \Delta \cup \Delta'\} \vdash_\infty \psi \to \varphi$, by **Cut**, $\Gamma \cup \{\psi \to \delta \mid \delta \in \Delta\} \vdash_\infty \psi \to \varphi$.

DT: From $\Gamma \cup \{\psi\} \vdash_\infty \varphi$, we have $\Gamma \cup \{\psi \to \psi\} \vdash_\infty \psi \to \varphi$ by **Cond**. From **Ax** and **W**, $\Gamma \vdash_\infty \psi \to \psi$, then by **Cut**, $\Gamma \vdash_\infty \psi \to \varphi$.

Raa, Con, Eqv are straightforward.

Lemma 11. *For any necessity form* $\hat{\varphi}$ *and formula* $[a]\varphi'$, $\vdash_\infty \hat{\varphi}([a]\varphi') \to \hat{\varphi}([a:\theta]\varphi')$.

Proof. Proof by induction on the complexity of $\hat{\varphi}$:

(#) $\hat{\varphi} = \#$. Guaranteed by [a]int from **Ax**. $\vdash_\infty [a]\varphi' \to [a:\theta]\varphi'$

($\to$) $\hat{\varphi} = \psi' \to \hat{\psi}$.
By IH, $\vdash_\infty \hat{\psi}([a]\varphi') \to \hat{\psi}([a:\theta]\varphi')$, by **RT**, $\{\hat{\psi}([a]\varphi')\} \vdash_\infty \hat{\psi}([a:\theta]\varphi')$, and by **Cond**, $\{\psi' \to \hat{\psi}([a]\varphi')\} \vdash_\infty \psi' \to \hat{\psi}([a:\theta]\varphi')$. Then we have $\vdash_\infty (\psi' \to \hat{\psi}([a]\varphi')) \to (\psi' \to \hat{\psi}([a:\theta]\varphi'))$ by **DT**.

($\square$) $\hat{\varphi} = [b:\chi]\hat{\psi}$.
By IH, $\vdash_\infty \hat{\psi}([a]\varphi') \to \hat{\psi}([a:\theta]\varphi')$, And then by **Ns**, $\vdash_\infty [b:\chi](\hat{\psi}([a]\varphi') \to \hat{\psi}([a:\theta]\varphi'))$. $\vdash_\infty [b:\chi]\hat{\psi}([a]\varphi') \to [b:\chi]\hat{\psi}([a:\theta]\varphi')$ from K: and **Eqv**.

4.2 Completeness

We now prove that S^∞ is strongly complete with respect to the class of all models. We will use a canonical model method; we can in fact use exactly the same canonical model used for completeness of pNAL in [21]. However, constructions and proofs, such as those for Lindenbaum's lemma, that are standard for finitary axiomatisations, can't be used directly for infinitary systems – typically because they are defined or proved by induction on the length of derivations. We start by proving a variant of Lindenbaum's lemma under the infinitary axiomatization S^∞, which is non-trivial, before proving a truth lemma (Lemma 15) and finally the completeness result (Theorem 16).

We say that a set of formulas Γ is *consistent* iff $\Gamma \nvdash_\infty \bot$ (where $\bot = \alpha \wedge \neg\alpha$ for some atomic proposition α); that it is *maximal* iff for any formula φ, either $\varphi \in \Gamma$ or $\neg\varphi \in \Gamma$. A maximal consistent set (MCS) is a set of formulas that is maximal and consistent.

Lemma 12 (Lindenbaum). *Let Γ be an consistent set of formulas. There exists an MCS Γ' such that $\Gamma \subseteq \Gamma'$.*

Proof Recall the rule **DiA**:

$$\{\hat{\varphi}([a:\theta]\psi) \mid \theta \in \mathcal{L}_{\text{PROP}}\} \vdash_\infty \hat{\varphi}([a]\psi)$$

A formula of the form $\hat{\varphi}([a]\psi)$, i.e., a formula that can be obtained by substitution of $[a]\psi$ on a necessity form $\hat{\varphi}$, will be said to be on **DiA-form**. If $\beta = \hat{\varphi}([a]\psi)$ is on **DiA**-form, then for any $\theta \in \mathcal{L}_{\text{PROP}}$, the formula $\beta(:\theta) = \hat{\varphi}([a:\theta]\psi)$ is called a **DiA-witness**. For example, given a formula $\alpha = \varphi \to [b]\psi$, and a $\theta \in \mathcal{L}_{\text{PROP}}$, then $\alpha(:\theta) = \varphi \to [b:\theta]\psi$ is a **DiA**-witness for α.

Let Γ be a consistent set of formulas. Enumerate all formulas in $\mathcal{L}_{\text{APNAL}}$ as $\psi_1, \psi_2, \cdots, \psi_n, \cdots$. We construct $\Gamma' \supseteq \Gamma$ inductively as follows:

- $\Gamma_0 = \Gamma$
- $\Gamma_{i+1} = \begin{cases} \Gamma_i \cup \{\psi_{i+1}\} & \text{if } \Gamma_i \vdash_\infty \psi_{i+1} \\ \Gamma_i \cup \{\neg\psi_{i+1}\} & \text{if } \Gamma_i \nvdash_\infty \psi_{i+1} \,\&\, \psi_{i+1} \text{ does not have the } \mathbf{DiA}\text{-form} \\ \Gamma_i \cup \{\neg\psi_{i+1}, \neg\psi_{i+1}(:\theta)\} & \text{if } \Gamma_i \nvdash_\infty \psi_{i+1} \,\&\, \psi_{i+1} \text{ has the } \mathbf{DiA}\text{-form, where } \psi_{i+1}(:\theta) \text{ is a } \mathbf{DiA}\text{-witness} \,\&\, \Gamma_i \nvdash_\infty \psi_{i+1}(:\theta) \end{cases}$
- $\Gamma' = \bigcup_{i \in \mathbb{N}} \Gamma_i$

The maximality of Γ' is easy to see from the construction. For the third case, if ψ has the **DiA**-form and $\Gamma \nvdash_\infty \psi$, then there must exists a **DiA**-witness, i.e., $\psi(:\theta)$ such that $\Gamma \nvdash_\infty \psi(:\theta)$, since $\vdash_\infty$ is closed under **DiA**. It remains to be shown that Γ' is consistent. First, we prove that every Γ_i is consistent, by induction on i. For the base case, Γ_0 is consistent by assumption. For the induction step, assume that Γ_i is consistent. We argue by the three cases in the definition of Γ_{i+1}.

C1: $\Gamma_{i+1} = \Gamma_i \cup \{\psi_{i+1}\}$ is obviously consistent.

C2: $\Gamma_{i+1} = \Gamma_i \cup \{\neg\psi_{i+1}\}$. If $\Gamma_{i+1} = \Gamma_i \cup \{\neg\psi_{i+1}\} \vdash_\infty \bot$, then $\Gamma_i \vdash_\infty \psi_{i+1}$ by **Raa**, which is a contradiction.

C3: Let $\psi_{i+1} = \hat{\varphi}([a]\psi)$ be the **DiA**-form, $\psi_{i+1}(:\theta) = \hat{\varphi}([a:\theta]\psi)$ be a **DiA**-witness. Suppose that $\Gamma_{i+1} = \Gamma_i \cup \{\neg\hat{\varphi}([a]\psi), \neg\hat{\varphi}([a:\theta]\psi)\} \vdash_\infty \bot$, by **Raa**, $\Gamma_i \cup \{\neg\hat{\varphi}([a:\theta]\psi)\} \vdash_\infty \hat{\varphi}([a]\psi)$. $\Gamma_i \cup \{\neg\hat{\varphi}([a:\theta]\psi)\} \vdash_\infty \hat{\varphi}([a]\psi) \to \hat{\varphi}([a:\theta]\psi)$ by Lemma 11 and **W**. Then by **RT**, $\Gamma_i \cup \{\neg\hat{\varphi}([a:\theta]\psi), \hat{\varphi}([a]\psi)\} \vdash_\infty \hat{\varphi}([a:\theta]\psi)$. By **Cut**, $\Gamma_i \cup \{\neg\hat{\varphi}([a:\theta]\psi)\} \vdash_\infty \hat{\varphi}([a:\theta]\psi)$, and thus $\Gamma_i \vdash_\infty \neg\hat{\varphi}([a:\theta]\psi) \to \hat{\varphi}([a:\theta]\psi)$ by **DT**. As by **Ax**, $\vdash_\infty (\neg\hat{\varphi}([a:\theta]\psi) \to \hat{\varphi}([a:\theta]\psi)) \to \hat{\varphi}([a:\theta]\psi)$, then by **W** and **Imp**, $\Gamma_i \vdash_\infty \hat{\varphi}([a:\theta]\psi)$, which contradicts the assumption that $\Gamma_i \nvdash_\infty \psi_{i+1}(:\theta)$ and the induction hypothesis that Γ_i is consistent.

Thus, each Γ_i is consistent. To show that Γ' is consistent, we first show the following claim. For any Γ'' and φ such that $\Gamma'' \vdash_\infty \varphi$,

$$\Gamma'' \subseteq \Gamma' \Rightarrow \varphi \in \Gamma'. \tag{1}$$

The proof is by induction on the definition of $\Gamma'' \vdash_\infty \varphi$. We only show **DiA** and **Na** here. Others are similar to the cases in [4].

DiA: We have that $\Gamma'' = \{\hat{\psi}([a:\theta]\xi) \mid \theta \in \mathcal{L}_{\text{PROP}}\}$, $\varphi = \hat{\psi}([a]\xi)$. Assume that $\Gamma'' \subseteq \Gamma'$. Proof by contradiction. Assume that $\varphi \notin \Gamma'$. Let $i \geq 1$ be such that $\varphi = \psi_i$ (φ is the i-th formula in the enumeration). If $\Gamma_{i-1} \vdash_\infty \varphi$ then $\varphi \in \Gamma_i$ by construction, but then $\varphi \in \Gamma'$. So $\Gamma_{i-1} \nvdash_\infty \varphi$. Thus, Γ_i is constructed by the third case in the definition: $\Gamma_i = \Gamma_{i-1} \cup \{\neg\varphi, \neg\varphi(:\theta)\}$ for some $\theta \in \mathcal{L}_{\text{PROP}}$. Now we claim that

$$\text{For any } j \in \mathbb{N}, \varphi(:\theta) \notin \Gamma_j. \tag{2}$$

If $j < i$, then by the construction, $\Gamma_j \nvdash_\infty \varphi(:\theta)$ as $\Gamma_{i-1} \nvdash_\infty \varphi(:\theta)$; if $j \geqslant i$, by the structure of Γ_j, we have $\Gamma_j \vdash_\infty \neg\varphi(:\theta)$, as $\Gamma_i \vdash_\infty \neg\varphi(:\theta)$. By the fact that Γ_j is consistent, we have $\varphi(:\theta) \notin \Gamma_j$. Therefore, claim (2) is proved. It implies that $\varphi(:\theta) \notin \Gamma'$ by the construction of Γ'. But we have that $\varphi(:\theta) \in \Gamma''$, which contradicts the assumption that $\Gamma'' \subseteq \Gamma'$.

Na: We have that $\Gamma'' = \varnothing$, $\varphi = [a]\varphi'$. Let $i \geq 1$ be such that $\varphi = \psi_i$. From $\vdash_\infty [a]\varphi'$ and **W** we have that $\Gamma_{i-1} \vdash_\infty \varphi$, so $\varphi \in \Gamma_i$ by construction and thus $\varphi \in \Gamma'$.

We have thus proved that (1) holds for any Γ'', φ such that $\Gamma'' \vdash_\infty \varphi$, particularly, for $\Gamma'' = \Gamma'$ and $\varphi = \bot$. Thus, if Γ' is inconsistent then $\bot \in \Gamma_j$ for some $j \in \mathbb{N}$, which contradicts the consistency of Γ_j.

Given the Lindenbaum lemma and the other properties of the system shown above, we can now use a canonical model technique to prove completeness. In fact, we can use exactly the same definition of the canonical model as for the sub-logic pNAL in [21], and extend the corresponding truth lemma.

For any MCS Γ, F_Γ and ω_Γ are defined as follows [21]:

$$bF_\Gamma a \quad \text{iff} \quad [\vec{c}][a:\theta]B_b\theta \in \Gamma \text{ for all } \vec{c} \text{ and } \theta$$

$$\omega_\Gamma(a) \;=\; \bigcap\{[\![\theta]\!] \mid B_a\theta \in \Gamma\}.$$

We also define the following, when Γ, Γ' are MCSs:

- Let $\langle a:\theta\rangle\Gamma = \{\varphi \mid \}\langle a:\theta\rangle\varphi \in \Gamma$.
- Let $\Gamma \trianglelefteq \Gamma'$ iff $B_a\theta \in \Gamma$ and $\Gamma'=\langle a:\theta\rangle\Gamma$ for some a and θ.
- Let $\leq$ be the transitive closure of $\trianglelefteq$

The truth lemma makes use of the following two lemmas[4]:

Lemma 13 ([21]). *If Γ is an MCS and $\Gamma \leq \Gamma'$ then*

1. *Γ' is also an MCS and*
2. *there is a $\vec{c}$ such that: (a) $\Gamma' = \langle\vec{c}\rangle\Gamma$, and (b) $[\overleftarrow{c}]\varphi \in \Gamma$ iff $\varphi \in \Gamma'$ for all φ (where $\overleftarrow{c}$ is the reversal of $\vec{c}$).*

Lemma 14 ([21]). *If $\Gamma \leq \Gamma'$ and $B_a\theta \in \Gamma'$ then $[F_\Gamma a \uparrow \theta]\omega_{\Gamma'} = \omega_{\langle a:\theta\rangle\Gamma'}$.*

The proof of the truth lemma extends the truth lemma for pNAL [21] with the clause for the new modalities.

Lemma 15 (Truth Lemma). *$F_\Gamma, \omega_\Gamma \models \varphi$ iff $\varphi \in \Gamma$, for any φ and Γ.*

Proof. Let Γ be an MCS. We prove by induction on formulas φ that, for any MCS Γ', if $\Gamma \leq \Gamma'$ then

$$F_\Gamma, \omega_{\Gamma'} \models \varphi \text{ iff } \varphi \in \Gamma'.$$

In each of the cases, we assume that $\Gamma' \geq \Gamma$. By Lemma 13.1, Γ' is a MCS. We show the new case; the others are exactly as in the proof for pNAL [21].

<u>$\langle a:\theta\rangle\psi$</u> The following are equivalent:

$F_\Gamma, \omega_{\Gamma'} \models \langle a:\theta\rangle\psi$	
$F_\Gamma, \omega_{\Gamma'} \models B_a\theta$ and $F_\Gamma, [F_\Gamma a \uparrow \theta]\omega_{\Gamma'} \models \psi$	by semantics
$B_a\theta \in \Gamma'$ and $F_\Gamma, [F_\Gamma a \uparrow \theta]\omega_{\Gamma'} \models \psi$	by the $B_a\theta$ case, above
$B_a\theta \in \Gamma'$ and $F_\Gamma, \omega_{\langle a:\theta\rangle\Gamma'} \models \psi$	by Lemma 14, since $\Gamma \leq \Gamma'$
$B_a\theta \in \Gamma'$ and $\psi \in \langle a:\theta\rangle\Gamma'$	by I.H., since $\Gamma \leq \langle a:\theta\rangle\Gamma'$
$B_a\theta \in \Gamma'$ and $\langle a:\theta\rangle\psi \in \Gamma'$	by definition of $\langle a:\theta\rangle\Gamma'$
$\langle a:\theta\rangle\psi \in \Gamma'$	by Sinc and closure of Γ'

<u>$\varphi = [a]\psi'$</u>

($\Rightarrow$) Proof by contraposition. Assume that $[a]\psi' \notin \Gamma'$,, then by **DiA**, there is a $\theta \in \mathcal{L}_{\text{PROP}}$ such that $[a:\theta]\psi' \notin \Gamma'$. By maximality, $\langle a:\theta\rangle\neg\psi' \in \Gamma'$. The induction hypothesis is that, for any Γ'' such that $\Gamma \leq \Gamma''$, $F_\Gamma, \omega_{\Gamma''} \models \psi'$ iff $\psi' \in \Gamma''$, which implies, by maximality, that $F_\Gamma, \omega_{\Gamma''} \models \neg\psi'$ iff $\neg\psi' \in \Gamma''$. Now we can use exactly the same reasoning as in the case for $\langle a:\theta\rangle\psi$, with $\psi = \neg\psi'$ (as just mentioned, the induction hypothesis, that proof relies on, holds for $\neg\psi'$), to conclude that $F_\Gamma, \omega_{\Gamma'} \models \langle a:\theta\rangle\neg\psi$, which means that $F_\Gamma, \omega_{\Gamma'} \not\models [a:\theta]\psi$. It follows that $F_\Gamma, \omega_{\Gamma'} \not\models [a]\psi$.

[4] Strictly speaking the corresponding lemmas in [21] don't say exactly the same thing since the notion of an MCS is different. However, they can be proven in exactly the same way.

($\Leftarrow$) Assume that $[a]\psi' \in \Gamma'$, then by [a]int and the fact that Γ' is an MCS, $[a : \theta]\psi' \in \Gamma'$ for all $\theta \in \mathcal{L}_{\text{PROP}}$, which, by consistency, means that $\langle a : \theta\rangle\neg\psi' \notin$ for all θ. Like in the ($\Rightarrow$) case, we can now reason exactly like in the case for $\langle a : \theta\rangle\psi$, with $\psi = \neg\psi'$, and conclude that $F_\Gamma, \omega_{\Gamma'} \nvDash \langle a : \theta\rangle\neg\psi'$ for any θ (again, our induction hypothesis for ψ' implies that it also holds for $\neg\psi'$). That is, $F_\Gamma, \omega_{\Gamma'} \vDash [a : \theta]\psi'$ for all $\theta \in \mathcal{L}_{\text{PROP}}$. It follows that $F_\Gamma, \omega_{\Gamma'} \vDash [a]\psi'$.

This completes the inductive proof. Finally, let $\top$ be any tautology. Then $B_a \top \in \Gamma$ by Nec_B and $\Gamma = \langle a : \top\rangle\Gamma$ by Null. Thus $\Gamma \trianglelefteq \Gamma$ and so $\Gamma \leq \Gamma$.

Theorem 16 (Strong Completeness). *For any set of formulas Γ and formula φ, if $\Gamma \vDash \varphi$ then $\Gamma \vdash_\infty \varphi$.*

Proof. Let $\Gamma \nvdash_\infty \varphi$. If $\Gamma \cup \{\neg\varphi\}$ was inconsistent, then $\Gamma \cup \{\neg\varphi\} \vdash_\infty \bot$, which by **DT** means that $\Gamma \vdash_\infty \neg\varphi \to \bot$ and by Taut, **W**, and **Imp** that $\Gamma \vdash_\infty \varphi$. But that is not the case, so $\Gamma \cup \{\neg\varphi\}$ is consistent. From Lemma 12 there is an MCS Γ' such that $\Gamma \cup \{\neg\varphi\} \subseteq \Gamma'$, and by Lemma 15 we have that $F_{\Gamma'}, \omega_{\Gamma'} \vDash \neg\varphi$ and $F_{\Gamma'}, \omega_{\Gamma'} \vDash \Gamma$. Thus, $\Gamma \nvDash \varphi$.

5 Discussion

We extended PNAL, a basic logic for reasoning about the belief dynamics of tweets in a social networks, with "ability" operators of the form $\langle a\rangle$ quantifying over the possible tweets agent a truthfully can make. We studied the logical properties of this modality and its interaction with explicit tweeting modalities. In particular, we provided a sound and strongly complete infinitary Hilbert-style axiomatic system.

Since the logic is not semantically compact, it is not possible to obtain a strong completeness result with a *finitary* axiomatisation. The possibility for finitary *weak* completeness is left for future work. Standard finitary methods such as using PDL-like closures in the construction of the canonical model, do not seem to work directly however. It has recently been shown that weak finitary completeness is possible for APAL restricted to propositional announcements [9].

Like both APAL and GAL, the APNAL modalities satisfy both the standard modal logic axiom 4 and the Church-Rosser property. For the former the CR property reads as $\Diamond\Box\varphi \to \Box\Diamond\varphi$, for both GAL and APNAL the more general variant $\langle a\rangle[b]\varphi \to [b]\langle a\rangle\varphi$ hold for any a, b[5].

Another obvious direction for future work is relaxing the simplifying assumptions in the framework, in particular to allow modelling of higher-order beliefs and tweets. This is true already for PNAL, see [21] for a general discussion. It is perhaps of particular interest in the context of APNAL as it would put the relationship between knowledge and ability with potential subtleties [3] on the table in the analysis of tweeting scenarios. Yet another natural direction would be to look at *group ability*, with GAL-like modalities of the form $\langle G\rangle$ where G is a group.

[5] For GAL the even more general variant $\langle G\rangle[H]\varphi \to [H]\langle G\rangle\varphi$ holds for any *sets* of agents G, H.

Acknowledgments. We are indebted to Jeremy Seligman for extensive discussions about the arbitrary tweeting modalities, and in particular the non-compactness observation. The first author is supported by the Project of MOE Liberal arts and Social Sciences Foundation under research no. 20YJC7204002.

References

1. Ågotnes, T., Balbiani, P., van Ditmarsch, H., Seban, P.: Group announcement logic. J. Appl. Logic **8**(1), 62–81 (2010)
2. Ågotnes, T., van Ditmarsch, H.: Coalitions and announcements. In: Padgham, L., Parkes, D., Muller, J., Parsons, S. (eds.) Proceedings of AAMAS, pp. 673–680 (2008)
3. Ågotnes, T., Goranko, V., Jamroga, W., Wooldridge, M.: Knowledge and ability. In: van Ditmarsch, H., Halpern, J.Y., van der Hoek, W., Kooi, B. (eds.) Handbook of Epistemic Logic, pp. 543–589. College Publications (2015)
4. Ågotnes, T., Walicki, M.: Strongly complete axiomatizations of "Knowing at Most" in syntactic structures. In: Toni, F., Torroni, P. (eds.) CLIMA 2005. LNCS (LNAI), vol. 3900, pp. 57–76. Springer, Heidelberg (2006). https://doi.org/10.1007/11750734_4
5. Balbiani, P., Baltag, A., van Ditmarsch, H., Herzig, A., Hoshi, T., de Lima, T.: What can we achieve by arbitrary announcements?: A dynamic take on fitch's knowability. In: Proceedings of TARK, pp. 42–51. ACM (2007)
6. Balbiani, P., van Ditmarsch, H.: A simple proof of the completeness of APAL. Stud. Logic **8**(1), 65–78 (2015)
7. Baltag, A., Christoff, Z., Rendsvig, R.K., Smets, S.: Dynamic epistemic logic of diffusion and prediction in threshold models. Studia Logica **107**(3), 489–531 (2019)
8. Bozzelli, L., van Ditmarsch, H., French, T., Hales, J., Pinchinat, S.: Refinement modal logic. Inf. Comput. **239**, 303–339 (2014)
9. van Ditmarsch, H., French, T.: Quantifying over boolean announcements. ArXiv abs/1712.05310 (2017)
10. van Ditmarsch, H., French, T., Pinchinat, S.: Future event logic - axioms and complexity. In: Beklemishev, L.D., Goranko, V., Shehtman, V.B. (eds.) Proceedings of AiML, pp. 77–99. College Publications (2010)
11. Galimullin, R., Alechina, N.: Coalition and group announcement logic. In: Lang, J. (ed.) Proceedings of TARK, EPTCS, vol. 251, pp. 207–220 (2017)
12. Goldblatt, R.: Axiomatising the Logic of Computer Programming. Springer, New York (1982)
13. Hales, J.: Arbitrary action model logic and action model synthesis. In: Proceedings of LICS, pp. 253–262. IEEE Computer Society (2013)
14. Kooi, B.: Hybrid logics with infinitary proof systems. J. Logic Comput. **16**(2), 161–175 (2006)
15. Kuijer, L.B.: Unsoundness of $R(\Box)$ (2015). http://personal.us.es/hvd/APAL_counterexample.pdf
16. Renardel de Lavalette, G.R., Kooi, B.P., Verbrugge, R.: Strong completeness for propositional dynamic logic. In: AiML2002-Advances in Modal Logic, pp. 377–393 (2002)
17. Morrison, C., Naumov, P.: Group conformity in social networks. J. Logic Lang. Inf. **29**(1), 3–19 (2020)
18. Seligman, J., Liu, F., Girard, P.: Facebook and the epistemic logic of friendship. In: Schipper, B.C. (ed.) Proceedings TARK, pp. 229–238 (2013)

19. Studer, T.: On the proof theory of the modal mu-calculus. Studia Logica **89**(3), 343–363 (2008)
20. Xiong, Z., Ågotnes, T.: On the logic of balance in social networks. J. Logic Lang. Inf. **29**(1), 53–75 (2020)
21. Xiong, Z., Ågotnes, T., Seligman, J., Zhu, R.: Towards a logic of tweeting. In: Baltag, A., Seligman, J., Yamada, T. (eds.) LORI 2017. LNCS, vol. 10455, pp. 49–64. Springer, Heidelberg (2017). https://doi.org/10.1007/978-3-662-55665-8_4

Author Index

Printed in the United States
By Bookmasters